PUBLICATIONS OF THE NEW CHAUCER SOCIETY

THE NEW CHAUCER SOCIETY

Studies in the Age of Chaucer, the yearbook of The New Chaucer Society, is published annually. Each issue contains substantial articles on all aspects of Chaucer and his age, book reviews, and an annotated Chaucer bibliography. Manuscripts, in duplicate, accompanied by return postage, should follow the *Chicago Manual of Style,* 14th edition. Unsolicited reviews are not accepted. Authors receive free twenty offprints of articles and ten of reviews. All correspondence regarding manuscript submissions should be directed to the Editor, David Matthews, English and American Studies, Humanities Lime Grove Building, The University of Manchester, Oxford Road, Manchester M13 9PL, United Kingdom. Subscriptions to The New Chaucer Society and information about the Society's activities should be directed to David Lawton, Department of English, Washington University, CB 1122, One Brookings Drive, St. Louis, MO 63130. Back issues of the journal may be ordered from The University of Notre Dame Press, Chicago Distribution Center, 11030 South Langley Avenue, Chicago, IL 60628; phone: 800-621-2736; fax: 800-621-8476, from outside the United States: phone: 773-702-7000; fax: 773-702-7212.

Studies in the Age of Chaucer

Thomas Hoccleve's personal seal (Kew, National Archives E 43/554, detail. Reproduced by permission. See p. 317)

Studies in the Age of Chaucer

Volume 29
2007

EDITOR

FRANK GRADY

PUBLISHED ANNUALLY BY THE NEW CHAUCER SOCIETY

WASHINGTON UNIVERSITY IN ST. LOUIS

The frontispiece design, showing the Pilgrims at the Tabard Inn, is adapted from the woodcut in Caxton's second edition of *The Canterbury Tales*.

ISBN 0-933784-31-7
ISSN 0190-2407

CONTENTS

CONTENTS

CONTENTS

CONTENTS

Studies in the Age of Chaucer

The PRESIDENTIAL ADDRESS
The New Chaucer Society
Fifteenth International Congress
July 27–31, 2006
Fordham University

The Presidential Address

New Chaucer Topographies

David Wallace
University of Pennsylvania

HOW IS CHAUCER DOING? Will our New Chaucer Society generations and constituencies hang together, as congenial souls,[1] as we plow deeper into the new millennium? We seem to be in a much less secure timeframe, now, in 2006. At York in 1984 there seemed a comforting if illusory congruence between the 1380s and 1980s. As we advanced through the 1990s, we knew that Chaucer would die, tidily enough, in London in 2000; we duly assembled in Westminster Abbey with the poet laureate. Since then, even the illusion of comfort in historical parallelism has gone awry. Several things happened: September 2001 turned out to supply the moment of millenarian change that was planned for, but yet failed to arrive, on 1 January 2000. And then, in our own modest sphere, the Linne Mooney discoveries of 2004 meant that we could not simply assume a structured path toward 2006 and 2008, years that we might associate with the copying of Hengwrt and Ellesmere and the orderly formation of Chaucerian textual afterlife. In a way we have been thrown back into the 1980s and 1990s, imagining a Chaucer who now looks much more like Petrarch or Christine de Pisan

This essay represents a slightly modified form of the lecture given at New York on 28 July 2006 as part of the 15th New Chaucer Society congress. Material on *Le feminine et le sacré* was added later and included in the joint presentation with Marilyn Nelson at the University of Connecticut on 12 October. I would like to thank Daniel Hoffman for his good offices and Marilyn Nelson for her inspiration and encouragement.
    [1] The most intensive investigation of Chaucer-reading communities to date is that of Stephanie Trigg, *Congenial Souls: Reading Chaucer from Medieval to Postmodern* (Minneapolis: University of Minnesota Press, 2002); see esp. pp. xx, 37–38. See now additionally Jennifer Summit and Nicholas Watson, "Response to the New Chaucer Society Conference, July 27–31, 2006," in *NCS Newsletter* 28 (Fall 2006), pp. 1–9; http://www.artsci.wustl.edu/~chaucer/congress2006.html.

as part-shaper of his own textual corpus. We are, conceptually if not organizationally, all at sea: a good place for a New, now not so new, Chaucer Society to be in its thirty-ninth year.

In the very last days of 1999, at the MLA Chaucer Forum, Lee Patterson observed that all prior *fins de siécle* had seen major figures arise to engage and revitalize Chaucer: William Morris, William Blake, John Dryden, Edmund Spenser, William Caxton. Public celebrations for Chaucer seemed fairly muted as 2000 came and went, especially when compared to those of 1900.[2] A sign of powerful poetic engagement with Chaucer *did,* however, appear in 1998; it is just taking us a while to digest it. I speak here of *Birthday Letters,* and more broadly of the ill-starred Ted Hughes/Sylvia Plath relationship.[3] The first of the two Chaucerian *Birthday* poems, "St Botolph's," replays the *innamoramento* scene of *Troilus and Criseyde,* as young Ted first sees Sylvia; the second, called simply "Chaucer," opens with Plath reciting the General Prologue, and later the Wife of Bath, to a field of cows. These two poems bespeak profound engagement not just with the texture of Chaucer's language but also with his multiple, nonlinear temporalities: the kind of thing that Paul Strohm and Carolyn Dinshaw are just now teasing out.[4] As Chaucerians, Plath and Hughes merit places on the smartest of NCS panels. But they feature no further in this presentation, for their engagement with Chaucer seems to me peculiarly *inward,* mystical in a Julian-like sense, tethered to the dynamics of interpersonal relationship rather than to the qualities of particular locales. In *Birthday Letters,* Chaucer becomes almost a third party to the disastrous, love-struck *agon* of two poets; this, then, might be regarded as the twentieth century's most fitting, one might say classical, rendition of a *fin de siécle* Chaucer. What appears out there now, in our new century, seems quite different. Chaucer now evokes spatial frameworks that are powerfully local, yet global. These

---

[2] Not so muted, however, as the centennial celebrations for Fame-hungry Francesco Petrarca in 2004. On Chaucer celebrations in 1900, which were actually considered relatively disappointing (particularly outside London), see Steve Ellis, *Chaucer at Large: The Poet in the Modern Imagination* (Minneapolis: University of Minnesota Press, 2000), pp. 17–19. For an intriguing complement to Ellis's work, see now Candace Barrington, *American Chaucer* (New York: Palgrave Macmillan, 2007).

[3] Ted Hughes, *Birthday Letters* (London: Faber, 1998).

[4] See Strohm, *Theory and the Premodern Text* (Minneapolis: University of Minnesota Press, 2000), esp. pp. 51–96; Dinshaw, "Never, Always, Now, Again: The Temporalities of Medieval Studies," NCS Conference, 27 July 2006.

new Chaucer topographies, while playing to broader publics, hold particular resonance for us, a *New* Chaucer Society: for we are both globally dispersed, from Melbourne to Hiroshima, *and* now continually connected through the World Wide Web. In these new circumstances, the traditional act of coming together every two years seems newly strange.

In speaking of new Chaucer topographies, I bypass the Chaucer blogger (whoever you are: some say a Langlandian ABD).[5] In 2003 and 2004, Peter Ackroyd, the prolific biographer of London and Londoners, passed through Chaucer at high speed, generating a "Brief Life" of the poet and his *Clerkenwell Tales*.[6] Ackroyd has evidently worked out a lucrative scheme whereby he immerses himself in the life of a poet, producing a brief and derivative biography, then gets paid again (by the same publisher) for much more interesting fictional pastiche.[7] One of Ackroyd's earliest works was a history of transvestism; his best novel is *Chatterton,* the saga of a medievalist *pasticheur;*[8] his *Clerkenwell Tales* offers a kind of voguing[9] in Chaucerian language.[10] Each of the first twenty-two chapters is named after a Chaucerian pilgrim: "The Prioress's Tale," "The Friar's Tale," and so on; the twenty-third and last chapter, "The Author's Tale," is footnotes. But this is a pilgrimage text that never

---

[5] http://houseoffame.blogspot.com

[6] See Peter Ackroyd, *The Clerkenwell Tales* (London: Chatto and Windus, 2003); *Chaucer* (London: Chatto and Windus, 2004). Ackroyd's Chaucer is, *in nuce,* a poet of hybridity and translation, of water and of London: see his *Albion: The Origins of the English Imagination* (London: Chatto and Windus, 2002), pp. 149–59.

[7] See further Ackroyd, *The Lambs of London* (London: Chatto and Windus, 2004); *Shakespeare* (London: Chatto and Windus, 2005). Charles and Mary Lamb are famous chiefly for their *Tales from Shakespeare.*

[8] See *Dressing Up: Transvestism and Drag: The History of an Obsession* (London: Thames and Hudson, 1979); *Chatterton* (London: Hamish Hamilton, 1987).

[9] "Vogue is a form of modern dance characterized by photo model-like poses integrated with angular, linear and rigid arm, leg, and body movements. Although often associated with Madonna's efforts to introduce it to mainstream popular culture, vogue as a subculture was in existence long before the release of her song, also titled 'Vogue.' This particular style of dance arose from the Harlem ballrooms back in the early 1930s. It was first called 'performance' and has since evolved into the more intricate and illusory form that is now commonly referred to as 'vogue' ": (http://en.wikipedia.org/wiki/Vogue_(dance).

[10] See, for example, p. 30 (part of "The Merchant's Tale"): in this part, apprentice Janekin dallies with Anne Strago, wife of Radulph Strago, haberdasher. Having "played at hazard" with other apprentices, Janekin "engaged in a violent game known to them as 'breaking doors with our heads.' " Anne bathes his broken head, and a neo-courtly exchange follows: " 'They say, mistress, that pity runs swiftest in a gentle heart.' 'But I have no gentle heart. I have no heart at all.' 'Then fortune is my foe.' " After their first lovemaking, the wife complains that her husband "did not keep me in proper estate. 'Other women,' she said, 'go gayer than I.' "

leaves the city: movement and narrative tension, which assume a millenarian quality, are supplied from without as Henry of Lancaster advances to reclaim his patrimony. The history of New Chaucer Society
conferences, over the last two decades, has been a succession of backfor-
mations: first the Arundel/Lollardy complex cast its shadow, then the
greater fifteenth century; next will be the Reformation. It is fascinating
to observe the congruence of Ackroyd's fiction with the first of these
backward steps: in his "Clerk's Tale," for example, a woman cries out,
" 'They pray to Our Lady of Falsingham. They do reverence to Thomas
of Cankerbury!' " (p. 37). But this observation may be flipped around:
it is fascinating to observe how congruent Arundel and Lollardy Studies
are with the genre of Gothic urbanism exemplified so well by Ackroyd,
by painter John Virtue,[11] or by the comic-book inventors of Gotham
city.[12] Chaucer, notoriously, wrote little about London.[13] For Ackroyd,
nonetheless, Chaucer forms part of a London pantheon that includes
Blake, Turner, and Dickens: "All of them," Ackroyd says, "were preoccupied with light and darkness, in a city that is built in the shadows of
money and power."[14] This association of Chaucer with urban Gothic

[11] John Virtue's large-scale paintings of London, produced in black and white, are
particularly preoccupied (like Ackroyd's fiction) with the Thames. Virtue worked as
Associate Artist of the National Gallery for two years and exhibited his work there from
9 March–5 June 2005: see http://www.nationalgallery.org.uk/education/artist/john_
virtue/default.htm. Virtue had a long career as a landscape painter of the Exe before
coming to the Thames. One constant of his work (which associates him with Ackroyd)
is ceaseless tracing of river courses: see Paul Moorhouse, "John Virtue's Art: The Image
of Man and Nature," in John Virtue, *New Work, 1998–2000* (St. Ives: Tate St. Ives,
2000), 7–22. This compulsion to record the crossing of landscape, seen differently in
the work of Somerset artist Richard Long, accounts in part, I would argue, for the
timeliness of Chaucer's *Tales* as expressive vehicle.
[12] "Gotham City," *The Superman Homepage* explains, "is a major American center of
commerce and culture. It is one of the nation's three largest cities (smaller than Metropolis, but tying New York City in population), and continually rivals The Big Apple
and The Big Apricot for status as the nation's spiritual center, as well as capital of the
free world." Its Gothicism, while suggesting something of a Reformation view of the
Middle Ages, recalls the *chiaroscuro* effects of Ackroydian and other contemporary fictional Londons: "What distinguishes Gotham City is its elaborate and uniformed architecture. Massive and ornate, the Gothic structures of the Gotham skyline are both
breathtaking and foreboding. As Metropolis is called the City of Tomorrow, Gotham
City's persona is far more dubious. Its dark alleys and chaotic corners continually draw
people and repel them in simultaneous revolutions of humanity" (http://www.super
manhomepage.com/comics/who/who-intro.php?topic=gotham).
[13] But see, most recently, Derek Pearsall, "How English Is Chaucer?" *TLS,* 12 January 2007, pp. 12–13 (13); Marion Turner, *Chaucerian Conflict: Languages of Antagonism
in Late Fourteenth-Century London* (Oxford: Oxford University Press, 2007).
[14] "London Luminaries and Cockney Visionaries," the LWT London Lecture 1993,
BL YA.1994.b.8928, p. 7. Ackroyd does not actually refer to Chaucer in this passage,
pace John O'Mahoney, "London Calling," *The Guardian,* 3 July 2004 (http://books.guar-
dian.co.uk/departments/generalfiction/story/0,,1252722,00.ht ml). But Ackroyd's asso-

perhaps explains why The Canterbury Tales "Medieval Misadventures" attraction at Canterbury, featuring grotesquely ugly animated puppets, opens (to amend Sylvia Plath) with horsepiss in darkness.[15]

Containment *and* restless movement are the most striking aspects of Ackroyd's *Tales*. Although hardly leaving London, it tracks constant movement *across* the city. "The Shipman's Tale," chapter 20, contrives to traverse London by water just to find a dead body. Such paradoxical compounding of containment and restless movement also characterizes the recent and ongoing two-part *Canterbury Tales* of the Royal Shakespeare Company.[16] This production also sustains distinctive commitment to topography: to articulating the many and different locations accruing as the tales unfold. At the same time, these locations are pretty much always articulated at the *same* place, theatrically speaking: center stage. So the great difference of spaces in *The Man of Law's Tale,* for example, must be acted out at the same central location: there is much hasty waving of scimitars behind scrim. Such centralized staging doubtless anticipates the demands of touring into the great unknown: following the opening run at Stratford-upon-Avon, the show set up shop, the

---

ciation of Chaucer as a Londoner with the Gothic qualities he evokes elsewhere in his writing docs qualify him to figure in this company. For Ackroyd, the Gothic lies perennially just below the surface of London. In speaking of the supposed absence of theater in nineteenth-century London, he remarks: "If some one had just scratched the surface they would have found penny gaffs, music halls, patent theatres, blood tubs, Gothic dramas" (p. 4).

[15] http://www.canterburytales.org.uk/home.htm; see further Sylvia Plath, "Ariel," in Plath, *Ariel* (New York: Harper and Row, 1966), pp. 26–27 (line 1: "Stasis in darkness"). The strange impulse to begin a Canterbury Tales experience in the huddled semidarkness of a tavern, reeking of urine, runs curiously counter to the *Tales'*s actual opening (with regenerative planetary motion). Analogous motifs are explored in *Urban Gothic,* a TV series that premiered on Channel 5 (UK) in 2000 and ran to thirteen episodes; a second series followed in 2001. Initial promotional material ran as follows: "Behind the facade of London's shiny dockside developments, its designer boutiques and coffee bars lie forgotten dark corners and darker secrets. It's a city where anything can happen and being young and pretty won't always save you. This cult smash hit follows scary stories and chilling episodes, from vampire documentaries to alien-infested supermarkets, from teenage necromancy to ghostly East End gangsters. In Urban Gothic, you'll find thirteen tales of the city to chill the blood" (http://www.imdb.com/title/tt0300602/plotsummary; see also http://myweb.tiscali.co.uk/davidjhowe00/main .htm). Both series are available on DVD. See further "The City" in the spin-off volume *Urban Gothic,* ed. David J. Howe (Tolworth, Surrey: Telos, 2001), which opens: "Walk the streets of the City, and what do you feel? Despair? Hopelessness? A feverish desire to escape? Certainly what you *won't* feel is safe. Around every gritty corner, danger lurks" (p. 11).

[16] The slowness of *The Knight's Tale* spells death to popular drama; it therefore passes as a furious romp that almost collapses it, generically speaking, into the *Miller's Tale* that chases it from the stage. See Geoffrey Chaucer, *The Canterbury Tales,* an adaptation in two parts by Mike Poulton (London: Nick Hern Books, 2005).

program note says, "in leisure centers across the UK, in places as far apart as Barrhead in Scotland and St Austell in Cornwall."[17]

This exercise in cultural integration, outreaching the Pardoner's "from Berwick unto Ware," creates new kinds of Chaucer topography. The show itself organizes around a stable performing center, yet that center itself continuously changes place. This *Canterbury Tales* has already exceeded the bounds of Britain by spending a month at the Kennedy Center in Washington, D.C., and there are plans to take it to Spain. The Spanish itinerary, however, is foundering on the fact that the *Tales* are too smutty and irreligious for the Dominican friars of Almagro—bare bums *do* appear in *The Miller's Tale*.[18] One also wonders how *The Prioress's Tale* went down in D.C. At Stratford-upon-Avon, at the Swan Theatre, *The Prioress's Tale* was played straight and unusually slow. The actors playing Jews wore caricature masks with long noses; the actors playing Christians, wearing no masks, were much given to ecclesiastical chanting by torchlight. Containment in darkness and centralization of space intensified all these effects. The audience was here targeted for double interpellation, caught between identification (with the beauties of Anglican choral tradition) and denial (of Christian anti-Semitism). Jews figure here somewhere between graphic, caricatural presence and shadowy absence. Such paralysis of over- and under-signification is solved *theatrically* by bringing on *The Nun's Priest's Tale:* ethical complexities wash away in a furious barnyard romp; the curtain then descends on Part I. This strategy, I think, is Chaucerian. It is *The Tale of Sir Thopas,* rather than the Nun's Priest, that follows the Prioress in Ellesmere order, but the *effect* is the same: comic performativity releases the audience from depression, or congestive sobriety; ethical misgivings go by the board. All this must play differently as non-British and non-Gentile audiences come to constitute new topographies for this Chaucerian drama.[19]

Another project currently carrying Chaucer into new locales is Cana-

---

[17] Program for Royal Shakespeare Company, *The Canterbury Tales* by Geoffrey Chaucer, new adaptation by Mike Poulton (2006), inside cover (not paginated). At the time of the 2006 NCS conference, this production was playing at the Gielgud Theatre, Shaftesbury Avenue, London.

[18] See Giles Tremlett, "Please do not fart at the festival," *The Guardian,* 20 June 2006, *G2,* p. 2.

[19] It is worth noting, however, that a high percentage of English theatergoers, especially in London and Stratford, are Americans (specifically young USers, "studying abroad.").

dian Baba Brinkman's *Rap Canterbury Tales*. Brinkman's Web site shows him rapping his way from Adelaide to Aberdeen; he also works in many English schools.[20] Again, this project is both centered and diffuse: the Web site forms a stable core, whereas Brinkman himself furiously tours and travels. The enabling conceit of the *Rap Canterbury Tales* CD is that Brinkman was at a hiphop show, a rap concert with star performers "bustin rhymes." Brinkman, or the narrator, sneaks onto the tour bus, where he remains mysteriously "unnoticed and invisible"; the performers arrive and begin rapping rhymes, and Brinkman promises to "tell you what I saw." He mimics African American diction for the opening exchanges between the Host and the Knight, but resorts to his own voice once the tale-rapping begins.[21] White rapping is by now, of course, commonplace: at the University of Pennsylvania 2006 commencement, we heard Jody Foster rap lyrics from Eminem.[22] Baba Brinkman is no Pat Boone, but the enabling appropriative gesture of his *Rap Canterbury Tales is* problematic: he's the white invisible man in a bus of black Chaucer rappers.

It is, nonetheless, worth pondering *why* Chaucer seems so amenable to rapping. One obvious answer is that it is pretty difficult *not* to fall into rapping rhythm while reciting *The Tale of Sir Thopas*. Another might be that the distance in *time* separating us from Chaucer is finding expression as distance in *culture*. This holds true for the BBC's six-part *Canterbury Tales* of 2004. The best of these sees Constance wash up on the eastern English coast as a political refugee from Nigeria. This works brilliantly, since Nigerian Constance *is* the one woman of true faith in a contemporary England that now actually *is* more pagan than fifth-century Northumberland; and nobody can be *more* wicked than a middle-class English Caucasian mother-in-law set to avert an unsuitable marriage. Racial differences here accentuate the geographical differences of the BBC *Man of Law's Tale*. The *Sea Captain's Tale* unfolds among a prosperous Anglo-Indian community; *The Knight's Tale* features actor

---

[20] See http://www.babasword.com; Baba, *The Rap Canterbury Tales* (CD, 2004).

[21] The absence of counter-rapping or alternative voicing is another curious aspect of Brinkman's one-man show. In his school presentations, however, he does invite competition from his audience; and he does rap Chaucer in inner city spaces where New Chaucerians, as yet, are seldom seen.

[22] See http://www.upenn.edu/almanac//volumes/v52/n34/commence06-jf.html. This was Penn's 250th commencement, in the year of the 300th birthday of Penn's founder, Benjamin Franklin (1706–90); the choice of speaker thus sparked some campus controversy.

9

Chiwetel Ejiofor as one of the two young prisoners yearning for Emily. Some synergy flows between marking the cultural and historical difference of Chaucer and this recourse to actors and communities of color: both are found different from and constitutive of contemporary English culture. Something of this informs David Dabydeen's engagement with Middle English texts in his semi-autobiographical novel of 1991, *The Intended.*[23] Dabydeen describes his first-person narrator surrogate as "Indian West-Indian Guyanese." For him, the study of Chaucer promises cultural capital of several kinds. First, he attempts to seduce nice white A-level student Janet through demonstrated mastery of *Troilus and Criseyde:* unfortunately, her examination board has set the *General Prologue,* so this comes to nought. Second, he uses his possession of a *Canterbury Tales* text to impress his landlord, Mr. Ali: " 'It's about a group of religious people going on a pilgrimage to a holy shrine,' " he says, " 'like Muslims to Mecca.' " Mr. Ali *is* impressed: " 'I got relatives in Canterbury,' he said, 'cousin own grocery. He settled there from Kenya ten years now. Sell fruit and veg. Good business, make much money' " (p. 97). This sense of Chaucer's forming part of a freshly complex urban terrain is sustained by Darcus Howe's evocation of Brixton topography. Darcus Howe is a Trinidadian, the son of an Anglican minister and nephew of C. L. R. James; he came to London at nineteen and in 1970 was arrested for riot and affray; his acquittal at the Old Bailey was celebrated by Linton Kwesi Johnson in his poem *Man Free.*[24] "Old Brixton is celebrated," Darcus Howe says, "in the names of the streets which cross Railton into Mayall on the left and Dulwich on the right. First Chaucer, then Spenser; Shakespeare and Milton follow."[25] This impeccably canonical space, laid out by Brixton's Victorian planners, is now punctuated by other cultural institutions and literary histories. But it is worth noticing that Chaucer is still voiced in this place: "Between Chaucer and Shakespeare," Darcus Howe says, "sits the Methodist church with its resident youth club, and Sheppards, which poet Linton Kwesi Johnson evoked in metaphor and simile in his poem 'Five nights of Bleedin.' Here on Railton Road in the quiet of the sabbath's morning," Howe continues, "Chaucer's ghost breaks silence as he recites the *Complaint of Troilus:*

[23] See Dabydeen, *The Intended* (London: Vintage, 2000).
[24] http://en.wikipedia.org/wiki/Darcus_Howe; http://www.awigp.com/default.asp?-numcat = darcus. For "Man Free (for Darcus Howe)," see Johnson, *Inglan is a Bitch,* 2nd ed. (London: Race Today Publications, 1981), 16–17.
[25] "Black Sabbath," in *"Time Out" London Walks,* vol. 1, 2nd ed. (London: Penguin, 2002), pp. 166–73 (169).

From thennesforth he rideth up and down,
And everything come him to remembrance,
As he rode forby places of the town
In which he whilllom had all his pleasiance.

(p. 170)

The eccentricity of orthography here, in this citation from the last Book of *Troilus and Criseyde*,[26] suggests that Howe works from memory: which is to say that Chaucer's mapping of past pleasures upon urban, neo-London landscape forms part of the fabric of Howe's Brixton, his home in London for some forty-odd years. David Dabydeen accords comparably magical memory functions to medieval texts: in fact, it is his engagement with far-off Middle English, in a university library, that connects or reconnects him with the creole or native vernacular of his far-off, native Guyana.[27] The narrator of his novel *The Intended* spends many "solitary hours—trying to master the alien language of medieval alliterative poetry, the sentences wrenched and wrecked by strange consonants, refusing to be smooth and civilized" (p. 195). In the midst of this struggle he is visited imaginatively by Joseph: an artist who gouges letters in mud with a stick, a figure associated both with African culture and with the Maroons living inland from the Guyanese coastal strip. It was, in fact, Dabydeen's undergraduate engagement with Middle English alliterative poetry at Cambridge that turned him to writing the excoriating Guyanese lyrics of his *Slave Song* (published in 1984).[28] Which is to say that the *temporal* alterity of Middle English resonated with the *cultural* alterity of Guyanese.[29] The "brokeness and rawness" of this creole

[26] 5.561–64. The eccentric orthography may owe something of course to the *Time Out* typesetters. For "Five Nights of Bleeding," see Linton Kwesi Johnson, *Dread Beat and Blood* (London: Bogle-L'Ouverture Publications, 1975), 15–17. For a wider range of work, see Johnson, *Mi Revalueshanary Fren: Selected Poems* (London: Penguin, 2002).

[27] Salikoko S. Mufwene thus ponders the difference between creoles and vernaculars: "The main implicit criterion, which is embarrassing for linguistics but has not been discussed, is the ethnicity of their speakers. Most hypotheses proposed in creolistics to account for the development of creoles would have been better thought out, had it not been partly for this factor" (*The Ecology of Language Evolution* [Cambridge: Cambridge University Press, 2001], p. xiii). See further Johnson, "If I Woz a Tap-Natch Poet," in *Mi Revalueshanary Fren*, 94–97, which bears the following epigraph from the *Oxford Companion to Twentieth-Century Poetry*: "dub poetry has been described . . . as 'over-compensation for deprivation'" (p. 94).

[28] *Slave Song* (Mundelstrup, Denmark: Dangaroo Press, 1984).

[29] Middle English alliterative poetry is often presented as embodying a poetic tradition *alter* or alternative to that of Chaucer (which benefited from congruence with Chancery Standard) that could not outlive the Middle Ages (or the Percy Folio); that, plus

perfectly expresses the extreme physical demands of cutting sugar cane. Until recently, the Guyanese plantations were owned by Bookers, provisioners both of sugar and the literary prize: "Booker own me patacake," says Dabydeen in *Slave Song.* "Booker own me pickni'" (p. 17).

In 2002, poet Marilyn Nelson received a fellowship enabling a group of "Americans of slave descent" to travel to "some place sanctified by the Negro soul," in a kind of "reverse diaspora."[30] The fruit of this collective journey is *The Cachoeira Tales,* of 2005; its formal and metrical model is *The Canterbury Tales.* Deciding the *telos* for this "pilgrimage" proves difficult: they might choose Zimbabwe to honor the black Anglican martyr Bernard Mizeki; perhaps the singing monastery of Keur Moussa in Senegal; or Jamaica, or Trinidad. Finally they choose the church of Senhor do Bonfim, or Lord of the Good End, a site in the Bahia region of Brazil, "sacred," Marilyn Nelson says, "to Christians and followers of Candomblé" (p. 12). Candomblé is a religion passed on by African priests and followers, brought to Brazil as slaves between 1549 and 1850; many Brazilian Catholics also participate in Candomblé practices. The *seemingly* arbitrary choice of destination makes an important point about black diaspora, in which pilgrimage can begin and end pretty much anywhere on the planet. There is no Mecca (except for black Muslims), no single sacred site.[31] Bonfim in Bahia works well for Nelson, since the possibilities of syncretism, religious and cultural, are rehearsed throughout her poem. Bahia also happens to be the place where Marilyn Nelson's son, Jacob, is studying and teaching; he contacts his mother by e-mail. The endurance and adaptability of family is one of the great wonders of African American culture; the "fellowship" that Nelson's poem realizes mixes family, friends, and people met *en route.* The pilgrim descriptions in the poem's "General Prologue" are

---

its consonantal, percussive rhythm, might have suggested sympathetic vibration with sugar-cutting, Guyanese creole.

[30] Marilyn Nelson, *The Cachoeira Tales and Other Poems* (Baton Rouge: Louisiana State University Press, 2005), p. 11.

[31] The Bahia region of Brazil is, nonetheless, of particular significance in the history of African slavery. Its major port, Salvador, which figures strongly in Nelson's poem, lay only 40–45 days' sailing time from West African coastlines in the seventeenth and eighteenth centuries. Emancipation did not come to Brazil until 1888, and some one million slaves were shipped there in the nineteenth century. Reproductive rates were low, due in part to a high preponderance of male slaves; this meant that slave communities retained more distinctively *African* characteristics here than elsewhere. See James Walvin, *Atlas of Slavery* (Harlow: Pearson Longman, 2006), pp. 85–91 and map 51; David Wallace, *Premodern Places: Calais to Surinam, Chaucer to Aphra Behn* (Oxford: Blackwell, 2004), pp. 239–302.

highly if complexly Chaucerian. There is a JAZZ MUSICIAN, a retired PILOT, and an ACTIVIST. And there is "the DIRECTOR of a small black theater," who seems at first reminiscent of Chaucer's Clerk, since she lives poor and for art, but finally proves more like the Wife of Bath:

> She was an ample sister, middle-aged,
> a champagne cocktail of faith and outrage,
> with one tooth missing from her ready smile,
> a close Afro, and a bohemian style.
>
> (p. 13)

The poem's first-person "I," or Marilyn Nelson-*persona* (to adopt proper Chaucerian etiquette), herself later has a Wife of Bath moment: "But I digress. / Where was I? Oh yes, Africa" (p. 28). This ostensibly simple Q&A, "Where was I? Africa," couched as a moment of mental aberration, speaks to a complex cultural situation: Nelson and her "fellowship" *were* once, in a sense, of Africa. Now they are African Americans in Latin America, discovering how the power of the dollar makes them (to locals) godlike. This moment occurs in "Baixa Mall," the poem's longest section. Here the issues of history, identity, and syncretism are worked out within the bonds of African American fellowship. That sounds solemn, hence misses the spirit of the poem: for although hard historical cases of enslavement and bigotry are laid out, the whole is oiled by drinking and there is much verbal play with strange terms such as "spoogly" and "Creole Swahili."[32] Medieval guild get-togethers, we might recall, were known as *drinkings;* here fellowship bonds through beverage, featuring the slave products of sugar and rum. There is talk of the Middle Passage, of languages and chants carried over, and of African gods surviving "by putting on white masks"; and there are tales of Anansi, the Ashanti King of all Stories who switches "his tool / for the tool of his friend, the elephant bull."[33] Elsewhere *Cachoeira Tales* sees peeing by night, bare bums comically displayed, arses that whistle and

---

[32] "When it comes to AAVE [African-American vernacular English], the 'boyz in the hood' do not have a corner on the market' (Geneva Smitherman, "Word from the Hood: the Lexicon of African-American Vernacular English," in *African-American English: Structure, History and Use,* ed. Salikoko S. Mufwene, John R. Rickford, Guy Bailey, and John Baugh [London: Routledge, 1998], pp. 203–25 [204]).

[33] "Baixa Mall," in Nelson, *Cachoeira Tales and Other Poems,* pp. 25–26. Marilyn Nelson tells me that although the "Trickster" stories may masquerade as Anansi tales, they are actually Nanabush tales from the Lakota tradition.

fart, and cursing "by two turds." There is also contemplation of slave blood flowing downhill from the punishment pillory, still part of local topography, to "Our Lady of the Rosary of Blacks" (p. 19). This *can* return us to Chaucer: to reconsider the role of the comic, oath-edged, and profane in a culture grounded upon reverence for tortured human deity.

Following the "Baixa Mall section" of the poem, the African American fellowship engages in a series of encounters with local, Bahian groups while continuing to reflect on histories, shared and discrete. The section called "Da Blues" stages the supper for thirty provided for by the terms of Nelson's "fellowship" (p. 39). This is a move like and unlike Chaucer: for whereas Chaucer's Host envisages a supper for thirty returned pilgrims, *The Cachoeira Tales* stages it, so to speak, on the road. Nelson's son Jacob, identified as "host," works to integrate this group of Brazilians and USers, assuming the role (for the rest of the poem) of syncretic commentator. Much is expected of the local Bahian musicians, but they actually play something likened to "grocery store Muzak." The pilgrims then take their turn, playing Blues "with the raunch / of a nightclub on Chicago's South Side / in the fifties"; the narrator's brother sings "like one possessed / by Maceo Merryweather or Leroy Carr" (p. 41). It is ironic that African Americans travel so far in order to discover the transcendent sound of their *own,* at-home music, although being *possessed* in such a way accords perfectly with local experiences of Candomblé. And the jazz musician's evocation of what jazz is like achieves a mystical quality that—in its involvement in the body, breath and death—suggests something of Julian: "And time stood still, for one long, soaring breath, / As I transcended injury or death" (p. 40). The poem's next section, "Music Monastery," toys with the idea that there *is* a music monastery, "very ascetic, very strict" (p. 43), that takes in only the very best. This explains Ornette Coleman's missing years. Next comes "In Memoriam," in which e-mail (e-mail again) brings news of the death of "two great Tuskegee Airmen" (p. 44). Marilyn Nelson, herself the daughter of a Tuskegee airman, writes in the spirit of Candomblé: "Colonel Wilson, General Davis: Live in me" (p. 44). "Olodum" then carries the process of integration between Brazilians and black USers to its furthest point through drumming, and dancing to drumming. Its epigraph is *"where there is dancing, there is hope"*(p. 45). And then *The Cachoeira Tales* has just two sections left: "Cachoeira" and "A Igreja do Nostra Senhor do Bonfim." This pilgrimage poem thus

14

ends by attempting to reach its declared destinations. This move proves difficult and unsatisfactory—which again seems Chaucerian, since we never do reach Canterbury (except in *The Tale of Beryn*). Cachoeira is home to "the famous Sisterhood of the Good Death," a community of older women, all formerly mothers and wives, who form "a sisterhood of sages in matronage" (p. 49). This group seems to blend *beguinage,* anchorhold, and Candomblé: for the eldest sister, "a black / ninety-odd-year-old woman facing death" (p. 51) becomes the bridge for the Virgin Mary's crossing back. Nelson and her fellow "visiting rich American descendants of slaves" (p. 50) never meet these sisters: the sisters are busy, "in solitude," preparing for the Feast of the Assumption. The trip to Bonfim Church proves similarly frustrating. It happens on the last day, with the company already splitting up with an eye to catching planes. A mad taxi dash en route to the airport allows only a quick rush into the sanctuary for a prayer "that all of us would meet good ends" (p. 53); Nelson's son then offers a concluding syncretist meditation on "Oxala and his twin, / the Christian Christ" (p. 54) as they race for the plane. It is in this belated rush for the shrine, and in her *not* meeting the "Sisterhood of the Good Death," that Marilyn Nelson seems most our contemporary, most (might we say?) like a universal modern subject. *The Cachoreia Tales* includes three epigraphs, all from Frantz Fanon's *Black Skin, White Masks.* The third of them explicitly resists premature universalizing of experience: "*I have barely opened eyes that had been blind-folded,*" says Fanon, "*and someone wants to drown me in the universal?*" (p. 8). But the very last couplet of Nelson's poem does open out to the common and unfinished history of our here and now, its openness expressed through a hyphenation that anticipates a subordinate or clinching clause that never comes: "Our pilgrimage ended, we left Salvador, / Meanwhile, our President cheered us toward war—" (p. 54).

I'd like to end myself here by considering how Marilyn Nelson's poem invites reflection upon our own current practices as Chaucerians, on how Cachoeira glosses Canterbury. Nelson, like a medievalist, dedicates much energy to the reading of fragments. Medieval English culture was fragmented by the furious violence of the Reformation. We look for finials in farmhouses, suggesting where a monastery might once have been; we guess at monastic library holdings from pastedowns and bric-a-brac; we read the *Canterbury Tales,* a poem in ten Fragments. Marilyn Nelson, while committed to syncretism, is also thrilled by the prospect of carried-over fragments of a true African culture, as when she contemplates young people practicing "*capoeira* kicks" (p. 35). *Capoeira,* Nelson explains, is a martial art that compares with tai-chi, "self-defence disguised as dance / That is another slave inheritance" (p. 35). Here, as so often in this poem, she is walking by the sea. A little later, after the Blues event, she is half-immersed in it: "Wading in the waves, / I thought of Matthew Arnold. Then, of slaves" (p. 43). Marilyn Nelson is an English professor: her mind turns to Arnold's "distant northern sea" as it had turned to Wordsworth's a few pages before (p. 37).[34] *As* an English professor, she knows syntax: the comma after the "then" of "Then, of slaves" is (like the unrequited hyphen that ends the poem) killer punctuation. The "blue Atlantic," Nelson says elsewhere, is "a bone highway" (p. 36). Matthew Arnold's "melancholy, long, withdrawing roar," compared to this, but whimpers; his ocean is figurative of time, rather than physically a means of transportation, exile, and enslavement.[35] Nelson's lines might thus also serve to keep our own histrionics, our proneness to medievalist melancholy as we contemplate Reformation outrages, within bounds.[36] Some historical violence fragments literary heritage; some fragments people.

The Cachoeira Tales understands superlatively well how a bonded

[34] Nelson's lines "The world was too much / with us" in her "Southern Cross" section (p. 37) echo Wordsworth's "The World is too much with us," an often-anthologized sonnet first published in 1807. Wordsworth's seaside poem sees him agonizing over his inability, in this world of "getting and spending," to be moved by "Nature." Wordsworth would rather "be / A Pagan suckled in a creed outworn," if only his jaded spirits could be revived by seeing "Proteus rising from the sea; / Or hear old Triton blow his wreathed horn" (http://rpo.library.utoronto.ca/poem/2380.html). Nelson, for her part, cites the Wordsworthian line on buying "American canned sodas from / a burdened woman who opened them with her thumb," and who then waits for the empties" (p. 37). Her beachside poem is thus both distanced from Wordsworth's (her sea is a "bone highway," p. 36, rather than a site for melancholic, neoclassical musings) and complicit with it; Wordsworth is part of her *Tales*'s fabric.

[35] Channel-gazing Arnold hears an "eternal note of sadness" in the sea-drawn motion of pebbles. He thinks of Sophocles, the Aegean and "human misery": but not of slavery, as his mind turns to the retreating "sea of faith." "On Dover Beach" first appeared in *New Poems* (London: Macmillan, 1867): see http://rpo.library.utoronto.ca/poem/89.html. For a new, British Asian (Punjabi) take on this poem, see Dalgit Nagra, *Look We Have Coming to Dover* (London: Faber, 2007).

[36] Lamenting a ruined Middle Ages can modulate into lament over the passing of Medieval Studies as a disciplinary force: see L. O. Aranye Fradenburg, *Sacrifice Your Love: Psychoanalysis, Historicism, Chaucer* (Minneapolis: University of Minnesota Press, 2002), which speaks of "how we skirt the edge of extinction" (p. 252). James Simpson, in the session following this presentation at the NYC NCS, declared his vigorous opposition to institutionalized Medieval Studies, thus curiously aligning himself with the Reformation wrecking crews whose work he elsewhere laments: see *Reform and Cultural Revolution* (Oxford: Oxford University Press, 2002), pp. 35–36, and, on Simpson's *jouissance*, David Wallace, "Oxford English Literary History," *JMEMS* 35.1 (2005): 13–23.

group, a *compagnye,* a Fellowship is made: no other contemporary neo-Chaucerian work—play, musical, or novel—shows equivalent understanding. Chaucer integrates the *felaweship* of his *Canterbury Tales* through shared adherences of religion, language, nationality, and sexuality. Each of these qualities, internal to the group, supposes qualities external and perhaps hostile to it; the ideological inside implies an alien outside. The qualitative outside to Marilyn Nelson's traveling African American Fellowship might be supposed to be *whiteness,* but such is not the case; *auctoritees* such as Shakespeare, Wordsworth, and Arnold prove integral to her poem's fabric. Nelson stages her keynote Chaucerian scene halfway through the text, in her "Baixa Mall" section. But she then goes beyond it by integrating her group *into* the local Brazilian milieu: it is here, in this mixing of cultures, that the celebratory meal for thirty is consumed. This is not a black-white thing, nor is it hardly just a black-brown thing, but a process to challenge the imperialist grand narrative adumbrated by Chaucer's *Canterbury Tales.* For the keynote movement of English colonialism has been to go out as a group, stay together as a group, and not to integrate with local populations. This principle of English nonintegration has a long history: for as *The Man of Law's Tale* suggests, and as linguist Salikoko Mufwene confirms, Germanic invaders of Britain did not mingle with native Celts[37] but rather displaced them—thus inventing Welshness and Wales, Wallaces and *foreigners.*[38] This way of apartheid was not the way of Portuguese or Spanish colonialism, and it is not the way of *The Cachoeira Tales.*

Marilyn Nelson's gaze out to sea and to Africa is returned, fortuitously and instructively, by Catherine Clément at the beginning of *The Feminine and the Sacred.*[39] A black Catholic mass in Senegal is punctuated by ecstatic female cries: "a fulminating access to the sacred," Clément

[37] See Mufwene, *Ecology,* p. 114. This pattern of nonmingling, Mufwene notes, also characterizes patterns of European (chiefly Germanic) settlement in North America. British speakers in early medieval Wales, Helen Fulton observes, did not know that they were Welsh. Until Anglo-Saxons told them otherwise, they thought they were British ("Negotiating Welshness: Multilingualism in Wales before and after 1066," Conceptualizing Multilingualism in England 800–1250, a conference at the Centre for Medieval Studies, University of York, 14–17 July 2006).

[38] See *Welsh, OED,* 1a: "belonging to the native British population of England in contrast to the Anglo-Saxons." Walter W. Skeat, citing Anglo-Saxon *welisc,* notes that "*Welsh* properly means 'foreign'" (*An Etymological Dictionary of the English Language,* 2nd ed., ed. Skeat (Oxford: Clarendon, 1924), *Welsh* (p. 707b)).

[39] Catherine Clément and Julia Kristeva, *The Feminine and the Sacred,* trans. Jane Marie Todd (New York: Columbia University Press, 2001), pp. 5–10; *Le féminin et le sacré* (Paris: Stock, 1999), pp. 13–21. Citations in the text are to the English edition.

says, "similar to that of their African-Brazilian cousins in Bahia."[40] Here
in Senegal, there is *less* tolerance for such "trances of the candomblé"
than Nelson has found in Brazil:[41] the screaming African women are
strapped down and stretchered away by "first aid workers" (p. 7). Clément is describing this scene to Julia Kristeva; *Le féminine et le sacré* unfolds
as an epistolary exchange between these two Parisian academic *galac-
ticos*.[42] Epistolarity is an archaic form: there are moments in their exchange when the women think of e-mail (p. 91) or resort to fax (p. 163).
But it also provides, as a literary form, intimacy that grounds common
exploration of "the feminine and the sacred." Marilyn Nelson, herself
invested in these topics, also pursues them through contemporary relations evocative of archaic form: that of "fellowship," based on the Chaucerian model. Kristeva, in responding to Clément, recounts her recent
"vision of American 'Africanness'": "black ladies who manage the store
racks, the department offices of universities, the branch offices of banks,
and even, sometimes, the panels at symposiums" (p. 11).[43] There is little
sense here of personal encounter with "dames noires." Kristeva's account remains at a level of distanced abstraction typical of much French
writing on contemporary America.[44] Intimacy, following epistolary pro-
tocols, is reserved for Clément, Kristeva's French addressee. Nelson, by
contrast, takes her "fellowship," and all its expressive and intellectual

---

[40] *Feminine and the Sacred,* p. 7. "Sans doute parce que j'imagine une porosité particu-
lière aux femmes noires, je crois deviner chez elles un accès foudroyant au sacré, analogue à celui de leurs cousines afro-brésiliennes pendant les ceremonies 'candomblés' à
Bahia" (*Le féminin and le sacré,* p. 16).

[41] This counter-intuitive discovery might be compared to that of Nelson and company in her "Da Blues" section, where the music of the U.S. visitors is found to be *more*
authentic than that of the Bahian locals.

[42] Kristeva, in particular, writes in the aftermath of major lectures at major venues.
On 4 February 1997 she is at "the French House" at Oxford: "So ugly! So depressing!
A sort of seedy motel on the outskirts of the city, which makes me yearn desperately
for the old Gothic or Renaissance stones I had just left, the splendors of the Bodleian
Library, the sumptuous guest room at New College where I stayed on my first visit
here, and the 'Voltaire Room' in which I just gave my paper" (*Feminine and the Sacred,*
p. 42).

[43] "Elles ne sont nullement en transe, ces dames noires qui dirigent les rayons des
magasins, les administrations des universités, les agences bancaires et même, parfois, les
panels des symposiums et autres célébrations télévisuelles ou culturelles" (*Le féminin et le
sacré,* p. 23). Kristeva has just returned to Paris from delivering a lecture to the New
School, New York, "Hannah Arendt and the Concept of 'Life.'"

[44] Thus Jean Baudrillard: "Why do people live in New York? There is no relationship
between them" (*America,* trans. Chris Turner [London: Verso, 1988], p. 15). Such abstracted detachment extends to discussions of *blackness:* see Baudrillard, pp. 16–17;
Kristeva in Clément and Kristeva, *Feminine and the Sacred,* p. 21.

resources, with her on the road. The Chaucerian form thus proves a less distanced, more immediate means of encountering unfamiliar cultures. It also proves capable of creative adaptation as Nelson throws her party for thirty en route, dissolving differences between travelers and locals, natives and pilgrims. This is her most brilliant amendment of Chaucerian structure.

Geoffrey Chaucer might have been disappointed, in 2000, not to have merited a new bust at the London Guildhall or a memorial window in Southwark cathedral (such as he received in 1900).[45] But he might now relish his escape from such institutional and official memorializations: the figuration of cultural difference as historical distance, or the confusion of these categories, frees Chaucer up (or cuts him loose). Something about *The Canterbury Tales* does resonate with the Web-tracked globalism of our present time; this makes it wonderfully amenable to poets like Marilyn Nelson. Actors and rappers, poets and novelists, are reimagining our poet in new locales. The uncharted 2000s can be welcomed as the epoch of these new Chaucer topographies.

---

[45] See Ellis, *Chaucer at Large*, pp. 18–19. The reading of Chaucer by poet laureate Andrew Motion at Westminster Abbey in 2000, under the auspices of the New Chaucer Society, did attract about eight hundred people.

THE BIENNIAL CHAUCER LECTURE
The New Chaucer Society
Fifteenth International Congress
July 27–31, 2006
Fordham University

The Biennial Chaucer Lecture

For the Birds

Susan Crane
Columbia University

MY TITLE'S DISMISSIVE CLICHÉ, "that's for the birds," re-flects the low status that creatures other than human have held in liter-ary and wider cultural studies. At the same time, my title claims a contribution on this low-status question, which I think gets set aside because it's so complex, rather than so unimportant. Animals (conven-tional shorthand for animals other than human) have myriad, sometimes contradictory uses in medieval as in modern culture. A swan can be a dish at dinner, or an ancestor represented in a crest and seal, or a sign of good luck for sailors.[1] In *The Squire's Tale,* Chaucer draws on the genre of romance as a way into thinking about the cultural place of falcons. He presents the peregrine falcon of this tale as richly symbolic, but also as a living bird, raising the issue of species difference and the question of how to respond to this difference—what Chaucer would call differ-ence of "kynde."

For such a project, the genre of romance has several facilitating strengths. The genre's appreciation for exotic encounters, its worldly rather than theological commitments, and its easy suspension of ordi-nary realities allow for presenting contact with animals in positive terms. *Bevis of Hamtoun* and *Guy of Warwick,* both cited in *Sir Thopas,*

For their insightful comments on a preliminary draft of this lecture, I am grateful to Chris Chism, Rita Copeland, Karl Steel, and Paul Strohm.

[1] Peter Hammond, *Food and Feast in Medieval England* (Phoenix Mill, Gloucestershire: Sutton, 1993, rev. ed. 2005), pp. 135–36, 144–45; Anthony Richard Wagner, "The Swan Badge and the Swan Knight," *Archaeologia* 97 (1959): 127–38; Isidore of Seville, *Etymologies: Livre XII, Des animaux,* ed. and trans. Jacques André (Paris: Belles Lettres, 1986), pp. 236–39 (swans as signs of good luck: this information is repeated in most of the insular Bestiaries).

provide typical examples of such contact. Bevis's horse Arundel is not only his partner in battle but an independent actor on Bevis's behalf. At one point Arundel is nearly hanged for murdering one of Bevis's enemies, but Bevis prefers exile with his horse to life in England without him. Bevis names his principal manor after his horse, and he, horse, and wife die on the same day.[2] Guy of Warwick makes an alliance with a lion he rescues from a dragon. The lion follows Guy everywhere, fasts when Guy is ill, and drags himself to Guy's side to die of an enemy's wounds: "His hondes he gan to licky: þat was his loue, sikerly." Guy's sorrow nearly splits his heart, and he very soon splits the killer "Fram þe heued doun to þe fot."[3] In these romances, a powerful animal's devotion reflects well on the hero, and the hero's responding devotion also reflects well on him, even when it puts his life and his patrimony at risk.

Romances' opportunities for thinking about animals come with restrictions on the kinds of thinking they welcome. The genre's discursive and ideological limitations are as evident as its strengths: elite and secular in its orientations, narrative rather than scientific or philosophical in approach, romance is as partial as any other genre. Romance would not endorse the peasant's perspective on a nobleman's hawk, "Ha! that kite will eat a chicken tonight that would have sated my children."[4] Nor do romances adopt the clear distinctions of patristic and scholastic writing on animals: as Thomas Aquinas puts it, "irrational creatures can have

[2] *The Romance of Sir Beues of Hamtoun,* ed. Eugen Kölbing, 3 vols., EETS, e.s. 46, 48, 65 (London: Trübner, 1885, 1886, 1894), 1:165–218. *Bevis* and *Guy* appear in many manuscripts, including Edinburgh, Advocates' Library MS 19.2.1 (the Auchinleck MS). "Romances of prys . . . Of Beves and sir Gy": Geoffrey Chaucer, *The Canterbury Tales,* in *The Riverside Chaucer,* 3rd ed., ed. Larry Benson (Boston: Houghton Mifflin, 1987), p. 216 (*Sir Thopas,* VII 897–99). Subsequent references to Chaucer's works in my text are cited in parentheses from this edition, by line number or fragment and line number.

[3] *The Romance of Guy of Warwick: The First or 14th-century Version,* ed. Julius Zupitza, EETS, e.s. 42, 49, 59 (London: Oxford University Press, 1883, 1887, 1891), 1: 236–55: quotations at Auchinleck lines 4335–36, 4393. "When Gij þat lyoun wounded seþ, / For sorwe him þouȝt his hert clef": Auchinleck lines 4337–38.

[4] Edmond Faral, "Des vilains, ou des XXII manières de vilains," *Romania* 48 (1922): 251 ("Ha! fait il, cil huas mangera enquenuit une geline et mi enfant en fuissent tuit saoul!") The peasant of this thirteenth-century satire is called "canine" for his ignoble perspective, not least in conflating a sparrow-hawk with the inferior kite, but his point that captive hawks were fed on domestic birds is entirely accurate. On the diet and expense of keeping hawks, see Robin S. Oggins, *The Kings and Their Hawks: Falconry in Medieval England* (New Haven: Yale University Press, 2004), pp. 22, 25, 30, 109–17, 129–30. On the "noble" falcon and "ignoble" kite, see Dafydd Evans, "The Nobility of Knight and Falcon," in *The Ideals and Practice of Medieval Knighthood III: Papers from the Fourth Strawberry Hill Conference, 1988* (Woodbridge, Suffolk: Boydell, 1990), pp. 79–99.

no share in human life, which of its nature is rational, and therefore no friendship [*amicitia*] is possible with them."[5] In this dichotomizing spirit, an English sermon condemns a man for weeping not over Christ's sacrifice but over *Guy of Warwick*, "when he came to the place where it dealt with the gratitude of the lion and how it was cut into three."[6] Closer to romance's sensibilities than official science and theology were pervasive lay convictions about animals' similarities to humans. Birds were conceived (and, according to Claude Lévi-Strauss, were still conceived in modern France) as making up a society with a metaphoric relation to human society, in which birdsong fills the function of human language.[7] Each section of *The Squire's Tale* begins by invoking this commonplace of courtly and romantic poetry: all the birds "songen hire affectiouns" at the arrival of spring; the next morning, Canacee understands their songs as she wears her magic ring (V.55, 398–400). Italian and Provençal poets describe birds singing "ciascuno in suo latino," each in its own Latin; Chaucer writes that Canacee understands her "haukes *ledene*" (V.478), a term for both Latin and language.[8] The reference to "Latin" strikes an analogy between birdsong and human speech, on the one hand, and Latin and vernaculars, on the other. "Hawk Latin" gets its plausibility from the differences among human languages: why not an animal language that is similarly obscure to humans, but similarly functional for its own speakers? The communicative, resourceful animals of romance express, in highly imaginative terms, a widespread convic-

[5] Thomas Aquinas, *Summa Theologiae*, vol. 34, ed. and trans. R. J. Batten (New York: McGraw-Hill, 1975), pp. 88–89 (2a2ae. 25, 3).

[6] Andrea Hopkins, *The Sinful Knights: A Study of Middle English Penitential Romance* (Oxford: Clarendon Press, 1990), p. 75; cited in Melissa Furrow, "Radial Categories and the Central Romance," *Florilegium* 22 (2005): 133.

[7] Claude Lévi-Strauss, *The Savage Mind* (London: Weidenfeld and Nicolson, 1966), pp. 204–8; examples of birds' vocalization represented as speech abound in Chaucer's *Parliament of Fowls, Complaint of Mars,* and *Nun's Priest's Tale.* Scientific and philosophical works argue against the analogy between birdsong and human speech, but their resistance is another indication of the analogy's currency: see the first chapter of Elizabeth Eva Leach, *Sung Birds: Music, Nature, and Poetry in the Later Middle Ages* (Ithaca: Cornell University Press, 2006).

[8] Guido Cavalcante, *Rime,* ed. Domenico de Robertis (Turin: Giulio Einaudi, 1986), p. 5, line 11 and n. citing the same expression in Bonagiunta da Lucca ("ciascun canta in suo latino"); William IX of Aquitaine, *Poesie,* ed. Nicolò Pasero (Modena: S.T.E.M.-Mucchi, 1973), p. 250, line 3 ("chanton chascus en lor lati") and p. 254 n. citing the same expression in lyrics of Cercamon, Marcabru, Arnaut Daniel, and others. *Middle English Dictionary,* ed. Hans Kurath et al. (Ann Arbor: University of Michigan Press, 1952–), *ledene:* (1) the Latin language; (2) (a) a language (b) speech, utterance; (3) (a) birdsong; also, the language of birds.

tion that humans and animals share contiguities beyond their mere physicality. These contiguities, like other preoccupations of romance such as chivalry, nation, adventure, and sexuality, deserve scholars' attention despite the challenge of romance's peculiar tone, by turns idealizing and critical, committed and ironic.

In scholarly circles, it's a good moment for *The Squire's Tale*. Emerging from a few decades of disrepute as no more than the clumsy utterance of its youthful teller, this tale is looking much more substantial as scholars consider its representations of an eastern kingdom and of womanhood as interpenetrating kinds of difference.[9] Animal difference interpenetrates these two, I will argue, as *The Squire's Tale* draws on both romance's preoccupation with animal allegiances and the courtly complaint's preoccupation with the perils of love: in Alfred David's memorable phrase, *The Squire's Tale* is Anelida's story "recycled—with feathers."[10] Some scholars dismiss the issue of cross-species contact in *The Squire's Tale* by proposing that the female peregrine, the formel, is probably an enchanted princess.[11] This view is neither sustainable nor refutable, given the tale's irresolution; but whether the formel is or is not *also* a human hardly makes her "kynde" less problematic. Indeed, it redoubles the species question, by taking her to be not only different from Canacee as bird from woman, but divided within herself as woman and bird. Most evidently, she's not simply human within, and animal without, since her heart belongs to a tercel, a male falcon, along with her feathers. The question of animal difference could only be dismissed by declaring every bird in the tale to be no more and no less than human.

Instead, Chaucer presses the species question by installing the peregrine in frameworks of gentility, femininity, and adventure that are central to romance. Her animal difference may seem compromised in her

---

[9] The turn from centuries of admiration to disrepute is most marked in Gardiner Stillwell, "Chaucer in Tartary," *RES* 24 (1948): 177–88. The argument against thinking of this tale as a function of its teller gets substantial articulation in David Lawton, *Chaucer's Narrators* (Woodbrige, Suffolk: D. S. Brewer, 1985), pp. 106–29. Critical attention to gender as a function of the exotic in this tale begins with John Fyler, "Domesticating the Exotic in the *Squire's Tale*," *ELH* 55 (1988): 1–26. For a complete overview, see *Chaucer's Physician's, Squire's, and Franklin's Tales. An Annotated Bibliography, 1900–2000*, ed. Kenneth Bleeth (Toronto: University of Toronto Press, forthcoming 2007).

[10] Alfred David, "Recycling *Anelida and Arcite*: Chaucer as a Source for Chaucer," *SAC, Proceedings* 1 (1984): 105–15 (quotation at p. 110).

[11] See *A Variorum Edition of the Works of Geoffrey Chaucer*, vol. 2, *The Canterbury Tales*, pt. 12, *The Squire's Tale*, ed. Donald C. Baker (Norman: University of Oklahoma Press, 1990), pp. 15–17.

several analogies with the tale's human characters, but I will argue that Chaucer's interest in animals encompasses his interest in how they are enmeshed in human culture. Specifically, the tale's representation of the falcon is crucial to its representation of difference within human societies, yet her species remains salient as Canacee takes pity on her and attempts to shelter her. I'll divide the question of species difference into three parts, the first concentrating on the peregrine's symbolic functions, the second on her relation to the exotic, and the third on her "kynde" and cross-species compassion.

A Symbolic Loop

Naturalists along the East Coast are elated that, less than a mile from this room, two red-tailed hawks have built their nest on the 35th-floor ledge of an apartment tower overlooking Central Park. Coverage of this nesting in the *New York Times* quotes the building's current owner, Donald Trump: "I am honored by their choice of my building." He explains that the hawks honor him by endorsing his eye for real estate: "They know a lot about location." And there's more than location at issue: we can be certain that The Donald would not feel honored if pigeons nested on his buildings. Yet of the nesting hawks, Trump concludes with pride, "This could only happen to me."[12]

In medieval cultures as well as today, honor is accrued from association with some animals, and dishonor from association with others. These associations pass the real animal through a symbolic process imputing to it qualities such as nobility or courage, that are then transferred to humans who associate with it. *The Sibley Guide to Birds* notes that the peregrine falcon "has long been considered the embodiment of speed and power. . . . It hunts . . . from high above in spectacular stoops."[13] Woodford's *Manual of Falconry* calls the female peregrine "the most spectacular bird to be employed in falconry," giving her extraordinary value in this elite and enclaved sport.[14] For her importance in

---

[12] Thomas J. Lueck, "Four Hawks, Two Nests, One Empty," *New York Times,* April 21, 2006, Late Edition (East Coast), p. B 5.

[13] David Allen Sibley, *National Audubon Society: The Sibley Guide to Birds* (New York: Alfred A. Knopf, 2000), p. 133.

[14] Michael Woodford, *A Manual of Falconry* (London: Adam & Charles Black, 1960), p. 3; similarly Philip Glasier, *Falconry and Hawking* (Woodstock, N.Y.: Overlook Press, 1998), p. 24: "For performance of the very highest quality, the peregrine leaves all the others far behind. Her most valuable trait is undoubtedly her persistence. I know of no other falcon which has this virtue to so great a degree."

hawking and her showy aggression, medieval writers call her "noble" and "molt cortois et vaillans" (very courtly and brave); in medieval iconography, a bird of prey on the fist conveys high social status.[15] This "circular loop of symbolic transfer," as anthropologist James Howe calls it, may begin in subjective judgments about which species have merit, but the circularity obscures this founding subjectivity so that it becomes unclear where the assertion of merit originates.[16] The catalogue of birds in Chaucer's *Parliament of Fowls* provides a condensed example in "the gentyl faucoun, that with his feet distrayneth / The kynges hand" (lines 337–38). Is the falcon "gentil" because it is preferred by kings, or is the king's gentility secured by his association with this "noble" and "valiant" bird? When we can no longer answer one way or the other, the symbolic loop neatly closes.

A specific kind of totemic thinking informs this use of birds for marking human status. Lévi-Strauss's reassessment of earlier work argued that totemism's primary usefulness is not to connect humans to animals, but to make analogies between species differences, on the one hand, and human status differences, on the other.[17] Totemic thought explains lineal and social distinctions among humans by reference to species distinctions. The evident difference between sparrows and falcons is recruited to make the difference between peasants and princes look natural. The superior merit of female falcons, formels, who are larger and bolder than the male tercels, is appropriate for an adventure illustrating female excellence.

The naturalizing power of totemic thought is certainly in play in *The Squire's Tale,* as well as in Donald Trump's remark that "this could only happen to me." But *The Squire's Tale* is also fascinated by cross-species affinity. Poststructuralist expansions of Lévi-Strauss's work have recuperated totemism's cross-species connections. Its claims are metonymic, not just analogous. In specific late medieval cases, the blood of a serpent

---

[15] *Variorum Edition,* ed. Baker, p. 207 (quoting the *Tresor de Brunet Latin*); Baudouin van den Abeele, *La fauconnerie dans les lettres françaises du XIIe au XIVe siècle* (Louvain: Presses Universitaires de Louvain, 1990), pp. 194–97; Evans, "Nobility of Knight and Falcon." Calling a falcon "noble" elides the hundreds of hours of labor required to tame and train a hawk to sit on a noble fist and hunt at a noble's bidding. Canacee's immediate rapport with the formel similarly elides the practical work of falconry, as if their connection were entirely natural.

[16] James Howe, "Fox Hunting as Ritual," *American Ethnologist* 8 (1981): 291.

[17] Claude Lévi-Strauss, *Totemism,* trans. Rodney Needham (Boston: Beacon Press, 1963).

or a swan distinguishes Melusine's and Elias's descendants from other lineages.[18] The falcon's first words to Canacee articulate both kinds of totemic connection—both an analogous superiority and a metonymy of hearts—that link woman to bird:

> That pitee renneth soone in gentil herte,
> Feelynge his similitude in peynes smerte,
> Is preved alday, as men may it see,
> As wel by werk as by auctoritee;
> For gentil herte kitheth gentillesse.
>
> (V.479–83)

Canacee's "similitude" to the falcon is a mutually reinforcing proof of their shared superiority. This symbolic loop is appropriately expressed in the virtually pleonastic "gentil herte kitheth gentillesse." A cross-species connection supplements their analogous excellence in the falcon's assertion that her "gentil herte" is her point of similitude with Canacee. This metonymy of gentle hearts elides the physical difference between princess and peregrine. Hearts connect them if appearances do not.

Metonymy's fragmentary, prosthetic enhancements can have awkward side effects. It's risky using animals to accrue merit to humans. In James Howe's example from modern hunting, foxhounds are said to be the "aristocrats" and "noble animals" of their species, so that their superiority among canines can reflect well on the huntsmen in contact with them, but Howe specifies that "the humans involved keep the identification partial and controlled. They do not wish to suggest inadvertently that they eat horsemeat, sniff each others' rear ends, or tear foxes apart with their teeth."[19] Rather than playing it safe with princess and peregrine, *The Squire's Tale* veers beyond their gentle hearts into their bodily differences. This falcon is superior to all others "as wel of plumage as of gentillesse" (V.426). She grows up not in a palace but "in a roche of marbul gray" (V.500): it's the right stone, but oddly un-

---

[18] Anthropologists such as Stanley Tambiah, J. C. Crocker, and John Borneman acknowledge the differentiating work of totemism, but they also refocus attention on the connection with animals that totemism often asserts: see Susan Crane, *The Performance of Self: Ritual, Clothing, and Identity During the Hundred Years War* (Philadelphia: University of Pennsylvania Press, 2002), pp. 107–25; on descendants of Melusine and Elias, see pp. 108–11.

[19] Howe, "Fox Hunting," p. 290.

dressed into architecture. She takes her faithless lover's hand just before he flies away (V.596, 605). Why this persistent emphasis on her status as a creature? Her totemic connections to Canacee are only part of the answer. As I've been outlining, the falcon's species difference is crucial to her enhancement of Canacee's status, validating her human merit from beyond the realm of the human. In the second and third sections of this talk, I'll suggest that the falcon's difference from humankind comments as well on the category of the "straunge," the foreign and exotic, and on the concept of "kynde," natural species and sympathies.

"Straunge"

Helen Cooper has compared the two parts of *The Squire's Tale* to a chapter from Jules Verne, followed by a chapter from Henry James.[20] The first part teems with strange sights and smells and wonders of science and magic; the second, in comparison, is intimate, confessional, and reflective. Yet the two parts are also analogues of each other. By keeping the falcon's beak and feathers in view, Chaucer aligns species difference with cultural difference. In each part of the tale, a visitor from afar brings Mongol royalty an unexpected invitation to encounter the "straunge" on adventure. The "strange knyght . . . of Arabe and of Inde" who presents Canacee's father with adventure provoking gifts is echoed in the "faucon peregryn . . . of fremde land" who presents Canacee with her feminine adventure (V.89, 110, 428–29). Since "peregrine" already means "coming from foreign parts," adding that she is "of foreign land" is emphatic.[21] The structural parallel between the tale's first and second parts suggests that the species differences of the latter comment on the cultural differences of the former.

One helpful way of thinking about difference in *The Squire's Tale* has been to notice how well romance serves orientalism. I'll briefly evoke this important argument, but moving beyond it is my purpose. Whether we think of the tale's narrating voice as the Squire's or Chaucer's, its position is unmistakably within masculine courtesy, within Christianity, and well to the west of Tartarye. From this position, the narration tends to represent cultural difference in positive terms, as ex-

[20] Helen Cooper, *The Canterbury Tales,* Oxford Guides to Chaucer, 2nd ed. (Oxford: Oxford University Press, 1996), pp. 222–23.
[21] *Chaucer: The Squire's Tale,* ed. Dorothy Bethurum (Oxford: Clarendon Press, 1965), p. 44, line 428 n.

otic but finally unthreatening. The Mongol king Cambyuskan keeps an unnamed religious law peculiar to his birth, yet he manifests at least eight virtues conventional to kingship, such as wisdom, mercy, courage, honor, and justice (V.17–27). Of the "straunge" foods consumed at Sarraye, only the familiar delicacies swan and heron are named (V.67–68). The yet more "straunge" Mamluk emissary from Middle India "out-Easts the East," in Kathryn Lynch's phrase, yet both his decorum and the Mongol court's are said to match perfectly the courtesies of Gawain and Lancelot.[22] The tale can look entirely orientalizing at such points: that is, entirely committed to evoking an Eastern strangeness in order to master and incorporate it. Anthropomorphism translates orientalism into cross-species terms: the falcon is rendered so like a courtly lady that her alien species appears to be accessible and even familiar.

Orientalism and romance have much in common: the genre's very heartbeat is difference encountered and then encompassed so as to enhance the prestige of gentilesse. In romance, whatever might appear alien turns out to be accessible, even as a residual strangeness preserves its special value.[23] The feminine is orientalism's most recurring image for the exotic East and romance's most characteristic ground for adventure. In *The Squire's Tale,* the narrator's expansive favoring of women both sets them apart and claims to know them, in categorical pronouncements on women: Canacee is "ful mesurable, as wommen be"; her encounter illustrates the "trouthe that is in wommen sene" (V.362, 645). Canacee's Mongol birth doubles her exotic femininity; her intimacy with a falcon redoubles it; and yet their encounter is coded in a familiar courtly idiom of pledges and deceptions, honor and despair.

[22] Kathryn L. Lynch, "East Meets West in Chaucer's Squire's and Franklin's Tales," *Speculum* 70 (1995): 530–51 (quotation at p. 541). See also Kenneth Bleeth, "Orientalism and the Critical History of the Squire's Tale," in *Chaucer's Cultural Geography,* ed. Kathryn L. Lynch (New York: Routledge, 2002), pp. 21–31; and Jenna Mead, "Reading by Said's Lantern: Orientalism and Chaucer's *Treatise on the Astrolabe,*" *Medieval Encounters* 5 (1999): 350–57. On the political complexities pertaining at the time of the tale's composition, see Carolyn P. Collette and Vincent J. DiMarco, "The Matter of Armenia in the Age of Chaucer," *SAC* 23 (2001): 317–58; and Alan S. Ambrisco, "'It lyth nat in my tonge': Occupatio and Otherness in the *Squire's Tale,*" *ChauR* 38 (2003–4): 205–28.

[23] *The Squire's Tale* does preserve whiffs of the exotic: the Tartar king's alien law is conventionally virtuous, but it remains undescribed and unassimilated to the tale's narrative position inside Christianity. The magical birthday gifts are susceptible to learned explanation, but finally they remain unexplained, and those who attempt explanation get little sympathy from the narrator. The narrator champions women with categorical praise, setting them above and apart from men: see Richard Firth Green, "Chaucer's Victimized Women," *SAC* 10 (1988): 3–21.

Chaucer's tale reflects romantic orientalism but moves beyond it as well. Sara Suleri Goodyear points out that analysis of literature on India can be constrained when it simply adopts orientalism's dualities of West and East, center and margin, and its ideology of appropriation and control. Suleri argues that British narratives about India by Kipling, Forster, and others betray some contradictory aspects of India's relation to Britain, such as a decentering inherent in the encounter, a disturbing breakdown of alterity, and a discovery of congruence in the opposing cultures' economies of desire.[24] Suleri's argument would question whether romantic orientalism in *The Squire's Tale* accounts for all its concerns. Here, I believe, is the revision that the tale's second part works on the first. It raises the alterity quotient, from cross-cultural relations to cross-species relations, but it turns from emphasizing alterity to exploding and collapsing it, in a tangle of connections, analogies, and migrating sensibilities. Part of the effect here is surely to complicate the question of cross-cultural difference, and part of the effect is just as surely to raise the question of cross-species difference. In *The Squire's Tale*'s second part, the orientalized "other" shifts from the Eastern to the animal realm. At the same time, differences here proliferate and dissolve, loosening orientalism's hold on species difference and Eastern exoticism alike.

I stressed at the outset that the tale's peregrine falcon, the formel, either is simply not human or is herself divided between human and bird—and this indeterminate condition is a first refusal of species dichotomy. Another refusal of dichotomy overlaps her language and Canacee's. At first it seems Canacee will need the magic ring, a perfect manifestation of animal orientalizing, a decoder of strange avian meanings. Instead, Canacee and the formel turn out not entirely to need it. The falcon begins by shrieking rather than speaking: "ever in oon she cryde alwey and shrighte" (V.417). Yet Canacee "hath understonde what this faucon *seyde*" before she asks the falcon to explain her cries in words (V.437). The formel's shrieks preserve a specific peculiarity of hawks: they have no song, but if fowlers do not handle them with caution, they imprint on humans and become "screamers." Fredrick II's *Art of Falconry* advises on ways to avoid this behavior.[25] Chaucer grafts

---

[24] Sara Suleri, *The Rhetoric of English India* (Chicago: University of Chicago Press, 1992).

[25] Latin *clamorosi:* Frederick II, *De arte venandi cum avibus,* ed. Carl Arnold Willemsen (Leipzig: in aedibus Insulae, 1942), pp. 136, 145; *The Art of Falconry, Being the De Arte Venandi cum Avibus of Frederick II of Hohenstaufen,* trans. Casey A. Wood and F. Marjorie Fyfe (Stanford: Stanford University Press, 1943), pp. 129, 136. Modern manuals agree,

courtly complaint onto peregrine screams, and Canacee "hath understonde" both of them. I've argued elsewhere that the two creatures share a feminine language of embodiment, and here I'd only add that their shared language undercuts the magic ring's dichotomous premise.[26]

The formel's cross-species allegiance with a princess joins in her ongoing experience of wrenching redefinitions, which she characteristically figures as interspecies migrations: she is an example for other creatures as the whipped dog is an example for taming lions; her lover is a tiger but one with knees to fall on in fake humility; he is a snake hidden under flowers who longs to eat worms like a captured songbird.[27] The caged bird passage is the formel's fullest expression of her disorientations:

> I trowe he hadde thilke text in mynde,
> That "alle thyng, repeirynge to his kynde,
> Gladeth hymself;" thus seyn men, as I gesse.
> Men loven of propre kynde newefangelnesse,
> As briddes doon that men in cages fede.
> For though thou nyght and day take of hem hede,
> And strawe hir cage faire and softe as silk,
> And yeve hem sugre, hony, breed and milk,
> Yet right anon as that his dore is uppe
> He with his feet wol spurne adoun his cuppe,
> And to the wode he wole and wormes ete;
> So newefangel been they of hire mete,
> And loven novelries of propre kynde,
> No gentillesse of blood ne may hem bynde.
>
> (V.607–20)

John Fyler has brilliantly detailed the ways in which this exemplum's "tenor and vehicle, number and gender keep reversing and dissolving

---

e.g., Glasier, *Falconry and Hawking,* p. 112: "a 'screamer'. . . is most undesirable, particularly so in the case of falcons, who tend to have extremely penetrating voices and will sometimes scream for hours on end without apparently getting the slightest bit hoarse."

[26] Susan Crane, *Gender and Romance in Chaucer's "Canterbury Tales"* (Princeton: Princeton University Press, 1994), pp. 73–76.

[27] On taming lions by whipping dogs (*Squire's Tale,* V 491), see John S. P. Tatlock, "Chaucer's Whelp and Lion," *MLN* 38 (1923): 506–7; Calvin S. Brown Jr. and Robert H. West, "'As by the Whelp Chastised is the Leon,'" *MLN* 55 (1940): 209–10; and Grace Frank, "As by the Whelp Chastised is the Leon," *MLN* 55 (1940): 481. On the tiger's doubleness (*Squire's Tale,* V 543–44), see Melvin Storm, "The Tercelet as Tiger: Bestiary Hypocrisy in the Squire's Tale," *ELN* 14 (1977): 172–74.

into each other."[28] The false *tercel* is one of those *men* who love novelty "of propre kynde," as captive songbirds love worms. The tercel joins humans on the comparison's literal plane, and the caged bird becomes figurative. Gender distinction cuts at right angles across the falcon's species conflation. "Men" slides from designating humanity and falcons in general to designating the specifically masculine flightiness of the tercel, the caged bird, and faithless male humans.[29] Gender difference is more persistent, and more perilous, than species difference.

The queasily shifting distinctions of the formel's desperate complaint run counter to orientalism, in which "the exotic" is foundationally different, and then appropriated. As the tale's second part comments on the first, difference becomes less secure, and managing it looks less certain. Most notoriously, an unassimilated suggestion of incest (or is it bigamy?) closes the summary of the events to come; further, Cambalo will confuse the formel's dichotomous view of the sexes by siding with her to win back her lover (V.651–70).[30] To be sure, romantic orientalism does mark Canacee and the formel, especially when their affiliation with each other is expressed as their difference from all male creatures. But even as their cross-species affinity exoticizes them, affinity also transcends the species difference that could distinguish them from each other, contributing to the formel's general experience of disorientation. The falseness of male creatures has united them in one dangerous "kynde," leaving her a helpless migrant in a "fremde land." Soon, Ca-

---

[28] Fyler, "Domesticating the Exotic," p. 17. The caged bird passage has received commentary too ample to document adequately here; see Bleeth's annotated bibliography (note 9 above).

[29] In *Gender and Romance,* pp. 66–73, I trace this passage's shifting gender alignments in relation to Chaucer's source passages from the *Consolation of Philosophy* and the *Roman de la Rose.*

[30] *Variorum Edition,* ed. Baker, pp. 241–42, summarizes commentary on incest, bigamy, or authorial/editorial lapse in these closing lines; recently Elizabeth Scala has argued for incest over bigamy or lapse: *Absent Narratives, Manuscript Textuality, and Literary Structure in Late Medieval England* (New York: Palgrave, 2002), pp. 71–98. The *Squire's Tale*'s compact plot summary at V 651–70 suggests that the tale is deliberately fragmentary. Abbreviation may have had some practical appeal for Chaucer (such as evasion of the genre's bulk, reticence about the plot, or dissatisfaction with his execution of the tale). More evident than any practical strategy in the tale's fragmentariness is the aesthetic of its evocative but disorienting projections: William Kamowski, "Trading the 'Knotte' for Loose Ends: The *Squire's Tale* and the Poetics of Chaucerian Fragments," *Style* 31 (1997): 391–412, aligns the tale with Coleridge's "Kubla Khan," another evocation of Eastern wonders that resorts to suspension in order to escape containment. He cites Marjorie Levinson on Romantic fragments: "A work that is never consumed can never be exhausted" (p. 398).

nacee will attempt a healing reconfiguration of the formel's shattering experience. Now, as the formel faints away in Canacee's lap, her best hope lies in the kindness of strangers.

"Kynde"

A long-standing argument in ethics seeks to determine how we should distribute our compassion. Should we care most for those most proximate? Do our particular nation, estate, sex, faith, or species have superior claims to those of others? Unchecked, the argument from proximity sustains practices that may be thought unappealing, such as misogyny, slavery, and oppression of the poor, so that a countercurrent in ethics presses for extending compassion to all living creatures, or at least to all humans.[31] The contradictory pressures in this ethical problem are encapsulated in the term "kynde." When Canacee swears to help the falcon "as wisly help me grete God of kynde" (V.469), she invokes both the divisions and hierarchies of created things (their kinds and species) and the loving disposition that unifies created things (kindness and benevolence).

Boethius's *Consolation of Philosophy* is Chaucer's closest source for the argument that God's creation is both diverse and united in love. In the *Parliament of Fowls,* for example, Nature declares to all the birds that the eagle will first choose a mate, because he is the worthiest, "And after hym by ordre shul ye chese, / After youre kynde," that is, according to

---

[31] In this debate, creatures other than human are considered from ancient Greek philosophy onward, but are typically set aside as too different from humans to be of ethical concern: a fine overview is Richard Sorabji, *Animal Minds and Human Morals: The Origins of the Western Debate* (Ithaca: Cornell University Press, 1993). Recent debates on ethical relationships between humans and animals tend to take place through utilitarianism, environmental ethics, and revisions to contractarian philosophy: see, for example, *Singer and His Critics,* ed. Dale Jamieson (Oxford: Blackwell, 1999), especially the essays of Richard J. Arneson, Colin McGinn, and Richard Holton and Rae Langton; Cora Diamond, *The Realistic Spirit: Wittgenstein, Philosophy, and the Mind* (Cambridge, Mass.: MIT Press, 1991), pp. 319–34 ("Eating Meat and Eating People"); and Martha C. Nussbaum, "Beyond 'Compassion and Humanity': Justice for Nonhuman Animals," in *Animal Rights: Current Debates,* ed. Cass Sunstein and Martha Nussbaum (Oxford: Oxford University Press, 2004), pp. 299–320. By the logic of the argument from proximity, human groups deemed unworthy of compassion are often aligned with animals: see, for example, Paul H. Freedman, "The Representation of Medieval Peasants as Bestial and as Human," in *The Animal/Human Boundary: Historical Perspectives,* ed. Angela N. H. Creager and William Chester Jordan (Rochester: University of Rochester Press, 2002), pp. 29–49; Marjorie Spiegel, *The Dreaded Comparison: Human and Animal Slavery* (New York: Mirror Books, 1996).

a hierarchy of species (lines 400–401). The birds' love for their mates expresses their "kynde" in its other aspect, reflecting God's unifying love. Boethius explains that the world's "chaungynges" and "contrarious qualites" are bound in harmony by the same love that "halt togidres peples joyned with an holy boond, and knytteth sacrement of mariages of chaste loves; and love enditeth lawes to trewe felawes. O weleful were mankynde, yif thilke love that governeth hevene governede yowr corages."[32] Thus it's doubly appropriate for Canacee to swear by the "grete God of kynde" as she addresses another species, and expresses a bond between them: "Ye sle me with youre sorwe verraily, / I have of yow so greet compassioun" (V.462–63).

Chaucer resists the simple clarity of Boethius's position on "kynde." In the *Parliament of Fowls,* the hierarchy of species is not evidently just, despite Nature's endorsement, and the closing song of love only partly counteracts the tensions among species. Boethius, in contrast, praises natural order in his exemplum of the caged bird, which rightly longs for its created place in the woods.[33] Chaucer's two revisions of the caged bird exemplum (the other from *The Manciple's Tale*) place little faith in "kynde" in its sense of natural characteristics. Instead, the caged bird's "propre kynde" misleads it into desiring "wormes and swich wrecchednesse" (IX 171). Mistrusting the "kynde" of physical nature, Chaucer prefers its complement in creation, the lovingkindness that can unite one creature to another. The falcon's opening remark to Canacee, "pitee renneth soone in gentil herte," specifies that her "pitee" is fellow-feeling or empathy:

> I se wel that ye han of my distresse
> Compassioun, my faire Canacee,
> Of verray wommanly benignytee
> That Nature in youre principles hath set.
> (V.483–87)

---

[32] *Riverside Chaucer, Boece,* Book II, Metrum 8 (pp. 420–21). This "kynde" love that unites is exemplified in "Christ's mooder meeke and kynde" (*Prioress's Tale,* VII 597).

[33] *Boece,* Book III, Metrum 2 (p. 423): "Alle thynges seken ayen to hir propre cours, and alle thynges rejoysen hem of hir retornynge ayen to hir nature." Lady Philosophy uses the term "kynde" in her teaching that "Alle kende tendeth" to God, the beginning and end of all things: *Boece,* Book I, Prosa 6 (p. 406). See Lynn Sadler, "Chaucer's *The Book of the Duchess* and the "Law of Kinde," *Annuale Mediaevale* 11 (1970): 51–64; Hugh White, *Nature, Sex, and Goodness in a Medieval Literary Tradition* (Oxford: Oxford University Press, 2000), pp. 68–109, 220–55.

Canacee's natural compassion for a fellow creature opposes the tercel's natural disposition for "newefangelnesse." Her cross-"kynde" empathy is a remarkable extension of anything in Boethius. For Boethius, as for medieval philosophy in general, human compassion expresses God's love *within* humankind.[34] Yet *The Squire's Tale* presses us to take Canacee's compassion seriously by setting up a structural parallel between the Mamluk emissary in the tale's first part and the peregrine "of fremde lond" in the second part. The emissary is warmly entertained at court following his presentation of gifts; the falcon is also sheltered at court following her long complaint. Both are shown hospitality, a highly valued practice in romances, but part two raises the stakes on part one.[35] Kindness, if it truly reflects the love unifying creation, should move across human differences and across species lines as well. The shift from part one's masculine register to the feminine register of part two renders Canacee's hospitality as a dependent, quite literally diminutive, version of her father's hospitality. Perhaps only this feminine register could entertain a concept so counter-hegemonic as cross-species empathy.

Hospitality, in its compassionate welcome to the stranger, expresses the unifying and differentiating tensions of "kynde" in a specific social practice. The stranger is welcomed into a space that is unfamiliar and potentially constraining. This contradiction within hospitality was so salient for Jacques Derrida that he renamed the practice "hostipitality," to recall the discredited but appealing medieval French etymology connecting *hospes,* host-guest-stranger, with *obses,* hostage. The perceived connection between "host" and "hostage" continued from Old French

---

[34] Similarly: "The love of charity extends solely to God and our neighbor, but 'neighbor' cannot be understood to include irrational creatures, because they do not share man's rational life. Therefore charity does not extend to them": Aquinas, *Summa Theologiae,* 34: 88–89 (2a2ae.25, 3).

[35] For the early Christian as for the medieval period, *hospitalitas* referred especially to welcoming, sheltering, and protecting travelers and strangers, in contrast to the *caritas* shown to neighbors. *MED,* s.v. *hospitalite,* attests emphasis in both secular and religious literature. On hospitality in romances, see Matilda Tomaryn Bruckner, *Narrative Invention in Twelfth-Century French Romance: The Convention of Hospitality, 1160–1200* (Lexington, Ky.: French Forum, 1980). On biblical exhortations to hospitality (e.g., Matthew 25:34–46, Romans 12:13, Hebrews 13:2, 1 Peter 4:9), see Andrew E. Arterbury, *Early Christian Hospitality in Its Mediterranean Setting* (Sheffield: Sheffield Phoenix, 2005), pp. 94–132. On medieval and early modern practices, see Hans Conrad Peyer, *Gastfreundschaft und kommerzielle Gastlichkeit im Mittelalter* (Munich: Stiftung Historisches Kolleg, 1983); Felicity Heal, *Hospitality in Early Modern England* (Oxford: Clarendon Press, 1990).

into Middle English.[36] Derrida points out that hospitality's welcome is based in the host's control of the household, so that the stranger enters "the internal law of the host . . . which tends to begin by dictating the law of its language . . . which is to say, its own concepts as well."[37] Because her strangeness is the precondition for extending hospitality to her, the hosted falls hostage to the strange ways of the host. Derrida wrote primarily in relation to human displacements, but he argued that the limit cases for hospitality would cross beyond the human to hosting divinities or animals: to Lot receiving angels for the night, Noah taking animals on board, and even Jonah's painful sheltering in the whale.[38]

The second part of *The Squire's Tale* engages the contradiction of hospitality more fully than the first part's enthusiastic orientalizing. Cambyuskan's hospitality to the Mamluk emissary appears unproblematic, their differences both evident and transcended in a chivalric code linking Mongol, Mamluk, and Arthurian knights in one big brotherhood.[39] To take up the most literal aspect of the law of the host that begins "by dictating the law of its language," the emissary speaks "After the forme used in his langage," yet also "withouten vice of silable or of lettre" (V.100–101): the narrator can accommodate an occulted Mamluk rhetoric as easily as Cambyuskan accommodates the emissary himself. Canacee's hosting would also seem an easy task, not a limit case, since she shares so many qualities with the peregrine and since their totemic relationship so enhances her status. But species difference sharpens the challenge to hospitality.

The little mews Canacee constructs is a wonderfully complex attempt at hosting without taking hostage. It makes a number of false starts, and perhaps never succeeds except in the persistence and resourcefulness of its attempts at cross-species compassion. In size, it recalls the birdcage

---

[36] Jacques Derrida, "Hostipitality," trans. Barry Stocker with Forbes Morlock, *Angelaki* 5:3 (December 2000): 3–18; *The Oxford English Dictionary,* 2nd ed. (Oxford: Clarendon Press, 1989), *host* (sb.[1] and sb.[2]) and *hostage* (sb.[1]).

[37] Derrida, "Hostipitality," *Angelaki,* p. 7.

[38] Derrida, "Hostipitality," trans. Gil Anidjar, in *Acts of Religion,* ed. Gil Anidjar (New York: Routledge, 2002), pp. 363–65. Despite their identical titles, the two Derrida essays cover some different ground.

[39] Christine Chism suggests in correspondence that the gifts may hint at a less than congenial relation between Mongol and Mamluk, because they could endanger their users; Cambyuskan could be responding to this danger "by locking up the 'masculine' chivalric gifts, and allowing the 'feminine' ones to play out only domestically." This reading intensifies the differences within the "exotic east," and discovers a tension within hospitality between welcome and constraint that is analogous to the tension expressed in Canacee's mews.

of the falcon's exemplum, as scholars have pointed out, so that the falcon appears quite radically appropriated, indeed captured and turned into a house pet.[40] Here we see "the internal law of the host" slide toward taking the guest hostage. If, however, this mews recalls the falcon's exemplum, it must also recall that the falcon imagined the birdcage as a good place, a place of comfort and tender care that the songbird was perverse to leave behind. Another contradictory image emerges in the overlay of the exemplum's "cage" with the contrasting term "mewe" (V.613, 643). The cage had a "dore" (V.615), but this structure called a mews may not have one, if it resembles a conventional mews with many openings or open sides to imitate the breezy nesting conditions of hawks in the wild.[41] This unclarity around whether Canacee's "mewe" has a door evokes Derrida's conundrum that hospitality requires and repudiates the door: "It does not seem to me that I am able to open up or offer hospitality, however generous, even in order to be generous, without reaffirming: this is mine, I am at home. . . . For there to be hospitality, there must be a door. But if there is a door, there is no longer hospitality."[42] Calling Canacee's little structure a "mews" elides the uncomfortable question of the door, as if to imagine that the falcon can be taken in without reservation.

In a further attempt at welcome, Canacee's mews is a miniature bedchamber framed within her own:

> And by hire beddes heed she made a mewe
> And covered it with veluettes blewe,
> In signe of trouthe that is in wommen sene.
> And al withoute, the mewe is peynted grene,
> In which were peynted alle thise false fowles,
> As ben thise tidyves, tercelettes, and owles.

[40] "The velvet cage is still a cage, positioned only some twenty lines after the caged bird gloss, a reminder that the falcon loses": Leslie Kordecki, "Chaucer's *Squire's Tale:* Animal Discourse, Women, and Subjectivity," *ChauR* 36 (2001–2): 291. Ruth Evans proposes the memorable image of "Canacee nursing the falcon like a young girl with a new Barbie," in her congress paper "The Perverse Nature of Charity and Chaucer's 'Squire's Tale,'" New Chaucer Society, Glasgow, 2004.

[41] Frederick II, *De arte venandi cum avibus,* ed. Willemsen, pp. 137–38; *Art of Falconry,* trans. Wood and Fyfe, pp. 129–30 and plates 67, 68, 134, 141. The usual way to keep hawks in halls and chambers was on perches. In Theseus's palace, "haukes sitten on the perche above" (*Knight's Tale,* A 2204); Oggins cites evidence of perches in bedrooms, *Kings and Their Hawks,* p. 109. Trained hawks were restrained with jesses, not free to fly about; *The Squire's Tale* is silent on jesses as well as on the door.

[42] Derrida, "Hostipitality," *Angelaki,* p. 14.

> Right for despit were peynted hem bisyde
> Pyes, on hem for to crie and chyde.
>
> (V.643–50)

Like the interior walls of an aristocratic bedchamber, the mews has cloth hangings in an emblematic color, here blue to signify the falcon's troth-keeping. Imitating the architectural space of her own chamber, Canacee offers the falcon an open equivalence between host and stranger. At the same time, this velvet chamber rather comically ignores their physical differences: is the falcon to recline on a tiny featherbed? The mews is not simply a cage, but neither does it resemble the falcon's native "roche of marbul gray."

The painted exterior of the mews makes a final, double effort at a hosting that transcends appropriation. The outer walls, colored green and decorated with images of false birds chided by magpies, seem to represent the formel's home in leafy nature, acknowledging the falcon's strange origins even as the mews' interior declares her equivalence with Canacee. In relation to each other, interior and exterior attempt a kind of hybrid space poised between woods and chamber, a space that might express the falcon's peregrinations. Even as it evokes nature, this green is also emblematic, answering the blue of "trouthe" with the color that represents lovers' fickleness.[43] Now the outer walls not only represent a leafy refuge, they also reimagine the walled garden in the *Romaunt of the Rose,* painted with personifications of qualities incompatible with "al the art of love."[44] Each painted figure expelled from love's garden has its living opposite inside the walls: skinny yellow Sorrow painted outside, dancing elegant Mirth inside; spiteful Villany painted outside, welcoming Courtesy inside.[45] Canacee transposes the *Romaunt of the Rose* into avian terms in painting "alle thise false fowles" on the outside and sheltering the faithful formel inside. Most important for responding to the formel's plight, Canacee's transposition refuses the conventional metaphoric relation of birds to humans, taking birds instead as the literal subject of a courtly narrative. The magpies' chiding assigns *them* the interpretive voice, in place of the dreaming lover in the *Romaunt of the*

[43] *Variorum Edition,* ed. Baker, lines 644–50 n., provides several examples of blue representing faithfulness, and green fickleness.
[44] *Riverside Chaucer, The Romaunt of the Rose,* line 40; "craft of love," line 2164.
[45] *Riverside Chaucer, The Romaunt of the Rose,* lines 166–80, 301–48, 729–846.

Rose.[46] The figurative relation collapses, or runs in reverse, recalling how the formel earlier figured her pain in a series of collapsing alterities.

Canacee's inspired bricolage subsumes prior models of interspecies constraint, birdcage and mews, into an unprecedented structure that is simultaneously human bedchamber, avian tree, and garden of love. In this structure, Canacee moves her relation to the falcon from totemic, symbolic, and allegorical terms toward literal and physical terms. Yes, Canacee's empathy is contradictory. It recognizes species difference and declares it transcended. Holding this contradiction in place, the mews expresses the opposition inherent in "kynde" between differentiation and lovingkindness.

The Squire's Tale insists on its parallel between cultural difference and species difference by giving the tale's two parts so many structural symmetries. Hospitality is its optimistic focal point for imagining cross-cultural and cross-species relations. Canacee's awkwardly strange and sheltering mews explores hospitality's tensions more fully than the neat integration of Mamluk emissary into Mongol feast. But I don't want to end this paper exclaiming that the falcon reveals so much about the tale's human protagonists. Both parts of the tale begin with a chorus of birds singing background music for noble Mongols (V.52–57, 395–400). Chaucer's innovation is going on from these conventional openings to depict birds as the protagonists, not just the setting, for a love narrative. I'd like to imagine that Canacee condenses Chaucer's artistic project into her mews. Sitting at her workbench, she says to herself, "As I make this mews, how can I evoke the symbolic associations that give a peregrine her high status? Can I represent both the strangeness and the proximity of another species? As strangeness shifts and slides, can I put a positive spin on the terror of deracination? Can I express compassion for a bird?"

---

[46] Magpies appropriately voice the condemnation of "false fowles" since they can learn words: "*Picae* quasi *poeticae,*" writes Isidore, "quod uerba in discrimine uocis exprimant, ut homo" (They are called mag*pies* as if *poetic,* because they can say words with distinct sounds, like men): *Etymologies,* pp. 258–59 (my italics; the association of *pica* and *poetica* continues in the insular Bestiaries). See also W. B. Yapp, "Birds in Captivity in the Middle Ages," *Archives of Natural History* 10 (1982): 482.

Chaucer's Volumes:

Toward a New Model of Literary History in the *Canterbury Tales*

Karla Taylor
University of Michigan

THE BATTLE BETWEEN the Wife of Bath and her fifth husband, Jankyn, in which she "rente out of his book a leef, / For which he smoot me so that I was deef,"[1] enacts the spectacular failure in transmission that results when a coercive literary tradition collides with an audience whose resistance finally wells over into violence. In addition to its commentary on the effects of antifeminist writings in the Wife's autobiographical prologue—the focus of most recent criticism on the Wife of Bath—the battle also figures the very structure of literary tradition, whose motive force is the dynamic interaction of repetition (emulation, imitation) and rupture,[2] as an overt rivalry. As she tells it, the Wife

It gives me great pleasure to acknowledge those whose responses to this essay (or to the papers it draws on) have shaped my thinking: Elizabeth Allen, Piero Boitani, Denise Boulange, Catherine Brown, Warren Ginsberg, Frank Grady, Teresa Kennedy, Ashby Kinch, Winthrop Wetherbee, and the anonymous readers for *Studies in the Age of Chaucer*.
    [1] Wife of Bath's Prologue, III.685, 667–68. All references to the *Canterbury Tales* are to Larry D. Benson, et al., *The Riverside Chaucer*, 3rd rev. ed. (Boston: Houghton Mifflin, 1987).
    [2] In the enormous literature on literary tradition, I have found particularly helpful Gian Biagio Conte, *Memoria dei poeti e sistema letterario: Catullo, Virgilio, Ovidio, Lucano* (Turin: Einaudi, 1974); Conte, *The Rhetoric of Imitation: Genre and Poetic Memory in Virgil and Other Latin Poets,* ed. and trans. Charles Segal (Ithaca: Cornell University Press), pp. 23–95; Conte, "Concluding Remarks" in *Genres and Readers: Lucretius, Love Elegy, Pliny's Encyclopedia,* trans. Glenn W. Most (Baltimore: Johns Hopkins University Press, 1994), pp. 129–43; and Stephen Hinds, *Allusion and Intertext: The Dynamics of Appropriation in Roman Poetry* (Cambridge: Cambridge University Press, 1998). For penetrating comments on Chaucer's "translation" of prior traditions, see Helen Cooper, "After Chaucer," *SAC* 25 (2003): 1–25. Cooper stresses the "ideological supersession" (p. 5) involved in translating tradition into new cultural contexts; Conte asserts that reuse is "the fundamental condition for the formation of an active tradition" (*Rhetoric of Imitation,* p. 41).

triumphs over Jankyn and his relentlessly repetitive antifeminism. After plucking one (or three) pages from the book, she makes him cast the whole thing into the fire, and takes control in all other ways as well. In her account, utter rupture prevails: the book destroyed, its audience partially deafened.

But the Wife's triumph obscures the continuities that also shape and finally delimit her refusals. Not only does the book continue to influence her represented life—it has provided the terms by which she understands herself, and she continues to reiterate its contents to her listeners—but her refusal itself appropriates the words and signifying structure of a different poetic predecessor. For, in summarizing the nightly recitals from the antifeminist book with which Jankyn regales her, the Wife borrows a rhyme from Dante's *Paradiso* XXXIII:

> bookes many on,
> And alle thise were bounden in o *volume.*
> And every nyght and day was his *custume,*
> Whan he hadde leyser and vacacioun
> From oother wordly occupacioun,
> To reden on this book of wikked wyves.
> (III.680–85, emphases mine)

Startlingly, the source of the rhyme is the culminating metaphor with which Dante describes the universe and its creator as a bound book:[3]

> Nel suo profondo vidi che s'interna,
> legato con amore in un *volume,*
> ciò che per l'universo si squaderna:
> sustanze e accidenti e lor *costume*
> quasi conflati insieme, per tal modo
> che ciò ch'i' dico è un semplice lume.

[In its depth I saw ingathered, bound by love in one single *volume,* that which is dispersed in leaves throughout the universe: substances and accidents and

---

[3] For the widespread metaphor of the universe as a book (with biblical, twelfth-century, and Dantean instances), see E. R. Curtius, *European Literature and the Latin Middle Ages,* trans. Willard R. Trask, Bollingen Series 36 (Princeton: Princeton University Press, 1953), rpt. 1973, pp. 302–47.

their *relations,* as though fused together in such a way that what I tell is but a simple light.][4]

The two books—Dante's metaphor for the divine unity of creator and creation, and Jankyn's narrowly self-interested polemic—could scarcely differ more. Yet the evidence supports the proposition that Chaucer draws on Dante's *volume* here, for the rhyme not only persists through translation but also brings with it the vehicle of the metaphor in which it originally appeared. The original context of the rhyme is not so much reproduced as answered in the subsequent narrative action of the Wife of Bath's Prologue.[5] In as neat (and literal) a deconstruction of Dante as one might wish for, the borrowed rhyme suggests that the Wife later "dis-quartoes" ("squaderna") Jankyn's book, and thus pointedly reverses the import of Dante's vision, in which the fragments of creation are bound together in one volume.[6]

[4] *Paradiso* XXXIII, 85–90; emphases mine. Unless otherwise noted, all references to and translations of the *Commedia* are to Dante Alighieri, *The Divine Comedy,* ed. and trans. Charles S. Singleton, 3 vols. in 6 parts, Bollingen Series 80 (Princeton: Princeton University Press, 1970–75). Seth Lerer originally called my attention to this rhyme as a possible Dantean borrowing; see my discussion in "Chaucer's Uncommon Voice," in Leonard M. Koff and Brenda Deen Schildgen, eds., *The "Decameron" and the "Canterbury Tales": New Essays on an Old Question* (Madison, N.J.: Fairleigh Dickinson University Press, 2000), pp. 52–54. Lerer himself has now commented on the borrowing in "Medieval English Literature and the Idea of the Anthology," *PMLA* 118 (2003): 1251–67.
[5] In the Wife's *volume/custume* rhyme, "volume" is uniquely stressed on the second syllable, perhaps as a result of the stress patterns of Dante's Italian or of the similarly stressed French *volume.* All other fourteenth-century English attestations stress the first syllable; see the on-line *Middle English Dictionary,* http://ets.umdl.umich.edu/m/med, s.v. *volume.* The unusual stress marks the word here. My analysis is based on the MED's unpublished lexical files as well as those published in the entry on "volume." I thank Robert E. Lewis, Editor-in-Chief, and the editors of the Middle English Dictionary Project for permission to consult the files. The relatively common *custume,* in the French-derived sense of "custom, habit, usage," differs from Dante's philosophical meaning of "nature, character, condition," "mode of conduct or relation." Vide *costume,* in Salvatore Battaglia and Giorgio Squarotti, eds., *Grande dizionario della lingua italiana,* 17 vols. (Turin: UTET, 1962–).
[6] The use of a rhyme filched from Dante to characterize the Wife's destroyed volume lends further evidence to support Helen Cooper's memorable formulation of Chaucer's response to Dante, especially concerning the access of human poetry to the divine. Cooper describes "two massively strong responses to Dante on Chaucer's part: first, that he was awesomely, mind-blowingly great as a poet; and second, that he was *wrong.*" Chaucer's "translation" of the Italian poet is "Dante turned inside out and upside down, not because Chaucer misunderstood Dante—because he translates the *Comedy* inaccurately—but because he understands it all too well"; I quote from "After Chaucer," pp. 12, 13. See also Cooper, "The Four Last Things in Dante and Chaucer: Ugolino in the House of Rumour," *NML* 3 (1999): 39–66.

The Wife's destruction of Jankyn's book, this essay will argue, comes at the midpoint and nadir of a series of encounters between resistant readers and authoritative literary traditions in the *Canterbury Tales*. The series is structured by "volumes": the Wife's *volume/custume* rhyme completes a paired Dantean appropriation begun in the Man of Law's Introduction with Chaucer's only other use of the word "volume."[7] These volumes shape the experience of their represented readers, who are supplemented by a second kind of textual reader emerging from the readerly roles written into the Miller's Prologue and the Midas story in *The Wife of Bath's Tale*. Taken together, these represented and implied textual readers address the difficulties Chaucer faced in transposing the classical literary tradition (defined by Virgil and Ovid) into English. They depict the empirical audience Chaucer had—the new readers to whom he sought to introduce the newly Englished classical tradition—and inscribe the potential audience he needed in order to realize his poetic ambitions.

The textual readers in the series—disgruntled, skeptical, disorderly, and above all deaf—model a dynamic process by which empirical readers as well might be transformed and linked to the classical literary tradition through open and hidden rehearsals of Ovid, Virgil, and Dante. The Wife's destruction of Jankyn's book threatens to rupture the continuities necessary to literary tradition—"la memoria dei poeti," as Gian Biago Conte has called it[8]—and thus to thwart Chaucer's effort to join new English readers to the classics. Yet a less rivalrous model of the relation between tradition and the new reader emerges from the dynamics of transmission in her tale of Midas. This new model of literary dynamics, I will argue, registers and accommodates the resistance of Chaucer's new English readers, and by doing so, suggests how he might more successfully transpose the classical tradition into his particular English vernacular context.

In pairing the Man of Law's Wife of Bath's volumes, I will also argue, Chaucer writes into the *Canterbury Tales* the central literary narrative of

---

[7] I thank Piero Boitani for drawing my attention to this use of "volume."

[8] From "La memoria dei poeti e arte allusiva," in *La memoria dei poeti e sistema letterario*. For Conte, poetic memory is among the "constitutive elements of poetic discourse" (*Rhetoric of Imitation*, p. 23) which, since it comprises "the recall of past forms, styles, mood, and atmosphere as well as of specific phrases or images—is not a casual but a ubiquitous and a necessary feature of the arts" (Segal, "Introduction," *Rhetoric of Imitation*, p. 11).

the *Commedia,* Dante's supersession of Virgil. The stark economy of this appropriation raises one of the enduring historical problems in Chaucer's uses of Dante: their inaccessibility to any known fourteenth-century English audience.[9] Without such recognition, what role might Chaucer's Dantean appropriations play in his effort to transform his readers?[10]

To address this problem, I rely on the complex temporality of literary appropriation, which looks not merely back to past tradition and texts—Conte's poetic memory—but also forward to future readers who have been preshaped by its dynamic presence.[11] Writers are quite capable of foreseeing future readers, whose responses they can also seek to influence or model in the texts themselves. Dante, for instance, defends his startling willingness to pass eternal judgment on souls by appealing to "coloro / che questo tempo chiameranno antico" (those who shall call this time ancient, *Paradiso* XVII, 119–20); if Dante's judgments are bitterly unwelcome to his contemporaries, these ideal future readers de-

---

[9] As far as scholars have been able to determine, fourteenth-century English readers would not have been capable of recognizing his Dantean appropriations. A. C. Spearing, deftly summarizing the lack of surviving written evidence for English knowledge of trecento Italian literature aside from Chaucer, draws this provisional conclusion in *"Troilus and Criseyde: The Illusion of Allusion," Exemplaria* 2 (1990): 263–77 (272). Distinguishing between "use" and "allusion" (pp. 264–65) and then (somewhat inconsistently) acknowledging "the possibility that from time to time Chaucer may make private allusions to Dante, for his own satisfaction, not expecting his readers to recognize them" (p. 271), he also registers the skeptic's discomfort with the idea of private allusion; his approach proceeds from his conviction that "in respect of his relation to his Italian sources . . . Chaucer is a much simpler and more accessible poet than the act of allusion would require" (p. 272). Although I take a different approach to Chaucer's use of his Italian reading, no one has stated the problem of audience more cogently.

[10] These uses thus cannot be called allusions. As traditionally defined, allusion differs from other kinds of intertextuality in requiring both intention from the poet and recognition of both echo and source from the audience. It requires a community of knowledge between poet and readers (or sorts readers into in-groups and out-groups according to their capacity to recognize the allusion), and assumes that both sides prize literary tradition. See *The New Princeton Encyclopedia of Poetry and Poetics,* ed. Alex Preminger and T. V. F. Brogan et al. (Princeton: Princeton University Press, 1993), pp. 39–40.

[11] I have assumed, with Conte, that one of the primary effects of a literary work is to invent its own competent reader—the "fit audience, though few" Milton imagined for *Paradise Lost.* Conte argues that an author not only "presupposes the competence of his (or her) own Model Reader" but also *"establishes"* that competence" (*Rhetoric of Imitation,* p. 30, original emphasis). In a note, he adds that H. R. Jauss's concept of literary genre as a horizon of expectation has proven too static to accommodate the far more dynamic textual processes that constitute the literary text: "If, instead, the textual process is rendered dynamic, then in the dialectic between author and reader a renewed authorial responsibility emerges that even goes beyond the expectations of the public and extends them while conquering new spaces of meaning" (p. 30).

mand his forthright truth-telling.[12] The contemporary and future audiences constructed here differ mainly in their capacities for recognition and discernment, qualities the poem itself seeks to transform in its empirical readers as well.

As historical audiences change, their capacity to recognize literary appropriations may also change. Chaucer's efforts to engender such change are sometimes obvious. The two explicit references to Dante in the *Canterbury Tales,* for example, suggest that Chaucer did not expect his contemporary English readers to recognize the Italian poet. When the Wife of Bath cites "the wise poete of Florence / That highte Dant" (*Wife of Bath's Tale,* III.1125–26) and the Monk refers his audience to "the grete poete of Ytaille / That highte Dante" (*Monk's Tale,* VII.2460–61), each identifies Dante in a *that*-complement that does not presuppose prior knowledge of the new information it presents. The laudatory adjectives "wise" and "grete" nevertheless entice readers to seek Dante out, as does Chaucer's inclusion of him as one of only two modern writers (the other is Petrarch) in the otherwise classical category of "poete." Although Chaucer's English contemporaries would not have recognized the Dantean source of his volumes, these enticements seem designed to engender their curiosity, and thus in turn to summon greater knowledge from future readers. For such hoped-for empirical readers, discovery might be only a matter of time.

Because readers' capacity for recognition can change over time, the initial unfamiliarity of a literary appropriation may not always be (or remain) a deficit. Citing *Anelida and Arcite*'s "vois memorial in the shade" (18), Helen Cooper describes how Chaucer's intertextuality makes "central . . . claims about poetry as fusing speech and memory, the contemporary and the traditional, the private voice of the poet given a public function."[13] In this dynamic fusion, what is originally private can and does become public to those who learn to recognize it. In particular, I suggest, even unrecognized appropriations can work their effects instrumentally on readers who, unaware, are changed by them. The very inaccessibility of Chaucer's Dantean usages to his fourteenth-century audiences may paradoxically promote their effectiveness in the new

---

[12] The textual reader modeled in this passage is of course part of Dante's effort to engender similar empirical readers. His equation of his own judgment with divine judgment is one of the reasons that Chaucer was both "fascinated and appalled" by the Italian poet, according to Cooper, "The Four Last Things," p. 42.

[13] Cooper, "After Chaucer," p. 4.

model of literary dynamics described in this essay. In this case, the provisionally unshared status of Chaucer's Dantean volumes—their temporality—plays an important role in deflecting any skepticism on the part of contemporary readers toward his broader poetic ambitions. The temporality of the appropriation thus contributes to a central purpose of the *Canterbury Tales:* to introduce Chaucer's chosen classical tradition and his new English audience to one another.

Rehearsing the Muses in the Man of Law's Introduction

Chaucer first uses the word "volume" (Man of Law's Introduction, II.60) to refer to the partial canon attributed to him by his own creation, the Man of Law. The context in which the word appears is profoundly literary. The bravura astronomical exordium at the beginning of the Man of Law's Introduction, which tells time according to the sun "Phebus" (by the arc of the artificial day and the length of "the shadwe of every tree," II.11, 7), initiates a multilayered linkage between the *Canterbury Tales* and the classical tradition it rehearses.[14] Framed first and last by Apollo and "the Muses that men clepe Pierides" (II.92), the Introduction alerts us to the topic of poetry.

At issue in the Man of Law's Introduction are the two fictional premises of the *Canterbury Tales:* rehearsal (my immediate focus) and literary competition. In the General Prologue, Chaucer's commitment to record the tales verbatim had seemed the most unpoetic undertaking imaginable. But it is profoundly poetic. Its poesis emerges most clearly in retrospect as it successively recast in the Miller's Prologue and the Man of

---

[14] The astronomical opening of the Man of Law's Introduction looks back to the astronomical opening of the General Prologue. In addition, compare references to morning in General Prologue, I.822–24 and the Man of Law's Introduction, II.1–15; the establishment and reiteration of the conditions of the tale-telling game at General Prologue, I.777–834 and the Man of Law's Introduction, II.33–45; and the fiction of rehearsal at General Prologue, I.725–23. Helen Cooper suggests that the astronomical exordium here (especially since it is matched by that of the Parson's Prologue) may have been the original beginning of the storytelling; see *The Structure of the Canterbury Tales* (London: Duckworth, 1983), p. 63. For the Man of Law's Introduction as a new beginning, see Carleton Brown, "The Man of Law's Headlink and the Prologue of the *Canterbury Tales*," *SP* 34 (1937): 8–35; John Fisher, *John Gower: Moral Philosopher and Friend of Chaucer* (New York: New York University Press, 1964), p. 286; and Alfred David, *The Strumpet Muse* (Bloomington: Indiana University Press, 1976), pp. 124–33. David argues that the Man of Law's Introduction is a central statement of Chaucer's poetic purposes; for the response to Gower on the relation of poetry and morals, see also Elizabeth Allen, "Chaucer Answers Gower: Constance and the Trouble with Reading," *ELH* 63 (1997): 627–55).

Law's Introduction. Initially the fiction of rehearsal is the basis of Chaucer's claim to imitate a prior reality truthfully:

> But first I pray yow, of youre curteisye,
> That ye n'arette it nat my vileynye,
> Though that I pleynly speke in this mateere,
> To telle you hir wordes and hir cheere,
> No thogh I speke hir wordes proprely.
> For this ye knowen al so wel as I:
> Whoso shal telle a tale after a man,
> He mot reherce as ny as evere he kan
> Everich a word, if it be in his charge,
> Al speke he never so rudeliche and large,
> Or ellis he moot telle his tale untrewe,
> Or feyne thyng, or fynde wordes newe.
>
> (GP, I.725–36)

Here rehearsal seems to promise a naively faithful transcription of the external world in words, of history "wie es eigentlich gewesen." The word "reherce" in the General Prologue constructs the voice of the chronicler as the recorder of a past he did not invent and does not distort.[15] When it is reiterated in the apology in the Miller's Prologue, the fiction of rehearsal stresses Chaucer's pose as a *compilator*.[16] Here it compels him to include the Miller's Tale: "M'athynketh that I shal reherce it heere" (II.3170). Omitting the tale would break his promise to tell "everich a word"; "shal" registers his sense of regretful obligation. Rehearsal as *compilatio* still purports to transmit an undistorted prior reality, but it differs from chronicle transcription in the explicitly verbal/textual status of the prior events it transmits. *Compilatio* stresses copying, transmission, transcription; although recognizably imitative, it does not overtly suggest departure.

Departure, however, is what the Man of Law has in mind when he takes up the topic of rehearsal. Here it imitates not the words of the pilgrims, but a prior textual reality, the classical tradition, which is given a distinctly Ovidian cast. In this wry account of a reader's revolt from

---

[15] I use Barbara Nolan's terms, from "'A Poet Ther Was': Chaucer's Voices in the General Prologue to *The Canterbury Tales*," *PMLA* 101(1986): 154–69.

[16] Rather than an *auctor*, as Alastair Minnis has shown in *The Medieval Theory of Authorship: Scholastic Literary Attitudes in the Latin Middle Ages*, 2nd ed. (Philadelphia: University of Pennsylvania Press, 1988), pp. 201–3.

his author, the Man of Law complains that Chaucer has already used up all the good stories, wrecking them with his incompetent English. Although rehearsal is clearly a long-standing Chaucerian habit, he sees no point in further repetition:

> "I kan right now no thrifty tale seyn
> That Chaucer, though he kan but lewedly
> On metres and on rymyng craftily,
> Hath seyd hem in swich Englissh as he kan
> Of olde tyme, as knoweth many a man;
> And if he have noght seyd hem, leve brother,
> In o book, he hath seyd hem in another.
> For he hath toold of loveris up and doun
> Mo than Ovide made of mencioun
> In his Episteles, that been ful olde.
> What sholde I tellen hem, syn they been tolde?"
>   II.46–56)

His slighting description of "lewed" English and twice-told tales introduces the selected writings to which Chaucer, under the charming guise of criticism by one of his readers, asserts authorship.[17] Prominent in this canon is Chaucer's first "volume," the collection of largely Ovidian stories assembled in *The Legend of Good Women* to which the Man of Law directs his audience: "Whoso that wole his large volume seke, / Cleped the Seintes Legende of Cupide" (II.60–61), he says, will find "Lucresse" and "Tesbee" among the list of Cupid's martyrs.[18] He grudgingly praises Chaucer for omitting the Ovidian topics of incest and rape—unlike Gower's "unkynde abhomynacions," the stories of Canacee and Machaire and Apollonius of Tyre[19]—and resolves not to "reherce" such tales himself (II.88, 89). Even so, the "cursed stories" (II.80) seem to

---

[17] David Wallace calls this moment the second authorial signature of the *Canterbury Tales,* and connects it to a poetic ambition modeled on Dante; see *Chaucerian Polity: Absolutist Lineage and Associational Form in England and Italy* (Stanford: Stanford University Press, 1997), p. 201.

[18] For good measure, his list is a little larger than any we know from the unfinished *Legend.* According to Fisher, it is deliberately inaccurate (*John Gower,* p. 288); Wallace suggests that such inaccuracies are characteristic of legal pleading (*Chaucerian Polity,* p. 204).

[19] See *Confessio Amantis,* III.143–360 and VIII.271–2008 in G. C. Macaulay, ed., *The English Works of John Gower,* 2 vols., EETS, e.s. 81–82 (Oxford: Clarendon Press, 1900–1901). The *Legend of Good Women* mentions Canace at FProl.265/GProl.219, without, however, narrating her story.

exert a certain fascination for him; he does not stop at naming them, but continues past the bare minimum of identifying detail with one extra line about Apollonius: "Whan he hir threw upon the pavement" (II.85). Just a touch too much information, the final detail does not so much shut off the narrative as make palpable its pull.[20] For all his protestations, then, the Man of Law's attitude toward rehearsal is not straightforward.

The literary framing of the Introduction is completed when, in a final refusal of the poetic, the Man of Law renounces the Muses themselves:

> "Me were looth be likned, doutelees,
> To Muses that men clepe Pierides—
> Metamorphosios woot what I mene;
> But nathelees, I recche noght a bene
> Though I come after hym with hawebake.
> I speke in prose, and lat him rymes make."
>
> (II.91–96)

Throughout the Introduction, the dominant issues have been rehearsal and the tension between writers and readers. The idea of repetition recurs in the ambiguous reference to the "Muses that men clepe Pierides." As a cognomen, "Pierides" designates the Muses' birthplace in Pieria as well as one of the mountains sacred to them, Pierus.[21] More telling in this context, the name recalls—and confuses—the contest between the Muses and the nine daughters of Pierus in *Metamorphoses* V.[22] As Urania

[20] This detail is absent from Gower's version. As Elizabeth Scala suggests, the Man of Law's denial "foregrounds what he desires most ardently to avoid narrating"; see "Canacee and the Chaucer Canon: Incest and Other Unnarratables," *ChauR* 30 (1995): 15–39 (22). The Man of Law's attraction to incest has been a frequent topic of recent commentary on the tale; see, for example, Elizabeth Archibald, "The Flight from Incest: Two Classical Precursors of the Constance Theme," *ChauR* 20 (1986): 259–72; Winthrop P. Wetherbee, "Constance and the World in Chaucer and Gower," in R. F. Yeager, ed., *John Gower: Recent Readings* (Kalamazoo: Western Michigan University Press for the Medieval Institute, 1989), pp. 65–93; and Dinshaw, *Chaucer's Sexual Poetics,* p. 101, which describes the Man of Law's Tale as a "narrative structured by incest."

[21] See Ovid, *Tristia* 5.3.10, in Arthur Leslie Wheeler, *Tristia, Ex Ponto* (London: W. Heinemann; New York, G. P. Putnam's Sons, 1924).

[22] See Ovid, *Metamorphoses,* V. 250–678, ed. and trans. Frank Justus Miller (Cambridge, Mass.: Harvard University Press; and London: William Heinemann, 1977), vol. 1, pp. 254–85. The Man of Law can't even be bothered to get his references straight; Maura Nolan cites this confusion as part of a pattern of error exposing the Man of Law as a "careless reader"; see "'Acquiteth yow now': Textual Contradiction and Legal Discourse in the Man of Law's Introduction," in Emily Steiner and Candace Barrington, eds., *The Letter of the Law: Legal Practice and Literary Production in Medieval England* (Ithaca: Cornell University Press, 2002), pp. 136–53 (149–50).

recounts the story to Minerva, the nine human Pierides criticize the Muses for misleading the "indoctum . . . vulgus" (unsophisticated rabble, *Metamorphoses* V.308) and challenge them to a storytelling contest. The human contestants lead off insultingly by telling how the giants defeated the gods, who then, in a parody of metamorphosis, disguise themselves as various animals and birds. Calliope, representing the nine Muses, answers with the rape of Proserpina, masterfully weaving other stories into her main narrative. The divine Pierides defeat their arrogant mortal challengers—the Pierides—and the Muses then punish them by turning them into chattering magpies that "imitate any sound they please" ("imitantes omnia picae," *Metamorphoses* V.299), the very figures of indiscriminant imitation.[23] The Ovidian descriptor "Pierides" thus melds together both fictional premises of the *Canterbury Tales:* rehearsal and the storytelling competition.

In rejecting the "Pierides," the Man of Law reduces the Muses' storytelling to magpie chatter, and levels the difference between the winners and the losers in this model for all literary competitions. Goddesses of the arts or human pretenders, they all just repeat a bunch of old stories, and he hopes to avoid comparison with the lot of them. Like the "indoctum vulgus" for whose favor the Pierides originally competed, the Man of Law is apparently incapable of telling a Muse from a magpie.

His dismissal of Chaucer's hand-me-down stories is thus widened to include literary rehearsal generally. In his rejection, the Man of Law figures a potential audience in need of transformation if the classic tradition is to find an English home.[24] And indeed, he shifts his ground

[23] The story of Proserpina suggests that narratives of rape, far from being banished, may condition the Man of Law's refusal to resemble the Muses here. But the meaningless iteration of magpie speech is scarcely more acceptable. Dante writes of the latter: "And if it should be argued to the contrary what Ovid says in the fifth book of the Metamorphoses (lines 294ff.) about the speaking magpies, I would reply that this is said figuratively, meaning something else. And if it is said that even in the present magpies and other birds speak, I would reply that this is false, because these acts are not speech, but rather a certain imitation of the sound of our voices; which is to say that they succeed in imitating us insofar as we make sounds, not insofar as we speak. Thus if someone enunciates distinctly 'magpie' to one of them, and he answers 'magpie,' this would be nothing but a reproduction or imitation of the sound made by the person enunciating." See *De vulgari eloquentia,* Book I, chaps. 2, 7, from *Literary Criticism of Dante Alighieri,* ed. and trans. Robert S. Haller (Lincoln: University of Nebraska Press, 1973), pp. 4–5.

[24] The Man of Law's shortcomings as a reader have been well catalogued; see, for instance, William L. Sullivan, "Chaucer's Man of Law as a Literary Critic," *MLN* 68 (1953): 1–8; Chauncey Wood, "Chaucer's Man of Law as Interpreter," *Traditio* 23 (1967): 149–90; Rodney Delasanta, "And of Great Reverence: Chaucer's Man of Law,"

significantly during the preamble to his tale. At first he complains that Chaucer has exhausted the limited supply of "thrifty" (II.46), or profitable, stories, whose value has moreover been depleted by retelling: "What sholde I tellen hem, syn they been tolde?" he demands (II.56). Perhaps he regards stories as perishable commodities good for one telling only—or perhaps he bridles at Chaucer's success in cornering the market for "thrifty" stories[25] (or even flooding it with cheap knockoffs). Either possibility suggests a commercial frame of reference at odds with the dynamic of literary tradition. Such "thrift" would moreover disrupt the commercial exchange of the merchants he praises in his Prologue; their livelihood, like literary tradition, depends on the value added in transmission. The Man of Law's own story of Constance, which he has learned from a merchant, accumulates value in this way. The layers of fictional transmission related at the end of the Man of Law's Prologue mirror the frequent historical retellings of this widespread story, one of the most popular in medieval literatures.[26]

These inconsistencies portray the Man of Law less as an incorrigibly "indoctum vulgus" than as a well-prepared but skeptical reader whose hostility toward the literary is neither straightforward nor absolute. His skepticism about rehearsal is related to his legal profession, described in

---

ChauR 5 (1971): 288–310; and Peter Nicholson, "The *Man of Law's Tale:* What Chaucer Really Owed to Gower," *ChauR* 26 (1991): 153–74. Maura Nolan, in the course of a significant argument for the centrality of the Man of Law's Introduction to Chaucer's poetic ambitions in the *Canterbury Tales,* concurs with this traditional reading of the Man of Law's inadequacies as a reader ("'Acquiteth yow now,'" pp. 149–50). More broadly, however, she reads the Introduction as a competition between legal and poetic discourses dramatizing the appeal and danger of the "historical tension" (p. 151) revealed by late fourteenth-century legal discourse. Her argument is largely complementary to the one I present here, especially since she too associates the challenge of authoritative Latin legal discourse with Chaucer's effort to establish an English vernacular tradition: "For a vernacular poet such as Chaucer, seeking to establish not only his own authority but also the authority of poetic and secular discourse itself, the language of the law could provide an essential vocabulary of legitimacy" (p. 152).

[25] Wallace describes the Man of Law as a "monopolist of one kind of discourse" (the law) who "comes to recognize the achievement of another" (Chaucer in literary discourse); see *Chaucerian Polity,* p. 203.

[26] For the story, see Margaret Schlauch, *Constance and Accused Queens* (New York: New York University Press, 1927). Chaucer relies chiefly on Nicholas Trivet's Anglo-Norman version, available in Schlauch, "The Man of Law's Tale," W. F. Bryan and Germain Dempster, eds., *Sources and Analogues of Chaucer's Canterbury Tales* (Chicago: University of Chicago Press, 1941), pp. 165–81; and most likely knew Gower's version in *Confessio Amantis,* II.597–1612. For an illuminating discussion of the Man of Law, his tale, mercantile culture, and Boccaccio's version of the Constance story (*Decameron* V.2), see Wallace, *Chaucerian Polity,* pp. 182–211.

his General Prologue portrait and recalled in the legal diction with which he and the Host restate the conditions of the tale-telling competition.[27] This deflection into the legal sphere, I suggest, provides Chaucer with a way of imagining one of the chief obstacles he faced in transplanting an old literary tradition into new soil: the wariness of readers like the Man of Law, whose legal profession grants him an insider's knowledge of the problems of repetition.

Legal and literary traditions are carefully linked in the Man of Law's portrait, especially as it touches on the parallel value of reuse in the practice of both realms. His promise as a reader emerges from the intellectual and professional habits described here. Although the portrait's instability of tone and perspective renders his ethical status uncertain,[28] he has clearly mastered the legal tradition. Learned in the history of

---

[27] The legal discourse with which the storytelling competition is formulated in the General Prologue and revised in the Miller's Prologue and the Man of Law's Introduction has been treated thoroughly by Maura Nolan in "'Acquiteth yow now,'" pp. 145–47. In addition, I note especially how extensively recursiveness dominates the exchange between Man of Law and Host (compare General Prologue, I.769–821, 828–34, 848–52; repeated words are in italics):

> "Sire Man of Lawe," quod he, "so have ye blis,
> Telle us a tale anon, as *forward* is.
> Ye been submytted, thurgh youre free *assent,*
> To stonden in this cas at my *juggement.*
> Acquiteth yow now of youre beheeste;
> Thanne have ye do youre devoir atte leeste."
>   "Hooste," quod he, "depardieux, ich assente;
> To breke forward is nat myn entente.
> Biheste is dette, and I wole holde fayn
> Al my biheste, I kan no bettre sayn.
> For swich lawe as a man yeveth another wight,
> He sholde hymselven usen it, by right;
> Thus wole oure text."
>   (II.33–45)

The exchange is both verbally repetitive (*biheste,* for instance, occurs three times in six lines) and about recursiveness (as in the legal principle of equity at the end). For a treatment of the General Prologue agreement as associational language typical of guilds, see Wallace, *Chaucerian Polity,* pp. 83–104. For the Man of Law's legal language, see also Fisher, *John Gower,* p. 288.

[28] As Jill Mann has pointed out, this is one of the portraits that praises professional skill as if it were the same as moral excellence; see *Chaucer and Medieval Estates Satire: The Literature of Social Classes and the General Prologue to the Canterbury Tales* (Cambridge: Cambridge University Press, 1973), p. 91. The observation pertains to the Physician, but clearly is intended to extend to the whole class of professional pilgrims of uncertain ethical value and social position. Mann discusses the Man of Law's portrait on pages 86–91.

statutes and cases since the Conquest, he skillfully transposes ancient precedent into new contexts in his own real estate practice:

> In termes hadde he caas and doomes alle
> That from the tyme of kyng William were falle,
> Therto he koude endite and make a thyng,
> Ther koude no wight pynche at his writyng;
> And every statut koud he pleyn by rote.
>
> (GP, I.323–27)

Strikingly, the words describing legal art—*endite, make, writyng*—are those Chaucer elsewhere uses to describe his own poetic practice.[29] The shared lexicon lends significance to the Man of Law's later reluctance to embrace the parallel structuring repetitions of literary tradition. Instead, his professional and social position, in granting him the capacity to recognize literary rehearsal, prompts his skepticism. To judge from the company he keeps (the Franklin in the General Prologue; the merchant from whom he learned his tale in his own Prologue) or from the historical people he resembles (newly professional laymen with legal training once available only to clerics),[30] his skill serves the "new men" of the *Canterbury Tales,* the group of substantial bourgeois and professional pilgrims whose combination of social position, education, and wealth marks the emergence of a new social formation and potential audience for English writing. A "new man" himself, the Man of Law is in the business of conveying the perquisites of ancient lineage to other "new men." Pragmatic skepticism toward claims of its inherent charisma would serve him well, even as he tacitly accommodates ancient aristocratic privilege to new social groups eager not only for the land but also for its cachet of exclusivity. Small wonder, then, that he brings a similar skepticism to claims of the accrued value of literary reuse—even as he

---

[29] See Glending Olson, "Making and Poetry in the Age of Chaucer," *CL* 31 (1979): 272–90; and Anne Middleton, "Chaucer's 'New Men' and the Good of Literature in the *Canterbury Tales,*" in Edward W. Said, ed., *Literature and Society: Selected Papers from the English Institute,* n.s., no. 3, 1978 (Baltimore: Johns Hopkins University Press, 1980), pp. 15–56. I borrow Middleton's term "new men" in the analysis below.

[30] See Ann W. Astell, *Chaucer and the Universe of Learning* (Ithaca: Cornell University Press, 1996), pp. 32–60, on the increasingly lay character of intellectual and professional education in the fourteenth century, with a useful bibliography. See also Wallace, *Chaucerian Polity,* pp. 196–99, for the education and social position of lawyers between lay and clerical status.

cites Ovid to refuse him. What he cannot countenance, in literature as in law, is an old tradition that cannot be accommodated to the new.

In short, the Man of Law's refusal to be summoned as a reader for Chaucer's fictions is not absolute, but contingent, conditioned by the conservative tendency of the status quo to replicate itself to the exclusion of the new. The fact is that most literary production *is* magpie chatter; it exists to repeat predictably, comfortingly, without challenging settled expectations or making unseemly demands. In this light, the Man of Law's refusal to repeat the same old stories accords with the revolt staged in the Miller's Prologue, where the drunken Miller intervenes to prevent the Monk from heaping more tragedies on top of the Knight's tale of fortune. The Miller's brilliant parody instead translates the Knight's classical themes to an English village setting; the redirection decisively prefers variety to untransposed iteration. In disparaging Chaucer for his retold stories, the Man of Law likewise styles himself a modern who wants to tell something completely different. He needs only to reconceive the new as the kind of transposition that can revivify the muses' tradition.

The Man of Law's resistance to iteration helps to transform the Canterbury fiction of rehearsal from magpie chatter ("imitantes omnia picae") into song fit for the Muses. Indeed it is his refusal to rehearse Ovid that most clearly recasts rehearsal as the fundamental form of literary imitation. Throughout, he has evoked Ovid and the Ovidian tradition in gathering richness: he recalls storytelling contests, of both the *Canterbury Tales* and the *Metamorphoses* V (II.33–45, 92); names Ovid and two of his story-collections, the *Heroides* and the *Metamorphoses* (II.54, 55, 93); summarizes a number of Chaucer's Ovidian stories (II.57, 62–76); and complains about tales of rape and incest drawn from the Ovidian tradition. But his dissociations effectively link the Man of Law to a chain of reuse. Through the friction provided by a recalcitrant reader, we can now see the two premises of the Canterbury fiction—to rehearse a storytelling competition—as a revisionary imitation of Ovid's artful poetic collection rather than as an unpoetic commitment to chronicle the facts of the pilgrimage just as they happened.

It's tempting just to invert everything the Man of Law says here into a backdoor assertion of authorial ambition, at the expense of a reader invented as straw man, but such inversion would miss the value his refusals bring to the dynamic interplay of a living literary tradition. Even his final rejection of verse revivifies what he ostensibly refuses.

Since the Man of Law obviously does not "speke in prose" (II.96), either in the Introduction's recounted exchange or in his subsequent Prologue and Tale,[31] I take his "forme of speche" instead as a marker of rehearsal: it suggests a prior Man of Law, who, like Monsieur Jourdain, habitually speaks prose even if his words are recorded in couplets or rhyme royal. Whatever the referential status of his claim, it introduces a new angle on the problems of rehearsal. Unlike verse, prose implied factual truth in the later Middle Ages.[32] Prose suggested the mimesis of reality, of prior events as they actually happened, rather than of the continuously recycled words of a poetic tradition. Strikingly, however, the Man of Law also calls merchants (including the one from whom he learned his tale) the "fadres of tidynges / And of tales" (II.129–30). Defined in the *House of Fame* as "novelries" (*HF*, II.686), tidings are for Chaucer the very figure of replication; distorted in the process of transmission, they are the wayward stuff from which literary tradition is made.[33] Although perhaps not exactly true, tidings are at least up to the minute and recognizably involved in the exchanges of daily life. They suggest that the Man of Law objects not to rehearsal *tout court,* but only to iteration without change. Dialectical rather than stubbornly recalcitrant, the "tidyng" he offers instead promises something new and relevant—the in-

[31] "I speke in prose" is usually explained as a trace of incomplete revision; the Melibee is most commonly suggested as the tale originally assigned to the Man of Law. The verb form can also express habitual action: "I usually speak in prose"; for this argument, which I rely on below, see Tauno Mustanoja, *A Middle English Syntax,* Mémoires de Société néophilologique, 23 (Helsinki: Société néophilologique, 1960–), pp. 482–83; and Ralph W. V. Elliott, *Chaucer's English* (London: Deutsch, 1974), p. 96. For a summary of scholarship, see Benson's introductory note to the Man of Law's Introduction in the *Riverside Chaucer,* p. 854. Maura Nolan treats the claim to "speke in prose" as one of the inconsistencies indicating Fragment II's centrality to the Canterbury project; see "'Acquiteth yow now,'" pp. 141–42 and 150–51.

[32] For prose as the formal vehicle for "the literature of fact," see Gabrielle M. Spiegel, *The Past as Text: The Theory and Practice of Medieval Historiography* (Baltimore: Johns Hopkins University Press, 1997), pp. 179–94 (193).

[33] The merchants' tidings, associated with a tale told in prose, may obliquely glance at the *novelle* of Boccaccio's merchant epic, the *Decameron.* For tidings in the *House of Fame,* see Donald R. Howard, "Flying Through Space: Chaucer and Milton," in Joseph Anthony Wittreich, ed., *Milton and the Line of Vision* (Madison: University of Wisconsin Press, 1975), pp. 3–23; and Taylor, *Chaucer Reads the "Divine Comedy"* (Stanford: Stanford University Press, 1989), pp. 20–49. Wallace links the Man of Law's mercantile "tidynges" to Boccaccio, see *Chaucerian Polity,* pp. 205–9. See too Robert Hanning, "Custance and Ciappelletto in the Middle of It All: Problems of Mediation in The *Man of Law's Tale* and *Decameron* 1.1," in Leonard M. Koff and Brenda Deen Schildgen, eds., *"The Decameron" and the "Canterbury Tales": New Essays on an Old Question* (Madison, N.J.: Fairleigh Dickinson University Press, 2000), pp. 177–211.

novation that renews the tradition. (Whether the Man of Law's Tale actually delivers is a different issue altogether.)

His skepticism honed by skilled use of legal precedent, the Man of Law figures not only the audience Chaucer found ready to hand, but also the one he seeks to engender. The Man of Law's unwillingness registers a genuine obstacle to transposing the classical tradition into English. His reference to the Pierides intimates a dynamic structure that makes only unwelcome roles available to any but the Muses and their privileged "poetes." As a disgruntled reader of Chaucer's works, the Man of Law can be belittled as one of the *indoctum vulgus.* As a storyteller in his own right, he wishes to avoid destructive competition against an overwhelming foe capable of reducing him to a chattering magpie—a fate, he implies, that has already befallen Chaucer. Underlying this dismal version of tradition—in which emulation and innovation become inimical rivalry and senseless iteration—is a sense that English soil may be too stony to support the fragile new transplant: the language undeveloped, the writers unworthy of competing, the readers incapable as yet of discernment. The Man of Law's resistance cannot be magically purged as the error of a textual reader invented to be scorned or silenced. It must be answered.

The answer is buried in Chaucer's "volumes": imitation at one remove. To elude and transform readerly resistance to a classical tradition structured as Ovidian rivalry, Chaucer links the *Canterbury Tales* to Virgil as well.[34] Rather than asserting the connection directly with recognizable Virgilian allusions, however, he slips it in through the intermediary of Dante's reading of Virgil in the *Commedia.* Chaucer's appropriation of a Dantean pretext unknown to his contemporaneous English readers does not divide them into *doctum* and *indoctum vulgus,* according to their capacity to recognize both pretext and appropriation; and it cannot trigger anyone's sense of inadequacy to the classical tradition. Such appropriation of unshared material from a modern vernacular Italian poet is well suited to elude the skepticism modeled by the Man of Law: what he does not recognize he is less likely to dismiss out of hand. In principle neither private nor secret, the Dantean pretext is for the moment simply

---

[34] Chaucer's relationship with Gower may also spur him to elide rivalry as a model for literary dynamics. Chaucer's possible competition with Gower has been a frequent focus of criticism on the Man of Law and his tale; see, for instance, Nicholson, "The *Man of Law's Tale*"; Scala, "Canacee and the Chaucer Canon," p. 20; and Allen, "Chaucer Answers Gower."

unshared, and for that reason it is more likely to mediate effectively between the classical tradition and a new English audience.

"Whoso That Wole His Large Volume Seke"

This, then, is the function of Chaucer's borrowed volumes. As I will show in this section, the Man of Law's Ovidian "volume" rehearses Dante's first encounter with Virgil in the *Commedia;* together with the Wife of Bath's echo of *Paradiso* XXXIII's *volume,* this passage signals the role of Dante's competitive emulation of Virgil in shaping the Canterbury fiction of rehearsal. Reading through Dante's volumes, Chaucer imagines a version of literary tradition whose dynamic processes are not structured, as they are in his Dantean pretext, by the polarized Ovidian alternatives of too-faithful imitation and rivalrous displacement.

These alternatives frame the Man of Law's refusals of Chaucer's "volume." From the initial new morning to the final reference to the Muses and (or as) the Pierides, the terms of the literary context invoked in his Introduction are derived from *Purgatorio* I, where Dante emerges from the "l'aura morta" (dead air) of hell into the new Easter dawn:

> Ma qui la morta poesì resurga,
> o sante Muse, poi ch vostro sono;
> e qui Caliopè alquanto surga,
> seguitando il mio canto con quel suono
> di cui le Piche misere sentiro
> lo colpo tal, che disperar perdono.
> (*Purgatorio* I, 17, 7–12)

[But here let dead poetry rise again, O holy Muses, since I am yours; and here let Calliope rise up somewhat, accompanying my song with that strain whose stroke the wretched Pies felt so that they despaired of pardon.][35]

As preoccupied with rehearsal as the Man of Law's Introduction, *Purgatorio* I revises detail after detail of *Inferno* I, where Dante's otherworldly journey had begun in his rereading of Virgil. This rereading, represented

[35] "Le Piche" are the magpies into which the daughters of Pierides were transformed; see above for discussion. The new dawn of Easter morning at *Purgatorio* I, 13–21, revises Dante's failed reach for the sun's light on Good Friday at the beginning of the *Inferno,* and moreover, through the verb "resurgere" (*Purgatorio* I, 7), associates Dante's poetry with Christ's resurrection.

in Virgil's entry into the *Commedia* as the embodiment of the *Aeneid,* provides the specific pretext for Chaucer's first "volume."

For Dante as for Chaucer, "volume" signals the classical tradition and the modern poet's relation to it. The word maps the arc of the *Commedia* as Dante journeys from Virgil's material, human *volume* to the sacred *volume* of *Paradiso* XXXIII. When Virgil first appears in *Inferno* I, he identifies himself as the poet of the *Aeneid:*

> "Poeta fui, e cantai di quel giusto
> figliuol d'Anchise che venne di Troia,
> poi ch 'l superbo Iliòn fu combusto."
> *(Inferno* I, 73–75)

[I was a poet, and I sang of that just son of Anchises who came from Troy after proud Ilium was burned.]

Recognizing Virgil from this periphrasis, Dante offers an homage that is gradually tempered into something else:[36]

> "Or se' tu quel Virgilio e quella fonte
> che spandi di parlar sì largo fiume?"
> rispuos' io lui con vergognosa fronte.
> "O de li altri poeti onore e lume,
> vagliami 'l lungo studio e'l grande amore
> che m'ha fatto cercar lo tuo volume.
> Tu se' lo mio maestro e 'l mio autore,
> Tu se' solo colui da cu' io tolsi
> lo bello stilo che m'ha fatto onore."
> *(Inferno* I, 79–87)

["Are you, then, that Virgil, that fount which pours forth so broad a stream of speech?" I answered him, my brow covered with shame. "O glory [honor] and light of other poets, may the long study and the great love that have made me search your volume avail me! You are my master and my author. You alone are he from whom I took the fair style that has done me honor."]

[36] For discussion and bibliography, see Anthony K. Cassell, *Lecturae Dantis Americana Inferno* I (Philadelphia: University of Pennsylvania Press, 1989), pp. 77–93. Robert Hollander has treated this passage most thoroughly; see *Studies in Dante* (Ravenna: A. Longo, 1980), pp. 39–89, and *Il Virgilio dantesco: Tragedia nella Commedia* (Florence: Olschki, 1983), pp. 127–29.

In a classic expression of the trope of influence, Virgil is both the source ("quella fonte") and the river ("sì largo fiume") of poetry that flows into Dante and many other later poets. Casting Virgil as the teacher ("maestro") and author ("autore") who made him a poet, Dante praises Virgil's "bello stilo," the beautiful style whose emulation has done Dante "onore"—the same "onore" that earlier described Virgil himself (line 87, line 82). Despite the literal and figurative language of influence, then, this passage accomplishes poetically what it takes Dante three cantiche to accomplish narratively: supersession. Virgil begins the passage as the honor of other poets himself, and ends it by doing honor to Dante with that which Dante took from him: "lo bello stilo che m'ha fatto onore."

This passage initiates the intricate parallels between the *Aeneid* and the *Commedia* as well as Virgil's role as guide through the first two realms of the otherworld. The relation between Dante and Virgil is mimetic, built upon repetition and imitation. From "onore" to "onore"; from Anchises embracing Aeneas to Dante embracing Casella and Cacciaguida greeting his descendent Dante in the Heaven of Mars (*Aeneid* VI, 700–702; Purgatorio II, 76–81; Paradiso XV, 13–31);[37] and from Orpheus's haunting poetic disintegration into the Thracian landscape, with the threefold reechoing of Eurydice's name, to Virgil's own disappearance with the same threefold repetition of his name (*Georgics* IV, 525–27; *Purgatorio* XXX, 49–51),[38] the *Commedia* defines itself by emulating and going beyond the classical tradition—mainly Virgil and the plot of the *Aeneid,* but also Ovid and the figures of metamorphosis. In order to carve out its place in poetry's palace, the *Commedia* repeats those who have gone before; in order to arrive at its imitatio Christi, it imitates the Roman poets and their traditions.

[37] Imitating *Aeneid,* VI, 684–88 and quoting 835, where Anchises addresses Julius Caesar. Dante's meeting with Cacciaguida recalls *Purgatorio* I's reference to the muses: "Sì pïa l'ombra d'Anchise si porse / se fede merta *nostra maggior musa,* / quando in Eliso del figlio s'accorse" (With like affection did the shade of Anchises stretch forward [if *our greatest Muse* merits belief], when in Elysium he perceived his son, *Paradiso* XV, 25–27); by "nostra maggior musa" Dante means Virgil himself. For a definitive discussion, with full bibliography, of the role of Virgil in Dante's self-definition as a poet, see Teodolinda Barolini, *Dante's Poets: Textuality and Truth in the "Comedy"* (Princeton: Princeton University Press, 1984), pp. 188–286.
[38] See Robert Ball, "Virgil's *Pietas* and Dante's *Pietà,*" in Rachel Jacoff and Jeffrey T. Schnapp, *The Poetry of Allusion: Virgil and Ovid in Dante's "Commedia"* (Stanford: Stanford University Press, 1991), pp. 32 and 258. Virgil's disappearance, in which he is displaced by Beatrice, recalls *Inferno* I with the "chiaro fonte" (clear fount, *Purgatorio* XXX, 76) in which Dante, seeing himself, once again feels shame: "tanta vergogna mi gravò la fronte" (so great shame weighed on my brow, *Purgatorio* XXX, 78).

However much Dante depends on the *Aeneid* as a model, his relation to its author is also competitive. Virgil as a guide is replaced by Beatrice at the end of *Purgatorio*. Dante imagines the dynamic mimesis and departure of literary tradition through the same Pieridian competition cited by the Man of Law: the opening of *Purgatorio* (quoted above) aligns the *Commedia* with the "sante Muse" and the song of the victorious Calliope rather than with that of the "Piche misere," the wretched, defeated magpies. In his model of literary history, Dante continues the classical tradition represented by Virgil's "volume" in order to displace it with his own.

This displacement culminates in the *Commedia*'s metaphor of the universe and its creator as a bound book. The "volume" of *Paradiso* XXXIII establishes Dante's claim to derive poetic authority from his imitation of the universe as God's book; it also measures the chasm between the theological poetry of the *Commedia* and the secular poetry of Dante's chief models and rivals, especially Virgil and Guido Cavalcanti.[39] In Dante's fourteenth-century Italian, *volume* could refer both to the heavenly spheres and the products of bookmaking; both meanings converge in the metaphor of the universe as a book.[40] Dante's heavenly *volume* is

---

[39] With this metaphor Dante also supersedes his "primo amico" and chief modern rival, Guido Cavalcanti. Dante had previously echoed the rhyme scheme of Cavalcanti's most famous canzone, "Donna me prega" ("A Lady Asks Me") in *Inferno* X, 65–69 (*nome/come/lume*). The highly abstract "sustanze e accidenti e lor costumi" (substances and accidents and their relations) echoes the same passage along with the signature rhyme (*lume/costume*). Here Dante distances himself for the last time from Cavalcanti's pathbreaking vernacular poetry, which uses the language of secular Aristotelian philosophy to construct love as a finite, created, knowable product of the sensible faculty, rather than (as in the *Commedia*) of the rational faculty with its transcendent participation in divine being: "elli è creato—ed ha sensato—nome, / d'alma costume—e di cor volontate" ([Love] is a created thing, and takes its name from its perception through the senses; it is a habit [*costume*] of the soul and a desire of the heart; lines 19–20); Gianfranco Contini, ed., *Poeti del duecento* (Milan: Riccardo Ricciardi, 1960), vol. 2, pp. 524–25; translation mine. For Dante's "need to define himself as not (*inter alios*) Guido Cavalcanti," see Teodolinda Barolini, "Dante and the Lyric Past," in *The Cambridge Companion to Dante*, ed. Rachel Jacoff (Cambridge: Cambridge University Press, 1993), p. 22. For a recent treatment of Cavalcanti's "synthesis of philosophy and vernacular lyric," see Alison Cornish, "A Lady Asks: The Gender of Vulgarization in Late Medieval Italy," *PMLA* 115 (2000): 165–80 (170).

[40] Derived from *volvere*, to roll, *volumen* had originally meant a scroll, but by the fourteenth century this had changed along with the technologies of bookmaking. The meanings of *volume* as a book by itself, and as a constitutive part of a work, began to appear in Italian texts in the early fourteenth century, primarily but not exclusively in Italian translations of the works of the Latin Church Fathers; see Manlio Cortelazzo and Michele A. Cortellazzo, eds., *Dizionario etimologico della lingua italiana*, 2nd ed. (Bologna: Zanichelli, 1999). Dante uses the word in each sense separately elsewhere in the *Para-*

clearly a codex consisting of quires bound together ("legato," *Paradiso* XXXIII, 86) to overcome the usual incompleteness of both universe and manuscripts, which are fragmented respectively into substances and accidents or separately circulating fascicles; the entropic tendencies of both are captured in the neologism "si squaderna" (dis-quartoes itself, 87).[41] The *Commedia*'s last, most capacious *volume* answers its first: the material, human, classical *Aeneid,* introduced in *Inferno* I as "lo tuo volume," is superseded by the sacred "volume" of *Paradiso* XXXIII.

Chaucer's first "volume" takes up Dante's first *volume,* and through it the Virgilian tradition. Despite the Man of Law's offhanded contempt toward Chaucer's works, his words—"Whoso that wole his large *volume seke*" (Man of Law's Introduction, II.60)—echo Dante's loving, assiduous study of Virgil: "'l lungo studio e 'l grande amore / che m'ha fatto *cercar il tuo volume,*" the long study and great love that have made me search your volume, *Inferno* I, 83–84). Chaucer had appropriated the scene of Dante's encounter with Virgil once before, in the *Parlement of Foules* in the early 1380s, without, however, using the word *volume.* New to English in the 1380s and still rare, the word is distinctive enough to point us toward the issues involved in its two appearances in the *Canterbury Tales.* A comparison between the two adaptations can illuminate the stakes of Chaucer's choice of words. In the *Parlement,* Chaucer adapts Dante's trope of the embodied text, with a characteristically different exchange of speaker and addressee. Thus the speaker is "Affrican," who has been conjured into the dream from the poet-dreamer's bedtime reading material, Macrobius's *The Dream of Scipio.* Affrican promises to reward the reader for his diligent labors:

---

diso. Thus, in a metaphorical usage, "volume" refers to the book of God's future judgments in "leggendo del magno volume" (reading in the great volume, *Paradiso* XV, 50), where the verb clarifies the nature of the metaphor. The Primum Mobile is a "volume" in its astronomical meaning, a revolving sphere (*Paradiso* XXVIII, 14); see too *Paradiso* XXIII, 112, referring to "tutti i volumi," all the heavenly spheres. Elsewhere the two meanings are conjoined; see *Paradiso* II, 76–78, which figures the moon's sphere as the verso and recto of a vellum manuscript: "sì come comparte/lo grasso e'l magro un corpo, così questo/nel suo volume cangerebbe carte" (just as fat and lean are distributed in a body, it would alternate the pages in its volume); similarly *Paradiso* XVII, 37 refers to the sublunary world with a pun on "quaderno" as fascicle and as the four spheres of earth, water, air, and fire.

[41] For the analogy between the universe as God's book and the material circulation of Dante's books in manuscript, see John Ahern, "Binding the Book: Hermeneutics and Manuscript Production in *Paradiso* 33," *PMLA* 97 (1982): 800–809.

"Thow hast the so wel born
In lokynge of myn olde bok totorn,
Of which Macrobye roughte nat a lyte,
That sumdel of thy labour wolde I quyte."
(*Parlement of Foules*, 109–12)

In this earlier adaptation, Chaucer uses a lexically more distant phrase to translate "cercar il tuo volume."[42] The new English word *volume*, reasonably accessible from both Latin and French, began appearing a few years after the *Parlement of Foules* in two kinds of texts: Wycliffite sermons and the Bible translation, and the English translation of Ranulf Hidgen's *Polychronicon*.[43] A brief excursion through its emerging English usages during the 1380s will help to frame Chaucer's two *volumes* when, a decade or so after the *Parlement*, he returned to Dante's scenes of reading in the Man of Law's Introduction and the Wife of Bath's Prologue.[44]

In its earliest, Wycliffite, attestations, *volume* refers to a book, either scroll or codex.[45] It was used consistently for inclusive and authoritative codifications of sacred law; when the reference is to a object, it is invariably a scroll. Thus a Wycliffite sermon uses the metaphor of a huge rolled-up scroll to mock the fraternal orders as new Pharisees for their superfluous additions to scripture: "men algatis don wrse nou, for in stede of philateries, men maken gret uolyms of new lawes þat been not

---

[42] In the *Commedia*, Dante is the speaker, summoning Virgil (and the *Aeneid*) into his poem and praising him in the second person; in the *Parlement*, Chaucer imagines Affrican speaking in the first person, laying claim to Macrobius's book as his own and summoning his own reader.

[43] For French *volume*, see Adolf Tobler, *Altfranzösisches Wörterbuch*, ed. and rev. Erhard Lommatzsch and Hans Helmut Christmann (Wiesbaden: Franz Steiner, 1995), s.v. *volume;* Tobler-Lommatsch cites attestations of the word in Brunetto Latini's *Trésor* and Jean Froissart's *Prison d'amour*. For Anglo-Norman French, see William Rothwell with Stewart Gregory and D. A. Trotter, *Anglo-Norman Dictionary* (London: Mondern Humanities Research Association, 1992), s.v. *volume*. For English, see the online *Middle English Dictionary*, http://ets.umdl.umich.edu/m/med, s.v. *volume*. My analysis is based on the *MED*'s unpublished lexical files; see note 5. The French historical dictionaries are not comparably comprehensive.

[44] The precise dates of the Man of Law's Introduction and the Wife of Bath's Prologue are uncertain. The Introduction's use of Nicholas of Lynn's *Kalendarium* dates it after 1386; the discussion of Gower's *Confessio Amantis* suggests a date after 1390. The Wife of Bath's Prologue is usually dated in the early- to mid-1390s; see Benson, *Riverside Chaucer*, p. 864.

[45] The spatial meanings of the word did not enter English until the seventeenth century; see the online *Oxford English Dictionary*, http://ets.umdl.umich.edu/cgi/o/oed, s.v. *volume*.

Goddis comaundementis."[46] The word also appears in the Wycliffite translations of the Bible. In the 1382 translation of Ezekiel 3:1–3, where God commands Ezekiel to eat a "volumen," the English "volum" refers to a scroll (the "involutus liber," rolled-up book, Ezekiel 2:9); thus God's word is put into the prophet's mouth. More literally, I Ezra 6:2 uses "volume" for an item in the "bibliotheca librorum" (library of books); similarly, the "volume of moises" in Nehemiah 13:1 is read aloud to the people of Israel. In both passages the English word translates Latin *volumen*. The 1382 version of Deuteronomy 28:58 reads: "But if þow keep and do alle þe wordes of þis lawe, þat been wryten in þis volym"; the 1388 version changes the syntax and ends "in þis volym ether book"—the gloss perhaps suggesting that the new English loan word in the 1382 translation had not been sufficiently clear, or more likely distinguishing between part (the book Deuteronomy) and whole (the volume of the entire Bible).[47] This meaning also accords well with its most common French usage, in which *volume* refers to a book consisting of several parts or works.

The meaning of a gathering of parts or works also informs the other early attestations of *volume,* a group of six found in John Trevisa's 1387 translation of Hidgen's *Polychronicon.* Trevisa's volumes are large collections: the laws of Justinian (V.535), the works of Hippocrates (V.27) and Eusebius (IV.109), and the capacious reading of Jerome (IV.109).[48] Although the works in a volume need not be sacred (they are also medi-

[46] Sermon 154, in Anne Hudson and Pamela Gradon, *English Wycliffite Sermons,* 5 vols. (Oxford: Clarendon Press, 1983–96), vol. 3, ed. Hudson (1990), p. 89. The English Wycliffite sermons probably belong to the last two decades of the fourteenth century; see Gradon's analysis, vol. 3, pp. xcix–cii.

[47] All citations from the Wycliffite translations of the Bible and the *Polychronicon* are taken from the *MED*'s lexical files or the online *MED.* Citations of the 1382 Wycliffite Bible, except those from Ezekiel are from *The Earlier Version of the Wycliffite Bible,* ed. Conrad Lindberg, 6 vols., *Stockholm Studies in English* (1959–73); Oxford, Bodleian Library MS Bodley 959 (1382) is the preferred MS for Deuteronomy and Ezra. For Ezekiel, the *MED* prefers later Cambridge University Library MS Corpus Christi College 4 (1425). See *The Holy Bible by John Wycliffe and His Followers,* ed. J. Forshall and F. Madden, 4 vols., Rolls Series 41 (Great Britain Public Record Office: 1850), vol. 3.

[48] Typical of secular and sacred volumes are these two citations: "Iustinianus . . . gadrede þe lawes of þe Romayns . . . into a volym of twelf bookes and cleped þat volym Iustinianus his code"(V.535); and "Of hym [Jerome] Eusebius writeþ þat he hadde as if were an þritty þowsand volumes of bookes in his librarie" (IV. 109), quoted from *Polychronicon Ranulfi Hidgen,* ed. C. Babington and J. R. Lumby, 8 vols. (London: Longman, 1865–86). The text is edited from Cambridge University Library MS St. John's College H.1, dated 1387.

cal, historical, legal, or other secular writings), they are consistently authoritative and ancient. John Trevisa modestly contrasts the ancient authorities to their modern digest, his own *Polychronicon;* the purpose of the present work, he writes, is to make it possible "þat they mowe be enformed . . . by þis short tretys, þat haveþ nouȝt i-seie þe grete volyms and large, þat beeth of stories i-write" (I.15). The *Polychronicon* is a summary compilation of ancient authorities for those to whom these sources, contained in large volumes, are inaccessible. Its own authority, here implied more modestly, is derived from the ancients. *Volume,* in its earliest English usages, thus referred to large books, usually collections of ancient, authoritative, and often sacred works.

In Chaucer's two uses, *volume* likewise means a codex in which shorter works are collected. Given the other fourteenth-century uses of the word, in particular those of the 1380s, its use here suggests that the place of Chaucer's works should be sought among ancient, even sacred authorities. Contemporary English readers could have grasped the implications of Chaucer's word choice even without knowing how closely it renders Dante's *volume.* But any link to an authoritative classical tradition forged by "volume" must be treated cautiously. The "volume" sniped at by the Man of Law compiles works that are scarcely sacred, authoritative, or ancient; rather, they are the modern works of a hack writer. The delicious comic misrepresentation—Chaucer taken to task by his disgruntled reader—dismantles (or unmasks) the scene it rehearses, in which Dante honors Virgil as a prelude to displacing him.

Nevertheless, "volume" registers serious literary ambition. It suggests that Chaucer, as so frequently, was provoked to work out ideas about the classical tradition and his own poetic aspirations in contrast to those he found in Dante.[49] Hidden beneath the Ovidian affiliations of Chaucer's first "volume" are glimpses of another book: Virgil's *volume* and the twisted chain that links it, through Dante, to the *Canterbury Tales.* It is to the *Aeneid* that I now turn.[50]

[49] For a parallel argument with respect to *Troilus and Criseyde,* see Winthrop P. Wetherbee, *Chaucer and the Poets: An Essay on "Troilus and Criseyde"* (Ithaca: Cornell University Press, 1984).

[50] For Virgil's readership in England, see Christopher Baswell's *Virgil in Medieval England: Figuring the "Aeneid" from the Twelfth Century to Chaucer* (Cambridge: Cambridge University Press, 1995). Baswell's study of the manuscript evidence shows how narrow the chiefly clerical English Virgilian tradition was during the three centuries before Chaucer's own writing.

67

"Nec Revocare Situs Aut Iungere Carmina Curat"

Because Chaucer's "large volume" points through his own Ovidian works and Dante's words back to Virgil's "volume," it signals a broad engagement with the multilayered dynamics of the classical tradition, of which Dante's supersession of Virgil is but one layer. The stark polarities of the Man of Law's Introduction—magpies and muses, competition and rehearsal—come to open combat in the Wife of Bath's Prologue. These polarities, as I will argue, are ultimately tempered by an alternative model in which literary history is generated from the waywardness of readers. Surprisingly, this waywardness is initially anchored in the *Aeneid*.

The way back to the *Aeneid* proceeds through Dante's supersessory narrative. Since the Man of Law's and Wife of Bath's volumes incorporate both *termini* of this narrative into the *Canterbury Tales,* they point to Chaucer's awareness of Virgil's spectral presence at the end of the *Commedia.* Virgil as an embodied character has long since disappeared when Dante envisions the universe "legato con amore in un volume" (bound with love in a single volume, *Paradiso* XXXIII, 86). Yet Virgilian echoes do not disappear, and the poem's final vision glances back at the *Aeneid* in two ways. First, it recalls both Virgil's "volume" and the "amore" with which Dante had studied it (Inferno I, 83–84). Second, the bound volume counters the *Commedia*'s last verbal echo of the *Aeneid,* in which Dante compares his vanished vision to the scattered leaves of the Cumaean Sibyl:

> Così la neve al sol si disigilla;
> così al vento ne le foglie levi
> si perdea la sentenza di Sibilla
> (Paradiso XXXIII, 64–66).

[Thus is the snow unsealed by the sun; thus in the wind, on the light leaves, the Sibyl's oracle was lost.]

Both images work together to contrast Dante's final vision to the *Aeneid.* The melting snow ("si disigilla")[51] anticipates the dissolution of "si

---

[51] Battaglia and Squarotti, eds., *Grande dizionario della lingua italiana,* s.v. *dissigillare* and *sigillare. Dissigillare* means "to open, to break the seal of a letter." The reflexive form *si disigillare* is Dante's metaphorical coinage, and is defined as "perdere la propria forma, perdere l'impronta ricevuta" (to lose one's proper form, to lose the stamped impression).

squaderna" (*Paradiso* XXXIII, 87); more centrally, the wind-scattered leaves provide the point of departure for Dante's bookbinding metaphor.

In linking the dispersed state of the universe to the Sibyl's leaves, *Paradiso* XXXIII revisits the third book of the *Aeneid,* where Helenus urges Aeneas to consult the Sibyl, and warns him to get her prophecy in spoken words rather than on the leaves on which she usually writes the future. Customarily, having marked signs on the leaves, she orders and seals them in her cave; but when the door turns, the wind scatters the leaves. As they flutter about, disarranged and disjoined, the prophecy is lost forever:

> "illa manent immota locis neque ab ordine cedunt;
> uerum eadem, uerso tenuis cum cardine uentus
> impulit et teneras turbauit ianua frondes,
> numquam deinde cauo uolitantia prendere saxo
> nec reuocare situs aut iungere carmina curat."

["These remain unmoved in their places and quit not their rank; but when at the turn of the hinge a light breeze has stirred them, and the open door scattered the tender foliage, never does she thereafter care to catch them, as they flutter in the rocky cave, nor to recover their places, nor to unite the verses."][52]

When Aeneas later gets the Sibyl's prophecy in spoken form, the sequential sounds of speech and syntax order the sense usually lost to the wind: "foliis tantum ne carmina manda, / ne turbata uolent rapidis ludibria uentis; / ipsa canas oro" (*Aeneid* VI, 74–76) ["Only trust not thy verses to leaves, lest they fly in disorder, the sport of rushing winds; chant them thyself, I pray"]. Thus the Sibyl's chanted prophecy of the Trojans' future in Italy is preserved in Virgil's own heroic song ("Arma virumque *cano*") and in the leaves of his *volume.* The Sibyl becomes Aeneas's guide to the underworld, just as Virgil later becomes Dante's guide to the afterlife. Her wind-blown leaves come to stand for the dispersed universe when at last (and only at the last) he leaves Virgil's book behind. Compared to Dante's heavenly volume, the *Aeneid* now appears not bound together, but scattered "ab ordine" (*Aeneid,* III, 447), out of its order, by a reader who supersedes his classical model.

---

[52] *Aeneid* III, 447–51; *P. Vergili Maronis Opera,* ed. R. A. B. Mynors, Oxford Classical Texts (Oxford: Clarendon Press, 1969; rev. ed. 1977); *Eclogues, Georgics, Aeneid,* ed. and trans. H. R. Fairclough, Loeb Classical Library (London: William Heinemann; and Cambridge, Mass.: Harvard University Press, 1968), vol. 1, pp. 378–79.

Chaucer's alternative to Dante's vaunting supersession begins to emerge by the end of the Introduction, where the Man of Law's refusal to rhyme reaches for a surprising link to the classical tradition. Coming directly after rejection of the Ovidian Pierides, his "hawebake," an image of impoverishment, contrasts prose to everything literary:

> "But nathelees, I recche noght a bene
> Though I come after hym with hawebake.
> I speke in prose, and lat him rymes make."
> (II.94–96)

Yet this passage also echoes the Virgilian tradition. Behind the scanty nourishment of beans and "hawebake" (baked haws) lurks a shadowy resemblance to Statius humbly coming after Virgil in the envoy to the *Thebaid:* "vive, precor; nec tu divinam Aeneida tempta, / sed longe sequere et vestigia semper adora" (O live, I pray! nor rival the divine *Aeneid,* but follow afar and ever venerate its footsteps).[53] The Virgilian reverberation is distant, mediated not only by Statius but also by Dante and by Chaucer in two of his own earlier works. The envoy of the *Thebaid* had already formed the cornerstone of the house of poetic fame at the end of *Troilus and Criseyde,* where Chaucer bids his poem to "kis the steppes where as thow seest pace / Virgile, Ovide, Omer, Lucan, and Stace" (*Troilus and Criseyde,* V.1791–92). This earlier homage to the classical tradition, Helen Cooper reminds us, was an idea also cribbed from Dante.[54] The Man of Law's resemblance to Statius is fainter, visible only in the outline of a reader following behind his author with humbler offerings, and only through the mediation of a second and more attenuated Chaucerian reuse in the Prologue to the *Legend of Good Women.* In that poem (the object of the Man of Law's disdain), Chaucer, represent-

[53] *Thebaid,* XII.816–17; *Statius,* ed. and trans. J. H. Mozley (London: William Heinemann; and Cambridge, Mass.: Harvard University Press, 1969), vol. 2, pp. 504–5.

[54] Helen Cooper, "After Chaucer," p. 16. The passage is borrowed from Dante's encounter with the virtuous pagans, in which he is the "sesto tra cotanto senno," the sixth among such lofty intellects, *Inferno* IV, 102. Wallace, *Chaucerian Polity,* pp. 80–82, takes the recurrent "sixth of six" in Chaucer's works as "authorial signatures" (along with the more obvious naming of himself in the Man of Law's Introduction, II.47) signaling both "ambitions of European magnitude" and "misgivings about the ethical value of such writing" (p. 81); one such signature is the Wife of Bath's invitation to a sixth husband to step forward ("Welcome the sixte, whan that evere he shal," Wife of Bath's Prologue, III.45).

ing himself as a gleaner in fields already harvested by earlier writers, had figured his relationship to his chosen traditions as belated rehearsal:

> And I come after, glenyng here and there,
> And am ful glad yf I may fynde an ere
> Of any goodly word that ye han left.
> And thogh it happen me rehercen eft
> That ye han in your fresshe songes say,
> Forbereth me, and beth nat evele apayd
> (*Legend of Good Women,* FProl.75–80)

Thus for one last time the Man of Law rehearses his author in the act of refusing him. Although the poverty of scanty forage and "hawebake" registers a certain diffidence—or better, an ambivalence toward the fact that a poet's ambitions are finally subject to the revisions of readers— the Man of Law has been transformed into a reader more cooperative than his refusals of the poetic otherwise suggest. The humbleness of the fare reveals its exalted lineage, which is traced back through Chaucer's previous reuses to its ancestor in Statius's reverent adoration of Virgil. As with Chaucer's unrecognized appropriation of Dante, the indirection of the Virgilian connection helps to circumvent readerly resistance to literary reuse. In effect, the Man of Law models the potential for an initially unpromising reader—apparently a representative *indoctum vulgus*—to "come after," and to become the reader Chaucer needs. His refractoriness enacts the sobering truth that a literary tradition survives in its readers as well as in its writers—and that competent readers transpose as well as imitate. Writers need readers, even those like Dante, who glorify themselves at the expense of their predecessors. Though the Man of Law does not exactly cover himself in glory when he snipes at Chaucer, surprisingly it is through his final refusal of the poetic that he achieves a vital emulation of the classical tradition. In the scene of reception figured in the Man of Law's Introduction, Chaucer emerges not as a "Daunt in Inglissh" but as an English Virgil. Far from thwarting Chaucer's effort to introduce the classics to his new English audience, the Man of Law's irreducible waywardness instead presages its success.

"Turne Over the Leef and Chese Another Tale"

But does the Man of Law really resemble Statius, humbly following in his author's footsteps? The reading I have just offered recuperates his resistance too neatly.[55] It is comforting but implausible to think that real readers so docilely imitate their textual models; as a textual invention, the Man of Law also registers the limits of a writer's control over reception. So where does Chaucer put the profoundly discomfiting waywardness of readers? My answer is familiar, though reframed by Chaucer's borrowed volumes: he builds it into the very structure of the *Canterbury Tales* as a consequence of its status as a rehearsal and a volume, a collection of parts. He does so, moreover, with the image Dante had used to supersede Virgil in the *Commedia:* the scattered leaves of the Sibyl's prophecy.

Chaucer was not alone in turning to the Sibyl as a metaphor to register the reading of Dante's *volume.* On 5 October 1402, Christine de Pizan began to compose *Le chemin de longue estude* (*The Path of Long Study*),[56] a Boethian dream vision whose title derives from the source of the Man of Law's "volume," the "lungo studio" (*Inferno* I, 83) with which Dante honors Virgil. The *Chemin*'s dream begins with a large-scale imitation of Virgil's advent in the *Commedia,* as a tall woman dressed in the ancient manner appears to guide Christine's visionary journey. The guide identifies herself through a long periphrasis as the seeress who guided Aeneas through the underworld (lines 596–600), and finally names herself as the "Sebille Cumee" (632), the Cumaean Sibyl whose scattered leaves inform not only Dante's last echo of Virgil's *volume* but also the narrative image of Chaucer's second "volume," the book rent apart by the Wife of Bath. As a woman writing in French, Christine addressed a different set of problems by constructing her relationship to the classical tradition through a Sibyl whom she is willing to follow.[57] Chaucer's appropriation of the action—not the figure herself—suggests a more refractory reading.

Chaucer's scattered leaves first appear well before the Wife of Bath's Prologue, in the authorial apology of the Miller's Prologue. The Miller's

---

[55] Maura Nolan warns that in resolving the textual and discursive difficulties of Fragment II, we risk the loss of history itself "in substituting an easy homology for the historical tension it reveals" (" 'Acquiteth yow now,' " p. 152).

[56] The date comes from the poem itself; see Christine de Pizan, *Le Chemin de longue Étude,* ed. Andrea Tarnowski, Lettres gothiques (Paris: Librairie Générale Française, 2000), lines 186–88.

[57] This parallel suggests that the intertextual relationship between Christine and Chaucer offers a fertile field for inquiry, as Theresa Coletti demonstrates in "Paths of Long Study: Reading Chaucer and Christine de Pizan in Tandem," *SAC* 28 (2007): 1–40.

Prologue is important not only for its recasting of the fiction of rehearsal but also for the Miller's disorderliness: his revolt against the Host's proposed order of tales. Although Chaucer distances himself from the "cherles tale" he is compelled to rehearse, his remedy in effect invites offended readers to imitate the Miller:

> M'athynketh that I shal reherce it here.
> And therfor every gentil wight I preye,
> For Goddes love, demeth nat that I sey
> Of yvel entente, but for I moot reherce
> Hir tales alle, be they better or werse,
> Or elles falsen som of my mateere.
> And therefore, whoso list it nat yheere,
> Turne over the leef and chese another tale.
>   (ProlMilT, I.3170–77)

The final line invites what resistant readers do anyway: disorder the work, in a discontinuous kind of reading especially viable with a volume comprised of leaves and parts. The ensuing preview (or content warning) of the generic and social variety of the collection ensures that readers can make informed choices. Chaucer twice abdicates responsibility for his rehearsed tales and shifts it explicitly to his audience: "Blameth nat me if that ye chese amys" (I.3181; repeated at I.3185). Long recognized as central to Chaucer's construction (or deconstruction) of his poetic authority in the *Canterbury Tales,* the apology not only articulates an internal authorial idea of (dis)order but also prefigures the external material history of the work. To judge from the manuscripts, Chaucer's scribes took the invitation quite literally, copying variously selected tales in any which order. Although the invitation does not itself cause the variety of manuscript orders, it does anticipate its inevitability, and finds a way to incorporate the inevitable as part of the plan rather than as its disruption.

We have traveled a long way from Dante's bound volume, through Virgil's scattered leaves, to the jumbled orders chosen by disgruntled (or even delighted) readers of Chaucer's Canterbury volume. Reframed as a response to Dante's displacement of Virgil, the shift of authorial responsibility in the Miller's Prologue takes on new significance as part of Chaucer's effort to link English to the classical tradition. By accommodating wayward readers in the plan of the work, Chaucer weighs

Dante's supersessory poetics against the practical literary and linguistic constraints of the English context within which he wrote. These constraints would have made nonsense of the ambitions of any poet who sought to make his place by overtly displacing his forebears. The early Italian vernacular traditions, and Dante's writings in particular, were defined by competition between Latin and vernacular; such competitive assertiveness makes sense for local vernaculars whose very name— *latino*—betrays an intimate filiation with their learned parent tongue.[58] The competition between languages for the authority to express Truth subtends Dante's dialectic treatment of Virgil, whom he both honors and supersedes; it also subtends his treatment of the earlier Italian vernacular poets, embodied in Guido Cavalcanti, whose fault (as Dante constructs it) is an insufficient connection to the Virgilian tradition: a lack of vernacular ambition.

But such competition could not address the particular situation of the even newer English vernacular literary writings. Like Pandarus, always hopping behind, English was later than French or Italian in developing the conditions for a full-blown literary language and public, largely because it had to displace the more prestigious sister vernacular, French.[59] For this reason, competition with Latin could not play the same formative role as it did in the development of Italian vernacular traditions; hence Chaucer could attempt to re-create an English classicism by resembling Virgil rather than by displacing him. It is a consequence less of tact than of nicely gauged tactics that the vernacular tradition Chaucer competes with isn't the familiar French, but the unfamiliar Italian: Who would care that he tears up Dante? No one resists a rupture that is slipped in unnoticed.

At issue here is nothing less than different models of literary history and vernacular poetic authority: neither Statius's reverent imitation nor

---

[58] An immediately relevant example (cited in Hanning, "Custance and Ciappelletto," p. 190) is in Boccaccio's version of the Custance story, in which Gostanza is addressed in "latino"—that is, Italian (*Decameron* 5.2, 16, in *Tutte le Opere di Giovanni Boccaccio*, vol. 4, ed. Vittore Branca [Milan: Mondadori, 1976]). For the competition between Latin and vernacular, see Barolini, "Dante and the Lyric Past," and *Dante's Poets;* and Cornish, "A Lady Asks"; see too Warren Ginsberg, *Dante's Aesthetics of Being* (Ann Arbor: University of Michigan Press, 1999), pp. 96–159. Dante's *De vulgari eloquentia* argues for a purified literary Italian as a worthy successor to Latin.

[59] Cooper cites the lack of fertile connection among the languages of England as part of Chaucer's literary context: "By the fourteenth century, French and Latin literatures tended to exist alongside English, rather than interbreeding with it. Chaucer radically changed that" ("After Chaucer," p. 11).

Dante's competitive supersession, but a model in which the necessary resistance of readers is accommodated as part of the authorial fiction of rehearsal. Dante, in claiming to surpass Virgil, arrogates all difference and innovation for himself; as a consequence of his powerful claim to vernacular authority, he also asserts an almost vatic power to dictate the reading of " 'l poema sacro." The reader's role is completely imitative; if you do not follow my grand "legno" (ship) in your "piccioletta barca" (little bark, *Paradiso* II, 3, 1), Dante warns, you will be a shipwreck, disqualified as a good reader.[60] In the Miller's Prologue and the Man of Law's Introduction, Chaucer reverses the roles: with his fiction of rehearsal, it is the poet who imitates; readers, on the other hand, refuse iteration, disorder the pages of the volume, and, out of their refusals, make the classical tradition live and speak in English. Chaucer instead builds his vernacular authority from refractory readers; the roles he constructs for them are skeptical, rebellious, destructive—everything but docilely imitative.

Loose Leaves and Deaf Ears

Literary history as active, competitive resistance reaches a crisis with Chaucer's second "volume," when the Wife of Bath reverses Dante's binding of his book by snatching page(s) from Jankyn's book. In a constitutive irony, however, her violent refusal necessarily rehearses the supersessory version of poetic imitation from which the *Commedia* is made. The Wife does to Jankyn's book, and Chaucer does to Dante, what Dante had done to Virgil: they all tear pages from their predecessors' carefully ordered and bound volumes. Like the Man of Law, the Wife of Bath is a refractory reader; her revolt from Jankyn's tyrannical "custume" becomes one of the cornerstones on which Chaucer builds both the innovations and the surprising classicism of the *Canterbury Tales*.

Much recent criticism has focused on the Wife's fictional battle with the antifeminist tradition gathered in Jankyn's "book of wikked wyves."[61] The *volume/custume* rhyme singles out quite precisely the qualities that come under critical scrutiny here. Like the volumes in the *Poly-*

---

[60] The classic treatments of Dante's addresses to his readers are Erich Auerbach, "Dante's Addresses to the Reader," *RP* 7(1954): 268–78; Leo Spitzer, "The Addresses to the Reader in the *Commedia*," in Spitzer, *Romanische Literaturstudien 1936–56* (Tübingen: Max Niemeyer, 1959), pp. 574–95; and Hermann Gmelin, "Die Anreden an den Leser in Dantes *Komödie*," *Deutsches Dante-Jahrbuch* 29–30 (1951): 260–70.

[61] See especially Carolyn Dinshaw, *Chaucer's Sexual Poetics*, pp. 113–31.

chronicon, Jankyn's compilation claims both inclusiveness and intellectual authoritativeness. Because it is also represented as a clerical tradition, this volume is also aligned with the sacred authority of Wycliffite usages. If the emergent English lexeme *volume* suggests the book's inclusive authority, the already familiar *custume* encodes its repetition. Jankyn's "custume"—as both the obnoxious personal habit of one bratty young clerk and the collective discourse of an entire tribe of scholars—illustrates the perils of a self-ratifying tradition, which derives cultural authority from its history of repetition.[62] The Wife relates enough of the book's content to suggest the oppressiveness of its repetitive prescriptions of her nature and moral capacity; its foreclosure of alternatives elicits her unexpectedly piercing response: "Who wolde wene, or who wolde suppose, / The wo that in myn herte was, and pyne?" (Wife of Bath's Prologue, III.786–87). Like the Man of Law, she is doomed to rehearse what she refuses, even as she diagnoses its shortcoming:

> Who peyntede the leon, tel me who?
> By God, if wommen hadde writen stories,
> As clerkes han withinne hire oratories,
> They wolde han writen of men moore wikkednesse
> Than al the mark of Adam may redresse.
>
> . . . .
>
> The clerk, whan he is oold, and may noght do
> Of Venus werkes worth his olde sho,
> Thanne sit he doun, and write in his dotage
> That wommen kan nat kepe hir mariage!
> (III.692–96, 707–10)

The Wife's memorable image drives her point home with considerable force: what purports to be the whole story, chorused in unison by a thousand voices, is instead only one story told from a very partial perspective.

Yet no matter how acutely she lays open the partiality of the antifeminist universal, her intellectual keenness has been blunted by Jankyn's "custume." Long before she is "beten for a book" (III.712) and deafened

---

[62] *Middle English Dictionary,* s.v. *costume;* the first two definitions, both attested by the early fourteenth century, concern, respectively, the traditional customs or usages of a nation or group, and the personal habit or usage of an individual.

physically for tearing it apart, she is deafened by listening to it. Her bodily damage is one of the first things we learn about her in the General Prologue: she is deaf in one ear because of the retaliatory blow Jankyn fetches her in the epic battle with which this essay began.[63] Her deafness also aptly figures her intellectual experience and rhetorical conduct as, for instance, she outtalks the composite "good" husband in her advice to "wise wyves" by overwhelming him/them with words kidnapped from the antifeminist tradition (III.193–451 [225]). Since she doesn't allow this husband a word in his own defense, it is she alone who speaks the words of the inimical traditions she has appropriated.

As a result, long after unleaving Jankyn's volume, she continues to repeat it. Her past haunts her present, and ours too. For the deafening tendency of a cultural script to reproduce itself becomes the chief interpretative question of the Wife of Bath's discourse: whether, far from achieving a real or imagined alternative to the antifeminist tradition, she might willy-nilly perpetuate it.[64] Despite their otherwise pronounced differences, then, the Wife of Bath shares the Man of Law's problem with rehearsal. And as we have already seen, rehearsal is also Chaucer's problem, both as the fundamental fiction of the *Canterbury Tales* and in the difficulties he faces in transposing his chosen literary traditions into English.

In the Wife of Bath's discourse, the destruction of the book is the first of two narrative images that address the problem of rehearsal. Embodying intellectual rebellion in violent physical action, the Wife tears one or three pages from the offending book and eventually has Jankyn cast its remains into the fire. The satisfying poetic justice both puts a

---

[63] See General Prologue, I.446: "But she was somdel deef, and that was scathe." The Wife mentions Jankyn's blow twice before she actually narrates the event; see Wife of Bath's Prologue, III.667–68, which refers to only one page torn from the book; III.711–12; and the full narrative at III.788–825, which refers to three pages torn from the book.

[64] This is widely recognized as the central question of the Wife of Bath's discourse. The dialectic between subversion and replication takes on cultural dimensions in feminist criticism, in which it is a question not of a fictional character's experience but of the poet's representational and discursive choices. For the argument for subversion, see Jill Mann, *Geoffrey Chaucer* (New York: Harvester Wheatsheaf, 1991), pp. 70–86. Both Dinshaw, *Chaucer's Sexual Poetics*, pp. 113–31; and Elaine Tuttle Hanson, *Chaucer and the Fictions of Gender* (Berkeley and Los Angeles: University of California Press, 1992), pp. 26–57, argue in very different ways that Chaucer does not escape from culturally controlling antifeminism in the Wife's discourse. My focus on rehearsal, as it is explored through several figures, suggests that Chaucer's transmission of received culture is not at all automatic or unconscious.

stop to and "quites" the book's claims to universal truth by fragmenting its material wholeness. The critical exposure of the antifeminism is accessible to readers unfamiliar with Dante—but the image pointedly reverses the trajectory and the values of Dante's original metaphor for sacral unity as one becomes three, and then books and scattered leaves alike are consigned to a domestic inferno. The unflattering requital turns its criticism of Jankyn's volume, with its claim to authoritative inclusiveness, back onto Dante's *volume* as well. The *Commedia*'s bookbinding metaphor heals the disjunctures of substances, accidents, and fascicles: the condition of the world in time. By ripping out the pages, the Wife reopens the wound for both bratty scholars and idealist poets, who only imagine that they have transcended the troublesome variability that makes the world—and readers—so stubbornly resist their strivings for universal truth.

Although the Wife of Bath's Prologue responds skeptically to Dante's vaulting claims to transcendence, the main point of Chaucer's appropriation is both broader and more available to his own first readers. The Wife counters an oppressively reiterated tradition with the same remedy as that offered in both the Miller's Prologue and the Man of Law's Introduction, for her rebellion also binds Chaucer to another tradition stretching from the Cumaean Sibyl to Virgil to Dante. The repetitive series of leaves and volumes, each remembering or dismembering its predecessor, constitutes Chaucer's chosen classical tradition of "poetes." Even rupture—the Wife's defiant refusal to hear a single story more—can be conceived only against the background of the tradition it unbinds.[65] As both Dante and Virgil had done before him, Chaucer now also scatters the once-bound quires of his predecessor's volume, and thus joins the reechoing line of the tradition Dante claims to supersede. The Prologue's treatment of the book typifies Chaucer's use of Dante, in which borrowing scarcely ever registers endorsement. Here Chaucer's

---

[65] Conte, among many others, argues throughout *The Rhetoric of Imitation* for the reciprocally constitutive dialectic of emulation and departure in literary tradition. Roman Jakobson, in *Language in Literature*, ed. Krystyna Pomorska and Stephen Rudy (Cambridge, Mass.: Belknap Press of Harvard University Press, 1987), describes this reciprocity as the major contribution of the Prague Circle and Russian Formalism: "The reader of a poem or the viewer of a painting has a vivid awareness of two orders: the traditional canon and the artistic novelty as a deviation from that canon. It is precisely against the background of the tradition that innovation is conceived. The Formalist studies brought to light that this simultaneous preservation of tradition and breaking away from tradition form the essence of every new work of art" (p. 46).

difference from Dante is palpable: the Wife, and Chaucer, find their voices not in completeness, but in fragmentation. Paradoxically, it is by taking Dante at his word and image that Chaucer also finds his own, different membership in the Virgilian tradition. In order to insert a new fascicle, one must first undo the bindings.

Thus Chaucer reaches back to Virgil with the leaves torn from Jankyn's book. The narrative image portrays literary tradition as a violent competition in which readers define themselves by displacing or destroying their authors. The fate of this Dantean volume, combined with its counterpart in the Man of Law's Introduction, suggests that Chaucer understood the narrative of literary supersession in the *Commedia,* and did not assent.[66] His demurral begins to take shape in the Miller's Prologue, where in casting himself as a rehearser of prior stories, he cedes the prerogative of resisting or disordering his pages to his own readers. The difference may be only one of role: whereas Dante redefines himself in the course of the *Commedia* from reader and imitator of Virgil's *volume* to poet and supersessor, Chaucer imagines himself as subject to the refractoriness of his own readers, for whom he must make space if he is to succeed as a classicizing "poete." But the Miller's Prologue does not go far enough in addressing the twin problems of rivalry and rehearsal. The alternative model of literary dynamics is developed fully only with the Wife of Bath's second narrative image: her story of Midas.

The story of Midas's hairy ass's ears in *The Wife of Bath's Tale* presents a considerably murkier narrative of literary history in which competition, imitation, and rupture become fused in such a way that they seem one snarled tangle. Like the Wife's first narrative image, the Midas story involves defects of the ear; unlike the destruction of Jankyn's book, this one does not evoke Dante and Virgil, but instead returns to Ovid. The second narrative image does not indict the competitiveness of the first, or even disavow it, so much as acknowledge it both as constitutive and

---

[66] Thus I differ with Howard H. Schless's assessment that Chaucer used Dante only in fragments, mostly for a memorable image or a stylistic decoration, but without regard for the full context from which he borrowed. The coherence of Chaucer's Dantean volumes suggests just the opposite: that he understood very well what Dante was up to, and demurred. For Schless's argument, see *Chaucer and Dante: A Reevaluation* (Norman, Okla.: Pilgrim Press, 1984), and "Transformations: Chaucer's Use of Italian," in D. S. Brewer, ed., *Geoffrey Chaucer: Writers and Their Background* (Athens: Ohio University Press, 1975), pp. 184–223. Warren Ginsberg's argument, that because of cultural differences Chaucer only partly grasped the poetic arguments of the Italian poets, is more compelling; see *Chaucer's Italian Translations* (Ann Arbor: University of Michigan Press, 2001).

as only part of a multilayered process always in flux. This Ovidian narrative lacks the dialectical clarity of Dante's supersession of Virgil—but it may more resonantly capture the real dilemmas of a poet seeking to introduce old tradition and new audience to one another, in a newly emergent literary vernacular as yet uncertainly suited for the role.

Ovid's story begins with another artistic competition,[67] with Midas as the *indoctum vulgus* who fails to recognize the superiority of Apollo's music to Pan's reedy piping. In the first of several layers depicting art and its reception, Apollo (like Calliope competing against the Pierides) punishes Midas by giving him ass's ears to match his capacity to hear. Having begun with the unequal competition between rustic pretender and the god of music and poetry, the story soon shifts from the cause of Midas's disfigurement to the consequences for a series of audiences. In the next layer, Midas tries to hide the embarrassing secret of his new ears. But it is spilled by his barber, who digs a hole in marshy ground, whispers the secret into it, and then buries his voice. The barber does not imitate Apollo or Pan, but transposes their musical competition into a story about its reception by Midas and the resulting punitive metamorphosis. He intends his story to be told once only—shades of the Man of Law's thrift!—but the secret is broadcast to the whole world the next year when the marsh reeds that grow on the spot retell his buried words ("obruta verba refert," *Metamorphoses* IX, 193) with their whispery rustling: Midas has ass's ears. In an irony typical of Ovidian poetic justice, the reeds—the material out of which Pan fashioned the pipes preferred by tone-deaf Midas—also become the instruments of his public exposure.[68] The final layer, then, depicts reception as a dynamic process in which a buried secret over time becomes public and widespread, in something like the temporal trajectory of literary appropriation. The reeds' windblown whispers figure as well the iterative side of literary reuse, although in a way baffled from the original competition: they don't tell the same story, but they do tell it on the same instrument. One might add that Ovid himself, now retelling the barber's secret, also resembles both reeds and pan-pipes; the poet's resemblance to his materials was no doubt compounded by the fact that both his pens and

---

[67] *Metamorphoses* XI, 146–93.
[68] Pan plays a song upon reeds joined with wax ("cerata modulatur *harundine* carmen," *Metamorphoses* XI, 154), and the barber's story is spread by a stand of trembling reeds ("*harundinibus* tremulis," *Metamorphoses* XI, 190).

the *volumen* publishing Midas's secret were made from reeds.[69] Finally, in each layer of transmission, the interests of the teller are thwarted in the reception. If one can speak of the motives of reeds, they are defined in this story as different from those of compulsively garrulous barbers; and the reeds tell on the barber just as surely as they tell on Midas.[70]

But somewhere in the mediated transmission of the story from *Meta-*

---

[69] In the technology of writing during Ovid's lifetime (43 B.C.E.–17 or 18 C.E.), pens were generally made from reeds; in addition, the *volumen*—the flexible scroll—was made from papyrus, an Egyptian marsh reed. Although parchment and the codex had supplanted papyrus and the *volumen* by the fourth century C.E., non-Christian writings were still usually written with the older technology through the third century. Martial (40–106 C.E.) refers to the codex with wonder, which suggests that the technology was new and uncommon. For papyrus, *volumen,* parchment, and codex, see Henri-Jean Martin, *The History and Power of Writing,* trans. Lydia G. Cochrane (Chicago: University of Chicago Press, 1988), pp. 45–60.

[70] One of the implications of Sergej Karcevskij's seminal description of communicative processes is that miscommunication is inevitable. Speakers (and poets) are inevitably frustrated to some degree by the incomprehensions or refusals of their audiences, as are audiences (or readers) by speakers (poets), because speaking and hearing involve different conceptual processes (the consequences of a fundamental disjunction between thought and language). Competition does not adequately explain most miscommunication; instead, speakers and hearers simply have different interests or cross-purposes, and mistakes may have no particular motivation. According to Karcevskij, every act of communication involves the "crossing of a synonymic and a homonymic series." That is, the speaker selects a sign most closely approximating her intended referential and connotative nexus from the set of all signs (whatever their phonic structure) that might have been appropriate to the situation and her intention; this involves selection among the "synonymic series." But the listener understands (also a form of intention), amidst of the syntactic live stream, by provisionally selecting the most plausible or appropriate possibility from a different set, that of all like-sounding words (whatever their designatory function), given this particular speaker and communicative situation; this involves selection among the "homonymic series." Karcevskij describes the fundamental instability of the linguistic sign thus: "The signifier (sound) and the signified (function) slide continually on the 'slope of reality.' Each 'overflows' the boundaries assigned to it by the other; the signifier tries to have functions other than its own; the signified tries to be expressed by means other than its sign. They are asymmetrical; coupled, they exist in a state of unstable equilibrium. It is because of this asymmetric dualism in the structure of its signs that a linguistic system can evolve: the 'adequate' position of the sign is continually displaced as a result of its adaptation to the exigencies of the concrete situation"; see "Du dualisme asymétrique du signe linguistique," *Travaux du Cercle linguistique de Prague,* 1 (1929): 88–92 (92); translated by Wendy Steiner as "The Asymmetric Dualism of the Linguistic Sign," in Peter Steiner, ed., *The Prague School: Selected Writings, 1929–1946,* pp. 47–54 (54). See also Wendy Steiner, "Language as Process: Sergej Karcevskij's Semiotics of Language," in Ladislav Matejka, ed., *Sound, Sign, and Meaning: Quinquagenary of the Prague Linguistic Circle,* Michigan Slavic Contributions, 6 (Ann Arbor: Department of Slavic Languages and Literature, University of Michigan, 1976), pp. 291–300. The unstable collisions of synonymy and homonymy not only provide a mechanism for diachronic semantic change but also suggest why we rarely say quite what we intend, and our listeners rarely (even with the best of will) understand quite what we thought we said.

morphoses to the Wife of Bath's *Tale,* someone mishears. Ovid's garrulous barber, a male "famulus" (slave, *Metamorphoses* XI, 183) in the new version becomes a female—Midas's wife—who compulsively shares her husband's secret. The Wife recounts the story as evidence for women's inability to hold their tongues, a common topic in proverbial wisdom about women's nature. In this case, however, it comes not from Ovid but from the *Roman de la rose:* "Car fame ne peut riens celer" (For a woman can hide nothing).[71] The change from barber to wife is necessary, of course, if the story is to have anything to do with women's garrulity; and the path to mishearing (or misprision) is eased by the phonic resemblance between "famulus" and "fame." The Wife herself betrays no awareness of the change. The defamatory antifeminist tradition has shaped what she apprehends and believes about women, and lack of awareness thus seems a marker of her impaired hearing. But the secret of revision will not stay buried in the marsh for long, since the Wife invites her audience to check the original: "The remenant of the tale if ye wol here, / Redeth Ovyde, and ther ye may it leere" (*Wife of Bath's Tale,* III.981–82). Anyone who reads Ovid will of course discover the rupture, and the invitation ensures that Chaucer's readers need not share the Wife's defective ear.

But the rupture also doubles the conflicted layers of transmission within the story, with its indistinct boundaries between tellers and audiences, whose resemblance to (even identity with) one another lies partly in the ways in which each thwarts the other's intentions. Barber/wife, reeds, Ovid, Wife—all exchange roles of teller and hearer; concealer, confidant(e), and spiller of secrets; and all share a garrulous compulsion to repeat the stories of others. The snarl of variously impaired and thwarted tellers and hearers captures the problems of rehearsal in the *Canterbury Tales.* Like the Wife, Chaucer shares something of each figure: the reeds, with their helplessly iterative rehearsals; the poet, who passes on twice-told tales and resembles (in his own self-representations) reedy Pan more than Apollo; and the barber, whose audience of reeds proves to have its own cross-purposes, and whose provisionally buried, as-yet-not-known secret is transformed into the widely known revelation: Midas has ass's ears. To the already tangled interchange of the Ovidian story, Chaucer adds the doubling of Midas and the Wife, who

---

[71] See Guillaume de Lorris and Jean de Meun, *Le Roman de la rose,* ed. Armand Strubel, Lettres Gothiques (Paris: Librairie Générale Française, 1992), l.19,224, p. 996.

shares a disfigurement of the ears with the tone-deaf audience whose humiliating secret she and all the other tellers make public.

Conclusion

As throughout the Wife's discourse, the relation of storytellers and readers—that is, literary tradition—is figured by defects of the ear. But Midas's (or the Wife's) impaired hearing doesn't prevent stories from being transmitted; and the conception of literary tradition to which this story gives voice differs significantly from the rivalrous model suggested by Chaucer's Dantean volumes. The Man of Law's Introduction, the Wife of Bath's Prologue, and even the Miller's Prologue (and, of course, the storytelling game of the whole *Canterbury Tales*) have constructed literary processes as competition: in Ovid's contest between Muses and mortal Pierides, in Dante's reading of Virgil's volume, in the Wife's destruction of Jankyn's volume. Clearly this figure imagines the defeat of the lesser poet by the greater; more surprisingly, it tends also to imagine a rivalry between poets and their audiences/readers for interpretative authority. Thus, although Dante reads Virgil in order finally to scatter the leaves of his volume, the addresses to the reader in the *Commedia* divide the *indoctum vulgus* from good readers who emulate Dante in interpreting correctly and converting. The work does not presuppose docility; quite the contrary, it invites resistance from some textual readers in order to quell it. But it also defines these resistant readers as without interpretative authority. The strikingly asymmetrical relation is tipped strongly toward the authority of the poet who seeks to rewrite past poets and future readers alike.

As we have seen from Chaucer's Dantean volumes, the *Canterbury Tales* stages readerly resistance more overtly and apparently shifts the balance of interpretative authority toward the reader. Even the Miller's Prologue, however, does not fundamentally depart from the competitive model. There, as in the Man of Law's Introduction, the reader's resistance is more apparent than real, for it is called forth in order to be accommodated, allayed—and perhaps waylaid. Chaucer's apology anticipates his readers' desire to depart from authorial designs, but in the same breath ingratiatingly subsumes such recalcitrance as part of his design. By embracing his magpie role as rehearser, Chaucer apparently attributes to his readers not just interpretative authority but also the creative authority to order and structure the work. But the usual effect of the apology in the Miller's Prologue is quite opposed to its overt meaning: it entices us to read the next story, not to skip over it. The apology's apparent concessions actually mask the conversion of readerly resistance into assent to Chaucer's own authority as poet. The taming of the reader culminates in the Wife's destruction of Jankyn's book, in which even in her greatest rebellion she helplessly emulates the volume that prescribes her being. When literary tradition is imagined as a contest—between poets, between poets and their readers—someone loses out, and the role for readers seems severely circumscribed.

But the Wife's story of Midas's hairy ears does not represent literary tradition—the rehearsal of stories—as a competition. Even in Ovid the contest between Apollo and Pan is quickly left behind in a process that continues without them; the Wife's version leaves competition out altogether. At every stage, audiences deflect, thwart, or frustrate authorial intentions. Yet here will is not set against will; the differences between storytellers and their audiences (and thus between one storyteller and the next) have no particular motivation, but are instead entailed by the very conditions of communication. The story imagines literary tradition less as competition than as friction sparked by the inertia of different materials rubbed together.

Such friction cannot be assimilated to or made complicit with authorial intent, but rather leaves a trace of the real differences between poets and their readers. It cannot be transformed or charmed away by inventing a fitter textual reader for real readers to emulate. Neither rivalrous nor imitative, each successive storyteller is simply different. The story of Midas's hairy ears makes no effort whatever to resolve the frustration; it is the condition of storytelling in the world. The story also retrospectively glosses the Man of Law's refusal to resemble the Pierides—his inability or refusal to distinguish muses from magpies, winners from losers—as a query about whether competition is the only or best way to figure the processes of literary transmission.

The Midas story figures a murky alternative to rivalry and too-faithful repetition that may indeed have been more effective in the specific circumstances of Chaucer's vernacular context. In its unresolved cross-purposes, frictions, and impairments, this figure of literary transmission is conditioned by a wealth of disconnection that Chaucer could neither ignore nor cater to in transposing the classical tradition into English. As we have seen, competitive supersession was an Italian vernacular response to a potentially smothering continuity with the more venerable, more prestigious Latin. In the English context, such continuity had to be established before it could be felt as overbearing. The problem confronting Chaucer was too much discontinuity, not too much sameness: a vernacular neither closely related to Latin, nor the native tongue of the muses, nor the traditional prestigious tongue of the social elite; and readers for whom Ovid or Virgil in Latin were a receding legacy, but who needed to be persuaded and accommodated before they would invest in English (rather than French) futures.

In such circumstances, the Midas story offers a measure of hope: despite all frustrations and impairments of the ears, stories are still passed on. If the intentions of poets and readers inevitably lie athwart one another, the indirection of Chaucer's borrowed classical volumes—their secret hidden only because not yet known—is a prudent and effective means of deflecting both rehearsal and rivalry. Rather than rending audiences into *doctum* (or at least docile) and *indoctum vulgus,* as a recognized allusion would do, the Dantean appropriation provisionally accommodates their resistance in order to get around it, to slip in connections to poetry of the most ambitious kind. It also provisionally buries the secret of rivalry (either leaves torn from Dante's bound volume, or the hairy ears of an unfit audience) in a hole in the ground. As a pedagogical strategy, the appropriation prepares the ground, supplying the wherewithal for discovery, or for letting the buried secret grow up into garrulous reeds whose whispering makes public the fait accompli of Chaucer's English classicism. Given the real discontinuities of Chaucer's literary and linguistic context, this temporal trajectory toward recognition offers a genuine tactical advantage because it does not prematurely trigger dismissal by (properly) skeptical, wary readers. The indirect, unshared appropriation makes possible a dynamic transmission of literary tradition that is not impelled by competitive supersession, but instead subsumes—perhaps even as its motive force—the inevitability of recalcitrant readers and mutually frustrated intentions. By inviting his readers to "Turne over the leef and chese another tale," Chaucer evades the violence of overt competition, with its perils of rejection. He may overtly imitate only magpies, millers, Pan, and Ovid, but under cover of such likenesses he also slips in the possibility, not wholly excluded, that he may also resemble Calliope, Apollo, and Virgil (or at least Dante's Virgil). Chaucer's magpies may be muses after all—but he doesn't force the choice upon his readers until they are ready to hear it. Before and after, both the frustrations and the ambition in the *Canterbury Tales* to link new English readers actively to the classical tradition are bound up in Chaucer's Dantean volumes.

Future Perfect:

The Augustinian Theology of Perfection and the *Canterbury Tales*

R. James Goldstein
Auburn University

A GENERATION AGO the most vigorous scholarly debates among Chaucerians in North America pitted the neo-Augustinian or exegetical critics, represented by D. W. Robertson and his followers, against New Critical formalist critics, represented most influentially by E. Talbot Donaldson.[1] In recent years, as older controversies over exegetical criticism recede into the ever more distant past, there have been signs that resistance to thinking seriously about the relation of Chaucer's writing to medieval theological discourses is waning. Indeed, current scholarship in the rapidly growing field of vernacular theology suggests that the time may be ripe to reexamine such a fundamental question as how the pervasive influence of Augustinian thought in the fourteenth century might matter to our reading of Chaucer, though such lines of questioning have long been taboo lest one be accused of harboring a reactionary Robertsonian agenda. By focusing on the theology of Christian perfection in *The Canterbury Tales,* the present essay aims to situate Chaucer's work within an Augustinian framework to offer an alternative

I would like to thank the College of Liberal Arts and Auburn University for summer grants in 2001 and 2002 that helped support research for this essay. Early versions of portions of this essay were read to the Chaucer Division of the Modern Language Association at the 2000 meeting in Washington, D.C., and at the New Chaucer Society Congress in Boulder, Colorado, in 2002; my thanks to the organizers and audiences. For helpful comments and suggestions on earlier drafts, I am grateful to Nicholas Watson, Britton J. Harwood, V. A. Kolve, and especially to the anonymous reviewers for *SAC* and to its editor.

[1] See Lee Patterson's still indispensable analysis of this debate in *Negotiating the Past: The Historical Understanding of Medieval Literature* (Madison: University of Wisconsin Press, 1987), pp. 1–39; for a contrasting account, see Alan Gaylord, "Reflections on D. W. Robertson, Jr., and 'Exegetical Criticism,'" *ChauR* 40.3 (2006): 311–33.

to suggestions in recent scholarship that locates convergences between *The Canterbury Tales* and reformist thought, sometimes of a radical or Wycliffite tendency.[2]

By focusing on the theology of perfection, this essay seeks to remedy the relative neglect of that topic by scholars who have generally not sought to appraise the cultural work performed by Chaucer's writing in terms of medieval ideas of perfection.[3] A notable exception is a recent essay by Nicholas Watson, who argues that Chaucer's self-consciously lay stance in *The Canterbury Tales* is best understood as "anti-perfectionist," or what he identifies as a "mediocrist" position.[4] The "public Christianity" that Chaucer displays in *The Canterbury Tales,* as Watson understands it, "is dismissive of the ideals of the professional religious orders," the religious who in the Church's traditional hierarchical thinking about personhood had claimed the privilege of being the *perfecti,* in contrast to the *mediocri,* those "virtuous lay Christians in active life."[5] While it is far from my intention to recuperate a Robertsonian herme-

---

[2] For examples, see Peggy Knapp, *Chaucer and the Social Contest* (New York: Routledge, 1990); Paul Strohm, "Chaucer's Lollard Joke: History and the Textual Unconscious," *SAC* 17 (1995): 23–42; David Aers and Lynn Staley, *The Powers of the Holy: Religion, Politics, and Gender in Medieval English Culture* (University Park: Pennsylvania State University Press, 1996); Alan J. Fletcher, "Chaucer the Heretic," *SAC* 25 (2003): 53–121. The list is by no means complete.

[3] Robertson barely mentions Christian perfection in his major work, though the idea received some attention in the work of his followers; see D. W. Robertson Jr., *A Preface to Chaucer: Studies in Medieval Perspectives* (Princeton: Princeton University Press, 1962), p. 350; Bernard F. Huppé, *A Reading of the Canterbury Tales* (Albany: SUNY, 1964), pp. 39, 113–17, 142–47, 228–29; Paul A. Olson, *The Canterbury Tales and the Good Society* (Princeton: Princeton University Press, 1986), who concludes that Chaucer "is preeminently the poet of perfection and discipline not only of the mind but of the imagination and affections" (p. 297). An anti-Robertsonian position was staked out in the early work of Donald R. Howard, who suggested that the "hierarchical view of perfection" in medieval Christianity "brought into the life of every Christian an inescapable tension: it demanded of him more than he could be expected to do" and made his or her life one of "unending struggle" (*The Three Temptations: Medieval Man in Search of the World* [Princeton: Princeton University Press, 1966], pp. 39–40; see also pp. 90–92); see also Howard, "The Conclusion of the Marriage Group: Chaucer and the Human Condition," *MP* 57 (1960): 223–32. Ironically, Howard's fierce opposition to the kind of neo-Augustinianism represented by Robertson rests on an insight that is anticipated in Augustine's anti-Pelagian discourse.

[4] Nicholas Watson, "Chaucer's Public Christianity," *Religion and Literature* 37.2 (2005): 99–114; on the self-consciousness of this lay persona, see pp. 100–101. When convenient, further citations to his essay appear parenthetically in the text.

[5] Ibid., pp. 100, 101. While acknowledging that his models "constantly overlap," Watson sketches three "alternative perfectionist models" available in the later fourteenth century to devout laypersons, which may be summarized thus: (1) a model that adapted the idea of the "mixed life" to the laity; (2) a "puritanical model" that in its more radical forms was Wycliffite but whose conception of the Christian life as "a strug-

neutic, I submit that Watson's argument seriously misreads Chaucer's stance toward perfectionism, foreclosing the possibility of reading *The Canterbury Tales* from within an Augustinian framework that was widely available in the fourteenth century. To help make that case, I propose to examine the contrasting lives of two secular wives who know a great deal about "wandrynge by the weye."[6] If Alisoun of Bath gleefully rejects the suitability of striving for Christian perfection in her own case, Custance is the only figure in *The Canterbury Tales* whom Chaucer explicitly describes as attaining perfection in this life. Chaucer's references to Christian perfection in relation to both fictional wayfarers suggest that the pair may be read as symbolic opposites in ways that cannot be fully appreciated either in terms of the old idea of a "marriage group" or of the reductive Robertsonian binary of *caritas* and *cupiditas*. Instead, I argue, the narratives of these two viators raise insistent questions about the relation between human and divine agency in the free will's cooperation or resistance to grace that Saint Augustine addressed in his anti-Pelagian tracts in the final decades of his career, arguments to which (ironically enough) the so-called exegetical critics paid virtually no attention, though the same cannot be said of fourteenth-century theologians.

My essay begins with a brief analysis of the conceptual foundations of Christian perfection, followed by a summary of Saint Augustine's argument in his anti-Pelagian tracts concerning the relation between the operations of divine grace and the fallen human will, and the constraints this dynamic places on the pursuit of Christian perfection. The Augustinian analysis continued to hold wide currency in Chaucer's day, as evidenced by the work of Oxford theologians as different as Thomas Bradwardine and John Wyclif, who both share, as we shall see, an Augustinian framework for thinking about grace, the will, and the meaning of Christian perfection. The second section offers a detailed rereading of *The Man of Law's Tale* to argue that in its portrayal of the operations of divine grace, Chaucer's revisions to his sources offer an implicit theological argument of a distinctively Augustinian character

---

gle against sin, undertaken in obedience to God's law," was broadly shared by less radical reformers like Langland; and (3) the "affective" model that stressed love (p. 102).

[6] *The Riverside Chaucer*, gen. ed. Larry Benson, 3rd. ed. (Boston: Houghton Mifflin, 1987), I.467; all quotations of Chaucer are from this edition. Chaucer alludes to medieval theologians' habit of describing life on earth as the time *in via*, defining the human person as a viator. See Gerhart B. Ladner, "Homo *Viator:* Mediaeval Ideas on Alienation and Order," *Speculum* 42 (1967): 233–59.

in ways that have not been properly appreciated before. The essay then turns in section three to reexamine the Wife of Bath's discussion of the evangelical counsels of perfection, which draws humorously on the distinction between the precepts and the counsels. Aquinas's analysis of this distinction in the *Summa Theologiae* provides a useful reference point, which allows us to contrast the method of the scholastic author with that of the fictional vernacular theologian who touches on such difficult "scole-matere" (III.1272). After analyzing the narrative uses Chaucer makes of the concept of perfection in this contrasting pair of lay secular wives, the fourth part of the essay widens its scope to sketch out what a rereading of *The Canterbury Tales* might reveal if we replace the idea of a "marriage group" with a "perfection group."

I

Late medieval philosophy and theology inherited the notion that human lives and experiences ought to be measured against an absolute standard of perfection supplied by God, the perfect being: "Be perfect just as your heavenly Father is perfect," said Jesus in the Sermon on the Mount (Matt. 5.48).[7] If absolute perfection can only be predicated of God and the kingdom of heaven, the idea of Christian perfection was applied in a relative sense throughout the Middle Ages to the *homo iustus,* the just man who by the grace of God could enjoy perfect charity to the degree to which it was possible in this life.[8] The connection made by theolo-

---

[7] The pursuit of perfection is a topic that is closely related to the idea of the *imitatio Christi;* for a comprehensive overview, see Giles Constable, "The Ideal of the Imitation of Christ," *Three Studies in Medieval Religious and Social Thought* (Cambridge: Cambridge University Press, 1995). Although it remains outside the scope of the present essay, Chaucer shows an interest in "perfect being theology," inspired by his reading of Boethius (cf. Troilus's predestination speech in Bk. 4, Theseus's final speech in *The Knight's Tale,* and Dorigen's soliloquy in *The Franklin's Tale*). Anselm's ontological proof of the existence of God, accepted by Bradwardine and Wyclif among others, is the most famous instance of arguing for the necessary existence of God as perfect being; for a recent discussion by a philosopher of religion, see Katherin A. Rogers, *Perfect Being Theology,* Reason and Religion (Edinburgh: Edinburgh University Press, 2000). A valuable overview of the overlapping senses of perfection is provided by Morton W. Bloomfield, "Some Reflections on the Medieval Idea of Perfection," *Franciscan Studies* 17 (1957): 213–37, rpt. in *Essays and Explorations: Studies in Ideas, Language, and Literature* (Cambridge, Mass.: Harvard University Press, 1970), pp. 29–55.

[8] See Saint Thomas Aquinas, *Summa Theologiae,* Blackfriars Edition, Latin text and English translation, vol. 47 (New York and London: McGraw-Hill and Eyre & Spottiswoode, 1973), II–II, q. 184, a. 1–2 (subsequent references will be to this edition). For an overview, see "Perfection" in *Dictionnaire de spiritualité, ascétique et mystique: Doctrine*

gians between perfection and justice indicates that the topic of Christian perfection overlaps with the theology of justification.[9] The relative perfection available on earth was traditionally understood to involve a hierarchy of different degrees, such as that represented by the well-known triad of the degrees of chastity or perfection, or the late medieval triad of the active, contemplative, and "mixed" life.[10] For most of the Middle Ages the pursuit of perfection was cultivated by the professional religious, especially in monastic tradition, within which develop arguments about different grades (*gradus*) of perfection.[11] The monastic reforms of the twelfth century, with their "interiorization of monastic values and spirituality," as Giles Constable observes, "eventually led to monasticizing everyone and destroying the special position held by monks in the early Middle Ages."[12] The theory and practice of Christian perfection became embroiled in controversy in the thirteenth century with the rise of the mendicant orders and the debates on religious poverty associated with the Spiritual Franciscan movement. Such debates provided occasions for articulating anticlerical positions to the extent that by the fourteenth century, traditional claims that the professional religious enjoyed a privileged access to the highest forms of perfection had lost much of their luster for lay audiences.[13] In England, it hardly needs stressing, the heterodox challenges to "private religion" by John Wyclif and his followers did much to tarnish the reputation of professional religious orders for perfection, putting them sharply on the defensive. The Benedictine monk Uthred of Boldon, an older contemporary of Chaucer's, wrote two treatises on perfection dated c. 1374–76, partly in response to Wyclif's

---

et histoire, vol. 12 part 1 (Paris: Beauchesne, 1984), cols. 1074–136. The fullest history in English is R. Newton Flew, *The Idea of Perfection in Christian Theology* (London: Oxford University Press, 1934).

[9] See Alister E. McGrath, *Iustitia Dei: A History of the Christian Doctrine of Justification,* 2 vols. (Cambridge: Cambridge University Press, 1986). I am grateful to an anonymous reader for supplying the reference and for the observation that many late medieval theologians disagreed with Augustine's doctrine of justification; see *Iustitia Dei* I, esp. pp. 172–79.

[10] See Howard, "Conclusion of the Marriage Group," p. 224; *The Idea of the Canterbury Tales* (Berkeley and Los Angeles: University of California Press, 1976), pp. 248–50.

[11] See Morton W. Bloomfield, *"Piers Plowman" as a Fourteenth-Century Apocalypse* (New Brunswick, NJ: Rutgers University Press, 1962), esp. pp. 44–97.

[12] Giles Constable, *The Reformation of the Twelfth Century* (Cambridge: Cambridge University Press, 1996), p. 7.

[13] On the emergence of anticlerical discourse from antifraternal polemic, see Wendy Scase, *"Piers Plowman" and the New Anticlericalism,* Cambridge Studies in Medieval Literature, 4 (Cambridge: Cambridge University Press, 1989).

attacks on the worldly corruption of and lack of scriptural basis for the regular orders; we shall return later to this debate concerning perfection by Chaucer's contemporaries.[14]

In short, Christian perfection was not a static concept but rather a highly contested category, serving as a kind of lightning rod through which some of the most charged theological and ecclesiological disputes were conducted during moments of institutional conflict at different times in the history of the medieval church. What was there about the idea of perfection, we might ask, that so readily lent itself to such a variety of uses? From the earliest years of Christianity, the discursive functions which the vocabulary of perfection was made to serve suggest that the concept itself marks out the site of certain unstable and even contradictory pressures. As Morton Bloomfield observes, from the beginning Christian perfection was understood as "both continual spiritual growth and spiritual attainment," though "theologians could stress either or both as they wished."[15] The difference between these two perspectives on perfection, as we shall see, creates a tension that writers attempt to work out in the form of two proto-narratives. The theme of the first story-type concerns moral and spiritual *amelioration*. Set in the present world, this narrative pattern tells of an individual's spiritual progress in a constant struggle against temptation.[16] The theme of what I designate the second proto-narrative is *transcendence* beyond the realm of temptation; set in the other world, this pattern narrates the story of an absolute *completion* projected into the future, perfection as *per-ficio* in the sense of bringing something to an end. These alternative patterns, I suggest, are evident in the full-fledged narratives about perfection in *The Canterbury Tales*.[17]

[14] See W. A. Pantin, "Two Treatises of Uthred of Boldon on the Monastic Life," in R. W. Hunt, W. A. Pantin, and R. W. Southern, eds., *Studies in Medieval History Presented to Francis Maurice Powicke* (Oxford: Clarendon, 1948), pp. 363–85. Cf. John Wyclif, *De perfectione statuum,* in *John Wiclif's Polemical Works in Latin,* ed. Rudolf Buddensieg, 2 vols. (London: Wyclif Society, 1883), 2:440–82, briefly discussed below.

[15] Bloomfield, *Piers Plowman,* p. 53. This double edge to perfection, I suggest, is closely paralleled by the different emphases in the concept of *imitatio Christi,* whether it is the divinity or humanity of Christ that is imitated; see Constable, "Imitation of Christ."

[16] The ameliorative proto-narrative roughly corresponds to Watson's "puritanical" model, the second of his three models of lay perfection he thinks Chaucer rejects (cf. note 5 above), though we should be clear that nothing specifically restricts this proto-narrative to laypersons.

[17] The narratological distinction I offer parallels what McGrath establishes is Augustine's sense that the sinner's justification is both an *event* and a *process,* though to distin-

In Saint Augustine's anti-Pelagian writings, the repeated oscillation between the first and second of these proto-narratives is symptomatic of a logical double bind for the Christian subject, which put in its starkest terms consists in the belief that no human being can fully attain perfection in this life, because "real" perfection, the one worth striving for, by definition takes place elsewhere, at some time in the future. Yet even the progressive path of relative perfection contains a structural instability or contradiction that becomes evident when the New Testament both demands that Christians strive to attain a perfect selfhood and at the same time insists that perfection is impossible without the operation of grace, a force radically alien to the self, without which the self can neither make progress nor attain the final reward. Augustine inherits this tension from the writings of Saint Paul, whose frequent references to his own spiritual struggles after his conversion developed his sense of life in this world as one of unending struggle against temptation in the pursuit of perfection.[18] The Pauline view of the Christian life as a progressive journey toward the goal of final perfection, a journey dependent on divine grace and requiring the vigilant conduct of spiritual warfare and self-discipline, received detailed articulation in Saint Augustine's response to the Pelagian heresy in a series of increasingly polemical works written from 412 to 430, when Augustine worked out his extraordinarily influential views on original sin, freedom, and grace, exploring at considerable length the implications of the concupiscence of the flesh for structurally flawed human beings.[19]

---

guish these two aspects clearly is a sixteenth-century development; see *Iustitia Dei,* I, p. 31, where he observes: "God's new creation is not finished once and for all in the event of justification, and requires perfecting, which is brought about by cooperative grace collaborating with the *liberum arbitrium liberatum.* Whilst *concupiscentia* may be relegated to the background as *caritas* begins its work of renewal within man, it continues to make its presence felt, so that renewed gifts of grace are required throughout man's existence, as sin is never totally overcome in this life." Since *The Canterbury Tales* are mostly narratives, not theological arguments, it is more useful for our purposes to describe these two aspects of Augustine's understanding of justification and perfection in narratological terms, as the story pattern of amelioration yielding to one of transcendence.

[18] The Apostle favors two metaphors that help shape both proto-narratives: the race where the winner is awarded the prize (*bravium*), and the defensive struggle against an inimical force (sin or the flesh). For running to attain the *bravium,* see 1 Cor. 9.24, Phil. 3.14; to attain the *corona,* 1 Cor. 9.25; for defensive struggle (*repugno, -are*), see Rom. 7.23, Heb. 12.4.

[19] For an excellent brief discussion of Augustine's views on grace and perfection and an account of the controversy, see Jaroslav Pelikan, *The Christian Tradition: A History of the Development of Doctrine, Vol. 1: The Emergence of the Catholic Tradition (100–600)* (Chicago: University of Chicago Press, 1971), pp. 307–18. See also Carol Harrison, *August-*

Augustine insists that baptism does not erase the inherited concupiscence of the flesh, against which the Christian must constantly struggle. So long as we occupy what Paul in Romans calls "the body of this death," human beings are self-divided along the fault line of the flesh and must engage in continuous spiritual warfare against concupiscence. Ascetic discipline, or the training of the concupiscent flesh through its mortification, provides the key strategy for the Christian who strives to fulfill the command to be perfect when the full attainment of that goal cannot take place in this world, not even by a saint.[20] Because it is always possible for the viator to make further progress in the journey toward perfection, to name perfection is to name both the struggle itself and the eventual reward for a transcendental desire or hunger that literally cannot be satiated in this world. Augustine's view of human nature after the Fall was pessimistic; the damage done as a consequence of original sin leaves us utterly dependent on God's grace, without which we can do nothing good. Thus to narrate the Christian's spiritual progress on the journey is to tell the story of God's grace.[21] Unlike the Pelagians, who claimed that it is within human ability to live without sin, for Augustine the moral life is far more complicated; as he argues in *De perfectione justitiae hominis* (On the Perfection of Human Righteousness), only Christ heals sinners and assists "those who believe and are making

---

ine: Christian Truth and Fractured Humanity, Christian Theology in Context (Oxford: Oxford University Press, 2000), pp. 79–114.

[20] Augustine frequently cites Paul's testimony in Philippians 3.12: "non quod iam acceperim, aut iam perfectus sim" (not as though I had already attained, or were already perfect); *Biblia sacra iuxta vulgatam clementinam,* 5th ed., Biblioteca de Autores Cristianos (Madrid: Edica, 1977); translations from the Vulgate are from the Douay-Rheims version, *The Holy Bible* (New York: P. J. Kennedy, 1914). In *De peccatorum meritis et remissione et de baptismo parvulorum* (The Punishment and Forgiveness of Sins and the Baptism of Children), Augustine comments about Paul: "He himself admits that he has not yet grasped the goal, that he is not yet perfect in the full righteousness which he longs to attain in Christ, but that he still deliberately struggles on. . . . For although he was a perfect wayfarer, he had not yet reached the end of the journey." For the Latin original, see *Patrilogiae cursus completus . . . Series (Latina),* ed. J.-P. Migne (Paris, 1844–64), 221 vols., 44, col. 163–64; henceforth cited as PL by volume number and column. Unless otherwise noted, translations from Augustine's anti-Pelagian writings are cited by volume and page number from *The Works of Saint Augustine: A Translation for the Twenty-first Century,* ed. John E. Rotelle, Part I, vol. 23–26: *Answer to the Pelagians,* Roland J. Teske, introduction, translation, and notes (Hyde Park, N.Y.: New City Press, 1997–99); the passage above is from *Works* 23, p. 94.

[21] "Proficientium est enim via: quamvis bene proficientes dicantur perfecti viatores" (This is the path of those who are making progress, and those who are making good progress are called perfect travelers). *On Nature and Grace, Works* 23, p. 230; PL 44, col. 253.

progress 'from day to day' through the renewal of the interior human being until perfect righteousness, which is like full health, is achieved."[22] Augustine shifts from the ameliorative to the transcendent narrative in an instant; our traveling may be on the correct path, but perfection cannot be completed until the journey ends.[23] God holds up the absolute standard of perfection that he knows in advance will be impossible to achieve in this life so that we will know through the commandments the direction in which to run.[24] The commandments thus create a moral road map for both the journey and the goal, though the human will alone is insufficient.[25] With the assistance of grace the viator's ameliorative narrative marks out progress yet cannot reach its final completion in the here and now. The residue of present imperfection can only be resolved with a future perfect tense: "It is, then, one thing to withdraw from every sin, for that is going on at present; it is something else to have withdrawn from every sin, for that will be attained in that perfection to come."[26]

In this ameliorative narrative of justification, Augustine affirms the interaction of human and divine agency while stressing that the free will needs to be assisted by grace. Although his tract *De gratia et libero arbitrio* (On Grace and Free Choice) addresses a specific monastic community whose members have rejected sexual desire, Augustine notes that his same general point about the dependence of the will on grace applies to those seculars who, not given the more perfect gift of continence, choose to marry and observe marital chastity by avoiding prohibited

---

[22] *Perfection of Human Righteousness, Works* 23, p. 291, quoting 2 Cor. 4:16. "Hoc fit in credentibus et proficientibus renovatione interioris hominis de die in diem, donec fiat perfecta justitia tanquam sanitas plena" (PL 44, col. 295). This treatise makes especially clear the extent to which Augustine's anti-Pelagian doctrine of justification provides an occasion to formulate his theology of perfection.

[23] "as many of us as run perfectly" should be mindful "that we are not yet perfect in order that we may become perfect in that place toward which we are running perfectly." *Perfection of Human Righteousness, Works* 23, p. 297; "quotquot perfecte currimus, hoc sapiamus, quod nondum perfecti sumus, ut illic perficiamur, quo perfecte adhuc currimus" (PL 44, col. 300).

[24] *Perfection of Human Righteousness, Works* 23, p. 298. "Cur ergo non praeciperetur homini ista perfectio, quamvis eam in hac vita nemo habeat? Non enim recte curritur, si quo currendum est nesciatur. Quomodo autem sciretur, si nullis praeceptis ostenderetur?" (PL 44, col. 301).

[25] *Perfection of Human Righteousness, Works* 23, p. 300; "nec juberetur, si nihil ibi nostra voluntas ageret; nec oraretur, si sola sufficeret" (PL 44, col. 303).

[26] *Perfection of Righteousness, Works* 23, p. 305. "Aliud est ergo, recedere ab omni peccato, quod nunc in opere est; aliud, recessisse ab omni peccato, quod in illa perfectione tunc erit" (PL 44, col. 308).

sexual practices.[27] Despite the focus on the moral choices of *monks*, Augustine insists that the general principle of the will assisted by grace applies to *ordinary* Christians too; in either case, God *prepares* the will, and by working with it (co-operating) perfects that which by working he begins.[28] Augustine finds it difficult to explain exactly *how* this operation takes place, though he affirms that God moves the will within the interior person.[29] What remains uncertain, however, is how free or autonomous the agency of the human will remains if it can move, whether for better or worse, only through the motion of a prior agency.[30]

In *De praedestinatione sanctorum* and *De dono perseverantiae* (On the Predestination of the Saints and The Gift of Perseverance), Augustine continues to place the primacy on God's operative grace, not on the natural ability of the free will.[31] In the first tract he argues that salvation cannot

---

[27] See *De gratia et libero arbitrio* (426 CE), where he advises the monks at Hadrumetum that the commandments against fornication and adultery demonstrate the existence of our free choice, but that without grace it is impossible to obey them: "Numquid tam multa quae praecipiuntur in lege Dei, ne fornicationes et adulteria committantur, indicant aliud quam liberum arbitrium? Neque enim praeciperentur nisi homo haberet propriam voluntatem, qua divinis praeceptis obidiret. Et tamen Dei donum est, sine quo servari castitatis praecepta non possunt" (PL 44, col. 886); *Grace and Free Choice, Works* 26, p. 76.

[28] "ille qui praeparat voluntatem, et cooperando perficit, quod operando incipit" (PL 44, col. 901). Teske notes that this discussion is the basis for the later theological distinction between *gratia operans* and *gratia cooperans;* see *Grace and Free Choice, Works* 26, p. 36 n. 26. As McGrath observes, "[o]nce justified by divine action, the sinner does not at once become a perfect example of holiness. . . . God *operates* upon man in the *act* of justification, and *cooperates* with him in the *process* of justification" (*Iustitia Dei* I, p. 28; italics in original). McGrath goes on to observe that Augustine denies that a sinner possesses merit before the act of justification but affirms merit after justification, so long as we recognize that merit is "a divine, rather than a human, work."

[29] "God works in the hearts of human beings to incline their wills to whatever he wills" (*Grace and Free Choice, Works* 26, p. 102); "Agit enim Omnipotens in cordibus hominum etiam motum voluntatis eorum, ut per eos agat quod per eos agere ipse voluerit" (PL 44, col. 908). The interiorizing of the actions of grace on the will, as Carol Harrison notes, is characteristic of Augustine's thought beginning around 418 (*Augustine*, p. 111 n. 90).

[30] Harrison, *Augustine,* p. 111, acknowledges that scholars have engaged in "herculean efforts . . . to retain meaningful reference to the freedom of the will in the context of his theology of grace."

[31] These two works from about 427 addressed monastic communities in southern France where Cassian was the leading intellectual figure, who worried that Augustine's theology of grace, free will, and especially predestination conflicted with the active pursuit of perfection through asceticism. See Saint Augustine, *Four Anti-Pelagian Writings: On Nature and Grace, On the Proceedings of Pelagius, On the Predestination of the Saints, On the Gift of Perseverance,* The Fathers of the Church, 86, trans. John A. Mourant and William J. Collinge (Washington, D.C.: Catholic University of America Press, 1992), p. 188.

depend on the unassisted human mind initiating faith but requires the divine gift of faith to move the will of those whom God has predestined for the kingdom to receive that gift. Augustine's "uncompromising doctrine of election and predestination" was thus the logical result of his insistence that man is wholly dependent on the operations of grace, not merit.[32] The very thoughts that from our vantage may appear to precede our giving the assent required for belief are actually given by God, not autonomously produced.[33] Although Augustine suggests it is futile to attempt to comprehend the justice of why God has chosen some sinners for salvation and not others, he insists that it is God who causes the predestined "to have good works when he makes them observe the divine commandments."[34] In short, the contingent nature of the perfected will implies a diminished agency for human beings. If *The Predestination of the Saints* concentrates on God's necessary role in initiating the conversion of the will to begin the faith of those he has predestined for salvation, *De dono perseverentiae* (On the Gift of Perseverance) focuses on the operation of the grace that assists those so predestined to remain on the right course until the very end—to persevere until death, the moment when the ameliorative proto-narrative gives way to the transcendent one. To tell either of these stories, however, is to tell of God's power and will and the radical insufficiency of the human mind after the Fall.[35] God's agency flows into the deepest recesses of the will, though his grace proves irresistible only to those whom he wishes to save.[36] God has

---

[32] Harrsion, *Augustine*, p. 113.

[33] *Predestination of the Saints, Works* 26, p. 158. "[N]on quia credere vel non credere non est in arbitrio voluntatis humanae, sed in electis praeparatur voluntas a Domino" (PL 44, col. 968).

[34] *Predestination of the Saints, Works* 26, p. 168. "[H]oc ipso quo eos facit habere deinceps opera bona, cum ipse facit ut faciant divina mandata" (PL 44, col. 977).

[35] Augustine recalls Saint Ambrose's observations that "our hearts and our thoughts are not in our power" (*Gift of Perseverance, Works* 26, p. 201; PL 44, col. 1003; cf. *Gift of Perseverance, Works* 26, p. 225; PL 44, col. 1024).

[36] Harrison argues that God's grace is irresistible not because it overpowers the will to do something it otherwise would not wish to do, but "because it unfailingly, irresistibly, calls forth a response which corresponds with man's deepest desires and motivations . . . so that he is able to respond to it freely, wholeheartedly, and in the way grace intends" (*Augustine,* p. 112). Yet because Augustine attributes the very movements of the heart and thoughts to God's agency, her account does not solve the problem but merely shifts the location of divine compulsion a step further back. Robertsonians who fault the Wife of Bath's misdirection of her will would do well to keep in mind this aporia in Augustine's late writings, which in my view neither Bradwardine nor Wyclif eliminates.

judged according to his inscrutable will that "it is better that some who will not persevere be mingled with the certain number of his saints."[37]

The experience of reading Augustine's predestinarian tracts can be a frightening one, since doubts may arise whether oneself is chosen for salvation or is one of those foreknown (*praesciti*) to damnation, as Augustine is well aware when he suggests that a preacher should exercise considerable caution in explaining predestination to his congregation lest he terrify them needlessly.[38] And yet, he insists, until the actual moment of death, no one can "say with a claim to certitude that any human being shares in this calling except when he has departed from this world," though how those who still remain *in via* might be granted this certitude remains unclear.[39] The Augustinian doctrine of predestination thus entails that from any perspective available in *this* life, the ameliorative narrative is liable to be short-circuited at any turn, since never can one be sure it is God's inscrutable will that an individual sinner is one of those chosen to keep up the good fight, to persevere on the path of perfecting righteousness until the end is attained. To everyone except God, therefore, the progress a person makes in life thus remains like an open book until the very end.[40] The Christian life of the viator takes place on the road between the conversion of the will and the final perseverance, though here, at least, Augustine does not offer a detailed road map of the progress of this long journey: "Between the extremes of the beginning of faith and the perfection of perseverance there are those in-between virtues by which we live correctly."[41] This underdeveloped, "in-between" portion of Augustine's narrative of amelioration will be worth recalling when we turn to examine the progress toward perfection of the two Chaucerian wives.

As Alister McGrath has observed, "[t]he characteristic medieval un-

---

[37] *Gift of Perseverance, Works* 26, p. 201. "Deus autem melius esse judicavit, miscere quosdam non perseveraturos certo numero sanctorum suorum; ut quibus non expedit in hujus vitae tentatione securitas, non possint esse securi" (PL 44, col. 1003).

[38] See *Gift of Perseverance*, chap. 22, 57–62 (*Works* 26, pp. 230–33; PL 44, cols. 1028–31).

[39] *Gift of Perseverance, Works* 26, p. 212. "Ad quam vocationem pertinere nullus est homo ab hominibus certa asseveratione dicendus, nisi cum de hoc saeculo exierit" (PL 44, col. 1012).

[40] Augustine acknowledges as much when he uses the progress he has made as an author, in correcting the erroneous views of his earlier books, as an analogy (or synecdoche) for spiritual progress; see *Gift of Perseverance, Works* 26, p. 229; PL 44, col. 1027–28.

[41] *Gift of Perseverance, Works* 26, p. 230. "Inter initium autem fidei et perfectionem perseverantiae, media sunt illa, quibus recte vivimus" (PL 44, col. 1028).

derstanding of the nature of justification . . . refers not merely to the beginning of the Christian life, but also to its continuation and ultimate perfection, in which the Christian is made righteous in the sight of God and the sight of men through a fundamental change in his nature, and not merely his status."[42] This essentially Augustinian framework, though modified in later centuries, continued to shape later theological understandings; indeed, "medieval theological tradition followed Augustine of Hippo in insisting that man has a positive role to play in his own justification."[43] One of the most important contexts for the later medieval debates over justification and its close conceptual link to the idea of perfection as both process and result occurs with the systematic development and institutionalization of the sacrament of penance. With the pivotal role played by Peter Lombard's *Sentences* in later theological debates and with the well-known canon of the Fourth Lateran Council (1215) enjoining annual confession on all Christians, "the justification of the sinner" became "firmly linked to the sacramental life of the church."[44] With this link established, it became difficult to think of the pursuit of Christian perfection outside the sacrament of penance.

Augustine's analysis of the relation of human and divine agency in the free will's cooperation or resistance to grace, and his startling claim that God predestined those who would maintain the grace of perseverance until the end, were matters of active controversy in England during the fourteenth century. The neo-Augustinian Thomas Bradwardine's *De causa Dei* revived such questions, which we know were broadly familiar to Chaucer's audience, since the humor of the philosophical joke in *The Nun's Priest's Tale* (VII.3242) depends on his readers associating Bradwardine's name with the apparent conflict between God's foreknowledge and human free will.[45] To support his view of the logical and

---

[42] McGrath, *Iustitia Dei,* I, p. 41.

[43] Ibid., p. 70; theologians differed in how they viewed "the precise nature of this human rôle in justification."

[44] Ibid., p. 99; see pp. 91–99 for fuller discussion.

[45] Thomas Bradwardine, *De causa Dei contra Pelagium,* ed. Henry Saville (London, 1618). Citations will be to book and chapter followed by page number. On Bradwardine, see Heiko A. Oberman, *Archbishop Thomas Bradwardine, A Fourteenth Century Augustinian: A Study of His Theology in Its Historical Context* (Utrecht: Kemink and Zoon, 1957); Gordon Leff, *Bradwardine and the Pelagians: A Study of His "De Causa Dei" and Its Opponents,* Cambridge Studies in Medieval Life and Thought, n.s. 5 (Cambridge: Cambridge University Press, 1957); McGrath, *Iustitia Dei,* I, pp. 116–17; 141–42. McGrath argues that Bradwardine's Augustinianism was not straightforward: despite the fact that "Bradwardine follows Augustine in discussing predestination within the context of the question of final perseverance, his explicit teaching on *double* predestina-

temporal primacy of grace over human free will, Bradwardine cites Augustine's affirmation in *De gratia et libero arbitrio* that God works in human hearts to incline their wills toward whatever he will, whether toward good or evil.[46] Even closer chronologically to Chaucer are the writings of that other influential Oxford scholar, John Wyclif, who maintains a recognizably Augustinian framework for his theology of grace, free will, merit, and their relation to the pursuit of moral and spiritual perfection. It is well known that Wyclif accepts the Augustinian argument for the predestination of the saved, and God's foreknowledge of those to be damned (*presciti*).[47] Short of divine revelation, according to Wyclif, no human being may possess absolute certainty whether someone was predestined to salvation or foreknown as damned, though one can tell with a high degree of probability if that person's life appears grossly in violation of the evangelical precepts.[48] Still, only God can know whether a sinner's contrition is genuine.[49] Perhaps less well known to literary scholars, however, is how Wyclif's conception of merit was clearly shaped by Augustinian tradition. In *De dominio divino* (1373–74), for example, he argues that because merit is wholly dependent on the grace of God, the creature can only merit relatively (*de congruo*), not absolutely or condignly; thus he can make himself worthy of reward only through God's gracious assistance.[50] The agency of the

---

tion at once distinguishes him from the authentic teaching of Augustine" (p. 141; emphasis in original). For McGrath's discussion of the complex question of what criteria we should use to determine if a late medieval theologian is "Augustinian," see pp. 173–79. On revived interest in Augustinianism in this period, see William J. Courtenay, *Schools and Scholars in Fourteenth-Century England* (Princeton: Princeton University Press, 1987), pp. 207–24.

[46] *De causa Dei*, II, c. 25, p. 563.

[47] See Anthony Kenny, *Wyclif,* Past Masters (Oxford: Oxford University Press, 1985), pp. 39–41; Richard Rex, *The Lollards,* Social History in Perspective (Basingstoke, Hampshire; and New York: Palgrave, 2002), pp. 38–39. Unlike Augustine, however, Wyclif went so far as to define the true church as comprising only the *congregatio predestinatorum,* those predestined for salvation; see Anne Hudson, *The Premature Reformation: Wycliffite Texts and Lollard History* (Oxford: Clarendon Press, 1988), pp. 314–15.

[48] Hudson, *Premature Reformation,* p. 315.

[49] Ibid., p. 294. For Wyclif on the necessary link between contrition and predestination, which only God can know, see *Trialogus cum Supplemento Trialogi,* ed. Gotthardus Lechler (Oxford: Clarendon Press, 1869), pp. 331–32. For his views on the grace of predestination, see *Trialogus,* pp. 150–54; he seems to treat *gratia predestinationis* and *caritas finalis perseverantie* as equivalent (p. 152).

[50] *De dominio divino,* ed. Reginald Lane Poole (London: Wyclif Society, 1890), pp. 226–27; all translations and paraphrases of Wyclif's Latin are mine. The dates of Wyclif's works are from Williell R. Thomson, *The Latin Writings of John Wyclyf: An Annotated Catalogue* (Toronto: Pontifical Institute of Mediaeval Studies, 1983), here p. 39; on Wyclif, cf. McGrath, *Iustitia Dei,* I, p. 117.

meritorious act thus cannot be separated from God's grace, thanks to which God is the main actor.[51] Wyclif draws on Grosseteste's distinction among three created or infused graces (*preveniens, iustificans, consumans*).[52] Throughout the discussion, perhaps what is most striking is the assumed currency of the early fifth-century controversy between Augustine and the so-called Pelagians; any attempt to historicize the theological implications of Chaucer's work must recognize the extent to which Augustine remains a towering presence in fourteenth-century debates, even if the "conceptual forms" employed in late scholasticism were unknown to Augustine.[53] The abstract story pattern of spiritual progress in the world of temptation, and of the final transcendent perfection achieved by those for whom God's "created grace" inclines the human will to perform meritorious acts and persevere until the end, takes on its most elaborate narrative form in *The Man of Law's Tale,* to which we now turn.

II

As many critics have observed, in *The Man of Law's Tale* Chaucer uses the historical setting of the tale to create a double focus on the inner spiritual life of the heroine and her place within a larger providential pattern of history.[54] I suggest that divine grace provides the thematic

[51] "Quod autem Dei gracia sit principalior in agendo, patet ex hoc quod creatura principalius disponitur ex Dei gracia ad merendum quam quacunque disposicione alia naturali" (*De dom. div.*, p. 241). Wyclif's argument clearly recalls that of Augustine in *De gratia et libero arbitrio;* indeed, Wyclif reads 2 Cor. 3.4–5 in a way that agrees with Augustine's exegesis in *De dono perseverantiae.*

[52] *De dom. div.*, p. 246. When God wills the sinner's will to turn toward the good, the operation of the divine will is prevenient grace. When the human will cooperates with the will of God and does not resist the offer of grace, this is *gratia gratificans.* Finally, when the will of God wants the justified sinner to keep his will turned toward the good, we may speak of *creata perseverancia* (p. 247), or what Augustine calls the gift of perseverance to the end.

[53] See McGrath's useful distinction between the dogmatic content and conceptual forms of Augustinian thought (*Iustitia Dei*, I, 175).

[54] John A. Yunck, "Religious Elements in Chaucer's *Man of Law's Tale, ELH* 27 (1960): 249–61. Some critics specifically associate the theme of Providence with Boethius; see, for example, Eugene Clasby, "Chaucer's Constance: Womanly Virtue and the Heroic Life," *ChauR* 13 (1979): 221–33; Stephen Manning, "Chaucer's Constance, Pale and Passive," *Chaucerian Problems and Perspectives: Essays Presented to Paul E. Beichner C.S.C.,* ed. Edward Vasta and Zacharias P. Thundy (Notre Dame: University of Notre Dame Press, 1979), pp. 13–23. In a more subtle essay, Jill Mann analyzes the Boethian resonance of the word "governance" in *The Man of Law's Tale;* see "Parents and Children in the *Canterbury Tales,*" *Literature in Fourteenth-Century England: The J. A. W. Bennett Memorial Lectures, Perugia, 1981–82,* ed. Piero Boitani and Anna Torti (Tübingen: Narr; Cambridge: Brewer, 1983), pp. 165–83 (at p. 168); see also Jill Mann, *Feminizing Chau-*

hinge that connects both aspects of the tale, which is both a narrative about the expansion of Christianity in the Roman Empire and the individual spiritual attainments of Custance.[55] In *The Man of Law's Tale,* Chaucer presents divine grace in terms that are consistently Augustinian in their orientation, a point that will become clearer when we analyze significant changes in Chaucer's adaptation of Nicholas Trevet's life of Constance from his Anglo-Norman *Cronicles,* the primary source for *The Man of Law's Tale.* The implicit theological argument of Chaucer's narrative, in other words, stakes out a distinctly Augustinian position on the relation between grace and will, which Chaucer's unique handling of the narrative helps us locate. By this reading, the often-remarked passive subjectivity of Custance offers a narrative analogue to the downgrading of human agency and free will that we have observed in Augustine's late work and which was reiterated in fourteenth-century England, as we have seen, by Bradwardine and Wyclif.[56] To describe Custance's life in terms of the proto-narratives we have analyzed in Saint Augustine's

---

cer (Woodbridge, Suffolk; and Rochester, N.Y.: Boydell Brewer, 2002), p. 104; rev. ed. of *Geoffrey Chaucer* [London: Harvester, 1991]). Though she does not specifically use Boethius, Helen Cooney, "Wonder and Immanent Justice in the *Man of Law's Tale,*" *ChauR* 33 (1999): 264–87, reads the tale as an exemplum of "the medieval Christian providential view of history" (pp. 266–67), which she suggests was also contained in Trevet.

[55] *Grace* is a key word in the tale, appearing eleven times, seven of which are clearly used in a specifically theological sense, as opposed to a political or purely human one. In Chaucer's entire canon, in fact, the only narrative whose total occurrences of the word in a theological sense approach those of *The Man of Law's Tale* is *Melibee,* which only minimally qualifies as a narrative. Not surprisingly, the only work in *The Canterbury Tales* whose theological use of *grace* surpasses *The Man of Law's Tale* is *The Parson's Tale,* with thirty-two occurrences, in addition to two in *The Parson's Prologue.* I base my analysis on Larry D. Benson, *A Glossorial Concordance to the Riverside Chaucer,* vol. 1 (New York and London: Garland, 1993), s.v. *grace. The Clerk's Tale,* interestingly, uses the word ten times, at least six of which occur in a nontheological sense.

[56] Critics who stress her passivity include Yunck, "Religious Elements"; Manning, "Chaucer's Constance"; Sheila Delany, "Womanliness in the *Man of Law's Tale,*" *ChauR* 9 (1974): 63–72, rpt. *Writing Woman: Women Writers and Women in Literature, Medieval to Modern* (New York: Schocken, 1983); page numbers cited from reprint. Some recent critics dispute readings that see Custance as passive. See Barbara Nolan, "Chaucer's Tales of Transcendence: Rhyme Royal and Christian Prayer in the *Canterbury Tales,*" in C. David Benson and Elizabeth Robertson, ed., *Chaucer's Religious Tales* (Cambridge: Brewer, 1990), pp. 21–38, esp. p. 25 n. 11; Jill Mann, *Feminizing Chaucer,* p. 102; Elizabeth Robertson, "The 'Elvyssh' Power of Constance: Christian Feminism in Geoffrey Chaucer's *The Man of Law's Tale,*" *SAC* 23 (2001): 143–80. The extent of Chaucer's knowledge of Bradwardine's work has not been studied in detail, though he could have gained a general knowledge of it from such friends as Ralph Strode; see J. A. W. Bennett, *Chaucer at Oxford and at Cambridge* (Oxford: Clarendon Press, 1974). My argument, however, does not hinge on whether the poet knew his work.

work, her spiritual journey on earth fleshes out the pattern of amelioration, and ends anagogically with her final perfection among the saints
in heaven.[57]

From the beginning of the tale, Custance evidently has attained a
high degree of perfection, as the Syrian merchants hear in reports about
her "vertu":

> "To alle hire werkes vertu is hir gyde;
> Humblesse hath slayn in hire al tirannye.
> She is mirour of alle curteisye;
> Hir herte is verray chambre of hoolynesse,
> Hir hand, ministre of fredam for almesse."
>
> (II.164–68)[58]

Although neither Trevet nor Gower provides this detailed portrait,
Chaucer's description makes it difficult to determine as yet whether we
should read the passage in Augustinian terms.[59] Yet what Chaucer omits
is as interesting as what he inserts. This is perhaps the first of countless
instances where Chaucer's adaptation deliberately downplays her
agency.[60] Trevet tells us about Constaunce's education; as an only child
Constaunce was instructed in the Christian faith and the seven "secular
sciences."[61] Yunck identifies this information as an example of the only
"religious element" Chaucer consistently omits: "the aggressive sanctity
of Trevet's Constance, that sort of militant, self-assured, often unpleas-
ant proselytizing fervor not uncommon in early saints' lives."[62] Indeed,

---

[57] On the anagogic sense of the tale, see V. A. Kolve, *Chaucer and the Imagery of
Narrative: The First Five Canterbury Tales* (Stanford: Stanford University Press, 1984), pp.
352–56.

[58] Delany, "Womanliness," assumes that Custance "is morally perfect from the start
of the tale" (p. 37), rejecting the possibility that the heroine's suffering is related to
struggling for perfection. The ameliorative proto-narrative crucial to both Paul's and
Augustine's discussion of the pursuit of perfection thus disappears from such an account.

[59] To use the technical language of the *moderni*, at this juncture we cannot tell
whether she performs her virtuous or meritorious works by doing *quod in se est ex puris
naturalibus* or whether her actions are assisted by the habit of infused grace. On *ex puris
naturalibus*, see Heiko A. Oberman, *The Harvest of Medieval Theology: Gabriel Biel and
Late Medieval Nominalism* (Grand Rapids, MI: Eerdman's, 1967), pp. 47–50; on the
axiom "facienti quod in se est Deus non denegat gratiam" (God will not deny grace to
one who does her best), see McGrath, *Iustitia Dei*, I, pp. 83–90.

[60] Cf. Yunck, "Religious Elements," p. 251.

[61] *Sources and Analogues of The Canterbury Tales, II,* ed. Robert M. Correale and Mary
Hamel (Cambridge: D. S. Brewer, 2005), p. 296; subsequent citations of Trevet will be
to this volume (henceforth *SA*).

[62] Yunck, "Religious Elements," p. 250.

in Trevet's account, when the Saracen merchants arrive in Rome, she "preached the Christian faith to them" (*lour precha la foi Cristiene*), to which they assent; thus "she had them baptized and instructed perfectly in the faith of Jesus Christ" (*les fist baptizer et enseigner parfitement en la foi Jhesu Crist*).[63] Though Trevet's grammatical construction leaves ambiguous the identity of the person or persons who teach the Saracens perfectly, this presumably refers to catechizing by a priest who takes over from where she leaves off. Gower omits the details of her education but retains her active role in the merchants' conversion: she "was so ful of feith" that "Sche hath converted" them.[64] Moreover, Gower, who unlike Trevet is writing under the shadow of Lollardy, does not describe Constance as preaching but merely informing them "with hire wordes wise."[65]

When it comes time for her to depart for Syria, Chaucer's heroine struggles to accept her father's will and is temporarily overcome with sorrow (II.264); she is, after all, only human.[66] But in what begins to look like a distinctly Augustinian emphasis, her grudging acceptance of her earthly father's will is subsumed by her submission to divine will as she prays that Christ might send her grace to fulfill his commands:

> "Allas, unto the Barbre nacioun
> I moste anoon, syn that it is youre wille;
> But Crist, that starf for our redempcioun
> So yeve me grace his heestes to fulfille!"
>
> (II.281–84)

The wording of her concise prayer precisely captures the Augustinian argument concerning the relation between grace and the fulfillment of the commandments; in *De praedestinatione sanctorum*, Augustine insists

[63] *SA*, pp. 296–97.

[64] *Confessio Amantis*, II, lines 598, 601. All citations of the *Confessio* (henceforth *CA*) are from G. C. Macaulay, ed., *The English Works of John Gower*, 2 vols., EETS, e.s. 81–82 (London: Oxford University Press, 1900–1901; rpt. 1957).

[65] *CA* II, 606.

[66] Edward A. Block, "Originality, Controlling Purpose, and Craftsmanship in Chaucer's *Man of Law's Tale*," *PMLA* 69 (1953): 572–616, describes Chaucer's Custance as more "human," with greater emotional depth than Trevet's heroine (pp. 591–92), though he nonetheless claims that she "remains too perfect to be a credible human being" (p. 592). Yunck, "Religious Elements," modifies Block's views, arguing that Chaucer's changes to Trevet create "a romantic homily on the virtues of complete submission to divine providence" that "stresses the activity of God and the passivity of all others," making God "the protagonist" of the tale (pp. 250, 251, 259).

that it is God who causes the predestined "to have good works when he makes them observe the divine commandments."[67] At the same time, Custance connects her adverse situation to her subservient status as a woman: "Wommen are born to thraldom and penance, / And to been under mannes governance" (II.286–87), evidently a reference to men's rule over women since Eve's curse.[68] Chaucer thus demands that we read her experience not only as an example of the general human dependence on divine grace to fulfill the will of God, but of the specifically feminine dependence on the will of the controlling authority of man.[69] Indeed, when the tales are read in the Ellesmere order, Custance's stance is soon to echo verbally in an inverted form with the Wife of Bath's gleeful declarations: "An housbonde I wol have . . . / Which shal be bothe my dettour and my *thral*"; of her first three husbands, she tells us, "I *governed* hem . . . wel, after *my lawe*" (III.154–55, 219; my emphasis).

When the Sultan's mother organizes the massacre, the evildoers place Custance "in a ship al steerelees" (II.439), steered only by the power of God. As she prays for grace she emphasizes the redemptive power of Christ's blood and her need for divine assistance to preserve her and protect her from the fiend: "Me kepe, and yif me myght my lyf t'amenden" (II.462), which suggests that she views herself as less than fully perfected, especially vulnerable to temptation during this crisis. Yet like Daniel in the den, Jonah in the fish's maw, the Israelites crossing the Red Sea, or Saint Mary in the Egyptian desert, Custance's preservation for three years and more becomes both a sign and an instrument of God's "wonderful myracle / In hire" (II.477–78).[70] In trying to make

[67] *Predestination of the Saints, Works,* 26, p. 168. "[H]oc ipso quo eos facit habere deinceps opera bona, cum ipse facit ut faciant divina mandata" (PL 44, col. 977).

[68] Mann, "Parents and Children," p. 167.

[69] *The Man of Law's Tale* has provoked a variety of feminist studies, few of which are sympathetic to its Christian ideology, including Delany, "Womanliness in the *Man of Law's Tale*"; Carolyn Dinshaw, "The Law of Man and Its 'Abhomynacions,'" *Chaucer's Sexual Poetics* (Madison: University of Wisconsin Press, 1989), pp. 88–112. Studies more sympathetic to its Christian ideology include Jill Mann, *Feminizing Chaucer,* pp. 100–112; Priscilla Martin, *Chaucer's Women: Nuns, Wives, and Amazons* (Iowa City: University of Iowa Press, 1990), who reminds us that despite being intended to serve as an example for all Christians, "her story is in many ways a tale of female suffering" (p. 139); E. Robertson, "'Elyvsshe' Power."

[70] Contrast Dinshaw, *Sexual Poetics,* who reads the tale as patriarchal ideology, since it presents women as especially "vulnerable to becoming Satan's 'instruments'" (p. 110). I agree that the tale is ideological in sexist ways, but in teasing out its Augustinian nuances I would locate its misogyny in the context of a more general antihumanist ideology. Mann, "Parents and Children," reminds us that "it is not women alone who are under governance . . . women attract attention because their subjection to male

sense of divine providence, the lay narrator reminds us that not even the theological experts fully understand God's inscrutable will in shaping human destinies: "By certeine meenes ofte, as knowen clerkis," Christ acts "for certein ende that ful derk is / To mannes wit, that for oure ignorance / Ne konne noght knowe his prudent purveiance" (II.480–83). The incomprehensibility of divine justice in God's predestining some sinners for salvation and foreknowing others to damnation, as we have seen, is a point reiterated by St. Augustine and stressed by Bradwardine and Wyclif.

Chaucer's Augustinian-inflected rhetoric continues in the Northumbrian episode, where a brief review of Trevet's version will help clarify what our poet accomplishes. The source is quite explicit about how Constaunce plays an active role in Hermengyld's conversion, through the example of "her noble and virtuous way of life" and her persuasive teaching of the elements of the faith.[71] Chaucer omits all this and instead has Custance sojourn long, "In orisons, with many a bitter teere, / Til Jhesu hath converted thurgh his grace / Dame Hermengyld" (II.537–39).[72] With this description of the agency of grace in Hermengyld's conversion, we might recall Augustine's observation that "no one is sufficient by himself either to begin to have faith or to bring it to completion."[73] Indeed, it is likely that Chaucer picked up a specifically Augustinian hint in this episode from Trevet, who describes his heroine "as one whom God had *predestined* for grace and virtue in temptation and joy," though Chaucer avoids referring to the controversial idea of predestination and omits reference to temptation, which might seem out of place here.[74] Although it is true that Chaucer presents Custance

---

'governance' is a model of the human subjection to God" (p. 168); see also Mann, *Feminizing Chaucer,* p. 104.

[71] *SA,* 304–5.

[72] Cf. Yunck: "What Trevet's heroine accomplished by preaching, Chaucer's accomplished by prayers and tears. Jesu brought about the conversion, the Hand of ever-watchful providence" (p. 251). Contrast Carolyn Dinshaw, "Pale Faces: Race, Religion, and Affect in Chaucer's Texts and Their Readers," *SAC* 23 (2001): 19–41, who misleadingly claims that despite being "utterly passive" Custance "manages to effect the conversion of the pagan Hermengyld" (p. 28).

[73] *Predestination of the Saints, Works,* 26, p. 151. "[N]emo sibi sufficit vel ad incipiendam vel ad perficiendam fidem, sed sufficientia nostra ex Deo est" (PL 44, col. 963).

[74] "E tut fut ele bele de merveil de corps, nepurquant ele passa en beauté de vertues come cele qe Dieux avoit *predestiné* a grace et vertue [en] temptacion et joie" (p. 304–5; my emphasis). I assume that Trevet presents Constaunce as not beyond temptation because he is writing the story for a nun; the perils of temptation constitute a traditional theme in both hagiographic and monastic literature. Although Block does not notice the specifically Augustinian rhetoric of either Trevet or Chaucer's version, he makes the general point that Chaucer's changes and additions heighten the religious element of

as playing an active role in the conversion of the constable ("so ferforth she gan oure lay declare / That she the constable, er that it was eve, / Converteth, and on Crist made hym bileve" [II.572–74]), her actions come in the context of advising Hermengyld to work "the wyl of Crist" (II.567) in response to the blind Briton's appeal for healing.[75] Furthermore, when the constable asks what all "this fare" amounts to, she explains: "it is Cristes myght, / That helpeth folk out of the feendes snare" (II.569–71). Once again Chaucer declines to follow Trevet's lead, who had described Hermegild and Constance as "preaching."[76] Writing at a time when some Lollards were affirming the right of lay persons and even women to preach, Chaucer seems to go out of his way *not* to describe Custance as preaching, unlike Trevet, who did not need to display such caution earlier in the century.[77]

Yet the pattern of Satanic temptation (and *concupiscentia carnis* as a consequence of the Fall) returns, for just as the serpent overcame the Sowdanesse (described as a descendant of Eve), he now attempts to prey on Custance: "Sathan, that evere us waiteth to bigile, / Saugh of Custance al hire *perfeccioun,* / And caste anon how he myghte quite hir" (II.582–84; my emphasis). Chaucer borrows from Trevet the idea of the devil instigating the knight to tempt the heroine to "consent to carnal sin."[78] However, only in Chaucer's version is the knight presented merely as Satan's instrument, whose object of assault is her *perfection,* though as we expect, the knight's attempt to seduce her "availleth noght; / She wolde do no synne, by no weye" (II.589–90). Although Chaucer declines to explain how her will withstands the temptation, the

---

the tale and both Custance and Alla show greater piety (pp. 587–89). Cf. Gower, who also puts an Augustinian spin on the narrative: "Thurgh grace of goddes pourveance / This maiden tawhte the creance / Unto this wif so parfitly" (*CA* II.753–55).

[75] In the corresponding passage in Trevet, Constaunce refers not to the will of God but to "la vertue qe Dieux te ad doné" (p. 307). Gower following Trevet narrates the miraculous restoration of sight to the blind Briton, which is enough to persuade the constable to convert (*CA* II.756–78).

[76] *SA,* pp. 306–7.

[77] Chaucer is more cautious than Elizabeth Robertson recognizes when she reads Custance as representative of a nonhierarchical, "apostolic Christianity" in some ways reminiscent of the Lollards: "A woman converting those around her through her prayers and explications of doctrine evokes one of Lollardy's cherished tenets: that anyone—even women and the uneducated laity—can preach" ("'Elyvsshe' Power," p. 169).

[78] "[U]n chivaler . . . estoit par privé temptacion suppris en l'amur la pucele Constance. . . . Et . . . par malveise emprise et temptacioun del diable ala susquere la pucele Constance de assent de pecché charnel" (pp. 307–9). Gower, unlike Chaucer, does not describe the knight's lust in terms of temptation, either his own or Constance's.

larger Augustinian pattern in the tale makes it unlikely that he conceives of her will as unassisted by grace; as Augustine reminds us in *De perfectione justitiae hominis,* we would not be commanded to avoid sin "if our will did nothing at all, and we would not need prayer, if our will alone were sufficient."[79] To put this point in terms of fourteenth-century scholastic debates, instead of her withstanding temptation by acting through the power of her unassisted will, *ex puris naturalibus,* Bradwardine holds that God is a "coefficient cause" of every human act; from this perspective, God is the first cause of Custance's acts of will.[80] Indeed, the emphatic rhetoric of the passage strongly implies she has received such grace that not only will she refuse the consent of reason; she does not even seem to experience delectation at the suggestion of sin. Bradwardine insists that God's special grace is required for a person to overcome temptation or avoid sin.[81] We thus might read the poet's explicit identification of her state of perfection—a moment unique in Chaucer's work—as implying that she is the recipient of what scholastics call *gratia gratum faciens,* the habit of justifying grace that makes the sinner acceptable to God, placing her in "a state of grace and inclined to meritorious works."[82]

After the lustful knight frames Custance for murdering Hermengyld, the pattern of direct divine agency that has been so strong in Chaucer's version of the story takes a remarkable turn when the hand of God smites the wicked knight and a voice from heaven miraculously declares his

---

[79] *Perfection of Human Righteousness, Works* 23, p. 300; "nec juberetur, si nihil ibi nostra voluntas nostra ageret; nec oraretur, si sola sufficeret" (PL 43, col. 303).

[80] On Bradwardine's doctrine of "divine coefficiency," see Oberman, *Bradwardine,* p. 77; as Oberman observes: "It is the Almighty who performs in men their movements of will, albeit in such a way that at the same time they do it entirely by themselves," because both "God and man are *similiter causa efficiens* of every act of will" (p. 81).

[81] "[Q]uod liberum arbitrium quantacunque gratia creata suffultum sine alio Dei auxilio speciali non potest temptationem aliquam superare" (II, c. 5, p. 477); "Quod nullus non tentatus, solius liberi arbitrii viribus, sine gratia quantacunque creata, absque alio Dei auxilio potest peccatum aliquod euitare" (II, c. 7, p. 490); cf. Leff, *Bradwardine and the Pelagians,* p. 72, and Oberman, *Bradwardine,* pp. 68–69. For an overview of Bradwardine's doctrine of grace, see Oberman, *Bradwardine,* pp. 135–42.

[82] I quote the definition from Oberman, *Harvest,* p. 470; see pp. 135–40. See also McGrath, *Iustitia Dei,* I, p. 189, for a similar definition and pp. 100–108 for medieval developments in the concept of grace. Cf. Wyclif, *De dominio divino,* p. 247, who comments on Grosseteste: "[V]idetur quod prius causaliter est gracie prime infusio quam peccatorum remissio, et per idem prius causaliter est peccati remissio quam medie gracie gratificantis infusio" (it seems that the infusion of the former grace [sc. *preveniens*] is causally prior to the remission of sins, and through it the remission of sin is causally prior to the infusion of the intermediate, justifying grace [i.e., in between *gracia preveniens* and *perseverentia*]).

guilt and her innocence. Moreover, unlike Trevet (whose divine voice speaks Latin), Chaucer has God manifest his will by speaking in the vernacular. To the best of my knowledge, this is the only instance in all of Chaucer in which the *vox dei* is heard to speak directly rather than through signs. If so, this is a uniquely powerful moment of theophany in the poet's work; because of this miracle, "by Custances mediacioun, / The kyng," along with many others who witnessed it, "Converted was, thanked be Cristes grace!" (II.684–86). Grace seems to operate the conversion; she is merely the instrument through which God directly manifests his grace, a point rhetorically emphasized by the strong stanza-final position, which stresses the importance of divine grace over human will.

Shortly afterward, it becomes clear that God's plan for the "hooly mayden" takes a new turn when Alla weds her: "And thus hath Crist ymaad Custance a queene" (II.692–93). The controversial stanza describing her wedding night expresses some anxiety over her need to step down from the highest grade of perfection as a virgin:

> They goon to bedde, as it was skile and right;
> For thogh that wyves be ful hooly thynges,
> They moste take in pacience at nyght
> Swiche manere necessaries as been plesynges
> To folk that han ywedded hem with rynges,
> And leye a lite hir hoolynesse aside,
> As for the tyme—it may no bet bitide.
>
> (II.708–14)

To be sure, the almost mocking tone of the passage evident in the description of wives as holy "thynges," the odd circumlocution for husbands with its flat-footed rhyme, and the qualifier "a lite" to describe how much the transition from virginity to lawful sexual activity matters to her degree of holiness: the tendency toward bathos here is of a piece with the frequently melodramatic, over-the-top voicing that Chaucer adds to his version of the tale, which is so frequently remarked by critics.[83] Once again, it may be helpful to gloss this moment with the Wife of Bath's discussion of holiness, especially her jocular rejection of virginity as the highest grade of perfection in favor of the lowest grade (even as she gleefully turns Augustine's key term *perseverentia* upside down):

[83] For example, Helen Phillips, *An Introduction to the Canterbury Tales: Readings, Fiction, Context* (New York: St. Martin's Press, 2000), p. 82.

> In swich estaat as God hath cleped us
> I wol *persevere;* I nam nat precius.
> In wyfhod I wol use myn instrument
> As frely as my Makere hath it sent.
>
> (III.147–50; my emphasis)

These two cases present nearly polar opposites. The Man of Law's melo-drama and mockery sporadically undercuts his serious presentation of the Augustinian theology of grace; the Wife of Bath's suggestion that she is only playing (III.192) invites us not to take her rejection of the theology of perfection too seriously. In exploring the contemporary rele-vance of traditional ideas of the grades of perfection, Chaucer character-istically exploits his fictional personae and their ironic voicings.[84]

Despite the ironic tone, Custance once more finds the grace to remain impervious to the concupiscence of the flesh on her wedding night. From a perspective that idealizes her perfection, even lawful marital sex is treated as one more trial that God in his providence sends her, along with the grace to endure "[s]wiche manere necessaries" with "pacience." Custance's patience and perseverance emerge clearly in the contrast be-tween her reaction to Donegild's wicked actions and the reaction of Alla's servant, who, faced with the forged order to set Custance adrift in the boat again, struggles mightily with a question familiar to Chaucer from Boethius, one that Bradwardine had recently revisited: How can God allow evil to flourish?[85] The messenger wonders aloud:

> "O myghty God, if that it be thy wille,
> Sith thou art rightful juge, how may it be
> That thou wolt suffren innocentz to spille,
> And wikked folk regne in prosperitee?"
>
> (II.813–16)

---

[84] Cf. Watson, "Chaucer's Public Christianity," p. 109, who describes Alisoun of Bath, with her "impassioned argument for an ethic of imperfection," as "one of the most ostentatiously indirect mouthpieces in *The Canterbury Tales;* indeed, she is as thickly swaddled in devices to distance the poet from his words as anything Chaucer wrote." We shall return to Chaucer's sometimes ironic distancing when he narrates the pursuit of perfection.

[85] Bradwardine takes an Augustinian position on evil as privation of good in I, c. 26; he discusses the senses in which God wills and does not will sin in I, c. 34; cf. Oberman, *Bradwardine,* pp. 123–34. Wyclif investigates whether evil is necessary in *Trialogus* III, c. 8.

Although Custance's "deedly pale face" (II.822) registers her very human (and especially female) susceptibility to fear, rather than question God's will as does the messenger, she fully embraces it, which we may read as a further sign of her grace: "she taketh in good entente / The wyl of Crist, and knelynge on the stronde, / She seyde, 'Lord, ay welcome be thy sonde'" (824–26).[86] Without questioning or attempting to understand God's will, she remembers what is most important: God preserved her throughout the last sea voyage. She measures her life in relation to the sovereign power of God, who is unchanging:

> "He that me kepte fro the false blame
> While I was on the lond amonges yow,
> He kan me kepe from harm and eek fro shame
> In salte see, althogh I se noght how.
> As strong as evere he was, he is yet now.
> In hym triste I, and in his mooder deere,
> That is to me my seyl and eek my steere."
>
> (II.827–33)

She does, however, question her husband's will as she addresses her innocent child: "Why wil thyn harde fader han thee spilt?" (II.857). Crossing herself, she boards the ship, and "with an hooly entente / She blisseth hire" (II.867–68). The provisions, we are told, are sufficient to meet her needs and those of her child, "heryed be Goddes grace!" (II.872).

Her triumph over the apostate knight who attempts to rape her serves as one more confirmation of the operation of God's grace in her life. Again, Chaucer's emphasis is significantly different from that of his source. In Trevet the knight is moved by Satan to tempt Constaunce to consent to sin, though we are told that God did not wish her to assent.[87] Yet in Chaucer's version, the very *expression* of the hypothetical possibility of Custance succumbing to temptation is literally written out. More-

---

[86] Yunck uses this passage to conclude: "In Chaucer's tale second causes fade into nothing in the majestic ubiquity of the great First Cause" ("Religious Elements," p. 259), a point Bradwardine would commend. Manning suggests that Yunck's comment "raises questions about Constance's free will" ("Chaucer's Constance," p. 20). On the implications of her fearful response, cf. Dinshaw, "Pale Faces."

[87] "E l'enemi, qi par tut s'afforsca de mal faire, moveit le chivaler renee a grevouse temptacion d'enticer la dame a consent de pecché. Mes Dieux, a qi ele avoit doné {son} queor de enfaunce, ne la voleit soeffrer assentier a tiel mal" (*SA,* p. 317).

over, as has often been remarked, in Chaucer's version Custance is much less actively involved in her defending herself than is the case in Trevet, where she tricks him into turning his back and pushes him overboard.[88] Instead, we are told: "The theef fil over bord al sodeynly . . . / And thus hath Crist unwemmed kept Custance" (II.922, 924). The *apo koinou* construction allows us to read the adjective *unwemmed* as applying equally to Christ and his servant; the adjective is also standard in Marian devotions, and indeed earlier in the stanza Mary's active role is mentioned. That Custance measures herself by the high standard set by Mary is clear when earlier she consoled herself by contrasting the degree of her suffering to Mary's far greater sorrow before the cross (II.841–47).[89] The homiletic rhetoric points the significance of the episode by denouncing the sin of lust, which weakens man's mind and destroys his body. However familiar the concupiscence of the flesh would be to most of Chaucer's readers at firsthand, the "foule lust of luxurie" (II.925) seems outside the heroine's lived experience. Instead, in the next two stanzas the emphasis is not on her constitutive weakness but on what God graciously offers her, affirming that she receives her strength from the same source as David and Judith, who both overcame more powerful foes: God sent all three the "spirit of vigour" (II.943).[90]

Custance evidently perseveres in a state of grace after her return to Rome, where she dwells a long time "In hooly werkes evere, as was hir grace" (II.980). The Augustinian implication is clearly that her works are deemed meritorious because God has justified and accepted her through his offer of grace. Alla, in contrast, at least in his own mind, has more to answer for and thus goes on pilgrimage to Rome to pray for Christ's forgiveness for "his wikked werkes" (II.994) after he "fil in swich repentance" (II.989) for executing his wicked mother. When Alla wonders about the identity of the child who reminds him of the wife he believes long dead, the senator affirms that she is "So vertuous a lyvere"

[88] Cf. Yunck, "Religious Elements," pp. 257–58. See also Cooney, who reads the episode as an instance that the narrator "attributes to providence as miracle something which Trevet unequivocally attributes to human agency" ("Wonder," p. 271). In Gower we are told "the myhti goddes hond" protected her (*CA* II.1124).

[89] On Custance's association with Mary, see Mann, "Parents and Children," pp. 73–74; Dinshaw, *Sexual Poetics,* p. 111.

[90] I suspect "spirit of vigor," not in Chaucer's source, is his interpolation of a theological term I have been unable to trace but that would be the opposite of *languor naturae,* a synonym for *lex membrorum* or *concupiscentia carnis* (see, e.g., *De causa Dei* I, 40, p. 364). The context suggests the spirit of vigor could also be described as the grace of perseverance.

that he has never seen or heard of a greater "Of worldly wommen, mayde, ne of wyf" (II.1024–26). For this witness, at least, Custance seems to have achieved in this life the highest degree of perfection available to a woman living in the world.

When she is finally reunited with her husband, the joyous communal feast, as V. A. Kolve has demonstrated, anagogically points to the eschatological feast of the saints, "the joye that lasteth everemo" (II.1076).[91] In terms of the Augustianian proto-narratives, her eternal glory marks the definitive end of the narrative of amelioration *in via* and the shift to fulfilled perfection or transcendence *in patria*. But the earthly joy of the reunited Alla and Custance soon comes to an end: "litel while it lasteth . . . / Joye of this world, for tyme wol nat abyde" (II.1132–33). And so, we are asked,

> Who lyved euere in swich delit o day
> That hym ne moeved outher conscience,
> Or ire, or talent, or som kynnes affray,
> Envye, or pride, or passion, or offence?
>   (II.1135–38)

We should note that the passage stresses not simply the transitory nature of worldly joy, but how it is daily disturbed by the temptations and struggles within the individual soul, precisely the kind of observation that Augustine repeatedly voices in his anti-Pelagian writings.[92] Although the reminder of daily internal struggles such as even Saint Paul and Saint Augustine acknowledge in the ameliorative narratives of their own lives hardly seems to describe Custance's experience, the stanza nonetheless reminds us that *no* human being is ever wholly immune to the inherited *poena* of original sin.[93] We should thus recall that many theologians, including Augustine, Bradwardine, and Wyclif, insist that

[91] Kolve, *Chaucer and the Imagery of Narrative*, pp. 352–56.

[92] Kolve thus seems slightly off the mark when he suggests that with this stanza the "story is adjusted to accord with what we know about all human lives. The joy that is possible within this world . . . must prove finite, unstable, and impure" (*Chaucer and the Imagery of Narrative*, p. 339). The passage on brief joy is based on Innocent III, *De miseria condicionis humane* I.20, as the Latin gloss to line 1135 indicates (*Riverside Chaucer*, p. 862), though the thought is Augustinian.

[93] In terms of Watson's three "models" for lay perfection that he believes Chaucer rejects, Custance most clearly is situated within the second, the so-called puritanical one; as should be abundantly clear by now, I think a more accurate descriptor for this framework is "Augustinian."

no one can know with certainty whom God predestined for salvation or foreknew to be worthy of damnation.[94] Does Chaucer wish us to believe that God graciously justifies and accepts Alla? The poet will not say: he only invites his readers to "prayen God his soule blesse" (II.1146). About Custance and her father there may be excellent reasons for hope, though not certainty: when Custance returns to spend the rest of her earthly days in Rome, we hear that they both live "In vertu and in hooly almus-dede" (II.1156) until death parts them. The narrator concludes with a prayer for Christ "of his myght" to send joy and to "governe us in his grace" (II.1160, 1161).

As my reading of *The Man of Law's Tale* demonstrates, Custance represents a very high standard of perfection indeed (it is not for nothing that the tale is generally conceived as a hagiographical romance), even if, when measured by an absolute standard of fulfillment, completion, and reward for the race well run, she sometimes "pales" with earthly fears while still on the road.[95] Subject to the temptations of the world, the flesh, and the devil but situated in history after the Redemption, the viator requires divine grace at every moment, and for every meritorious act, according to the implicit Augustinian argument delineated far more sharply in Chaucer's retelling than in Trevet's version.

III

In the Ellesmere order, the next figure Chaucer's readers encounter after Custance is Alisoun of Bath, who stands, as we have already begun to

[94] Bradwardine insists that no one knows what end he will have, "nec vtrum sit praedestinatus finaliter filius vitae vel mortis" (I, c. 39, p. 338). In *De statu innocencie,* Wyclif argues that we should suppose that our neighbor will be saved when we see him do well, and that those who do the contrary will be damned. *De mandatis divinis and De statu innocencie,* ed. Johann Loserth and F. D. Matthew (London: Wyclif Society, 1922), p. 515. In *De civili dominio,* he affirms that no one can know whether someone is in a state of grace without special revelation (II, p. 211); in book three of that work he reiterates that no one can know if they are in a state of grace, though we can make intelligent conjectures on the basis of probable signs (IV, p. 525).

[95] Watson dismisses *The Man of Law's Tale* as "redolent of the desert ideal" in its "evocations of an ancient world of holy living . . . an age of miracles whose lessons cannot be directly translated into the present"; "Christian Ideologies," *A Companion to Chaucer,* ed. Peter Brown (Oxford: Blackwell, 2000), pp. 75–89 (quotations from pp. 85, 77). He maintains the same stance in "Chaucer's Public Christianity," claiming that the tale "belongs to a past so distant that few of its wonders can be expected to recur in the present" (p. 107). However, Chaucer and his audience, whether orthodox or Wycliffite, would surely view the operation of divine grace in the soul as wondrous. Cf. Morton W. Bloomfield, "*The Man of Law's Tale:* A Tragedy of Victimization and a Christian Comedy," *PMLA* 87 (1972): 384–90, esp. pp. 388–89.

appreciate, as the symbolic inverse of Custance. Like the Wycliffites, the Wife of Bath satirizes the pretensions of the friars to imitate gospel perfection, as her subversive remarks about the practice of *glosing* and her digression into antifraternal satire at the beginning of her tale both suggest. Unlike Wyclif and his followers, however, Alisoun never challenges the distinction between evangelical counsels and precepts, never suggests that the pursuit of perfection as it was traditionally conceived by clerical authorities should no longer be taken seriously by anyone.[96] Indeed, she seems rather more interested in discussing the ideal of perfection than Wyclif tended to be. If the heterodox theologian's contribution to late medieval thinking about perfection as a topic in its own right remains sparse and underdeveloped, Wyclif's relatively shallow interest may be explained by his animosity toward followers of what he came to call "private religion" (monks and, after 1380, especially the friars); the Wife's satirical swipes, on the other hand, are mild by comparison. As Wyclif's views toward the "new sects" grew more vehement, the idea of perfection came to have too many bad associations for him to have much explicit interest in the concept, except of course when he polemically challenged his opponents' claims to be pursuing it.[97]

Yet at the same time, the scriptural admonitions to be perfect and a millennium of theological thought about the topic guaranteed that in some contexts, at least, Wyclif found it impossible to avoid speaking in such terms. Given that he was a university-trained cleric writing primarily for other clerics, it should come as no surprise that like other theologians of the time, Wyclif betrays a clear bias toward the professional religious life in a way that tends to leave relatively underdeveloped the space reserved for the secular life of the faithful lay Christian. In *De civili dominio* (late 1375 to late 1376), for example, he affirms the superiority of virginity to marriage.[98] Moreover, unlike some of the more radical

---

[96] On the possible convergence of *The Wife of Bath's Prologue* with Lollardy, see Alcuin Blamires, "The Wife of Bath and Lollardy" *MÆ* 58 (1989): 224–42. On the broader question of Chaucer's "indeterminate" relation to Wycliffite thought, see Fletcher, "Chaucer the Heretic."

[97] On the polemic by Wyclif and his followers against "private religions" of the so-called new sects, see Hudson, *Premature Reformation*, pp. 347–51. See David Aers, "John Wyclif's Understanding of Christian Discipleship," *Faith, Ethics, and Church*, pp. 119–48, esp. pp. 125–26 on Wyclif's rejection of the distinction between counsels of perfection and the commands to be obeyed by all Christians.

[98] *De civili dominio*, ed. Reginald Lane Poole and Johann Loserth, 4 vols. (London: Wyclif Society, 1885–1904) 1:167; date from Thomson, *Latin Writings of John Wyclyf*, p. 48. Cf. Rex, *Lollards*, p. 46. As Anne Hudson remarks, if Wyclif at times "castigated the requirement of sacerdotal celibacy," he never seems to "commit himself in positive terms to a married clergy" (*Premature Reformation*, p. 357).

Lollards, Wyclif did not explicitly argue for the priesthood of all believers, even if some of his reasoning tended in that direction.[99] Yet he also argues that evangelical counsels like suffering injuries are not just for heroes or saints, but that everyone is bound by them.[100] Wyclif thus believes all viators are obligated to follow the counsels at least under pain of venial sin; each man must judge for himself, considering how neglect of the counsels easily leads to temptation.[101] Unlike imperfect human vows, ceremonies, and sects, the doctrine of Christ in his precepts and counsels—the Christian religion in the form it is handed down in the Gospel—is the most perfect of all.[102] Christ, he suggests, knew that it was not expedient that everyone should be monks or friars; indeed, it would be better for the church if this diversity of orders did not even exist.[103]

[99] See Hudson, *Premature Reformation,* p. 325, who suggests that the anti-Lollard polemicist Thomas Netter was correct to attribute the fully developed idea not to Wyclif but to some of his followers.

[100] *De civili dominio* II, p.156. Contrast Rex, *Lollards,* p. 37, who observes that Wyclif viewed Christ's injunction of poverty as a counsel of perfection, not a precept.

[101] *De civili dominio* II, p. 163.

[102] "[R]egula ac religio christiana secundum formam in evangelio traditam est omnium perfectissima et sola pro se bona. Unde vota et religiones humanitus adinvente sapiunt quandam imperfeccionem; ideo in quantum sunt plures in ecclesia talis ordinis" (II, p. 163).

[103] *De civili dominio* II, p.165. Wyclif continued to harp on these themes with increasing vehemence later in his career. For example, in the *Trialogus* (from late 1382 or early 1383 [dated Thomson, *Latin Writings of John Wyclyf,* p. 79]), he suggests that all viators should be content in their own grade, in imitation of those "perfect" men the apostles, who did not have excess in their food or in their clothing (*Trialogus,* p. 195). The Supplement to the *Trialogus* refutes the claims of perfection by monastics; the more perfect Christian religion rests with those living in the world than with those private orders where the obligation is greater but the fruits fewer (*Trialogus,* pp. 429–33). In *De perfectione statuum* from May 1383 (Thomson, *Latin Writings of John Wyclyf,* p. 293), Wyclif contrasts the true perfection of the Christian order to that claimed for themselves by the private orders, especially the friars (*John Wiclif's Polemical Works in Latin,* ed. Rudolf Buddensieg, 2 vols. [London: Wyclif Society, 1883], 2:440–82, at pp. 451–52).

For a taste of the kind of dissident preaching on perfection that may have circulated in the vernacular while Chaucer worked, perhaps the closest we can get is the recently edited Lollard sermon *Omnis plantacio,* probably written by the second decade of the fifteenth century, which offers an account closely resembling Wyclif's of the false claims to perfection by members of the "new sects" who ignore the perfection of gospel precepts by establishing "newe rulis not expressid in þe gospel" and impudently claim "þat þer stondiþ þe plente of perfit lyuyng, þei menen in her doing and seiyng þat Crist was fauti [i]n his ordynaunce, and þat he and hise apostlis and oþir perfit men at sueden Crist wiþoute ony addiciouns of newe ritis or rulis of religioun kept not perfitli Goddis lawe, siþ þei weren not of suche ordris ne kepten þe priuat newe foundun rulis of such religioun. For, if Crist tauȝte fulli þe rule of perfeccioun and lyuede þeraftir, it hadde be ynow for a man þat wolde haue be perfit, as þis maistir was, for to haue sued his rule and his lyuyng. But þese sectis, menynge þat Crist shulde haue be vnperfit in his loore

In attempting to divorce themselves from self-justifying claims to perfection by the religious orders, the radical reformers thus offered a model that even lay women could choose to pursue if they wished, one based on the life and teaching of Jesus Christ. In this highly charged environment, the theological significance of Alisoun's lifestyle choices may be far more complicated than previous criticism has acknowledged, least of all criticism of the exegetical variety. Whatever else she may represent—and perhaps no other figure in Chaucer's poetry has represented more diverse things to more readers—the Wife of Bath surely dramatizes in highly symbolic ways the difficulties that possessing a will poses for the viator. Fully embracing the secular life of living in the world, the fictional viator of whom we are told "she koude muchel of wandrynge by the weye" (I.467), the Wife narrates a story informing us that her most distinctive form of "wandering" consists in a marital history of passing through a succession of husbands. As she tells us early on, she intends to remarry for a sixth time because, as she explains with characteristic brio, "I *wol* nat kepe me chaast in al" (III.46; my emphasis). Indeed, marriage is so central to her constitution as a "social person" that the history of Chaucer criticism has been much concerned since Kittredge to viewing her performance as initiating a marriage group.[104] Few critics, however, have attended to the question of her choice to marry in the context of Christian perfection, and the possibilities for attaining perfection in this life as a person living in the world. Marriage and conducting business affairs—the two things that most constitute the kind of person the Wife represents—are unmistakable marks of the secular life. In the discussion of marriage in her prologue, as Alisoun ponders the choices that face a woman living in the world, she raises some of the central issues for what it might mean to live ethically in the world, rather than to seek the more demanding life of withdrawing from it. She represents, according to Watson, "the poem's

---

and his lyuyng, han cloutid up a rule þe which conteyneþ al þe perfeccioun of Cristis rule—and sumwhat of perfeccioun ouer as þei seien. And so, as her rule passiþ in perfeccioun Cristis rule þe which he kepte, so þei þat kepen þis rule passen Crist in perfit lyuyng." *The Works of a Lollard Preacher: The Sermon* Omnis plantacio, *the Tract* Fundamentum aliud nemo potest ponere, *and the Tract* De oblacione iugis sacrificii, ed. Anne Hudson, EETS o.s. 317 (Oxford: Oxford University Press, 2001), pp. 17–18.

[104] I borrow the useful concept of "social person" from Elizabeth Fowler, *Literary Character: The Human Figure in Early English Writing* (Ithaca: Cornell University Press, 2003).

117

most important attempt to articulate a mediocrist religiosity outside *The Parson's Tale.*"[105] For that reason alone she deserves our careful attention.

The Wife of Bath's portrait in *The General Prologue* informs us that if any other wife goes before her in making offerings at her parish church, "certeyn so wrooth was she / That she was out of alle charitee" (I.451–52). Earlier generations of exegetical critics read these lines as evidence of her moral hypocrisy, but when reading the pilgrim portraits, it is always worth asking who is speaking. Instead of assuming this comment represents Chaucer's moral judgment on her character, we might consider that the poet's source for this insight may be the Wife herself, whose language of moral self-criticism the poet may be citing in free indirect discourse. Although Robertson offered a superficial allegorical interpretation of the Wife as representing feminine carnality itself, the issues her performance raises, when read within the discursive field of Augustinian theology, are far more complex than such self-assured monological readings allow.[106]

In justifying her decision at the age of twelve not to remain a virgin, or, the next best thing, not to complete her days after the death of her first husband as a chaste widow, Alisoun observes that both Christ and the Apostle Paul accept the place of marriage within the divine scheme. Indeed, she proceeds to defend her lifestyle choices in terms of a crucial theological distinction, ultimately based on Saint Paul, between what God mandates or prohibits by his commandments and what he recommends: that is, the difference between a "precept" (*praeceptum*) and a "counsel" (*consilium*). The distinction proves crucial for theologians who wished to understand the scriptural demand for Christians to seek perfection. In claiming that it is possible to attain a measure of holiness (III.58) even in the state of matrimony, the Wife introduces the distinction thus:

> Wher can ye seye, in any manere age,
> That hye God *defended* mariage
> By expres word? I pray yow, telleth me.
> Or where *comanded* he virginitee?
> I woot as wel as ye, it is no drede,
> Th'apostel, whan he speketh of maydenhede,

[105] Watson, "Chaucer's Public Christianity," p. 109.
[106] Cf. Robertson, *Preface to Chaucer,* p. 321; Olson, *Canterbury Tales and the Good Society,* p. 243.

He seyde that *precept* therof hadde he noon.
Men may *conseille* a womman to been oon,
But *conseillyng* is no *comandement*.
He putte it in oure owene *juggement;*

. . . .

Poul dorste nat *comanden,* atte leeste,
A thyng of which his maister yaf noon *heeste.*
The dart is set up for virginitee;
Cacche whoso may, who *renneth* best lat see.
> (III.59–68; 73–76; emphasis added)

At stake in her argument is nothing less than the nature of divine law, the moral obligations it creates, and the relation of free will—the ability to make rational moral choices through the exercise of what medieval theologians refer to as *liberum arbitrium*[107] (cf. *juggement* in the passage quoted above)—and the grace and justice inherent in God's system of reward and punishment based on merit and demerit. In other words, far more is theologically at stake than a simplistic description of the Wife as a carnal sinner who promotes the reign of *cupiditas* over that of *caritas.* Moreover, the Wife's adaptation of Saint Paul's metaphor of a competitive foot race anticipates her introduction of the idea of Christian perfection a few lines later.[108] As the Wife explains—and her theological reasoning on this point carries a great deal of authority—the prize for virginity "is nat taken of every wight, / But ther as God lust gyve it of his myght" (III.77–78). The final verse of this couplet thus refers to God's pleasure or will (*voluntas*), his gift (*donum*), and his power (*potentas*). No wonder scholars in recent years have adduced the Wife as participating in the late fourteenth-century English phenomenon of vernacular theology: we are only a few verses into her theological argument and already she has implicitly raised fundamental questions that occupied Saint Augustine, as we have already seen, in his response to Pelagius and his followers, namely, the nature of grace as God's gratuitous, unmerited gift, and the relation among grace, free will, and the predestina-

---

[107] See McGrath, *Iustitia Dei,* I, pp. 18–23, who indicates that the Eastern church adopted the nonbiblical Greek term *autexousia* from the Stoics, which Tertullian then introduced to the Western church as *liberum arbitrium.*

[108] The heavily glossed manuscripts of *The Wife of Bath's Prologue* identify Chaucer's immediate source here and throughout much of the *Prologue* as Saint Jerome's *Adversus Jovinianum;* the text from Saint Paul used by Jerome is 1 Cor. 15.8; see *Riverside Chaucer,* p. 866 n. line 75.

tion of the saints, questions that also occupied Wyclif only a decade or so before Chaucer created the Wife of Bath. As Augustine might remind us, "God works in the hearts of human beings to incline their wills to whatever he wills."[109] If the Wife were a real person, no one could know with certitude whether her heart was to remain hardened (if that even accurately describes her condition), or whether she was predestined to have God prepare her will to respond to his gracious call, and to persevere to the end.

The Wife's immediate concern, however, is the place in God's scheme of salvation that might be available to a lesser vessel such as herself, whom God manifestly has not called to the higher standard of virginity, to whom God has not offered that admirable gift. Her answer, again, hinges on Paul's personal example and his distinction between counsel and precept. Although he himself was a virgin and expressed the desire that everyone could be like him, "[a]l nys but conseil to virginitee" (III.82). Thus the Wife of Bath relishes the freedom to remarry, because Paul gave permission "[o]f indulgence" to be a wife (84).[110] The distinction between precept and counsel leads her to articulate the idea of Christian perfection: because Paul states in 1 Corinthians that it is "good no womman for to touche" (87), she concludes, the Apostle "heeld virginitee / Moore parfit than weddyng in freletee" (91–92). Yet not all the vessels in a lord's household can be of gold, she observes; even wooden and earthen ones do service (99–101). There must be a place for diverse callings in the divine plan: "God clepeth folk to hym in sondry wyse, / And everich hath of God a propre yifte" (102–3). We might say that her optimism about the possibility for ordinary Christians who choose the lesser path to reach salvation is, to use one of her favorite words, refreshing.

Having introduced the notion of relative degrees of perfection based on the grades of chastity, the Wife soon enlarges the concept of Christian perfection and its relation to the most disciplined forms of imitating Christ available to those who would attain the highest form of perfection not as a matter of precept but of counsel:

---

[109] *Grace and Free Choice, Works* 26, p. 102. "Agit Omnipotens in cordibus hominum etiam motum voluntatis eorum, ut per eos agat quod per eos agere ipse volueri" (PL 44, col. 908).

[110] Cf. 1 Cor. 7.6. Robertson, *Preface to Chaucer,* p. 322, cites Lombard, *Sententiae* 4.26.1–3 on marriage as indulgence, not commandment in the New Law.

Virginitee is greet perfeccion,
And continence eek with devocion,
But Crist, that of perfeccion is welle,
Bad nat every wight he sholde go selle
Al that he hadde, and gyve it to the poore,
And in swich wise folwe hym and his foore.
He spak to hem that wolde lyve parfitly;
And lordynges, by youre leve, that am nat I.
(III.105–12)

Thus the Wife of Bath in fashioning a story about herself performs the historically important task of imagining a space for the integrity of ordinary life against the backdrop of the elitist "ethic of supererogation" that gave rise to medieval monasticism.[111] In returning to Jerome's *Adversus Jovinianum* as his primary source for the ethical debate in which the Wife engages, Chaucer stages a return to a foundational moment in establishing institutional supports for an ethical elite, implicitly diagnosing the causes behind the theoretical underdevelopment of a viable domain for moral excellence capable of being lived out by the ordinary lay person.[112] Unlike Watson, however, who believes that perfectionist ideology, or "the pursuit of purity as a serious and workable contemporary ambition for those living in the world, is . . . nowhere extolled in *The Canterbury Tales,*" I do not believe that Chaucer seriously abandoned the Augustinian model of lay perfection. Nor do I believe that "Chaucer's ecclesiology is . . . anti-perfectionist" (a point to which I shall return in the fourth section of this essay), or that the poet ultimately wished to contest what is admirable about an ascetic ethic of supereroga-

---

[111] I take the phrase from Charles Taylor, *Sources of the Self: The Making of Modern Identity* (Cambridge: Harvard University Press, 1989), p. 26. In Catholic moral theology, "works of supererogation" are "acts which are not enjoined as of strict obligation, and therefore are not simply good as opposed to bad, but better as opposed to good"; thus the counsels of evangelical perfection (poverty, chastity, obedience) were taken to be not universal obligations but supererogatory; see *The Oxford Dictionary of the Christian Church,* ed. F. L. Cross and E. A. Livingstone, 2nd cor. ed. (Oxford: Oxford University Press, 1983), p. 1324. The term, based on Luke 10.35, only appears to have emerged in this technical sense in the Middle Ages. Aquinas employs it several times in *Summa theologiae* II–II, 186–87.

[112] It is worth noting that Pelagius sided with Jovinian against Jerome, though he "was not endorsing [Jovinian's] attempt to find the ideal Christian life in that led by the married majority, but on the contrary, was advocating the ascetic life as the standard which *all* Christians ought to be aiming for; he did not advocate mediocrity as the norm, but perfection" (Harrison, *Augustine,* p. 102).

tion (as Wyclif and his followers most certainly did).[113] Nonetheless, we can be confident that the comic figure of the Wife provides an important supplement to the narrow framework typical of medieval theologians' attempts to work out the implications of scriptural admonishments to moral perfection that are coupled with reminders of the limitations to human agency: the moral choices made by the free will depend on the quality of God's assistance to that will.

For an example of what I call the relatively underdeveloped domain for moral excellence by ordinary persons (*mediocriter boni*) that is an unintended consequence of theologians' focus on questions of perfection, we may turn briefly to the *Summa Theologiae,* where this problem emerges with illustrative clarity. Thomas focuses on the state of perfection for those who undertake perpetually binding vows, such as bishops and monastics.[114] Within this conceptual framework, the relation of Christian perfection to the vows of poverty, continence, and obedience is examined in the question devoted to the religious state.[115] In a move that is not at all surprising, he confirms the traditional theological view that perfection consists principally in charity (II–II.184.1), or that out of which the Wife sometimes finds herself, according to *The General Prologue.* Although it may at first appear that perfection in this life is not possible, Thomas maintains that it is possible to be perfect in this life in two limited senses. The first occurs when "everything incompatible with charity, i.e. mortal sins, is excluded from the will of a man" (p. 25). Since charity cannot thrive without the exclusion of mortal sin from the will, perfection is necessary for salvation (*sine tali perfectione caritas esse non potest. Unde est de necessitate salutis*). Because Aquinas is not such an ethical elitist as to believe that *only* the professional religious are likely to be saved, however, his observation about the necessary relation between

[113] Watson, "Chaucer's Public Christianity," p. 108.

[114] Saint Thomas Aquinas, *Summa theologiae,* Latin text and English translation, vol. 47 (New York and London: Blackfriars, 1973), II–II.183.1. When convenient, citations appear parenthetically. Thomas devotes questions 185 (the episcopal state) and 186 (the essential elements of the religious state) to the instituted states of perfection.

[115] Defining perfection in terms of states of being risks excluding a dynamic notion of spiritual progress. To avoid such an exclusion, Thomas employs a tripartite terminology based on Augustine; states are not all equidistant from the goal and may be distinguished "according to beginners, advanced, and perfect" (*secundum incipientes, proficientes et perfectos* [*ST* II–II.183.4]). As the Blackfriars editors note, "Thomas preferred the terminology of Augustine because it better described the psychological aspects of growth in Christian perfection and was more expressive of the dynamism of charity" (p. 13).

perfection and salvation potentially maps out a theoretical space for lay persons to seek Christian perfection. Yet Thomas's bias toward the professional religious reemerges when he defines the second limited sense in which perfection in this life is possible, when "the will of a man rejects not only what is incompatible with charity, but even that which would prevent the affection of the soul from being directed totally to God" (p. 25). These two pathways toward perfection hinge on the distinction between the willing transgression of the law and the voluntary removal of those obstacles that stand in the way of the proper direction of the *affectus mentis* toward the perfecting of charity.[116] The difference is between staying on the road until reaching the destination (the moment at the end of life when what I have called the ameliorative narrative cedes to the transcendental one) instead of taking a different road, and using tools that might prove instrumental toward reaching that end, pushing aside the obstacles on the road that might otherwise have led the traveler astray.

On the basis of this distinction, Thomas considers the relation of the precepts and the counsels, inquiring whether perfection in this life consists in observing not only the precepts but also the counsels. Such may appear to be the case from Jesus' admonition to the young man in Matt. 20.40: "If thou wilt be perfect, go sell what thou hast, and give to the poor, and come, follow me." This text, of course, is the same one that attracts the Wife of Bath's interest: "Crist, that of perfeccion is welle, / Bad nat every wight he sholde go selle / Al that he hadde, and gyve it to the poore. . . . / He spak to hem that wolde lyve parfitly" (III.107–11). In his attempt to solve this theological problem, Thomas observes that there is no limit to the commandment to love God and one's neighbor, since one can always strive for more charity. In this ameliorative narrative, whatever "goes beyond" (*quod est plus*) the charity enjoined in the commandment is thus the domain of the evangelical counsels.[117] If the purpose of the precepts is to remove those things contrary to charity (which he previously identified with mortal sin), the counsels are designed to "remove those impediments to the exercise of charity which

[116] Aquinas cites Augustine: "venenum caritatis est cupiditas, perfectio nulla cupiditas" (covetousness is the poison of charity; the perfection of charity is the absence of all covetousness), LXXXIII *Quæstiones* 36 (PL 40, col. 25).

[117] "Perfection consists essentially in the precepts," but secondarily and instrumentally "it consists in the counsels, all of which, like the precepts, are ordained to charity, but in different ways" (*ST* II–II.184.3. *resp.*).

are not incompatible with charity, *such as marriage, secular occupations, etc.*"[118] Here it becomes readily apparent how little space Thomas in fact leaves in his moral scheme for exploring the possibilities for ordinary Christians to make spiritual progress worthy to be described as "perfection." Shrewd businessmen or women for whom marriage is a sound investment (like the Wife of Bath) evidently need not apply. Yet the relatively underdeveloped concept of spiritual perfection for ordinary Christians in Thomas is, I suggest, precisely the theoretical weakness within medieval theology that the Wife of Bath, in a late fourteenth-century context, playfully wishes to expose. If the abstract modalities and clerical subjectivities interpellated by theological discourse from Augustine to Aquinas and beyond left a relatively underdeveloped theoretical space for the texture of lived experience by a layperson, a space that the fictional figure of the Wife of Bath jocularly fleshes out (as it were), Chaucer's achievement points to his awareness of the need to conceptualize in greater detail the possibilities for perfection by lay persons who live in the world.

Such a need was also apparent to Chaucer's older contemporary, the Benedictine monk Uthred of Boldon, author of *De substantialibus regule monachalis* (On the Vows of the Monastic Rule) and *De perfectione vivendi in religione* (On the Perfection of Living in a State of Religion), two closely related treatises written c. 1374–76, partially in response to Wyclif's attacks on monastic orders.[119] In the second work Uthred affirms that personal perfection is indeed available in principle not just to professional religious but also to lay persons since it consists in the practice of the theological virtues, which may be regained through penitence. Therefore, a man may be perfect in any walk of life, whether secular, regular, or ecclesiastic, though as we might expect from a monastic writer, he believes that attaining a higher form of perfection is more likely for someone nonsecular like himself.[120] Although, as Pantin suggests, we

---

[118] "[C]onsilia autem ordinantur ad removendum impedimenta actus caritatis, quae tamen caritati non contrariantur, *sicut est matrimonium, occupatio negotiorum saecularium, et alia hujusmodi*" (p. 28, my emphasis).

[119] Pantin, "Two Treatises of Uthred of Boldon," pp. 363- 85; translations from Uthred are mine.

[120] "Nec gradus aliquis nec status in Christianismo secularis, religiosus aut ecclesiasticus qualiscumque reddit aut efficit hominem sic perfectum esse, sed eius conversacio virtuosa, quamvis gradus et status huiusmodi multum iuvent . . . et quanto gradus superior, tanto perfeccior, quia Deo propinquior, occupans debet esse" (In Christianity, it is not any secular, regular or ecclesiastic grade or state whatsoever that makes a man perfect in this way, but his virtuous way of life, though the grade or state helps many

might view Uthred's concessions to the possibility of perfection among ordinary Christians as "reflect[ing] the growing desire to open up the spiritual life to the devout laity" (p. 384), it is clear where his allegiances lie when he continues to treat as normative the monastic rules based on the evangelical counsels. He may sense the need to respond to critics like Wyclif, but he is not prepared to make a radical break. In her own way, the Wife of Bath wishes to expose the same limitation in the theology of perfection as it was developed by celibate clerics. If perfection is admirable but no more than supererogatory, why should anyone bother with the counsels any more? Orthodox theologians like Uthred grudgingly admit that choosing the more elitist pursuit of perfection offers no guarantee of success, and conversely, that choosing to live within the world as a lay person is not necessarily a recipe for spiritual disaster. Such an admission points to a theological blind spot that a lively questioning mind like the Wife of Bath's has exposed to daylight. Indeed, we might even conclude that Chaucer uses the Wife of Bath as his most richly imagined figure to represent the double bind encountered by a fourteenth-century laywoman when confronted by traditional demands for Christian perfection. But this hardly means that Chaucer is signaling, through his playful fiction, his willingness to jettison the traditional norms underpinning the discourse of Christian perfection entirely, any more than do these orthodox theologians.

Indeed, neither Alisoun's frank enjoyment of sensuality ("In wyfhod I wol use myn instrument / As frely as my Makere hath it sent," 149–50) nor her recognition that market values have permeated fourteenth-century social relations ("Wynne whoso may, for al is for to selle," 414) implies that Chaucer believed the Augustinian theology of perfection should not apply to her life story. It is, of course, her keen awareness of her individual life as a *process* that her autobiographical confession reveals:

> "But—Lord Crist!—whan that it remembreth me
> Upon my yowthe, and on my jolitee,
> It tikleth me aboute myn herte roote.

. . . and the higher the grade, the more perfect the one occupying it ought to be, since it is closer to God [Pantin, "Two Treatises," p. 376; his ellipses]). Although the *regula paradisi* (the domain of the evangelical counsels) may help men attain perfection, "it does not therefore follow that the life of regulars is generally to be called more perfect than that of seculars, who may perhaps be more discerning and stronger in resisting temptations," since perfection is a matter of interior habits of virtue, not of corporeal observances (quoting Pantin's summary, "Two Treatises," p. 379).

Unto this day it dooth myn herte boote
That I have had my world as in my tyme."

(III.469–73)

One need not be part of a Robertsonian rearguard action to insist that we have not properly heard the implications of her use of the word *world* unless we recognize it as equivalent to *seculum:* the time-bound world that is passing away. In other words, as the Man of Law reminds us at the very moment his ameliorative narrative shifts to the transcendent, anagogical one, "joye of this world" only lasts for a short while, "for tyme wol nat abyde" (II.1133). Alisoun's process of recollecting enjoyment past offers a mirror image of the Augustinian paradigm for the right use of memory in *The Confessions;* her movement on the road appears to reverse his directions for the journey toward the future perfect: "Between the extremes of the beginning of faith and the perfection of perseverance there are those in-between virtues by which we live correctly."[121] In short, the direction of Alisoun's wandering seems the reverse of Custance's symbolic movement, of whom we are told upon first meeting her *in via:* "Hir herte is verray chambre of hoolynesse" (II.167). On the other hand, unlike the Robertsonians, I do not believe Chaucer implies that the reader's most appropriate response to her "ticklish" heart is to castigate her for hardening it against the offer of prevenient grace. Indeed, it is not at all a matter of succumbing to Robertson's cardinal sin of sentimentality to recognize that her performance is carefully calculated to appeal to the lay reader's sympathetic identification with the difficulties and temptations she faces while living "in between."[122]

In short, for all the frivolity of her holiday mood, the Wife's story of her will to imperfection contains a serious point; as Augustine observes, "God works in the hearts of human beings to incline their wills to whatever he wills."[123] Moreover, human intelligence is incapable of understanding God's inscrutable decision that "it is better that some who will

[121] *Gift of Perseverance, Works* 26, p. 230. "Inter initium autem fidei et perfectionem perseverantiae, media sunt illa, quibus recte vivimus" (PL 44, col. 1028).

[122] For a parallel Augustinian sense of human life in the middle used by Chaucer, see V. A. Kolve, "'Man in the Middle': Art and Religion in Chaucer's *Friar's Tale,*" *SAC* 12 (1990): 5–46.

[123] *Grace and Free Choice, Works* 26, p. 102; "Agit Omnipotens in cordibus hominum etiam motum voluntatis eorum, ut per eos agat quod per eos agere ipse voluerit"(PL 44, col. 908).

not persevere be mingled with the certain number of his saints."[124] Yet who is to say how the Wife of Bath might respond to the Parson's call to contrition, the way of "refresshynge for youre soules" (again, one of the Wife's favorite words), in short, the "ful noble wey . . . which may nat fayle . . . and this wey is cleped Penitence" (X.77, 79–80). As we saw in the first part of this essay, with the well-established link between the justification of the sinner and the sacraments of the Church, it was difficult to think of the pursuit of Christian perfection outside the sacrament of penance. Yet even within the temporal boundaries established by the fiction of *The Canterbury Tales,* the Wife of Bath's story is not over, though if she were a real person, only God could know with certitude, Chaucer would doubtless agree, how that story would end.[125]

IV

As the previous section suggests, if *The Wife of Bath's Prologue* offers readers one of the most detailed and persuasive narratives in medieval literature of what the textured experience of living in the world feels like, this is in large part because, as Elizabeth Fowler has brilliantly argued, it is not the theologians but the poets who perform the important cultural work of producing a recognizable interiority: Chaucer, she proposes, "presents poetic character as a more moving and compelling vehicle for these insights than is the theological discourse about penance." In reading his fiction we "become habituated to a world in which person, passion, and cognition can work the way they do when we read Chaucer."[126] Alisoun of Bath and Custance, with their manifestly different relation to the ideal of perfection, thus offer richly textured insights into what it is like for an embodied being in the world who must struggle with temptation (or with one's fifth husband over the indignities of misogynistic clerical authority).[127] Yet at the same time, the aporia Saint

---

[124] *Gift of Perseverance, Works* 26, p. 201. "Deus autem melius esse judicavit, miscere quosdam non perseveraturos certo numero sanctorum suorum; ut quibus non expedit in hujus vitae tentatione securitas, non possint esse securi" (PL 44, col. 1003).

[125] As for the ending of *The Wife of Bath's Tale,* it would probably be too much of a stretch to read the magic of its happy ending as a fairy tale analogue of the Augustinian aporia implicit in the dialectic between the sovereign human will responding to the gratuitous offer of supernatural grace.

[126] Fowler, *Literary Character,* pp. 36, 92.

[127] Although Watson believes Custance lives in a world too distant to have relevance to the fourteenth century, he recognizes that "her mode of selfhood (like her devotion) is more familiar than Griselda's" ("Chaucer's Public Christianity," p. 107).

Augustine reaches when he interiorizes the actions of grace on the will, where even "our hearts and our thoughts are not in our power," suggests that what we habitually experience as most intimate within ourselves could also be viewed as a force radically alien to the self.[128]

If Chaucer was more engaged by the theology of Christian perfection than previous criticism has acknowledged, what might a reading of *The Canterbury Tales* begin to look like if instead of assuming that Chaucer deliberately created a "marriage group," we consider the possibility that he has created, in effect if not conscious intention, a "perfection" group? As the contrasting marriages of Custance and Alisoun of Bath suggest, such a group would include those tales in which marriage is an important concern, though it need not be limited to them. It might also include tales that use in thematically important ways lexical items sharing the root derived from the Latin verb *per-ficio* and its French derivatives.[129] But there is no need to restrict the group to tales that employ the vocabulary of perfection, since other works demonstrate a significant thematic concern with perfection. For example, we should include *The Canon Yeoman's Tale* because of the centrality of the idea of perfection to alchemical writings.[130] In what follows, then, let us briefly sketch out a reading of *The Canterbury Tales* as unfolding a narrative of both the progress and completion of perfection.[131]

[128] *Gift of Perseverance, Works* 26, p. 201; PL 44, col. 1003. I do not suggest, of course, that this represents Augustine's own understanding of the logic of his argument.

[129] As a specialized term from philosophical and theological inquiry, the Latin *perfectio* and related words entered French and then Middle English, where the earliest recorded instance in the *MED* is from the early thirteenth-century *Ancrene Wisse*. See *MED,* s.v. *perfeccioun,* for examples under definitions 1 (d) from *Ancrene Wisse* (c. 1230 [?a1200]), and examples under 1 (c) and 1 (d) from *Ayenbit of Inwit* (1340). It is only with Chaucer's generation of vernacular writers that the vocabulary of perfection seems fully naturalized in the language, both as an everyday term so common as barely to attract scholars' notice, and also as part of an emerging lexicon of theological and philosophical vocabulary. Unfortunately, the word is not included in J. D. Burnley, *Chaucer's Language and the Philosophers' Tradition,* Chaucer Studies 2 (Cambridge and Totowa, N.J.: D. S. Brewer, 1979).

[130] The link between alchemy and perfection is clear from Gower's frequent use of the word in his discussion of alchemy in *Confessio Amantis,* Bk. 4. It is worth recalling the relevance of the doctrine of alchemical marriage to *The Canon Yeoman's Tale.* On the pursuit of perfection in that work, see Lee Patterson, "Perpetual Motion: Alchemy and the Technology of the Self," *SAC* 15 (1993): 25–60, esp. pp. 51–50; he cites Roger Bacon's claim that the elixir could re-create the perfection of Adam and Eve before the Fall (p. 51).

[131] My discussion omits Fragment I, though it is worth noting that Theseus's speech about the First Mover bases its argument for marriage on perfect being theology (I, 3007–9). Theseus counsels that Palamon and Emily should "make of sorwes two / O parfit joye, lastynge everemo" (I, 3071–72). However, his view of the perfect joy of

Not long after the Wife of Bath's discourse is concluded, the fourth fragment offers *The Clerk's Tale* and *The Merchant's Tale,* a pairing that deserves to be reconceived as variations on the central theme of the perfection group. Certainly any reading of *The Clerk's Tale* must come to grips with the critically vexed problem created by the clashes between the surface narrative of Walter's gratuitous cruelty toward his wife and the Clerk's allegorical interpretation after the story ends, or "the disunity of the tale's two levels of meaning."[132] However, to describe Griselda's patience, rather than her husband's cruelty, as "monstrous" seems to give less credit to her perfectionism than her exemplum demands.[133] To read the tale from within an Augustinian framework, however, would be to contrast the operation of divine grace on Griselda's unfathomable interiority with the way Walter succumbs to temptation as he "in his herte longeth so / To tempte his wyf" (IV.451–52). Indeed, Walter's wonderment at Griselda's patient endurance is filtered through the vocabulary of perfection: if he did not know that his wife *parfitly* loved her children, he would have thought her steadfastness was some kind of trick (IV.690). I certainly do not mean to suggest that reading *The Clerk's Tale* within an Augustinian framework exhausts that tale's significance.[134] Instead, I am suggesting that the apparent dissonances within the tale are greatly amplified by the way it engages in a dialogue with other versions of Christian perfection in *The Canterbury Tales;* Griselda's "inportable" humility (IV.1144) offers a narrative analogue to the aporia within the deepest recesses of the will in Augustine's interiorization of divine agency within the soul. *The Clerk's Tale,* in short, presents Griselda as one who by all appearances seems likely to enjoy the

---

erotic love—an idea paralleled in Chaucer's other romance of antiquity, *Troilus and Criseyde* (II, 891) and in *The Wife of Bath's Tale* (III.1258)—must seem inadequate when read retrospectively from the Augustinian perspective on history introduced by *The Man of Law's Tale,* since there is no possibility for the lovers to experience transcendence to eternity, notwithstanding Theseus's claim. If we read the sequence of fabliaux that follow the first tale as initiating from the Miller's repudiation of the Knight's idealism, Theseus's lofty vision of marriage as an imitation of divine perfection exactly names the specific ground of his philosophical ideal.

[132] Aers and Staley, *Powers of the Holy,* p. 235.

[133] Watson, "Chaucer's Public Christianity," p. 107. Cf. Kathryn L. McKinley, "The *Clerk's Tale:* Hagiography and the Problematics of Lay Sanctity," *ChauR* 33 (1998): 90–111, who faults the tale for its theology of perfection (p. 106) and regrets that Chaucer fails to submit the tale's notion of sanctity to more critical scrutiny (p. 109).

[134] I do not wish to ignore the political significance of the tale as a study of Lombard tyranny as described by David Wallace, for example. Indeed, the other-worldly perspectives of the tale provide a tense contrast with its critical analysis of authoritarian polity.

grace of perseverance until the end. If from the vantage point of a viator who finds the interior acts of the will more difficult to sustain than does patient Griselda, her evident progress in the ameliorative narrative serves as a reminder of how dependent we are on divine assistance.

The Merchant's Tale, on the other hand, explores the theology of perfection in the context of marriage in a consistently burlesque fashion, offering a comically inverted image of Griselda's patient endurance. The grotesque wedding night between January and May contrasts with the one in *The Man of Law's Tale* examined earlier. January's desire to regain paradise through marriage to a twenty-year-old bride is presented as a mock version of an eleventh-hour conversion, his repentance at death's brink for a life of sensual enjoyment (IV.1400–404). His repentance is a sham, of course; to the extent that the tale is as much about the human longing for transcendence as it is about marriage, it makes a mockery of the pursuit of perfection in the Fallen world. In his fantasy, January believes that transcendence is possible on earth: "I shal have myn hevene in erthe heere" (1647), though his garden marks the site not of a return to prelapsarian justice but of his blind participation in May's adultery. The moment of January's miraculously restored vision provides a witty parody of the beatific vision, a satirical narrative of transcendence, an upside-down version of what Dante provides his readers at the end of *Paradiso.* When his wife persuades him that his vision is only a foretaste of what is to come, only "som glymsyng, and no *parfit* sighte" (IV.2383; emphasis added), we laugh heartily as we imagine the future imperfect of their marriage. The pairing of the two tales of Fragment IV, then, explores the pursuit of perfection by running the gamut from the sublime to the ridiculous.

Lest the exemplum of Griselda's patience fade from memory, however, Fragments V and VII offer at least two recapitulations of key portions of its argument in different generic and modal contexts. Kittredge, we recall, famously thought *The Franklin's Tale* ended the "marriage debate" with Chaucer's own ideal solution; for our purposes, we need only to observe that the Franklin's core moral argument extols the "heigh vertu" of patience (V.773), a necessary virtue because, in comparison to the absolute perfection of God (an axiomatic principle that initiates Dorigen's philosophical conundrum [V.871–72]), no one can measure up to that highest of standards:

> Lerneth to suffre, or elles, so moot I goon,
> Ye shul it lerne, wher so ye wole or noon;

> For in this world, certein, ther no wight is
> That he ne dooth or seith somtyme amys.
>
> (V.777–80)[135]

The link between perfection and the need for patience is also made by Prudence in *The Tale of Melibee,* a point likely to be lost on a reader who does not remain alert to the way the theme of perfection is carefully woven through the *Tales*. In reply to Prudence's scriptural text that "pacience is a greet vertu of perfeccioun" (VII.1517), Melibee takes an aggressively antiperfectionist stance:

> "Certes," quod Melibee, "I graunte yow . . . that pacience is a greet vertu of perfeccioun; / but every man may nat have the perfeccioun that ye seken; / ne I nam nat of the nombre of right parfite men, / for myn herte may nevere been in pees unto the tyme it be venged."
>
> (VII.1518–21)

But of course we know that Prudence will ultimately prevail by rhetorically shaping the movement of Melibee's will. The grace that Melibee is finally willing to extend to his enemies is explicitly described as an imitation of God's mercy to sinners and points hopefully to the future perfect, when the story not only of Melibee's life but of all Christians who have perseverance to the end reaches the transcendent state of eternity (VII.1881–88). Guided by the counsel of Prudence, Melibee thus provides another variation on the ameliorative narrative of perfection as a work still in progress. As we observed in the first section of this essay, the Augustinian framework for understanding justification, with its close conceptual link to the idea of perfection as both process and result, was inseparable from the sacrament of penance, which after 1215 was equally enjoined on both lay and religious orders of society. In precisely this sense, the closing gesture of *The Tale of Melibee* anticipates the summative role of *The Parson's Tale* for *The Canterbury Tales* as a whole.

Although this preliminary sketch of a perfection group thus far has retraced the marriage debate according to the Ellesmere order, not all

---

[135] On this passage as the core moral argument of the tale, see Derek Pearsall, *The Canterbury Tales* (London and Boston: Allen & Unwin, 1985), pp. 159–60; to Pearsall's illuminating remarks on how Chaucer adds "a new meaning to a moral commonplace" about patience (p. 160), I would add that the moral framework provided by the topic of perfection, no less than that of marriage, enables him to achieve that new meaning.

of Chaucer's concern with the theology of perfection coincides with his interest in marriage. Indeed, after the Wife of Bath's performance, the next tale that explicitly raises the issue of perfection is *The Summoner's Tale,* Chaucer's most extended piece of antifraternal satire.[136] Chaucer's treatment of the hypocritical friar clearly calls into question his vocation, and rewards him with the well-deserved indignity of a fart in the face. The friar claims special privileges not only for his order, but for himself individually. When Thomas complains that he has donated "many a pound" to various friars "yet fare I never the bet" (III.1951), the friar questions the layman's need to seek other friars when he himself is "a *parfit* leche" (1956; emphasis added). About twenty years ago, Paul Olson provided compelling evidence that Chaucer's satire against the friars pointedly draws on arguments first made by Spiritual Franciscans against Conventuals and later taken up by secular clerics, including Wyclif.[137] On the other hand, Watson concludes from Chaucer's use of anticlerical satire in *The General Prologue* and in certain tales that "[i]n the most general terms, the poem is *dismissive of the ideals* of the professional religious orders."[138] To be sure, the satirical material raises legitimate questions about Chaucer's ecclesiology. Though I claim no originality here, satire traditionally works by signaling to readers that a large gap ironically separates an ideal definition of a stable norm (for example, the Benedictine rule that the Monk in *The General Prologue* cavalierly dismisses) from the aberrant behavior of the individual or group targeted by the satire. Chaucer, like Langland, continues to value the *ideal* of religious perfection that members of the regular orders

[136] For an exegetical reading, see John V. Fleming, "Gospel Asceticism: Some Chaucerian Images of Perfection," in David Lyle Jeffrey, ed., *Chaucer and Scriptural Tradition* (Ottawa: Ottawa University Press, 1984), pp. 183–95.

[137] See Olson, *The Canterbury Tales and the Good Society,* pp. 214–34. Olson concludes that although Chaucer agrees with Wyclif's diagnosis of what has gone wrong with the "the four sects of the Church," "[h]e does not accept the Wycliffite call for abolition and disendowment of the new orders" (p. 292).

[138] Watson, "Chaucer's Public Christianity," p. 100 (my emphasis). At the same time, he asserts that Chaucer's conservative religious views imply he has "no direct truck with Lollardy or other radical contemporary discourses" (p. 112). See Fletcher, "Chaucer the Heretic," p. 111 n. 165: "In *The Canterbury Tales,* it is not so much contested theological issues that are foregrounded than [sic] the ecclesiological ones to which the theological issues, to be sure, have given rise. Broadly speaking, the 'new sects' of the Church . . . come off badly in *The Canterbury Tales,* but not the seculars, the only wing of the clergy having members evangelically sanctioned and of whom Wyclif therefore approved." Fletcher believes, in short, that Chaucer *did* have " 'direct' truck"; he devotes the final section of his essay to considering the full range of possible explanations.

sought to emulate, even if what is most striking to a fourteenth-century observer is the failure of so many professional religious to live up to those ideals. Logically, to satirize hypocritical individuals is not at all to imply that the ideals they fail to live up to are themselves contemptible. When the Prioress describes the abbot in her tale as "an hooly man, / As monkes been—or elles oghte be" (VII.642–43), it is the failure by many monks to live up to the ideal of holiness that Chaucer targets, not the status of the claim that monks ought specially to pursue perfection. Indeed, this is precisely the distinction that Chaucer recalls in the address to canons regular that interrupts *The Canon's Yeoman's Tale:*

> But worshipful chanons religious,
> Ne demeth nat that I sclaundre youre hous,
> Although that my tale of a chanoun bee.
> Of every ordre some shrewe is, pardee,
> And God forbede that al a compaignye
> Sholde rewe o singuleer mannes folye.
> To sclaundre yow is no thyng myn entente,
> But to correcten that is mys I mente.
>
> (VIII.992–99)

If the shoe fits, wear it: this may be an ancient rhetorical topos for satirists, but I see no reason to read it ironically instead of taking Chaucer at face value here.[139] If the poet's reformist ecclesiology were as radical as Wyclif's, to insist on the distinction between individuals and species would only confuse the issue. In short, if Chaucer, like the Wycliffites, thought it was the existence of "new sectes" themselves that was illegitimate, it would be far more difficult to explain the Yeoman's or Prioress's continuing to value the ideals that hypocrites immorally fail to embody. If we wonder why Chaucer loses no opportunity to satirize members of the religious orders in the poem, one obvious reason might be that the growing vernacular literature of anticlerical satire offered greater satisfactions to writers and readers with a taste for satire than do stories about friars ministering to lepers in the spirit of Saint Francis, or about devoutly prayerful monks. Borrowing from Fletcher, we might even consider the possibility that Chaucer wanted to demonstrate, through his mastery of anticlerical satire, that he "could simply be a club member for whom the belonging was what mattered."[140]

[139] See Watson's discussion of satire in "Chaucer's Public Christianity," pp. 110–12.
[140] Fletcher, "Chaucer the Heretic," p. 113.

The Second Nun's Tale is a tale that some critics have wished to add to the list of members of the marriage group, because of Cecilia's chaste earthly marriage and her spiritual espousal to Christ, which links her with the fictional Second Nun. However, in introducing us to the only canonized saint to whom an entire narrative is devoted, *The Second Nun's Tale* also provides Chaucer's most detailed instance of Christian perfection as both process and achievement. Her narrative culminates at the moment of her transcendence, a moment that literally takes place outside of secular time in the gap between two stanzas, since the exact moment of her death is never described (VIII.546–47). That moment of the end of her life's journey is anticipated by the martyrdom of Valerian and Tiburce, whom she prepares by exhorting them through the familiar Pauline-Augustinian imagery of *bravium* and *corona,* of the race and battle won and the victor's crowning:

> "Ye han for sothe ydoon a greet bataille,
> Youre cours is doon, youre feith han ye conserved.
> Gooth to the corone of lif that may nat faille;
> The rightful Juge, which that ye han served,
> Shal yeve it yow, as ye han it deserved."
>
> (VIII.386–90)

From the vantage of the Augustinian framework that I have argued Chaucer quietly and unostentatiously advances in *The Canterbury Tales,* the two brothers' preservation of their faith is due to the gift of final perseverance; their works are deemed meritorious because God has justified and accepted them through his offer of grace, which they accept. The saint's life demonstrates, as the Second Nun reminds us in her prologue, the biblical proposition "that feith is deed withouten werkis" (VIII.64). Moreover, the close conceptual link between Saint Cecilia and the theology of perfection is demonstrated by the last of the several meanings assigned to her name, which contains the ideas of "good *perseverynge,* / And brennynge evere in charite ful brighte" (117–18; emphasis added). Although it is easy to miss the Augustinian resonance of *perseverance,* or indeed how Cecilia's grace of perseverance rights the Wife of Bath's reversal of it (III.148), we need to take seriously the proposition that the Second Nun and her performance represent the poet's celebration of the dignity and worth of the ideals of monasticism, the supererogatory works of those called to the path of higher perfection, however troubled the institution clearly seemed to critical fourteenth-century observers. There is no reason to read *The Second Nun's Tale* as expressing Chaucer's "despair" over the lost currency of traditional monastic ideals, rather than his cautiously optimistic sense of the possibility of reform by individuals and their collective institutions, and his sense of urgency that fourteenth-century monastic orders would do well to return to the pristine ideals embodied by Cecilia and the Second Nun.[141] The traditional motive employed by Chaucerian satire, as the direct address in *The Canon Yeoman's Tale* reminds us, is the correction of vice, not for the radical project of abandoning a millennium of monasticism as wrong from the start. The respect he clearly bestows on the Second Nun strongly suggests that Chaucer is no Wycliffite.

Before Chaucer turns to the Parson, we may turn briefly to consider what the Augustinian reading of perfection might do to our understanding of what exactly is at stake in *The Canon's Yeoman's Tale*. Many critics have pointed out the infernal symbolism of the fruitless labors in the alchemist's laboratory in the first part of the Yeoman's tale, with the "smel of brymstoon" (VIII.885), and the hellish discord that breaks out when the pot is shattered (916–31). What I wish to add is the suggestion that the unexpected and dramatic encounter of the pilgrims with the Canon and his servant near the final stages of the journey is literally about the "roadness" of the road itself, which allegorically represents the symbolic space of the progress narrative, the course of a lifetime of exercising the free will, with the assistance of infused habitual grace, to make good choices: "Between the extremes of the beginning of faith and the perfection of perseverance there are those in-between virtues by which we live correctly," as Saint Augustine wrote late in his career.[142] If Augustine provides no detailed road map of the progress of this long journey, that is precisely what Chaucer offers in his fictions of the human figure. As we are approaching the end of the road to Canterbury, the Yeoman boasts that his master can "clene turnen up-so-doun" the road to Canterbury (VIII.625), an image that anticipates the anagogical, infernal imagery of the alchemist's laboratory. What perhaps deserves not-

---

[141] Watson believes that "the very lack of thematic contact between the simple evangelical faith of the catacombs and the Canon's messy fraudulence suggests something like despair over the modern relevance of the learned purity Cecilia represents" ("Chaucer' Public Christianity," p. 108).

[142] *Gift of Perseverance, Works* 26, p. 230. "Inter initium autem fidei et perfectionem perseverantiae, media sunt illa, quibus recte vivimus" (PL 44, col. 1028).

ing in this context is that the dress of the Canon clearly identifies him as a Canon Regular of Saint Augustine.[143] Rather than imagining that the poet was taking revenge on an individual Augustinian canon who had swindled him as used to be suggested, it is worth considering the possibility that Chaucer has deliberately chosen an Augustinian canon at precisely the moment when he wanted to dramatize the *viatas* of the *via,* to coin a scholastic term. For it is here that the Yeoman apparently decides, before our very eyes, to change the direction of his life by abandoning his master of the last seven years, when that least likely instrument of divine grace, none other than Harry Bailey, encourages him to continue his story without fear of his earthly master. In other words, the drama of *The Canon's Yeoman's Prologue* reads like an exemplary conversion narrative along the lines adumbrated by Augustine in *The Predestination of the Saints,* which concentrates on God's necessary role in initiating the conversion of the will to begin the faith of those he has predestined for salvation. The failed enterprise of alchemy ("For evere we lakken our conclusioun" [VIII.672]) thus symbolizes the infernal reversal of the workings of the Holy Spirit on human hearts. What remains impossible to determine, however, is whether the Yeoman's conversion is genuine, for there are many signs that he still feels the attractions of the old life; even if we assume that his conversion is real, we cannot say whether Chaucer would have us imagine his fictional character receiving the gift of final perseverance.

The roadness of the road as an allegorical symbol, of course, recurs in its more familiar guise in *The Parson's Prologue,* with the final speaker's prayer for divine assistance in his task:

> And Jhesu, for his grace, wit me sende
> To shewe yow the wey, in this viage,
> Of thilke parfit glorious pilgrymage
> That highte Jerusalem celestial.
>
> (X.48–51)

Penance is the "siker wey" (X.94) for the viator's ameliorative narrative of perfection to reach its transcendent completion, the very "conclusioun" that the Yeoman so far lacks. *The Parson's Tale* itself helps establish the continuing influence of Augustinian doctrines about justification or

---

[143] See *Riverside Chaucer,* p. 948 n. 557.

the perfection of righteousness on the penitential theology of the later Middle Ages:

But nathelees, men shal hope that every tyme that man falleth, be it never so ofte, that he may arise thurgh Penitence, *if he have grace;* but certeinly it is greet doute. For, as seith Seint Gregorie, "Unnethe ariseth he out of his synne, that is charged with the charge of yvel usage." / And therfore repentant folk, that stynte for to synne and forlete synne er that synne forlete hem, hooly chirche holdeth hem siker of hire savacioun. And he that synneth and verraily repenteth hym in his laste, hooly chirche yet hopeth his savacioun, by the grete mercy of oure Lord Jhesu Crist, for his repentaunce; but taak the siker wey. (X.90–93; my emphasis)

The Parson is describing three different categories of sinners, each with its own degree of certainty of salvation. The first group is the largest, comprising those Christians (whether lay or clerical is totally irrelevant) who, thanks to the residual effects of the Fall, sin again and again but undergo the sacrament of penance at *least* once a year, as required by the canon of 1215—the historical backdrop to the pastoral literature Chaucer employs as his two main sources in the tale. However, the more often concupiscence (or the *pena* of original sin according to Augustine) becomes habitually acted upon, burdening the sinner with its oppressive *charge* (in Saint Gregory's words), the greater the risk of failure. The second group is a far more select one, comprising precisely those sinners, even Saint Paul in Saint Augustine's analysis, who "are running perfectly" and are well on their way to crowning glory but have not yet attained the future perfect when the race and the victory are finally won. Such sinners enjoy as much certainty of salvation as is possible from a human perspective in this life, though only God possesses absolute certainty whether they will persevere to the end. The final group, small but not so select (unless we mean in the strict Augustinian sense of those chosen or predestined for salvation), comprises those eleventh-hour penitents who risk damnation day after day, year after year, in the event they meet the sudden kind of accidental death about which the Pardoner so offensively warns his fellows after concluding his exemplum (VI.935–36). Because of the great danger that the habit of sin will be ever more difficult to dislodge and replace with the habit of justifying grace (*gratia gratum faciens,* in scholastic terminology), the first group is living in "greet doute." We should also notice that such repentance is presented as entirely conditional upon divine grace: without it, according to Augustinian thinking about grace and free will, including the views of Bradwardine and Wyclif, the will cannot move by itself to repent.[144]

However, the best way I know to demonstrate Chaucer's unostentatiously Augustinian position in the concluding tale is to notice how effortlessly he summarizes Augustine's anti-Pelagian position in the second part of *The Parson's Tale* in a crucial passage that does not rely on one of the tale's main sources. As we saw in part one above, so long as they occupy what Saint Paul calls in Romans "the body of this death," or as Chaucer translates it here, "the prisoun of my caytyf body" (X.343), human beings are self-divided along the fault line of the flesh and must engage in continuous spiritual warfare against temptation: "Therfore, al the while that a man hath in hym the peyne of concupiscence, it is impossible but he be tempted somtime and moeved in his flessh to synne. / And this thyng may nat faille as longe as he lyveth; it may wel wexe fieble and faille by vertu of baptesme and by the grace of God thurgh penitence, / but fully ne shal it nevere quenche, that he ne shal som tyme be moeved in hymself."[145] The pursuit of perfection thus requires self-discipline against an unruly aspect of the inner self that lies at the deepest core of one's being. But once again, Chaucer emphasizes that without divine grace there can be no effective penance. For this reason, it is important to reinstate the unanimous manuscript order of the last two couplets of *The Parson's Prologue*, because Chaucer deliberately has the *Prologue* conclude with the word *grace* (we may in fact read

---

[144] Contrast Watson's comment on this passage: "This passage distinguishes two levels of certainty of salvation: the confidence of those who succeed in shaking off their sins in their lifetimes (who are 'siker of hire savacioun'), and the hopeful fear of those who repent only after they are incapable of sin in 'greet doute' of mercy" (p. 103). I remain baffled by Watson's analysis of these less certain sinners for three reasons: first, because even on one's deathbed one still remains capable of sin (though not every category of sin); second, because even if we stipulate that someone is already "incapable of sin," there would then be nothing to repent; and third, because no one but Jesus, the one perfect man, is incapable of sin (cf. X.1007, X.955). We should remember, in other words, as Saint Augustine frequently reminds us when discussing the perfection of human righteousness, that not even Saint Paul describes himself as *incapable* of sinning (the note to line 93 in *Riverside Chaucer*, p. 957, is somewhat misleading, though it does clearly connect the passage to Augustinian thought).

[145] X.338–41. The sentence concludes by listing exceptions: sickness, sorcery, or cold drink can each cool the concupiscent flesh. The passage is not translated from one of Chaucer's main sources; *Riverside Chaucer*, p. 959, cites Peter Lombard for a condensed version of this Augustinian view of original sin transmitting concupiscence of the flesh.

the couplet as spoken by the Parson, praying that his listeners receive the grace "to do wel" (X.72).[146] The prayer for grace that concludes the *Prologue* thus anticipates the ending of *The Parson's Tale,* creating symmetrical balance between the two endings by concluding the tale with the negation of sin from the transcendent perspective of the future perfect; the gorgeously composed cadences of the final sentence of the final tale provide the right-side-up description of the beatific vision that was so savagely parodied in January's garden: in heaven the final "fruit" of penance will be "every soule replenyssed with the sighte of the *parfit* knowynge of God . . . and the lyf by deeth and mortificacion of synne" (X.1079–80; emphasis added). This eloquent finale stands in effect as the poet's more humble equivalent of Dante's final prophetic vision at the end of *Paradiso,* without the ego.

Near the end of his life, when Chaucer finally speaks in his own voice outside *The Canterbury Tales* in his Retractions, his petitionary prayer to Jesus, Mary, and the saints is fully consistent with the Augustinian emphasis that receiving prevenient grace is a necessary precondition to sincere repentence: "from hennes forth unto my lyves ende sende me grace to biwayle my giltes and to studie to the salvacioun of my soule, and graunte me grace of verray penitence, confessioun and satisfaccioun to doon in this present lyf . . . so that I may been oon of hem at the day of doom that shulle be saved" (X.1089–91). If his prayers were answered, Chaucer's own narrative of the self has completed the shift from the ameliorative to the transcendental one and achieved his future perfect in communion with the saints.

In this essay I have assumed the desirability and possibility of answering questions long avoided until fairly recently, questions about the "opinions, beliefs, prejudices, and passions" that Chaucer's "writings about religion express or take for granted in his earliest readers," and I share Nicholas Watson's conclusion that Chaucer's view of Christian community was "traditional, even conservative."[147] Where we part company is in my belief that Chaucer demonstrates an ongoing interest in understanding the requirements for Christian perfection by both clerical and lay orders of fourteenth-century society, though as a layman writing primarily for other lay readers, it is not surprising that he was especially

---

[146] On the unanimity of the manuscripts, see *Riverside Chaucer,* p. 1134 n. 73–74.
[147] Watson, "Chaucer's Public Christianity," pp. 99, 112.

interested in the opportunities and temptations presented to those who have chosen to live as fully active participants in worldly affairs. Moreover, I have argued that the soteriology assumed and given narrative embodiment throughout *The Canterbury Tales* places sufficient emphasis on revealing the dialectical relation between human and divine agency in the free will's cooperation or resistance to grace as to deserve being described as "Augustinian," so long as we understand that both Bradwardine and Wyclif share such a framework, for all their other differences. Finally, I have joined those who suggest that Chaucer's ecclesiology was broadly reformist rather than radical like that of the Wycliffites, even though he agrees with their diagnoses of ecclesiastical corruption. As Alan Fletcher has recently observed, there is no reason to assume that Chaucer's opinion of the Lollards remained fixed over time.[148] The same should be said of his views about those who claimed to pursue the highest perfection as a special vocation. However difficult a time the poet may have had making up his mind about the validity of the Lollards' various claims, I see no reason to conclude that he ever seriously doubted that all Christians had an obligation to follow Saint Augustine's exhortations to pray for God's gracious assistance and hope to be enabled through their cooperative striving to make progress on the road to the future perfect, despite the many obstacles temptation places in the way. Whether Chaucer, like both Augustine and Wyclif, believed his outcome was predestined, neither *The Canterbury Tales* nor the Retractions allows us to answer with confidence. But as we know from *The Nun's Priest's Tale,* it was a question he thought both worth raising and, at least at that point in his life, worth celebrating with laughter.

[148] Fletcher, "Chaucer the Heretic," p. 109.

140

The Gender of Song in Chaucer

Nicolette Zeeman
King's College, Cambridge

Madame, ye ben of al beaute shryne
As fer as cercled is the mapamounde,
For as the cristal glorious ye shyne,
And lyke ruby ben your chekes rounde.
Therwith ye ben so mery and so jocounde
That at a revel whan that I see you daunce,
It is an oynement unto my wounde,
Thogh ye to me ne do no daliaunce.

For thogh I wepe of teres ful a tyne,
Yet may that wo myn herte nat confounde;
Your semy voys that ye so smal out twyne
Maketh my thoght in joy and blis habounde.
So curtaysly I go with love bounde
That to myself I sey in my penaunce,
"Suffyseth me to love you Rosemounde,
Thogh ye to me ne do no daliaunce."

Nas never pyk walwed in galauntyne
As I in love am walwed and ywounde,
For which ful ofte I of myself devyne
That I am trewe Tristam the secounde.
My love may not refreyde nor afounde,
I brenne ay in an amorous plesaunce.
Do what you lyst, I wyl your thral be founde,
Thogh ye to me ne do no daliaunce.[1]

IN THE *BALLADE* "To Rosemounde," we are in the realm of desire and its substitutions, of Freudian narcissism and the Lacanian imagi-

My thanks to Jonathan Burt, Christopher Cannon, Rita Copeland, Sarah Kay, David Wallace, and the *SAC* readers.
[1] *The Riverside Chaucer,* gen. ed. Larry D. Benson, 3rd ed. (Boston: Houghton Mifflin, 1987), p. 649; for verbal parallels to this subtly comic poem in other lyrics, see Rossell Hope Robbins, "Chaucer's 'To Rosamounde,'" *Studies in the Literary Imagination* 4

nary. The lady is variously described in the glittering language of the fetish (*shryne, mapamounde, cristal*); in her the singer fantasizes his own completeness and identity (she is the all-enclosing shrine of the "world," the "ointment" to his "wound"); she represents a kind of pregendered "sufficiency" from whom he cannot imagine separation ("Suffyseth me to love you," "Do what you lyst, I wyl your thral be founde"). And the singer repeatedly attributes the impossibility of his desire to the distant lady, who never ceases to demonstrate his irrelevance, not so much by refusing him, as by ignoring him entirely. The singer himself has an unstable and even amorphous quality. His self-figuration in terms of lack contradicts the claims he makes about his imagined satisfactions (he is "wounded" but cured, weeping but full of *blis*, marginalized but *bounde*); his very form and size seem to oscillate (his tears fill "a barrel," he compares himself to Sir *Tristam*, he is like a fish); he is marginalized and apparently irrelevant to the lady and her social scene, but he is also peculiarly self-contained, if diminutized, by his contentment with small satisfactions ("So curtaysly I go . . . That to myself I sey . . . 'Suffyseth me . . .'"). This is the fantasy and the narcissism, but also the contradictory and uncertain shape of the "lover."

This comic poem also draws on a tradition of love song in which varying degrees of social awareness, irony, and humor play a substantial role. Its subtle exaggerations archly situate the singer as a solipsistic and nonintegrated member of courtly society. This social awareness is reinforced by the recognition of threatening "others," the evocation of a crowded social scene ("at a revel whan that I see you daunce"); in this scene the lady is the most mobile figure of all, engaging in implied *daliaunce* with unspecified others. As the *ballade* proceeds and Rosemounde is named, repetition of the refrain increases its pointed comment on her lack of interest, especially in contrast to the hypnotized watcher with his immobilizing imaginary of love ("Maketh my thoght in joy and blis habounde . . . with love bounde . . . in my penaunce, / 'Suffyseth me to love you'"; "My love may not refreyde nor afounde, / I brenne ay in an amorous plesaunce . . . I wyl your thral be founde"). All this culminates in the last stanza with the mock-heroics of "trewe Tristam the secounde" and its bathetic counterpart, the fish on a dish:

(1971): 73–81 (74–77); also V. J. Scattergood in A. J. Minnis, with V. J. Scattergood and J. J. Smith, *Oxford Guides to Chaucer: The Shorter Poems* (Oxford: Clarendon Press, 1995), pp. 479–80.

"Nas never pyk walwed in galauntyne / As I in love am walwed and ywounde."

I want to pause over this pike, *walwed* and *ywounde* in sauce (both words can mean either "steeped" or "turned," "stirred"), presumably looking up from the plate with its dead eye at those who are going to eat it.[2] I propose that this eccentric image is emblematic of Chaucer's treatment of songs and singers in his later writing. Of course, at one level the pike alludes to a traditional portrayal of the (usually masculine) persona of many medieval love lyrics, gazing transfixed and helpless, under the eyes of the (usually feminine) love "object"—in fact, often ignored by her—and of the unnamed others of the court. For the singer and lover, these eyes are always potentially threatening, ridiculing, devouring. But Chaucer takes this idea a stage further. His grotesque suggestion that Rosemounde's admirer might be physically consumed by those around him is the first of many instances in his later poetry where the singer is graphically and aggressively reminded of his own bodiliness. Insofar as Chaucer may be construed to be writing this lyric in his own voice, he not only reidentifies himself (the subject of lack, the lyrical "I") as bodily matter but also threatens himself with carnivalesque ingestion by another body altogether.[3] Underlying the poem's imaginary desire for undifferentiated identity with the lady, in other words, is the possibility of a very different, destructive bodily undifferentiation, here conceived as one of physical incorporation.

Singing, Affect, and Sexual Identity

The subject of the essay is the vulnerability of male singers in Chaucer's later poetry, or rather the abjective and brutal things that happen to them. Chaucer's unfortunate artists of song include Nicholas, Absolon, Januarie, the "litel clergeon," and Chantecleer, but also a number of others, the Pardoner, the Summoner, the Friar, the Manciple's crow, even the teller of the "ballad" Sir Thopas.

This Chaucerian phenomenon of the unfortunate singer could be read poetically. Chaucer could be laying out a *mise-en-abîme* of the dangerous

[2] See MED, s.v. "walwen" v, 2b; "winden" v (1), 2–5; Robbins, "Chaucer's 'To Rosamounde,'" p. 76.
[3] Is this a carnivalesque version of the Old French "coeur mangé"? See Ardis Butterfield, *Poetry and Music in Medieval France from Jean Renart to Guillaume de Machaut* (Cambridge: Cambridge University Press, 2002), p. 240.

predicament of the poet—always at the mercy of an ill-disposed community of hearers, readers, and competitors. The singer, with his preoccupied vulnerability, could stand for the generic category of "the poet"; song is an essential element in much of the courtly vernacular love literature of the later Middle Ages, and, in this tradition at any rate, it is perhaps "the" emblematic poetic form.[4] A more specific variant of this reading might be that Chaucer's singers represent a specific group of poets, the "makers" of courtly vernacular love literature (emblematized by song). Chaucer may be repudiating this group in order to shore up his identification with another literary community, one that is more oriented to an archival textuality, the classics, and philosophical concerns.[5] In his later writing, after all, Chaucer situates himself in a conceptually more ambitious and international poetic tradition.

However, although something poetic is almost certainly at issue, the violence and obscenity of Chaucer's treatment of his masculine singers suggests that something more psychosexually invested may also be occurring. This seems to be corroborated by features of the singers and their songs foregrounded by Chaucer. These are features that can certainly be found in courtly singers and songs prior to Chaucer (see below, pp. 153–55); however, Chaucer develops, even caricatures, them in such a way as to suggest that they represent for him a special focus of analysis and anxiety. First among these features is the subject of the songs. Driven by sublimated affect, these songs are hyperbolic expressions of pleasure but also of sexual desire, "love," or religious devotion; however, Chaucer highlights, often to comic effect, the "self-dissolving" and boundary-confusing nature of the language of emotional identification, frequently exaggerating its blurred distinctions between the erotic and religious. Second, Chaucer emphasizes the artfulness, and even "clericalism," of his singers. They tend to be full of self-delight, busily engaged

---

[4] James I. Wimsatt, *Chaucer and His French Contemporaries: Natural Music in the Fourteenth Century* (Toronto: University of Toronto Press, 1991), chap. 1 and passim; on the lyric grounding of the *Romance of the Rose* and thirteenth- and fourteenth-century "lyrical" narrative, see Sylvia Huot, *From Song to Book: The Poetics of Writing in Old French Lyric and Lyrical Narrative Poetry* (Ithaca: Cornell University Press, 1987), esp. pp. 4–6; on the lyric as "authority" in romance, see Butterfield, *Poetry and Music,* chaps. 13–15; for Chaucer as a lyric poet, see Rossell Hope Robbins, "Geoffroi Chaucier, Poète Français, Father of English Poetry," *ChauR* 13 (1978–79): 93–115; Scattergood, in Minnis, *Shorter Poems,* pp. 455–512.

[5] This is the view of Chaucer argued for in Winthrop Wetherbee, *Chaucer and the Poets. An Essay on "Troilus and Criseyde"* (Ithaca: Cornell University Press, 1984), intro. and chap. 1.

in the activity of song and self-importantly identifying with its craft (reinforced by the fact that they are usually also "artists" of knowledge, rhetoric, clothing, or manners). Third, Chaucer's singers tend to be characterized by a very unstably differentiated sexual identity; they can be highly sexed, infantilized, aged, effeminized, implied to have same-sex desire, or they can have a combination of these attributes. It is my proposition that for Chaucer the arts of affect—and in particular the performance of secular and religious love song—are a means of staging the unstable differentiations of sexual identity.

And Chaucer also usually commits an act of narrative violence on his singers. He simulates (often humorously) the capacity of affective song to perturb the categories of gender and then aggressively repudiates it. Although he has been celebrated in much recent criticism for his espousal of the instability and even "feminization" of masculine gender and sexuality,[6] this does not seem to be what we are seeing here. Rita Copeland has argued similarly about Chaucer's representation of the Pardoner as "Rhetoric": she claims that the homology between the man and his art produces a two-way dynamic, simultaneously staging the Pardoner's uncertain sexuality in terms of his anxiety-making art of rhetoric and reflecting on that art through his sexuality. Copeland links this to the conflicted institutional history of rhetoric.[7] In a similar way, I propose that Chaucer is attuned to the problematics of sexual identity written into the medieval arts of affect and affective song. The violence with which he responds to these problematics suggests something of the difficulty they pose for him.

Tools with which to understand this dynamic are to be found in psychoanalytic theories about how sublimated affect, narcissism, the imaginary, the "maternal," and song have the capacity to unsettle sexual identity. Medievalists who have used Freud and Lacan to discuss the literatures of love and religious devotion include Sarah Kay and Aranye Fradenburg.[8] Although neither has focused directly on the way that

[6] See Jill Mann, *Feminizing Chaucer,* 2nd ed. (Cambridge: D. S. Brewer, 2002), chaps. 3 and 5; Susan Crane, *Gender and Romance in Chaucer's "Canterbury Tales"* (Princeton: Princeton University Press, 1993), chap. 1.

[7] "The Pardoner's Body and the Disciplining of Rhetoric," in *Framing Medieval Bodies,* ed. Sarah Kay and Miri Rubin (Manchester: Manchester University Press, 1994), pp. 138–59 (138).

[8] Sarah Kay shows that in "courtly love" the illusory securities of affect and the imaginary work in a dynamic relation to desire, which, by contrast, never finds its end: "Desire and Subjectivity," in *The Troubadours: An Introduction,* ed. Simon Gaunt and Sarah Kay (Cambridge: Cambridge University Press, 1999), pp. 212–27 (for the imagi-

psychoanalytic theories of narcissism and the imaginary undermine the sexual identity of the secular "lover," Fradenburg, in an influential study of what she calls the "disincarnational poetics" of *The Prioress's Tale,* has described how the undifferentiating and reiterative language of miracle or praise elides speakers and devotees with the object of devotion, melding "men" and "children," the Prioress, the "litel clergeon," the Virgin Mary, and God.[9] Subsequent somatic readings of *The Prioress's Tale* by Elizabeth Robertson, Corey Marvin, Robert Sturges, and Bruce Holsinger have also variously used Kristevan theories about affect, the embodied "maternal," and the semiotics of material language and song to analyze these cross-identifications and the relations between the "litel clergeon" and a semiotics of the maternal or feminine culture.[10] In this essay, focusing on both religious and secular affect, and its expression in song, I shall develop these analyses. What is more, psychoanalytic recognition of the gender-perturbing implications of affect, narcissism, and the imaginary also explains why discourses of religious and secular affect are for Chaucer an object, first, of critical scrutiny and, second, of aggression. In this last respect I will also draw on Freudian and Kristevan explorations of the intimate relation of narcissism to defensiveness, aggressivity, and abjection. Fradenburg has in fact also explored this phenomenon in several of the *Canterbury Tales,* showing how affect, narcissism, and the imaginary mask, but also facilitate, aggressive urges toward the other, whether this is (in *The Manciple's Tale*) "the sovereign" or (in *The Prioress's Tale*) the Jews.[11] In this essay, however, I shall argue

---

nary, see pp. 217, 221–22); L. O. Aranye Fradenburg traces another version of this dynamic in the literature of both love and religion: *Sacrifice Your Love: Psychoanalysis, Historicism, Chaucer* (Minneapolis: University of Minnesota Press, 2002), intro. (for the imaginary of the group, see pp. 28–41).

[9]"Criticism, Anti-semitism, and the Prioress's Tale," *Exemplaria* 1 (1989): 69–115 (93).

[10]Elizabeth Robertson, "Aspects of Female Piety in the Prioress's Tale," in *Chaucer's Religious Tales,* ed. C. David Benson and Elizabeth Robertson (Cambridge: D. S. Brewer, 1990), pp. 145–60; Corey J. Marvin, "'I will thee not forsake': The Kristevan Maternal Space in Chaucer's *Prioress's Tale* and John of Garland's *Stella maris,*" *Exemplaria* 8 (1996): 35–58; Robert S. Sturges, *Chaucer's Pardoner and Gender Theory* (Basingstoke: Macmillan, 2000), pp. 92–96; Bruce W. Holsinger, *Music, Body, and Desire in Medieval Culture: Hildegard of Bingen to Chaucer* (Stanford: Stanford University Press, 2001), chap. 6.

[11]Louise Fradenburg, "The Manciple's Servant Tongue: Politics and Poetry in The *Canterbury Tales,*" *ELH* 82 (1985), 85–118. According to Fradenburg, in *The Manciple's Tale* the court servant (Manciple/crow) of this "obsessional court text" cannot resist using the courtly discourse of the sovereign (Apollo) to offend him; however, the servant is at the same time subject to the exercise of the sovereign's power, trapped by his deadening discourse (citation, "Manciple's Servant Tongue," 109).

that in Chaucer the gender-perturbing affective language of the masculine singer draws the phobic and abjective urge back onto the singer—and poet?—himself.[12]

Freud's "Three Essays on Sexuality" implicitly acknowledges that the achievement of sexual difference is an uncertain process, in which "numerous deviations" occur: the first essay catalogues these "deviations" and the second and third essays identify their origins in the many wrong turns possible in the course of infantile and pubescent development.[13] For Lacan, identity is by definition incomplete, "split"; there is no genital drive, and therefore "no straightforward biological sequence" and no "complete and assured sexual identity."[14] For Lacan, moreover, anatomical difference does not determine sexual difference, merely offering a figure for it; even if sexual difference cannot be entirely overthrown (it is part of the structure of the Symbolic), subjects can find themselves on either side of the gender divide, regardless of their biological sex.[15] Among a series of feminist revisions of Lacan is that of Rose, who insists that in fact the imposition of cultural prohibitions inevitably produces reactive fantasies that undermine them: "The unconscious constantly reveals the 'failure' of identity. . . . There is a resistance to identity at the very heart of psychic life."[16] As a result of the very modes of its own production, in other words, sexual identity is insecure.

Idealized affect or "love" exaggerates this insecurity. Freud argues that love, wherever it is directed, is narcissistic and identificatory; love is a form of sublimatory secondary narcissism (part of the ego's attempt to recover the state of primary narcissism), so that either the subject

[12] In this essay I am in a sense psychoanalyzing "Chaucer" in that I attribute the aggression of the tale primarily to the poet and claim that it derives from Chaucer's recognition of himself in the boundary-blurring forms of song. Compare H. Marshall Leicester, *The Disenchanted Self: Representing the Subject in the "Canterbury Tales"* (Berkeley and Los Angeles: University of California Press, 1990); against the use of psychoanalysis in reading medieval literature, see Lee Patterson, "Chaucer's Pardoner on the Couch: Psyche and Clio in Medieval Literary Studies," *Speculum* 76 (2001): 638–80.

[13] Sigmund Freud, "Three Essays on Sexuality," in *The Standard Edition of the Complete Psychological Works,* gen. ed. James Strachey (London: Hogarth Press, 1966–74), 7:123–243 (136); and Juliet Mitchell, in *Feminine Sexuality: Jacques Lacan and the école freudienne,* ed. Juliet Mitchell and Jacqueline Rose (Basingstoke: Macmillan, 1982), pp. 12–13.

[14] See Jacques Lacan, *The Four Fundamental Concepts of Psycho-analysis,* trans. Alan Sheridan (Harmondsworth: Penguin, 1979), pp. 161–89; citation, Mitchell, in *Feminine Sexuality,* p. 35.

[15] See Jacques Lacan, *Ecrits. A Selection,* trans. Alan Sheridan (London: Tavistock, 1977), 149–53; Jacqueline Rose, in *Feminine Sexuality,* pp. 42–43; Jacqueline Rose, *Sexuality in the Field of Vision* (London: Verso, 1986), p. 67.

[16] Rose, *Sexuality in the Field of Vision,* pp. 89–91.

loves an idealized object that it imagines will love itself in return, or the subject turns the love object into something the subject would like to be, idealizing the love object through the transference of its own ego ideal onto it.[17] Such identificatory mechanisms, moving between the poles of infantile pleasure and idealized or sublimatory affect, inevitably undermine the categories of identity. Freud also notes a related "oceanic" experience, in which the subject feels at one with external phenomena to the point of feeling dissolved into them, an experience that he says he has been told characterizes religious experience.[18]

Lacan concurs that "the element of idealising exaltation that is expressly sought out in the ideology of courtly love . . . is fundamentally narcissistic"; it is an exploration of the realm of the imaginary, where the subject, necessarily divided at the point of its entry into culture, comforts itself with consoling fantasies of identity and unity. However, troubadour love poetry ("a scholastics of unhappy love"), with its endless bars to satisfaction, also expresses the divagations of desire and the impossibility of the sexual relation.[19] Nor is this merely a matter of the sublimations of courtly love, moreover, for the woman (the "petit object a" that stands in for the object of desire) can be confused with God in that he "has not yet made his exit." Rose comments, "As negative to the man, woman becomes the total object of fantasy . . . elevated to the place of the Other and made to stand for its Truth. Since the place of the Other is also the place of God, this is the ultimate form of mystification."[20] Affect has the capacity, in other words, to blur the identity of the "lover" but also to mystify the various "objects" to which desire attaches itself—in extreme circumstances it is not possible to separate erotic from divine affectivity.

[17] Sigmund Freud, "On Narcissism. An Introduction," in *Standard Edition*, 14:73–102 (90, 94, 100); see also Rose, *Sexuality in the Field of Vision*, pp. 180–82; "Group Psychology and the Analysis of the Ego," *Standard Edition*, 18:65–143 (112–13).

[18] *Civilisation and its Discontents, Standard Edition*, 21:57–145 (64–73).

[19] Jacques Lacan, *The Ethics of Psychoanalysis 1959–1960*, trans. Dennis Porter, *The Seminar*, ed. Jacques-Alain Miller, Book 7 (London: Routledge, 1992), chap. 11 (citations 151, 146). Later, Lacan claims that "courtly love" is an explicit acknowledgment of the impossibility of the sexual relation, a "highly refined way of making up for [its] absence" (*On Feminine Sexuality. The Limits of Love and Knowledge. Encore 1972–1973*, trans. Bruce Fink, *The Seminar*, ed. Jacques-Alain Miller, Book 20 (New York: W. W. Norton, 1998), chap. 6, "God and Woman's Jouissance," [citation 69]); see also Rose, *Feminine Sexuality*, pp. 46–47, and *Sexuality in the Field of Vision*, pp. 174–78; Sarah Kay, "Desire and Subjectivity," pp. 217–19.

[20] Lacan, *On Feminine Sexuality*, chap. 7, "A Love Letter" (84); Rose, *Sexuality in the Field of Vision*, p. 74.

Kristeva concurs that love occurs between the two poles of narcissism and idealism.[21] In *Tales of Love,* she too explores the ways that the category of "love" contains not only erotic but also religious affect—Christianity, she says, understands love as a fantasy "homologisation," whether between Christ and the Father, the subject and God, or the subject and the neighbor. Like Lacan, she distinguishes desire from affect: "desire . . . emphasizes the lack, whereas affect, while acknowledging the latter, gives greater importance to the movement toward the other and to mutual attraction."[22]

Central here too is the connection of affect, narcissism, and the imaginary with aggressivity. The connection arises partly because, according to Freud, narcissistic disorders are a defensive, and therefore also aggressive, response to trauma or anxiety, but also because of ambivalence, the mutual dependence of love and hate.[23] "No-one," says Freud, "can tolerate a too intimate approach to his neighbour"; in every emotional attachment of any length there is a "sediment of . . . aversion and hostility," an expression of self-love or narcissism. Lacan plays out this ambivalence as a development of the aggressive anxiety of the subject recognizing that his uncoordinated body does not correspond to his imaginary and idealizing self-image.[24] In her distinctively visceral way, Kristeva describes how narcissism hides an underlying emptiness, hatred, and the death drive itself: "Is it not true that the narcissist, as such, is precisely someone incapable of love?" She adds, "The fragility of the narcissistic elaboration, underpinning the ego image as well as ideal cathexes, is such that its cracks immediately reveal the negative of our image sequences. . . . Narcissism and its lining, emptiness, are in short our most intimate, brittle and archaic elaborations of the death drive."[25] However, Kristeva goes further. "A precondition of narcissism"

---

[21] Kristeva, *Tales of Love,* pp. 6, 33–36.

[22] Ibid., pp. 139–69; citation p. 155, where she also cites Aelred of Rievaulx to the effect that "affect is a spontaneous affinity with someone."

[23] See Freud, "Mourning and Melancholia," *Standard Edition,* 14:237–58 (256); Annie Reich, "Pathological Forms of Self-Esteem Regulation," in *Essential Papers on Narcissism,* ed. Andrew P. Morrison (New York: New York University Press, 1986), pp. 44–60.

[24] Freud, "Group Psychology and the Analysis of the Ego," pp. 101–2, 121; Lacan, "Aggressivity in Psychoanalysis," in *Ecrits. A Selection,* trans. Alan Sheridan, pp. 8–29 (17–21); see Rose, *Sexuality in the Field of Vision,* pp. 174–75.

[25] Kristeva, *Tales of Love,* pp. 33–44, 123–25 (citations pp. 33, 43–44, translation altered); Kristeva claims that even primary, pre-Oedipal narcissism is formed under the shadow of "an" other.

is the abject, the phobic object that, despite attempts to repudiate it, is always "within"; as soon as repression is relaxed, it is this that breaks up "the more or less beautiful image in which I behold or recognise myself." A further definition of the abject makes clear why this notion is particularly helpful: the abject is "what disturbs identity, system, order. What does not respect borders, positions, rules. The in-between, the ambiguous."[26] Because it perturbs sexual identity, the urge of idealizing affect can itself become a phobic object.

Love, then, is a fragile and potentially aggressive substitution for originary losses, and its fantasies are ones of merging and completion by the other. Insofar as it involves a narcissistic identification with an imagined love object, it blurs the boundaries of identity and sexual difference; not only does it entail its own underlying aggressivity, but its consequences in the undermining of subjecthood and sexual identity produce new sites of anxiety and abjection.

Some of these psychoanalytic theories about the fluidity of sexual identity were anticipated in the ancient and premodern periods. According to medical teaching, the inscription of sexual difference on the body was unstable; many texts subscribed to the Galenic view that masculine and feminine genitalia were identical, merely inversions of each other.[27] Biological engenderment was understood to be subject to a range of variable conditions, and prone to failure or confusion; doctors recognized the biological categories of the "virile woman," the "effeminate man," as well as the hermaphrodite.[28] Writers recognized same-sex sexual desire (mainly for men)[29] and recent studies of premodern homophobic or antisodomitical literature have revealed a subtext to much of this writing, according to which same-sex sexual orientation is inevitable or even part of the order of "grammar" and nature.[30] There is also evidence that, as in the early modern period, heterosexual desire was thought to

[26] Julia Kristeva, *Powers of Horror: An Essay on Abjection,* trans. Leon S. Roudiez (New York: Columbia University Press, 1982), pp. 13, 4 (see also chap. 3).
[27] See Danielle Jacquart and Claude Thomasset, *Sexuality and Medicine in the Middle Ages,* trans. Matthew Adamson (Cambridge: Polity Press, 1988), pp. 17–18, 36–37; Joan Cadden, *Meanings of Sex Difference in the Middle Ages: Medicine, Science, and Culture* (Cambridge: Cambridge University Press, 1993), pp. 34–35.
[28] Cadden, *Sex Difference,* pp. 202–27.
[29] Ibid., pp. 214–19.
[30] See Mark D. Jordan, *The Invention of Sodomy in Christian Theology* (Chicago: University of Chicago Press, 1997), chap. 4; William Burgwinkle, *Sodomy, Masculinity, and Law in Medieval Literature: France and England, 1050–1230* (Cambridge: Cambridge University Press, 2004), chap. 5.

be "feminizing" and to undermine masculine sexual identity. "Excessive love" ("nimius amor"), according to Isidore of Seville, is *femineus;* medical texts saw the lovers' disease of "amor hereos" (usually attributed to men desiring women) as "unmanning" in the sense that it disempowered and infantilized men, depriving them of appetite and words. Innocent III wrote of "most base sexual desire, that not only feminises but also wastes the body."[31] Certainly many sexual practices such as same-sex sexuality or cross-dressing were connected with heightened sexuality,[32] and, whether excessive or not,[33] heterosexual activity was widely seen as feminizing for men: for Vincent of Beauvais, Robert Holcot, Gower, and Lydgate, the prime example was Sardanapalus.[34] Romance literature also explored the way that love of women "feminized" knights, rendering them passive and drawing them away from chivalric activities.[35] Many "nature texts," despite their overt imprimatur for heterosexuality, were in fact preoccupied with same-sex sexuality, and often also saw aspects of sexuality (whether Nature, Venus, or Pleasure) not just as feminized, but as hermaphroditic, thus throwing sexual differen-

[31] Isidore cited in Mary Frances Wack, *Lovesickness in the Middle Ages: The "Viaticum" and Its Commentaries* (Philadelphia: University of Pennsylvania Press, 1990), pp. 13, 65; see also pp. 151–52; Wack argues that the love of women returns men to a Kristevan pre-Oedipal maternal (152). Innocent III cited in Richard Firth Green, "The Sexual Normality of Chaucer's Pardoner," *Mediaevalia* 8 (1982): 351–58 (354).

[32] Jordan, *Invention of Sodomy,* chap. 2; Vern L. Bullough, "On Being a Male in the Middle Ages," in *Medieval Masculinities: Regarding Men in the Middle Ages,* ed. Clare A. Lees, with the assistance of Thelma Fenster and Jo Ann McNamara (Minneapolis: University of Minnesota Press, 1994), pp. 31–45 (35); Burgwinkle, *Sodomy, Masculinity, and Law,* p. 191.

[33] Bowers, Kelly, and Minnis argue that the issue is excessive sexuality, not sexual orientation (John M. Bowers, "Queering the Summoner: Same-sex Union in Chaucer's *Canterbury Tales,*" in *Speaking Images: Essays in Honor of V. A. Kolve,* ed. Robert F. Yeager and Charlotte C. Morse [Asheville, N.C.: Pegasus Press, 2001], pp. 301–24 (302); Henry Ansgar Kelly, "The Pardoner's Voice: Disjunctive Narrative and Modes of Effeminisation," in *Speaking Images,* pp. 411–44; Alastair Minnis, "Chaucer and the Queering Eunuch," *NML* 6 (2003): 107–28 (126–27]).

[34] See Green, "Sexual Normality," pp. 354–56; Kelly, "Pardoner's Voice," pp. 415–16; Minnis, "Chaucer and the Queering Eunuch," p. 114.

[35] See E. Jane Burns on the "gender indeterminacy that lies at the heart of courtliness" in "Refashioning Courtly Love: Lancelot as Ladies' Man or Lady/Man?" in *Constructing Medieval Sexuality,* ed. Karma Lochrie, Peggy McCracken, and James A. Schultz (Minneapolis: University of Minnesota Press, 1997), pp. 111–34 (129); see also Roberta L. Krueger, "Questions of Gender in Old French Courtly Romance," in *The Cambridge Companion to Medieval Romance,* ed. Roberta L. Krueger (Cambridge: Cambridge University Press, 2000), pp. 132–49 (144–45); James A. Schulz, "Bodies That Don't Matter: Heterosexuality before Heterosexuality in Gottfried's *Tristan,*" in *Constructing Medieval Sexuality,* ed. Lochrie, pp. 91–110.

tiation completely into question.[36] In many contexts, then, affect—even heterosexual affect—was thought to subvert the categories of gender.

In song, of course, affect is cultivated and excited through the art of poetry and sometimes instrumental or sung music.[37] It is true that the main medieval theories of instrumental and sung music are the mathematical, Boethian ones, which describe music and its pleasures as structured in terms of numerical and cosmological harmony; the pleasures of song and even poetry are often described in similarly Boethian, numerical terms.[38] However, there is also some (albeit contested) evidence that medieval theorists believe that instrumental or sung music can express specific forms of affect.[39] But, whether or not this is true, it is clear that some later medieval writers associate musico-poetical notions of "song" with the expression of affect. Later medieval commentaries on the *carmina, cantica* or "pars . . . decantativa*" ("sung part") of the Bible, for instance, extensively explore their articulation of love, praise, or sorrow.[40] There is even some evidence that Latin poetic commentators associate the affective genre of *elegia* with musical "song."[41] Above all, there

[36] See Cadden, *Sex Difference,* p. 222; Green, "Sexual Normality," p. 356; Burgwinkle, *Sodomy, Masculinity, and Law,* pp.185–92.

[37] On verse as a fourteenth-century "musique naturelle" that might, but need not be, accompanied or sung, see Glending Olson, "Deschamps' *Art de dictier* and Chaucer's Literary Environment," *Speculum* 48 (1973): 714–23; Wimsatt, *Chaucer and His French Contemporaries,* chap. 1.

[38] See David S. Chamberlain, "Philosophy of Music in the *Consolatio* of Boethius," *Speculum* 45 (1970), pp. 80–97; John Stevens, *Words and Music in the Middle Ages: Song, Narrative, Dance and Drama, 1050–1350* (Cambridge: Cambridge University Press, 1986), part 1 and chap. 12; Christopher Page, *The Owl and the Nightingale: Musical Life and Ideas in France, 1100–1300* (London: Dent, 1989), pp. 138–43; Wimsatt, *Chaucer and His French Contemporaries,* chap. 1.

[39] Although Stevens claims that medieval music does not "mimetically" express specific forms of affect, he in fact cites several "rhetorical" descriptions of the affective impact of music (*Words and Music,* pp. 300–304, 386–409). My comments are confined to descriptions of songs that contain verbally explicit articulations of affect.

[40] See Giles of Rome, Commentary on the *Song of Songs,* Prologue, trans. in *Medieval Literary Theory and Criticism, c.1100–c.1375. The Commentary-Tradition,* ed. A. J. Minnis and A. B. Scott, with the assistance of David Wallace (Oxford: Clarendon Press, 1988), pp. 243–47; Nicholas of Lyra, Commentaries on the *Psalms, Song of Songs* and *Lamentations* in *Biblia sacra cum glossis,* 7 vols. (Lyons, 1565), vol. 3, fol. 83v; vol. 5, fol. 354v; vol. 6, fol. 178r (partly translated in *Medieval Literary Theory,* ed. Minnis and Scott, pp. 271–74); *Petri Aureoli . . . Compendiosa in universam sacram scripturam commentaria* (Paris, 1585), fol. 22v.

[41] For the possibility of Latin elegiac verse set to music, see Christopher Page, "The Boethian Metrum 'Bella bis quinis': A New Song from Saxon Canterbury," in *Boethius: His Life, Thought, and Influence,* ed. Margaret Gibson (Oxford: Blackwell, 1981), chap. 12; for the influence of *elegia* on vernacular "song," see Nancy Dean, "Chaucer's Complaint: A Genre Descended from the *Heroides,*" *CL* 19 (1967): 1–27; James Simpson,

are long-standing genres of Latin and vernacular song devoted to the expression of affect: the sorrowful *planctus* or "complaint,"[42] and the love song, in which poets repeatedly claim that it is amorous "volunté et sentement" that makes them sing.[43] Certainly for Chaucer, also writing in this vernacular tradition, it is lovers, exemplified *par excellence* by Troilus, who can sing or "make of sentement."[44]

Is it possible that the use of song to express affect also intensifies the gender- and sexuality-troubling consequences of affect? Again, there are some analogies in performed music: Bruce Holsinger has shown that certain forms of music were understood to stage sexuality and gender; he has also argued that certain types of music, in particular ornate polyphony, were thought conducive to sexual irregularity or effeminization.[45] Such medieval anxieties may anticipate Kristeva's analysis of the way that the aural sounds and rhythms of language and music have a gender-troubling capacity to move between the poles of the prelinguistic, undifferentiated "maternal" and the sublimatory products of language, between what she calls *semiosis* and the symbolic.[46] It certainly seems likely that gender-disturbing effects of emotional identification may be intensified in "musique naturelle," poetic song.

There is every evidence that this was recognized in the courtly love

---

Reform and Cultural Revolution, 1350–1547: The Oxford English Literary History II (Oxford: Oxford University Press, 2002), chap. 4.

[42] See Peter Dronke, *Poetic Individuality in the Middle Ages: New Departures in Poetry, 1000–1150* (Oxford: Clarendon Press, 1970), pp. 26–31, 114–46; Stevens, *Words and Music,* chap. 4; Nancy Dean, "Chaucer's *Complaint.*"

[43] Olson, "Deschamps' *Art de dictier,*" p. 722; see also Nicolette Zeeman, "The Lover-Poet and Love as the Most Pleasing 'matere' in Medieval French Love Poetry," *MLR* 83 (1988): 820–42 (821–22); Stevens, *Words and Music,* pp. 392–96.

[44] *Legend of Good Women,* Prologue, F69; see also J. Stephen Russell, "Song and the Ineffable in the *Prioress's Tale,*" *ChauR* 33 (1998–99): 176–89 (179); Olson, "Deschamps' *Art de dictier,*" pp. 722–23. Other academically recognized arts such as theology, ethics, rhetoric, or "poetry" were certainly thought to possess a volitional or emotive dimension, functioning to excite specific affects: see *Medieval Literary Theory,* ed. Minnis and Scott, pp. 200–223. Similarly, excitatory impact may well have been attributed to other "practical" arts, such as etiquette, dress, acting, and even the "art of love" itself.

[45] Holsinger, *Music, Body, and Desire,* chaps. 3, 4, and 7. Some medieval writers also subscribed to the prejudice that other affect-inducing arts such as rhetoric, courtesy, dress, or the "art of love" were inherently feminizing (for rhetoric, see Copeland, "Pardoner's Body"; for courtesy and dress, see Burgwinkle, *Sodomy, Masculinity, and Law,* pp. 49, 189; for the view that any pleasurable art and even university learning can be corrupting, see pp. 47–48, 67–70; for the "art of love," see above).

[46] Julia Kristeva, *Desire in Language: A Semiotic Approach to Literature and Art,* trans. Thomas Gora, Alice Jardine, and Leon S. Roudiez (Oxford: Blackwell, 1980), chap. 5.

narratives and "dits amoureux" of premodern poets such as Machaut, Froissart, Gower, or Charles d'Orléans. Certainly in their works the identificatory language of sublimated affect goes hand in hand with a masculine persona constructed, whether explicitly or implicitly, in contrast to militaristic or chivalric versions of masculinity, and usually is seen within a feminine and "clericalized" culture of love and courtly "arts." The lover is usually portrayed as emotionally volatile, passive, dependent, timid, infantilized, and, in some texts, aged—as here with Amans, the mesmerized, sad/happy, young/old lover of Gower's *Confessio amantis:*

> Min herte, as I you saide er this,
> Som time of hire is sore adrad,
> And som time it is overglad,
> Al out of reule and out of space.
> For whan I se hir goodli face
> And thenke upon hire hihe pris,
> As thogh I were in Paradis,
> I am so ravisht of the syhte,
> That speke unto hire I ne myhte
> As for the time, thogh I wolde:
> For I ne mai my wit unfolde
> To finde o worde of that I mene,
> Bot al it is foryete clene.[47]

The blurring of Amans's psychic and sexual identity is reinforced by the narcissistic language of excess and religious "ravishment." And in this "feminizing" culture of intense love, even the most ordinary little song (predictably derived from the "cleric's cleric," Ovid), with its fantasy conflations of sorrow and gladness, willing and obeying, lassitude and "busy-ness," magnifies these perturbations of identity:

> And otherwhile I singe a song,
> Which Ovide in his bokes made,
> And seide, "O whiche sorwes glade,
> O which wofull prosperite

---

[47] *Confessio amantis* in John Gower, *English Works,* ed. G. C. Macaulay, 2 vols., EETS, e.s. 81, 82 (London: Oxford University Press, 1900), 4:676–88; for the contrast with chivalric, militaristic masculinity, see 4:1608–2199; for the discovery of Amans's age, see 8:2301–461.

Belongeth to the proprete
Of love, who so wole him serve!
And yit therfro mai noman swerve,
That he ne mot his lawe obeie."
And thus I ryde forth mi weie,
And am riht besi overal
With herte and with mi body al.
(4.1210–20)

Chaucer's singers derive from this "narcissistic *economy*" of later medieval courtly love song, with its staging of the uncertainties of sexual identity and its religio-erotic fantasies of "merging that is loss of otherness." Chaucer's exaggerated profiling of traditional features of the masculine and clericalized lover and singer submits this culture to sharp critical analysis. But repeatedly he also brutally repudiates his singers. Do "those uncertain spaces of unstable identity . . . [and] the non-separation of subject/object, on which language has no hold but one woven of fright and repulsion," produce in Chaucer an anxious and aggressive self recognition?[48]

Singers in the Fabliaux

My first two examples are Absolon and Nicholas in *The Miller's Tale,* two characters for whom gender is not at all a clear-cut matter.[49] Absolon, for instance, is diminutized, infantilized, feminized, and sentimentalized. The word *smal* recurs around him: while this has a specific meaning in each context, its repetition has a blurring effect and cumulatively its effect is to recall its more generally diminutizing meanings, "slender," "little," "thin": Absolon is clad "smal and proprely" ("tightly and handsomely"), and he sings with "his voys gentil and smal" ("refined and high-pitched") to a "smal rubible" ("little two-stringed fid-

---

[48] Kristeva, *Tales of Love,* pp. 267–68, 120; Kristeva, *Powers of Horror,* p. 58; on the subject of abjection as "eminently productive of culture," see also p. 45. Holsinger notes a similar visceral medieval anxiety about the myth of Orphean music and homosexuality: "Orphic fragmentation . . . adumbrates the . . . fate of this transgressively musical body in the hands of Latin Christendom"; Jean de Meun, for example, "wishes" that Orpheus be physically punished, castrated, and hanged by the source of song, "la gorge" (*Music, Body, and Desire,* pp. 301–2).

[49] See E. Talbot Donaldson, *Speaking of Chaucer* (London: Athlone Press, 1970), chap. 2; Elaine Tuttle Hansen, *Chaucer and the Fictions of Gender* (Berkeley and Los Angeles: University of California Press, 1992), chap. 8.

dle").[50] When Chaucer describes him as a "myrie child" ("pleasant young man"), again there is an echo of the alternative, infantilizing denotation "child."[51] "Myrie child" is also a common and semantically weak Middle English romance phrase that, like the Middle English lyric epithets *joly* and *gay* ("cheerful," "playful," even "amorous"), has the "soft-focus" effect of a sentimental commonplace and imputes an undifferentiated quality to Absolon.[52] As we have seen, even Absolon's apparently active heterosexual pursuit need not necessarily connote clear-cut sexual difference, but rather another possibility of effeminization; and the description of him as *daungerous* about language (in love texts the term is usually used about women) certainly associates him with a supposedly feminine "disdainfulness."[53]

It is Nicholas, however, not Absolon, who is described as looking "lyk a mayden meke for to see" ("meek" as a "girl" or "virgin," I.3202). Although Chaucer may be likening Nicholas to a virgin rather than a girl, the term also connotes femininity;[54] and even the appearance of "virginal" sexual inexperience must to some degree undermine Nicholas's supposedly keen heterosexuality.[55] Readers have also noted that, for Nicholas, art or trickery in many respects takes precedence over sex (on the day that John goes out, Nicholas and Alisoun could have got together, but instead Nicholas spends the day arranging his complicated plan); similarly, Nicholas's famous soubriqet, *hende,* another adjective drawn from Middle English verse, can mean not only "at hand" but

[50] I.3320, 3360, 3331; see MED, s.v. "smal" adj, 1–4.

[51] I.3325; compare VII, 484, 497, 501; also MED, s.v. "child" n, 1–5.

[52] See I.3339 and note; Donaldson, *Speaking of Chaucer,* p. 20; also MED, s.v. "gai" adj; s.v. "joli" adj; Chaucer not only associates *gai* with the musical instrument the *sautrie* (I.296, 3213), but also generally connects it with music and revelry.

[53] I.3338; see Guillaume de Lorris and Jean de Meun, *Le Roman de la rose,* ed. Armand Strubel, Lettres Gothiques (Paris: Librairie générale française, 1992), line 2825 etc; Middle English *Romaunt of the Rose* (*Riverside Chaucer,* pp. 685–767), lines 591, 2312, 3727. For the medieval-romance feminine connotations of his pink face, gray eyes, and "lovely looks" for the ladies, see Donaldson, *Speaking of Chaucer,* pp. 20–21; compare too Absolon's complaisant *curteisie* (I.3351) with "So curtaysly I go" in the "Balade to Rosemounde" (line 13).

[54] See MED, "maiden" n; also Chaucer's equally variable use elsewhere; Tuttle Hansen, *Chaucer and the Fictions of Gender,* p. 233 n. 44.

[55] Compare the Host's comment to the Clerk: "Ye ryde as coy and stille as dooth a mayde / Were newe spoused, sittynge at the bord" (IV.2–3; for mayde as both "girl" and "virgin," see MED, "maid(e" n and adj; and Chaucer's use elsewhere; for *coy* as a common romance epithet for women, see Donaldson, *Speaking of Chaucer,* pp. 15–16); although not a singer, the Clerk has clerico-lyric connections, telling a tale in rime royale, whose source is Petrarch, author of the original of the "Canticus Troili"; on rime royale, see below.

also "skilful, clever" (though this word's other, more bland meanings of "good-looking," "pleasant, courteous, gracious," or even "nice" also impute something "soft-focus" to Nicholas and his sense of himself).[56] Nicholas's sexual identity is thus undermined not only by his connotations of femininity, virginity, or sentimentalized courtliness, but even by the elaboration of the very skills that he exploits to secure sexual satisfaction. In fact, both Nicholas and Absolon have a whole range of "arts," which they use performatively and with much self-congratulatory delight to further the cause of pleasure and "love": astronomy, religious narrative, rhetoric, aromatics, fine manners, dress, music, and, of course, song.[57]

The Miller's Tale is also full of references to Middle English secular love lyric and the religious and erotic *Song of Songs,* along with its Latin and vernacular, religious and secular, tradition in liturgy, exegesis, and song.[58] Peter Dronke has shown that the secular erotic tradition of the *Song of Songs* to which it refers occurs in love songs in Latin, French, and English.[59] However, Kaske has shown how all kinds of narrative details, from Alisoun's "mouth . . . sweete as bragot or the meeth, / Or hoord of apples" (I.3261–62) to Absolon's hanging around Alisoun's house and his golden hair, "strouted as a fanne large and brode" (I.3315), directly echo the *Song of Songs* itself.[60] Donaldson interpreted these refer-

[56] See note to I.3199; Paul E. Beichner, "Characterization in *The Miller's Tale,*" in *Chaucer Criticism,* ed. Richard J. Schoeck and Jerome Taylor, vol. 2 (Notre Dame: University of Notre Dame Press, 1960), pp. 117–29.

[57] Chaucer's foregrounding of Absolon's pedantry in dress and manners (including his "squaymousness" about farting, I.3337) seems to exploit the prejudice against "feminizing" arts of etiquette.

[58] R. E. Kaske, "The *Canticum canticorum* in the *Miller's Tale,*" SP 59 (1962): 479–500; Jesse M. Gellrich, "The Parody of Medieval Music in the *Miller's Tale,*" JEGP 73 (1974): 176–88; as part of her analysis of Chaucer's intellectually and socially capacious literary vernacular, Katherine Zieman connects "Pilates voys" (I.3124) with music terminology derived from the rationalistic Boethian tradition of "medieval music theory" ("Chaucer's Voys," *Representations* 60 [1997]: 70–91). For a list of Chaucerian music references, see Nigel Wilkins, *Music in the Age of Chaucer* (Cambridge: D. S. Brewer, 1979), chap. 4.

[59] On the tradition of the *Song of Songs,* see Ann W. Astell, *The Song of Songs in the Middle Ages* (Ithaca: Cornell University Press, 1990); E. Ann Matter, *The Voice of My Beloved: The Song of Songs in Western Medieval Christianity* (Philadelphia: University of Pennsylvania Press, 1990), including chap. 7, on religious lyric; Peter Dronke, "The Song of Songs and Medieval Love Lyric," in his *The Medieval Poet and His World* (Rome: Edizione di Storia e Letteratura, 1984), pp. 209–36.

[60] See *Song of Songs,* 7.8–9, "the odour of thy mouth like apples. Thy throat like the best wine"; 5.2–6 on the lover at the door; 5.10–11, the lover's head "as the finest gold" and hair "as branches of palm trees"; see Kaske, "The *Canticum canticorum,*" pp. 487–90).

ences to song in terms of the tale's pastiche of the *"déclassé* and shop-worn" descriptive linguistic registers of earlier Middle English verse (both romance and lyric); this allowed him in turn to conflate the gender instability of the masculine protagonists with the relatively stable gender of the sensualized and commodified Alisoun, and to read them all as examples of aesthetic vulgarity and personal immorality.[61] However, it may be that Chaucer's commentary on song is not grounded in either aesthetics or morals, but in an exploration of the language of sentiment and song—and its implications for gender and sexuality.

Certainly Nicholas and Absolon's performances of Middle English song are without equivalent in the analogues. They are in fact remarkably full of echoes of other thirteenth- and fourteenth-century Middle English lyrics, to the degree that some readers have even asked whether one would hear them as comic if they did not appear in Chaucer's comic fables. They replay the Middle English lyric's rhetoric of "simplicity," "directness," even a certain appearance of "childlikeness," and they echo its language of affect, played out in the accessible and mundane vocabulary of orally transmitted song; they also re-create something of its underlying artfulness—its distinctive brand of clerico-vernacular *faux-naif.* While Donaldson may be right that they simulate an older lyric style and thus function as some kind of a social and literary joke at the expense of their singers, they also stage a rhetoric of sentiment—along with the questions that this raises about identity.

When we first meet him, Nicholas seems to be constantly singing, suffusing the whole place with song ("So swetely that all the chambre rong"); he himself is almost indistinguishable from his song:

> And al above ther lay a gay sautrie,
> On which he made a-nyghtes melodie
> So swetely that all the chambre rong;
> And *Angelus ad virginem* he song;
> And after that he song the Kynges Noote.
> (I.3213–17)

Nicholas's singing of the annunciation lyric, "Angelus ad virginem," comically juxtaposes angelic sexlessness and the highly sexualized

[61] Donaldson, *Speaking of Chaucer,* chap. 2 (citation, p. 18).

medieval fabliau tradition in which clerics disguise themselves as angels in a seduction ploy.[62] However, this conjunction of the sacred with the secular (reinforced by the apparently secular "Kynges Noote") also conflates two kinds of affectivity in a sublime sentimental fantasy that combines the religious and the erotic, the angel and the lover. This is the confusion made possible by the language of lovers' *sentiment* and song. Chaucer also tells us that Nicholas is an expert in the art of "deerne love" ("secret love," I.3200), again doing so with common Middle English lyric phraseology.[63] The passages of Nicholas's song that Chaucer re-creates for us also echo the short three- or four-stress lines common in these lyrics, and they mimic the lyrics' self-consciously simple, affective language, and their ability to mask a predatory agenda with the language of love. Even Nicholas's invocation of God mingles the language of eroticism with that of religion:

> And prively he caughte hire by the queynte,
> And seyde, "Ywis, but if ich have my wille,
> For derne love of thee, lemman, I spille."
> And heeld hire harde by the haunchebones,
> And seyde, "Lemman, love me al atones,
> Or I wol dyen, also God me save!"[64]

Later on, another blurring of categories occurs, occluding the body and its sexual activities, when the narrator uses the imagery of music for sex ("Ther was the revel and the melodye") and perhaps even for masturbation, when Nicholas "taketh his sawtrie, / And pleyeth faste, and maketh melodie."[65]

Chaucer tells us that Absolon sings in the contemporary style, with trilled or "broken" short notes, "brokkynge as a nyghtyngale" (an art

---

[62] On this song, see John Stevens, "*Angelus ad virginem:* The History of a Medieval Song," in *Medieval Studies for J. A. W. Bennett aetatis suae LXX,* ed. P. L. Heyworth (Oxford: Clarendon Press, 1981), pp. 297–328 (on its appearance in more secular MSS, see pp. 321–23); see also Gellrich, "Parody of Medieval Music," p. 178.

[63] See Donaldson, *Speaking of Chaucer,* pp. 19–20; also "Dame Sirith," in *Early Middle English Verse and Prose,* ed. J. A. W. Bennett and G. V. Smithers (Oxford: Clarendon Press, 1968), pp.77–95 (lines 127–32); Nicholas is also "sleigh and ful privee" (I.3201).

[64] I.3276–81; see "Dame Sirith," lines 232–34; the lyric term *lemman* also occurs in this text; see also note to *Canterbury Tales,* IX.204–6.

[65] I.3652; I,3305–6; see Gellrich, "Parody of Medieval Music," pp. 177, 179.

some contemporaries regarded as an affectation).[66] His first lyric, a deca-syllabic couplet or *refrain*[67] sung to the lutelike *gyterne,* is certainly less obviously marked by the registers of Middle English lyric and closer to "straight" Chaucerian pathos:

> He syngeth in his voys gentil and smal,
> "Now, deere lady, if thy wille be,
> I praye yow that ye wole rewe on me."
> (I.3360–62)

It is in his second song that Absolon's infantilism reappears, dramati-cally linked to the undifferentiated language of sublimated affect. Here Chaucer really goes to work with his vernacular re-creation of the *Song of Songs,* subtly distorting the simultaneously erotic and spiritual regis-ters of the *Song* and its textual legacy with the language of neediness and sentimentality:

> "What do ye, hony-comb, sweete Alisoun,
> My faire bryd, my sweete cynamome?
> Awaketh, lemman myn, and speketh to me!
> Wel litel thynken ye upon my wo,
> That for youre love I swete ther I go.
> No wonder is thogh that I swelte and swete;
> I moorne as dooth a lamb after the tete.
> Ywis, lemman, I have swich love-longynge
> That lik a turtel trewe is my moornynge.
> I may nat ete na moore than a mayde."
> (I.3698–707)

Kaske and Gellrich have found parallels in the *Song of Songs* and in Middle English liturgical or devotional writing for almost every aspect of this song. Absolon's *hony-comb* and *cynamome* echo *favus* and *cinnamo-mum* in the *Song of Songs* (4.11; 5.1; 4.14) and a liturgical description of the Virgin Mary "sicut cinnamomum"; Absolon's "love-longynge" re-calls the biblical phrase "quia amore langueo" ("because I languish with

---

[66] I.3377; see note; for Lollard criticisms, see Bruce W. Holsinger, "The Vision of Music in a Lollard Florilegium: *Cantus* in the Middle English *'Rosarium theologie'* (Cam-bridge, Gonville and Caius College MS 354/581)," *Plainsong and Medieval Music* 8 (1999): 95–106 (104).
[67] On the refrain, see Butterfield, *Poetry and Music,* chaps. 4 and 5.

love"), while the line "that for youre love I swete ther I go" echoes "for my head is full of dew, and my locks of the drops of the night" (*Song of Songs,* 2.5; 5.8; 5.2); Absolon's "I moorne as dooth a lamb after the tete" infantilizes the lamb of God's desire for the breasts "more beautiful than wine" (*Song of Songs,* 4.10) and the Middle English vocabulary of an antiphon to the Virgin Mary, "O Þow ioieful womman . . . wiseliche Þow ȝaf souke wiþ Þin hooli tete."[68] However, the subversive effect of Chaucer's caricatural versions of these biblical and liturgical passages comes from their disturbingly ambiguous conflation of the religious and the secular. As Donaldson illustrates, Absolon's song also invokes the registers of Middle English lyric by using a number of common lyric words and phrases (*love-longynge, lemman,* "faire bryd") and he will conclude his appeal with a package of lyric clichés: "Lemman, thy grace, and sweete bryd, thyn oore"; his "mourning" is "true" as that of the turtle dove (a comparison that, while it echoes *Song of Songs* 2.12, is usually made for women), and his acknowledgment of the lady's indifference sounds like petulance: "Wel litel thynken ye upon my wo."[69]

In Absolon's words, then, the *Song of Song*'s figures of animality and food have been transmuted into the narcissistic forms of a fantasy maternal. His desire is like the as-yet-undifferentiated desire of the baby for pleasure, honeycomb, and the breast, and it is described in the bodily language of fainting, sweating, and "mourning for the teat." In fact, he confusingly both uses the language of the body and also denies it, claiming that he wants to eat and that he is off his food—he is like an eager baby lamb and an appetiteless girl. Oscillating between childishness and artful affectation, between bodiliness and bodily denial, in Absolon's mouth the sacred/secular tradition of the *Song of Songs* is lyric kitsch. "Kiss me," he says in a climax of narcissistic undifferentiation, for the love of Jesus—and of me: "Thanne kysse me, syn it may be no bet, / For Jhesus love, and for the love of me" (I.3716–17).

This, then, is Chaucer's narrative dissection of the language of affect in song. Humiliation will follow. The uncertain gendering of the body as Alisoun will present it to Absolon will make explicit the sexual ambiguity with which Absolon has been portrayed; but Alisoun's action will also brutally confront Absolon's fantasy of self and beloved with the body, graphically revealed in all its obscenity and uncoordination. Re-

[68] Kaske, "The *Canticum canticorum,*" pp. 481–86; Gellrich, "Parody of Medieval Music," pp. 183–85; see also Donaldson, *Speaking of Chaucer,* p. 44.
[69] I.3726, 3706, 3701; see Donaldson, *Speaking of Chaucer,* pp. 26–27.

garded as part of an emerging pattern in Chaucer's poetry, what could otherwise have been seen as Alisoun's "fabliau gamefulness" can now be seen as a phobic and repudiatory gesture on Chaucer's part.

However, Chaucer also covers his tracks. He does so by exploiting, prior to the event, Absolon's blissful unawareness of his predicament and the people who are listening—an unawareness that turns out to be typical of Chaucer's singers. If all performers are made vulnerable by the very act of performance, Chaucer portrays his singers as unusually oblivious, entirely preoccupied by affect and art. In this respect they differ from the singer of the *ballade* to Rosemounde, who, like many earlier courtly singers, betrays considerable awareness of the threat posed by his social milieu. In a slightly Bergsonian move,[70] Chaucer makes the singers of his narratives so self-obsessed—it could be described as another form of narcissism[71]—that they seem to "ask for" victimhood. We could say that Chaucer uses the effects of narcissism doubly—not only as a central aspect of his portrayal of song and affect, but as that which serves to "naturalize" the aggression he visits on his singers: it is the singers, he implies, who are responsible for the disasters that befall them.

Absolon is always, for instance, monomaniacally serenading Alisoun when she is in bed with someone else. The first time, Alisoun is listening with her husband, and Chaucer reinforces the sense of Absolon as an outsider by reporting the marital conversation as Absolon sings— though John, presumably a churchgoing man and an uneducated musical listener, may ludicrously be mistaking Absolon's love songs, with their "broken," quick notes, for church "chaunting."[72] Chaucer invokes

---

[70] Henri Bergson claims that laughter is a response to "inflexibility" or automatism in the face of change; the obsessive-repetitive and the narcissist both demand their own victim-hood ("Laughter," in *Comedy. George Meredith, An Essay on Comedy. Henri Bergson, Laughter,* ed. Wylie Sypher [Baltimore: Johns Hopkins University Press, 1956], pp. 61–190 [66–71]).

[71] "Putting love into words . . . stresses the utterance more than the propositional act . . . [and] necessarily summons up not the narcissistic *parry* but what appears to me as the narcissistic *economy* . . . scription attracts us" (Kristeva, *Tales of Love,* pp. 268–69; also pp. 152–53). However, on the problematically capacious psychoanalytic category of *narcissism,* see Sydney E. Pulver, "Narcissism: The Term and the Concept," in *Essential Papers on Narcissism,* ed. Morrison, pp. 91–111 (91–92).

[72] That is, liturgical plainsong with its single line of melody and long notes; Gellrich claims more literalistically that Absolon is singing "in low tones as he would *chant* the office" ("Parody of Medieval Music," p. 183); Kaske proposes that the word refers us back to the "voice of my beloved," who speaks outside the wall (2.8–9), and perhaps to the *Song of Songs* itself (Kaske, "The *Canticum canticorum*," p. 492).

a little rustic pastoralism, and perhaps even a popular song, when he comments indifferently that, for all the attention Absolon will get from Alisoun, he "may blowe the bukkes horn" ("blow the deer-horn").[73] Absolon's second song is his secular *Song of Songs,* sung this time as she lies in bed with Nicholas. Alisoun roundly rebuffs Absolon, shouting with gameful brutality, "Go fro the wyndow, Jakke fool,"[74] but like one of Bergson's oblivious victims, Absolon does not give up. Consumed by his own fantasies, he utters a commonplace about love being "yvel biset" and hopes at least to get a kiss; Chaucer describes him preoccupied with his own elaborate procedures, down on his knees and busy wiping his mouth in preparation. But Chaucer also stresses the complicity of those around him—"Now hust, and thou shalt laughen al thy fille" (I.3722).

What follows is one of Chaucer's most aggressive and bodily repudiations of song; if Kaske is right that Absolon's *awaketh* echoes the *surge* of the *Song of Songs,*[75] then this is a very different "arising":

> And Absolon, hym fil no bet ne wers,
> But with his mouth he kiste hir naked ers
> Ful savourly, er he were war of this.
> Abak he stirte, and thoughte it was amys,
> For wel he wiste a womman hath no berd.
> He felte a thyng al rough and long yherd,
> And seyde, "Fy! allas! what have I do?"
>
> (I.3733–39)

Savourly is a deft final allusion to the lyric tradition of the *Song of Songs,* with its reference to real eating and the "taste" of the embodied kiss, but also, by the pun on *sapor* and *sapientia* ("taste" and "wisdom"), to spiritual "tasting" of God.[76] But it appears in the context of a violently reembodied acting of kissing/eating, a direct encounter with the "naked

---

[73] That is, "idle away time . . . like a shepherd" (Geoffrey Chaucer, *The Canterbury Tales,* ed. Jill Mann [London: Penguin, 2005], gloss to I.3387).

[74] I.3708; on the parody infantilism, and even the suggestion of a popular song, to be found in "com pa me," see note to I.3709; and *Canterbury Tales,* ed. Mann, note to I.3709.

[75] *The Miller's Tale,* I.3670; *Song of Songs,* 2.13; Kaske, "The *Canticum canticorum,*" p. 482.

[76] See Jean Leclercq, O.S.B., *The Love of Learning and the Desire for God: A Study of Monastic Culture,* trans. Catharine Misrahi, 2nd ed. (London: SPCK, 1978), pp. 39–44, 104–9, 233–86.

ers"; it is followed by a grotesque sequence of overlaid body images—anus/woman's mouth, anus/bearded man's face, anus/female pubic hair. And most important, the singer's own mouth is brought into direct encounter with—and silenced by—this carnivalesque imagined sequence of "lower" body parts. Nicholas and Alisoun, having witnessed the whole thing, now refuse to interact with Absolon, except to shout out to themselves obscenely, "A berd! A berd!"

> This sely Absolon herde every deel,
> And on his lippe he gan for anger byte,
> And to hymself he seyde, "I shal thee quyte."
> Who rubbeth now, who froteth now his lippes
> With dust, with sond, with straw, with clooth, with chippes.
>
> (I.3744–48)

Released by the violence of events, the aggressivity that underlies Absolon's narcissism is now made manifest. He grovels on the ground, biting and rubbing the mouth with which he sang his songs in the dirt; behind his sublimatory arts of love and song lies a substantial ambivalence about the body, now expressed in inwardly turned disgust. Soon he will angrily renounce aspirations to love (and song?), commit himself to Satan, and become a small "devil" with a hot *kultour* (I.3750, 3754–57, 3775–76).

Turning to Nicholas, Bergson's theory of the automatism or rigidity of the victim explains why Nicholas now changes from trickster to victim. He is so exhilarated by Alisoun's trick that he wants to repeat it, though this is the one thing you do not do, as "a really living life should never repeat itself."[77] Reincarnated as the trickster, Absolon now lures Nicholas by deceptively sending out all the signs of victimhood, repeating all his idiotic lyric tropes of courtship, "Spek, sweete bryd . . . ," and this time it is Nicholas whose backside parodically "rises" and "sings" in the dark,[78] only to receive the most violent "kiss" of the tale with the "hoote kultour." The "punishments" that Chaucer inflicts on Absolon and Nicholas confront the mouth of the singer with that other "mouth" at the other end of the body—the Chaucerian singer is reminded that

[77] Bergson, "Laughter," p. 82.
[78] See Gellrich, "Parody of Medieval Music," p. 186; also on the "music" of farting, see Valerie J. Allen, "Broken Air" (in the cluster of essays on "Medieval Noise"), *Exemplaria* 16 (2004): 305–22 (312–14).

the body, the mouth, and the intestine are continuous.[79] Once again, the lyric "I" is reduced to carnivalesquely brutalized "lower" body parts—and an appeal for a fantasy version of the "world upside down," a secular Noah's flood. Chaucer thrusts the grotesque body into the fantasy world of the narcissist.

The blurring of sexual identity that has been staged in the songs of these singers is again affirmed by the ambiguous sexual connotations of concluding events: Absolon's failure to have a heterosexual encounter, along with his subsequent repudiation of "love," and the anal "kiss" that both he and Nicholas receive raise the specter of alternative forms of sexuality, even male same-sex eroticism. The uncertain gendering of the two clerics receives dramatic confirmation.

The Merchant's Tale is also full of music (as in *The Miller's Tale,* its songs are without equivalent in the analogues). Januarie knows, for instance, that unsatisfied *bacheleris* such as Damyan "synge 'allas'" (IV.1274, 1881–82). The marriage of Januarie and May, in contrast, appears to be a Bacchic and Venerian carnival, whose music is both compared to and defined against the music of myth, bible, science, and philosophy:

> Biforn hem stoode instrumentz of swich soun
> That Orpheus, ne of Thebes Amphioun,
> Ne maden nevere swich a melodye.
> At every cours thanne cam loud mynstralcye
> That nevere tromped Joab for to heere,
> Nor he Theodomas . . .
> Hoold thou thy pees, thou poete Marcian,
> That writest us that ilke weddyng murie
> Of hire Philologie and hym Mercurie,
> And of the songes that the Muses songe!
> (IV.1715–20, 1732–35)

Insofar as the music of this marriage is secular, affective, and erotic, it brings Venus, who "laugheth upon every wight" and "with hire fyr-brond in hire hand aboute / Dаunceth biforn the bryde and al the route"; her firebrand certainly arouses the young Damyan (IV.1723,

---

[79] My thinking here has been influenced by conversations with Katie Walter, whose Ph.D. dissertation is "Discourses of the Human: Mouths in Late Medieval Religious Literature" (University of Cambridge, 2007).

1727–28, 1776–77). But there is little eroticism for the reader in Januarie, Chaucer's vision of a sexuality compromised by age: in the case of Venus's self-deceiving knight and "myrie . . . wedded man" (IV.1731), even the figure of the "music" of sensuality is undone, as Januarie's presence turns an indescribability topos into an expression of euphemism and disgust: "Whan tendre youthe hath wedded stoupyng age, / Ther is swich myrthe that it may nat be writen" (IV.1738–39).

Although Januarie himself is not so much ambivalent toward his body as in denial of it, this ageist tale with its unsparing detail ruthlessly incites readerly ambivalence about his body and sexual identity. Januarie is sexually ambiguous partly because he is old: the medieval commonplace that age removes passion and sexual desire underlines the assumption that age subverts the categories of sexuality.[80] However, Januarie has a rather youthful-seeming hyperactivity and has certainly not given up all pretensions to an erotic life. The effect of Januarie's sexual ambiguity really derives from the disturbing combination of bodily inadequacy with aspirations to eroticism and affect: Januarie's age, in other words, has a subversive effect similar to that of Absolon's infantilism. And of course Januarie has pretensions to "artistry"—he is a member of the minor gentry, who imagines himself skilled in the arts of biblical and secular ethics, counsel, rhetoric, and song. His particular combination of decayed sensualism and clerico-courtly affectation is emblematized in his singing.[81]

In this tale Chaucer returns to the ambivalently erotic and spiritual exegetical tradition of the *Song of Songs* and its appearance in Middle English lyric. The tale is, after all, about Januarie's attempt to have, and imaginatively to conflate, "parfite blisses two—/ This is to seye, in erthe and eek in hevene" (IV.1638–39), coitus and eternal bliss, polarized theological and ontological alternatives. His first postcoital outburst is a bizarre combination of the grotesque and the pretentious, the animalesque and the artful:

> And upright in his bed thanne sitteth he,
> And after that he sang ful loude and cleere,

---

[80] See Shulamith Shahar, "The Old Body in Medieval Culture," in *Framing Medieval Bodies,* ed. Kay and Rubin, pp. 160–86 (163, 167–69); Carol A. Everest, "Sex and Old Age in Chaucer's *Reeve's Prologue," ChauR* 31 (1996–97): 99–114.

[81] On Januarie as a parody "Solomon" of wisdom and song, see Bruce A. Rosenberg, "The 'Cherry-Tree Carol' and the *Merchant's Tale," ChauR* 5 (1970–71): 264–76 (271).

> And kiste his wyf, and made wantown cheere.
> He was al coltish, ful of ragerye,
> And ful of jargon as a flekked pye.
> The slake skyn aboute his nekke shaketh
> Whil that he sang, so chaunteth he and craketh.
>   (IV.1844–50)

Like Chaucer's best victims, Januarie is entirely indifferent to the opinions of those around him, whether divine or female ("God woot what that May thoughte in hir herte," IV.1851). This is even truer of his next song (though Donaldson claims that this song too, if read out of context, would be almost impossible to identify as a joke):[82] sung in the priapic/courtly walled garden, this song is a tissue of citations from the *Song* and incorporates all the sublime erotic/religious registers of the tradition, but this time shadowed by decayed sensualism:

> "Rys up, my wyf, my love, my lady free!
> The turtles voys is herd, my dowve sweete;
> The wynter is goon with alle his reynes weete.
> Com forth now, with thyne eyen columbyn!
> How fairer ben thy brestes than is wyn!
> The gardyn is enclosed al aboute;
> Com forth, my white spouse . . ."
> Swiche olde lewed wordes used he.
>   (IV.2138–44, 2149)

The narrator's "devastating anticlimax" of a response acknowledges the disturbing conflation of registers in the song: insofar as *lewed* signifies "stupid, uncouth, rude," it is a brutal admission of the crass sensuality, the "lewedness," if not of the song itself, then of Januarie's use of it; insofar as *lewed* signifies "uneducated, ignorant," it is an ironic allusion (but at whose expense?) to the extraordinarily learned, spiritual, and erotic exegetical tradition within which the song is composed.[83] The narrator's response points once again to sublimatory narcissism of song, its capacity to mystify the body and to confuse sexual identity.

Januarie is of course another "blind" victim. He sings this song sur-

[82] Donaldson, *Speaking of Chaucer,* p. 44; also Rosenberg, "'Cherry Tree Carol,'" pp. 269–70.
[83] See MED, s.v."leued" adj, 1 and 2; citation, Donaldson, *Speaking of Chaucer,* p. 44; see also Derek Pearsall, *The Canterbury Tales* (London: Allen and Unwin, 1985), p. 204.

rounded by a crowd of variously invested listeners, his wife, her lover, God (to whom Januarie and May refer, but who takes no part), and the gods of the underworld (whom they appear not to notice, but who will have a substantial role to play). All these protagonists have their own agenda—May is signaling to Damyan and Pluto and Proserpine are having an argument. At the climax of the tale, Januarie sings again, as if to ask for his punishment, "ful murier than the papejay, / 'Yow love I best, and shal, and oother noon.' "[84] Once again, there is more than "fabliau logic" to the events of *The Merchant's Tale*. Januarie's gender-disturbing humiliation is to service his wife's infidelity, as he abjectly bends over and allows his wife to put her foot on his back, while he embraces the tree in which she and Damian are indeed to "Rys up" for the sexual act. All the signs of his engenderment are contradictory:

> "But wolde ye vouche sauf, for Goddes sake,
> The pyrie inwith youre armes for to take . . .
> Thanne sholde I clymbe wel ynogh," quod she,
> "So I my foot myghte sette upon your bak.". . .
> He stoupeth doun, and on his bak she stood,
> And caughte hire by a twiste, and up she gooth.
> (IV.2341–42, 2344–45, 2348–49)

Not only is the description of sex that follows notoriously more brutal than anywhere else in Chaucer, but the violence done to Januarie is particularly exquisite in that Pluto, in what he claims is an act of kindness, makes the old man look at it. When the *smok* goes "up," once again the Chaucerian singer has "lower" body parts thrust in his face and the narcissist is faced with an outrageous body. What is more, in the last lines, Chaucer performs a new variation on the solipsism of the courtly lover and singer; Januarie not only connives in his betrayal, but, with a little persuasion from May, refuses to see what he has seen: "This Januarie, who is glad but he? He kisseth hire and clippeth hire ful ofte" (IV.2412–13). Januarie's solipsism is both the cause of his punishment and also the final punishment that Chaucer inflicts on him.

---

[84] IV.2322–23. On the tale's lyric connections and its parodic references to the spiritual desire of the Virgin Mary in the "Cherry-Tree Carol," see Rosenberg, " 'Cherry-Tree Carol.' "

Artful and Clerical Singers

This abjective Chaucerian response to the masculine singer in fact pervades the *Canterbury Tales*. The unlucky singers tend to be men of the arts—courtly lovers, literary men, small-time scholars, or clerics.[85] Suddenly the Pardoner's connections with music and song, observed most recently by Sturges and Holsinger, seem relevant.[86] Along with rhetoric, singing is one of several arts by which he stages his uncertain sexuality, though, as for rhetoric, it is simultaneously a means for Chaucer to reflect on the significance of song.[87] First, there is the Pardoner's polyphonic performance (with his possibly lascivious or homoerotic voice "as smal as hath a goot"[88]) together with the Summoner—and the narrator's phallic pun about the Summoner's "part":

> Ful loude he soong "Com hider, love, to me!"
> This Somonour bar to hym a stif burdoun;
> Was nevere trompe of half so greet a soun.[89]

As elsewhere in Chaucer, however, the gender-disturbing language of affect moves easily between the erotic and the religious sublimes, and the Pardoner also engages in buoyant liturgical singing:

> But alderbest he song an offertorie;
> For wel he wiste, whan that song was songe,

[85] On the affective arts, see note 45 above. The nonclerical Miller can only "blowe and sowne" the rustic music of the bagpipe with its erotic connotations (I.565); see Edward A. Block, "Chaucer's Millers and Their Bagpipes," *Speculum* 29 (1954): 239–43.

[86] Sturges associates him with a Kristevan notion of music as connected to the maternal semiotic and to medieval grammarians' notion of "confused speech" (*Chaucer's Pardoner,* chap. 5, esp. pp. 84–92); Holsinger connects him to the "homoerotic" art of polyphony (*Music, Body, and Desire,* pp. 175–87); for the "corrupt" music of the *Pardoner's Tale,* see Robert Boenig, "Musical Irony in the Pardoner's Tale," *ChauR* 24 (1989): 253–58.

[87] The debate about the Pardoner's sexuality is summarized in Sturges, *Chaucer's Pardoner,* chap. 2; also Leicester, *Disenchanted Self,* pp. 35–64, 161–94. On the Pardoner's rhetoric, see Copeland, "Pardoner's Body."

[88] I.688 (on this, see note to 1.688–89); this phrase also recalls the *smal* voice of Absolon (I.3360); note too the musical connotations of his preaching ringing out like a "bell," and his likening of himself to a "bird" (VI.331, 395–97).

[89] I.672–74. See John M. Bowers, "Queering the Summoner," p. 302.

> He moste preche and wel affile his tonge
> To wynne silver, as he ful wel koude;
> Therefore he song the murierly and loude.[90]

Readers have commented on the compulsive *bisynesse*—even the automaton-like manner—with which the Pardoner goes about his arts.[91] In his performance the various narcissisms of the artist and the lover (though what does he love?)[92] are superimposed on each other. And of course this hyperactivity also serves to naturalize one of Chaucer's more vicious and bodily rebuffs, the Host's simultaneously sacramental, homophobic, castratory, and excremental joke. What is it that drives the Pardoner to court disaster by addressing to the Host his religious and pornographic proposition that the Host "kisse the relikes everychon" and "unbokele anon [his] purs"? The Host of course replies with the language of the body:

> I wolde I hadde thy coillons in myn hond
> In stide of relikes or of seintuarie.
> Lat kutte hem of, I wol thee helpe hem carie;
> They shul be shryned in an hogges toord!
>
> (VI.952–55)

A violent echo of Jean de Meun's bodily repost to the lyric "love" of Guillaume de Lorris,[93] the Host's "joke" confronts the Pardoner with a vision of the obscene and fragmented body, imposing silence, at least temporarily, on the singer: "This Pardoner answerde nat a word; / So wrooth he was, no word ne wolde he seye" (VI.956–57).

Other instances across the *Canterbury Tales* suggest that this is a pervasive pattern in Chaucer's writing: for instance, the lascivious (and pos-

---

[90] I.710–14; this song is echoed in the (heterosexual) Pardoner's singing in "The *Canterbury Interlude* and the Merchant's *Tale of Beryn*" (in *The Canterbury Tales: Fifteenth-Century Continuations and Additions,* ed. John M. Bowers [Kalamazoo: Medieval Institute Publications, 1992], pp.55–196, lines 412–18).

[91] VI.399; Leicester, *Disenchanted Self,* pp. 39–44, 55–58; on the Pardoner as automaton, see Pearsall, *Canterbury Tales,* pp. 98–101; Sturges, *Pardoner's Body,* pp. 97–98.

[92] Carolyn Dinshaw claims that the Pardoner makes up for psychic lack by fetishism in *Chaucer's Sexual Poetics* (Madison: University of Wisconsin Press, 1989), chap. 6.

[93] VI.944–45; the lines refer to the relics/testicles discussion of Jean de Meun's *Reson:* see Guillaume de Lorris and Jean de Meun, *Le Roman de la rose,* lines 7102–38; see also Dinshaw, *Chaucer's Sexual Poetics,* pp. 168–81; Marijane Osborn, "Transgressive Word and Image in Chaucer's Enshrined *Coillons* Passage," *ChauR* 37 (2002–3): 365–84.

sibly bisexual) singing Summoner receives, at least by analogy, a carnivalesque reposte when the Summoner of *The Friar's Tale* is sent off to hell along with the old woman's *panne* (III.1629, 1635, 1639–41). And, again by analogy, infernal and anal rebukes are provided for the flirtatious Friar of *The General Prologue,* also skilled in the rhetoric of preaching and able to "synge and pleyen on a rote" (I.236); first, in the Prologue to *The Summoner's Tale* all friars are promised a place in hell under Satan's arse; and in the tale itself, the friar receives an anal "gift," including a vividly imagined method for making sure that the gift reaches the faces and noses of the whole convent, with the "firste fruyt" (III.2277) saved for the friar himself. With his own compulsive regularity, Chaucer brings the imaginary of the masculine singer, with his sublimating arts of love, rhetoric, and song, face to face with "lower" places and body parts.[94]

Something very similar occurs in *The Prioress's Tale.* Here the subversions of gender that occur round the "litel clergeon" seem to elicit violence from Chaucer in a way that those surrounding the Prioress do not; it is on the child, the Prioress's counterpart in the tale, rather than the Prioress, that Chaucer takes out his aggression. Nevertheless, the centrality of clerical song in the tale means that it was always bound to be a tale of martyrdom.

The Prologue to the tale is itself a song, written in rime royale (a song stanza extensively used by Machaut), and the Prioress describes the tale, also in rime royale, as her own hagiographical narrative *song.*[95] *The General Prologue* has already described the Prioress as a courtly lady, whose liturgical singing is fashionably "Entuned in hir nose ful semely," and whose motto refers to the undifferentiating effects of affect, *"amor vincit omnia"* (I.123, 162): once again, the posture of sentimentality espoused by the Chaucerian singer allows the secular and religious to blur. As noted above, the writings of Kristeva have shaped a number of readings of this tale.[96] Fradenburg has shown in detail how, in her opening

---

[94] See Allen, "Broken Air"; Peter W. Travis, "Thirteen Ways of Listening to a Fart: Noise in Chaucer's Summoner's Tale," *Exemplaria* 16 (2004): 323–48.

[95] VII.487; on rime royale, see Wimsatt, *Chaucer and His French Contemporaries,* pp. 16–17, 168–69; on Chaucer's exploitation of the "song effect" of the rime royale stanza in *Troilus and Criseyde,* see Barry Windeatt, *Oxford Guides to Chaucer: Troilus and Criseyde* (Oxford: Clarendon Press, 1992), pp. 164–65.

[96] See the comments on Fradenburg, "Criticism, Anti-semitism," above, page 146; for the place of a Kristevan presymbolic "maternal" in the "melodies, sounds and rhythms" of the songs of the Prioress and the *clergeon,* and the argument that the violent tale describes the *clergeon's* entry into symbolic culture, see Marvin, "'I will thee not

song, the Prioress identifies herself with children, and by implication with the masculine child of her tale, as when she likens herself to "a child of twelf month oold, or lesse." The opening song praises a male God in the language of primary and secondary narcissism, describing him as bountifully *ysprad* through the world and through the femininity of his mother, Mary.[97] As in other Chaucerian tales, the subversion of gender is staged in a language both erotic and spiritual, infantilizing and sublimatory.

However, many of the same features can be seen in the song of the *clergeon,* and it is on him that the tale enacts its violence. He is a seven-year-old boy, a "wydwes sone" and a devotee of the Virgin Mary, associated with the world of material and spiritual "mothers." Like that of the Prioress, the affectivity of this diminutized "litel clergeon" is both determined by infantilism and displaced by spiritualization, and his song of sublimated love for the heavenly mother once more enables him to conflate the two. The song's affective fantasies of immediacy and identification are further reinforced by the idea that the child's song is apparently divinely inspired, unlearned and even involuntary. Holsinger stresses the noninstitutional, intuitive nature of the child's discovery and singing of the song—"the *sound* of the antiphon enchants him well before he knows the meaning of the words."[98] The song is something that draws the child ineluctably to it: on first hearing the *Alma redemptoris,* "he drough hym ner and ner, / And herkned ay the wordes and the noote, / Til he the firste vers koude al by rote" (VII.520–22). Later the song appears to pass through his throat almost of its own accord—and eventually the miraculously intervening "sweetness" of the Virgin Mary means that he cannot stop singing:

> And thanne he song it wel and boldely,
> Fro word to word, acordynge with the note.
> Twies a day it passed thurgh his throte,
> To scoleward and homward whan he wente . . .

---

forsake'" (citation, p. 43); Holsinger claims that song in this tale possesses a sublimated, authoritative "voiceless immediacy" and exemplifies the "visceral promise of . . . salvation"; however, he also sees institutional music and its pedagogy as a mechanism of violence on the singer (*Music, Body, and Desire,* chap. 6, citations, pp. 265, 287); also Robertson, "Aspects of Female Piety"; Sturges, *Chaucer's Pardoner,* pp. 92–96; compare Kristeva, "Stabat Mater," in *Tales of Love,* pp. 234–63.

[97] VII.484, VII.453–73; see Fradenburg, "Criticism, Anti-semitism," pp. 91–94; Holsinger, *Music, Body, and Desire,* pp. 263–64.

[98] Holsinger, *Music, Body, and Desire,* pp. 265–72, 282–84 (citation, 266).

As I have seyd, thurghout the Juerie
This litel child, as he cam to and fro,
Ful murily than wolde he synge and crie
O *Alma redemptoris* everemo.
The swetnesse his herte perced so
Of Cristes mooder that, to hire to preye,
He kan nat stynte of syngyng by the weye.
                    (VII.546–49, 551–57)

The song, however, is also learned. Fradenburg, Marvin, and Holsinger all associate school and music teaching with violence, claiming that this violent pedagogy is repressed for much of the tale, but nevertheless is referred to obliquely and then reintroduced figuratively in the narrative of martyrdom at the end.[99] I want to take a different and slightly more positive view of song's "art": it is, after all, a central component of all Chaucerian song. Although young, the *clergeon* is indeed a schoolboy who "learns" the skills of clericalism and song, whether this is from his school, his school companions, or his mother (even love for the Virgin has been *ytaught* by his mother, VII.509). When he hears the song, he asks for it to be "construed" and says that he will use all *diligence* to "konne it al"; he learns it "by rote"; later, we might say, he is able to "construe" his miraculous singing to the abbot (VII.528, 539–40, 545, 642–69). In fact, the *clergeon*, who sings so "wel and boldely," is very pleased with his art indeed. I suggest that he has all the self-preoccupation that characterizes so many of Chaucer's singers, consumed as they are in the fantasy of their own song. Here again, in other words, the narcissism of the art of song runs parallel to the narcissism of affect expressed in the song.

And once more, this narcissism serves to naturalize the tale's violence. This violence (at the literal level attributed to, and then enacted on, the Jews) is surely connected less with musical pedagogy than with "Chaucer" and his attitude to song, affect, and the instabilities of gender. As in the other tales we have looked at, Chaucer sets up his narrative in such as way as to imply that the singer's narcissism contributes to his downfall. Like the fantasy of the song passing involuntarily through his

[99] Ibid., pp. 267–92; Fradenburg, "Criticism, Anti-semitism," p. 105; Marvin connects this learning with entry into the symbolic, but also sees it as mediated by the maternal, somaticism and song ("'I will thee not forsake,'" pp. 38–46). On this learning, see Carleton F. Brown, "Chaucer's *Litel clergeon*," *MP* 3 (1905–6): 467–91.

throat, the child is *murily* indifferent to the aggressive others who surround him, as he passes daily through the Jewish quarter, apparently involuntarily obliging the Jews to listen to his Christian song. As in other tales, Chaucer stresses the complicity and mutual dialogue of his listeners—*Sathanas* speaks from within the Jewish people, objecting to the singer's obsessive performance of affect:

> Is this to yow a thyng that is honest,
> That swich a boy shal walken as hym lest
> In youre despit, and synge of swich sentence,
> Which is agayn youre lawes reverence?
>
> (VII.561–64)

The Jews' revenge exemplifies the violent anality that characterizes many of Chaucer's treatments of the singer. In this tale of conduits (bodily and otherwise), the child is killed and cast into a sewer: "in a wardrobe they hym threwe / Wher as thise Jewes purgen hire entraille" (VI.572–73). It is another tale in which, imaginatively at any rate, Chaucer shits on the singer.[100]

However, even this is not the end of the tale, for, with a bit of divine aid, the child proves to be the most determined of all of Chaucer's singers:

> Ther he with throte ykorven lay upright,
> He *Alma redemptoris* gan to synge
> So loude that al the place gan to rynge.
>
> (VI.611–13)

Hagiographies tend to upend the terms of secular narrative, and this one is no exception, for here the compulsive singer is not the victim but the victor; in due course they carry him to the abbey, "syngynge his song alway," and salvation turns out to be an ever-repeating "song al newe" (VI.622, 584). And yet the child's abjection is not, I suggest, the sublimating "point where the scales are tipped towards pure spirituality," a vision of "perversion and beauty as the lining and the cloth of one and the same economy":[101] it is an extreme version of the blissfully

---

[100] For analogues to this, see *Sources and Analogues of Chaucer's Canterbury Tales,* ed. W. F. Bryan and Germaine Dempster (London: Routledge and Kegan Paul, 1941), pp. 447–85.

[101] Kristeva, *Powers of Horror,* pp.127, 125.

oblivious Chaucerian singer, the narcissistic child in the cesspit and still "asking for it," singing his love songs to the Virgin Mary.

There is a similar obliviousness and, for the Host, interminability to another, very different, Chaucerian tale, *Sir Thopas*. Although this is usually described as a comic version of a Middle English verse romance, can we regard this stanzaic, tail rhyme poem as a narrative "song" and its teller as a singer? The poem is certainly full of ballad motifs.[102] What is more, tail rhyme stanzas very similar to those of *Sir Thopas*, including the "bob" line, also appear in a number of shorter Middle English poems, carols, and lyrics.[103] I propose that Chaucer regards *Sir Thopas* as a narrative ballad, a form of song.[104] Much of *Sir Thopas*'s comedy, after all, derives from exaggerating effects found in both Middle English verse romance and lyric—poised and buoyant short lines and a cultivatedly simple, even "faux-naif," voice:

> Sire Thopas wax a doghty swayn;
> Whit was his face as payndemayn,
>   His lippes rede as rose;
> His rode is lyk scarlet in grayn,
> And I yow telle in good certayn
>   He hadde a semely nose.
>   (VII.724–29)

And if *Sir Thopas* is partly a ballad or song, then it can be no coincidence that its hero is so ambiguously gendered—as well as being given to a range of courtly arts and a great deal of amorphous sentimentality.

Like Absolon, Thopas takes the potentially infantilizing epithet *child* (VII.810, 830). His "lippes rede as rose," scarlet *rode,* and cute nose are just some of his traditionally feminine attributes; he has a girl's name, is "sweete as is the brembul flour" (746) and is cast in the commonly

---

[102] For the tale's connections with Middle English ballads such as the songs of Robin Hood or the ballad-like *Horn Child*, see *Sources and Analogues,* ed. Bryan and Dempster, p. 501; *Riverside Chaucer,* p. 917 and notes to VII.739, 740–41, 839; Donaldson also compares the vocabularies of *Sir Thopas, The Miller's Tale,* and Middle English romance and lyric (*Speaking of Chaucer,* pp. 14–29).

[103] See E. G. Stanley, "The Use of Bob Lines in Sir Thopas," *NM* 73 (1972): 417–26 (421–26); *Riverside Chaucer,* p. 917. On the comedy of stanzaic form in the tale, see Alan T. Gaylord, "Chaucer's Dainty 'Dogerel': The 'Elvyssh' Prosody of *Sir Thopas,*" *SAC* 1 (1979): 83–104 (esp. 93–98).

[104] The dialogue between the Host and Chaucer that precedes this tale, linking it with *The Prioress's Tale,* is also in rime royale.

feminine role of object of desire: "Ful many a mayde, bright in bour, / They moorne for hym paramour, / Whan hem were bet to slepe."[105] While Sir Thopas's repeated *priking,* and even a certain subsequent lassitude, may well connote active sexuality,[106] this, as we have seen, does not necessarily clarify sexual orientation or identity. And of course he is, like other Chaucerian men associated with song, an artful courtier, skilled in the business of dress, etiquette, food, and entertainment. He is also a lover, whose affect is of the most identificatory, "oceanic," or self-dissolving kind; as soon as he enters the pastoral landscape of plant and birdsong, he falls in love without a love-object in sight:

> Sire Thopas fil in love-longynge,
> Al whan he herde the thrustel synge . . .
>
> "O Seinte Marie, benedicite!
> What eyleth this love at me
>   To bynde me so soore?
> Me dremed al this nyght, pardee,
> An elf-queene shal my lemman be
>   And slepe under my goore.
>   (VII.772–73, 784–89)

Thopas so identifies with the imagined "elf-queene," who he fantasizes will "slepe under [his] goore," that she is virtually elided with the landscape into which he journeys in search of her; it is a landscape where the arts of "bataille and . . . chivalry" slip amorphously into the arts of "ladyes love-drury" (894–95).

And yet, it is not Sir Thopas who receives a Chaucerian rebuff. Although this "ballad-romance" is similar to *The Prioress's Tale* in that its hero has the unstable sexual identity and the narcissistic affect that Chaucer clearly associates with song, here the "singer" of the tale is a man, and it is this singer who is repudiated. He is of course the diminutized and feminized Chaucer figure himself: despite the size of his waist, he is described in feminized terms as an object of desire, "a popet in an arm t'enbrace / For any womman, smal and fair of face." Like Rosem-

---

[105] VII.742–44; see Donaldson, *Speaking of Chaucer,* pp.14–29; Pearsall, *Canterbury Tales,* pp. 163–64; for his name, see *Sources and Analogues,* ed. Bryan and Dempster, p. 493 n. 5.
[106] VII.754, 757, 774, 778–83; on the repetition of the apparently common romance term *priking,* see Gaylord, "Chaucer's Dainty 'Dogerel,'" p. 91.

ounde, he is capable of *daliaunce,* even if he chooses not to, and, like the "elf-queene," he is "elvyssh" ("mysterious, other worldly," VII.701–4). Geoffrey is the unsurely sexed singer from whom the tale of *Sir Thopas* springs—and it is on Geoffrey that the Host turns, disrupting his "song" of chivalic affect, sending it to the devil, and stuffing the mouth of the singer with the products of the other "mouth" of the body: "Thy drasty rymyng is nat worth a toord!" (VII.930). It is as close as Chaucer comes to acknowledging his fraught self-recognition in the figure of the singer.

The murderous *Manciple's Tale* enacts a rather different, "frustrated," variation on this theme.[107] Although the tale contains two singers, the bird (also a poet figure) and Phebus (the god of music and poetry), who are in their different ways punished, the tale contains no actual love song. Initially, Phebus is the "flour of bachilrie" (IX.125), his imagined song apparently a reflection of masculine sexual prowess:

> Pleyen he koude on every mynstralcie,
> And syngen that it was a melodie
> To heeren of his cleere voys the soun.
> (IX.113–15)

What is more, he has taught his crow to be an artist and a "counter-feiter" of speech and joyous, pleasure-giving song: "in al this world no nyghtyngale / Ne koude, by an hondred thousand deel, / Syngen so wonder myrily and weel" (IX.134, 136–38). But the crow witnesses the adultery of Phebus's wife and therefore sings not a joyful song but the sad "song" of "Cokkow! Cokkow! Cokkow!":

> "What, bryd?" quod Phebus. "What song syngestow?
> Ne were thow wont so myrily to synge
> That to myn herte it was a rejoysynge
> To heere thy voys? Allas, what song is this?
> (IX,243–47)

Phebus is not only unable to satisfy his wife, but he is also a self-deceiving woman killer and a destroyer of music. Having murdered his wife, he blames the crow, takes away the bird's white feathers and his song,

---

[107] See the brief remarks of Holsinger on music and violence in this tale, *Music, Body, and Desire,* p. 262; also Fradenburg, "The Manciple's Servant Tongue."

and destroys his own instruments. This Phebus is far more destructive toward music than in any of the analogues; only in Machaut's lyrical narrative of the *Voir Dit* does Phebus remove the bird's song—"Jamais ne feras que jangler"—and in none does he destroy his instruments.[108] Although the tale concludes with the Manciple's mother's grim advice not to speak and is widely read as Chaucer's farewell to fiction,[109] it is in fact also Chaucer's farewell to song. The tale also represents a new twist on the blinkered self-preoccupation of the Chaucerian singer, both in the figure of the foolish crow and in that of the unsinging god of music, who throughout sees only what he wants to see and imposes his own passions upon it. He quits the crow for his "false tale" by blackening him and sending him "Unto the devel":

> Ne nevere sweete noyse shul ye make,
> But evere crie agayn tempest and rayn,
> In tokenynge that thurgh thee my wyf is slayn.
> (IX.293, 307, 300–302)

Phebus is just one more self-deceiving and aggressive narcissist.

My final courtly and clerical singer from the *Canterbury Tales,* Chauntecleer the cock, escapes death only by the narrowest margin. Chauntecleer has "Sevene hennes for to doon al his plesaunce, / Whiche were his sustres and his paramours." *Soror* is the term of erotic affection in the *Song of Songs,* and in Middle English *sustres* can signify female "companions"; however, *sustres* also transgressively figures the hens as "sisters," both in the sense of siblings and of nuns.[110] Chantecleer's love relations already look a little unclear. Of the hens, moreover, his favorite is "damoysele Pertelote," whom he has loved since she was seven days old (VII.2866–67, 2870–73). I do not wish to labor Chauntecleer's high sexual drive, polygamy, incest, or taste for the younger chicken, but what initially looks like voracious chicken heterosexuality might be better described as sexual polymorphousness. Equally important,

---

[108] See note to IX.295–96; *Sources and Analogues,* ed. Bryan and Dempster, pp. 699–722 (711–16, citation 716).

[109] See Lee W. Patterson, "The 'Parson's Tale' and the Quitting of the 'Canterbury Tales,'" *Traditio* 34 (1978): 331–80 (370, 376–79); but see Pearsall on the single verse line, "and many a song and many a leccherous lay," in the Retraction (X.1086; *Canterbury Tales,* p. 293).

[110] See *Song of Songs* 4.10, 12; MED, s.v. "suster" n, 1, 3 and 4.

Chauntecleer expresses himself in the identificatory language of sublimated affect, "love":

> Syn thilke day that she [Pertelote] was seven nyght oold
> That trewely she hath the herte in hoold
> Of Chauntecleer, loken in every lith;
> He loved hire so that wel was hym therwith.
>
> (VII.2873–76)

Chauntecleer's identification with the love object is expressed in the lyric
commonplace that she "hath [his] herte in hoold"; her very "face" erases
any fear that might be in him: "Ye ben so scarlet reed aboute youre
yen, / It maketh al my drede for to dyen."[111] In the course of the tale,
she does indeed drive dreams and fears from his mind. Chauntecleer's
love language is also one of his many courtly/clerical arts, which include
his learning about dreams, Latin, diet and the bodily humors, and of
course his singing; once again, Chauntecleer's narcissistic artistic self-
imagining echoes the narcissism of his love language and his song.

In contrast to the analogues, the discussions of song in *The Nun's
Priest's Tale* are very elaborate. Chauntecleer's name means "sing-bright"
and his song, repeatedly described as *murie,* rivals church music:

> In al the land, of crowyng nas his peer.
> His voys was murier than the murie orgon
> On messe-dayes that in the chirche gon.
> Wel sikerer was his crowyng in his logge
> Than is a clokke or an abbey orlogge.
>
> (VII.2850–54)

Chantecleer may be a practitioner of the music of number (his crowing
is *siker,* "sure" as a clock), but his song is also the secular music of affect,
associated with the expression of, and the effects of, pleasure or love, as
here, singing with Pertelote:

> swich a joye was it to here hem synge,
> Whan that the brighte sonne gan to sprynge,
> In sweete accord, "My lief is faren in londe!"[112]

---

[111] VII.2874; 3161–62; see note 112 below.

[112] VII.2877–79; this lyric is reproduced in *Canterbury Tales,* ed. Mann, note to
VII.2879, where Mann also notes that the lyric is echoed by the narrator voice in
VII.2874–75, "trewely she hath the herte in hoold / Of Chauntecleer."

Later on he sings what could be an inset love lyric, again expressing the multiply overlaid identificatory pleasures to be derived by the lover from the landscape and the lady:

> "The sonne," he seyde, "is clomben up on hevene
> Fourty degrees and oon, and moore ywis.
> Madame Pertelote, my worldes blis,
> Herkneth thise blisful briddes how they synge,
> And se the fresshe floures how they sprynge;
> Ful is myn herte of revel and solas!"
>
> (VII.3198–203)

The narrator comically associates the singing Chauntecleer with the dangerously displaced sexuality of the *mermayde* when he says he sings "murier than the mermayde in the see" (VII.3270). Later the fox will associate his singing with the spiritually displaced sexuality of the angel:

> trewely, ye have as myrie a stevene
> As any aungel hath that is in hevene.
> Therwith ye han in musyk moore feelynge
> Than hadde Boece, or any that kan synge.
>
> (VII.3291–94)

Although the fox invokes Boethius, expert on musical "number," in fact he attributes to Chauntecleer not number, but "moore feelynge" than other singers.[113] The fox goes on to flatter the clerical *discrecioun, wisedom,* and *subtiltee* of Chantecleer's father, whom he has clearly eaten (VII.3309, 3311, 3319), and recounts the elaborate physical techniques by which song is perfected. But what is at stake here is still an art "of herte":

> Save yow, I herde nevere man so synge
> As dide youre fader in the morwenynge.
> Certes, it was of herte, al that he song.
> And for to make his voys the moore strong,
> He wolde so peyne hym that with bothe his yen

---

[113] Arguing that these lines are ironic and condemnatory, see David S. Chamberlain, "The Nun's Priest's Tale and Boethius's *De musica,*" *MP* 68 (1970–71): 188–91; but, albeit humorously, affective music is surely what interests Chaucer here.

He moste wynke, so loude he wolde cryen,
And stonden on his tiptoon therwithal,
And strecche forth his nekke long and smal.

(VII.3301–8)

It is difficult not to be reminded of Absolon, and even more of January, in this description of Chauntecleer's father up (postcoitally?) in the morning, standing on his toes, stretching out his neck "long and smal," shutting his eyes, and straining to sing "so loude."

Just like Januarie's blindness, the closing of Chauntecleer's eyes is emblematic of the state of mind of the Chaucerian singer, who is always in the grip of an art and an affect that render him oblivious to the predators around him. Consumed by the narcissistic image of himself offered by the fox ("So was he ravysshed with his flaterie," VII.3324), "Chauntecleer stood hye upon his toos, / Strecchynge his nekke, and heeld his eyen cloos, / And gan to crowe loude" (VII.3331–33). His replication of his father's actions demands comic victimhood—and for Chaucer, this is victimhood of the most bodily and abjectifying kind, as the fox grabs Chauntecleer by the source of song, his throat. Chaucer describes the throat here not with his usual neutral term *nekke,* but with the rare Middle English term *gargat:* this arresting and very physical-sounding word is French-origin (where it seems often to occur in narrative descriptions of military and chivalric violence).[114] Like the singer of the Rosamounde *ballade,* this singer may be eaten, and Chauntecleer, the impersonation of Chaucerian song, is on the point of entering the entrails of the beast.

Epilogue

Masked by high comedy, then, there is a dark side to Chaucer's relation with the sublimatory arts and affect of song. For him song seems to stage not only the vanity of the artist but also the instability of sexual identity that arises from the fantasy identifications and self-dissolvings of affect. Repeatedly, Chaucerian song elicits a brutal repudiation, a gross and abrupt reminder to the masculine singer that his song arises

---

[114] See Tobler-Lommatzsch, *Altfranzösisches Wörterbuch* (Berlin, 1925–36; Wiesbaden, 1954–), "gargate" n; MED, s.v. "gargat(e)" n, a; the word is not used in the analogues to the tale.

from the throat and therefore also from the "lower" body: Chaucer threatens forcibly to put it back there.

I want to end by reflecting on a very different Chaucerian singer, Troilus. Long described as an unusually "feminized" Chaucerian hero, Troilus also sings a splendid array of songs—not only the famous translations from Petrarch, Dante, and Boethius, but also a whole range of other small, inset lyrics or *refrains*.[115] Even his philosophical songs perform affect, staging all the psychosexual ambiguities of his love; they express his solipsism as an artist and lover, his refusal or incapacity to interact with the world around him, the crucially imaginary dimension of love. I do not wish to deny for a moment the tragedy of Troilus, or the many complex reasons for it; however, what happens to singers in the comic *Canterbury Tales* may give us a clue to the inevitability—and some of the comic mechanisms—of Chaucerian tragedy. When, in the face of loss, Troilus will still not give up on the fantasy of Criseyde's return, it is Pandarus who ventriloquizes the text's irritation at the solipsism of love: "Ye haselwode!" Interestingly, Pandarus seems to be invoking a more insouciant vein of medieval pastoral music in order to dismiss Troilus the lover and singer, as he makes clear later:

> "From haselwode, there joly Robyn pleyde,
> Shal come al that that thow abidest heere.
> Ye, fare wel al the snow of ferne yere!"

And when all is indeed lost, the narrator himself tells the lyric hero that he can, like Absolon, with his "bukkes horn," "est or west, / Pipe in an ivy lef, if that the lest."[116] From the moment he sang, perhaps, it was bound to end badly for Troilus.

---

[115] On song in *Troilus and Criseyde*, see Wimsatt, *Chaucer and His French Contemporaries,* pp. 141–61; Windeatt, *Troilus and Criseyde,* pp. 163–69.
[116] V.505, V.1174–76, 1432–33; compare V.1746–47.

Chaucer's Pardoner and Host—On the Road, in the Alehouse

Shayne Aaron Legassie
Columbia University

W E FIRST ENCOUNTER the Pardoner of Chaucer's *Canterbury Tales* in a sly passage steeped in images of Christian pilgrimage. Having come from Rome to Southwark in the company of the corrupt Summoner, the Pardoner makes a flamboyant entrance:

> With him ther rood a gentil PARDONER
> Of Rouncivale, his freend and his compeer,
> That streight was comen fro the court of Rome.
> Ful loud he soong "Com hider, love, to me!"
> This Somonour bar to hym a stif burdoun;
> Was nevere trompe of half so greet a soun.
>
> (I.669–74)[1]

As Melvin Storm and others have suggested, the "styf burdoun," which the Summoner is said to "bare," has the literal meaning of the bass line of the song of which the Pardoner sings the melody, but the word *burdoun* can also mean "staff," such as the kind used in pilgrimage, with all of its priapic connotations.[2] Although the Pardoner supposedly comes

---

[1] Citations of the *Canterbury Tales* refer to Larry D. Benson, gen. ed., *The Riverside Chaucer,* 3rd ed. (Boston: Houghton Mifflin, 1987). I would like to thank the following people for their questions, suggestions, objections, and support on earlier versions of this essay: Columbia University's Medieval Guild and Queer Student Alliance, Susan Crane, Joan Ferrante, Kamil Godula, Frank Grady, Robert Hanning, Derrick Higginbotham, Adnan Hussein, Ellen Kettels, Katherine Lewis, Asifa Malik, Brenna Mead, Margaret Pappano, Paul Strohm, and the two anonymous readers of *SAC.*

[2] Melvin Storm, "The Pardoner's Invitation: Quaestor's Bag or Becket's Shrine?" *PMLA* 97 (1982): 810–18. Indeed, the Old French word *bourdon* is the one used in the *Romance of the Rose* (2.21354), a text that inspired part of Chaucer's characterization of the Pardoner. The Pardoner's pilgrimage staff is also overtly phallic in the prologue to the anonymous *Tale of Beryn,* a fifteenth-century continuation of the *Canterbury Tales.* See "The Canterbury Interlude and Merchant's Tale of Beryn," in John M. Bowers, ed., *The Canterbury Tales: Fifteenth-Century Continuations and Additions* (Kalamazoo: Medieval Institute Publications, 1992).

from the pope's court in Rome, the *vernycle* (I.685), a pilgrim badge cast in the likeness of the veil that swabbed Christ's bloody face, marks him as a pilgrim rather than an ecclesiastical bureaucrat. In this brief introduction of the Pardoner, we see him heading from one pilgrimage center to another, intoning in hircine falsetto a love ballad with his hyperphallicized "freend," in language that intimates their sexual relationship through a pun involving one of the central symbols of the pilgrim enterprise. Moreover, the last time we hear of the Pardoner is after his conflict with the Host in Fragment VI, an altercation whose rhetoric also figures sodomy through images and practices associated with pilgrimage. Chaucer's linking of pilgrimage and homoeroticism could not be more straightforward and was not unusual in medieval Europe. This observation warrants a reconsideration of the Pardoner's place in the pilgrimage frame of the *Canterbury Tales*.

Most antihomophobic interpretations of the Pardoner that have drawn on a diverse group of texts collectively referred to as "queer theory" have seen him as a force that throws the heteronormative constitution of the pilgrim *compaignye* into crisis. These readings of the frame of the *Canterbury Tales* follow a similar narrative arc: from a not-quite-successful construction of a provisional but heteronormative social structure (the pilgrimage *compaignye*), to an return of the repressed element of that structure (in the form of the "queer" Pardoner) that calls into question its foundational assumptions, to a not-entirely-decisive containment of that "queer" epistemological challenge through the Pardoner's violent marginalization from and equivocal reintegration into the *compaignye*.[3] The assumption of a sexually normative pilgrimage is a heuristic convenience that has allowed scholars to impart crucial insights

---

[3] A list of the studies that have influenced me most includes: Carolyn Dinshaw, *Chaucer's Sexual Poetics* (Madison: University of Wisconsin Press, 1989), and *Getting Medieval: Sexual Communities Pre- and Post Modern* (Durham: Duke University Press, 1999); Glenn Burger,*Chaucer's Queer Nation* (Minneapolis: University of Minnesota Press, 2003); Robert S. Sturges, *Chaucer's Pardoner and Gender Theory* (New York: St. Martin's Press, 2000); H. Marshall Leicester Jr., *The Disenchanted Self: Representing the Subject in the "Canterbury Tales"* (Berkeley and Los Angeles: University of California Press, 1990); Michael Calabrese, "Make a Mark that Shows: Orphean Song, Orphean Sexuality, and the Exile of Chaucer's Pardoner," *Viator* 24 (1993): 269–86; and Steven F. Kruger "Claiming the Pardoner: Toward a Gay Reading of the *Pardoner's Tale*," *Exemplaria* 6 (1994): 112–39. All of these important analyses also draw on two pathbreaking views of the Pardoner by Monica McAlpine, "The Pardoner's Homosexuality and Why It Matters," *PMLA* 95 (1980): 8–22; and Donald Howard, *The Idea of the "Canterbury Tales"* (Berkeley and Los Angeles: University of California Press, 1976).

into the Pardoner's "performance" as they have called it, but it is an assumption that reveals the extent to which the metaphysics of queer theory have obscured a vital aspect of Chaucer's depiction of social space. One of the most remarkable characteristics of these analyses is that they consider the Pardoner's queer "performance" outside of any particular spatial context. Yet, as the language of the Pardoner's portrait suggests, the pilgrimage setting is essential to understanding Chaucer's depiction of the Pardoner's gender and sexuality.

Moreover, in the conflict that erupts between the Host and the Pardoner at the end of Fragment VI, one observes that the pilgrimage trail of the *Canterbury Tales* is used as a setting for an exploration of the technologies of masculine embodiment not just of the Pardoner, but also of the Host. The conflict between the Host and the Pardoner at the conclusion of Fragment VI asks readers to consider the relationships between sexual perversion, masculinity, and pilgrimage, an issue that has been obscured by a lack of attention to the discourses and social practices surrounding medieval devotional travel. The theoretical paradigm about pilgrimage that is most readily available to medievalists, the notion of pilgrimage as a "liminal" or "liminoid" phenomenon, does allow some insight into masculine self-fashioning, but like the notion of "normativity," its strong metaphysical orientation and its sheer heuristic power have the potential to displace a consideration of medieval social practice. Although they might seem to have little in common, both "normativity" and "liminality" owe a great debt to a branch of anthropological theory that likens events in social life to drama. This analogy has been criticized within anthropological circles precisely for its overinvestment in the form of social phenomena and its inability to discuss the content of those phenomena.[4] In the case of Chaucer, the "content" that might be better understood is precisely the gender and sexual politics that inform and surround the Pardoner's performance and the Host's reaction to it. This essay acknowledges the strengths of "normativity" and "liminality" while also providing an indication of how comparing the *Canterbury Tales'* representations of lived spaces to those of

---

[4] Clifford Geertz writes of this analogy: "It can expose some of the profoundest features of social process, but at the expense of making vividly disparate matters drably homogeneous." Geertz, *Local Knowledge: Further Essays in Interpretive Anthropology,* 3rd ed. (New York: Basic Books, 2000), pp. 26–30, at 28.

other medieval texts might generate new insights into Chaucer's treatment of gender and devotional travel.[5]

Strange Bedfellows

And smale foweles maken melodye,
That slepen al the nyght with open ye
(So Priketh hem nature hir corages),
Thanne longen folk to goon on pilgrimages
    —Chaucer, *Canterbury Tales* (I.9–12)

ROMEO Have not saints lips, and holy palmers, too?
JULIET Ay, pilgrim, lips that they must use in prayer.
—William Shakespeare, *Romeo and Juliet* (1.5.98–99)[6]

Carolyn Dinshaw has shown that the opening lines of the *General Prologue* (I.1–11) advance a vision of the cosmos as inescapably and pervasively heterosexual.[7] Dinshaw further suggests that, in shifting from the heterosexual cosmos to the pilgrimage trail in line 12 of the *General Prologue,* Chaucer's poem founds pilgrimage as a "humanly *heterosexual*" institution.[8] As David Wallace has observed of the same lines, the poem's abrupt shift from the unbridled cosmic eros of the dream vision to the finite spaces of Chaucer's England generates the "surprising" assertion that what "folk are said to 'longen' to do" is go on pilgrimage.[9] Both Dinshaw and Wallace alert us to the manner in which the juxtaposition of the abstract, universal space associated with courtly dream vision with the quotidian space of fourteenth-century England generates

---

[5] Morton W. Bloomfield was perhaps the first person to argue that reading the *Canterbury Tales* alongside nonfictional pilgrimage narrative might open up interesting vistas in his "Authenticating Realism and the Realism of Chaucer," *Thought* 39 (1964): 348. Donald Howard's *Writers and Pilgrims: Pilgrim Narrative and Its Posterity* (Berkeley and Los Angeles: University of California Press, 1980) and Christian K. Zacher's *Curiosity and Pilgrimage: The Literature of Discovery in Fourteenth-Century England* (Baltimore: Johns Hopkins University Press, 1976) took Bloomfield's lead and in the process showed the shortcomings of a narrowly allegorizing approach to the pilgrimage frame that reads it exclusively as a figuration of man's journey through life.

[6] Stephen Greenblatt, gen. ed., *The Norton Shakespeare* (New York: W. W. Norton, 1997), p. 888.

[7] Dinshaw, *Getting Medieval,* pp. 117–21.

[8] Ibid., pp. 272–73 n. 9, emphasis is Dinshaw's.

[9] David Wallace, *Chaucerian Polity: Absolutist Lineages and Associational Forms in England and Italy* (Stanford: Stanford University Press, 1997) p. 67.

the unexpected correlation of unbridled libidinous drive with the devotional practice of pilgrimage.

However, the "surprise" that Wallace detects in the yoking of *libido* and *peregrinatio* might not have constituted much of a novelty for Chaucer's readership. Reading the opening lines of the *General Prologue* alongside medieval representations of pilgrimage reveals a widespread association of holy travel with erotic desire, particularly types of desire that presented alternatives to clerical celibacy and marital monogamy. Rather than conceive of the Canterbury pilgrimage as an inherently heterosexual undertaking haunted by the marginalized figure of the Pardoner, I am interested in exploring what kind of readings of the Pardoner's place in the *Canterbury Tales* might result from denying ourselves recourse to the concept of "heteronormativity,"[10] and to a certain metanarrative in which the oppositional "queer" emerges from within and in opposition to an abstracted and unbounded "norm," the latter concept often serving to displace medieval texts' complex treatments of gender and desire as they relate to institutional and lived spaces, spaces like the road from Southwark to Canterbury.

Initially, there would seem to be considerable warrant to assume a view of pilgrimage as a metaphor for "heterosexual" erotics. Thanks in no small part to the celebrated first encounter between the two star-crossed protagonists of Shakespeare's *Romeo and Juliet,* pilgrimage has become linked in the modern mind to heterosexual romance. Indeed, Shakespeare was heir to a venerable literary trope that figured heteroerotic pursuit as a pilgrimage. Book IX of *The Romance of the Rose* allegorizes the violent conquest of a virgin as a peregrination along a stubbornly narrow trail. Both poet Eustache Deschamps and priest Olivier Maillard argued that women went on pilgrimage for the express purpose of cuckolding their husbands; the former wrote in his *Miroir de Mariage:* "If I say; keep the house / She objects with pilgrimage. / She

---

[10] Karma Lochrie has questioned the utility of the concepts of "heteronormativity" and even "heterosexuality," for the study of the European Middle Ages. Modern medical and sexological notions of "normal" sexuality and the ideology of heteronormativity (both of which focus exclusively on the gender of the subject's sexual partner) bear little resemblance to medieval notions of sodomy, in which the gender of one's sexual partner was but one of many factors defining "unnatural" vs. "natural" sex. See her *Heterosyncrasies: Female Sexuality When Normal Wasn't* (Minneapolis: University of Minnesota Press, 2005), especially "Introduction: the Heterosyncratic," pp. xi–xxviii.

has to go to St. Denis! / There they mock married men."[11] Chaucer's English contemporaries looked askance at pilgrimage for similar reasons. William Langland's *Piers Plowman* depicts "Eremites on a hep with hokede staues" that "Wenten to Walsyngham and here wenches aftir" (Prologue, lines 51–52).[12] In 1407, Wycliffite preacher William Thorpe ran afoul of the Archbishop of Canterbury when he objected that pilgrimage was spiritually insalubrious because of the money that pilgrims spent on the services of innkeepers and prostitutes.[13] Chaucer's Wife of Bath confesses that she travels on pilgrimage to engage in "daliance" (III.565), and the Host asks the drunken Cook why he is so fatigued on the pilgrimage trail: "Hastow had fleen al nyght, or artow dronke? / Or hastow with some quene al nyght yswonke" (IX.17–18)? Margery Kempe reports that she and her husband became the objects of local gossip when they were suspected of using pilgrimage as a smokescreen for sexual congress after they had taken vows of marital celibacy.[14]

Other forms of medieval travel, particularly mercantile travel (one need think of Boccaccio's *Decameron* or Marco Polo's description of Asian brothels), were also understood as presenting the chance to engage in types of sexual congress not available at home, but it was the gap between the holy intentions of the pilgrim and his or her actions that is perhaps responsible for the singling out of pilgrimage as a vehicle for sexual transgression. The notion that the practice of pilgrimage might thwart the intentions with which the pilgrim undergoes the hardships of travel is evident in Guibert of Nogent's twelfth-century autobiography. Guibert relates an early version of what became a popular miracle. A man goes on pilgrimage to Santiago to atone for his venial sins. Among the items he carries are two of his female lover's undergarments, which Guibert intimates serve as props in the traveler's autoerotic sports. The

---

[11] Quoted in Jean Verdon, *Travel in the Middle Ages,* trans. George Holoch (Notre Dame: University of Notre Dame Press, 2003), p. 218. Verdon assembles similar viewpoints, mostly from late medieval France, and also presents fascinating anecdotes about the sexual transgressions of actual pilgrims, including a group of pilgrims reprimanded in Orléans for dancing in a church with women, one of them a known prostitute (see p. 217). For numerous English examples of sexually transgressive female pilgrims, see Susan Signe Morrison, *Women Pilgrims in Late Medieval England: Private Piety as Public Performance* (New York: Routledge, 2000), pp. 106–27.

[12] George Russell and George Kane, eds., *Piers Plowman: The C Version* (London: Athlone Press, 1997).

[13] Alfred Pollard, ed., *Fifteenth-Century Prose and Verse* (New York: A. Constable, 1903), p. 140.

[14] *The Book of Margery Kempe,* trans. and ed. Lynn Staley (New York: W. W. Norton, 2001), p.31.

devil appears to the masturbating pilgrim disguised as Saint James and convinces him to castrate himself. The pilgrim dies as a result, but his corpse is revived thanks to the intercession of Saint James, although his sinful member is not.[15]

As the miracle of the masturbating pilgrim suggests, pilgrimage was frequently associated with sexual acts that would be grouped under the medieval category of sodomy, an expansive rubric, which, as Mark Jordan has shown, gathered under one umbrella term an astonishing array of previously unrelated sexual transgressions, including masturbation.[16] In tracing Shakespeare's use of the pilgrimage metaphor back to medieval poetic conventions and polemical concerns regarding the erotic opportunities available to pilgrims, it might be easy to lose sight of the fact that what all of these "heterosexual" conceptions of pilgrimage have in common is that they couple devotional travel with expressions of desire that transgress proper conjugal monogamy and sacerdotal celibacy: adultery, prostitution, clerical concubinage.

The link between sexual transgression and pilgrimage was pervasive in medieval Europe, and it is within this context that we should understand the "heterosexual" courtly poetics of pilgrimage to which Shakespeare is heir; they are part of a larger ideological armature that yoked together disparate forms of erotic transgression, many of them "sodomitical," with the practice of holy travel. In fact, nonfictional pilgrimage accounts frequently demonstrate a fascination with or intimate knowledge of sodomitical desire. Fifteenth-century knight and would-be international playboy Arnold Von Harff includes for his reader a series of phrases in Albanian, Turkish, Breton, Hebrew, and Arabic that should prove useful to the German-speaking traveler who might want to have sex with non-Christian women while having his clothes laundered.[17] In-

---

[15] Guibert of Nogent, *Self and Society in Medieval France,* ed. and trans. John F. Benton (Toronto: University of Toronto Press, 1996), pp. 218–19. The idea that traveling men might use their lover's garments to masturbate on the road could be at play in another twelfth-century text, *The Life of Christina of Markyate.* When Christina's companion and confessor Geoffrey is called to Rome, he asks her for two of her undergarments "not for his pleasure but to mitigate the hardships of his journey" [*non ad voluptatem sed ad laboris relevandum sudorem*]. Christina ultimately refuses his request. See C. H. Talbot, ed. and trans., *The Life of Christina of Markyate, Twelfth-Century Recluse* (Toronto: University of Toronto Press, 1998), pp. 160–61.

[16] Mark Jordan, *The Invention of Sodomy in Medieval Christian Theology* (Chicago: University of Chicago Press, 1997).

[17] Malcom Letts, trans., *The Pilgrimage of Arnold Von Harff, Knight, from Cologne through Italy, Syria, Egypt, Arabia, Ethiopia, Nubia, Palestine, Turkey, France, and Spain, which he accomplished in the years 1496–1499* (London: Palestine Pilgrims' Text Society, 1946), pp. 77, 90–91, 249, 284.

tercourse between Christians and Jews or Muslims was, like only the most "unnatural" of sexual transgressions, routinely prohibited in medieval civic and Canon law on pain of death.[18] Felix Fabri, also traveling to Jerusalem at the end of the fifteenth century, anxiously reports rumors that Venetian galley slaves have sex with one another,[19] and Pero Tafur, also traveling in the fifteenth century, reported seeing the ruins of three Mediterranean cities that were destroyed because of their inhabitants' sodomitical practices.[20] In fact, the invitation to imagine homosex among the ruins of ancient cities was institutionalized as part of the Christian pilgrimage to Jerusalem, which included an obligatory stop in Sodom and Gomorrah. The cities were such a must-see that when Tafur's company decided to bypass this part of their pilgrimage, he hired a guide to take him on a private tour of their ruins.[21]

The manner in which another text imagines the erotics of the pilgrimage trail, the *Codex Calixtinus,* which contains both an early version of the masturbating pilgrim miracle as well as a guide for pilgrims who wish to visit Santiago de Compostela, sheds light on some overlooked aspects of the *Canterbury Tales'* poetics of male embodiment. The *Codex* exists in thirteen copies, dating from around 1130 to the early sixteenth century.[22] The *Guide* provides practical information for the aspiring pilgrim: the major roads that lead to Santiago, the shrines that can be

---

[18] James A. Brundage, *Law, Sex, and Christian Society in Medieval Europe* (Chicago: University of Chicago Press, 1987), pp. 461–62; 518. See also David Nirenberg, *Communities of Violence: The Persecution of Minorities in the Middle Ages* (Princeton: Princeton University Press, 1996), pp. 125–65.

[19] Aubrey Stewart, trans., *The Wanderings of Felix Fabri* (New York: Palestine Pilgrims' Text Society, 1896), vols. 7–10, p. 46.

[20] Pero Tafur, *Travels and Adventures,* ed. and trans. Malcom Letts (London: George Routledge & Sons, 1926), pp. 53, 142. See also Benjamin Liu, "Affined to Love the Moor: Sexual Misalliance and Cultural Mixing in the *Cantigas d'escarnho e de mal dezir,*" in *Queer Iberia,* ed. Gregory S. Hutcheson and Josiah Blackmore (Durham: Duke University Press, 1999), pp. 48–72. Liu argues that travel to Muslim-controlled lands, including Jerusalem, was associated with sodomy in the satiric Galician-Portuguese poetry.

[21] Tafur, *Travels and Adventures,* p. 59.

[22] The *Codex* is also known as the *Liber Sancti Jacobi* and most copies of it contain the liturgy and miracles of Saint James, the pilgrim's guide, and the *Pseudo-Turpin Chronicle.* For the most part, copies of the earliest manuscript, housed at the cathedral of Santiago de Compostela, seem to have been commissioned by bishops and monastic communities. See Paula Gerson, Jeanne Krochalis, and Alison Stone, eds., *The Pilgrim's Guide: A Critical Edition* (London: Henry Miller Publishers, 1998), for their discussion of the possible origins and the reception history of the pilgrim's guide and its accompanying texts. All citations of the *Codex Calixtinus* in Latin and in English are drawn from this edition and translation and will be cited parenthetically in the body of the essay.

visited along each one, the best places to buy provisions, and a description of the city and its cathedral; in this regard, it offers its readers information not unlike other medieval texts written for those planning a pilgrimage. Chapter Seven of the *Guide,* however, makes an atypical move. Entitled *De nominibus terrarum et qualitatibus gencium que in ytinere sancti iacobi habentur* ["The Names of the Lands and the Characteristics of the Peoples on the Road to Santiago"], the chapter takes an ethnographic turn, casting a scandalized yet palpably enthralled eye on the sexual perversions of the Gascon, Basque, and Navarrese inhabitants whom the pilgrim can expect to encounter on his way to Compostela. Of the Gascons, the author observes: "They eat and drink liberally and are poorly dressed, and they all lie down together on a bed of dirty rotting straw—the servants with the master and mistress" (23). The Basque and Navarrese stand accused of much more sordid offenses such as eating without utensils and exposing their genitals to one another in public (29). Moreover: "Nauarri etiam utuntur fornicatione incesta pecudibus. Seram enim Nauarrus ad mule sue et eque posteriora suspendere dicitur, ne alius accedat sed ipse. Vulue etiam mulieris et mule basia prebet libidinosa" (28). [The Navarrese even practice unchaste fornication with animals. For the Navarrese is said to hang a padlock behind his mule and his mare, so that none may come near her but himself. He even offers libidinous kisses to the vulva of woman and mule (29)]. The rustic pleasures paraded before the view of the would-be pilgrim alert him to the perfidy he will encounter in his travels, suggesting that he minimize his contact with the populations along the trail. Yet, the vivid detail with which the author issues his alarm, ostensibly intended to help readers arrive at their destination unscathed, might possibly incite from the *Guide's* readership as much longing as it does loathing. One can well imagine to what use the information about the sexual mores of the countryside could be put by the enterprising reader and pilgrim.

Although the twelfth-century *Guide* seems less than concerned about the erotics of reader relations, its construction of ethnographic authority proves to be a much more delicate enterprise,[23] particularly as it involves

---

[23] By "ethnographic authority" I mean the rhetorical tactics through which travelers convert their partial and power-charged contacts with other peoples into an authoritative and purportedly impartial representation of an entire "culture." Anthropologists in particular have been concerned with the manner in which their discipline has established and fiercely guarded research and writing conventions that efface the power negotiations between the professional ethnographer and his or her objects of study. See Johannes

the body of the pilgrim-author. On the one hand, the author bases the authority of his description of the "peoples along the road to Santiago" on having seen and heard them himself, thus allowing him to claim: "Si illos comedere uideres, canibus edentibus uel porcis eos computares. Sique illos loqui audieres, canum latrancium memorare" (28). [If you saw them eat, you would think them dogs and pigs. If you heard them speak, you would be reminded of the barking of dogs (29).] Yet, as we have already seen, when reporting the Navarrese attraction to farm animals, the author bases the truth of what he reports not on having witnessed it, but on having heard of it from unspecified sources (i.e., "It is said that . . ."). The shifting strategies by which the author positions himself as an authority on the sexual customs of the Gascons, Basques, and Navarrese in part secures the integrity of his own body while denigrating the bodies of those whom he has encountered in his travels. The impersonal grammatical construction "It is said that" makes it clear that the pilgrim-author did not see, watch, or enjoy the sight of man-on-mule action, but it also occludes the possible processes of inquiry through which he may have secured such information. This same chapter also offers a list of Basque words that is intended to demonstrate the barbarity of their language and culture (29), yet it also suggests that the author had more than passing contact with Basque people. In fact, like his knowledge of the eating and dwelling habits of the Basques, this diminutive Basque lexicon suggests the author's active pursuit of information about the peoples he encountered. The nature of that pursuit is obscured by the impersonal construction of "what is said about" the sexual practices of Navarrese men, rhetorically absolving the author of active probing of these matters and insulating his own body from sodomitical contact with those he encountered on the road to Santiago.

Such rhetorical strategies work to allay the fear that forms of sodomy that take animals and women as their objects might expand to interpo-

---

Fabian, *Time and the Other: How Anthropology Makes Its Object* (New York: Columbia University Press, 2002), and two books by James Clifford, *The Predicament of Culture: Twentieth-Century Ethnography, Literature, and Art* (Cambridge, Mass.: Harvard University Press, 1988) and *Routes: Travel and Translation in the Late Twentieth Century* (Cambridge, Mass.: Harvard University Press, 1997). The most far-reaching consideration of how such theoretical concerns affect the study of the Middle Ages is Kathleen Biddick's "The Devil's Anal Eye: Inquisitorial Optics and Ethnographic Authority," in *The Shock of Medievalism* (Durham: Duke University Press), pp. 105–34. See also Claire Sponsler, "Medieval Ethnography: Fieldwork in the European Past," *Assays: Critical Approaches to Medieval and Renaissance Texts* 7 (1992): 1–30.

late the male pilgrim. This anxiety is suggested more directly at various points in the *Guide:* "Et si quis transceuncium secundum eorum peticionem nummos illis dare noluerit, et iaculis illum percuciunt, et censum ab eo auferunt, exprobantes illum et usque ad femoralias exquirentes" (24). [And if someone passing through does not want to give them money in accordance with their demand, they both beat him with sticks and snatch away the assessed sum from him, upbraiding him and searching him down to his underwear (25).] The Basques not only rob male pilgrims, but also "uerum etiam ut asinos equitare et perimere solebant [were wont to ride them like donkeys and slay them]" (pp. 25–26).

Given the catalogue of perversions attributed to these people, the assertion that they are accustomed to ride (*equitare*) men like donkeys raises doubts about the literal register of this final accusation. Was the author subjected to the fondling and groping that he describes? Was he treated like a mule? How closely did he observe the customary genital exposure that he reports? Just how feculent *was* the straw in which master, mistress, and servant slept? These questions are held at bay through rhetorical techniques that distance the pilgrim-author's vulnerable flesh from the scene of intercultural encounter, an encounter (or rather a series of encounters) whose prose afterlife is authorized by the paradoxical assertion of its author's bodily *proximity to* the people that the *Guide* describes. Adultery, fornication, prostitution, homosexual encounter, masturbation, miscegenation, bestiality: medieval pilgrimage made for strange bedfellows.

Although the *Guide* was written some three centuries before Chaucer began his *Canterbury Tales,* its concern to shield the pilgrim's body from the taint of sodomy alerts us to a long-standing set of medieval assumptions about the carnal pleasures available in devotional travel and their destabilizing effects on the traveler's sense of identity, assumptions that must be kept in mind as we think about the Pardoner. Pilgrimage raises the possibility that one might become the object, or perhaps even the subject of, unspeakable urges, urges so transgressive that they confound the hierarchical binaries through which the traveling subject thinks itself: masculine/feminine, urban/rustic, literate/barbaric, human/animal, celibate/sodomite. This is a very different and much more dire image of pilgrimage than we see in devotional and conduct literature, and one much more similar to the pilgrimage frame of Chaucer's *Canterbury Tales* than would initially appear. Moralistic literature objects to the false pilgrim who realizes a concealed passion far from the strictures of home, but the Santiago *Guide* suggests an awareness that the very same material conditions that enabled sexual experimentation on the pilgrimage trail also posed a challenge to one's sense of self as it had been cultivated through the ideologies and social practices of the traveler's home. Relative anonymity and distance from local forms of surveillance, improvisational social interactions, and ad hoc sleeping arrangements were just some of the factors that made pilgrimage so alluring, and so perilous.

Placing Chaucer's pilgrimage in the context of other medieval European depictions of devotional travel, it is hard to imagine a setting for the *Canterbury Tales* that would have been *less* conducive to a sexual or gender-normalizing project. The reading of the pilgrimage trail in the *Canterbury Tales* as "heteronormative" might obscure just how multiple, tentative, and fragile are the masculinities-in-transit that Chaucer's poem depicts. Granted degrees of social and erotic freedom unlikely to be had at home, yet also displaced from the institutional, civic, and domestic spaces under whose aegis they emerge, these pilgrim masculinities cannot rely on the familiar frames in which they are fashioned and validated, and must continue to rearticulate themselves, sometimes violently, on the road to Canterbury.

Masculinities on the Road

Voyaging smoothly is a becoming, and a difficult, uncertain becoming at that.
—Gilles Deleuze and Félix Guattari, *A Thousand Plateaus*

It must be our aim not to deny or disavow masculinity, but to disturb its manifest destiny—to draw attention to it as a prosthetic reality—a "prefixing" of the rules of gender and sexuality; an appendix or addition, that willy-nilly, supplements and suspends a "lack-in-being."
—Homi K. Bhabha, "Are You a Man or a Mouse?"

Glenn Burger observes two impulses that are more present in Fragment VI of Chaucer's *Canterbury Tales* than anywhere else: the display of the male body and the foregrounding of the pilgrimage to Canterbury.[24] This is true from the outset of the Pardoner's confessional prologue, when he stops the pilgrimage to declare: "heere at this alestake / I wol bothe drynke and eten of a cake" (VI.321–22). Although the pilgrimage

[24] Burger, *Chaucer's Queer Nation*, p. 121; p. 242 n. 3.

frame normally registers time through cosmic or astrological discourses (as in the case of the opening lines of the *General Prologue* or in the Introduction of Fragment II, 1–14), or through recourse to monastic or liturgical time, here the time that it has taken for the Pardoner to speak his *Prologue* is registered as the time it has taken him to eat a cake and drink his ale; time on the pilgrimage trail is reckoned through the Pardoner's body.[25] Indeed, the two thematic tendencies that Burger detects in Fragment VI collide spectacularly in the wake of the Pardoner's infamous overture to the Host to "Unbokele anon thy purs" (945) and kiss his "relikes everychon, / Ye, for a grote" (944–45). The Host, suspecting some lascivious word-play in the nouns *purs* and *relikes* unleashes his fury:

> "Nay, nay!" quod he, "thanne have I Cristes curs!
> Lat be," quod he, "it shal nat be, so theech!
> Thou woldest make me kisse thyn olde breech,
> And swere it were a relyk of a seint,
> Though it were with thy fundement depeint!
> But, by the croys which that Seint Eleyne fond,
> I wolde I hadde thy coillons in myn hond
> In stide of relikes or of seintuarie.
> Lat kutte hem of, I wol thee helpe hem carie;
> They shul be shryned in an hogges toord!"
>
> (VI.946–57)

The relics that the Pardoner offers up for the host's devotion are the forgeries that he carries over his crotch in his *male* (I.694). The violence of the Host's threat to sever the Pardoner's *coillons* and turn them into relics suggests that he understands the Pardoner's invitation to kiss all of his *relikes* to carry with it a sodomitic overture and in fact makes what is implicit in the Pardoner's address to him painfully concrete. Carolyn Dinshaw has demonstrated that Chaucer is drawing on an episode from the *Romance of the Rose* in which Raison and Amant dispute the former's glossing of "reliques" as "coilles."[26] Chaucer provides the modestly educated Host with a sensitive intertextual ear, and here the fiction of the

[25] This is especially interesting in light of Barbara Page's observation that it is the Host who is repeatedly depicted as obsessed with reckoning time on the pilgrimage trail, a characteristic that she suggests characterizes his bourgeois masculinity. See her "Concerning the Host," *ChauR* 4 (1970): 1–13.

[26] Dinshaw, *Chaucer's Sexual Poetics*, p. 169.

Canterbury pilgrimage is, as many critics have pointed out, complicit in what we might call homophobic violence. Whether or not the Pardoner offers his relics in this manner, the Host seizes on the possibility of sodomitic encounter on the pilgrimage trail (and significantly, as we shall see, in an alehouse) to provide himself with the occasion for a drama of masculine self-definition, a performance that, like the posturing of the author of the *Guide to Santiago,* relies on the repudiation of sodomitic pleasure to cement his identity in the uncertain climate of the pilgrimage trail. More important, the Host's performance of masculinity has much more in common with the Pardoner's than has been generally acknowledged.

Queer readings of the Pardoner have offered intriguing insights into his performance of masculinity. Dinshaw characterizes him as a "fetishist" who "surrounds himself with objects—relics, sealed documents; even words, regarded as objects—which he substitutes for his own lacking wholeness."[27] Sturges, drawing on Dinshaw's interpretation, has seen the Host's threat of violence to the Pardoner as "a threat of exposure or unveiling," that "undermines the Pardoner's masculine authority . . . that deconstructs performative masculinity."[28] In Sturges's view, the Host's exposure of the Pardoner's fetishistic claim to phallic authority (what Dinshaw, via Freud, describes as the simultaneously naive and skeptical belief that the objects he carries can magically make him whole), secures the Host's masculinity by discrediting the Pardoner's.[29] Sturges sees this episode as a "symbolic castration," and the way he uses that Lacanian term differs from the way it is developed in the work of Slavoj Zizek, who argues that "symbolic castration" occurs not when someone is ritualistically divested of his or her phallic prop, but rather at the very moment in which the subject is invested with the power-generating phallic supplement, since this investment points to the gap between one's body and the power claims that one makes through it.[30] As I will suggest, Zizek's exegesis of Lacan provides another way to look at the violent episode that concludes the Pardoner's performance, and especially its setting on the pilgrimage trail.

An assumption common to many analyses of the Pardoner is that

[27] Ibid., p. 159.
[28] Sturges, *Chaucer's Pardoner and Gender Theory,* p. 75.
[29] Also see Kruger, "Claiming the Pardoner," p. 136.
[30] *Organs Without Bodies: On Deleuze and Consequences* (New York: Routledge, 2004), pp. 87–93.

we can learn a lot about the construction of masculinity through his catastrophic bid for phallic authority, which brings to mind Judith Halberstam's observation that masculinity "becomes legible as masculinity when it leaves the white male middle-class body,"[31] that is to say, when it is claimed by bodies with which it is not routinely associated. Halberstam argues that the "naturalization" of masculinity, the manner in which it is seen to effortlessly inhere in the bodies of a small and empowered group of men, masks the manner in which that group's "heroic" masculinity depends "on the subordination of alternative masculinities"[32]—those of the poor, the nonwhite, the nonstraight, and the nonmale. One might see in the standoff between the Host and the Pardoner a gruesome allegory of Halberstam's theory. Readers of the *Canterbury Tales* could view the Host's threat as a window onto the more subtle strategies by which "heroic" or dominant masculinities parasitically feed on "alternative" ones. Although several analyses of the Host's tirade state that, as Halberstam demonstrates, there are multiple *masculinities,* they focus exclusively on the Pardoner's performance of masculinity as fetishistic, as stemming from a sense of bodily or psychological lack, while the Host's is read as antifetishistic, as following a much less tortuous path to self-realization. If, as both Halberstam and Bhabha have argued, dominant masculinities, like all masculinities, are essentially prosthetic, they secure their "manifest destiny" through denying their reliance on "prostheses" and projecting that reliance onto others. Following the logic of their compelling arguments, one must wonder if the critical propensity to focus on the "fetishistic" construction of the Pardoner's masculinity unintentionally perpetuates the ideologies that safeguard masculinity as the property of socially enfranchised, "biologically" male, bodies.[33] If modern Euro-American societies have strung a

---

[31] Judith Halberstam, *Female Masculinity* (Durham: Duke University Press, 1998), p. 2.

[32] Ibid., p. 1.

[33] In devoting an almost exclusive interest in the manner in which the Pardoner claims, or fails to claim, status as a masculine subject, antihomophobic readings run the risk of aligning themselves with inter- and trans-phobic assessments such as Eugene Vance's, who views the Pardoner's crotch as "deficient." Vance, "Chaucer's Pardoner: Relics, Discourse, and Frames of Propriety" in *NLH* 20 (1988–89): 741–43. In a fascinatingly sympathetic reading of the Pardoner, Lee Patterson argues that the Pardoner is "lacking sexual organs . . . that allow him to assert a straightforward gender identity," *Chaucer and the Subject of History* (Madison: University of Wisconsin Press, 1991), p. 397. Patterson seems to assume that sexual organs are the sole basis upon which one can "assert a straightforward gender identity"—in this case, masculinity, which aligns his reading of the Pardoner with the logic that Halberstam dismantles, a logic that has also been critiqued by intersex and transgender theorists and activists.

velvet rope around Masculinity for an elite few to enjoy by discrediting alternative masculinities as derivative and prosthetic, all the while denying Masculinity's own reliance on both prostheses and the masculine variations that it impugns, then it would seem worthwhile to consider to what extent the Host's masculinity participates in the same fetishistic fantasies as the masculinity that it "unmasks," and why it is that its prosthetic nature has for so long evaded critical scrutiny.

In attempting to answer this question, I return to Burger's observation that the pilgrimage frame is brought to the fore in Fragment VI to a peculiar degree, and this is especially so in the confrontation between the Pardoner and the Host. Not only does the language of the Host's threat draw on images related to the pilgrimage (relics, monstrances, processions—and in its reference to the Pardoner's *breech* it may even refer to Saint Thomas's venerated hair pants at Canterbury),[34] but the Pardoner's overture to the Host is prefaced by an effort to convince his fellow pilgrims of the benefits of making an offering to his relics by highlighting the perils inherent in travel:

> Paraventure ther may fallen oon or two
> Doun of his hors and breke his nekke atwo.
> Looke which a seuretee is it to yow alle
> That I am in youre felaweshipe yfalle,
> That may assoile yow, bothe moore and lasse,
> Whan that the soule shal fro the body passe.
>
> (VI. 936–40)

Here, the Pardoner brandishes with little subtlety his "male" full of fetishes in an attempt to secure a degree of masculine authority above both the "moore" and the "lasse" (VI. 939). Indeed, his "male" resting in his lap assumes the appearance of the phallus as explicated by Slavoj Zizek: "And one has to think of the phallus not as the organ that immediately expresses the vital force of my being, my virility, and so forth but, precisely, as such an insignia [i.e., a royal scepter] . . . phallus is an 'organ without a body' that I put on, which gets attached to my body, without ever becoming its 'organic part,' namely, forever sticking out as its incoherent, excessive supplement."[35] That the Pardoner makes his

---

[34] Daniel Knapp, "The Relyk of a Seint: A Gloss on Chaucer's Pilgrimage," *ELH* 39 (1972): 1–26.

[35] *Organs Without Bodies,* p. 87.

boldest bid for masculine authority by pointing to his relic-laden male, that excessive supplement, at the same time that he draws attention to the perils that pilgrimage poses to the body; that the Host threatens the Pardoner's body through a rhetoric laden with images of objects and practices associated with pilgrimage warrant a closer examination of the implications that the pilgrimage setting has for the interpretation of the Host and Pardoner's below-the-belt imbroglio.

The Pardoner's phallic push, so to speak, is reminiscent of an encounter narrated in the nonfictional pilgrimage account of Pero Tafur, a Castilian knight who traveled to Constantinople and back in the 1430s. On his way back to Spain, Tafur has an altercation with a German noble who has confiscated his sword and claimed later to have lost it. Although Tafur's German foe offers to replace the lost sword with one of his own, Tafur threatens to return to Germany with fellow Spaniards to avenge this affront. For readers of Pero Tafur's narrative, his uncompromising insistence on having his sword and no other seems odd in light of his flexibility in other sumptuary matters: he dons Muslim dress to enter a mosque in Jerusalem, grows a beard so lengthy that it offends his compatriots, and dons his king's livery at strategic moments. Tafur's conflict in Germany is best understood as an attempt to assert his status as a Knight by insisting on the inseparability of his sword from his body; the sword becomes, in Zizek's words, an "incoherent, excessive supplement." Like Tafur, the Pardoner as a traveling subject positions himself relative to those he encounters along the way by cleaving fetishistically to the objects through which he is invested with institutional and masculine authority; in fact, the sword was as inseparable from knightly identity in fifteenth-century Castile as pardons were from Pardoners.[36] Just as Tafur's sword takes on an almost incomprehensible

---

[36] For this episode, see Tafur, *Travels and Adventures,* pp. 205–8. In fifteenth-century Castile, the ritual of the investment of arms had become the single most defining mark of knighthood. N. R. Porro, *La investidura de armas en Castilla del Rey Sabio a los católicos* (Valladolid: Junta de Castilla y León, 1998), pp. 30–37. Relics are another question entirely. Sigfried Wenzel, "Chaucer's Pardoner and His Relics," *SAC* 11 (1989), argues that the association of pardoners with fake relics was not as uncommon as scholars of Chaucer have maintained. Alfred L. Kellogg and Louis A. Haselmeyer, "Chaucer's Satire of the Pardoner," *PMLA* 66 (March 1951): 251–77, made the influential but mistaken argument that Chaucer's coupling of his Pardoner with fake relics was unique. Jill Mann cited several continental examples of this association in *Chaucer and Medieval Estates Satire: The Literature of Social Classes and the General Prologue of the "Canterbury Tales"* (Cambridge: Cambridge University Press, 1973), pp. 149–51; and J. J. Jusserand, *English Wayfaring Life in the Middle Ages,* 2nd ed. (London: Unwin, 1920), cites several English examples on pp. 316–25.

importance in the dispute that he narrates, so too does the Pardoner's bag of tricks in the *Canterbury Tales*. Both travelers believe in the power of the objects that they annex to their bodies to constitute them as subjects and guarantee them recognition of their claims to social precedence on the basis of gender, estate, and other axes of social differentiation.

It might seem too obvious to cite Judith Butler's now-axiomatic assertion that gender identity is performative.[37] What is often not taken into account in elaborations of Butler's formulation is the fact that the gestures, utterances, and acts that create the illusion of a gendered subject rely crucially on the spaces in which they unfold.[38] In order for a

[37] Butler first explored these ideas in *Gender Trouble: Feminism and the Subversion of Identity* (New York: Routledge, 1989), but her subsequent work over the last fifteen years has continued to revise and expand on the implications of her insight, most recently in *Undoing Gender* (New York: Routledge, 2004).

[38] The community of literary scholars that has done so much to craft and advance queer-affirmative ways of reading Middle English literature faces a methodological challenge: some of the most heuristically powerful formulations of queer theory itself require a careful retooling when brought to bear on the embodied social practices of sexual dissidents and gender minorities. Judith Butler's argument about the performative nature of gender is essentially temporal: it seeks to revise the cause-and-effect narrative in which bodily "sex" precedes and provides the building blocks for "gender." The "disembodied" nature of much of Butler's theory has been discussed by her critics and acknowledged by Butler herself. See Butler's *Undoing Gender,* p. 198. Butler's influence on the study of gender and sexual desire in medieval literature has been, of course, enormous, and it is no coincidence that this body of criticism has focused to a great extent on questions of temporality rather than space. Carolyn Dinshaw's "touch across time" from *Getting Medieval* is a good example of the powerful way queer theory can be used to rethink affective sentiments across vast historical divides. See also the essays in *Queering the Middle Ages,* ed. Glenn Burger and Steven F. Kruger (Minneapolis: University of Minnesota Press, 2001), especially the editors' provocative introduction, pp. xi–xxiii. Equally influential in the study of Middle English literature has been Eve Kosovsky Sedgwick's *Epistemology of the Closet* (Berkeley and Los Angeles: University of California Press, 1990), a book whose arguments harness their force from a culturally potent domestic-spatial metaphor whose universality has been called into question by the work of Gayatri Gopinath and José Quiroga, among others. Gopinath and Quiroga demonstrate the manner in which the critical commonplaces of queer theory, such as the "epistemology of the closet," are ill-equipped to deal with manifestations of queer desire and social practice in other societies, which emerge in relation to culturally distinct practices of dwelling and travel. See Gayatri Gopinath, "Homo-Economics: Queer Sexualities in a Transnational Frame," in *Burning Down the House: Recycling Domesticity,* ed. Rosemary Marangoly George (Boulder, Colo.: Westview Press, 1998), pp. 102–26; and José Quiroga, *Tropics of Desire: Interventions from Queer Latino America* (New York: New York University Press, 2000). Quiroga demonstrates how Euro-American ideas about the space of the "closet," and particularly the coercive and normalizing injunction to "come out" of it, ignore the living conditions and cultural realities of queer Latin Americans and Latino/a immigrants, and Gopinath demonstrates how an uncritical acceptance of Western assumptions about the "closet" as a space of secrecy and abjection might lead to misrepresentations of the erotic practices of non-Western cultures. For a rare

core gender identity to congeal to the point that it assumes the appearance of the *cause* of all of the little performances of which it is actually the *effect*, those performances must be considered by a group of people familiar with the signifying conventions that the performances are, in various ways, exploiting. Travel removes the gendered subject from the spaces in which his or her gender identity is prompted, staged, interpreted, and confirmed, potentially leading to the traveler's disquieting awareness of the contingency of the quotidian—the ritualistic, routine, even boredom-inducing means through which certain men and women lay claim to and perform their power and prestige. In short, travel can reiterate one's own "symbolic castration," the yawning gap between one's body and the power that one claims, following Zizek, at the very moment that one annexes symbols of power to it. Under such circumstances, the prostheses of masculinity, "incoherent, excessive supplements" are liable to come under unprecedented scrutiny and need shoring up.

If becoming a man or a woman is difficult work, it is all the more so in transit. But it is not just the Pardoner who testifies to the varying degrees to which gender performance must be recalibrated according to one's location. Charting the Host's career in masculinity across the numerous spaces that it fugitively inhabits in the *Canterbury Tales* dramatizes this point. The *General Prologue* states:

> A semely man OURE HOOSTE was withalle
> For to been a marchal in an halle.
> A large man he was with eyen stepe—
> A fairer burgeys was ther noon in Chepe—
> Boold of his speche, and wys, and wel ytaught
> And of manhod hym lakkede right naught.
> (I.751–56)

Not only is the Host described in terms that index the distance between his robust "manhod" and that of the Pardoner, whose portrait precedes the Host's, but his masculinity is also made intelligible to Chaucer's

---

consideration of gender, sexual desire, and medieval space, see Susan Schibanoff's fascinating examination of one medieval woman's attempt to combat and come to terms with the patriarchally imposed separation from her female lover: Schibanoff, "Hildegard of Bingen and Richardis of Stade: The Discourses of Desire," in *Same Sex Love and Desire Among Women in the Middle Ages,* ed. Francesca Canadé Sautman and Pamela Sheingorn (New York: Palgrave, 2001), pp. 49–85.

reader through reference to the spaces in which he would excel as a man: the aristocratic or royal "hall" and more specifically, in "Chepe," (Cheapside) London. If the aristocratic household or the urban topography of London provide the framework within which the Host's masculine authority is understood, it is perhaps because it is difficult to make a case for it at his home in Southwark.

Dispersed throughout the pilgrimage frame are references to the Host's wife Goodelief. The Host wishes she could have heard the tale of exemplary wifehood offered by the Clerk (IV.1212a–g), and later on aborts his "tale" about her abuses for fear that she will learn of his unflattering disclosure from one of the pilgrim company (IV.2419–40). The Host's abrupt discarding of the matter of his *tale* is probably not what most readers would expect from a man of such *boold* speech, yet Goodelief's shadow looms large on the pilgrimage trail to Canterbury, silencing the Host in a manner not unlike the manner in which we see him silence the Pardoner at the end of Fragment VI. Goodelief's mysterious power over the Host is clarified in his final description of their home life. He tells the pilgrim company that, when he fails to thrash their servants or when he does not assault the neighbors who fail to defer to her when she goes to Mass, Goodlief's ire is stirred to a fever pitch:

> Whan she comth hoom she rampeth in my face,
> And crieth, 'False coward, wrek thy wyf!
> By corpus bones, I wol have thy knyf,
> And thou shalt have my distaf and go spynne!'
> Fro day to nyght right thus she wol bigynne.
>
> . . . .
>
> For I am perilous with knyf in honde,
> Al be it that I dar nat hire withstonde,
> For she is byg in armes, by my feith:
> That shal he fynde that hire mysdooth or seith—
> But lat us passe awey fro this mateere.
>   (VII.1904–8; 1919–23)

In yet another aborted speech regarding his wife, the Host reveals the phallic supplement through which he fetishistically supplements his "lack-in-being": his knife. Although in public, the Host is "perilous with knyf in honde," at home it not only does him no good, but it actually becomes his greatest liability. Goodelief undermines her husband's masculine performance by suggesting that it is his knife alone that grants the Host his authority as man and as husband, that his body itself, evidently slight alongside hers, is no guarantee of that authority. In threatening to divest the Host of his knife and force him to take up the distaff, Goodelief comes close to enacting domestic mutiny.

Yet, the threat of wifely insurrection does not "unveil" the Host's fetishistic will-to-sufficiency. The revelation that the Host's claim to masculinity rests on rather shaky foundations does not annul that claim. Rather than deflating the Host's faith in his phallic insignia and the inevitability of the domestic and civic power that he claims through it, Goodelief's domestic "rebellion," in making explicit the brittle logic of her husband's masculine self-constitution, redoubles the power accorded to his phallic prop in the public sphere. It is, after all, to get the Host to perform masculinity in a certain way, to use his knife against the neighbors who have slighted his wife, that Goodelief demonstrates how much her husband stakes on so little. Although the scene described by the Host would seem to constitute a subversion of the power he claims through his masculinity within the home, it is within the domestic world that his phallic authority is scripted, and he is, at most, only its co-author.

One final but crucial point: as the Host's boast suggests, were Goodelief not so "byg in armes" he would silence her with his blade. Goodelief's comic belittling of her husband is conservative—even reactionary—in that it harnesses and ultimately confirms the power of a violent masculinity. What Chaucer offers here is a comic variation on a much more sinister and pervasive cultural understanding, in which public masculinities depend on the confirmation of their power through the exercise of violence in the domestic realm. Goodelief constitutes a phobic distortion of a domestic sphere, traditionally gendered as the realm of the (compliant and submissive) feminine, in which women (and servants [knaves], as the Host makes clear) live with the reality of violent coercion and retribution by those who claim phallic authority in the public sphere, whose claim to that public authority rests, in part, on their roles as master, husband, father. This reading of the spatial constructions of the Host's masculinity should not overlook the way that Chaucer's poem creates a domestic threat to masculinity that is, in fact, no more of a threat than the incalculable number of women, children, and servants who have had and continue to suffer violence in the places they call "home."

Inscribed by the *General Prologue* as displacement from courtly and civic spaces, assuming its contours in its movements between household and city, the Host's masculinity, like those of the Pardoner and of Pero Tafur, finds itself at a loss on the road, unmoored from the sites in and through which it thinks, performs, and enacts its power. If the Host's masculine prerogative is acknowledged in Southwark, it is because he successfully shuttles his performance of masculinity back and forth between the masculinized sphere of the street and the feminized world of the home. On the pilgrimage trail, the Host is far away from these markedly local spaces in which he negotiates his power (Southwark home and street) and in which the poem defines it (aristocratic hall, Cheapside). Under these conditions of displacement, the Host's knife, like the Pardoner's *male*, this "organ without a body," takes on an almost unconscionable centrality to his self-definition. It is the process of this "difficult, uncertain becoming" between Southwark and Canterbury that a focus on the spatial practices of the Host's masculinity asks us to entertain when we return our attention to the explosive conclusion of Fragment VI.

What escapes the notice of most analyses of this scene is that it is not only the Pardoner whose reliance on props is exposed, but also the Host's. His threat to cut off the *coillons* of the Pardoner implies the use of the phallic supplement through and around which he negotiates his masculine authority at home and in the public world of Southwark. Yes, the Pardoner's body is not enough to claim masculinity, but this is not because of his anatomical anomalies or his erotic disposition. In reaching for his knife, the Host demonstrates that no body is sufficient to claim masculinity in and of itself. This claim is crucially dependent on phallic props and a fetishistic relationship to them, that is to say, one that believes in their power as a source of plenitude yet also refuses to acknowledge dependence on them. The Host insists on the trumped-up nature of the Pardoner's masculinity, but the manner in which this passage of Fragment VI implies the use of the Host's knife without ever actually bringing it into sight suggests Chaucer's complicity in the degradation of the Pardoner. As we have seen, the most cherished stratagem through which masculinities orchestrate their transparency is by exposing other masculinities' reliance on bodily supplements while disavowing their own. We see such a dynamic at work in the Host's silencing of the

Pardoner, and the implicit presence of the Host's knife is part of a textual optic that foregrounds the prostheses of the "weakest link" in the chain of masculinity, while bringing into sight only flickers of the prosthesis of its "superior." For all of this, it would be shortsighted to assume that the Host ensconces himself amid this phallic panoply on the throne of heroic masculinity. This dubious honor must go to the Knight, who, in breaking up this fight, not only points out the excessive nature of the Host's reliance on his knife, but seemingly does so without any discernable phallic propping up:

> But right anon the worthy Knyght bigan
> Whan that he saugh that al the peple lough,
> "Namoore of this for it is right ynough!
> Sire Pardoner, be glad and myrie of cheere;
> And ye, sire Hoost, that been to me so deere,
> I prey yow that ye kisse the Pardoner.
> And Pardoner, I prey thee, drawe thee neer,
> And, as we diden, lat us laughe and pleye."
> Anon they kiste, and ryden forth hir weye.
> (VI.960–68)

Initially, it would appear that the Knight saves the day through his appeal to good manners alone. Yet, the language of his intervention creates a textual echo that suggests that he is using much more than a call for decorum to put an end to this conflict. The heated argument between the Host and the Pardoner is halted by the Knight's "Namoore," an interjection that takes us back to the Knight's *Tale,* at the point in which Theseus puts an end to Palamoun and Arcite's near-fatal struggle:

> And at a stert he was bitwix hem two,
> And pulled out a swerd and cride, "Hoo!
> Namoore, up peyne of lesynge of youre heed"
> (1.1705–8)![39]

The repetition of the imperative "Namoore" represents the Knight's fantastic invocation of the authority of the "fictional" Theseus, whom he himself has created, and who brandishes his sword to squelch the

---

[39] I would like to thank Frank Grady for this suggestion.

conflict between Palamoun and Arcite. The Knight's role-playing and the linguistic repetition on which it is founded calls oblique attention to his own lethal skill in arms, something that the *General Prologue* dwells on at great length. Even more indirectly than the Host, the Knight claims authority through alluding to the phallic prop (his weaponry) on which his masculinity is founded. The Pardoner's Prologue, Tale, and Epilogue move from the Pardoner, who calls attention to the technologies that found his masculinity, to the Host, who alludes obliquely to the technologies of his masculinity through a threat of violence against the Pardoner, to the Knight, who might implicitly threaten the armed violence associated with chivalric masculinities through the textual citation of his own *Tale*. This progression represents an increasing subtlety of self-assertion and disavowal, and suggests an understanding that the force of any masculinity derives in no small part from the stealth with which it appeals to its fetishes.

Fragment VI invites a consideration of the masculine body as a traveling body, as a body suspended between the institutional, domestic, and civic spaces in which it symbolically and materially justifies and exercises its power, and stages the delicate attempts at maintaining and making sense of that power away from home. In charting the articulations of the Host's masculine authority across the spaces of the household, the city street, and the pilgrimage trail, we are able to view the fetishistic logic that provides its foundation. By highlighting the similarities of this logic with the logic that underwrites the Pardoner's, and even the Knight's, claims to masculinity, we challenge the often unspoken conceptions of what counts as a "real" man, which have historically bristled with racist, sexist, class-based, and homo- and transphobic, bias.

Yet, in spite of these similarities between the Pardoner's and the Host's phallicizing tactics, they enact them in and as very different spatial maneuvers. Characterized predominately by kinesis, the Pardoner's masculinity takes shape between and among far-flung rural, civic, and institutional spaces. If the Host's gender identity is one that is unsettled by his occasional movement away from the urban center and domestic space of its origin, the Pardoner's is one that, owing to the nature of his profession, exists in an almost permanent state of movement between spaces, none of which can be posited as a site of origin.[40] The Pardoner

[40] In fact, the depiction of the Pardoner's traveling practices, devotional and professional alike, is central to Chaucer's overall strategy of creating this corrupt figure. Christian Zacher argues that the seriousness with which each of the pilgrims undertakes the

and the Host are, in effect, two sides of the same coin; both are figures through which Chaucer stages the challenge that travel poses to socially recognized expressions of phallic authority, the latter as an example of the limitations of locally fashioned masculinities and the former as evidence of travel's ability to give rise to new, socially pernicious gender identities.

The sense of dizzying kinesis that attends the Pardoner's gender performance is mirrored structurally in the circularity of his con act. The credence accorded to his bulls and relics rests on his tales of where he has been, tales that, in turn, gain credence through his presentation of the bulls and relics. In the Host, the *Canterbury Tales* offers a version of masculinity so enmeshed in modes of urban dwelling that its chain of citation strains as it is pulled away from its accustomed spatial frame. In the Pardoner, one observes a masculinity without a spatial frame at all, one that emerges in the interstices of institutional and jurisdictional spaces, one whose chain of citation unabashedly and troublingly loops back on itself. The Pardoner is associated with Rouncivale, a hospital at Charing Cross, but unlike the Host, his *General Prologue* portrait as well as his confessional monologue focuses more on his movement between spaces than it does his mode of dwelling in the city; in fact, the allusion to Rouncivale, an institution that became the subject of scandal in the later fourteenth century, reveals less about the Pardoner as an occupant of a city or an institution than it does about his perambulations.[41] According to the *General Prologue,* the Pardoner travels the length and breadth of England swindling lay people and clerics alike:

> But with thise relikes, whan that he fond
> A povre person dwellynge upon lond,
> Upon a day he gat hym moore moneye

---

pilgrimage is a good index of how Chaucer meant to portray them, and thus argues that the Wife of Bath and the Pardoner, as "negative" examples of pilgrimage, are the most outré of the Canterbury company. Rather than viewing Chaucer as a conservative apologist for the embattled institution of pilgrimage who uses the character of the Pardoner as a negative example of devotional travel, my reading focuses on the spatial trajectory of the Pardoner, the networks of mobility, and the practices of dwelling, in which Chaucer accomplishes the embodiment of this singular literary creation. Zacher, p. 93. See also David Lawton's "Chaucer's Two Ways: The Pilgrimage Frame of the *Canterbury Tales,*" SAC 9 (1987): 3–40, who argues that the use of the pilgrimage frame dramatizes the immorality of pilgrims such as the Wife of Bath and the Pardoner (p. 33).

[41] Kellogg and Haselmeyer, "Chaucer's Satire," pp. 251–77.

> Than that the person gat in monthes tweye;
> And thus, with feyned flaterye and japes,
> He made the person and the peple his apes.
>
> (I.701–5)

Although the countryside that provides the stage for the Pardoner's sacramental graft is here gendered masculine through the phonetic convergence of *person* (a gender-neutral noun meaning "person") and *person* (an always masculine noun meaning "parson"), this same countryside and the poverty by which it is defined is gendered feminine in the Pardoner's confessional prologue through its association with women and children:

> I wol have moneie, wolle, chese, and whete,
> Al were it yeven of the povereste page,
> Or of the povereste wydwe in a village,
> Al sholde hir children sterve for famine.
> Nay, I wol drynke licour of the vyne
> And have a joly wenche in every toun.
>
> (VI.448–53)

The human face that the Pardoner puts on the poverty of the "village" indexes the exorbitance of his greed, but it also demonstrates the manner in which his livelihood and his claim to phallic authority relies on the exploitation of disempowered women and children scattered throughout England.[42]

Chaucer's Pardoner avails himself of a logic that has prevailed in almost every culture until the late twentieth century: the gendering of voluntary travel as masculine and of dwelling as feminine. As Eric J. Leed's survey of the Western literary tradition has shown, masculinity has traditionally been associated with, and even *defined by*, the ability to cross political borders at will, while the hallmark of femininity has been

---

[42] David Wallace, *Chaucerian Polity*, discusses Chaucer's representations of what he calls the "powers of the countryside," the violent and sometimes miraculous means by which country folk in the *Canterbury Tales* resist the exploitation of city dwellers. The Pardoner's self-presentation vis-à-vis the rural world is more in line with the examples of unchallenged urban supremacy from Boccaccio's *Decameron*, also analyzed by Wallace, pp. 125–55.

"sessility," rootedness in the home.[43] The Pardoner draws on the association of travel with masculine power and of dwelling with disempowerment to conceive of his claims to authority over his victims, whom he figures resolutely as *dwellers:*

> First I pronounce whennes that I come,
> And thane my bulles shewe I, alle and some.
> Oure lige lordes seel on my patente,
> That shewe I first, my body to warente,
> That no man be so boold, ne preest ne clerk,
> Me to destourbe of Cristes hooly werk.
> And after that thane telle I forth my tales;
> Bulles of popes and of cardynales,
> Of patriarkes and bishopes I shewe,
> And in Latyn I speke a wordes fewe,
> To saffron with my predicacioun,
> And for to stire hem to devocioun.
>
> (VI.335–46)

It is the Pardoner's purported access to distant centers of ecclesiastical power that opens the door of the parish churches in which he bilks the poor and naive, in the process diverting the offerings that would go to the local parish priest into his swelling coffers. The priests and clerks that would object to the Pardoner's diversion of their parishes' revenues are forced to acquiesce to him because he has visited bishoprics and papal courts. The Pardoner's various bulls and seals attest to his having traveled to the courts of the highest-ranking members of the ecclesiasti-

---

[43] Eric J. Leed, *The Mind of the Traveler: From Gilgamesh to Global Tourism* (New York: Basic Books, 1991); Teresa de Lauretis has argued that the masculine monopoly on travel has not simply made it difficult for women to leave home on their own accord, but has formatively shaped Western epistemology and narratology. See her *Alice Doesn't: Feminism, Semiotics, Cinema* (Bloomington: University of Indiana Press, 1984). Janet Wolff and Caren Kaplan have both argued against the widespread use of travel metaphors in critical theory on the basis that the masculinist history of travel compromises the theoretical tools that would explain and critique Western cultural production. Wolff, "On the Road Again: Metaphors of Travel in Cultural Criticism," in *Cultural Studies* 7 (May 1993): 224–39, and Kaplan, *Questions of Travel: Postmodern Discourses of Displacement* (Durham: Duke University Press, 1996). Pilgrimage, especially to local shrines, is an exception to this rule, as the figure of Chaucer's Wife of Bath suggests. What is important here is the manner in which the Pardoner's speech positions him as an institutional traveler, while Chaucer's narrative casts him as a devotional traveler, perhaps suggesting Chaucer's undermining of the Pardoner's masculine self-fashioning through travel.

cal elite. These documents, like the *vernycle* he wears on his cap, are material proof of a mobility that his victims do not share and to which they must, on pain of institutional violence, defer. The physical proof of his travels "warente," or guarantee, the safety of the Pardoner's body from the physical violence of the provincial prelacy; it secures his phallic authority through the disempowerment of local priests and clerks. The first thing I do, says the Pardoner, is "pronounce whennes I come"—the Pardoner's traffic in relics and indulgences is enabled by his traffic in travel narrative. In these rural settings, the Pardoner usurps the thoroughly masculine discourse of the sermon (*predicacioun*), complete with its Latin tag phrases, from parish priests through a phallicizing discourse of travel narrative.[44] The Pardoner, in spite of the physical vulnerability or possibly "deficient" anatomy of his body, fashions a masculine identity in and through travel from civic and ecclesiastical centers to a remote and emasculated world of villages and towns.

The Pardoner's performance and its aftermath provide the occasion for the *Canterbury Tales'* most sustained exploration of the vulnerability of the types of masculine self-constitution that rely on quotidian forms of violence to achieve their sense coherence and to enforce their social precedence. Although most explorations of the Pardoner's gender have focused on the question of his anatomy or his sexual disposition, his appearance in Fragment VI precipitates a consideration, if not exactly a critique, of masculinity's dependence on its unabashed dominance of femininity and its less frequently acknowledged dominance of other masculinities. Indeed, in the context of Fragment VI, the Pardoner's sexuality is subsumed under his desire for dominance: the "wenches" he claims to desire are just one more example of the goods and privileges that he commands in the course of his coercive journeys. The Pardoner's

[44] As Kellogg and Haselmeyer showed, the medieval Papacy was concerned about the abuses of the Pardoner's real-life counterparts. The Fourth Lateran Council (1215) forbade Pardoners from preaching, and canon law emphatically defined pardoners as messengers who linked ecclesiastical centers and rural peripheries, not as preachers. See "Chaucer's Satire," pp. 255–61. Pardoners were, in fact, subject to the violent repulsion of local clerics, who questioned the latitude of their powers. It is within this context that I read the Pardoner's sermon as an usurpation. See also Alan J. Fletcher, "The Preaching of the Pardoner," *SAC* 11 (1989): 15–36, who argues that the form of the Pardoner's sermon would have caused suspicion among Chaucer's readers in the England of the 1390s. Alastair Minnis has pointed out that the Pardoner also usurps the ability to absolve sinners, a prerogative that belonged exclusively to ordained priests. See Minnis, "Reclaiming the Pardoners" *JMEMS* 33 (Spring 2003): 311–34. One can see the performative speech act of absolution as yet another way in which the Pardoner constructs himself as a gendered subject.

clash with the Host and its resolution at the hands of the Knight suggest an understanding of masculinity that is not principally defined by anatomy or what we would call sexual preference, although both play a role in the two combatants' self-fashioning and their sparring with each other. In short, pilgrimage presents each character with unique opportunities and challenges in the articulation of his identity. Each has a distinct relationship to pilgrimage, and their differential positions vis-à-vis pilgrimage suggest that pilgrims' liberation from conventionally defined hierarchies does not necessarily contribute to social harmony. The alehouse row of Fragment VI complicates one of the most influential theories regarding the relationship between self-fashioning and devotional travel: Victor and Edith Turners' characterization of Christian pilgrimage as a "liminoid" or "liminal" social practice.[45] Although the concept of "liminality" is routinely and usefully invoked, it is yet another example of a powerful theoretical tool whose metaphysics tend to overshadow a consideration of the specific ways that Chaucer represents medieval uses of space, and to cloud an understanding of his depiction of the gender politics of devotional travel, especially the experiences of women.

The Absent Tapster (The Limits of "Liminality")

"Once traveling is foregrounded as a cultural practice, then dwelling too needs to be reconceived—no longer simply the ground from which traveling departs and to which it returns."

—James Clifford[46]

A pilgrim is one who divests himself of the mundane concomitants of religion—which become entangled with its practice in the local situation—to confront, in a special "far" milieu, the basic elements and structures of his faith in their unshielded, virgin radiance.

—Victor and Edith Turner.[47]

The "liminality" of pilgrimage is something that readers of Chaucer and other medieval representations of devotional travel have long taken for granted. Victor and Edith Turner influentially argued that pilgrimage is akin to primitive rites of initiation that dramatized and ratified a

---

[45] Victor Turner and Edith L. Turner, *Image and Pilgrimage in Christian Culture* (New York: Columbia University Press, 1978).
[46] Clifford, *Routes: Travel and Translation in the Late Twentieth Century*, p. 44.
[47] Witter and Turner, *Image and Pilgrimage in Christian Culture*, p. 15.

change in status, for example, the transition from boyhood to manhood. Taking their cue from anthropologist Arnold van Gennep, the Turners posited three stages for such "social dramas": separation, margin or limen, and reaggregation.[48] According to the Turners, the pilgrim experience is universal: pilgrims leave behind the social hierarchies and conflicts of their home to participate in a corporate spiritual enterprise. In the time between their departure from and return to home (i.e., the "liminal" phase), there is a potential for forms of self-fashioning that are not held in thrall to the power structures of the pilgrims' homes and, under certain circumstances, might even subvert them entirely. More specifically, the pilgrim company is offered as an example of *communitas,* a "spontaneous" "liminal phenomenon" conspicuous for its "undifferentiated" and "egalitarian" social bonds.[49] In literary studies, recourse to the idea of "liminality" is both routine and uncritical of the ways that the Turners' theories have been received, critiqued, modified, and adapted in other disciplines. Anthropologists and historians have made two far-reaching criticisms of the concept of pilgrimage-as-liminoid-phenomenon: (1) in the way that this theory focuses on the institutional intentions behind pilgrimage rather than on the social practice of actual pilgrims, it tends to homogenize the spaces that the pilgrim traverses in the course of his or her journey, rendering invisible the differences in the ways that pilgrims can and do use specific spaces;[50] and (2) it distorts the understanding of women's roles in purportedly "liminoid" social practices, which are qualitatively so different from men's that they often

[48] Ibid, p. 249.
[49] Ibid., pp. 250–51.
[50] The fieldwork of anthropologist Michael Sallnow at rural pilgrimage shrines in the Peruvian Andes suggests that the Turners' ideas about the status-leveling inherent in the liminoid experience of pilgrimage not only would have distorted the evidence he had gathered, but were—quite simply—wrong. Sallnow found that pilgrimage led to an *intensification* of pilgrims' claims to social precedence over one another and was characterized by power-charged conflicts between the elites responsible for the maintenance of the shrines and the pilgrims who came to worship at them, which is to say that the shrine, more than any other space, was the setting for the most contentious identitarian and social struggles. Sallnow's conclusions call into question both the hypothesis of the suspension social contest in Christian pilgrimage, and also the suggestion that all spaces through which the pilgrim passes are equally "liminal." See Michael J. Sallnow, *Pilgrims of the Andes: Regional Cults in Cusco* (Washington D.C.: Smithsonian Institution Press, 1987). A collection of essays by anthropologists has suggested ways to correct and expand on the Turners' view of pilgrimage as a liminoid phenomenon. See John Eade and Michael J. Sallnow, eds., *Contesting the Sacred: The Anthropology of Christian Pilgrimage* (New York: Routledge, 1991).

cannot be recognized as "liminal" at all.[51] Although each critic approaches the Turners' influential theory from a different disciplinary standpoint, collectively their work poses the question of what is left of that theory once we take into account the social forces and practices that militate against the suspension of social hierarchy in pilgrimage. Together they show that, if pilgrimage can be called a liminal experience, then it is liminal at specific junctures, under certain conditions, and for certain people.

These objections to the universal claims of the Turners' theory raise two important questions for evaluating the frame of Chaucer's fictional pilgrimage: Are certain spaces more "liminal" than others, and if so, then for whom? The alehouse of Fragment VI is a place where such questions might be productively advanced. Paul Strohm has singled out the alehouse as a space that could, like its cousins the inn and the tavern, serve as a fraught setting for "occasion[s] of social redefinition."[52] Per-

[51] Caroline Bynum has argued against the imposition of the Turners' concept of liminality on the life-stories of female saints, stating that the apparent universality of their theory masks the fact that it is a theory derived from evidence left behind by "educated elites, aristocratic elites, and male elites." See her "Women's Stories, Women's Symbols: A Critique of Victor Turner's Theory of Liminality," in *Fragmentation and Redemption: Essays of Gender and the Human Body in Medieval Religion* (New York: Zone Books, 1991), pp. 27–53. Bynum also observes that, while the writing of elite males often organizes the life of its subject as a series of dramatic transitions and upward changes in status, women's life-writing is not as formatively shaped by the themes of "climax, conversion, reintegration, and triumph," but are rather quite conspicuous for their emphasis on the continuity of women's status, which she interprets as a symptom of women's "insignificance" to many medieval power structures. "Women's lives," argues Bynum, "are not liminal to women" (p. 32). Darlene M. Juschka's anthropological research suggests that there are material and cultural reasons why medieval women such as Margery Kempe might not have produced a pilgrimage account that unfolded as a classic narrative of separation, limen, and reaggregation. See Juschka, "Who's Turn Is It to Cook? Communitas and Pilgrimage Questioned," *Mosaic* 36 (December 2003): 189–204. For Juschka, the concept of *communitas* presupposes "a self unfettered by history, capable of being cast off temporarily in the experience of a more universal humanity," a fantasy that Juschka argues is not attainable for women, who are, even on the pilgrimage trail, reminded constantly in ways both nettling and traumatic of their subordinate status as women.
[52] Paul Strohm, "Three London Itineraries: Aesthetic Purity and the Composing Process," in *Theory and the Premodern Text* (Minneapolis: University of Minnesota Press, 2000), p. 10. Strohm shows how taverns play a decisive role in social constitution in three late medieval English texts. On the technical-legal differences between inns, taverns, and alehouses (often blurred in reality), see Peter Clark, *The English Alehouse: A Social History, 1200–1830* (London: Longman, 1983), p. 20. Donald Howard argued that the unnamed alehouse was an "abstract" marker in the landscape; unlike other Fragments, Fragment VI has no references to towns that help place it before or after any other another fragment and thus belonged, with its unsavory Pardoner, "to the no-man's land where it is." While the reference to the alehouse does not allow us to deter-

haps because they brought together transient persons for brief periods of time into novel situations of intimacy, alehouses, taverns, and inns seem especially apt stages for the types of egalitarian social bonds that the Turners characterize as typical of Christian pilgrimage.[53] However, when we compare Chaucer's depiction of the alehouse conflict of Fragment VI to other medieval depictions of taverns, alehouses, and inns, it would seem that "liminality" or *communitas* fail to illuminate several troubling facets of the gender politics of self-fashioning and communal bonding on the pilgrimage trail. Indeed, by comparing Chaucer's alehouse to other literary representations of drinking and sleeping establishments, one appreciates just how little the frame of the *Canterbury Tales,* like the Turners' anthropological study, has to say about the way pilgrims inhabit specific spaces in the course of their travels or the difference that gender makes in the way one experiences "liminality" or *communitas.*

Like Fragment VI of Chaucer's *Canterbury Tales,* Day 2 Novella 3 of Giovanni Boccaccio's *Decameron* tantalizes its readers with the possibility that there is something queer afoot. It also offers what could be considered a textbook case of male self-fashioning in the liminal space of an inn. In Boccaccio's narrative, Alessandro, a young man from a finan-

---

mine the proper placement of Fragment VI, it does, however, represent the only time that the pilgrim company stops at a specified location to listen to one of the pilgrim's performances and is significant because it serves as the setting for the most violent conflict of the Canterbury pilgrimage. Howard, *The Idea of the Canterbury Tales,* p. 338.

[53] Taverns, alehouses, and inns provide a strategic way to evaluate the strengths and weaknesses of the Turnerian concept of liminality precisely because such institutions, frequented by almost all medieval travelers, confound easy distinctions between travel and dwelling, a strict division on which the Turners' theory depends. Victor and Edith Turner characterize medieval Europe as a culture of decided stasis, in which pilgrimage affords Christians one of the only opportunities to leave the confines of the feudal village. See the Introduction of their *Image and Pilgrimage in Christian Culture,* pp. 1–39. The Europe of the Middle Ages was, as the Turners point out, more "localized" than it was in the twentieth century, in the sense that it was, for the most part, a collection of societies that thought allegiance and exercised power in political units that might be called pre- or subnational. However, the Turners' conception of a "localized" medieval Europe has an Epcot-like quality, painting it as an archipelago of self-contained rural backwaters. Through this spatializing fiction, the Turners fashion a "native" for their anthropological consideration of medieval pilgrimage, a maneuver that, in the discipline of academic ethnography, has often served to erase the cosmopolitan experiences of the people studied in the process of creating an "authentic" *ethnos* uncontaminated by cross-cultural contact. For a critique of anthropology's desire for a culturally isolated and pure "native," see Arjun Appaduri, "Putting Hierarchy in Its Place," *Cultural Anthropology* 3, no. 1 (1988): 36–49. Appaduri observes, "Natives, people confined to and by the places to which they belong, groups unsullied by contact with a larger world, have probably never existed" (p. 39).

cially troubled Florentine family, marries the daughter of the King of England. He first encounters his future wife when she is on her way to Rome, while she is masquerading as an abbot. Like the young merchant protagonist of *Decameron* 2.3, the reader is not aware that there is more to this abbot than meets the eye. Boccaccio teases his unknowing readers with intimations that the abbot's exchanges with Alessandro on the road to Rome are not quite platonic: "eventually [the Abbot] found himself level with Alessandro, who was very young, exceedingly good-looking and well-built, and the most well-mannered, agreeable and finely-spoken person you can imagine. The Abbot's first glimpse of Alessandro gave him more genuine pleasure than anything he had ever seen in his life."[54] Things do not really heat up until the traveling companions come upon "a town not very richly endowed with inns" (131).[55] Alessandro eventually secures lodging in a small *albergo,* whose tight quarters make it necessary for him to lie down next to the Abbot:

The Abbot, far from being asleep, was locked in meditation on the subject of certain newly aroused longings of his. . . . Having firmly made up his mind, he waited for complete silence to descend on the inn, then called out to Alessandro in a low voice, and firmly brushing aside the latter's numerous excuses, persuaded him to undress and lie down at his side. The Abbot placed one of his hands on Alessandro's chest, and then, to Alessandro's great astonishment, began to caress him in the manner of a young girl fondling her lover, causing Alessandro to suspect, since there seemed to be no other explanation for this extraordinary behavior, that the youth was possibly in the grip of some impure passion. (132)[56]

Alessandro's groping of the Abbot reveals to both him and Boccaccio's reader that the Abbot is a she, and a comely she at that. The two travel-

---

[54] Giovanni Boccaccio, *The Decameron,* trans. G. H. McWilliam (London: Penguin, 1972), p. 130. Subsequent citations will appear in the body of this essay. The Italian reads: *gli venne nel cammino presso di sé veduto Alessandro, il quale era giovane assai, di persona e di viso bellissimo, e, quanto alcuno altro esser potesse, costumato e piacevole e di bella maniera; il quale maravigliosamente nella prima vista gli piacque quanto mai alcuna altra cosa gli fosse piaciuta.* Italian cited from *The Decameron,* ed. Vittore Branca (Milan: Mondadori, 1985), p. 108.

[55] *a una villa la quale non era troppo riccamente fornita d'alberghi,* p. 108.

[56] *L'abate, il quale non dormiva anzi alli suoi nuovi disii fieramente pensava. . . . E deliberatosi del tutto di prenderlo, parendogli ogni cosa cheta per l'albergo, con sommessa voce chiamò Alessandro e gli disse che appresso lui si coricasse: il quale, dopo molte disdette spogliatosi, vi si coricò. L'abate, postagli la mano sopra il petto, lo 'ncominciò a toccare non altramenti che sogliano fare le vaghe giovani i loro amanti: di che Alessandro si maravigliò forte e dubitò non forse l'abate, da disonesto amor preso, si movesse a cosí fattamente toccarlo,* pp. 109–10.

ing companions vow to marry one another and then spend the night making love. Upon reaching Rome, the disguised bride reveals herself as the daughter of the king of England, whom she has fled in order to avoid an unwanted marriage with the aged king of Scotland. The pope ratifies the princess's marriage to Alessandro, who then brings his merchant family out of debt and one day inherits and rules over his father-in-law's realm.

Although the road to Rome is where Boccaccio first raises the possibility of homoerotic desire, the inn is where an attempt to realize it is staged and repudiated, its containment bringing about a new social identity for its male protagonist and an entirely new political order in England. The inn is more or differently "liminal" than other spaces in *Decameron* 2.3—it is where people whose social stations would normally prevent their coming into such close contact come together to inaugurate an entirely new dynasty. Equally important, it is a space that is asymmetrically "liminal" for its male and female protagonists. Alessandro enters the inn a merchant and leaves it a king, a poster child for the revisionist potential of liminality (also, his sexual congress with a woman above his social station is made possible by the kind of suspension of social hierarchy that the Turners associated with liminality). The princess of England, on the other hand, experiences a different kind of change, one of life cycle rather than status[57]: from daughter to wife. As the reader experiences the events in the *albergo,* the very same vow and sexual act that effect Alessandro's dramatic social ascent reveal and restore his wife's gender identity. The inn is a stage for Alessandro's transformation, but for his wife it is the space in which she becomes, to borrow Caroline Bynum's phrase, "what [she] is most deeply."[58] More specifically, the *Decameron* makes the king's daughter part of the machinery of the liminality—as a mechanism, or perhaps insofar as she acts on her desire, an agent of liminality—not hers, but someone else's. Both Chaucer's alehouse and Boccaccio's *albergo* are the settings for the destabilization and rearticulation of masculine identity around a perceived

---

[57] Kim M. Phillips has discussed the drastic differences in medieval understandings of men's and women's life cycles. See her "Margery Kempe and the Ages of Women," in *A Companion to "The Book of Margery Kempe,"* ed. John H. Arnold and Katherine J. Lewis (Cambridge: D. S. Brewer, 2004), pp. 17–34. Phillips observes: "A male *puer, adolescens,* or *senex* is defined by nothing more than his own age in body and mind. Female life stages [maid, wife, widow], on the other hand, have meaning only in relationship to men" (p. 33).

[58] Bynum, "Women's Stories, Women's Symbols," pp. 48–49.

threat of sodomy. Neither author's comic tale is especially concerned about the manner in which its female characters fashion gender identity in spaces such as taverns or alehouses.

Depending on how we interpret the Knight's "resolution" of the argument between the Pardoner and the Host, we might see the alehouse as a space in which *communitas* that was forged in the Host's Tabard is put to the test and ultimately redeemed, or a space in which its illusory quality and its fragility are most emphatically underlined, a space that it must flee to remain intact. Rather different from Boccaccio's *albergo,* the extent to which the alehouse constitutes a liminal space for the male pilgrims involved in this conflict is an open question. In the case of the Pardoner's performance in Fragment VI, the relationship between women's roles in alehouses to the liminality that men might or might not experience in them is even less directly represented than it is in *Decameron* 2.3. Not only does Chaucer's episode make no reference to the female pilgrims of the company, but, in the Pardoner's mention of the ale and cake that he consumes, it also chooses to imply rather than directly represent women's work in the alehouse. The production and provision of ale and perhaps even the cakes that accompanied it was work that, in Chaucer's England, fell primarily to women.[59] In particular, the job of tapster was gendered female and carried with it a set of sexual prejudices.[60] The stigmatized labor of alewives and tapsters is purged from the alehouse of Fragment VI, and its omission suggests a larger cultural disavowal of the importance of that labor to what I would call the "liminality effects" that the Turners see as inherent to and inevitable in Christian pilgrimage. Turning to another fourteenth-century depiction of an alehouse, I want to question the assumption of the "spontaneity" and egalitarian nature of pilgrimage *communitas,* the "liminal" status of pilgrimage, and the meaning of "pilgrimage" itself.

In late September 1394, the town of Burford in Oxfordshire played host to an improbable visitor. Alighting in this provincial wool-market town, one Eleanor Rykener took up residence with a man named John

---

[59] Judith M. Bennett, *Ale, Beer, and Brewsters in England: Women's Work in a Changing World, 1300–1600* (Oxford: Oxford University Press, 1996).

[60] The character of Kit from the anonymous *Tale of Beryn,* a fifteenth-century interpolation into the *Canterbury Tales,* is a prime example. For a thorough list of Middle English depictions of taverns and tapsters, see Ralph Hanna III, "Brewing Trouble: On Literature and History—and Alewives," in *Bodies and Disciplines: Intersections of Literature and History in Fifteenth-Century England,* ed. Barbara A. Hanawalt and David Wallace (Minneapolis: University of Minnesota Press, 1996), pp. 1–18.

Clerk at a tavern called the Swan and worked there as a tapster. As she had done in Oxford for the previous five weeks, where she had found work as an embroideress, Eleanor supplemented her meager wages through sex work. In her six-week tenure at the Swan, Eleanor's services where solicited by two Franciscans, a Carmelite, and six foreign men. Unknown to at least some of her clients, Eleanor had learned both embroidery and prostitution in London, where she/he had lived as a man named John. What is implicit in the fictional confrontation between the Pardoner and the Host is made quite explicit by John/Eleanor's travels: in transient and erotically charged spaces such as alehouses, taverns, and inns, gender was remarkably open for negotiation, and not just for the men who passed through them.

The story of John/Eleanor Rykener is by now familiar to many medievalists through a memorandum produced at a legal inquest at the Guild Hall in London in 1394. This Latin document summarizes the interrogation of "John Britby, of the county of York, and John Rykener, who calls himself Eleanor, and who appeared before the Mayor and Aldermen in women's clothing."[61] According to the scribe's account, Britby and Rykener were "found last Sunday in a certain stall in Soper's Lane, committing that detestable, unmentionable and ignominious vice" (p. 111). At the hearing, John Britby (who seems to have been a visitor to London) confessed to propositioning Rykener, whom he had mistaken for a woman. Eleanor consented, but insisted that she be paid for her services. Britby agreed and the two repaired to the Cheapside market stalls where they were apprehended. What follows is a lengthy account of John/Eleanor's career as a prostitute, a confession that implicates numerous men, women, locals, foreigners, priests, monks, whores, wives, and nuns from England and the Continent. The result of the inquest is unknown.

The scribal account of John/Eleanor's confession has attracted scholarly attention in the excellent studies of Ruth Mazo Karras and David Lorenzo Boyd, and Carolyn Dinshaw.[62] These studies have analyzed the

---

[61] All citations of this document and its English translation come from Ruth Mazzo Karras and David Lorenzo Boyd, "Ut Cum Muliere: A Male Transvestite Prostitute in Fourteenth-Century London," in *Premodern Sexualities*, ed. Louise Fradenburg and Carla Freccero (New York: Routledge, 1996), pp. 99–116. The document is translated on pages 111–12. All other citations of this translation appear parenthetically in the body of the article.

[62] Karras and Boyd, "Ut Cum Muliere," and Dinshaw, *Getting Medieval*, pp. 100–142.

legal terms used in the memorandum and have contextualized its rhetoric within the uncertain political and theological environment of London in the 1390s. There is no doubt that this document must be thought of in the context of London politics and society, both because that is the environment in which it was written and in which it attempted to make some sort of social intervention, and also because it was in London that John acquired the skills and the dispositions that would motivate and make possible his future life as Eleanor. Yet, as the document makes clear, larger circuits of travel and exchange that exceed "London" and indeed "England" also gave rise to the conditions in which "Eleanor" emerged. The Guild Hall memorandum of the Rykener trial reveals that the unlikely existence of John/Eleanor was made possible by the intersection of at least three distinct but articulated vectors of human mobility: (1) the institutionally related travels of members of the clergy, both domestic and international; (2) regional and international mercantile travel to such places as Burford and London; and (3) the economically motivated migration of poor single women to cities and market towns.[63]

During her salacious stint in Oxfordshire, "Eleanor" engaged in the types of low-paying vocations (as an embroideress and a tapster) that migrant women frequently supplemented with the wages won in sex work. Even though it does not disclose the motives for the journey, her

---

[63] Indeed, an awareness of the working conditions of economically disenfranchised women affords an informative vista onto Rykener's career. Ruth Mazo Karras has shown that in late medieval England urban prostitutes did not make their living from sex work alone, but rather survived by working in several unskilled temporary positions at the same time, supplementing their anemic wages with prostitution. Karras, *Common Women: Prostitution and Sexuality in Medieval England* (Oxford: Oxford University Press, 1996). Furthermore, the work of Maryane Kowaleski on Exeter and P. J. P. Goldberg on York suggests that women who moved from the city of their birth were likely to engage in such temporary and poorly remunerated work, and therefore prostitution as well. Kowaleski, "Women's Work in the Market Town: Exeter in the Late Fourteenth Century," in *Women and Work in Preindustrial Europe,* ed. Barbara Hanawalt (Bloomington: Indiana University Press, 1986). Goldberg, *Women, Work, and Lifecycle in a Medieval Economy: Women in York and Yorkshire, c. 1300–1520* (Oxford: Oxford University Press, 1992). While migrant women's lack of access to steady employment might, as Goldberg has suggested, be explained by regional chauvinism, it seems an equally decisive explanation would lie the manner in which most women's participation in the late medieval economy was gained through the home, as Judith M. Bennett suggests. Bennett, *Ale, Beer, and Brewsters in England: Women's Work in a Changing World, 1300–1600* (Oxford: Oxford University Press, 1996). A single woman arriving in a market town or city where she did not have relatives also lacked economic opportunities, such as the production and sale of wool, eggs, ale, or bread, that were often available to daughters, wives, and widows who lived in households.

testimony suggests the complex manner in which Eleanor's erotic and wage-earning pursuits enabled and, on the other hand, were complicated by, his/her resourceful and strategic crossings of the gender binary that governed the social horizons of the migrant poor. John/Eleanor Rykener's life as a woman was dependent on a degree of anonymity, and by implication, mobility. The range of gender expression and erotic possibilities evident in Rykener's life in Oxford, Burford, and then London was not likely thinkable in the orbit of social formations such as his/her familial household, church, parish, or town. Rykener's choice of the name "Eleanor" may itself reveal his/her awareness of the manner in which his/her strategic movements across political boundaries authorized him/her to circumvent surveillance of his/her erotic desire and gender expression. Citing twelfth-century puns on Eleanor of Aquitaine's name, Carolyn Dinshaw has suggested that Rykener's adoption of the name "Eleanor" may have been a pun on "alien," someone or something foreign, strange, or, perhaps most interestingly, someone from far away.[64] John's reinvention as Eleanor was made possible by his/her ability to move from one place where she was known as John to another where she was not and by the hard-won self-sufficiency that characterized the tedious and undervalued labor of the migrant woman.[65]

[64] Dinshaw, *Getting Medieval,* p. 103. For a consideration of this pun on Eleanor of Aquitaine's name, see Margaret Aziza Pappano, "Marie de France, Aliénor d'Aquitaine, and the Alien Queen," in *Eleanor of Aquitaine: Lord and Lady,* ed. Bonnie Wheeler and John C. Parsons (New York: Palgrave, 2002), pp. 337–68. Karras notes that prostitutes sometimes worked under names that exotically positioned them as natives of a faraway place. She cites the example of "Spanish Nell," who perhaps traded on the eroticism of her Iberian origin to increase demand for her services. See *Common Women,* p. 56.

[65] Rykener's career gives us reason to qualify David M. Halperin's suggestion that the historical study of lesbianism, as opposed to the study of male homosexuality, must develop conceptual tools that take into account the historical continuity of men's traffic in women; as I have been suggesting, one cannot historicize "male homosexuals" like the Pardoner or John/Eleanor without taking into account the traffic in low-status women, a fact that would suggest the centrality of this traffic to the history of male and female "homosexuality" alike. Halperin in his *How to Do the History of Male Homosexuality* (Chicago: University of Chicago Press, 2004) writes: "To see the historical dimensions of the social construction of same-sex relations among women, we need a new optic that will reveal specific historical variations in a phenomenon that necessarily exists in a constant and inescapable relation to the institutionalized structures of male dominance. . . . Histories of lesbianism need to reckon with this quite specific dimension of lesbian existence, which has potentially far-reaching implications for how we understand the different temporalities of female and male homosexuality" (p. 79). Halperin draws on Gayle Rubin's essay, "The Traffic in Women: Notes on the 'Political Economy' of Sex," in *Toward an Anthropology of Women,* ed. Raina R. Reiter (New York: Monthly Review Press, 1975), pp. 157–210. One sees a similar interrelationship between poor, "effeminate" men and the world of female prostitution in many historical contexts. For a contemporary example from Brazil, see Don Kulick's *Travesti: Sex, Gender, and Culture*

In the way that Rykener's story complicates easy distinctions between dwelling and travel, being and becoming, old and new self, it poses a challenge to anyone who would try to parse it out by the light of the Turners' notion of liminality. One of the most fascinating things about the Guildhall document is that it suggests that the status-leveling and potential for self-reinvention that the Turners associated with pilgrimage also seem to characterize other forms of travel. But there is an important ethical point to make as well: "pilgrimage," like all forms of travel, is a social practice that is something unfathomably larger than the experience of the person who leaves his or her home. Although travelers and the people who write about them tend to define the experience of the person who crosses political boundaries *as* travel, the ability to get from place to place, to sleep, to eat, to drink abroad depends on the existence of workers who may never leave home. Without the labor of these people, who themselves gain vast amounts of cultural knowledge from their social interactions with travelers, there could be no travel. John/Eleanor's experiences with wayfaring men suggests the ways that "travel" provides enticements and chances for self-fashioning even for those who might be in the places in which they live. What the career and institutional discipline of John/Eleanor suggests is that the "local" gender and sexual norms of "home" exist in alternatively productive and defensive tension with the regional, national, and international movement of bodies. Ideal expressions of gender and desire, even when they appear culturally and spatially bound, are in transformative dialogue or even in competition with emergent alternatives generated by the social practices (some calculating and tactical, others improvisational and unknowing) of people in transit.

Chaucer, in saturating the depiction of his Pardoner with so many images of pilgrimage, seems to have understood the great potential for social innovation in travel. Yet, when the alehouse scene of the *Canterbury Tales* is read alongside the record of the Rykener inquest, it is clear that Chaucer, like the Turners, somehow stops short of imagining the potential that a journey might have for those who, like the absent tap-

---

Among Brazilian Transgendered Prostitutes (Chicago: University of Chicago Press, 1998). It is possible that Halperin doesn't make this connection because for him "women" functions as an analytical concept unmarked by race and class; Hortense Spillers has highlighted the limitations of Rubin's model of the traffic in "women" when it is brought to bear on the historical realities of U.S. slavery and particularly that institution's attempt to dismantle kinship structures. See Spillers, "Mama's Baby, Papa's Maybe: An American Grammar Book," *Diacritics* 17, no. 2 (1987): 65–81.

ster of Fragment VI, sustained the fragile lives of medieval pilgrims. Moreover, while the Pardoner rhetorically positions himself as a traveler and fixes women and poverty as immobile and inescapably provincial, John/Eleanor was able to think and live his/her gender differently thanks to the unprecedented mobility of the working poor after the Black Death and also the movements of men such as the Pardoner. To what extent does travel provide opportunities for social reinvention for women like the absent tapster of Fragment VI? To what extent is Christian pilgrimage "liminal" for the residents of any of the devotional centers about which the Turners write? The Turners' fieldwork provides such a convenient vantage point for reading Chaucer's fiction perhaps because both implicitly define the experiences of the pilgrim as "pilgrimage," and both suggest that the liminal effects of pilgrimage are set into motion by the pilgrim's departure from the place where he lives. A more ecological approach to theorizing pilgrimage would ask to what extent the people who mend pilgrims' clothing, prepare their food, serve their ale, who sustain some of the most "liminal" spaces of the pilgrimage trail, also participate in the social life of devotional travel. One perhaps might even argue that it is these people's labor that makes possible the *communitas* that, in the Turners' paradigm, seems to spring out of nowhere. Throughout medieval Europe many—perhaps even most—of these laborers were women.[66]

As I have been suggesting, the pilgrimage frame of the *Canterbury Tales* exhibits an almost exclusive interest in the undermining and forging of masculinities on the road and provides a much more limited vista onto the strategies of and dangers to feminine self-fashioning. The other character that Chaucer associates with pilgrimage is, of course, the Wife of Bath, who journeys in order to gratify her sexual urges. In the course

[66] Most eating and lodging establishments were owned by married couples probably because the labor involved would or could not have been performed by men. For a discussion of the everyday workings of medieval French inns, see Verdon, *Travel in the Middle Ages,* pp. 109–17. For a discussion of women's work in English taverns, see Barbara A. Hanawalt, "The Host, the Law and the Ambiguous Space of Medieval London Taverns," in *Medieval Crime and Social Control,* ed. Hanawalt and Wallace (Minneapolis: University of Minnesota Press, 1999), pp. 204–23, esp. pp. 206–10. As Rykener's tenure in a tavern suggests, another reason that women worked in medieval taverns and inns was because they provided sexual services. Such was the case in the medieval Arab Mediterranean as well, where the *funduq* (an inn and warehouse for merchants) was associated with drinking and prostitution. See Olivia Remie Constable, *Housing the Stranger in the Mediterranean World* (Cambridge: Cambridge University Press, 2003), pp. 100–103. The depiction of female workers in inns as loose in sexual virtue can be seen in a text as late as Cervantes's *Don Quixote.*

of her travels, she becomes more fully what she already is at home—a bad, lascivious wife. Unlike the Pardoner, whose perverse gender emerges within and thanks to devotional travel, the Wife of Bath does not need pilgrimage to become what she is; her wanderings are just another example of the wayward nature she exhibits at home. To articulate the difference in terms that look back to some of the texts we have already considered: the Wife of Bath's relationship to pilgrimage is drawn from the types of moralistic and conduct literature that condemn the hypocrisy of going on pilgrimage for false motives, while the Pardoner's is closer to the view of pilgrimage found in the *Guide to Santiago:* the sexual opportunities available in devotional travel are not simply immoral, but also pose the threat of the integrity of masculinity itself. The Wife of Bath is an example of what a dissolute woman will do if she goes on pilgrimage; the Pardoner is a cautionary embodiment of travel's socially destabilizing potential. Pilgrimage does not provide the Wife with the potential to revise her gender identity or to fashion a new kind of femininity. The potentiality that the Turners attribute to the liminal social practice of pilgrimage is just not there for the Wife of Bath, and seemingly much less so for the Prioress or Second Nun.

For the most part, the frame of the *Canterbury Tales* offers no consideration of the potential of pilgrimage or other forms of travel to expand the possibilities of femininity or to bring it into crisis—it is for masculinity that geographical displacement poses a problem. The one possible exception to this observation would be Goodelief, a woman whose body and role in her marriage defy gender expectations. Suggestively, she is the wife of an innkeeper. Yet, as a conceptual tool, "liminality," with its focus on those who leave home, who become members of a pilgrim *communitas,* and who return home transformed somehow by the experience, does not provide a vantage point from which we might begin to evaluate the way that Goodelief's lodging and provisioning of pilgrims—that is to say, the way "pilgrimage" itself—contributes to her unique gender performance. In the final analysis, liminality is better for talking about certain figures (Boccaccio's Alessandro and perhaps Chaucer's Pardoner and Host) than others (John/Eleanor Rykener, the Wife of Bath). The way in which and the extent to which the Turners' hypotheses will illuminate Chaucer's pilgrimage frame cannot be assumed in advance. There still seems much to be gained by supplementing our most venerated theoretical paradigms with a consideration of the ways that *The Canterbury Tales* depicts the uses—and abuses—of social space.

Affective Politics in Chaucer's *Reeve's Tale:*

"Cherl" Masculinity after 1381

Holly A. Crocker
University of South Carolina

C HAUCER'S *REEVE'S TALE* has been characterized as something of a letdown, a concessionary nod to ruling powers by a poet too invested in elite culture to engage in anything beyond a passing critique of social inequities.[1] If *The Miller's Tale* gave voice to the agrarian many, those *rustici* who were alienated from channels of government in post-rebellion England, then the privileged few need not worry, at least not for long: with his creation of a singularly odious character, whose profession involved administrative service to baronial interests, Chaucer comes closest to representing a "peasant consciousness" with his menacing, quarreling, sermoning Reeve.[2] This speaker, taken together with this story's pivotal position in the first fragment, makes *The Reeve's Tale* thoroughly deflating. Nevertheless, in this essay I argue that the tale's comedown derives from its engagement with late medieval politics of the countryside. Chaucer does not back away from contemporary issues of

Thanks to Harry Berger Jr., Alcuin Blamires, Greg Forter, Frank Grady, John Plummer, Tison Pugh, Elizabeth Robertson, Kathryn Schwarz, Nicole Nolan Sidhu, Dan Smith, and the anonymous readers for their suggestions on earlier drafts of this paper. Most of all, thanks to Tommy for rejecting my "best/worst Stanley Cavell."

[1] Lee Patterson, *Chaucer and the Subject of History* (Madison: University of Wisconsin Press, 1991), pp. 244–79; Steven Justice, *Writing and Rebellion: England in 1381* (Berkeley and Los Angeles: University of California Press, 1994), pp. 225–31.

[2] "Peasant consciousness," is Patterson's phrase. As everyone knows, especially Patterson and Justice, these characters are not really peasants. We are therefore dealing with a process of political identification, which is decidedly psychological. See Diana Fuss, *Identification Papers* (New York: Routledge, 1995), pp. 141–72, who explores identification's centrality to psychoanalytic conceptions of the political *and* its problematic relation to a colonial history of imperialism. Fuss's reading of Frantz Fanon's psychoanalytically inflected work is particularly useful to what follows, for she reminds us of the ways in which psychological identification—or the desire *to be* the other—facilitates historical formations of repression.

social struggle in *The Reeve's Tale;* rather, he uses this narrative to illustrate the affective turn of politics after the Rising of 1381. Though the tale never addresses the peasants' revolt directly, its masculine struggle shows that the post-rebellion dispersal of peasant identity *back into the countryside* is driven by a politics of affect.

To be attuned to such representational politics means developing a criticism that is sensitive to affect, in medieval contexts and in our own. Because affect is a sticky notion, however, it has often been considered an imprecise interpretive methodology.[3] Sometimes equated with emotion in contemporary discourse, affect's difficulty emerges from its uncharted categorical parameters, potentially accounting for Anne Hudson's recent dismissal of affect as an "unpredictable realm."[4] Yet medieval thinkers were definite about affect's content, so that writers including Augustine of Hippo, Bernard of Clairvaux, and Robert Grosseteste designated four *affects*—fear, love, sadness, and joy—as fundamental elements of the sensitive soul.[5] This taxonomy coexisted with a

[3] Sara Ahmed, *The Cultural Politics of Emotion* (New York: Routledge, 2004), pp. 44–49, persuasively argues that feelings become associated through their circulation. In her lexicon, emotions, sensations, and feelings are "sticky."

[4] Anne Hudson, "Langland and Lollardy," *YLS* 17 (2003): 93–106. Hudson gives a useful explanation of the affective valence of historically situated terms: "[They] have no fixed association, little firm semantic content, and can vary in usage unpredictably according to political events and the outlook of the speaker who uses them, and in understanding according to the views of the reader or listener who receives them." However, her modern examples—"fascist," "communist," "terrorist," and "freedom fighter"—empty this analysis by cutting it off from historicist inquiry (p. 96). As these extreme instances nevertheless indicate, affects inhere within certain terms because they are constructed that way in and through particular cultural practices and events.

[5] For invaluable historical accounts, see Simon Knuuttila, *Emotions in Ancient and Medieval Philosophy* (Oxford: Clarendon, 2004); Michel Meyer, *Le Philosophe et les passions: Esquisse d'une histoire de la nature humaine* (Paris: Hachette, 1991); and Thomas Dixon, *From Passions to Emotions: The Creation of a Secular Psychological Category* (Cambridge: Cambridge University Press, 2003), esp. pp. 1–61. Other specific discussions are also helpful: see Anastasia Scrutton, "Emotion in Augustine of Hippo and Thomas Aquinas: A Way Forward for the Im/passibility Debate?" *International Journal of Systematic Theology* 7 (2005): 169–77. Karma Lochrie, *Margery Kempe and Translations of the Flesh* (Philadelphia: University of Pennsylvania Press, 1991), pp. 21–23, traces the gendered relation of this classificatory system to the movements of the will and the governance of reason in the writings of Bernard. For an explanation of Grosseteste's interest in the affective aspects of understanding, see D. A. Callus, *Robert Grosseteste, Scholar and Bishop: Essays in Commemoration of the Seventh Centenary of His Death* (Oxford: Oxford University Press, 1955), pp. 21–22; A. J. Minnis, *Medieval Theory of Authorship,* 2nd ed. (Aldershot: Wildwood House, 1988), p. 120–22, helpfully chronicles Grosseteste's influence on other writers who explore the relation between *aspectus* and *affectus* using this fourfold scheme. As various scholars explain, this division was originally used by the stoics to condemn affect, but it was more widely adapted by later writers in defense of feelings.

Platonic division of the affects into concupiscent and irascible varieties, which Thomas Aquinas elaborated into eleven (and Jean Gerson expanded into one hundred!) inclinations.[6] Despite the specificity and complexity of these accounts, however, medievals are like moderns in their belief that affect traverses the boundary between inner and outer feelings.[7] Critical attention to medieval uses of affect, therefore, not only illuminates the construction of personal borders but also shows the ways in which differential categories such as gender and rank interanimate to create interpersonal associations with political significance.

By interweaving rank and gender, *The Reeve's Tale* creates a "cherl" masculinity to consolidate a group of lesser men. It does so, importantly, by using affective appeals, harnessing fear's partitioning and consolidating powers to figure a form of masculinity that is locally enabled, albeit culturally dispossessed. Instead of focusing on the social classifications that might divide its students from Symkyn, or the psychological affinities that might suggest Oswald the Reeve's similarity to Robyn the Miller, this tale focuses on the ways in which men use differences in affect to create categories of distinction for and within their communities.[8] Grouping men together through a starkly instrumentalist view of women, the capacity for affect is represented as a "feminine" trait,

[6] See Ruth E. Harvey, *The Inward Wits: Psychological Theory in the Middle Ages and the Renaissance* (London: Warburg Institute, 1975), for a lucid and compact explanation of the ways a Thomistic account of the soul relates to humoral theory and faculty psychology. Also see Knuuttila, *Emotions in Ancient and Medieval Philosophy*, pp. 226–55, 282–86.

[7] Brian Massumi, *Parables for the Virtual: Movement, Affect, Sensation* (Durham: Duke University Press, 2002), pp. 27–28, and Charles Altieri, *The Particulars of Rapture: An Aesthetics of the Affects* (Ithaca: Cornell University Press, 2003), p. 2, are most explicit in their insistence that affect is not reducible to emotion (Altieri's four basic categories—feelings, moods, passions, and emotions—seek to account for the cognitive, somatic, psychic, and quasi-spiritual dimensions of affect). Emotions, for these writers and those following, are forms of affect. Equally important for my thinking in this essay, Sara Ahmed, *Cultural Politics of Emotion,* and Eve Kosofsky Sedgwick, *Touching Feeling: Affect, Pedagogy, Performativity* (Durham: Duke University Press, 2003), emphasize affect's ability to put inner and outer states of feeling into contact with one another, particularly as the individual perceives herself in relation to (private) desires and (public) pressures.

[8] William F. Woods, "The Logic of Deprivation in *The Reeve's Tale,*" *ChauR* 30 (1995): 150–63, argues that the particularized space of the tale allows the Reeve to stage his own class struggle against ruling ideologies. For a late medieval expression of the common idea that society was divided into three estates—those who pray, fight, work—see Thomas Wimbledon, *Wimbledon's Sermon "Redde Rationem Villicationis Tue": A Middle English Sermon of the Fourteenth Century,* ed. Ione Kemp Knight (Pittsburgh: Duquesne University Press, 1967), pp. 61–66. Wimbledon's articulation of this structure is particularly interesting for my purposes in this essay because he associates Christ's authority with that of a "housholdere," suggesting that ultimate (masculine) authority is identified with the image of "a housholdynge man."

though it must also be emphasized that such a gendered association itself relies on negative affect—the fear of exposure and exclusion—to define this gathering of men.[9] By governing women, who are explicitly identified with affect in this tale, men distinguish themselves from one another.[10] Just like anything else, women become weapons in a competitive universe where a class of men, elsewhere called "cherls," vie for dominance over one another.[11]

Although this struggle is limited to a certain set of men, it has wider import, since it also shows that affective assemblages frequently obscure the ethical implications of political positions. In this essay's final section, I therefore urge medievalists to engage the ethical consequences of affective associations. By considering the junctures of feeling informing the political options on offer to different people at various historical moments, we frankly avoid the polarizations of "history vs. psychology" that have bedeviled medieval literary studies.[12] But freeing ourselves from this professional bind is only important because it allows literary medievalists to pursue the affective associations that pressure individual subjects in representations of late fourteenth-century English society. These choices, *The Reeve's Tale* demonstrates, have political consequences that are explicitly ethical even if they resist ideological classifications

[9] Joan Cadden, *Meanings of Sex Difference in the Middle Ages: Medicine, Science, and Culture* (Cambridge: Cambridge University Press, 1993), pp. 167–227.

[10] Essays in the volume *The Representation of Women's Emotions in Medieval and Early Modern Culture,* ed. Lisa Perfetti (Gainesville: University Press of Florida, 2005), explore women's associations with emotion in premodern medical, philosophical, and literary representations.

[11] *MED,* s.v. "cherl." Originating as it does from the Old English *ceorl,* which designated agrarian servitude after the Norman Conquest, this term could easily translate into "peasant." But it does not translate so easily, mainly because its development in Middle English also carries an affective intonation suggesting a lack of civility, a lack of morality, or sometimes, though not always, both. A survey of this term's usage in the *Canterbury Tales* equally suggests its multivalence during this period: in almost all instances "cherl" suggests a lack of social decorum, though this uncultivated simplicity sometimes exposes moral corruption in others. For example, in *The Summoner's Tale,* "cherl" functions to separate the bodily, common sense of the tale's "goode man" from the bookish, logical learning of its greedy friar (III. 2182; 2206; 2218; 2227; 2232; 2238; 2241; 2267; 2290). In *The Parson's Tale,* the term initially seems only to designate social rank: "As wel may the cherl be saved as the lord" (X.761). But then it takes a moral turn to indicate thralldom: "Every sinful man is a cherl to synne" (X.763). As pilgrim-Chaucer's usage of the term in the first fragment demonstrates ["The Millere is a cherl" (I.3182)], lower rank often indicates a boorish disposition.

[12] My phrasing here is indebted to Raymond Williams's moving essay, "Structures of Feeling," *Marxism and Literature* (Oxford: Oxford University Press, 1977), pp. 128–35, though my alteration marks my emphasis on what Williams called those "meanings and values as they are actively lived and felt" (p. 132).

or psychoanalytic excavations. Chaucer's representation of the affective power of a "cherl" masculinity in *The Reeve's Tale,* because it recognizes the moral compromises that group identities often demand of individuals, at least acknowledges the political limitations placed upon members of the laboring estate in the wake of the 1381 revolt. Though it would be wrong to conclude that Chaucer sympathizes with "cherl" masculinity, his willingness to present the exploitation of women that attends the marginalization of men argues for a reconsideration of political empathy, especially the ways in which social oppression fans out to divide members of a community who might otherwise find common ground.

Domesticating Affect

Critics who have examined the tale's particularization of space rightly note that there is not much room for common ground in *The Reeve's Tale.* Yet I suggest this narrowing reflects the restriction of politics during this period.[13] With a change in the broader political climate, struggles between men become increasingly localized, increasingly attuned to differences in individual performances of social roles and their attendant affects. The particular environs in which men define themselves are crucial during this period, for it is in relation to their personal situations that men form alliances with or vendettas against one another. Chaucer's *Reeve's Tale* engages this change in political outlook by suggesting that a man's social rank derives from his attention to local governance, over himself and his household. As a result, the tale's construction of a "cherl" masculinity is engaged with and indebted to larger discursive movements of the late Middle Ages.[14] More than the Miller's fabliau, *The Reeve's Tale* differentiates characters by drawing on medieval gender discourse, particularly as expectations from conduct books, legal formulae, and clerical writings *affected* local politics in late medieval England.[15]

[13] See Peter Brown, "The Containment of Symkyn: The Function of Space in *The Reeve's Tale,*" *ChauR* 14 (1980): 225–36; Woods, "Logic of Deprivation"; and Woods, "Symkyn's Place in *The Reeve's Tale,*" *ChauR* 39 (2004): 17–40.

[14] Carl Lindahl, *Earnest Games: Folkloric Patterns in the "Canterbury Tales"* (Bloomington: Indiana University Press, 1987), pp. 24–31, points out that the majority of pilgrims would have fallen into a middling station, distinguishable only by their claims to "gentil" and "cherl" status. Glenn Burger, *Chaucer's Queer Nation* (Minneapolis: University of Minnesota Press, 2003), p. 53, rightly notes the "elasticity" of "gentil," and thus presumably "cherl."

[15] Burger, *Chaucer's Queer Nation,* pp. 37–77, shows through an analysis of medieval conjugality that the household was increasingly becoming a locus of masculinity in the late medieval cultural imagination.

In the century following the peasants' revolt, instructional literatures detailing this type of domestic management become much more numerous. Yet the basic assumption that conduct books rely upon—men are ultimately responsible for domestic order—is a much earlier notion, and derives from the ways in which the affects were supposed to engender the bodies of men and women. Because the affects derived from the sensitive (or lower) part of the soul, they were ideally subject to the rational power of the will. When the affects were governed by the soul's intellectual (or higher) faculty, they were appropriately disposed. Because this arrangement was never purely a top-down process, but was also influenced by the body's habituations, it was always possible for the affects to become corrupt. Drawing on the Aristotelian model of gender difference, rational governance of the lower sensitive faculties (including the affects) was represented as a masculine enterprise.[16] Walter Hilton makes this division explicit, using gender hierarchy to explain the proper order of the rational and sensitive parts of the soul: "The overe is likned to a man, for it schulde be maister and sovereyne, and that is propirli the ymage of God, for bi that oonli the soule knoweth God and loveth God. And the nethere is likned to a woman, for it schulde be buxum to the overe partie of resoun, as a woman is buxum to man."[17] Here we see that the orderly arrangement of the soul aligns masculinity with reason and femininity with affect, since the lower part of the soul respects the higher part's authority on account of love.

Perhaps most famously, this gendered model of affective governance is domesticated in *Sawles Warde*: in this marital allegory, wit's control over his household is facilitated by the affects of fear and love. Without the help of these forces, the servants of this bodily edifice—the physical senses—would be corrupted by his unruly wife, Will.[18] Here the affects are pliant because, as messengers of death's fears and heaven's joys, they communicate the consequences of moral training. Writers who extol the positive potential of affect stress the necessity of moral training as a

---

[16]See Harvey, *Inward Wits;* and Perfetti, "Introduction," *Representation of Women's Emotions,* pp. 1–19; and Cadden, *Meanings of Sex Difference in the Middle Ages,* 180–83.

[17]Walter Hilton, *The Scale of Perfection,* ed. Thomas Bestul (Kalamazoo: Medieval Institute Publications, 2000), Book II, chap. 12, lines 663–66.

[18]*Sawles Warde, Medieval English Prose for Women: Selections from the Katherine Group and "Ancrene Wisse,"* ed. Bella Millett and Jocelyn Wogan-Browne (Oxford: Clarendon, 1990), pp. 86–109.

masculine responsibility.[19] Hilton's *Mixed Life* advises its addressee to govern himself because his spiritual fitness is connected to his ability to provide domestic order. Using the traditional figure of Martha to describe the active aspects of this "medeled" life, he explains: "For thou schalt oo tyme with Martha be bisi for to rule and governe thi houshoold, thi children, thi servantis, thi neighbores, thi tenauntes: yf thei doon yvel, for to teche hem and amende hem and chastice hem. And thou shalt also loke and knowen wiseli that thi thynges and thi wordeli goodes be rightfully keped bi thi servantes, govern[ed] and truli spended, that thou myght the more plenteousli fulfille the deedes of merci with hem unto thi even-Cristene."[20] Moreover, as Richard Rolle explains in his *Form of Living,* those who are involved in the "actife lyfe" are required "to ordayne thair meyne in drede and in the lufe of God, and fynd tham thaire necessaries."[21] Whether they are addressed to women or to men, religious writings suggest that virtuous laymen are supposed to govern the domestic body, regulating affect through a visible program of training that ultimately signifies masculine reason.

From the outset, Chaucer's *Reeve's Tale* shows that miller-Symkyn attempts to gain social respect through the manifest governance of his household. As a cultural model, we might say that this "housholdere" masculinity attempts to avoid affect by presenting masculine agency as a disciplined mode of regulation.[22] In the most dispassionate manner, a man must publicly mark his control over all elements of his estate. Symkyn's visible dominance over trade, property, and women therefore appears to actualize a fully legitimate fantasy of masculinity in the late medieval imagination of the gendered household. In later secular treatises, young men are told, often by fathers, that a carefully documented

---

[19] Callus, *Robert Grosseteste,* pp. 120–22.

[20] Walter Hilton, *Mixed Life, Walter Hilton's "Mixed Life" Edited from Lambeth Palace MS 472,* ed. S. J. Ogilvie-Thomson (Salzburg: Institut für Anglistik und Amerikanistik Universität Salzburg, 1986), lines 103–11.

[21] Richard Rolle, *The Form of Living, English Writings of Richard Rolle, Hermit of Hampole,* ed. Hope Emily Allen (Oxford: Clarendon Press, 1931), chap. 12, lines 20–22.

[22] I take this phrasing from Wimbledon (note 8 above); also relevant is the entry from the *MED,* s.v. "housholder(e)," (a)–(b): "The head of a household or family; one who manages a household" and "the owner or occupant of a house [often difficult to distinguish from (a)]." The most familiar Chaucerian example of this term appears in *The General Prologue,* which describes the Franklin as a "housholdere" (I.339). Perhaps coincidentally, *The Franklin's Tale* is a story chronicling marital reciprocity and its inherent challenges.

regimen of household authority will secure the masculine control that Symkyn seems to possess.[23] For example, in *Myne Awen Dere Sone,* the father stresses that a man's personal authority derives from the way he rules those who will be subject to his dominion in the fluctuating domestic domain. A man owes certain responsibilities "To thame that soulde be thy seruand[s]," which means his wife and daughters: he should guard the chastity of his daughters and he should protect the good name of his wife.[24] Furthermore, in terms that resonate particularly with Symkyn's failures in this tale, the speaker warns, "Delay thou nevere [your daughter's] maryage / For covatise of heritage."[25] This text suggests that a man's ordered regulation of women and children (particularly daughters) provides a public account of his masculine character.

Conduct literature for women, too, indicates social expectations for masculine governance that separate domestic management from affective investment. A man needs to indicate his control over all affairs under his familial authority through visibly regularized gestures, which the husband in the late fourteenth-century *Le ménagier de Paris* accomplishes through his careful and exhaustive instructions to his young wife. Demonstrating the performative requirement that accompanies lay masculinity in the late Middle Ages, the *ménagier* offers public documentation of his control over his young wife's administration of minute details through the book itself. When he offers his wife advice concerning cooking, gardening, and servants, he shows that his wife's agency is a product of his measured power. Although the *ménagier* worries to his wife that his meticulous instructions will "cause [her] to hold [him] unreasonable," he nevertheless believes it will lessen her burden if he tells her "what help and what folk you shall take and how you shall set them to work, for in these affairs I would that you should have only the ordering thereof, and the supervision and the care of setting others to perform

[23] See, for example, *How the Wise Man Taught His Son, The Minor Poems of the Vernon MS.,* ed. Frederick Furnivall, EETS 117 (London: Paul, Trench, and Trübner & Co. for EETS, 1892–19), pp. 522–53; and *The Consail and Teiching that the Wys Man Gaif His Sone, Ratis Raving and other Moral and Religious Pieces in Prose and Verse,* ed. J. R. Lumby, EETS 43 (Oxford: Oxford University Press for EETS, 1870). *Walter of Henley's Dite de Hosebondrie,* ed. Elizabeth Lamond (London: Longmans, Green, & Co., 1890), illustrates the popularity of father-son advice as a literary frame: this treatise deals with agriculture and cattle-breeding, suggesting that all matters of husbandry respond to the visual imperative that makes display part of management.

[24] *Myne Awen Dere Sone,* ed. Tauno F. Mustanoja, *Neuphologische Mitteilungen* 49 (1948): 145–93, vj.100.

[25] *Myne Awen Dere Sone,* vij.131–32.

them at your husband's cost."[26] His wife is supposed to order his house-hold, because his comprehensive governance makes her agency a reflection of his domestic regulation.

Young men were supposed to internalize this rationally ordered relational hierarchy of gender, as we see from the advice contained in the fifteenth-century didactic treatise *How the Goode Man Taght Hys Sone:* "Wyrche with thy wyfe, as reson ys; / Thogh sche be sirvunt in degree, In some degree sche fellowe ys."[27] According to this model, a woman should work for the good of her husband, as the advice the father gives his daughters in Caxton's translation of *Le Livre du chevalier de La Tour Landry* indicates: "[E]uery good woman / al be it so that she haue neuer so peruers and euylle husbond / yet this notwithstondyng she ne oughte to leue the seruyse of god . . . atte leste she ought to be more humble and deuoute for to Impetre and get the grace of god for her and her husband."[28] The middling female speaker in *The Goodwife Taught Her Daughter* urges its addressee to respect husbandly authority: "Loke that thou him bowe and loue ouer alle thing. / Mekeli him answere and noght to atterling / And so thou schalt slaken his mod and been his derling. / Fare wordes wrath slaketh."[29] Similarly, admonitory literature for men, such as *The Consail and Teiching that the Wys Man Gaif His Sone,* suggests that a man shows his wisdom by treating his wife with the respect he owes himself: "Be war, my weddyt sone, for-thy / And treit thi wyf recht tendyrly; / And gyf hir cau[se] of gud bounte, / Sa that defalt be nocht in thee."[30]

As advisory literatures illustrate, "actife" masculinity is founded on a man's ability to make his household a public sign of his individual regulation. Furthermore, instructional discourse—secular and religious—

[26] *The Goodman of Paris: A Treatise on Moral and Domestic Economy by a Citizen of Paris,* ed. Eileen Power (London: Routledge, 1928), p. 193. *Le Mesnagier de Paris,* ed. Georgina E. Brereton and Janet M. Ferrier, trans. Karin Ueltschi, Lettres Gothiques (Paris: Librarie Générale Française, 1994), p. 409: [cause de moy tenir pour outrageux]; Power, p. 194, Brereton, p. 410: [quelles aydes et quelles gens vous prendrez, et comment vous les embesoignerez; car de ce ne vueil je que vous ayez fors le commandement, la visitacion, la diligence de le faire faire par autres et aux despens de vostre mary].

[27] *How the Goode Man Taght Hys Sone, The Trials and Joys of Marriage,* ed. Eve Salisbury (Kalamazoo: Western Michigan University for TEAMS, 2002), lines 130–32.

[28] William Caxton, trans., *The Book of the Knight of the Tower,* ed. M. Y. Offord, EETS, supp. series 2 (London: Oxford University Press for EETS, 1971), p. 133.

[29] *The Good Wife Taught Her Daughter, The Good Wyfe Wold a Pylgremage, The Thewis of Gud Women,* ed. Tauno F. Mustanoja (Helsinki: Suomalaisan Kirjallisuuden Seuran, 1948), E. V.24–27.

[30] Lumby, III.1800–803.

institutes gender difference by suggesting that masculine power derives from reasoned control, while feminine influence emerges from affective submission. Symkyn's departure from this gender ideal is evident early in the tale, insofar as his governance is more a product of affect than reason. Symkyn controls the borders of the domestic, but his purchase over this masculinity, as is apparent even from his portrait, is tenuous at best, suggesting his potential vulnerability while demonstrating his conspicuous hostility:

> Ay by his belt he baar a long panade,
> And of a swerd ful trenchant was the blade.
> A joly poppere baar he in his pouche;
> Ther was no man, for peril, dorste hym touche
> A Sheffeld thwitel baar he in his hose.
>
> (I.3929–33)

Because Symkyn is capable of immoderate violence (not because he exercises rational control), he compels submission from those who reside in his domain. His fortified demeanor affirms the deportment books' suggestion that gender-order needs constant cultivation; however, the poem does not attribute Symkyn's regimen of control to the duties accompanying disciplined masculine regulation. The tale attributes Symkyn's show of strength to personal pride, an impassioned overflow that diminishes his regulatory reason.[31] Associating this behavior with anxious confidence therefore suggests that Symkyn compensates for a lack of reason with a surplus of affect.

More broadly, Symkyn's authority is problematic because it exposes the contingency of the affects and the various identities they situate. Even as comportment books of the late Middle Ages suggest that an appropriate program of training for the self can instill the virtues associated with social betterment, their "how to" orientation potentially suggests such characteristics can be feigned by anyone who presumes to put on such airs. By detailing the lengthy and fundamental commitment their programs of moral virtue and social manners require, religious and secular advice literatures seek to resolve the cultural anxiety their very

---

[31] See Tison Pugh, *Queering Medieval Genres* (New York: Palgrave Macmillan, 2004), pp. 53–56, whose analysis of the portrait convincingly suggests that Symkyn's conspicuously "phallic" masculinity is presented as an affective show that foregrounds his lack of sexual potency.

existence bespeaks. Conduct books are quick to insist that simulated shows of identity will be transparent, even though an older discourse of training also claims that a person's environmental circumstances can alter the complexion. The notion that a person's internal disposition is structured by external situation is evident in the *Secretum secretorum,* which administers advice regarding grooming habits and choice of secretaries alongside considerations of planetary motions and seasonal characteristics.[32] A weaker version of this regulatory program features in Chaucer's *Tale of Melibee,* when Prudence advises her husband to define himself through the company he assembles (VII.1155–65).[33] By teaching individuals to manage their environs, admonitory literatures potentially suggest that personal circumstances can be changed to further individual ambitions.

Such advice reinforces the cultural privilege of the prince in the *fürstenspiegel* tradition, but Chaucer's *Reeve's Tale* reveals the social threat inherent within this discourse: if an identity may be cultivated through the management of material resources, it opens the possibility that social rank is fluid. Indeed, it is clear that Symkyn can simulate a more respectable masculinity, since he has the possessions that will allow him to climb the social ladder: "Greet sokene hath this millere" (I.3987). Moreover, through his graft he has also made the local connections that give his daughter a respectable dowry. Ultimately, though, the tale addresses the risks associated with cultivating social roles, suggesting that internal qualities are shaped by a lifelong process of affective habituation. As we see through the ridiculous spectacle that Symkyn and his wife make of themselves as they parade through town, the occasional ability to wear expensive clothing does not confer social legitimacy:

[32] *Secretum Secretorum: Nine English Versions,* ed. M. A. Manzalaoui, vol. 1, EETS, o.s., no. 276 (Oxford: Oxford University Press, 1977). As Judith Ferster, *Fictions of Advice: The Literature and Politics of Counsel in Late Medieval England* (Philadelphia: University of Pennsylvania Press, 1996), p. 44, remarks regarding this tradition, "Virtues are disciplines."

[33] In a fascinating irony, John of Salisbury captures Symkyn's view of marriage with his cynical reflection: "A daughter at all comely . . . is merchandise displayed for sale to attract the customer." John of Salisbury, *Frivolities of Courtiers and Footprints of Philosophers: Being a Translation of the First, Second, and Third Books of the "Policraticus" of John of Salisbury,* trans. Joseph B. Pike (Minneapolis: University of Minnesota Press, 1938), p. 199. See Larry Scanlon's discussion of the *Policraticus* and the *Melibee*'s relation to the *fürstenspiegel* in his *Narrative, Authority, and Power: The Medieval Exemplum and the Chaucerian Tradition* (Cambridge: Cambridge University Press, 1994), pp. 81–118 and 206–15. I am most intrigued by his claim, p. 212, that the *Melibee* defines an emergent secular authority, which relates to "the intersection of documentary culture and gender visibility."

A ful fair sighte was it upon hem two;
On halydayes biforn hire wolde he go
With his typet wounde aboute his heed,
And she cam after in a gyte of reed;
And Symkyn hadde hosen of the same.

(I.3951–55)

Likewise, the newfound capacity to form a marital alliance with the local parson does not sanctify Symkyn's base origins, which are clearly signaled by cues from physiognomy: "Round was his face, and camus was his nose; / As piled as an ape was his skulle" (I.3934).[34] Because a person's affective inclinations were expressed through the body, Symkyn's elementary disposition belies his inferiority.

In other words, Symkyn's baseness is evident despite his attempts to emulate a respectable masculinity. In fact, his attempt to fit social prescriptions works to underscore his difference from the model of masculinity he seeks to emulate. He expresses a "proper" attitude concerning the choice of a bride—"For Symkyn wolde no wyf, as he sayde, / But she were wel ynorissed and a mayde, / To saven his estaat of yomanrye" (I.3947–49)—echoing advice literature with patent accuracy. Yet Symkyn's choice of the parson's illegitimate daughter only verifies Andreas Capellanus's misogamous jibe: "Moreover, no woman can be found of such low stock as not to maintain that she has notable parents and is descended from a family of high-ranking men, and who does not use all sorts of boasting to exalt herself."[35] That Symkyn would buy such a line suggests that he does not understand the discursive construction of masculinity promoted in advice literatures. His social illiteracy, importantly, is due to his affective deficiency. Although Symkyn's masculinity emerges in contrast to a cultural model of individual training, his personal misgovernment implicates all those who occupy his household. The tale's use of affect, therefore, not only intensifies the humiliation of its haughty miller but also facilitates the construction of a "cherl"

---

[34] *Physiologus, The Epic of the Beast: Reynard the Fox and Physiologus,* trans. and intro. James Carlill (London: Routledge), p. 185. Walter Clyde Curry, "Chaucer's Reeve and Miller," *PMLA* 35 (1920): 189–209, argues that physiognomy is very important to the characterization of the miller's base status in the tale.

[35] Andreas Capellanus, *The Art of Courtly Love,* trans. P. G. Walsh (London: Duckworth, 1982) III.96: [Sed et nulla mulier inveniture ex tam infimo genere nata, quae se non asserat egregious habere parentes et a magnatum stipite derivari, et quae se omni iactantia non extollat].

masculinity through its representation of the women as "sensitive" aspects of Symkyn's domestic body.

The clerks come to Trumpington to see if they can put a stop to Symkyn's cheating ways, but as the beginning of the tale indicates, it is the miller's "family business" that makes his corruption too much to tolerate. More than his personal habits, the women in the tale represent Symkyn's affective mismanagement. Because the two women complete the miller's character, the tale suggests that Symkyn converts the profit he gains from milling into social respect within his community.[36] But here too Symkyn cheats. As a production of her father and supplement to her husband, Symkyn's wife forms the perfect bond between movable goods and symbolic capital: "A wyf he hadde, ycomen of noble kyn; / The person of the toun hir fader was" (I.3942–43).[37] And as a bizarre admixture of noble and base stock, "With kamus nose and eyen greye as glas, / With buttokes brode and brestes rounde and hye" (I.3974–75), Malyne's body figures the masculine fraud from which Symkyn extracts social gain. Because these two women represent Symkyn's faulty pretensions, they become the sites of his punishment. In order to prove that Symkyn's masculinity is a sham, therefore, the tale dispassionately depicts the women as ungoverned aspects of the miller's gender identity.

Feminine Feeling

As my discussion of the portraits indicates, neither Malyne nor her mother has the potential to be anything other than a component of Symkyn's corrupted disposition. Yet all appears well in this domestic domain, which is to say that Symkyn is able to pass off his version of masculine authority as governed reason as long as the women remain obedient to his command. When the clerks come to Trumpington, the women are on display as markers of Symkyn's masculine governance, visible only insofar as they offer public witness to his cultivation of the domestic as his proprietary domain. Flaunting his control, Symkyn enfolds the clerks' humiliation into an ostentatious display of superiority.

[36] Susanna Greer Fein, "'Lat the Children Pleye': The Game Between the Ages in *The Reeve's Tale*," in S. G. Fein, D. Raybin, and P. C. Braeger, eds., *Rebels and Rivals: The Contestive Spirit in the Canterbury Tales* (Kalamazoo: Medieval Institute Publishers, Western Michigan University, 1991), pp. 73–104 (80).

[37] Pierre Bourdieu, in his classic formulation, "The Market of Symbolic Goods," *Poetics* 14 (1985): 13–44, argues that symbolic goods maintain cultural distinctions by marking their producers and consumers with legitimacy.

Like a perfectly timed machine, Symkyn appears to control the flows of agency that keep his household running smoothly. According to the hierarchy Symkyn relies upon for his position, any agency the women display is a figuration of the miller's power and an index of his control. But when Symkyn sets free the clerks' horse, he loosens the ties binding masculine authority in this universe, unleashing a competition he cannot reign in through a programmatic exercise of household discipline.[38] The miller sets in motion a chain of events enabling the clerks to play him at his own game, beat him on his home turf, and turn his possessions against him.

Symkyn's oversight, which the clerks utilize, is women's alignment with affect as it is represented in the misogamous tradition of the Middle Ages. Now, it should be acknowledged that this belief was part of the medieval outlook more generally, since works extolling women equally suggest their expansive capacities to feel joy, sadness, fear, or love. As didactic literature demonstrates, women's submission derives from an intensity of feeling: the affection that they harbor for their spouses compels women to obey their husbands. Men are encouraged to love their wives, but this fondness translates into a responsibility for order, as both religious and secular advice literatures attest. On the contrary, in the misogynist clerical tradition, a woman's affective propensity makes her an easy target for (male) exploitation. The miller thinks he has his women under control, and indeed, the women do their part to remain faithful to Symkyn. However, according to misogamous literatures, woman's mutability, her lack of reason, and her carnal appetite make it impossible for her to exercise her intention, or her "will," for a man's good.[39] In order to reduce the women to what Ian Lancashire aptly describes as currency in a men's market, this tale invokes clerical as-

[38] V. A. Kolve, *Chaucer and the Imagery of Narrative: The First Five Canterbury Tales* (London: Edward Arnold, 1984), pp. 235–48, argues that the two episodes of duping in this tale are joined through the image of the clerk's horse running wild through the fens. As he illustrates, such episodes of "loosening" often suggest diminished rationality and heightened sexual desire in men.

[39] See *MED*, s.v., "wil(le)," particularly 2(a), which identifies "will" with the appetitive or volitional part of the soul. Lochrie, *Margery Kempe*, pp. 19–23, explores the will's relation to the flesh in gendered terms. See also Elizabeth Robertson, *Early English Devotional Prose and the Female Audience* (Knoxville: University of Tennessee Press, 1990), pp. 130–42, who discusses the feminization of will in *Sawles Warde*. Her essay, "Souls that Matter: Gender and the Soul in *Piers Plowman*," in *Mindful Spirit in Late Medieval Literature: Essays in Honor of Elizabeth D. Kirk*, ed. Bonnie Wheeler (New York: Palgrave Macmillan, 2006), pp. 165–86, extends this line of inquiry.

sumptions about gender difference, devaluing Symkyn's model of masculinity for his inability to regulate feminine *affectus*.[40]

As the Wife of Bath knows well, clerical discourse rates marriage a second-best to celibacy, because it is a necessary concession to the appetitive pull of the volitional flesh: "[Paul] heeld virginitee / Moore parfit than weddyng in freletee" (III.91–92). Writers from Augustine to Heloise assert that marriage imposes weakness on a man because it necessarily depletes his reason.[41] Ruth Mazo Karras argues that the most important threshold for defining clerical masculinity is the faculty of reason, which divides the educated man from irrational creatures, namely, beasts and women.[42] Although clerics might be expected to have "more" reason than laymen, all men were associated with reason in the Middle Ages. The divide between celibate and conjugal masculinities, then, turns on the clerisy's formal separation from women. When a man married, he was yoked to another, who, according to the misogamous tradition, was associated with the debilitating appetites of the willful, *feeling*, flesh.[43] According to antimatrimonial literature, a married man has less reason than his celibate counterpart. Even Augustine, who is sympathetic to marriage, claims that a man hides his conjugal intimacy because his procreative organs are not fully ruled by reason during sexual intercourse.[44] But he also associates reason with the order a husband provides, for in his allegorical rendering of the encounter between Christ and the Samaritan woman, her five husbands signify her five senses (over which she has no control) and her "true" husband is the reason that Christ calls forth in order to enable her to recognize the salvation on offer.[45]

---

[40] Ian Lancashire, "Sexual Innuendo in the *Reeve's Tale*," *ChauR* 6 (1972): 159–70.

[41] See Katharina Wilson and Elizabeth M. Makowski, *"wykked wyves and the woes of marriage": Misogamous Literature from Juvenal to Chaucer* (Albany: SUNY Press, 199), esp. chap. 4, for a survey of materials that express this view. See also examples in G. R. Owst, *Literature and the Pulpit in Medieval England* (1933; London: Blackwell, 1961), pp. 378–79.

[42] Ruth Mazo Karras, *From Boys to Men: Formations of Masculinity in Late Medieval Europe* (Philadelphia: University of Pennsylvania Press, 2003), pp. 67–108.

[43] Lochrie, *Margery Kempe*, pp. 13–55; See also Peter Brown, *The Body and Society: Men, Women, and Sexual Renunciation in Early Christianity* (New York: Columbia University Press, 1988), pp. 341–47, for an account of the flesh's unruly willfulness in Augustine.

[44] Augustine, *City of God*, trans. Henry Bettenson (London: Penguin, 1972), XIV.16–18.

[45] Augustine, "Homilies on the Gospel of John; Homilies on the First Epistle of John Tractate VIII," *Nicene and Post-Nicene Authors*, vol. 7, ed. Philip Schaff (Grand Rapids, Mich.: Eerdmans, 1991), pp. 58–59.

Because they are associated with reason, then, laymen have the responsibility to govern their less capable household counterparts in measured fashion. Clerks, especially those at university, have no such burdens placed on their rational capacities. To distinguish himself as a man, a clerk only had to compete with other (educated) men. This competition, however, often involved women, at least at an instrumental level. As Karras points out, clerical disputation often used women as "tools to think with, or stimuli to the larger discussions."[46] Representations of women as passive in sexual encounters that naturalized violence, she explains, dovetailed with the clerical establishment's attempts to keep students away from marriageable women. Although the celibate imperative would have made all sexual contact with women off limits, Karras suggests that the university authorities "thought of [students] as sexual beings and called for them to relate to women in that way alone."[47] Clerical literature admits that women have will, but only as it enables them to seek sexual contact with men. According to the misogynist clerical tradition, then, feminine willfulness is always a threat to the kind of masculine governance Symkyn attempts to perform, because its exercise and its administration is infused with undisciplined affect.

Unless a man is the genuine article, a householder whose rational control brings all members of the domestic under the comprehensive scope of his programmatic discipline, the unruly affects of those "lesser" inhabitants of his private space are almost guaranteed to overthrow his measured governance. In an example of what happens to a cleric turned husband, the Wife of Bath's fifth husband, Jankyn, reads Alisoun the stories of Livia and Lucilla in an effort to contain her will. The Wife has been well schooled in Jankyn's primer of wifely wickedness, explaining that Livia and Lucilla were women who brought about their husbands' deaths, albeit from different motives: "That oon for love, that oother was for hate" (III.749). She reproduces accurately the story and the sentence of Walter Map's version, which universalizes the claim that feminine willfulness is detrimental to man: "Take the experience of these two as an example of the fact that a woman will put everything at risk, both what she loves and what she hates, and is skilled in bringing harm when she wants to, which is always; and often she does harm when she is trying to help, and so it turns out that she brings harm even when

[46] Karras, *From Boys to Men*, p. 88.
[47] Ibid., pp. 79; 80.

she does not want to. You have been put in a furnace: if you are gold, you will emerge more pure."[48] These exempla suggest that a woman's intention is unconnected to the consequences of her act. If she acts at all, she will cause her partner's demise, mainly because she feels too intensely to exercise discretion. Furthermore, the fact that Alisoun doesn't listen to Jankyn provides a particular instance of a husband's inability to govern wifely will: "I sette noght an hawe / Of his proverbes n'of his olde sawe" (III.659–60).

This strain of clerical discourse insists that men cannot stake their claims to authority on careful household governance. As Jehan le Fèvre's translation of *The Lamentations of Matheolus* suggests, the smart man does not deal with women except as instruments for short-term gain: "[W]oman is not rational. . . . She entrusts her honour openly to her eyes, yet they can't help but fail to protect it, since folly animates her gaze . . . all her actions are stupid and foolish. Woman can do no good; indeed, goodness is destroyed and obliterated by her."[49] This attitude, which is echoed by Andreas Capellanus, Jacques de Vitry, and Jean de Meun, suggests that men can direct feminine will only to where it is already going.[50] This literature does not claim that men necessarily control women; rather, as Aleyn and John demonstrate, "rational" clerks use women for bodily satisfaction only. Jeffrey Baylor rightly points to the anti-intellectual methods of domination the clerks use to avenge themselves upon Symkyn and his family.[51] Even so, their university training instilled the notion that "real" men manage affect through the detached governance of masculine reason, which in this context translates into the idea that "genuine" men dominate women through the adaptive manipulation of feminine will.

[48] Walter Map, "Dissuasio Valerii ad Rufinium," in *Jankyn's Book of Wikked Wyves*, ed. Ralph Hanna III and Traugott Lawler, The Chaucer Library, The Primary Texts, vol. 1 (Athens: University of Georgia Press, 1997), pp. 242–51: [Exemplo harum experimentum cape, quod audax est ad omnia quecumque [amat vel odit] femina, et artificiosa nocere cum vult, quod semper est; et frequenter, cum iu[v]are parat, obest, unde fit ut noceat, et nolens, In fornace positus es; [fol. 81} si aurum es, exibis purior].

[49] Jehan le Fèvre, *The Lamentations of Matheolus, Woman Defamed and Woman Defended: An Anthology of Medieval Texts*, ed. Alcuin Blamires (Oxford: Clarendon, 1992), pp. 194–95.

[50] Capellanus, III.83; III.107; Jacques de Vitry, *Sermons for All, Sermon 66*, Blamires, p. 146; In Jean de Meun's continuation of the *Roman de la Rose*, vv. 8608–28, Lucretia's suicide is blamed on her stubborn refusal to be convinced by her male relatives that she had not been violated.

[51] Jeffrey Baylor, "The Failure of the Intellect in Chaucer's *Reeve's Tale*," ELN 28:1 (1990): 17–19.

The clerks and Symkyn therefore share the belief that men should direct women, but they differ when it comes to their views of feminine agency and a man's ability to contain womanly will. While the misogamous tradition represents feminine agency as a purely sexual force that cannot *really* be harnessed or regulated by masculine reason, the conjugal discourse of lay masculinity suggests that womanly will is an undisciplined force that *needs* to be harnessed and regulated by masculine wit.[52] These masculine perspectives differ over whether or not feminine will can be turned to masculine good. Despite his corrupted practice, Symkyn subscribes to a model of manliness that depends on the positive potential of feminine affect for its authenticity. While secular writers, including Christine de Pizan and *Le ménagier de Paris,* discuss wives' positive influence on their husbands, there is also a type of clerical writing that suggests a wife's will can do her husband good.[53] Sharon Farmer explains that this ideal of conjugal mutuality urged women to use their influence to better their husbands' spiritual conditions.[54] As Thomas Chobham's *Summa confessorum* illustrates, this discourse concomitantly suggests a man's control over his wife, "as a part of his own body," and her power over him, "For no priest can soften a man's heart as a wife can."[55] Similarly, in the Wycliffite treatise, *Of Weddid Men and Wifis, and of Here Children Also,* wives are advised to exert softening influence over their husbands.[56] This ideal of gender difference, which is performatively

---

[52] There is a medieval tradition of debate poems between wit and will that express spiritual order in gendered terms, with the husband serving as wit and the wife, will. In a variation on this motif, a poem in MS. Jesus Camb 22, Palm Sunday Service, printed in M. R. James, *A Descriptive Catalogue of the MSS in the Library of Jesus College Cambridge* (London: C. J. Clay and Sons, 1895), p. 24, also sets the conflict within marriage, but interestingly alters the traditional alignments: Will advises the young man to marry, while Wit warns him against its perils.

[53] See also Christine de Pizan, *A Medieval Woman's Mirror of Honor: The Treasury of the City of Ladies,* trans. Charity Cannon Willard, ed. Madeleine Pelner Cosman (New York: Persea Books, 1989), who claims that a wife's practice of femininity will reform her husband, which will then in turn improve her domestic condition: "No man is so perverse that in the end his conscience and reason will not say to him: 'You have wronged and sinned against your good, honest wife.' Consequently, he may reform and love her as much or even more than if he had never strayed from the path of virtue" (p. 100).

[54] Sharon Farmer, "Persuasive Voices: Clerical Images of Medieval Wives," *Speculum* 61 (1986): 517–43.

[55] Thomas Chobham, *Thomae de Chobham: Summa Confessorum,* ed. F. Broomfield (Louvain, 1968), p. 375: {sicut parti corporis sui. . . . Nullus enim sacerdos ita potest cor viri emollire sicut potest uxor}.

[56] John Wyclif, *Of Weddid Men and Wifis, and of Here Children Also, Select English Works of John Wyclif,* ed. Thomas Arnold, vol. 3 (Oxford: Clarendon, 1971), pp. 188–201 (198).

realized through marriage, gives both partners agency through reciprocally inflected affective attachments.

If we agree that this relationship represents an idealized model of
medieval marriage, it is clear that Symkyn's practice of lay manhood is
its debased double. Mixing assumptions about women from the misogamous tradition with the authority of conjugal discourse, Symkyn treats
the women of his household like disinterested commodities before the
clerks arrive at his mill. Effacing the feeling that either might express,
Symkyn leaves no room for the feminine improvement of his house.
Thomas Chobham claims that a confessor should advise a woman to
work to correct her husband's faults, even to the point of giving away
his property "for pious causes" ("in pias causas").[57] For each masculine
ill, he claims there is a feminine corrective: "[I]f he is hard and merciless
and an oppressor of the poor she ought to incite him to mercy, if he is a
plunderer to detest his plundering; if he is a grasping man, let her inspire generosity in him and let her secretly give alms from their common
property and let her make good the alms which he fails to give."[58]
Under the ideal of conjugality, which, according to Glenn Burger, entails the "feminization of the female (as Aristotelian body and recepta-
cle, mother, helpmeet, needing male protection and regulation) and the
masculinization of the male (as possessing the vital seed in procreation,
head of the household, agent of outward action)," a woman marks her
presence through the softening affect she applies to her husband's hard
governance.[59] Symkyn makes no room for such feminine intervention,
because he regards each expression of womanly affection as an opportunity for exploitation.

On this point, therefore, Symkyn's estimation converges with the
opinion of the two clerks, revealing the elementary affinity between
"cherls" in this tale: while Symkyn treats the women like inert tools he
may use for gain, John and Aleyn view the women as passive instruments they may employ for advantage. The conduct of Malyne and her
mother, however, at least offers a passing possibility that this reductive
view of femininity lacks credibility. The women of this fabliau hold open

---

[57] Chobham, *Thomae de Chobham*, p. 375.
[58] Ibid., p. 375: [et si durus est et immisericors et oppressor pauperum, debet eum
invitare ad misericordiam; si raptor est, debet detestari rapinam; si avarus est, suscitet
in eo largitatem, et occulte faciat eleemosynas de rebus communibus, et eleemosynas
quas ille omittit, illa suppleat].
[59] Burger, *Chaucer's Queer Nation*, p. 73.

the possibility that that there is an alternative to this world of grasping manly competition. Unlike their counterparts in the Old French analogue, the wife is not complicit in her husband's theft and the daughter does not facilitate her sexual initiation.[60] Regardless of the wife's introduction, she never again manifests the haughtiness her snobby education supposedly instilled; as Nicholas Orme speculates, her training at the nunnery, which would have focused primarily on manners, may ironically contribute to the courtesy with which she treats her husband's guests.[61] And, notwithstanding a great deal of critical effort to associate Malyne with a "lusty" disposition, she never exhibits traits suggesting sexual immodesty.[62] These women are the only characters who attempt to do good: the wife alerts the clerks to their missing horse and the daughter directs her lover to his stolen grain. In fact, Chaucer's version of the story omits characteristics that would associate these women with the guile and lustiness that generally define women of the fabliaux.

Despite the tale's generic departures, though, the women's potential for ethical agency is foreclosed in order to alienate Symkyn through its construction of a "cherl" masculinity. Indeed, the tale incorporates its appeals to feminine affect into a broader and therefore more devastating representation of women as potent weapons in an exclusively masculine contest. The problematic consequences of the tale's instrumentalist view of feminine feeling become particularly apparent during the plunder of Malyne's body. The scene describing Aleyn and Malyne's union raises doubts about Aleyn's view of feminine will because his "seduction" suggests that he considers Malyne as an object lacking investment in her sexual availability:

> And up he rist, and by the wenche he crepte.
> This wenche lay uprighte and faste slepte,
> Til he so ny was, er she myghte espie,
> That it had been to late for to crie,
> And shortly for to seyn, they were aton.
> Now pley, Aleyn, for I wol speke of John.
>
> (I.4193–98)

---

[60] "Le Meunier et les II Clers," *The Literary Context of Chaucer's Fabliaux,* ed. Larry D. Benson and Theodore M. Andersson (New York: Bobbs-Merrill, 1971), pp. 100–115.

[61] Nicholas Orme, *English Schools in the Middle Ages* (London: Methuen, 1973), p. 54.

[62] W. A. Turner, "Chaucer's 'Lusty Malyne,'" *N &Q* 199 (1954): 232; and Katherine T. Emerson, "The Question of 'Lusty Malyne,'" *N &Q* 202 (1957): 277–78, work hardest to establish Malyne's sexual looseness.

While the issue of women's consent is foreclosed in many clerical disputational pieces, medieval rape law in many respects made compliance a decisive nonissue in legal appeals.[63] As legal scholars point out, most rape cases that made it to pleading failed on technical grounds, many because a woman failed to make her protest public by raising the "hue and cry."[64]

In cases of rape, both in legal and spiritual terms, a woman's moral disposition is at issue. Failure to make a display of resistance, according to the law, indicated an internal attitude, which for moralists was the key index of a maiden's complicity in such an incident. Augustine claims that there is room for a woman to remain pure as long as she refuses such violation, at least at the level of spiritual agency: "Purity is a virtue of the mind . . . it is not lost when the body is violated. Indeed, when the quality of modesty resists the indecency of carnal desires the body itself is sanctified . . . because the will to employ the body in holiness endures."[65] But for jurists, the evidence of resistance must be easier to see. Glanville advises that "a woman who suffers in this way must go, soon after the deed is done, to the nearest vill and there show to trustworthy men the injury done to her, and any effusion of blood there may be and any tearing of clothes."[66] Bracton likewise says that an appeal of rape must indicate "whether garments were torn and whether blood was shed by the ravishment."[67] As many scholars point out, it is possible, even likely, that Aleyn rapes Malyne. Yet in the legal context of

[63] For an example of the connection between this attitude and training in the trivium, see T. J. Garbaty, "Pamphilus, De Amore: An Introduction and Translation," *ChauR* 2 (1967): 108–34. This text, which involves an attempted rhetorical seduction and ensuing rape of the beautiful Galatea by her suitor Pamphilus, is commonly thought to have been used as a Latin primer. See Anne Schotter, "Rhetoric Versus Rape in the Medieval Latin *Pamphilus*," *PQ* 71 (1992): 243–60; see also Marjorie Curry Woods, "The Teaching of Writing in Medieval Europe," in *A Short History of Writing Instruction*, ed. James J. Murphy (Davis, Calif.: Hermagoras Press, 1990), pp. 77–94.

[64] Joseph Allen Hornsby, *Chaucer and the Law* (Norman, Okla.: Pilgrim Books, 1988), p. 140.

[65] Augustine, *City of God*, I.18.

[66] George D. G. Hall, ed. and trans., *Tractatus de Legibus et Consuetudinibus Regni Anglie qui Glanvilla Vocatur, The Treatise on the Laws and Customs of the Realm of England Commonly Called Glanvill* (London: Nelson, 1965), p. 175: [Tenetur autem mulier que tale quid patitur mox dum recens fuerit maleficium uicinam uillam adire, et ibi iniuriam sibi illatam probis hominibus ostendere et sanguinem si quis fuerit effusus et uestium scissiones].

[67] Henry Bracton, *De Legibus et Consuetudinibus Angliae, On the Laws and Customs of England (c. 1250)*, ed. George E. Woodbine, trans. Samuel E. Thorne, Selden Society (1968; Cambridge, Mass.: Harvard University Press, 1977), pp. 394–95: [tunc de scissione vestimentorum et de sanguinis effusione per corruptionem].

rape appeals, unlike others invoked by the tale, a woman's resistance must be manifest, because here her physical struggle indicates the purity of her will.

This tale deploys legal standards for determining the crime of rape, not just to besmirch Malyne's sexual modesty but also to impugn her affective disposition more broadly. Aleyn seizes Malyne before she can cry out, but clearly by morning he wins her consent. Between Aleyn's stealth and Malyne's affection, neither the girl nor Symkyn has a legal claim to rape.[68] Any appeal she might make is vitiated by her open dedication to the clerk's cause. Returning the stolen grain, therefore, affirms Malyne's consent more than it displays her decency. While modern critics rightly point to the vicious consequences that would ensue from Malyne's sexual violation, I suggest that her debasement here is more comprehensive than previously acknowledged: compounding the physical, psychological, and social damage that echoes as the aftermath of the encounter's dawn-song, this tale additionally suggests that Malyne's *affectus* is corrupt.[69] It does so, moreover, by using one of the only ethical acts of the tale to indict her character. In a bitter irony, then, the ethical innocence of Malyne's affection reduces her to a stock character of the fabliau, the type of easy "wenche" who wants Aleyn to use her for sexual pleasure.[70] Here as elsewhere, feminine feeling is reduced to

[68] Tamarah Kohanski, "In Search of Malyne," *ChauR* 27 (1993): 228–38, argues that this episode should be read as a rape; also, Elaine Tuttle Hansen, *Chaucer and the Fictions of Gender* (Berkeley and Los Angeles: University of California Press, 1992), p. 242, uses the word "rape" casually to refer to the encounter between Malyne and Aleyn.

[69] Pamela Barnett, "'And Shortly for to Seyn They Wer Aton': Chaucer's Deflection of Rape in the 'Reeve's' and 'Franklin's Tales,'" *WS* 22 (1993): 145–62, is particularly helpful on the tale's mystification of rape through Malyne's stereotypical consent. See also Cadden, *Meanings of Sex Difference*, p. 95 n. 130, who cites the pre-Galenic text *On Human Generation* to illustrate the theory of the two wills in cases of rape: "Displicet rationi et placet carni. Et si igitur in rapta non est voluntas rationis, est tamen delectationis carnis" [{What} is displeasing to reason is pleasing to the flesh. And if, therefore, there is not the rational will in the raped women, there is nevertheless {the will} of carnal pleasure]. Ovid makes this attitude so common that Christine de Pizan feels she must answer it in her *Book of the City of Ladies,* trans. Earl Jeffrey Richards, foreword Natalie Zemon Davis (New York: Persea Books, 1998), 2:44–47. See also Corinne Saunders, *Rape and Ravishment in the Literature of Medieval England* (Cambridge: D. S. Brewer, 2001), who gives a history of the development of and changes in rape law and the ecclesiastical responses the issue generated.

[70] Emerson, "The Question of 'Lusty Malyne,'" pp. 277–78, concludes that Chaucer usually employs "wenche" to designate a "loose woman." Kohanski, "In Search of Malyne," p. 229, points out that in all other cases, an adjective that suggests traits about the character's "essence" is verified by the actions of the character. Emerson's alternative definition of "wenche," "female servant" or "lowborn woman," works more clearly to insult Symkyn's pretensions for his daughter's marriage. Chaucer uses the term "wen-

sexual complicity, making rape a crime that men commit against one another in a world where women are simply instruments for social gain.[71]

Malyne's ethical separation from her father's moral corruption is therefore presented as a sign of Symkyn's weakness, not her independent worth.[72] Similarly, the wife is not a challenging conquest, but the ease John has in taking her does not arise from her complicity. Like Malyne, the wife's inability to distinguish between male players allows another man to commandeer her for use against her husband. With the cradle moved, John lies in wait for the miller's wife to place *herself* in a position where he can use her for his own profit. When she finds the cradle at the foot of the clerks' bed, she makes an ironic exclamation confirming her intention to remain faithful to her husband: " 'Allas!' " quod she, " 'I hadde almoost mysgoon; / I hadde almoost goon to the clerkes bed. / Ey, benedicte! Thanne hadde I foule ysped!' " (I.4218–20). Her desire to remain faithful, however, allows the most able masculine player to direct her for his use. John thus defines his masculine ability by procuring Symkyn's wife despite her wish to stay true to her husband. Her inability to differentiate between men is consistent with the tale's treatment of feminine will: she cannot tell who is the *better* man because she cannot even tell who is the *right* man. The contest, the tale's account insists, remains one between men who use women as implements to distinguish themselves from one another.

The wife's pleasure in her encounter, like Malyne's affection for her

---

che" to designate a "low-born" woman in another fabliau. In *The Miller's Tale,* when carpenter-John is preparing for the flood, his female house-servant is referred as his "wenche" (I.3631). *MED,* s.v. "wenche," easily suggests a social rather than sexual connotation: "an unmarried girl . . . occasionally with disparaging overtones." This term affectively associates the social and moral status of a woman much in the same fashion that "cherl" does for a man.

[71] Daniel Pigg, "Performing the Perverse: The Abuse of Masculine Power in the *Reeve's Tale,*" in *Masculinities in Chaucer,* ed. Peter Beidler (Cambridge: D. S. Brewer, 1998), pp. 53–61, is right to claim that this tale is one of male-on-male violence, suggesting as he does that it performs a "symbolic rape" of Symkyn and thereby the Miller (p. 60). See Slavoj Žžek's discussion of rape as a weapon, *The Metastases of Enjoyment: Six Essays on Woman and Causality* (London: Verso, 1995), p. 74, which he claims is meant to expose the father "in his utter impotence, which makes him guilty in his own eyes as well as in those of his daughter; the daughter is guilty for causing her father's humiliation; and so on."

[72] Sheila Delany, *Medieval Literary Politics: Shapes of Ideology* (Manchester: University of Manchester Press, 1990), p. 110, claims that Malyne's act undoes the logic of economic exchange involved in the aims set out for her marriage, but also notes the ineffective challenge her act poses since she devalues herself.

clerk, shows the dangers that women's affective capacities pose to masculine regulation. Even if she intends to consolidate Symkyn's masculine prowess, the wife's sexual desire overflows the boundaries of his management, further weakening his control. Since the tale never suggests that the wife is unhappy with her marriage because Symkyn is a poor lover, it is unreasonable to assume that she is just waiting for any man to come along to satisfy her keen sexual longing. But the tale does suggest Symkyn's ineptitude, drawing a very clear distinction between the miller "That as an hors he fnorteth in his sleep," and John, who fervently works on her body, "He priketh harde and depe as he were mad" (I.4163; 4231). As Elaine Tuttle Hansen points out, "Mrs. Symkyn's pleasure is referred to only in a line that clearly serves to cast aspersions on the husband's sexual capacity."[73] Her function as a tool that measures masculine worth, however, also allows John to equal his partner in the revenge they extract from another man. Taking delight from an encounter with a man she thinks is her invigorated husband, the wife's pleasure makes the two clerks equal in sexual ability while it simultaneously excludes Symkyn from their more "rational" kind of masculinity.

All Politics Is Local

If this episode is to remain a competition between men, the particulars of the clerks' vengeance must continually be recast in relation to Symkyn alone. The tale invokes a contemporary model of masculinity to suggest that the women in the tale are part of the miller's identity, but this model may be used to uncase the miller's social pretensions only if it pairs with the misogynist assumption that feminine affect is universally detrimental to male authority. While Symkyn seeks to pass off this debased fusion as socially legitimate, the clerks' conduct threatens to expose this position as an ethical counterfeit. Indeed, through their independent acts of kindness, the women "almoost" (I.4248) emerge from this tale as exemplars of an ethics of reciprocity. But I emphasize *almost* here, to acknowledge that the women are always compromised by the tale's values; like Malyne, whose sentimental fondness for Aleyn becomes the object of derision, the women's attempts to do right in this domain makes *Symkyn* a target of mockery. To be sure, ridiculing isolated acts of kindness in an otherwise vengeful world suggests that this

---

[73] Hansen, *Chaucer and the Fictions of Gender,* p. 243.

tale's universe is as choleric as its teller, the Reeve, who is often described as bitter and vindictive.[74]

But I want to go one step further, because I believe the tale's meanness points to Chaucer's exploration of affect's impact upon dissident politics, within the first fragment and beyond. The Miller perhaps means to smooth the joinings of voluntary association with his cheery suggestion that the detrimental potential of feminine affect may be contained through a calculated project of selective perception: "An housbonde shal nat been inquisityf / Of Goddes pryvetee, nor of his wyf" (I.3163–64). Yet the Reeve will have none of it: he rejects the Miller's plenteous universe, readjusting the social frame of struggle to focus upon the wranglings that distinguish men within local communities. Structured by what William Ian Miller calls the "contagious" affect of fear, the schooling Symkyn receives is meant to transfer from one pretentious miller to another.[75] Even as Symkyn learns the hard lesson that he should not presume to identify with his social betters, his exposure presses the point that Robyn should think twice about pretending to represent his social peers, especially against those of higher rank. This deflation achieves fear's purpose as Sara Ahmed describes it, because in separating the Miller from his fellow men, it "re-establishes distance between bodies."[76] The Reeve's attack reframes Robyn's challenge to the Knight as its own form of social imposture, alienating him socially by identifying the Miller as a political phony. By using fear's estranging capacity, this attack associates the Miller with social fraud in a way that cannot be undone by tracing the historical alliances that actual millers forged with their more visibly servile neighbors in instances of rural resistance in the late Middle Ages.[77]

This tale's method *is* therefore psychological, as Lee Patterson argues, but only to the extent that it collapses the boundary between self and other that modern theories of psychology maintain.[78] Moreover, because

[74] Bruce Moore, "The Reeve's Rusty Blade," *MÆ* 58 (1989): 304–12, and Edward Vasta, "How Chaucer's Reeve Succeeds," *Criticism* 25 (1983): 1–12.

[75] William Ian Miller, *The Mystery of Courage* (Cambridge, Mass.: Harvard University Press, 2000), pp. 92–105; 201–19. See also his discussion of vicarious experience of emotion in *The Anatomy of Disgust* (Cambridge, Mass.: Harvard University Press, 1997), pp. 194–96.

[76] Ahmed, *Cultural Politics of Emotion,* p. 63.

[77] Patterson, *Chaucer and the Subject of History,* pp. 256–58.

[78] See Gail Kern Paster, Katherine Rowe, and Mary Floyd-Wilson, "Introduction," *Reading the Early Modern Passions: Essays in the Cultural History of Emotion,* ed. Gail Kern Paster, Katherine Rowe, and Mary Floyd-Wilson, pp. 13–15, for a survey of studies

this tale refuses the border between inner and outer states of feeling, its stakes are deeply political. At issue in this tale is the scope of the political, the very site of contest where persons mete out differences and find commonalities that form the basis of community itself. These grounds are necessarily inflected by historical situation, but they are not reducible to cultural circumstance. As William Ian Miller explains of emotions, "[they] are connected to ideas, perceptions, and cognitions and to the social and cultural contexts in which it makes sense to have those feelings and ideas."[79] The affective dimension of the tale, then, emphasizes what Brian Massumi provocatively calls "the passage" between outward and inward conditions of feeling.[80] By representing what it feels like to be subjected to certain social conditions, the Reeve's narrative attack shows Chaucer's awareness that an appeal to peasant consciousness is a politically belated act. While it might promote a unifying sense of nostalgia, this group identity offers few advantages to those individuals who actually make up this set after the failure of the rebels to assert its authority. Though members of the rising undoubtedly attempted to declare their political legitimacy as a group through adaptive appropriations of documentary culture, Richard's infamous dismissal enacts the alienation of the "lowest" cultural order: "Rustics you were and rustics you are still; you will remain in bondage, not as before but incomparably harsher."[81]

Designated as visibly invisible members of the body politic, the luckiest of the rebels and their supporters washed back into their local communities, taking with them knowledge of the tactical advantage that discursive appropriation may yield.[82] This localization of politics should

---

that illustrate psychoanalysis's involvement in defining and maintaining a border between inward and outward states as a condition of modern consciousness. See also Patterson, "'No Man His Reson Herde,'" p. 161, for his devaluation of this tale's "psychological" priorities.

[79] Miller, *Anatomy of Disgust,* p. 8.

[80] Massumi, *Parables for the Virtual,* p. 217, expresses affect's mobility this way: "As processional as it is precessional, affect inhabits the passage."

[81] Walsingham, *Historia Anglicana,* quoted in R. B. Dobson, ed., *The Peasants' Revolt of 1381* (London: Macmillan, 1970), p. 311. For the Latin, see Thomas Walsingham, *Historia Anglicana,* ed. H. T. Riley, 2 vols. (London, 1863–64), 2:18: "Rustici quidem fuistis et estis; in bondagio permanebitis." It should be noted that Walsingham's "rustici" could also be translated "churls."

[82] Justice, *Writing and Rebellion,* pp. 38–39, suggests that once the explosive events of the rebellion subsided, there was a long period of petty unrest in rural communities, of "local violence and theft only occasioned or colored, rather than motivated, by political complaint" (p. 39).

be at least vaguely familiar to Chaucer scholars, for the poet's own service in the countryside as Knight of the Shire (1386) and Justice of the Peace (1385–89) has long been viewed as a savvy retreat from the court factionalism that fatally embroiled many of his contemporaries on the larger political stage.[83] But as Kellie P. Robertson points out, when Chaucer served on the Peace Commissions, he was responsible for enforcing some of the most divisive statutes of the era alongside some of the most hated men in England.[84] Moreover, social and legal historians of the late Middle Ages are quick to remind us that during this period the country provided no idyllic escape from vindictive infighting or manipulative intrigue. In an attempt to express the widespread use of intimidation and favoritism in Peace Commissions, Alan Harding characterizes the precipitous downfall of Robert Tresilian, who served with Chaucer in Kent before he was tried, then hanged, for treason, "as the application of local methods to national politics."[85] *The Reeve's Tale* is not a depoliticized retreat to petty infighting between individuals. Instead, it offers a representation of English politics in the years after the failed rising with which Chaucer would have been intimately, experientially, familiar.

Chaucer's involvement, I suggest, also entangles us, showing the ways in which affect moves between bodies, precipitating an unmediated, uninitiated, and often-unwanted form of contact. We could assert our distance from the simple historical fact that Chaucer was intimately implicated in the post-rebellion politics of the English countryside with a pithy declaration, "Chaucer was the police."[86] In drawing this comparison, it is immediately clear that David R. Carlson identifies Chaucer with the oppressive apparatus of state power.[87] Yet in characterizing Chaucer's position between crown and country as involving "cognate

---

[83] Donald Howard, *Chaucer: His Life, His Works, His World* (New York: Fawcett Columbine, 1987), pp. 383–400; Derek Pearsall, *The Life of Geoffrey Chaucer* (Oxford: Blackwell, 1992), pp. 202–9.

[84] Kellie P. Robertson, "Laboring in the God of Love's Garden: Chaucer's Prologue to *The Legend of Good Women*," *SAC* 24 (2002): 115–47. Robertson makes this point on p. 116, but her entire article convincingly adjusts the view that Chaucer's service in the countryside was a retreat from politics, particularly politics involving the legibility of laborers as a group in late fourteenth-century England.

[85] Alan Harding, *Law Courts of Medieval England* (London: George Allen and Unwin, 1973), p. 94.

[86] David R. Carlson, *Chaucer's Jobs* (New York: Palgrave Macmillan, 2004), p. 1.

[87] The first sentence of Carlson's book reads: "Chaucer was the police, not in an attenuated or metaphoric sense: in the better part of his mature employments, he was an official of the repressive apparatus of state" (p. 1).

varieties of surveillance," Carlson puts Chaucer in uneasy contact with his abusive manager, the Reeve, whose overseeing power derives just as much from exploiting as enforcing elite power.[88] This touching, and the discomfort that accompanies it, indicates the ways that affect infuses the politics of representation, both Chaucer's and our own.[89] In these concluding pages, therefore, I put the affective politics of Chaucer's *Reeve's Tale* in contact with similar appeals from our own culture to argue that an empathy based on touching—however discomfiting, however disaffecting—offers a way to see another's political position without identifying with it, at least not fully.

This version of empathy takes full advantage of the tension that Karl Morrison so famously and effectively explores through the gripping address, *I Am You,* for it preserves a difference between subjects who nevertheless rub up against one another in an uneasily shared awareness.[90] As Chaucer's tale of a miller and two clerks demonstrates, this contact can be quite competitive, even coercive, in its consolidating processes. In drawing attention to affect as a crucial element in representation, therefore, I am also acknowledging the negativity inherent to many such mobilizations. In other words, not all affects, or their analyses, deal in terms of love or joy. In fact, if we return to medieval classifications, it seems that many affiliations base their claims to subjects on the ability to inspire divisive feelings. Thus, while I join Nicholas Watson in his desire to formulate and practice a medievalism attentive to affect, here I am suggesting that we must also do so in contexts where we leave ourselves unprotected from the negative feelings we engage through such study.[91] For it should be acknowledged, in the terms that have

[88] Carlson, *Chaucer's Jobs,* p. 8. Although this phrase refers specifically to Chaucer's work in customs, when discussing Chaucer's service as Justice of the Peace, Carlson comments, "Chaucer worked in surveillance again, on behalf of the crown again, though in a way more directly to be associated with modern-day police work" (p. 15).

[89] My discussion of touching's connection to affect in the remainder of this essay is heavily indebted to Sedgwick's discussion, pp. 3–17, where she argues that a shift in inquiry from epistemology to phenomenology might lead us to ask different questions of affective relations: "what motivates performativity and performance, for example, and what individual and collective effects are mobilized in their execution?" (p. 17). Carolyn Dinshaw's *Getting Medieval: Sexualities and Communities, Pre- and Postmodern* (Durham: Duke University Press, 1999), pp. 16, 39–40, 150–52, 163, explores the pleasurable possibilities of touching in a way that I find particularly helpful in considering our relations to medieval texts and their communities.

[90] Karl Morrison, *"I Am You": The Hermeneutics of Empathy in Western Literature, Theology, and Art* (Princeton: Princeton University Press, 1988).

[91] Nicholas Watson, "Desire for the Past," *SAC* 21 (1999): 59–97. Watson's inspiring article demonstrates the ways that our critical practice must remain open to feelings of love and joy, and the risks and difficulties involved in doing so. Perhaps unsurprisingly,

galvanized debate over feminist historiography, that *The Reeve's Tale* is "not a story to pass on" if we are seeking to separate ourselves from the vicious exploitation of women that enable many formations of masculinity, in medieval culture or since.[92]

In fact, after reading an earlier draft of this paper, a generous colleague wanted to know why a feminist scholar like myself would be "for" affect, since my analysis attempts to show that such appeals can be used to promote oppressive and domineering forms of gender identity. I take the point: if affective appeals consolidate repression, wouldn't it be my critical duty to resist that abuse by uncovering affect as something to be eliminated in gender/class negotiations? Maybe so, but I think risking the protected distance a critical posture affords is worth taking, and for reasons that are just as pressing now as they were in the late fourteenth century. First, were I to mark my resistance to affect in Chaucer's *Reeve's Tale* by condemning it, I would only be saying something about myself, mostly for myself. That is certainly one purpose of criticism, and by now I hope it is clear that I fully believe this tale's abuse of women is appalling. Nevertheless, I also know that this tale will be passed on, for the simple fact that its affective dynamism *works*. Appeals that are brazenly mean are often effective—we all know this from our playground years. And, if we need a refresher in our cynics lessons, we need only look to the arena of modern politics to confirm affect's pervasive success in mobilizing feelings that exceed rationality, such as fear.[93]

---

his analysis suggests that feelings expressive of positive affects are often more difficult to sustain in professional disciplinary settings than those negative currents I trace here.

[92] This phrase derives from Kathleen Biddick's quotation of Toni Morrison's *Beloved* in her article, "Genders, Bodies, Borders: Technologies of the Visible," *Speculum* 68 (1993): 389–418, where she uses it to critique Caroline Walker Bynum's *Holy Feast and Holy Fast: The Religious Significance of Food to Medieval Women* (Berkeley and Los Angeles: University of California Press, 1987) for Bynum's intense investment in her matter. My interest in this phrase as it relates to the debate over what constitutes a properly disciplined feminist historiography was piqued by Watson's discussion in his article, "Desire for the Past," especially p. 65.

[93] Though it may seem like an extreme example, *The Reeve's Tale*'s deployment of gender to situate rank resonates with Louisiana governor Edwin W. Edwards's legendary electoral confidence: "The only way I can lose this election is if I'm caught in bed with either a dead girl or a live boy." His assertion baldly recognizes that members of a community will overlook a public figure's transgression of broad moral prohibitions as long as he achieves political goals they find desirable. The amazing arc of Edwards's career might be said more broadly to illustrate affect's peculiar influence over American politics: he served in all three branches of government before winning his fourth term as governor in 1991. After several indictments, Edwards was finally convicted on seventeen counts of racketeering involving casino licenses in 2000. In the run-off election for governor in 1991, when Edwards faced David Duke, former leader of the Ku Klux

But it is not just that *The Reeve's Tale* reveals the persistent efficacy of fear as a politically unifying force during historical periods characterized by great social and economic inequities.[94] Rather, the operation of affect in modern political life further elucidates the social stakes of *The Reeve's Tale,* and our critical responses to its gendered politics. In pondering the question, "What's the Matter with Liberals?" Thomas Frank extends his thesis that affective mobilizations of class are currently informing the trend toward conservative moral values in American politics with a crowning example of "one of the most ill-conceived liberal electoral efforts of all time."[95] By this he refers to a campaign sponsored by the British *Guardian,* in which readers of the newspaper wrote letters to voters in Ohio in a personal attempt to persuade them not to vote for George W. Bush. As Frank explains, "Unsurprisingly, the Ohioans strongly resented being lectured to on the foolishness of their national leader by some random bunch of erudite Europeans."[96] This episode is relevant to the Reeve's deflation of a pretentious miller, because the error of liberals in Frank's example is their assumption that members of "lower" social strata do not formulate methods for constructing and regulating their own. As Oswald's narrative illustrates, members of so-called "lesser" cultural groups have finely tuned internal mechanisms for differentiation. These tactics may partake of political strategies fa-

---

Klan, bumper stickers summed up the community's feeling that its political choices were ethically limited with the snappy injunction: "Vote for Crook—It's Important."

[94] See Ahmed, *Cultural Politics of Emotion,* pp. 62–81, for a discussion of the ways that appeals to fear promise to establish distance between the self and the threats one feels.

[95] Thomas Frank, "What's the Matter with Liberals? The Election of 2004," *New York Review of Books,* vol. 52, no. 8, 12 May 2005, pp. 46–51 (48). This essay is based on the afterword to the paperback edition of his book, *What's the Matter with Kansas? How Conservatives Won the Heart of America* (New York: Henry Holt, 2005). Tom Mertes, "A Republican Proletariat," *New Left Review* 30 (November–December 2004): 37–47, engages Frank's oeuvre in terms that resonate with the priorities of my argument, pointing out that blue-collar American workers apparently have "learned that they have very little to gain from the [Democratic] party" (47). This disaffection, Mertes contends, arises from an awareness that both parties promote economic policies that benefit wealthy elites. Mertes thus connects the earlier indictment of Clintonian economic policy in Frank's 2001 book, *One Market Under God,* to the "backlash" against liberal politics that Frank traces in *What's the Matter with Kansas?* in explicitly affective terms: "In this situation [*What's the Matter with Kansas?*], workers who vote Republican may be less deluded than Frank seems to believe. Putting it in sociological language, since there is so little to choose 'instrumentally' between the two parties, each of them dedicated to capital unbound, why not at least get the satisfaction of voting 'expressively' for the one which seems to speak for their values, if not their interests?" (46).

[96] Frank, "What's the Matter with Liberals? p. 48.

miliar from official discourse, but often they gain traction from their localized calibrations of affect.

I am therefore arguing for the alterity of peasant consciousness, even as I suggest its centrality to Chaucer's *Reeve's Tale*. Let me emphasize, however, that I am not following the reasoning of Alcuin Blamires, who suggests that Chaucer scapegoats the Reeve in order to allow the Knight to float free from a baronial perspective.[97] When he categorizes both Miller and Reeve as "cherls," Chaucer defines these characters, at least morally, as a political class unto themselves. The Reeve and the Knight inhabit parallel universes, which are characterized by separate discourses of affective training. Even so, these spaces touch one another in marginal yet important ways, for it can equally be argued that the *Knight's Tale* depicts the combination of domestic governance and sexual exploitation required to secure masculine power. The Reeve's attack against his fellow "cherl," therefore, reveals even more fundamentally the ways in which the sublimation of women, which Robyn initially challenges with his lusty Alisoun, covers men's instrumental relations in elite fictions of identity. Nevertheless, the failure of Symkyn's masculine regimen does not subject Theseus's modes of affective governance to scrutiny. Instead, this tale's deflationary movement more centrally exposes the ethical alienation of "lesser" men, those "cherls" who do not have access to the cultural institutions that entitle their modes of exploitation.

Acknowledging "cherl" masculinity's ethical alienation, therefore, opens up the possibility for political empathy, even if we recognize that this position depends for its very coherence on denying empathy to others.[98] In their abuse of the two women, the men in the tale demonstrate

[97] Alcuin Blamires, "Chaucer the Reactionary: Ideology and the General Prologue to the *Canterbury Tales*," *RES*, n.s., 51 (2000): 254–539. Blamires is right to suggest that the Reeve is presented as an odious manager, and to point out that historically reeves were hated representatives of seigneurial control among their villein-peers. But to suggest that Oswald's bitter disposition is connected to an idealization of the Knight, and then to assume that this binary reveals Chaucer's own attitude in an opposition between aristocratic and rural sympathies, is to polarize the politics of both Chaucer and the *Canterbury Tales* in ways that cannot be sustained. That Chaucer presents a portrait of peasant consciousness complex enough to admit differences among individual members of the group certainly does not automatically mean that his political ideology was aristocratic. It is clear that Chaucer had *some* aristocratic tendencies, but the socially nebulous collection of pilgrims in *The Canterbury Tales* suggests that Chaucer is interested in complicating oppositional reductions based on traditional social divisions.

[98] My conception of this version of political empathy is indebted to Sedgwick's theory of touching, particularly her meditations on the preposition "beside," in which "a number of elements may lie alongside one another, though not an infinity of them" (p. 8). Judith Butler's discussion of becoming "undone by each other," or living "beside ourselves," equally speaks to the sense of "ethical enmeshment" (Butler's phrasing) that I

the menacing potential of the phrase, "I am you," for in acting upon the assumption that the women are fully incorporated elements of masculine identities, the men deny the women's claims to presence, both in terms of gender and class.[99] Yet this tale also founds its abuse in terms that are explicitly gender- and class-coded, suggesting as it does that men repress women to prevent their exploitation by other men. The tale thus presents the violation of the two women as justified punishment because in this locale social pretension is figured as the greatest trespass against community. Furthermore, by asserting that gender is a register that ranks various men, this narrative devalues feminine agency except as it enables men to differentiate themselves. The women are therefore allowed no empathy in this tale, mainly because they are already assumed to be lesser members of a domain where *men* must vie for superiority. And, because social station is the ultimate priority in this context, the tale compels its audience to make an ethical choice, the conclusion of which is affectively foregone: though it never acknowledges this demand, the tale asks its audience to excuse sexual violation because it punishes class counterfeit.[100]

If we look to Chaucer to expose *this* instance of political misprision for its ideological inconsistency or psychic pathology, we will simply confront the frustrating efficacy of affect's influence over localized politics. The Reeve's strategy succeeds with his immediate audience, affectively uniting "those who work" through its instrumental appropriation of feminine agency for masculine gain. The Cook *loves The Reeve's Tale,* and subsequently begins a tale in which women's will is even more explicitly equated to their sexual utility in ways that profit men: "And hadde a wyf that heeld for contenance / A shoppe, and swyved for hir sustenance" (I.4421–22). It might be comforting to assume that the

seek to capture here (pp. 19, 20, 25). See Judith Butler, *Undoing Gender* (New York: Routledge, 2004).

[99] See Morrison, pp. 69–136. Watson, "Desire for the Past," pp. 73–76, helpfully discusses this phrase's malevolent potential in relation to postcolonial critiques such as that by Diana Fuss (see note 2 above), though Watson's analysis does not address Fuss's argument directly.

[100] Anne McClintock makes this precise point in her critique of postcolonialism's effacement of women's experience, but she does not admit that men are also subject to similar colonizing gestures, which frequently essentialize, then privilege, certain masculinities as substitutions for social rank. See her article, "The Angel of Progress: Pitfalls of the Term 'Post-Colonial,'" *Social Text* 31/32 (1992): 84–98, for the most precise articulation of this position, which she elaborates in her book, *Imperial Leather: Race, Gender, and Sexuality in the Colonial Contest,* (New York: Routledge, 1995).

following breakdown of the first fragment is Chaucer's attempt to expose this narrative trajectory for its problematic use of gendered politics. But Chaucer neither challenges nor affirms the Reeve's machinations, allowing the Cook's intervention to extend and limit Oswald's political appeal to members of a "lower" estate. And, even if we would like to assert our distance from the masculine community that emerges as a result of this tale's instrumental abuse of women, a pithy formalist declaration—"Chaucer's *Reeve's Tale* is a fabliau"—does not account for this narrative's reductive representation of feminine feeling.[101] By acknowledging and exploiting the affections of the female characters, this tale fashions a masculine collective united through its grasping manipulations of others.[102] Nevertheless, because Symkyn is finally excluded from this grouping, the tale's formulation of a "cherl" identity further demonstrates the ethical and political limitations imposed on men who enjoy less formal access to conventions of dominance during this period.

Depending as it does on affect to gather, rank, and punish different members, "cherl" masculinity ultimately exceeds traditional forms of critique in medieval literary studies. Since historicism and psychoanalysis similarly rely on exposing social formations or psychological structures, these methods collectively fail to engage the affective morality

[101] The generic conventions of the fabliaux are notoriously difficult to chart with precision, as my recent attempt continues to illustrate: Holly A. Crocker, "The Provocative Body of the Fabliaux," *Comic Provocations: Exposing the Corpus of Old French Fabliaux,* ed. Holly A. Crocker (New York: Palgrave Macmillan, 2006), pp. 1–14. Nevertheless, it is generally agreed that fabliau characters are one-dimensional, lacking in emotional depth and gravity. As Lesley Johnson memorably argues, "Women on Top: Antifeminism in the Fabliaux?" *MLR* 78 (1983): 298–307, and Lisa Perfetti wittily demonstrates, "The Lewd and the Ludic: Female Pleasure in the Fabliaux," in *Comic Provocations,* pp. 17–32, women of the fabliaux are often depicted as sexually available, but their exploits nearly always arise from a volitional betrayal that illustrates their cleverness. For examples of such fabliaux, see *La Saineresse* and *De Berengier au lonc cul, Nouveau Recueil Complet des Fabliaux,* ed. Willem Noomen and Nico van den Boogaard, 10 vols. (Assen: Van Gorcum, 1983–98), vol. 4. In fabliaux depicting the sexual initiation of a seemingly naïve young woman, the girl's adherence to conventional morality usually makes her a target of seduction. In many cases, however, the girl's naïveté is so extreme that she appears to be in collaboration with her lover. The most familiar example of this type of fabliau is probably *La Damoisele qui ne poot oïr parler de foutre* (*NRCF,* vol. 4). Other variations include *L'Esquiriel* (*NRCF,* vol. 6), and both manuscript traditions of *Cele qui fu foutue et desfoutue* (*NRCF,* vol. 4).

[102] Generally, husbands who seek absolute domination of their wives themselves become dupes. Kyril Petkov illustrates the ways in which "arrogance" reverses gender polarities across a wide cross section of fabliaux in his essay "Mobility and Resentment in a World of Flux: Arrogance in the Old French Fabliaux," in *Comic Provocations,* pp. 113–27.

that subtends and distorts much political discourse, including that of *The Reeve's Tale*.[103] As an alternative to exposure as a model of analysis, Chaucer's *Reeve's Tale* issues a call to confront the ethical consequences of affective appeals *within* their social contexts, which have psychological *and* historical dimensions that continue to affect us. Consequently, acknowledging our sustained involvement in the ethical cynicism of this fabliau allows us to consider the tale's gendered negotiation of a laboring identity as it potentially addresses the political alienation of "peasant consciousness" in the years after the rebellion. Though *The Miller's Tale* might cast a nostalgic glance backward to a time when the traditionally dispossessed could assert political legitimacy through group action, by the late1380s Chaucer knew as well as anyone that those days in June were a distant memory. And, since Chaucer is not a particularly sentimental poet, it is hard to believe that he would neglect the affective wrangling ushered into English politics more broadly when Richard quashed the rebels' petition for political recognition. Indeed, if there is a hint of sentiment in Chaucer's presentation of the dispute between Oswald and Robyn, it lies in an awareness that the ethical grounds over which men like these could contend were politically limited to the domain of affect after 1381.

---

[103] See Bruno Latour, "Why Has Critique Run out of Steam? From Matters of Fact to Matters of Concern," *Critical Inquiry* 30 (2004): 225–48. Latour argues for "renewing empiricism" by recognizing that "reality is not defined by matters of fact" (232). Instead, he suggests that the critical enterprise should pursue what he calls "matters of concern," the *ways* in which objects, things, facts accrue reality. Instead of accepting at face value the conditions of existence for an object, thing, or fact, Latour imagines a role for the critic that includes affect: "The critic is not the one who lifts the rugs from under the feet of the naïve believers, but the one who offers participants arenas in which to gather. The critic is not the one who alternates haphazardly between antifetishism and positivism like the drunk iconoclast drawn by Goya, but the one for whom, if something is constructed, then it means it is fragile and thus in great need of care and caution" (p. 246). For a helpful sketch of what she has since called "affect-critique," see Linda Charnes, "Styles that Matter: On the Discursive Limits of Ideology Critique," *ShakS* 24 (1996): 118–47.

Chaucer's Dorigen and Boccaccio's Female Voices

Michael Calabrese
California State University-Los Angeles

T
HE SPECIFIC BOCCACCIAN ANALOGUES for Chaucer *Franklin's Tale* have received detailed critical treatment. Scholars consider Menedon's story in the *Filocolo* the likely source, and even though there is no absolute critical consensus that Chaucer knew the *Decameron,* the version of the story in that collection (10, 5) has nonetheless fruitfully been compared to Chaucer's tale. Over the past twenty years, in fact, the complex relations between Boccaccio and Chaucer have been receiving ever expanding and dynamic treatment, without critics compelling themselves to determine whether Chaucer actually read the *Decameron* and employed it as a source.[1] I want to further these inquiries by engag-

I offer thanks to Frank Grady, to the anonymous readers at *SAC,* and to Tracy Adams, Albrecht Classen, R. W. Hanning, Roberta Morosini, and Bonnie Wheeler; I also thank Orlando and Joseph Calabrese, who were there on the banks of Loch Lomond.
[1] The essential critical studies include David Wallace, *Chaucer and the Early Writings of Boccaccio* (Cambridge: D. S. Brewer, 1985), and *Chaucerian Polity: Absolutist Lineages and Associational Forms in England and Italy* (Stanford: University Press, 1997); Leonard Michael Koff et al., *The Decameron and the Canterbury Tales: New Essays on an Old Question* (Madison, N.J.: Fairleigh Dickinson University Press, 2000); Karla Taylor, "Chaucer's Uncommon Voice: Some Contexts for Influence," in Koff, 47–82. Robert R. Edwards, "Rewriting Menedon's Story: *Decameron* 10.5 and the *Franklin's Tale,*" in Koff, 226–46, traces the shifts in both authors' versions of the *Filocolo* source. The essay is reprinted in his comprehensive assessment of the two poets, *Chaucer and Boccaccio: Antiquity and Modernity* (New York: Palgrave, 2002), pp. 153–72; see also his "Source, Context, and Cultural Translation in the *Franklin's Tale,*" *MP* 94, no. 2 (1996): 141–62. N. S. Thomson, *Chaucer, Boccaccio, and the Debate of Love* (Oxford: Clarendon Press, 1996), esp., pp. 318–21 , describes Chaucer's potential exposure to the *Decameron;* Nick Havely, *Chaucer's Boccaccio* (Cambridge: D. S. Brewer, 1980), offers an anthology of the primary Boccaccian works that directly influenced Chaucer, whose relationship with the Italian author Havely calls "a working partnership between equals" (p. 12). An important overview of the issue of sources, including editions of all the relevant texts, is conveniently found in Robert M. Correale and Mary Hamel, *Sources and Analogues of the Canterbury Tales I* (Cambridge: D. S. Brewer 2002), 211–65, which also includes a succinct critical and bibliographical summary of Chaucer's potential use of the *Decameron,* in Helen Cooper, "The Frame," pp. 7–13. Most recently, Warren Ginsberg, "Gli scogli neri il niente che c'è: Dorigen's Black Rocks and Chaucer's Translation of Italy," in

ing the *Decameron* beyond the obvious analogue at 10, 5 to include other *novelle* that reflect the conflicts and dramas of Chaucer's difficult tale, primarily concerning male desire and woman's language. I will also consider Boccaccio's understudied *Elegy of Lady Fiammetta,* a festival of woman's language and desire that offers striking parallels to the discourse of Chaucer's heroine.[2] I make no historical case for Chaucer's knowledge of the *Fiammetta,* but I believe Chaucer was familiar with the *Decameron* and thus align myself with those critics who treat it as an analogue, however firmly one defines that term.[3] However, my argu-

---

Reading Medieval Culture: Essays in Honor of Robert W. Hanning, ed. Robert M. Stein and Sandra Pierson Prior (Notre Dame: Notre Dame University Press, 2005), pp. 387–408, has examined the Franklin's adaptation of Menedon's tale as a cultural translation of Boccaccio's world of social self-interest into the narrator's own social project as an "arriviste" into gentility. On *The Franklin's Tale* itself, the criticism is vast; see Kenneth Bleeth, *Chaucer's Physician's, Squire's, and Franklin's Tales, An Annotated Bibliography, 1900–2000* (Toronto: University of Toronto Press, forthcoming); I thank Professor Bleeth for providing me an advanced copy. A pre-1979 survey of opinions on Dorigen and marriage is supplied by Janemarie Luecke, "Dorigen: Marriage Model or Male Fantasy," *Journal of Women's Studies in Literature* 1 (Spring 1979): 107–21. R. W. Hanning is currently preparing a major study of Chaucer and Boccaccio entitled *Poetics of Deliberation: Prudential Fictions in the Decameron and the Canterbury Tales.* Concerning the very nature of source study, Wallace, "Early Writing," p. 1, discusses going beyond line-by-line comparisons to address "abstract questions of cultural enterprise." Thompson, *Chaucer, Boccaccio, and the Debate of Love,* p. 313, suggests making thematic comparisons "beyond the search for verbal parallels." Peter Beidler, in Koff, pp. 25–46, addresses the issue in the very title of his essay, "Just Say Yes, Chaucer Knew the *Decameron:* or Bringing the *Shipman's Tale* out of Limbo." See also Janet Levarie Smarr, "Mercury in the Garden: Mythographic Methods in the *Merchant's Tale* and *Decameron* 7, 9," in *Classical Fable and the Rise of the Vernacular in Early France and England,* ed. Jane Chance (Gainesville: University Press of Florida, 1990), pp. 199–214, which defends studying Chaucer and Boccaccio comparatively, whether or not Chaucer directly knew the *Decameron.*

[2] On woman's language, satire, and potential feminism in the *Fiammetta,* see Victoria Kirkham, "Two New Translations: The Early Boccaccio in English Dress," *Italica* 70 (Spring 1993): 79–89; Michael Calabrese, "Feminism and the Packaging of Boccaccio's *Fiammetta,*" *Italica* 74 (Spring 1997): 20–42; and Janet Levarie Smarr, *Boccaccio and Fiammetta* (Urbana: University of Illinois Press, 1986), pp. 129–48, exploring the work as a study of "obsessive passion."

[3] On the distinction between source and analogue, see Beidler, "Just say Yes." Thomas J. Farrell, "Source or Hard Analogue? *Decameron* X, 10 and the *Clerk's Tale,*" *ChauR* 37, no. 4 (2003): 346–64, applies Beidler's definitions to the various "sources" behind the *Clerk's Tale* and argues, pp. 350–51, that Boccaccio's *Decameron* version is, in Beidler's terms, a "hard analogue," i.e., a work with narrative but not necessarily verbal parallels to Chaucer's poem and one that Chaucer may have read and knew but did not necessarily use in his own composition. Farrell also brings Christine's work to bear, deeming it, in Beidler's terms, a "soft analogue," a work Chaucer could not have read but one from which we can learn "something about the horizons of discourse in the later Middle Ages" from a "writer who was writing close to Chaucer in time and place" (p. 360).

ment does not require explicit historical evidence of Chaucer's reading, for I attend not so much to direct sources as to the textual environment or the horizon of expectation against which we can read Dorigen. In fact, even Christine de Pizan, whose discourses on marriage and language obviously postdate Chaucer, can help us understand Dorigen's predicament and the tense love triangle in *The Franklin's Tale*.

Studying these analogues also allows us to adjust recent critical assessment of Dorigen's emotional and ethical status, for if we consider *The Franklin's Tale* in comparison to the exempla of female verbal power offered by Boccaccio and Christine, we begin to see Dorigen as a woman who, in a moment of crisis when invited to commit adultery, uses words recklessly to court calamity, when she could have used them to bring order both to her own marriage and to the emotional life of her lovesick friend and neighbor, Aurelius. We need not prove that Dorigen's promise is rash; everyone, including her, knows this. But we comprehend better the particular workings of mischief in the tale and also its unlikely resolution of the problems of abandonment, insecurity, and flirtation when we witness how other amatory poets crafted female voices that negotiate dangers differently from Dorigen. Put another way, I want to see who Dorigen's literary sisters are and what they did rhetorically in similar circumstances. I hope, too, to raise the stock of the men in the tale, who are far from perfect but whose critical fortunes have suffered as Dorigen's have risen. To this end, I explore the role of male competition in the tale. That the men, however driven by a kind of competitive urge, actually do inspire and ignite one another's virtue may very well be one of the most gracious and miraculous aspects of the tale.[4]

I begin the essay with an overview of these conflicts in *The Franklin's Tale* itself. Then, as a specific prelude to studying Boccaccio's speakers, I will look at theories of rhetoric that Boccaccio and Chaucer would have shared and also at discussions of marriage and propriety in two works by Christine, *Le livre des trois vertus* and her *Livre du duc des vrais amans*. Christine's work bears the influence of the Italian poet and testifies to the shared conceptions that Christian, Humanistic poets would

---

[4] A convincing defense of at least one of the men is offered by Colin Wilcockson, "Thou and Tears: The Advice of Arveragus to Dorigen in Chaucer's *Franklin's Tale*," *RES* 54 (2003): 308–12. Stephen Knight, "Rhetoric and Poetry in the *Franklin's Tale*," *ChauR* 4, no. 1 (1970): 14–30, sees Arveragus as the first character who "sets aside self-indulgence for an intangible reason" and notes that "[f]rom this grand moment on, honour is triumphant" (p. 28).

have had about ethics, danger, and careless speech, particularly women's speech. I will then turn to a number of related *Decameron novelle,* beginning with I, 5, where we read of a wife who uses language keenly, cleverly, yet unambiguously to reject an unwanted love and restore order to her suitor's emotional life. In 6, 3 we meet a clever woman who extinguishes the base advances of a pimpish Archbishop and his friend the Marshall, who she knows has paid for sex with another man's wife. 9,1 will show how a widow confounds two unwanted suitors, and in 6, 7, we will hear how, at a critical moment, Madonna Filippa, by speaking wisely, undoes an old law that prohibits her from having an affair, displaying how woman's speech silences men and defeats their ambitions of control, whether that control means having sex with or denying sexual freedom to the woman. I will then move to the *Fiammetta,* an extended study of narcissistic female speech and emotionalism, inspired by an abandonment that leads to an empty threat of suicide. Fiammetta, like Dorigen, is a maker of lists, and the rhetorical style of each woman undermines her moral and emotional authority. At the end of the essay, I will turn briefly to the more apparent analogues of Chaucer's tale, *Filocolo* 4 and *Decameron* 10, 5 as a way of recapitulating my argument through comparisons to these more familiar renditions (one a direct source) of *The Franklin's Tale.*

Language, Danger, and Competition in *The Franklin's Tale*

As we listen to all that Dorigen says, we would be wise to keep in mind the words of Boccaccio's Gilberto, the husband in the *Decameron* version of the tale, who tells his wife that "Le parole per gli orecchi dal cuore ricevute hanno maggior forza che molti non stimano, e quasi ogni cosa diviene agli amanti possibile" [the power of words received by the heart through the ears is greater than many people think and to those who are in love nearly everything becomes possible].[5] In the sequence below, Dorigen, motivated by her suitor's piteous complaint, speaks words powerful enough to compel him to attempt the impossible:

[5] All references to the *Decameron* are to Giovanni Boccaccio, *Decameron,* ed. Vittore Branca (Turin: Einaudi, 1980), here p. 1152. For short phrases quoted in Italian, I occasionally offer my own gloss, but I have most often provided translations from *Giovanni Boccaccio, The Decameron,* trans. G. H. McWilliam (Penguin: New York, 1972), here p. 728.

She gan to looke upon Aurelius;
"Is this youre wyl," quod she, "and sey ye thus?
Nevere erst," quod she, "ne wiste I what ye mente.
But now, Aurelie, I knowe youre entente,
By thilke God that yaf me soule and lyf,
Ne shal I nevere been untrewe wyf
In word ne werk, as fer as I have wit;
I wol been his to whom that I am knyt.
Taak this for fynal answere as of me."
But after that in pley thus seyde she:
"Aurelie," quod she, "by heighe God above,
Yet wolde I graunte yow to been youre love,
Syn I yow se so pitously complayne.
Looke what day that endelong Britayne
Ye remoeve all the rokkes, stoon by stoon,
That they ne lette ship ne boot to goon—
I seye, whan ye han maad the coost so clene
Of rokkes that ther nys no stoon ysene,
Thanne wol I love you best of any man;
Have heer my trouthe, in al that evere I kan."

Critics do not agree upon the significance of this offer.[6] In an important reading that maintains starkly that Dorigen does not, in fact, ever make

[6] References to Chaucer are to Larry D. Benson, *The Riverside Chaucer* (Boston: Houghton Mifflin, 1987), henceforth cited in the text. In the vast sea of criticism on Dorigen's promise, Alan Gaylord, "The Promises in the *Franklin's Tale*," *ELH* 31 (1964): 331–65, questions the authority of the promise "that no one really keeps" and that "was never really made!" (p. 348); Carol A. Pulham, "Promises, Promises: Dorigen's Dilemma Revisited," *ChauR* 31, no. 1 (1996): 76–86, focuses on the historical nature and gravity of the oral contract; Conor McCarthy, "Love, Marriage, and Law: Three Canterbury Tales," *ES* 83 (2002): 504–18, examines the legal aspects of the pledge, concluding that "she should not have made [it]" (p. 516). See also Joseph Hornsby, *Chaucer and the Law* (Norman, Okla.: Pilgrim Books, 1988), pp. 51–56, on the "complex relation of promise and intention," and the tension between the false "trouthe" of Dorigen's pledge, a "clearly invalid agreement" (p. 54), and the true "trouthe" of marriage. Hornsby concludes that "language for Chaucer is a powerful and dangerous tool, one that must be used with care because the consequences extend beyond any earthly hardship to those ultimately affecting the soul" (p. 56). Edwards, "Rewriting," p. 235, notes that "whatever Dorigen says about her intent and however much medieval ethics may have privileged intent over the literal language of promises, Dorigen wrongly assumes that she can quibble with language, just as Dianora [in the *Filocolo*] can dissemble with it." See also James I. Wimsatt, "The Wife of Bath, the Franklin, and the Rhetoric of St. Jerome," in *A Wyf Ther Was: Essays in Honour of Paule Mertend-Fonck*, ed. Juliette Dor (Liège: Université de Liège, 1992), pp. 275–81. Phyllis Hodgson, *The Franklin's Tale* (London: Athlone, 1960), p. 90, identifies Dorigen's prom-

any promises to Aurelius at all, Bonnie Wheeler argues for a particular significance to Dorigen's final comments in this scene: "What deyntee sholde a man han in his lyf / For to go love another mannes wyf, / That hath hir body whan so that hym liketh?" (V.1003–5). Wheeler argues that here Dorigen "unmasks Aurelius's courtly appeals for *mercy* and *grace* as barely veiled attempts at sexual theft as well as indelicacy," while, at once, "speaking to her own powerlessness, to her own disablement by rhetorical codes."[7] I read Dorigen's words, rather, as an inflammation of the male rivalry that Aurelius is conducting. The term "deyntee" is particularly telling; it may mean "state of honor, being held in high esteem, dignity," making for a good question, considering the themes of the tale and Aurelius's perceived station: "what honor is there in pursuing a married women?" But Dorigen's references to sexual access cast a prurient valence on the term, which in this case would mean "delight, pleasure," as the Franklin himself uses it when praising the Squire's tale as he interrupts it.[8] She is asking, therefore, in what sounds like a leading rhetorical question to a man in love, "what delight could you possibly have in loving a woman whom another man can have whenever he likes?" By reminding him in sexually suggestive terms that her body *is* being freely enjoyed, but not by him, she only encourages Aurelius to commit himself to achieving the "impossible" and to have what his rival freely enjoys. What she offers in play he commits himself to in earnest.[9]

---

ise as a "common human weakness, that of not being able to give a flat refusal where it would cause pain." Cynthia A. Gravlee, "Presence, Absence, and Difference: Reception and Deception in the *Franklin's Tale*," in *Desiring Discourse: The Literature of Love, Ovid through Chaucer,* ed. James J. Paxson and Cynthia A. Gravlee (Selinsgrove, Pa.: Susquehanna University Press, 1998), pp. 177–87, argues (p. 170) that Dorigen "plays a game with Aurelius" and that therefore (p. 180) "the nobility of character inherent in gentillesse is not present" in her. R. D. Eaton, "Narrative Closure in Chaucer's *Franklin's Tale*," *Neophilologus* 84 (2000): 309–21, argues that Dorigen has "however innocently, bartered with her sexual favors," "has acted weakly and indecisively when cornered" (p. 310), and is a "victim of her own desire and her own sensuality" (p. 320). In an inventive and dynamic reading, Kathryn L. Lynch, "East Meets West in Chaucer's Squire's and Franklin's Tales," *Speculum* 70 (1995): 545–47, reads Dorigen's flirtation with Aurelius as a flirtation with the feminine and the exotic, both associated with the East.

[7] Bonnie Wheeler, "*Trouthe* without Consequences: Rhetoric and Gender in Chaucer's *Franklin's Tale*," *Representations of the Feminine in the Middle Ages,* ed. Bonnie Wheeler (Dallas: Academia, 1993), p. 107; Wheeler sees Dorigen as a crafty and capable rhetorician, who ultimately denies Aurelius "with a firm, categorical *no.*"

[8] *MED* s.v. deinte, 2 a, 1 a; *Canterbury Tales,* V.681.

[9] Gerald Morgan, "Boccaccio's *Filocolo* and the Moral Argument of the *Franklin's Tale*," *ChauR* 20, no. 4 (1986): 285–306, argues, p. 297, that the task and promise offered "in play" are attempts "to restore the situation to its proper level of pleasantness and good cheer." Elizabeth A Dobbs, "'Re-Sounding' Echo," *ChauR* 40, n. 2 (2006):

The exigencies of male competition do, in fact, drive the tale. The very vocabulary of Dorigen's initial promise betrays comparison and competition: she promises, by God no less, to love Aurelius the "best" of any man. Even Aurelius's initial revelation to her bespeaks competition and comparison: he tells her he wishes that the day Arveragus "hadde wente over the see" that he himself "hadde went ther nevere [he] sholde have come again" (V.869–71). The explicit terms of competition, including sexual competition, that inform Dorigen's speech compel an ongoing response and plant a seed that cannot be uprooted: "Be your love," "love you best," "another man has my body whenever he wants." These are taunts. However adorned Dorigen's performance may be throughout the tale with tears and sorrow, Chaucer wants us to see the engine of desire and the moral culpability beneath her "play," her colorful lamentation, and her perpetual complaint. The comic movement of the tale, however, unfolds when Aurelius converts the terms of his own competition from sexual to social, once he knows that sexual conquest would constitute a loss of honor and thus no victory over Arveragus. If he sleeps with her, Aurelius realizes, he will not really be the "best" in any sense of the term, but he can "better" Arveragus by courteously absolving Dorigen and freely denying himself that body that he has so long coveted. Dorigen's taunting question has thus set in motion a dangerous competition that foreshadows a redemptive tussle of gentility. As Arveragus's own chivalric travels, which take him away from his wife and into the world of men and violence, clearly establish, men in this tale are bound to compete. The one-upmanship that ends the tale may not be spiritually pure, but it does not have to be; it *works* to heal what can be healed in the combative world of honor, desire, sex, and money.[10]

289–310, offers an excellent study of the relations of Dorigen and Aurelius to Narcissus and Echo, sparked by Chaucer's allusion to the pair at V 951–52; this reference betrays, says Dobbs, p. 302, Chaucer's "heightened interest in acts of speaking" in comparison to the two Boccaccian analogues to the tale. In the Ovidian mythological source, differences of meaning come into play, Dobbs notes, p. 303, because "what is echoed has been separated from its original context." Dobbs sees this phenomenon manifested in Aurelius's fragmented, partial, and selective interpretation of Dorigen's words and of her promise, until, dramatically, the end of the tale, when he responds, she says, p. 306, "to the larger meaning revealed by her grief" and "releases her from her promise."

[10] Edwards, "Cultural Translation," p. 154, studies the economic vocabulary of Chaucer's tale, noting that the "dominant aristocratic ethos of the Love Questions {in the *Filocolo*} is rephrased, hence revised in some measure, within the idiom of mercantile culture."

In fact, even before the tale begins we witness some one-upmanship between the veteran Franklin himself and the young Squire. The older man's interruption establishes the very theme of masculine competition while it also explores the issues of youth, rhetoric, and excess that the Franklin will embody in Dorigen, the most prolific speaker in the tale, Squire-like in her prolixity. The Franklin coyly anticipates Dorigen's rhetorics, her bathetic apostrophe, her endless amplification, and her amorous play, in his unconvincing disavowal of rhetoric, where he promises that, since he never studied Cicero, he will only speak "bare and pleyn" (V.717–28):[11]

> At my bigynnyng first I yow biseche,
> Have me excused of my rude speche.
> I lerned nevere rethorik, certeyn;
> Thyng that I speke, it moot be bare and pleyn.
> I sleep nevere on the Mount of Pernaso,
> Ne lerned Marcus Tullius Scithero.
> Colours ne knowe I none, withouten drede,
> But swiche colours as growen in the mede,
> Or elles swiche as men dye or peynte.
> Colours of rethorik been to me queynte;
> My spirit feeleth noght of swich mateere.
> But if yow list, my tale shul ye heere.

These odd claims provoke us to examine the emotional and stylistic disconnections in Dorigen's life and words. The colors, such as they are, that inform much of her language create the turmoil that drives the tale and betrays what Stephen Knight has termed her "emotional excesses."[12] Dorigen, both in her flirtation and in her overwrought laments

---

[11] James J. Murphy, "A New Look at Chaucer and the Rhetoricians," *RES* 15 (1964): 10, reads these terms to mean " 'uncomplicated' rather than 'low' or 'humble,' which is the meaning of [John of] Garland's *humilis stylus* or the *extenuatus* of [Cicero's] *ad Herrenium*." Challenging the notion of the "interruption" and summarizing the past scholarship is David Seaman, " 'The Wordes of the Frankeleyn to the Squier': An Interruption?" *ELN* 24 (1986): 12–18. See also Lynch, "East Meets West," pp. 542–43.

[12] Knight, "Rhetoric and Poetry," pp. 21–22, provocatively studies Dorigen's "rather unstable mentality" and her "hyperbolic character," as revealed in her own and in her narrator's rhetoric, that is, in the specific formal features of presentation and also in the rhythms and syntax of the poetry itself. Phyllis Hodgson, *Franklin's Tale*, pp. 103, 104, considers the allusions in Dorigen's catalogue "not equally pertinent," perhaps reflecting the "immoderation and illogicality of a frenzied woman," perhaps related to Chaucer's

and exempla, abuses rhetoric. The Franklin is often wry or dismissive of her words and emotions, treating her with somewhat less respect than he does that young person whom he cannot bear listening much to, the Squire. The young man, speaking of Apollo in pompous words that anticipate Aurelius's upcoming prayer to the god, plans to continue his tale, we might say, for another "day or twaye," when the Franklin ambushes him with a complex piece of interruption rhetoric. He softens the blow by commending the young man's great "wit," which is remarkable despite his "yowthe"; he then congratulates him for speaking "feelyngly" and claims that he has had "greet deyntee" in the young man's speech. The Franklin then contrasts him to his own son, who is more apt to "pleye" at dice than to act like a man "virtuous withal" or to show proper "gentillesse." He exclaims further that he would rather see his son reform than have "twenty pound" worth of land.

The Franklin has left some clues in his interruption here, for some of his words playfully anticipate the tale to follow: "twenty pound" for "a thousand pounds" to have the impossible happen; "deyntee" here and in Dorigen's question to Aurelius; the term "gentilesse," obviously, throughout the tale. "Doom" anticipates the "question" of judgment with which the Franklin ends his tale, the host's reference to "biheste" recalls the theme of contract that binds the pilgrims and will bind Dorigen, his son's failure to "entende" to virtue anticipates the themes of intention and morality that will permeate the tale, and finally the Franklin's pledge to "obeye" the host's will reflects the themes of *maistrie* and lordship that we are about to hear about. In short, Chaucer saturates the introduction with an anticipatory vocabulary that sets up the Franklin's own narrative. However, the specific terms of the interruption also reveal an important sentiment that will help us understand the Franklin's treatment of Dorigen: when we put his various polite phrases together, we see that the Franklin thinks that young people feel, speak, and play too much. He claims that the Squire has no peer, but he is about to present one in Dorigen, whom, he implies, could very well have been interrupted without much loss: "thus pleyned Dorigen a day or tweye, / Purposynge evere that she wolde deye"(V.1457–58). This gentle barb—the "day or tweye" is anticipated by the Franklin's

---

attempt to "ridicule a common rhetorical practice [elaboration through exempla] by reducing it to an absurdity."

claim to the Host that he should be allowed to offer the Squire a "word or two"—characterizes his tone throughout the narrative.[13] The Franklin has interrupted one young, naive, feeling speaker to make room for one of his own, pulling rank on the Squire in a move that anticipates the class competition between men within the tale. Dorigen not only recalls the voluble young Squire but also the Franklin's own son, who has not quite mastered the virtues of "gentility," something more valuable than "twenty" or, we might add, "a thousand pounds" both in the Franklin family economy and in his tale. Chaucer loves the follies of both young and old, and it comes as no accident that the Franklin initiates a discussion of verbosity, emotion, and youth while Dorigen is waiting in the wings.

Modern Advocacy and Medieval Analogues

To criticize the behavior of Dorigen opposes much of the critical treatment that she has received within the last twenty years, which tends to argue that Dorigen is so constrained by patriarchal circumstance— expressed through genre, law, custom, character, economics, sexual inequality—that she cannot produce a "no" that Aurelius will hear or respect.[14] A related critical move sees Dorigen not so much as a victim

[13] *Canterbury Tales,* V.700–701. Contributing to this tone, the Franklin mocks his own rhetorical excesses: "But sodeinly bigonne revel newe / Til that the brighte sonne loste his hewe, / For th'orisonte hath reft the sonne his light, / This is as muche to saye as it was night" (V.1015–18).

[14] The tendency to locate Dorigen's oppression can be observed in a number of essays. Nina Manasan Greenberg, "Dorigen as Enigma: The Production of Meaning and the *Franklin's Tale" ChauR* 33, no. 4 (1999): 329–49, explores Dorigen's "absence" and how the question of "who is most free" excludes her. Dorigen is caught, she argues, in a "phallogocentric power structure," a "masculinist sexual economy" and in the "commodification" of women within male discourse" (see pp. 335, 336, 338, 345). Her "exclusion is *intrinsic* to an order from which nothing escapes: the order of 'man's' discourse." Despite this exclusion, Greenberg nonetheless notes that "what is so exciting" is that Chaucer gives Dorigen the power to save or slay a man with one word. Mary R. Bowman, " 'Half as She Were Mad': Dorigen in the Male World of the *Franklin's Tale," ChauR* 27, no. 3 (1993): 239–51, argues that Dorigen is "reduced to an object of exchange between Arveragus and Aurelius"; she is a "commodity" and the counterpart of a "sum of money" who still, in her long lament, is able to "shape self-expression within the discursive materials of [the male] world"; Bowman casts her lamentations as "the only surviving testament to the woman who is otherwise denied personhood by the tale," with even the male narrator himself "unsympathetically" and unkindly mocking her speech (see pp. 241, 242, 248, 250). Most recently, Ginsberg, "niente che c'è," p. 403, reads the lament as evidence of Dorigen's cultural entrapment: "If the terrain Boccaccio gave women to express their selfhood was limited, the room they can call their own in the *Franklin's Tale* has shrunk to the size of a tomb." Eve

but as a gifted and morally evolved heroine, responsible for resolving the tale's conflicts through her own powerful agency.[15] Insofar as they are both Dorigenocentric, both camps produce exculpatory readings, resulting in a strong critical orthodoxy. Characteristic of the former perspective is Crane's account in *Gender and Romance in Chaucer's Canterbury*

Salisbury, "Chaucer's 'Wife,' the Law, and the Middle English Breton Lays," in *Domestic Violence in Medieval Texts,* ed. Eve Salisbury, Georgiana Donavin, and Merall Llewelyn Price (Gainesville: University Press of Florida, 2002), pp. 73–93, sees Dorigen as the victim of "psychological abuse," an "abandoned," "unprotected" "target" and "virtually pimped" (see pp. 86–88). Pamela E. Barnett, "'And shortly for to seyn they were aton': Chaucer's Deflection of Rape in the *Reeve's* and the *Franklin's Tales,*" *WS* 22 (1993): 145–62, calls the feminist literary project "one of recovery," concerned with "retrieving marginal voices and deflected gender issues"; she argues pointedly that the *"Franklin's Tale* is motivated by an attempted rape" and that "consent is not an adequate basis on which to rule out the existence of a rape scenario." In this reading, Aurelius forces himself on Dorigen sexually, appealing to "a patriarchal discourse on female sexuality in which 'no' means 'yes.'" The overall goal of this critical project, concludes Barrett, is "to locate what we consider to be rape according to our feminist standards," voicing the "woman's protest" and the "man's intent to harm" (see pp. 145, 155, 158, 161, 162). Francine McGregor in "What of Dorigen? Agency and Ambivalence in the *Franklin's Tale,*" *ChauR* 31, no. 4 (1997): 365–78, argues, p. 376, that Dorigen sees Aurelius as a "potential violator" and the proposed assignation as threatened rape. M. C. Boden, "Disordered Grief and Fashionable Afflictions in Chaucer's *Franklin's Tale* and the *Clerks Tale,*" in *Grief and Gender: 700–1700,* ed. Jennifer C. Vaught (New York: Palgrave Macmillan, 2003), p. 61, argues that Dorigen's catalogue of model suicides that capitulated to a male imperative for female purity displays a "classical muting of the oppressed group representing their condition in the discourse of the dominant group."

[15] A number of essays depict Dorigen heroically, often noting as well the circumstances of her oppression. David Raybin, "'Wommen of Kinde Desiren Libertee': Rereading Dorigen, Rereading Marriage," *ChauR* 27 no. 1 (1992): 65–86, sees in Dorigen "true courage" and "moral purity" and thinks her the "most important, sympathetic and convincing character in the tale," praising her "independent agency," how she "makes the bottom line choices" and "orchestrates the tale's delicate movement, both determining her own behavior and encouraging the generous responses of the two men" (see pp. 65–66). She does all this despite the fact that her "men may think they are in control—men usually do." Emilio Englade, "'Straw for Youre Gentilesse!' Masculine Identity, Honor, and Dorigen," *PMAM* 5 (1998): 34–57, argues, p. 50, that "the honor [the men] have retained has little to do with personal virtue; only Dorigen has consistently acted out of selflessness." In a detailed and productive source study, Warren S. Smith, "Dorigen's Lament and the Resolution of the *Franklin's Tale,*" *ChauR* 36, no. 4 (2002): 374–90, reads Dorigen's lament specifically through its source in Jerome's *Against Jovinian* and argues that Chaucer "transforms the tone of Dorigen's complaint to make her consistently sympathetic with the suffering women of the examples and contemptuous of the violent men, thus reassuring us that her final decision about her fate will rest on a compassionate and morally upright basis" (p. 386). See also Andrea Rossi-Reder, "Male Movement and Female Fixity in the *Franklin's Tale* and *Il Filocolo,*" in *Masculinities in Chaucer: Approaches to Maleness in the Canterbury Tales and Troilus and Criseyde,* ed. Peter Beidler (Cambridge and Rochester, N.Y.: D. S. Brewer, 1998), pp. 105–16. Dorigen, she writes "[a]s a medieval woman . . . has little access to the mobility and to the credit for deeds that men in her society enjoy." Because of this handicap, Dorigen has to use her mind more ands thus "plays more of a moral role than any of

Tales, where she explores Dorigen's "ultimate failure to deflect Aurelius's courtship." Opposing the reading famously offered by R. E. Kaske, who spoke of Dorigen's "feminine flightiness," Crane locates her failure, rather, in the difficulty of "expressing resistance to courtship in romance" and of "being heard to speak against courtship." "That Dorigen finds herself ventriloquizing encouragement," Crane reasons, "as she attempts resistance reveals that there is no vocabulary of refusal in this generic context. . . . The only way for Dorigen to communicate refusal to Aurelius would be to relocate herself altogether outside of sexual circulation, and the many stories she later recalls can only imagine that outside as death."[16] But contemporary models for successful defense of the sort that Dorigen requires—the generic resource that Crane says does not exist—can indeed be found in Boccaccio, in works in fact that Chaucer may have known firsthand. Boccaccio demonstrates the existence of a high standard, and a high success rate, for a deflective female rhetoric. We see confirmation that Boccaccio is not unique in offering such models of the art of refusal in the works of Christine, obviously influenced by her countryman in this matter.

But the critical adjustments I exhort here, which oppose the tendency to see Dorigen either as a victim or a hero, are not meant simply to condemn Dorigen morally. Her sufferings, however artificial and hyperbolic in her monologues, are at other times trenchant and real, and by the end of the tale this woman has been ordered by her husband to sleep with another man and to keep it secret on pain of death. Chaucerian morality is never simplistic or even overt, but we must temper our sympathy, which can be a deceptive reader response to Chaucer, with an awareness of the poet's sense of ethics and language and also his sense, drawn in part from Boccaccio, that language, used well, can heal and

---

the men, thereby deserving recognition for her morally grounded generosity" (pp. 108, 115).

   [16] Susan Crane, *Gender and Romance in Chaucer's Canterbury Tales* (Princeton: Princeton University Press, 1994), 62, 63, 66, 65. See R. E. Kaske, "Chaucer's Marriage Group," in *Chaucer the Love Poet,* ed. Jerome Mitchell and William Provost (Athens: University of Georgia Press, 1973), pp. 45–65, esp. page 61 for the discussion of flightiness and Kaske's further contention that Dorigen is "certainly one of Chaucer's more attractive heroines and is portrayed with obvious sympathy." Complicating Crane's notions about the near impossibility of Dorigen finding a language of rejection, John A. Pitcher, "'Word and Werk' in Chaucer's *Franklin's Tale,*" *L&P* 49, nos. 1–2 (2003): 77–109, argues that her "speech act also gives expression to a portion of her desire"(p. 90). Luecke, "Marriage Model," argues that Dorigen "is at best an adolescent; certainly a child by the standard of [Margaret] Paston and [Christine] de Pizan's documentary evidence of an adult woman" (p. 113).

can thus become its own form of personal advocacy against many forms of patriarchy.

Ethics, Rhetoric, and Female Speech in Boccaccio and Christine de Pisan

How exactly can the *Decameron* and the amatory work of Christine help us understand Dorigen's plight and performances? Chaucer, always interested in human speech as a manifestation of morality, ethics, and social relations, would have seen in the *Decameron* various examples of reckless, dangerous speech, committed by both men and women. But he would also have seen that women can speak well and wisely to various but related ends: to defeat the sexual ambitions of cads; to chasten, educate, and heal weak men; and to combat authority, law, and constraint, with the goal, in all cases, of maintaining freedom and self-determination.[17]

Some have seen in Boccaccio's gendering of desire little more than an unending, insidious misogyny.[18] But we do not have to adjudicate this

[17] Thompson, *Chaucer, Boccaccio, and the Debate of Love,* pp. 69–70, writes most eloquently about Boccaccio's moral arts: "Into the general framework of an anatomy of moral failings, Boccaccio introduces the emergent theme of the power of words: they can be used to disguise reality, in which case a man may be fooled, but not God; they may also be used to convey a reforming message in disguise." On the issues of feminism and masculism in Boccaccio, see Michael Calabrese, "Men and Sex in Boccaccio's *Decameron,*" *M&H* 28 (2002): 45–72, and "Male Piety and Sexuality in Boccaccio's *Decameron,*" *PQ* 82 (2005): 257–76. See also Laura Di Sisto, "Boccaccio Friend or Foe? An Examination of the Role of Women in the *Decameron,*" *Spunti e Recerche* 10 (1994): 63–75, arguing that Boccaccio "restricts *Decameron*ian women to sexual activity" and "hardly gives them credit for anything else" (p. 63). Of central importance to an understanding of the *Decameron*'s moral universe is Victoria Kirkham, *The Sign of Reason in Boccaccio's Fiction* (Florence: Olschki, 1993).

[18] Marilyn Migiel, *A Rhetoric of the Decameron* (Toronto: University of Toronto Press, 2003), exposes what she sees as misogynist regulation and suppression of women beneath any apparent empowerment or expression of agency. Migiel argues that "rhetorical victories do not necessarily point to gains for women" (p. 119). See also her "Domestic Violence in the *Decameron,*" in Salisbury et al., pp. 164–79. See also Mihoko Suzuki, "Gender, Power, and the Female Reader: Boccaccio's *Decameron* and Marguerite de Navarre's *Heptameron,*" *CLS* 30, no. 3 (1993): 231–52, which indicts the *Decameron* as a "consistent presentation of masculine drives and judgments, which largely accord with the dictates of patriarchy"(p. 240). Kurtis B. Hass's "*The Franklin's Tale* and the Medieval *Trivium:* A Call for Critical Thinking," *JEGP* 106.1 (2007): 45–63, was published while this essay was in press; Hass examines how Dorigen and Aurelius deficiently employ the *trivium*, leaving then "vulnerable to the Orleans clerk's corruptions of the *quadrivium*" (p. 45). Though Hass also sees Aurelius's actions as constituting "an attempted rape," his conclusion that *gentilesse* must be "girded by careful, moral thought processes (p. 63) is complementary to my own.

problem, for studying Chaucer's debt to the Italian poet does not depend upon determining definitively how Boccaccio treats women but rather upon engaging the *Decameron* in the broader context of medieval amatory literature.[19] For in medieval narrative of all kinds (including, in addition to the *Decameron* and the *Canterbury Tales,* both the *Roman de la Rose* and the *De Amore* of Andreas Capellanus), men act carnally, usually as if their lives depended on sexual success. Women seem, from a common misogynist perspective, the tempting cause of all this male anxiety, but the frequent Patristic association of man with "reason" and woman with "sensuality," though often related to an allegorical understanding of the Fall from Paradise, is seldom transferred wholesale into amatory narrative.[20] In fact, we often see, as, for example, in Chaucer's *Tale of Melibee,* the *Man of Law's Tale,* and the *Second Nun's Tale,* that *man* represents sensuality and error, while woman embodies reason, self-mastery, and the wisdom that inspires virtue and order. Women remind men of their better selves, and even, at times, make chaste brothers and friends out of sexual pursuers. These women, as they confront and heal men, summon the power of language and sometimes invoke what Boccaccio's Lauretta terms "biting" wit, an image that recalls the power of the saints as teeth that "cut men off from error," and soften them by biting and chewing, in Saint Augustine's exegesis of the Song of Songs.[21]

[19] Concerning issues of gender, feminism, voicing, and authorial intention in the *Decameron,* see Regina Psaki, "Women in the *Decameron,*" in *Approaches to Teaching Boccaccio's Decameron,* ed. James H. McGregor (New York: Modern Language Association of America, 2000), pp. 79–86, which offers an important caveat, "No single pronouncement [about gender] is definitive, even when we might want it to be; each will be contradicted sooner or later, tacitly or explicitly" (p. 80). And see Psaki, " 'Women Make All Things Lose Their Power': Woman's Knowledge, Men's Fear in the *Decameron* and the *Corbaccio,*" *Heliotropia* 1.1 (2003): 26 December 2005 (http://www.brown.edu/ Departments/Italian_Studies/heliotropia/01-01/psaki.shtml). On Boccaccio and women more generally, see the various listings in *Women in the Middle Ages: An Encyclopedia* (Westport, Conn.: Greenwood, 2004), pp. 103–17.

[20] For an overview of readings of the Fall, see Pierre J. Payer, "The Fall, Original Sin, and Concupiscence," in *The Bridling of Desire: Views of Sex in the Latter Middle Ages* (Toronto: University of Toronto Press, 1993), pp. 42–60; on man and woman in relation to reason and sensuality, see Augustine, *The Trinity,* trans. Edmund Hill (New York: New City Press, 1991), pp. 322ff. (Book 12).

[21] "È il vero che, se per risposta si dice e il rispenditore morda come cane, essendo come da cane prima stato morso non par da riprender come, se ció avvenuto non fosse" [It is of course true, in the case of repartee, that when someone bites like a dog after having, so to speak, been bitten by a dog in the first place, his reaction does not seem as reprehensible as it would have been had he not been provoked] Branca, pp. 726–27; McWilliam, p. 452. Augustine writes that he contemplates the saints in the image of sheep, "more pleasantly" when he sees them as "dentes Ecclesiae . . . praecidere ab erroribus homines . . . emollita duritia, quasi demorsos mansosque" [the teeth of the

This wit, and all the arts of repartee and verbal combat, is identified as particularly suited to women throughout the *Decameron*. In addition to Lauretta, two other female narrators, Pampinea and Filomena, whom Lauretta cites with praise, also lament their contemporary sisters' deficiency in these important arts.[22] Pampinea, a powerful organizing figure in the introduction and the *brigata*'s the first queen, describes concision and wit as beautiful adornments that function like "flowers in a green field" or "bright stars on a cloudless night." She recommends this skill specifically to women "in quanto più alle donne che agli uomini il molto parlare e lungo, quando senza esso si possa far, si disdice" [for it is more unseemly for a woman to speak at inordinate length, when this can be avoided, than it is for a man].[23] Women have of late, Pampinea continues, neglected verbal arts in favor of decorating themselves with dress, a superficial adornment in contrast to the more meaningful and productive adornments of language.[24] These remarks on language and dress contrast ignorant, supercilious indulgence to a better form of adornment attained through wisdom and wit. In fact, we observe such relations between speech and virtue throughout the *Decameron* not only in women but in whoever speaks wisely and inspires goodness in others, a prevalent theme in the last day of storytelling, as displayed in the eloquent Titus and in Count Guy, who reminds the sexually enflamed King Charles of the importance of self-control.[25] As Victoria Kirkham has written, Boccaccio knew that "speech, the intellectual instrument by which man is distinguished from the beasts, comports a powerful ethical valence. What we say and how we say it is the measure of our humanity."[26] Regardless of the speaker's gender, all speech reflects morality,

---

church . . . cutting off men from their errors . . . after their hardness has been softened as if by being bitten and chewed], *De Doctrina Christiana, II, vi, PL* 34, p. 38; translation from Saint Augustine, *On Christian Doctrine,* trans. D. W. Robertson Jr. (Indianapolis: Bobbs-Merrill, 1958), p. 37. References below to the *Filocolo* are to *Il Filocolo,* ed. Antonio Enzo Quaglio, vol. 1 of *Tutte le opere di Giovanni Boccaccio,* ed. Vittore Branca (Milan: Mondadori, 1964–83), excerpted in Correale and Hamel, *Sources and Analogues,* to which I refer throughout this essay.

[22] See the nearly identical passages at 1, 10 and 6, 1, discussed below.

[23] Branca, p. 116; McWilliam, p. 63.

[24] Note also that in such *novelle* as 3, 4 and 7, 1 and throughout the eighth day, women use language to deceive, though often as the heroines of the story; the relationship between morality and language in these *novelle* needs to be studied independently.

[25] See *Decameron* 10, 8 and 6; see especially the king's reaction in 10, 6 (Branca, p. 1165), which recalls the healing moments of self-knowledge, shame, and reason that we have been observing in Boccaccio's men.

[26] Kirkham, *"Sign of Reason,"* p. 175; see all of pp. 173–97, exploring the theme of communication in the *Decameron* in relation to "the philosophical teachings on human locution inherited by the later Middle Ages" (p. 174).

related not only to Christian ethics but also to a Classical sense of decorum as expressed in the rhetorical handbooks of Cicero and Quintilian and in their many medieval adapters and translators, including Brunetto Latini and Petrarch.[27] The frame narrative of the *Decameron,* therefore, constructs a rhetorical poetics that both informs the *novelle* themselves and provides for an interested reader like Chaucer the models and doctrines with which he can shape his own female speakers.

Another discourse relevant to interpreting both Boccaccio's and Chaucer's female speakers is the book of manners, such as *Le livre des trois vertus* (*Book of the Three Virtues, aka, The Treasury of the City of Ladies*) of Boccaccio's French disciple Christine de Pizan. As Christine guides married women through the dangerous waters of male aggression, she outlines how a chaperon must carefully guard a young married woman against the "divers semblans et manieres" [various signs and gestures] of male flirtation, "comme hommes scevent bien en tel cas" [as men well know how to do in such a case]. The situation is dangerous espe-

---

[27] On the influence of Cicero as Boccaccio would have received him, perhaps though Brunetto Latini's adaptations, see James Murphy, *Rhetoric in the Middle Ages* (Tempe: ACMRS, 2001), pp. 89–132, esp. p. 112 on *De Inventione* and the legal curriculum in Italy and pp. 10–15 for an outline of Cicero's rhetorical models. See also Murphy's "Cicero's Rhetoric in the Middle Ages," *Quarterly Journal of Speech* 53 (1967): 334–41. One can multiply passages from classical rhetoric that point to decorum and the virtue of the speaker, but this passage from Quintilian is apt: "Nature, in the very gift to man by which she shows herself to have been particularly generous to him and particularly to have separated him from the other animals, Nature herself will prove to have been no parent but a stepmother if she designed the power of speech to be the companion of crime, the opponent of innocence and the enemy of truth" (*Institutio* XII, 1 1–2, quoted by M. Winterbottom, "Quintilian and Rhetoric," in *Empire and its Aftermath: Silver Latin II,* ed. T. A. Dorey [London and Boston: Routledge and Kegan Paul, 1975], pp. 79–97; here 97). Despite the "mutilated" state of Quintilian's texts in the Middle Ages, Winterbottom reports (p. 94) that Petrarch found and glossed at least books 1 and 12 of the *Institutio.* See also Dominic A. LaRusso, "Rhetoric in the Italian Renaissance," and John O. Ward, "Renaissance Commentators on Ciceronian Rhetoric," in *Renaissance Eloquence: Studies in the Theory and Practice of Renaissance Rhetoric,* ed. James Murphy (Berkeley and Los Angeles: University of California Press, 1983), pp. 37–55, 126–73. LaRusso (p. 40) quotes a critical summary of Italian Humanist thought from Nancy Stuever, *The Language of History in the Renaissance* (Princeton: Princeton University Press, 1970) p. 116: "rhetoric was a coherent body of knowledge of human behavior with a special focus on the relation of discourse to action. For [the Humanists] rhetoric functioned as a psychology which stressed the sophisticated analysis of problems of will and choice, motivation and compulsion; which developed a concrete self-consciousness in the author of the relation of meaning to intention; and which placed a high value on a sense of *opportunità* (*kairos*), a grasp of the relation of choice to circumstance." On Boccaccio's prose style in relation to the *ars dictandi,* see Judith Serafini-Sauli, *Giovanni Boccaccio* (Boston: Twayne, 1982), pp. 88–94, who observes that in the *Decameron* "the proper or improper use of language . . . identifies persons and determines events" (p. 92).

cially when the wife "ne soit mie de tel savoir ne constance qu'elle puisse ou sache ou vueille resister aux amonnestemens de celui qui met toute peine [a l'attraire] a s'amour" [is so lacking in knowledge or constancy that she is unable, does not know how or does not wish to resist the appeals of the man who is trying his best to attract her].[28] A wise woman in waiting should guard her charge so as to fend off the entreaties of a suitor. Dances and social events, such as the one that proves nearly fatal for Dorigen, are not forbidden because social duty demands it, but they are recognized as danger zones.[29]

Christine focuses on the chaperon's watchful verbal art, not the wife's, but once the man has slipped through the defenses, she too must know the craft of fending him off. The strategy of denial recommended here does not contain any impossible tasks but rather proposes a constant refusal to see the suitor or to entertain his overtures. The wife must inform him time and again that she is sleeping or busy in order to douse his hopes: "Et ainsi lui face dire par pluseurs fois tant que par la continuacion de tenir telz manieres longuement il aperçoive bien qu'il perdroit sa peine de plus y muser" [When she has told him this sort of thing several times and continues to take such an attitude over a long period, he may at last realize that he would be wasting his time to keep trying]. Of course, aware of the power of a playful word to sustain male hopes, Christine also recommends that the chaperon urge that she "se garde bien que de yeux, de parole, de ris ne de contenance quelconques ne lui face nul semblant par quoy le puist attraire ne lui donner aucune esperance" [be very careful that she does not, by any look in her eyes, or by speech, smile, or manner, give any indication to him by which she may lead him on or raise his hopes].[30]

Christine then takes the pleasure of quoting herself and includes an exemplary letter of advice from her *Livre du duc des vrais amans* (the *Book of the Duke of True Lovers*) sent by one *Sebile* advising her lady to maintain her honor, virtue, and discretion by resisting the allure of a flirtation. The letter (quoted here from the source text) reads in part:

"Ma dame, j'ay entendu aucunes nouvelles de vostre gouvernement teles que j'en suis dolente de tout mon cuer pour la paour que j'ay du decheement de

---

[28] Christine de Pizan, *Le livre des trois vertus,* ed. Charity Cannon Willard, with Eric Hicks (Paris: Librairie Honoré Champion, 1989), pp. 104–5; translation is from *The Treasure of the City of Ladies,* trans. Sarah Lawson (New York: Penguin, 1985), p. 95.

[29] See Willard, "*Le livre,*" p. 97; Lawson, p. 90.

[30] Willard, "*Le livre,*" p. 103; Lawson, p. 94.

vostre bon los; et sont teles, comme il me semble, que comme il soit de droit et raison que toute princesse et haulte dame . . . se doyent riuler . . . parlant a dongier, non trop accointable . . . ne croye n'adjouste foy a flateurs ne a flateuses, ains les congnoisce et chace de soy; ne croye de legier paroles raportees; n'ait coustume de souvant conseiller a estrange ne privé en lieu secret ne a part, mesmement a nul de ses gens ou de ses femmes, si que on ne puist jugier que plus sache de son secret l'une que l'autre, et ne die devant gens a personne quelconques, *en riant,* aucuns moz couvers que chacun n'entende, affin que les oyans ne supposent aucun nice secret entre eulx." (my emphasis)

[My lady, I have heard certain rumors touching your conduct which grieve me from the bottom of my heart because of the fear I have of the ruin of your good name, to the which, as it seems to me, they tend, for it is right and fitting for every princess and high-born lady . . . [to] regulate [her] conduct . . . [she should be] in speech restrained and not too familiar . . . not trusting in flatterers, but recognizing them, and driving them from her, not lightly believing gossip, not given to the habit of whispering either to stranger or to intimate friend in any secret or solitary place . . . [and] never saying *in jest* to anyone whomsoever, in the presence of others, aught which may not be understood of all, so that those hearing it may not imagine there to be some foolish secret between them.][31]

Further, a noble lady should not appear "plus veult our parler d'amours" [more willing to listen to amorous discourse] than is her wont, because people will say she is in love.[32] Christine would have approved of Dorigen's denial of Aurelius and would have praised whatever attendant she may have had, until, however, some words "in play" [*en riant*] almost strip her of all she has. In Pisanian perspective, Dorigen's offer is a failure of status and station in a young, high-born, married woman.

Keeping in mind these various standards of manners, rhetoric, and virtue, specifically when defined as female practices and imperatives, let

---

[31] Christine de Pizan, *Le livre du duc des vrais amans,* ed. Thelma S. Fenster (Binghamton, N.Y.: MRTS, 1995), pp. 172–73, 174; translation (with my adjustments to suture the ellipses) from *The Book of the Duke of True Lovers,* trans. Alice Kemp-Welsh (London: Chatto and Windus, 1909), pp. 104–5. A more recent but very similar translation is *The Book of the Duke of True Lovers,* trans. Thelma Fenster (New York: Persea, 1991); see pp. 111–20 for the text of Sebile's letter.

[32] Christine de Pizan, "*Le livre du duc*" p. 174; Kemp-Welsh, p. 108. More exactly, as Sebile warns, when a lady shows such interest in love talk and then suddenly changes, then people will know that she was in love, for her every public move is monitored as a reflection of her social, ethical behavior.

us turn to the *novelle* of the *Decameron* and look more closely at how Boccaccio shapes women's language. Esther Zago has sensitively described the great power that Boccaccio attributes to his female characters in her study of the medically healing powers of the *Decameron* women who promote "healthy sexuality and secular morality" by "speak[ing] in self-defense [and] thus challenging male authority both in the private space of the home and in the public space of the court of law." This craft is the unique result of woman's particular "ability to diagnose the symptoms of lovesickness in themselves and others."[33] The *Decameron* is not a mirror for women like Christine's book, which, one could argue, tends more toward restriction than autonomy in an effort to impress virtue. But though Christine and Boccaccio may differ in their conception of who and what a woman's enemies are, the *Decameron* nonetheless places a similar premium on self-mastery and on rhetorical cultivation, and its women employ all manner of verbal craft in order to guarantee for themselves their own versions of safety, freedom, and control.

Crafty Women in the *Decameron* and One Other

In 1, 5, Fiammetta tells the story of the Marchesana di Monferrato, who stays home while her husband goes off to the Crusades, not completely unlike the masculine voyage of chivalric adventure Arveragus takes in Chaucer's tale. King Phillip hears that the two make, like Arveragus and Dorigen, an ideal match and that the lady's beauty is without compare: "non esser sotto le stelle una simile coppia a quella del marchese e della sua donna: però che, quanto tra' cavalieri era d'ogni virtú il marchese famoso, tanto la donna tra tutte l'altre donne del mondo era bellissima" [there was not a wedded couple under the sun to compare with the Marquis and his lady; for just as the Marquis was a paragon of all

---

[33] Esther Zago, "Women, Medicine, and the Law in Boccaccio's *Decameron*," in *Women Healers and Physicians: Climbing a Long Hill,* ed. Lilian R. Furst (Lexington: University Press of Kentucky, 1997), pp. 64–78; here 76, 65. 67. Of the *novelle* I am here addressing, only 6, 7 is also studied by Zago, who also, in arguments that I find compatible to my own, addresses 2, 8; 10, 7; 4, 1; 4, 5; and 2, 2. Zago laments, understandably, that "these [positive] views could only prosper in the greenhouse of literary imagination" (p. 76) as Boccaccio's own work moves toward the extreme misogyny of the *Corbaccio,* but work in progress by Michaela Paasche Grudin promises to reread that text in light of a political allegory that has nothing to do with women; that idea was offered by Grudin's "Another Look at the Black Crow of Boccaccio's *Il Corbaccio,*" Annual Meeting of the Medieval Association of the Pacific, San Francisco State University, March 12, 2005.

the knightly virtues, so the lady was more beautiful and worthy of esteem than any other woman in the world].[34] So he redirects and ceremoniously delays his departure in order to visit her, in an obvious and vulgar blunder. Being "savia e avveduta" and acting "come valorosa donna," she promises to entertain the king with a banquet, in an act that a woman of her station should perform. But, being wise and well mannered, she senses why he has come and immediately takes action to protect herself. We can compare her awareness to the obliviousness of Dorigen, for though Aurelius looked at her so many times as a "man that asketh grace," "nothying wiste she of his entente"(V.958–59).

When at the banquet the Marchesana serves only chicken, variously dressed, and the king inquires, suggestively, whether there are any roosters in this region, she takes the occasion to cut his passion to the quick by answering, "no, ma le femine, quantunque in vestimenti e in onori alquanto dall'altre variino, tutte per ciò son fatte qui come altrove" [no, but our women, whilst they may differ slightly from each other in their rank and the style of their dress, are made no differently here than they are elsewhere],[35] an oblique but unambiguous notice that he should expect no frivolity, no "play" if you will, from her. The effect is much as in the (differently achieved) dénouement of *The Franklin's Tale,* an instantaneous ignition of virtue, for at this point, "Il re, udite queste parole, raccolse bene la cagione del convito delle galline e la vertú nascosa nelle parole" [the king saw clearly the reason for the banquet of chickens and the virtue that lay concealed beneath her little homily] and, realizing that she could not be charmed and that he would not use force, "cosí come disavedutamente acceso s'era di lei, saviamente s'era da spegnere per onor di lui il male concetto fuoco" [in the same way that he had foolishly become inflamed, so now he wisely decided that he was honor-bound to extinguish quickly the ill-conceived fires of his passion].[36] She felt no tedious despair at her man's parting, and, however artful, her "no" is still clear and absolute. Accordingly, the king is transformed by her words, as an innate sense of shame and self-regulation is activated. The lady is finally merciful and wishes him well, per-

[34] Branca, p. 91, next quotation, p. 92; McWilliam, p. 49; the opening of the *Franklin's Tale* stresses among other things Arveragus's "worthynesse" and Dorigen's great beauty.

[35] Branca, p. 93; McWilliam, p. 51.

[36] Branca, p. 94; McWilliam, p. 51. Migiel, "Rhetoric," p. 39, will answer in the negative her own rhetorical question, "This is indisputably a pro-woman story, is it not?"

haps perceiving that he recognizes his error, for the king leaves quickly, Fiammetta tells us, to balance the shame of his having come at all ("acciò che il presto partirsi ricoprisse la sua disonesta venuta"), and the Brigata all praise the valor and the incisive chastisement of the triumphant lady ("Il valore e il leggiadro gastigamento della marchesana").[37] Fiammetta's goal in telling the story is, accordingly, to show "come e con opere e con parole una gentil donna sé da questo [an inappropriate love] guardasse e altrui ne rimovesse" [how through her words and actions a gentlewoman avoided this pitfall and guided her suitor clear of its dangers].[38] The rocks and their removal in Chaucer's tale might seem the most dramatic image of all the stories at hand, but the removal of dangerous passion is the true magic of Boccaccio's various *novelle* and of *The Franklin's Tale* itself. Aurelius had asked Dorigen for "grace," but the grace that he finally receives is actually of a higher order, of a kind that brings an emotional cleansing and a satisfaction that sexual "grace" cannot.

In Lauretta's story (6, 3) we witness another woman who uses wit to chill the base advances of a man, Dego della Ratta, marshal to King Robert of Naples, a man famous for an act of adulterous prostitution, worsened, if it can be made worse, by the fact that he welshed on the deal, paying in inferior coin, *popolini,* which he deceptively gilds or "decorates" (*dorare*). Critics of *The Franklin's Tale* have argued that the men in the tale treat Dorigen as a commodity, trafficking in women, but that vocabulary is much better applied to Boccaccio's story; the *novella* is low and raw, and Lauretta makes clear that the woman was forced by her husband into the night of prostitution "against her will" ("come che contro al piacer di lei fosse").[39] It merits comparison to Chaucer's story exactly because it is such an antiversion of the courtly *Franklin's Tale.*

The crux of the story comes when the marshal, accompanied by an amoral archbishop who is, stunningly, a relative of the woman he had violated, eyes a woman in a public square, monna Nonna de' Pulci; the bishop, essentially pimping, asks the woman if she likes this fellow and

---

[37] Branca, pp. 94, 95.
[38] Ibid., p. 90; McWilliam, p. 49. We have to acknowledge that the issue is slightly different from in Chaucer, because the question is here one of rank: a man of higher nobility breeds danger for a woman; "da questo" here means not only an adulterous love but an inappropriate one with a man of higher rank, who is likely to exploit the advantage. But the contrast with Dorigen nonetheless obtains, and rank plays its own important role in Chaucer's tale as well.
[39] Branca, p. 728.

thinks she "can make a conquest of him" [Nonna, che ti par di costui? crederestil vincere?].[40] The vocabulary is well chosen, for conquer she does, but not in the sense intended by the men. This woman knows, despite the talk of her "conquering," that she is a potential victim and must quickly find a way to win victory. She speaks bitingly, as Lauretta has recommended in her peroration, and cuts clearly to the heart of the matter: "Messere, e' forse non vincerebbe me; ma vorrei buona moneta." [In the unlikely event, my lord, of his making a conquest of me, I should want to be paid in good coin].[41] These words defeat the men, silencing and driving them away, without their being able even to look at one another: "senza guardar l'un l'altro vergognosi e taciti se n'andarono, senza piú quel giorno dirle alcuna cosa." Thus, reports Lauretta with satisfaction, "essendo la giovane stata morsa, non le si disdisse il mordere altrui mottegiando" [since the girl was bitten first, it was not inappropriate that she should make an equally biting retort].[42] Significantly, Nonna is said to have been well known to the *brigata* as a "fresca e bella giovane e parlante e di gran cuore," who sadly died in the recent pestilence.[43] By invoking the frame narrative of plague, Lauretta highlights the power of a woman, once "fresh and vital" to chasten and cleanse foul male lust, which serves throughout the *Decameron* as a plague of its own.[44]

Not one but two men are routed in 9, 1, where a widow undoes the desires of a pair of suitors who assail her after, as Filomena recounts, "unwisely on several occasions, she listened to them" [avendo ella a esse men saviamente piú volte gli orecchi porti]. Regrouping after this seemingly innocuous error and "wisely wishing to extricate herself and not being able to" [volendosi saviamente ritrarre e non potendo], she defeats the foolish pair with wit and with an impossible request, which serves here as remedy rather than, as in *The Franklin's Tale*, as encouragement.[45] The widow devises a task that they will both fail at, even though it is not technically impossible, as she makes one suitor take the place of a dead body in a tomb with the other carrying the body away.

---

[40] Ibid.
[41] Branca, p. 729; McWilliam, p. 453
[42] Branca, p. 729; McWilliam, p. 454.
[43] Branca, p. 728.
[44] See Calabrese, *"Men and Sex,"* passim, and see Jessica Levenstein, "Out of Bounds: Passion and the Plague in Boccaccio's *Decameron," Italica* 73 (Autumn 1996): 313–35, focusing on these themes as they are manifested in Day Four in particular.
[45] Branca, p. 1034.

The fools try but fail to perform it fully, as the absurd graveyard procession is busted up by the police. When she then sends them packing—because they agreed to her terms, they do not argue—they leave her in peace, however ridiculous the task really was. Impossible tasks are supposed to be constructed to get rid of idiots, not encourage them with a project, and Francesca de' Lazarri successfully "rids herself of both [se gli tolse da dosso]."[46] All she did was listen, but women who wish to be left alone must be careful to a fault, for the male imagination can build a dream from very little.

In Filostrato's story on Day Six (6, 7), we hear of another woman who outwits men, not spurning suitors this time but confronting both her husband and a law that would condemn a wife for practicing sexual independence. Like 6, 3, this *novella* depicts male attempts to control women and valorizes a woman who successfully combats those restrictions through assertive wit. Filostrato begins:

Valorose donne, bella cosa è in ogni parte saper ben parlare, ma io la reputo bellissima quivi saperlo fare dove la necessitá il richiede; il che sí ben seppe fare una gentil donna della quale intendo di ragionarvi, che non solamente festa e riso porse agli uditori, ma sé de' lacci di vituperosa morte disviluppò, come voi udirete.

[Worthy ladies, a capacity for saying the right things in the right place is all very well, but to be able to say them in a moment of dire necessity is, in my opinion, a truly rare accomplishment. With this ability, a certain noble woman of whom I propose to speak was so liberally endowed, that not only did she provide laughter and merriment to her listeners, but, as you shall presently hear, she disentangled herself from the meshes of an ignominious death.][47]

The connections between this *novella* and *The Franklin's Tale* are oblique but significant. Madonna Filippa finds herself, like Dorigen, entrapped in a nexus of law and marital obligations on the one hand and, on the other, her own desires and obligations with a suitor. Her husband, Rinaldo, finds her in the arms of her lover Lazzarino and brings her up on a charge of adultery, punishable, ahistorically in the fictive world of the tale, with death. In *The Franklin's Tale,* the heroine faces death as well as a result of her (however unconsummated) relations with her suitor,

---

[46] Branca, p. 1041; McWilliam, p. 655
[47] Branca, p. 745; McWilliam p. 461–62.

perhaps to come by her own hand or by the hand of her husband, who swears her to silence. This threat of death, however differently manifested in each story, relates to the women's dual debt, both to their husbands and also to their suitors. Dorigen has made a pledge of truth to Aurelius for which she may have to die, and Filippa so loves her suitor that she would rather die than flee into exile and therefore prove herself unworthy of such a man (negarsi degna di cosí fatto amante), to whom she is bound "per buono e per perfetto amore."[48] In both stories women must struggle to integrate personal emotions and desires while confronting the strictures of "law," as expressed in either statute or contract, laboring to preserve the marriages that they want while also negotiating formal public bonds of obligation and "trouthe" that they have made independent of their husbands.[49] Madonna Filippa, for her part, routs patriarchy, husband, and law by employing, much like the Wife of Bath, a "who painted the lion?" perspective; that is, in this case, who made the law against adultery? The women whom it rules were not consulted when the law was forged, and thus it does not satisfy the requirements for communal good, as she tells the potestà, "le leggi deono esser comuni e fatte con consentimento di coloro a cui toccano."[50]

---

[48] Branca, p. 747.

[49] See the important study of "illicit consequence" in the chapter "Rash Promises," in Richard Firth Green, A Crisis of Truth: Literature and Law in Ricardian England (Philadelphia: University of Pennsylvania Press, 1999), pp. 326–35: "Many medieval people might well have felt that an unmarried Dorigen would have been obliged to honor her oath," but "Dorigen's marital status, however, complicates the problem considerably," for promises constituted a "kind of private law," and many would have felt that it was "up to Dorigen and her husband . . . to try to resolve the conflicting obligations that bound her" (pp. 329, 332).

[50] Branca, p. 748. Kenneth Pennington, "A Note to Decameron 6:7: The Wit of Madonna Filippa," Speculum 52 (October 1977): 902–5, explores the legal tradition of quod omnes tangit as it pertains to her defense. Though Pennington discards the argument that Filippa's speech reflects classical models of rhetoric as found in Quintilian (see 902 n. 3 where he cites Carlo Muscetta, Boccaccio [Bari: Laterza, 1972], pp. 251, 303), the progress of her argument clearly reflects any number of such models; see, for example, Cicero, De Inventione I, VII, 9 (Cicéron, De Invention, ed. G. Achard [Paris: Les Belles Lettres, 1994], p. 64), laying out the structure of Invention, Arrangement, Expression, Memory, and Delivery. On Boccaccio's possession of Quintilian's Institutio Oratoria and use of it in Genealogia Deorum Gentilium, see Cornelia C. Coulter, "Boccaccio's Knowledge of Quintilian," Speculum 33 (1958): 490–96. Muscetta, p. 251, discusses the origins of the story: "Alla novella di monna Filippa non sono state ritrovate fonti, perché essa è nata da suggestioni quintilianee, da aggiungere agli insegnamenti che Boccaccio aveva ben serbati nella memoria, per quanto riguardava la caratterizzazione e localizzazione della dicacitas" [For the story of Filippa no sources have been found, because it was born from the tradition of Quintillian, joined to other particulars that Boccaccio had kept in mind in regard to the characterization and localization of dicacitas].

She then claims ownership and control over the "excess" beyond that which she renders to satisfy her husband, who admits, in fact, that he has no complaint about her abundant attention to his needs.[51]

Just as in 6, 3, here a woman succeeds through ready, calm, incisive, rational, and powerful speech. Filippa, whom all the town exclaims "was right and spoke well" (gridarono la donna aver ragione e dire bene), wins her case, with male forces stunned and in retreat: "Per la qual cosa Rinaldo, rimaso di cosí matta impresa confuso, si partí dal giudicio; e la donna lieta e libera, quasi dal fuoco risuscitata, alla sua casa se ne tornò gloriosa" [After making such a fool of himself, Rinaldo departed from the scene feeling quite mortified; and his wife, now a free and contented woman, having, so to speak, been resurrected from the flames, returned to her house in triumph].[52] As Roberta Morosini has argued, through a "dislocated" but purposeful display of logic and eloquence, Filippa soundly routs both jealous husband and unjust law while saving both her life and her marriage.[53]

---

[51] Migiel, "Rhetoric," p. 121, dismisses the perceived victory, noting, by reference to contemporary law, that Madonna Filippa's "arguments would have been considered specious in the fourteenth century." Psaki, "Woman's Knowledge," convincingly studies the tale as one of Boccaccio's frequent critiques of the "male desire for dominance" arising from projected fears of woman's secret knowledge and power. Nella Giannetto, "Madonna Filippa tra 'casus' e 'controversia,' Lettura della novella VI, 7 del *Decameron,*" *Studi sul Boccaccio* 32 (2004): 81–100, draws attention to the entire discourse of the heroine and away from the final moment of confrontation: "Ed è quanto mai scorretto ridurre il discorso di Filippa alla sua battuta finale, perchè le argomentazioni da lei svolte nella prima parte non sono di poco conto e fra l'altro esprimono una posizione assolutamente rivoluzionaria per il loro tempo, dando alle donne dignità di soggetti che possono e debbono contare quanto gli uomini, almeno nel caso dell'emanazione di una legge che riguardi anche loro" [It would be wrong to reduce the discourse of Filippa to her final battle alone, for the arguments that she develops in the first part of the story are not to be discounted; among other things, they express an absolutely revolutionary position for her time, giving to women the dignity of subjects that can and, in fact, ought to count as much as men, at least in the case of one particular law that directly concerns them] (p. 86). Filippa's own drama and also its structural relation to the work as a whole, with passive Griselda as her antithesis, reflect, Giannetto argues, the complex structures of contradiction that dynamically drive the *Decameron,* themes Boccaccio possibly derived from texts in Latin juridical literature that depict the rhetorical arts and legalistic arguments of "controversia."

[52] Branca, p. 749; McWilliam, p. 464.

[53] Roberta Morosini, "Bone Eloquence *e mondo alla rovescia nel discorso* semblable al la reisun *nella novella di Madonna Filippa (Decameron VI.7),*" *Italica* 77 no. 1 (2000): 1–13, studies the *novella* as an analogue to Marie de France's Fable 47, *De equo vendito,* for both tales explore the power of "logica dislocata," a rhetoric that appears reasonable but ingeniously masks a different reality. However, though Filippa rationalizes her adultery, her act of reasoning involves both a personal triumph over her husband and the proper modification of the indiscriminate statute against adultery (see pp. 4–5).

Of course not all of Boccaccio's women are models of rhetorical brilliance. And though we have seen a number of Boccaccian women whom Dorigen fails to emulate, she does successfully fulfill the model of another female speaker, one of Boccaccio's many Fiammettas, the heroine of the *Elegy* that bears her name.[54] Fiammetta, a married woman abandoned by her lover, rails against him for some eighty pages and even falsely accuses him of rape. This may not seem much like *The Franklin's Tale,* yet the similarity between the two female speakers lies in the bathos and excess of their monologues, which flirt with suicide with little real result, foiled in Fiammetta's case when, on the way to hurl herself from a precipice, her skirt gets caught on a stray piece of lumber. In one of Boccaccio's deflatingly ironic touches, she reports that her laments are often so loud that they wake up her husband.[55] She piles up historical analogues to her own woe and contemplates models, such as Dido's, for her own ever-impending suicide. Her laments defy paraphrase, but even a short excerpt reveals what they have in common with those of Dorigen; each discourse, however supposedly passionate, proceeds in a certain cataloguing and accruative way; the goal in both cases seems to be pure compilation. These excerpts from Fiammetta's rejection of poison and from her survey of those men and women, including at one point Hecuba, whose sorrows, though substantial, cannot compete with her own, represent her self-aggrandizing style well:

"Vennermi poi nel pensiero li velenosi sughi, li quali per addietro a Socrate e a Sofonisba e ad Annibale e a molti altri prencipi l'ultimo giorno segnarono, e questi assai a' miei piaceri si confecero; ma veggendo che a cercare d'averli tempo si convenia interporre, e dubitando non in quel mezzo si mutasse il mio proponimento, di cercare altra maniera imaginai."

[Then I thought of poisonous drinks which in the end had brought an end to the days of Socrates, Sophonisba, Hannibal, and of many other princes, and these means suited my tastes well, but because I realized it was necessary to have time to obtain them, and believing that in the meantime my resolution might waver as I was searching, I tried to devise another way.][56]

---

[54] Citations are to *Elegia di Madonna Fiammetta* in *Opere di Giovanni Boccaccio,* ed. Cesare Segre (Milan: Mursia, 1978), pp. 943–1080. Translations are from *The Elegy of Lady Fiammetta,* ed. and trans. Maria Causa-Steindler and Thomas Mauch (Chicago: University of Chicago Press, 2000), which is based in part on Segre's edition.

[55] Segre, p. 1036; Causa-Steindler, p. 105.

[56] Segre, p. 1048; Causa-Steindler, p. 120.

"Dopo tutti questi, quasi da se medesimi riservati, come molto gravi mi si fanno sentire i guai d'Isifile, di Medea, d'Oenone e d'Adriana, le lagrime delle quali e i dolori assai con le mie simiglianti le giudico; però che ciascuna di queste, dal suo amante ingannata, cosí come io, sparse lagrime, gittò sospiri, e amarissime pene senza frutto sostenne; le quali, avvegna che, come è detto, sí come io si dolessero, pure ebbero termine con giusta vendetta le lagrime loro, la qual cosa ancora non hanno le mie. . . . Sí che, ogni cosa pensata, io sola tra le misere mi trovo ottenere il principato, e piú non posso."

[After all these {Sophonisba, Cornelia Cleopatra, Ulysses, and others} the tribulations of Hypsipyle, Medea, Oenone, and Ariadne strike me as if they were to be set apart from the rest for their great severity, and I find their tears and pains very similar to mine because each one was betrayed by her lover, as I was, and each wept, sighed, and suffered bitter and fruitless pain; but, as I have said, even though they suffered as they did, their tears ended with a fair vengeance, which mine do not have yet. . . . Therefore, all things considered, I alone find myself achieving first place among suffering women, and I can do no more.][57]

Fiammetta's monologues, like Dorigen's, reveal a presumptuous self-promotion into Classical and epic history.[58] They spill forth learning that serves no social, communal, or spiritual end but rather only inflates the puny self as if its amatory woes were of paramount importance in the sweep of human history. Compare the content and texture of Dorigen's catalogue in this brief excerpt (V.1443–56):

"What seith Omer of goode Penalopee?
Al Grece knoweth of hire chastitee.
Pardee, of Laodomya is written thus,

[57] Segre, p. 1076; Causa-Steindler, p. 154.
[58] On Fiammetta's use (and misuse) of classical models, see Suzanne Hagedorn, "Abandoned Women and the Dynamics of Reader Response," in *Abandoned Women: Rewriting the Classics in Dante, Boccaccio, and Chaucer* (Ann Arbor: University of Michigan Press, 2004), pp. 102–29; and Janet L. Smarr, "Boccaccio's *Elegia* on the Use of the Classics," *Italian Culture* 11 (1993): 127–34. Fiammetta, writes Smarr, p. 132, "seeks explicitly the glory of seeing herself the most wretched of all," while she "miss[es] the obvious element of moral and social criticism implicit in these examples" (p. 133). Renato Barilli, "La retorica nella narrative del Boccaccio: L'"*Elegia di Madonna Fiammetta,*" *Quaderni d'italianistica* 6, no. 2 (1985): 241–48, recognizes the bathetic, bourgeois character of her mythic complaints and tiresome self-inflation, which nonetheless serve Boccaccio's ethical goals to move, to teach, and to delight through exposing Fiammetta's shame and dishonor.

That whan at Troie was slayn Protheselaus,
Ne lenger wolde she lyve after his day.
The same of noble Porcia telle I may;
Withoute Brutus koude she nat lyve,
To whom she hadde al hool hir herte yive.
The parfit wyfhod of Arthemesie
Honured is thurgh al the Barbarie.
O Teuta, queene, thy wyfly chastitee
To alle wyves may a mirour bee.
The same thyng I seye of Bilyea,
Of Rodogone, and eek Valeria."

We are compelled here to agree with Jamie Fumo's mordant characterization of the exempla as "increasingly forced" and with Knight's observation that the catalogue trails off easily into a series of "etcetera's."[59]
By having Dorigen hyper-trope her trauma, Chaucer disables or at least
seriously compromises our tolerance and emotional engagement with
her, and at this point in the narrative she is in danger of becoming the
object of satire.

Among the women in Boccaccio that we have seen, therefore, Fiammetta provides the closest analogue to Dorigen and her expansive rhetorical displays. But Chaucer's satire strikes me in places as less broad
and more subtle than Boccaccio's, and, without attempting a full psychological analysis of Dorigen's motives, I would like to return to the
critical exchange with Aurelius and speculate about what she might
desire from him, in this, the very event that inspires the long rhetorical
displays that follow. Dorigen misses a chance to distinguish herself as a
potent female speaker, in the analogous contexts I have been exploring,
by offering Aurelius hope, a hope that may be veiled in a wifely concern
for her Arveragus's return, but which nonetheless may also represent
her need to have a man of worth, one not unlike her husband in many
respects (and who can dance as well), at the ready. Aurelius is "yong,
strong, virtuous, and riche, and wys, / And wel biloved, and holden in
gret prys" plus "Oon of the best faringe man on lyve"(V.933–34, 932).
The Franklin makes him just as attractive as Arveragus, and we are
certainly supposed to recognize his appeal, even if Dorigen suppresses
it. As the Miller reports, the man close to hand has an advantage over

[59] Jamie Fumo, "Aurelius' Prayer, *Franklin's Tale* 1031–79: Sources and Analogues,"
Neophilologus 88 (2004): 623–35; here 626. Knight, "Rhetoric and Poetry," p. 27.

the one who has gone far away: "Alwey the nye slye / Maketh the ferre leeve to be looth" (I.3393–94).[60] Arveragus had won Dorigen with "many a labour, many a greet empryse"(V.7332), and by extension she makes the same demands on Aurelius: for the unspoken import of the contract is "show me how much you love me," "show me your worth." Courtly service compels him to obey, as Dorigen replicates, perhaps even unconsciously, the same process that attained her husband. Why, for instance, does she speak to Aurelius in "play"? She has refused quite strenuously to play up to this point in the tale, despite all that her friends have done. For their part they *"pleye* hem al the longe day" after leaving the beach "for to *playen* somewher elles" as they all do their best to make merry "save Dorigen alone, / Which made alwey hir compleint and hir mone" (V.905, 897, 919–20). She has moped for 175 lines and now, when faced with an offer of adultery, she begins to play? We have to face the possibility that she simply may be enjoying the attention.

Analogues Revisited and Conclusions

We have been listening to female voices exclusive of the apparent analogues of *The Franklin's Tale* in order to expand the context for interpreting Dorigen's words and actions. But I want to summarize and to end the essay by turning our attention to Menedon's story and to *Decameron* 10, 5, looking specifically at the issue of female agency at two critical moments in *The Franklin's Tale*'s closest analogues: the moment of the promise, which I have just glossed in part as courtship *redux,* and also the final release of the heroine from her pledge. As for the first, in Boccaccio's stories the intentions of both wives are unambiguous. In Emilia's version in the *Decameron,* Dianora "desires to rid herself of [Ansaldo] once and for all by requesting him to do something for her that was both bizarre and as she thought impossible" [con una nuova e al suo giudicio impossibil domanda si pensò di volerosi torre da dosso]. Her motive is clear, and Ansaldo knows that she did this "per torlo dalla sua speranza" [to dash his hopes].[61] She also threatens Ansaldo's go-between with exposing his suit to her male kinfolk, employing a traditional method of defense against unwanted sexual aggression. In Menedon's

---

[60] Morgan, "Boccaccio's *Filocolo,*" while locating Aurelius as the locus of sin in the tale, nonetheless remarks on the similarities of the courtships, a device to "fix in our minds a sense of the moral equality in the making of the two promises" (p. 292).

[61] McWilliam, p. 727; Branca, pp. 1150, 51.

story, the lady employs a strategy akin to that recommended by Christine de Pizan, in the hope that her indifference sends her suitor the message: "Poi che questi s'avedrà che da me né buona risposta né buona atto puote avere, forse elli si rimarrà d'amarmi e di darmi questi stimoli" [Once this man realizes that he can obtain no favorable response or good act from me, perhaps he will stop loving me and bothering me].[62] She almost tells her husband about it but fears, wisely, that she may create a feud or unjustly implicate herself, though she, like her *Decameron* counterpart, does finally append a threat to her impossible task, telling Tarolfo that she *will* inform her husband if he keeps pestering her after failing to produce the garden in winter. She certainly considers the task she invents a device to get rid of him, with no implication of flirtation, conscious or otherwise, detectable in her words "Questa è cosa impossibile: io mi leverò costui da dosso per questa maniera" [this is something impossible: I shall rid myself of him in this way]. Tarolfo, for his part, understands the strategy as a form of rejection: "egli conoscesse bene perché la donna questo gli domandava" [he understood perfectly why the lady had requested it].[63]

Both Boccaccian women are clearly trying to send someone packing. Dorigen's tone, however, fluctuates; her motivations remain suspect, and the Franklin certainly does not explicitly frame her actions as crafted to rid herself of Aurelius. Though she has no clear motive, the result is tangible, and her dangerous play abuses the affections of a man by doing the single most dangerous thing a wife can do with an unwanted suitor. She gives him hope. As Ovid famously notes and as Boccaccio explicitly states in the *Filicolo,* men live on hope, however oblique and ridiculous. When the *donna* in the *Filocolo* tells herself that the garden mission will save her from further harassment, Menedon observes that this is but foolish optimism on her part, however clear she thought her refusal: "Ma già per tutto questo Taralfo di ciò non si rimanea, seguendo d'Ovidio gli amaestramenti, il quale dice l'uomo non lasciare per durezza della donna di non perseverare, però che per continuanza la molle acqua fora la dura pietra" [But through all this Tarolfo still did not stop, following the teachings of Ovid, who said that a man should not stop persevering because of a lady's hardness, since by persistence soft water works its way through hard rock].[64] If this applies to Boccac-

---

[62] *Sources and Analogues,* pp. 221, 220.

[63] Ibid., pp. 223, 222.

[64] Ibid., pp. 221, 220; note 25, p. 221, cites *Ars Amatoria* 1, 475–76, and *Epistulae ex Ponto* 4.10.5.

cio's story, where the "no" was earnest, it applies even more so to Chaucer's, where the "no" is wrapped up in play.

Turning to the scenes of final resolution in the versions, we see in Menedon's tale how the *donna,* preparing to keep her bargain, "adorned herself and made herself beautiful" [ornatasi e fattasi bella], arriving at Tarolfo's home "painted with shame" [di vergogna dipinta].[65] These details depict the *donna* as an assertive and bold agent, perhaps undone by the magic she failed to anticipate, but meeting the moment with power and grace, standing tall and beautiful, not unlike the biblical Judith and very much like the well-born and virtuous woman she is. She cannot control the blush of shame, a disarming, deeply humanizing image, but she can summon up the civil dignity and personal grace to fulfill her ill-conceived obligation.[66] In the corresponding scene in Chaucer's version, we see no such personal preparation by the "half mad" Dorigen, and the text highlights, instead, the specifically male agency that is working out the problems of the tale: Arveragus himself summons an entourage for his wife, commanding them, "Gooth forth anon with Dorigen." Aurelius, when deciding that "fro his lust yet were hym levere abyde," does consider Dorigen and her lamentation for a line and a half, but thinks of Arveragus for three, deeply moved by this "worthy knight, / That bad hire holden al that she had hight" (V.1517–18). This man's actions are dictated not by Dorigen but by another man.[67] Accordingly, *The* Franklin's summation, after warning wives to remember Dorigen and "be war of hire beheeste," highlights this purified, nonsexual form of competition that resolves, and will continue to resolve, the conflicts of the tale. "Thus can a squire doon a gentil dede," says the Franklin, "As wel as kan a knight, withouten drede (V.1543–44), a narrative sentiment echoed later in the tale itself when the clerk displays his own, very self-conscious *gentillesse.*[68] With all of Dorigen's wit and energy de-

---

[65] *Sources and Analogues,* pp. 230, 231.

[66] In a more skeptical reading of the gendered social relationships in this episode, Ginsberg, "niente che c'è," argues that the story as a whole, and in particular Menedon's *questione* and Fiammetta's pro-husband adjudication of it, reveals Menedon's own wish "to preserve and justify masculine predominance over the maidens and wives who threaten it" (p. 401).

[67] Taylor, "Uncommon Voice," p. 71, addresses well the social competition that motivates Aurelius but judges him more severely than I; Aurelius, she writes, "coarsens the spirit of inward nobility by adapting aristocratic forms to his opportunistic motives," as he displays throughout the tale, p. 72, "persistently contractual thinking" and "self-interested opportunism."

[68] Concerning the attribution of these lines and for the argument that they rightly belong to the Franklin and not to Aurelius, see Paul Franklin Baum, "Notes on Chaucer," *MLN* 32 (1917): 377. In a scene that redramatizes Aurelius's compassion for

voted either to reckless "play" or to long, unproductive displays of earnest, it is left, ironically, to the forces of patriarchy, embodied in the dynamic of male competition, to resolve the tale's central conflicts.

Compare also the climactic moment in the *Decameron* version. After receiving Dianora and hearing of Gilberto's generosity, Ansaldo refuses to take his prize, as "il suo fervore in compassione cominció a cambiare" [{his} ardor began to turn to compassion], and "spento del cuore il concupiscibile amore" [{his} heart was purged of the lustful passion] he had harbored for the lady," leaving only an "honest charity" for her ["onesta carità"].[69] Once Ansaldo is cured and comes to his senses, releasing her from her bond, Dianora tells him, in essence, that she knew he had it in him, though her register is loftier and more eloquent: "Niuna cosa mi poté mai far credere, avendo riguardo a' vostri costumi, che altro mi dovesse seguir della mia venuta che quello che io veggio che voi ne fate; di che io vi sarò sempre obligata" [Nothing could ever make me believe, in view of your impeccable manners, that my coming to your house would have any other sequel than the one which I see you have made of it, for which I shall always remain in your debt].[70] Chaucer gives no such confident, mature, active speech to Dorigen at the corresponding point in his tale, and, accordingly, Aurelius departs without forging a future relationship of brotherhood with either Dorigen or with Arveragus; he has acted well but gives no indication that he wants to be part of the family. We see, then, both in the assigning of the task and in the critical moment of final confrontation, that Chaucer has crafted Dorigen as weaker and less stable than her Boccaccian counterparts. The rhetorical products of this young mind generate, but can never resolve, the sexual, emotional, and legal conflicts of the tale.

What may we finally conclude from these disjunctions? Clearly, from all the texts at hand, both the hard and the "soft" analogues, we see that Chaucer, like Boccaccio and Christine, explores how women's language can harm or can heal. But though Chaucer knew the *Filicolo* and explicitly based Dorigen on Boccaccio's character, and assuming for a moment that he knew the *Decameron,* he ultimately chose not to embody

---

Dorigen and his desire to respond to Arveragus's gentility, the clerk follows suit and frees Aurelius himself from his debt: "Leeve brother, / Everich of you dide gentilly til oother. / Thou art a squier, and he is a knight; / But God forbede, for his blisful myght, But if a clerk koude doon a gentil dede / As well as any of yow, it is no drede!" (V.1607–12).

[69] Branca, pp. 1154, 55; McWilliam, p. 730.
[70] Branca, p. 1154; McWilliam, p. 730.

the positive rhetorical models he found in those texts in creating his Dorigen. In *The Franklin's Tale* he has labored to distance himself from the scenario, so frequent in Boccaccio, in which wives successfully rout the advances of unwanted suitors who could compromise their morals and their marriages. And even with both hard and soft analogues left aside, Chaucer himself was certainly aware of the specific power of woman's language, which he incarnates so frequently in the *Canterbury Tales* in such characters as the Wife of Bath, Prudence, and St. Cecelia.[71] He has made Dorigen a different kind of speaker, a different agent, a different woman, one who, alone, cannot heal. The reasons Chaucer choose to incarnate in Dorigen not the language of craft, insight, and success but the language of desire and disruptive danger must lie in part in the larger social and rhetorical ethics of the *Canterbury Tales.* Throughout the *Tales,* Chaucer studies the languages not only of *caritas* but also of treachery, graft, seduction, adultery, abuse, and greed. Dorigen will never rank near the Pardoner or the Summoner on a moral continuum, but if Chaucer does not encode vice in her speech, he does encode danger and the inflammation of anxious desire in herself, her neighbor, and her husband. These anxieties rage until a movement of healing, also characteristically Chaucerian, occurs in the tale, arising ironically, as I have argued, from the tensions of male competition. Of course Chaucer's *narrative* motivation reflects a convention well expressed in an adage employed by Pandarus in the *Troilus,* "And next the derke nyght the glade morwe."[72] That is, without Dorigen's disruption or her failure to heal the lovesick Aurelius, the movement of grace and gentilesse, so precious to the Franklin, and, in a less-socially conditioned way, to Chaucer, could never occur.[73] But to understand this movement of grace, we have to understand the matter from which Chaucer shaped

[71] I would like to add Griselda to this list, but we know her origins. On Prudence's powerful, guiding speech in particular, see Wallace, "Chaucerian Polity," 211–46 (in his chapter "Household Rhetoric"); throughout this chapter and the next, Wallace, focusing on various *Tales* that are set in "a household dominated by a powerful, irascible, and violent male," explores how "those located or trapped in such discursive space" must "find a language that will hold off, divert, or dissipate the immediate threat of masculine violence" (p. 212). Working from Wallace and others, Monica McAlpine, "Criseyde's Prudence," *SAC* 25 (2003): 199–224, argues that Criseyde as well "displays many of the characteristics these scholars associate with a female-gendered prudence" (p. 209).

[72] *Troilus and Criseyde* I, 951.

[73] On the Franklin's social status and ambitions, see the discussion and bibliography in Paul Strohm, *Social Chaucer* (Cambridge, Mass.: Harvard University Press, 1989), pp. 105–9.

Dorigen, and we have to understand her words and desires in the Boccaccian context from which she emerges, at Chaucer's hand, into *The Franklin's Tale*. Put another way, because of the choices before Chaucer, based on his reading and his comprehensive embrace of Boccaccio as a storehouse of rhetorical models, we see his construction of Dorigen more clearly when she is placed in direct juxtaposition to the paradigms that he finally eschewed when making her.

I would not claim that the Boccaccian context, aided by Christine de Pizan, is the only context or the finest context in which to view Dorigen, but I would argue that it is an important context and one that compels us to reconsider what I have depicted as both a victim and a hero-centered critical approach. And I hope to have shown that an exculpatory assessment of Dorigen has isolated Chaucer's character from the moral and rhetorical worlds of her origins, to which I have attempted to return her. Dorigen is a voice; she has no *culpa* to excuse, but to understand what she is and what she is not demands an interrogation of her speech acts as social, ethical, and moral human performances. The situation recalls an event narrated by Boccaccio's friend Petrarch. In his letter to Pulice di Vicenza, the poet records a tense debate with an aged scholar who objects to his criticism of the revered Cicero, in whom Petrarch has detected fickleness and error: "More gently, I beg of you," pleads the old man, "more gently with my Cicero" [Parcius, oro, parcius de Cicerone meo] and "Alas! Alas! Is my beloved Cicero accused of wrong doing?" [Heu michi, ergo Cicero meus arguitur?].[74] In studying Dorigen, as in studying all of Chaucer's women and men, we have to resist the impulse to overprotect those characters whose struggles and concerns seem to reflect our own. Doing this may require us to go a little *less* gently with Dorigen than might be comfortable.

---

[74] *Ad Familiares*, xxiv, 2, Francesco Petrarcha, *Opere, Le Familiari*, vol. 4, ed. Umberto Bosco (Florence: G. C. Sansoni, 1942), p. 223; translation from *Petrarch: The First Modern Scholar and Man of Letters*, ed. James Harvey Robinson (New York: Greenwood, 1969) (reprint of G. P. Putnam's, 1919), p. 245, with adjustment.

Some New Light on Thomas Hoccleve

Linne R. Mooney
University of York

As JOHN BURROW POINTS OUT in his 1994 biography of Thomas Hoccleve, the large number of documents concerned with grants and payments to Hoccleve, together with the autobiographical passages in his poems, "enable us to know more about Hoccleve than about most vernacular writers of the period."[1] Burrow's biography sets forth what we know of Hoccleve from these sources, and its appendix lists not only the manuscripts identified as written by Hoccleve's hand but also the sixty-nine documents that name him as recipient of grants, annuities, or payments from the Exchequer. These latter Hoccleve life records are written by various clerks of royal government, and have been connected with Hoccleve because they name him. But since Hoccleve served as a Clerk in the Office of the Privy Seal for more than thirty-five years, we might expect to find among the surviving documents of that Office some samples of Hoccleve's own handwriting, that is, documents written by him in the course of his work for the Privy Seal. Two such documents were identified by A. I. Doyle and M. B. Parkes in 1978.[2] These are National Archives E 28/29 (temp. Henry IV–V, draft of a document among letters written to and from Robert Frye, Clerk of the Offices of the Privy Seal and Signet) and E 404/31/322 (issue warrant, commanding the Exchequer to pay wages to 24 "vad-letz" of the royal household for accompanying Henry V on his forthcom-

---

[1] John Burrow, *Thomas Hoccleve*, Authors of the Middle Ages series, 4 (Aldershot, Hants: Variorum, 1994), p. 1.

[2] A. I. Doyle and M. B. Parkes, "The Production of Copies of the *Canterbury Tales* and the *Confessio Amantis* in the Early Fifteenth Century," in M. B. Parkes and A. G. Watson, eds., *Medieval Scribes, Manuscripts, and Libraries: Essays Presented to N. R. Ker* (London: Scolar, 1978): 163–210, esp. 82; repr. Parkes, *Scribes, Scripts, and Readers: Studies in the Communication, Presentation, and Dissemination of Medieval Texts* (London: Hambledon Press, 1991), pp. 201–48, esp. 222.

ing expedition to France, dated 27 May 1415).[3] Doyle and Parkes concluded: "Doubtless there are more unidentified specimens of [Hoccleve's] handwriting preserved among the collections in the P.R.O. and elsewhere."[4]

There are indeed many more documents written by Hoccleve's hand in the collections of the National Archives, as I discovered when I went to examine the two named by Doyle and Parkes. The almost 150 documents written by Hoccleve that I have discovered so far survive in the following categories of documents at the National Archives (formerly called the Public Record Office, or P.R.O.): E 404, Warrants for Issues of the Exchequer of Receipt, or Lower Exchequer; E 208, King's Remembrancer / *Brevia Baronibus* files of the Exchequer; and E 28, King's Council and Privy Seal records of the Exchequer of Receipt.

By far the greatest number of documents (132) I have identified as written by Hoccleve are in E 404 files, which are documents written by Clerks of the Wardrobe and Clerks of the Privy Seal instructing the Exchequer of Receipt to make payments out of the royal treasury. Those written by the Clerks of the Privy Seal command such payments in the name of the king and are stamped on the back with the Privy Seal in red wax. Those written by Clerks of the Wardrobe command such payments in the names of the Barons of the Exchequer, and were authenticated by the Clerks' signatures. These latter documents, by far the most numerous in these files, are written on small slips of parchment often little more than 4 cm in height (by ca. 30 cm in width) because they simply record the warrant for payment in a few lines of script. The former are written on larger slips of parchment at least 9–12 cm in height (and ca. 30 cm in width), even if only recording a few lines of script, in order to allow space enough on the dorse for the stamp of the Privy Seal. These two types of document, written by clerks of two distinct Offices, are filed together because they were both received and kept by the Clerks of the Receipt of the Exchequer, who paid out the

---

[3] Pierre Chaplais, *English Royal Documents, King John—Henry VI, 1199–1461* (Oxford: Clarendon, 1971), plate 22(a) (illustrated on page 74, described and transcribed on page 75). The first, E 28/29, is one document in a collection of letters principally written by Robert Frye, Hoccleve's contemporary at the Privy Seal, and it is a first draft of a letter addressed to a bishop, *"reverent pere en dieu,"* asking for support for Henry's war in France. It is not illustrated in any published work, at least to my knowledge. The second document is, as Doyle and Parkes note (footnote 40), illustrated in Pierre Chaplais, *English Royal Documents, King John—Henry VI, 1199–1461*, plate 22.

[4] Doyle and Parkes, "The Production of Copies," p. 182, n. 40.

sums to the persons named in the documents. The Clerks of the Receipt of the Exchequer then recorded on the Issue Rolls (now E 403 files at the National Archives) that the sum named had been paid on a certain date to a certain person. The Issue Rolls of the Exchequer have been previously quite thoroughly searched for references to Thomas Hoccleve (that is, annuity and other payments made to him) and these comprise the bulk of the documents listed in Burrow's appendix. They survive on rolls, one for each half year of each reign, with entries organized in chronological order down the roll, usually one line per entry. The Issue Warrants, now E 404 files, covering the period from ca. 1154 to 1837, are now arranged in chronological order and bound into soft-backed booklets of twenty-five documents each. They are fullest for the years 1399 to 1485, for which period they are stored as one box of booklets per regnal year, and numbered in order from the first document received in a regnal year to the last.[5]

Some of the E 404 issue warrants are not only written by Hoccleve but also name Hoccleve as the proposed recipient of payments from the Exchequer: they instruct the Receipt of the Exchequer to repay him for purchases of ink, parchment, and wax purchased for use in the Office of the Privy Seal; these would have initiated the payments to Hoccleve entered in the Issue Rolls (E 403 documents) that have been noted by previous scholars (items 13, 19, 22, 24, 31, 35, 39, 43, 50, 56, 62, and 68 of Burrow's appendix). However, the E 404 Privy Seal warrants that *instruct* the Exchequer to repay Hoccleve, and therefore name him as recipient, have not until now been included in the published list of documents in which Hoccleve's name occurs,[6] and it follows, of course, that

[5] For example E 404/31/322 represents E (Exchequer), 404 files for the warrants of Privy Seal and Wardrobe, the second number designating the box, that is, 31 for the box containing documents dated in the third regnal year of Henry V, 21 March 1415–20 March 1416, and the third number designating the document, that is, 322 for the 322th document in this box, dated 27 May, 3 Henry V.

[6] Frederick J. Furnivall, "Appendix of Entries About Grants and Payments to Hoccleve, from the Privy-Council Proceedings, the Patent- and Issue-Rolls, and the Record Office," *Hoccleve's Works: The Minor Poems,* ed. Frederick J. Furnivall and I. Gollancz, EETS, e.s. 61 (1892), pp. li–lxx; H. C. Schulz, "Thomas Hoccleve, Scribe," *Speculum* 12 (1937): 76–81; Jerome Mitchell, "Thomas Hoccleve: His Traditionalism and His Individuality: A Study in Fifteenth-Century English Poetic" (Ph.D. diss., Duke University, 1965), Appendix 2 (not included but cited in his published *Thomas Hoccleve: A Study in Early Fifteenth-Century English Poetic* (Urbana: University of Illinois Press, 1968), p. 1, n. 1). These lists instead include the Exechequer entries that make the payments to Hoccleve, which would have resulted from the Exchequer's receipt of the instructions written under the Privy Seal that I have newly identified as written in Hoccleve's hand.

no one has previously identified them as having been written by Hoc-cleve.

In addition to the E 404 files, nine documents written by Hoccleve survive in E 208, the King's Remembrancer / *Brevia Baronibus* files, which, according to the National Archives catalogue, "contain writs sent to the Treasurer and Barons of the Exchequer under the great and privy seals sending or requiring information, giving general administrative orders, or directing them to grant discharge of an account or particular debt or debtor."[7] These writs were then "enrolled on the *Brevia directa* section of the King's Remembrancer's memoranda rolls" (now E 159 files at the National Archives).[8] The E 208 files for this period are uncatalogued, and stored in bundles of parchment documents measuring ca. 10 × 30 cm., in boxes according to regnal years.[9]

A further five documents written by Hoccleve survive in E 28 files, the King's Council and Privy Seal Records of the Receipt of the Exchequer. One is the draft of a document written by Hoccleve, which is described above as having been identified by Doyle and Parkes; that is, E 28/29, item 30, a draft of a letter from Henry IV requesting aid for fighting the war with France, surviving in a bundle of letters to and from Robert Frye.[10] Another four are in a single file, E 28/97, comprising Privy Seal writs for military service and returns from the seventh year of the reign of Henry V (all four dated 29 December 1419).

One document survives in the E 43 files, a varied collection of debentures, receipts, warrants, and writs that have been set aside in this category because of the excellent condition of their seals. This is a receipt for his annuity written by Hoccleve, to which is attached his own personal seal.

Appendix A describes the characteristics of Hoccleve's handwriting by which these documents have been identified as his. A typical E 404 document by Hoccleve's hand is E 404/33/223, dated 7 March, 5 Henry V (1418), commanding the Exchequer to pay Thomas Hoccleve 42 shil-

---

[7] www.nationalarchives.gov.uk/catalogue/displaycataloguedetails.asp?CATID = 51 99&CATLN = 3&Highlight = %2CKING%2CKING%2CKING%2CKING%2CKI NG&accessmethod = 0, 20 June 2006.

[8] Ibid.

[9] Because these are uncatalogued, my references to them below and in the appendices name which box and bundle they occur in, then specify them by date of the document and sometimes by position in the pile that constitutes the bundle, but this positioning may have changed since my examination in the case of loose bundles.

[10] A final copy of this document is copied by Hoccleve into the Formulary (British Library Additional MS 24062), addressed to the Prior of the Grand Chartreuse. I am indebted to Dr. Doyle for this reference.

lings, 9 pence for expenses of purchasing wax and ink from Walter Lucy of London, for use in the Office of the Privy Seal:

Figure 1   Kew, National Archives E/404/33/233 (reduced), dated 7 March, 5 Henry V (1418). Reproduced with permission.

These documents show Thomas Hoccleve to have been an active clerk in the Office of the Privy Seal from at least 25 July 1391 until 29 June 1425, less than a year before 8 May 1426, by which date he is presumed to have died.[11] Virtually from the beginning of Henry IV's reign onward we find Hoccleve writing the documents that instruct the Exchequer to pay suppliers for purchase of parchment, paper, ink, and wax used by the clerks of the Office of the Privy Seal,[12] often going to the Exchequer to receive the payment that would be passed on to the suppliers by

[11] Scholars have dated the beginning of Hoccleve's service at the Privy Seal to about 1387, since he states in the *Regiment of Princes* (lines 802–5) that he had been writing for the Office for twenty-four years come Easter, and this is assumed to have been written in 1411 (see Burrow, *Thomas Hoccleve*, p. 2). The earliest document I have identified as definitely being written by his hand is dated 25 July, 15 Richard II (1391). Schulz corrected earlier scholars' estimates of the date of death (they had estimated near 1450), pp. 76–81, and more recent scholarship has more precisely dated it to sometime early in 1426: see Burrow, *Thomas Hoccleve*, p. 30 and note 121: "[Hoccleve's] annuity was last paid for the period to Michaelmas 1425," which "proves . . . that he was not alive to receive that due at Easter 1426, since the grant was for life."

[12] The series of such documents by Hoccleve's hand or naming him as recipient for purchases of ink, wax, parchment, and paper for use in the Office of the Privy Seal begins with E 404/15/45, written 30 October in the first year of Henry IV's reign, that is, very early in the reign, asking simply that the clerks be paid as accustomed for parchment purchased by them for use in the Office; this is followed by E 404/16/325, dated 13 January 1401, the first asking for payment specifically to the haberdasher William Surcestre of London, who has supplied the Office with ink, wax, and paper since Christmas 1399: in little over a year the Office had purchased (and presumably used) 46 pounds of red wax at 10 d. per pound; 2 gallons, 1 pottel, and 1 quart of ink at 40 d. per gallon; 4 quires of ordinary paper at 8 d. per quire, and ½ quire of 'papier royale' at 12 d. per quire. Presumably at this time the clerks were still purchasing parchment themselves, though later they purchase parchment as well from Surcestre. Thereafter there are several more payments either requested by Hoccleve for payment to William Surcestre or Exchequer records of payments to Hoccleve to be passed on to Surcestre, or later to Walter Lucy, another haberdasher:

E 404/17/254, dated 1 November 1401 to pay Surcestre
E 404/18/260, dated 3 December 1402 to pay Surcestre
E 403/574, m. 15 dated 23 February 1403, recording payment to Surcestre by Hoccleve's hand (Burrow, *Thomas Hoccleve*, item 13 in Appendix)

his hand; and from 1406 onward receiving these payments himself as repayment for supplies he has purchased over a period of time, up to a year and sometimes longer. Because he seems to have been in charge of supplies from 1399 onward, it seems clear that by then he must have been a full-fledged clerk of the Privy Seal and more than the others apparently in charge of the day-to-day running of the Office. This role fits well with his having created toward the end of his life the formulary of Privy Seal documents now preserved in British Library, Additional 24062, as if he understood the workings of the Office better than anyone and could record for future reference the correct forms that clerks ought to use in putting into words the various kinds of royal commands.

His supervisory role, or his seniority in the Privy Seal, is also demonstrated by his capacity to choose to write the documents for the highest-ranking people who were to be remunerated by the Exchequer, thus

---

E 404/18/564, dated 15 June, 1403 to pay Surcestre

E 404/19/450, dated 18 June 1404 to pay William Surcestre and John Pountfreit, haberdashers of London

E 404/20/164, dated 18 February 1405 to pay Surcestre

E 403/587, m. 14, dated 14 August 1406, recording payment to Hoccleve (Burrow, *Thomas Hoccleve,* item 19 in Appendix)

E 403/591, m. 10, dated 15 July 1407 recording payment to Hoccleve (Burrow, *Thomas Hoccleve,* item 22 in Appendix)

E 403/594, m. 10, dated 16 January 1408 recording payment to Hoccleve (Burrow, *Thomas Hoccleve,* item 24 in Appendix)

E 404/24/293, dated 21 February 1409 to pay Hoccleve

E 403/605, m. 6, dated 23 June 1410 recording payment to Hoccleve (Burrow, *Thomas Hoccleve,* item 31 in Appendix)

E 405/24, dated 5 November 1412 recording payment to Hoccleve (Burrow, *Thomas Hoccleve,* item 35 in Appendix)

E 403/619, m. 10, dated 17 January 1415 recording payment to Hoccleve (Burrow, *Thomas Hoccleve,* item 39 in Appendix)

E 403/627, m. 27, dated 14 February 1417 recording payment to Hoccleve (Burrow, *Thomas Hoccleve,* item 43 in Appendix)

E 404/33/223, dated 7 March 1418 to pay Hoccleve for supplies bought from Walter Lucy haberdasher of London

E 404/35/131, dated 10 June 1419 to pay Hoccleve for supplies from Lucy

E 403/640, mm. 10–11, dated 10 July 1419 recording payment to Hoccleve for the expenses named in the previous item (Burrow, *Thomas Hoccleve,* item 50 in Appendix)

E 403/652, m. 18, dated 23 February 1422 recording payment to Hoccleve for purchase of supplies from Lucy (Burrow, *Thomas Hoccleve,* item 56 in Appendix)

E 404/39/303, dated 19 May 1423 to pay Hoccleve for supplies from Lucy

E 403/660, m. 6, dated 20 May 1423 recording payment to Hoccleve for purchase of these supplies from Lucy (Burrow, *Thomas Hoccleve,* item 62 in Appendix)

E 403/673, m. 16, dated 4 March 1426, recording payment to Hoccleve to be delivered by Lucy's hand, for repayment for purchase of supplies (Burrow, *Thomas Hoccleve,* item 68 in Appendix)

ensuring for himself the best rewards. For instance, in 9 Henry V, on 3 June 1421, he writes two documents requesting the Exchequer to pay Louis, Duke of Bavarre, and Henry Percy, Earl of Northumberland, their annuities (E 404/37/102 and /103). These two documents are followed by several more requests for payments to other, lesser individuals written by several clerks or underclerks of the Privy Seal. In other words, Hoccleve first wrote the requests for the two highest-ranking individuals to be paid at the time, and other clerks or underclerks were presumably assigned to copy the form he had used to write similar requests for lesser individuals.

The collection of fees or rewards from men of high ranks for whom the clerks wrote out official copies of writs, grants, and so on is an issue Hoccleve raises in *The Regiment of Princes,* when he tells the Old Man that he was often swindled of his fees by middlemen, the great men's servants, but dared not complain to the great men about it (lines 1499–1547).[13] Especially toward the end of his career, one finds Hoccleve repeatedly writing the instructions for the Exchequer to pay certain prominent people; it is not that they are the only ones being paid by the Crown out of the Lower Exchequer accounts, but the instructions regarding these important individuals' payments are more often than not being written by Hoccleve. This choice of only the highest-ranking people is especially true in the 1420s, in his last years in the Privy Seal, when fewer documents written by his hand survive. In 1422 the only E 404 document written by Hoccleve is the instruction to pay Geoffrey Young, Warden of Leeds Castle in Kent (E 404/38/90). In 1423 he writes three documents in this category: three to pay John Radclif Seneschal of Guyenne, John Duke of Bedford, and Edmund Mortimer Earl of March and Lieutenant of Ireland (E 404/39/268, /269, /285, respectively). In 1424 he writes the warrants to pay John Shilley and Thomas Denney, Esquires, serving in France with Humfrey Duke of Gloucester (E 404/40/162) and at the end of that year to pay Henry Percy Earl of Northumberland (E 404/41/158). Finally, in 1425 he writes the requests for the Exchequer to pay Roger Fienes, knight; John Grey, knight; and Geffrey Whightyngton, esquire, who are serving in France under John Duke of Bedford (E 404/41/190, /191, /192); to pay James Butler ("le Botiller") Earl of Ormond and Lieutenant of Ireland (E 404/

---

[13] Thomas Hoccleve, *Hoccleve's Works: The Regement of Princes . . . and Fourteen of Hoccleve's Minor Poems,* ed. Frederick J. Furnivall, EETS, e.s. 72 (1897; repr. Kraus 1988), p. 55.

41/197); and to pay Sir Robert Ogle, Custodian of Roxburgh Castle (E 404/41/344), the latest identified surviving Privy Seal document by his hand.

In spite of his importance in keeping the office running and perhaps in training younger clerks, Hoccleve did not rise to hold more lucrative posts than that of one of the four (or five to six in these years) chief Clerks of the Privy Seal.[14] By contrast, as A. L. Brown points out, "Robert Frye [who] began at the bottom of the ladder like Hoccleve . . . was promoted to the important and lucrative post of Clerk (or Secretary) of the King's Council, and later became the secondary, or second in command, of the Office of the Privy Seal."[15] Hoccleve's never being promoted may have simply been because Frye beat him to the post of Secretary to the Council and thence Secondary at the Privy Seal, for the still-higher office of Keeper of the Privy Seal was very rarely filled from

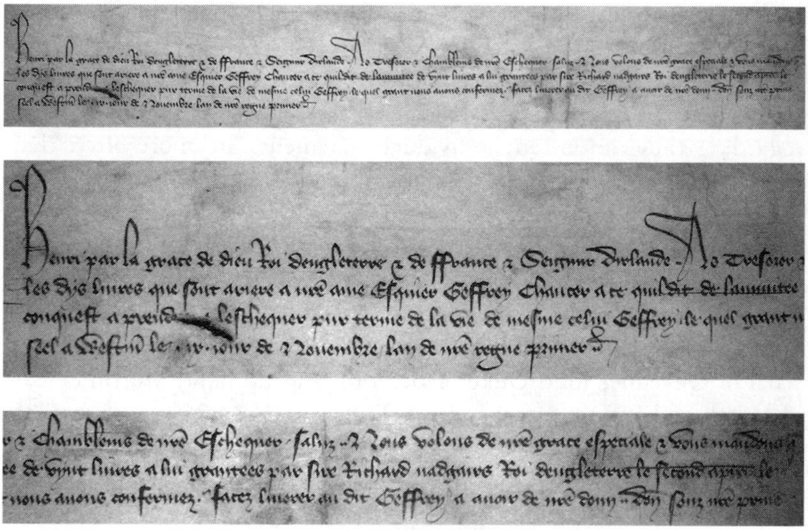

Figure 2   Kew, National Archives E 404/15/62, dated 9 November, 1 Henry IV (1399), entire document, reduced, and right and left sides, reduced. Reproduced with permission.

[14] A. L. Brown, "The Privy Seal Clerks in the Early Fifteenth Century," in *The Study of Medieval Records: Essays in Honour of Kathleen Major,* ed. D. A. Bullough and R. L. Storey (Oxford: Clarendon, 1971), pp. 260–81; on the number of clerks in this period, see p. 262.
[15] Ibid., p. 260.

within the Office. During the years Hoccleve served, the Keepers were promoted from Keeper of the Rolls of Chancery, Secretary to the King's Council, Keeper of the King's Wardrobe, other members of the king's personal household, and men who held high office in the Church (sometimes while also holding one of these bureaucratic offices as well).[16] Hoccleve himself was never given a benefice, though he might well have expected one based on the wording of his first annuity grant, offered annually throughout his life or until the king had granted him a benefice without cure of souls worth 20 pounds per year (*"quousque ipse ad beneficium ecclesiasticum sine cura valoris viginti librarum per annum per nos fierit promotus*).[17] Hoccleve says in his *Regiment of Princes* (written ca. 1410–11) that he often hoped for a benefice but was never given one, and so married, by which he made himself ineligible for one.[18]

Besides giving clues to Hoccleve's position within the Office of the Privy Seal, the newly identified documents written by his hand help us with dates, both of his service in the Office and of his "wild infirmyte." With regard to the latter, Hoccleve describes his illness thus in the "Complaint":

> Witnes uppon the wyld infirmyte
> Which that I had, as many a man well knewe,
> And whiche me owt of my selfe cast and threw
> (ed. Furnivall and Gollancz, lines 40–42)

[16] See *Handbook of British Chronology*, ed. F. Maurice Powicke and E. B. Fryde, 2nd ed. (London: Royal Historical Society, 1961), pp. 92–93.

[17] Burrow, *Thomas Hoccleve*, Appendix, no. 6, p. 34. The grant of larger annuity on 17 May 1409 (Burrow, Appendix, no. 28, pp. 39–40) does not include this clause, and its absence may indicate that Hoccleve had already married by then, or was about to be married, as suggested by J. H. Kern, "Een en ander over Thomas Hoccleve en zijn werken," *Verslagen en Mededeelingen der Koninklijke Akademie van Wetenschappen*, vol. 1 (1915), 340. See Burrow, *Thomas Hoccleve*, p. 12 and n. 44.

[18] As Hoccleve remarks in his dialogue with the Old Man in the prologue to the *Regiment*,

> I gasyd longe firste, & waytid faste
> After some benefice; and whan non cam,
> By proces I me weddid atte laste;
> And god it wot, it sore me agaste
> To bynde me, where I was at my large;
> But done it was; I toke on me that charge.
> (ed. Furnivall, lines 1451–56; p. 53.)

Brown, "Privy Seal Clerks," p. 268, notes that Hoccleve's colleague John Bailly did receive ecclesiastical benefice(s).

For date and duration he only suggests,

> But althowghe the substaunce of my memory
> Wente to pley, as for a certayne space,
> Yet the Lorde of vertew, the Kynge of Glory,
> Of His highe myght and his benynge grace,
> Made it to returne into the place
> Whennes it cam, whiche at All Hallwe Messe,
> Was five yeere, neyther more ne lesse
> ("Complaint," lines 50–56).

These clues from Hoccleve tell us to look for a period of inactivity from his work lasting several months and ending around 1 November, All Saints' Day. Scholars have disagreed as to the date of writing of the "Complaint" and "Dialogue with a Friend." Thanks to new and convincing arguments by John Burrow, the whole *Series* beginning with the "Complaint" and "Dialogue" is now thought to have been written between late 1419 and sometime in 1421, perhaps continuing into 1422, rather than beginning in that year.[19] Burrow claims that since the "Complaint" and "Dialogue" come first, Hoccleve must have written them at the beginning of this period, in late 1419, thus the illness would have occurred in the summer and autumn of 1414, with its cure on All Saints' Day 1414. Burrow argues in favor of 1414 on the ground that the *Series* must have been written during Humfrey Duke of Gloucester's first Regency (30 December 1419–2 February 1421) rather than the second, since in praising Gloucester, Hoccleve refers only to his military feats in the second campaign in France, 1417–19 (which preceded the first Regency), not to those of the third campaign. This dating to the first Regency, after return from second campaign, is confirmed by a marginal note of the holograph copy of Hoccleve's "Dialogue," Durham University Library, Cosin V.iii.9, which notes beside lines 542–43 ("As blyue as that I herde of his comynge / ffro ffrance") that this refers to the second return from campaigning in France (*"scilicet de secundo reditu suo de ffrancia"*) to distinguish it from the third. Therefore the return of sanity on All Saints' day to which Hoccleve refers in his "Complaint" must have occurred five years before this date, in 1414.[20]

---

[19] Burrow, *Thomas Hoccleve*, pp. 22, 27; Burrow, "Thomas Hoccleve: Some Redatings," *RES* 46 (1995), 366–72.
[20] Burrow, "Redatings," 370–72.

M. C. Seymour (and others) had argued for dating the illness to the summer and autumn of 1416, based on a 1421 dating of the "Complaint,"[21] though Seymour's principal argument for a 1416 dating rested on the unusual collection of Hoccleve's Easter annuity, paid in July 1416 not to Hoccleve himself but to his underclerk, John Welde and two others.[22] Burrow acknowledges that this payment was irregular, but points out that

Hoccleve may have made over some parts of his annuity to creditors (a common practice, see *Chaucer Life-Records,* 142) and left the rest to be collected by his clerk; or he may have been abroad: see n. 22 [where the text to which note 22 is attached suggests, "Henry V passed much of his reign across the Channel, and between 1417 and 1422 a section of the Privy Seal office followed him there. Yet nothing in the documentary or poetic evidence shows the poet as anything but a confirmed Londoner."][23]

Among the newly discovered documents, none suggests that Hoccleve went abroad with the king in 1415–16, and on the other hand there is a Hoccleve-written document dated at *Westminster* on 1 September, 1415 that suggests otherwise.[24]

[21] M. C. Seymour, ed., *Selections from Hoccleve* (Oxford: Oxford University Press, 1981), p. 133.

[22] Ibid., 133.

[23] Burrow, *Thomas Hoccleve,* p. 22, n. 88, and p. 7 for the text to which note 22 is attached. See also Burrow, "Redatings," 371–72.

[24] Kew, National Archives, E 404/31/452. In fact there are very few documents written by Hoccleve that are written from outside Westminster. For instance, when Henry V went to Leicester to hold Parliament there in the spring of 1414, he took three Privy Seal clerks with him (to judge by the number of different hands writing the twenty-two Privy Seal documents from Leicester) but not Thomas Hoccleve. For dates of Henry's travel to and from Leicester, see E 404/30/96 dated Westminster on 3 May; E 404/30/98 dated Leicester on 4 May; and for the return, see E 404/30/128 dated Leicester on 29 May and E 404/30/136 dated Westminster on 10 June. One document in this period is dated from Westminster, E 404/30/176, when perhaps the king made a quick trip back to the metropolis, but neither is this one written by Hoccleve. I have identified only four Privy Seal documents by Hoccleve's hand that are written anywhere but Westminster: (1) E 404/17/377 dated at Eltham, 28 December, 3 Henry IV (1401) demonstrates that Hoccleve was at Eltham for the Christmas festivities in 1401 (see John Lavan Kirby, *Henry IV of England: A Biography* [London: Constable and Co., 1970], p. 132). This writ requests the exchequer to pay two men of Sandwich £24 for purchasing a ship called "Juliane' from John Kent and delivering it to mariners of Brittany at the king's commandment. (2) E 404/19/163, dated at Cirencester 1 November, 5 Henry IV (1403), showing that Hoccleve was in Henry's entourage for at least part of the campaign in the West country in that autumn: Henry had been in Bristol on 23 October and had intended to hold a Parliament at Coventry on 30 November, but then postponed it to Westminster in the following year (Kirby, *Henry IV,* pp. 160–61). (3) E 404/19/285, dated at Abingdon Abbey on 27 December, 5 Henry IV (1403), showing

While accepting the earlier dating of the *Series* to 1419–21, I would argue with Ethan Knapp that the 1416 (rather than Burrow's 1414) dating for Hoccleve's illness makes more sense not only because of the irregular payment of his annuity in 1416 but also because, as Knapp points out, "the discussion in the 'Dialogue' of Hoccleve's desire to take up writing again fits best a scenario in which his infirmity fell after his composition of the 'Address to Sir John Oldcastle'" and "revision of the *Series* continued through at least 1421."[25] If Hoccleve began writing only after he had heard of the duke's return in very late November or in December (the Regency began on 30 December, not before), then Hoccleve's reference to the healing on All Saints' Day occurring five years ago, "neither more ne less," would have been written at least a month after All Saints' Day 1419 by the time Gloucester returned, so not quite "neither more ne less." Since even Burrow argues for Hoccleve's continuing to work on and make changes to *The Series* after its inception in very late 1419 or early 1420,[26] we cannot know whether the single word "five" ("Complaint," line 56) might not also have been changed to update the poem at the time it was presented to the duke. Thus the 1419 start-date for *The Series* cannot be taken as conclusive evidence of a 1414 illness.

Besides these arguments based on dates of Hoccleve's other writings and references in the "Complaint" and "Dialogue," the dates of the newly identified documents also support the 1416 dating of Hoccleve's illness. For one thing, Hoccleve's burst of activity in the summer of 1415 in writing documents to see that members of Henry V's army were paid for their roles in the campaign in that year, his most intense

---

that Hoccleve was again present during the king's Christmas festivities, this year held at Abingdon (Kirby, p. 162). (4) E 404/20/294, dated at Leicester 16 August, 6 Henry IV (1405), showing that Hoccleve was in the king's entourage or had joined him at Leicester as he returned from Pontefract, where he had been negotiating with the Earl of Northumberland (Kirby, p. 172) and before moving on to Lichfield, where on 27 August he confirmed his agreement with Northumberland for the surrender of Berwick: Kirby writes, "After a long stay at Pontefract Henry had made his way to Leicester by the end of July, then curved southwards through the midlands, and come to Lichfield in the second half of August" (p. 173); this document shows him to have been still at Leicester on the 16th.

[25] Ethan Knapp, *The Bureaucratic Muse: Thomas Hoccleve and the Literature of Late Medieval England* (University Park: Pennsylvania State University Press, 2001), p. 159 n. 1.

[26] Burrow himself makes a similar argument for continued changes and correction of the *Series* over this period when he argues for insertion of the passage on coin-clipping after May 1421 ("Redatings," p. 369).

activity as judged by the surviving E 404 documents, does not fit with the portrait of someone recovering from serious illness or nervous break-down. (Nor does his writing the balade "To Sir John Oldcastle" in the summer of 1415.) For another, there is a lengthier hiatus of activity in 1416 than in 1414. In the earlier year, 1414, records show Hoccleve still writing a document for the Privy Seal as late as 17 April (E 404/30/63) and collecting his own annuity as late as 2 May (E 403/617, m. 4). We have no further documents by his hand or annuity collected by him until 29 January of the following year (E 404/30/191), but Hoc-cleve himself has told us that he was cured on or around All Saints' Day, that is, 1 November. So in all there are only six months, from 2 May until 1 November in 1414, for which we cannot account for Hoccleve's activities.

By contrast, there is a much longer period in late 1415 and through most of 1416 in which we cannot account for Hoccleve's activities. He was very active in spring and summer of 1415, writing eighteen surviv-ing documents in a single month in May–June 1415. The last of these, E 404/31/383 (dated 13 June, 3 Henry V [1415]), is written only two days before Henry V "[rode] through London and formally [took] his leave of the mayor and sheriffs" as he set out for the south coast.[27] After this, in July–August 1415, Hoccleve writes "To Sir John Oldcastle" while Henry and his army paused at Southampton in preparation for the crossing to Harfleur, as he notes by way of heading in the holograph manuscript, Huntington Library HM 111, folio 1r: "Ceste feust faicte au temps que le Roy Henri le Vth (que Dieu pardoint) feust a Hampton sur son primer passage vers Harflete." He is still active on 1 September 1415, writing the document, Kew, National Archives E 404/31/452 (dated at Westminster 1 September, 3 Henry V) to pay Richard Berall, esquire, who is made Custodian of Roxburgh Castle for a quarter year, taking over the Wardenship from Robert Dumfrauill Knight, previous Custodian of the Castle (so that D'Umfraville could accompany Henry on the campaign), and giving him rights to arm the castle with as many men as needed to safeguard it if it is attacked by the king's enemies.[28]

But after Agincourt on 25 October 1415, there is a period of inactiv-ity in late 1415 and most of 1416 in which no documents by Hoccleve's

[27] Christopher Allmand, *Henry V* (London: Methuen, 1992), p. 73.
[28] It must be coincidence only that Hoccleve's last issue warrant involved Roxburgh, too: in 1425 he wrote the Issue Warrant for payment of its Custodian, Sir Robert Ogle (E 404/41/344).

hand survive in the E 404 files or elsewhere in similar files I have examined. After 1 September 1415, his name next appears in the records on 29 February 1416, when he receives his annuity from the Exchequer *"per manus proprias per assignacionem factam isto die"* (E 403/622, m. 11). On 18 July 1416, as noted by previous scholars, his annuity is collected not by Hoccleve himself but by John Welde, together with two other Clerks, John Burgh and Robert Welton (E 403/624, m. 9). He appears next writing a document for the Privy Seal on 9 December 1416 (E 404/32/262), little more than six weeks after All Saints' Day. Thus in the fourteen months between 1 September 1415 and All Saints' Day (1 November) 1416, Hoccleve makes only a single appearance in the records, on 29 February 1416, even then perhaps not appearing in person. Out of forty payments of Hoccleve's annuity recorded by Burrow in his Appendix,[29] twenty-six were paid *"per manus proprias,"* which means Hoccleve appeared in person at the Exchequer to receive the payment.[30] One, in Trinity term 1415, is recorded simply as being paid *"de certo suo annuo,"* which does not tell us whether he appeared in person (this was the very busy time when Hoccleve and others at the Office of the Privy Seal were preparing the documents related to the French invasion, and Hoccleve was writing "To Sir John Oldcastle").[31] One is the unusual collection by John Welde and two other clerks in July 1416, discussed above, each collecting a portion with the remainder to be paid to Hoccleve by the hands of John Welde.[32] Another five were paid *"per assignationem factam isto die,"* that is, the payment is not made directly by the Exchequer, but the Exchequer assigns some other royal income-collector—like the wool tax, for instance—to pay the money, giving the awardee (Hoccleve) a tally or another issue warrant.[33] This was a common practice when money in the royal exchequer was tight, and twice when Hoccleve is paid in this way other Privy Seal clerks, Baillay and Offorde, are as well.[34] Finally, seven payments, including that on 29

---

[29] Burrow, *Thomas Hoccleve,* Appendix, pp. 33–49.
[30] Burrow's numbers 12, 15, 16, 17, 18, 20, 21, 22, 25, 26, 27, 29, 32, 34, 37, 38, 44, 47, 49, 51, 52, 53, 59, 61, 65, and 66 (*Thomas Hoccleve,* pp. 36–49).
[31] Burrow's document number 40 (*Thomas Hoccleve,* p. 42).
[32] See p. 303. Burrow's document number 44 (*Thomas Hoccleve,* p. 43).
[33] Burrow, Appendix, numbers 8, 10, 33, 45 and 48 (*Thomas Hoccleve,* pp. 35–44). For assignments, see Burrow, note 46 on page 12, citing Martin M. Crow and Clair C. Olson, *Chaucer Life-Records* (Oxford: Clarendon, 1966), pp. 136–37.
[34] Burrow, Appendix, number 45 (p. 44), E 403/630, m. 7, dated 25 May 1417, and numbers 46 and 48 (p. 44), E 403/633, mm. 6 and 13, E 403/638, m. 9

February 1416, were made *"per assignationem factam isto die per manus proprias"* or *"per manus propriasper assignationem factam isto die."*[35] The last of these specifies that the payment is being made *"per manus proprias, videlicet, per assignationem factam isto die,"* which suggests that we are to interpret this combination as a payment made to Hoccleve in person but giving him an assignment to collect from some other source. Perhaps those made only *per assignationem factam isto die* are simply assignments made without Hoccleve coming to the Exchequer, or perhaps it is the other way around, in the longer wording specifying that the payment is to be made to Hoccleve although it is assigned in his absence. If he does appear, this walk to the Exchequer to collect his annuity—then being foiled by being given an assignment instead—on 29 February 1416 seems to be the only sighting of Hoccleve either writing documents at the Privy Seal or collecting his annuity at any time in the fourteen months between the beginning of September 1415 and mid-December 1416.[36] In this period he produces no poetry, and at least once assigns others to collect his annuity for him. Thus this longer period in 1415–16 seems more likely to mark the period of Hoccleve's illness.

John Burrow has noted that "Hoccleve represents himself in his writings as a great worrier, especially about money,"[37] and it may be that the poet's financial difficulties, particularly acute at this period, contributed to his "wyld infirmyte." Hoccleve states in his "Dialogue" that it was long illness that caused his mind to go astray[38] and certainly illness

---

[35] Burrow, Appendix, numbers 11, 30, 41, 46 (recording two payments), 54, 55 and 57.

[36] By contrast, in other periods when there is a gap in the Hoccleve-written documents in these files, Hoccleve does unambiguously appear in person to collect his annuity at least once. For instance, there is a gap in the Hoccleve-written Privy Seal documents between 23 February 1410 (E 404/25/201) and 10 October 1412 (E 404/28/77), but Hoccleve appears in person to collect his annuity (*"per manus propprias"*) on 17 July 1410 and 26 February 1412, with a third payment ambiguously stating only that the payment was assigned to be paid by another office of royal government (*"per assignacionem factam isto die"*) on 11 July 1411 (Burrow, Appendix, documents 32 and 34 and 33, respectively, *Thomas Hoccleve*, pp. 40–41); and again there is a gap of over a year between 7 March 1418 (E 404/33/223) and 21 May 1419 (E 404/35/119), but Hoccleve appeared in person on 1 July 1418 to collect his annuity (*"per manus propprias"*), with another payment ambiguously only reassigned (*"per assignacionem factam isto die"*) on 7 December 1418 (Burrow, Appendix, documents 47 and 48, *Thomas Hoccleve*, p. 44).

[37] Burrow comments on Hoccleve's financial worries (*Thomas Hoccleve*, p. 8); and actual financial difficulties (ibid., pp. 11–12).

[38] *Dialogue*, line 426.

could well have followed from the overwork at the Privy Seal in the spring and summer of 1415. But there were also financial difficulties. Burrow has noted that there is a missed annuity payment in 1414.[39] Hoccleve had recently prepared presentation copies of his *Regiment of Princes* for noble patrons,[40] and he may have been asked about this time also to prepare a volume of his balades for Edward Duke of York. An envoy he wrote to conclude and dedicate this volume of balades survives in one of the autograph manuscripts (San Marino, California, Henry E. Huntington Library, HM 111, fols. 32v–34), which Furnivall and Gollancz entitled "Balade to my gracious Lord of York":

> Go, little pamflet, and streight thee dresse
> Unto the noble rootid gentillesse
> Of the myghty Prince of famous honour,
> My gracious Lord of York, to whos noblesse
> Me recommande with hertes humblesse,
> As he that have his grace & his favour
> Fownden always, for which I am dettour,
> For him to preye & so shal my symplesse
> Hertily do unto my dethes hour.
>
> Remembre his worthynesse, I charge thee,
> How ones at London desired he
> Of me that am his servant & shal ay
> To have of my balades swich plentee
> As ther weren remeynynge unto me;
> And for nat wole I to his wil seyn nay,
> But fulfille it as ferfoorth as I may,
> Be thow an owter of my nycetee,
> For my good Lordes lust and game & play.
> ("Balade to my gracious Lord of York," lines 1–18)[41]

The Duke of York to whom this volume was to be presented was Edward, Duke of York 1402–15.[42] The volume of balades therefore

---

[39] *Thomas Hoccleve*, p. 22.

[40] Of the two surviving copies, British Library MSS Arundel 38 and Harley 4866, Burrow remarks, "These two manuscripts (the earliest surviving copies of any of Hoccleve's works) are both expensive products, and one may wonder whether the recipient paid for them" (*Thomas Hoccleve*, p. 19).

[41] From the edition of Furnivall and Gollancz, p. 49.

[42] Furnivall and Gollancz assumed that this balade was addressed to Richard Plantagenet, Duke of York, father of King Edward IV, and so dated Hoccleve's poem to midcentury and followed George Mason in assuming therefore that Hoccleve had lived

should be dated after 1402 and before Edward's death at Agincourt in October 1415. But since Edward had asked for a volume collecting together "of my balades swich plentee / As ther weren remeynynge unto me" and Hoccleve wrote the balades and *Male Regle* to which we believe he refers in the first decade of the century, the request by Edward must date from a period of years well after their composition. This period seems unlikely to have been 1409–11, when Hoccleve's resources had already gone into the commissioned presentation copies of the *Regiment,* so it seems likely that the volume of balades was requested and prepared after that. Thus, if after paying for the presentation copies of the *Regiment,* Hoccleve also prepared a volume of balades for the Duke of York sometime in 1412–15, then the latter's death at Agincourt would have created some financial hardship for the poet, just as he had hoped to be rewarded for preparing a requested volume. Of course without means of closer dating of this lost volume of balades, we cannot know whether Hoccleve had been paid for it already, but it remains one additional possible reason for acute financial difficulties at this time.

The newly identified E 404 and E 208 documents probably witness only a small fraction of Hoccleve's work at the Office, since the Office of the Privy Seal was responsible for composing, writing, and issuing documents relaying all of the decisions of the king and the King's Council, and sometimes those of other royal officials as well. A. L. Brown describes its functions:

> It was primarily a writing-office where decisions by the king, the Council, and royal officials were translated into formal royal letters and authenticated with the privy seal. It was a "clearing-house," sending out formal warrants to Chancery, Exchequer, and other offices, sending "missive" letters to royal officials in England, Wales, Ireland, Gascony, and Calais, to individuals, towns, cathedral chapters, universities, and all manner of people, and sending diplomatic letters to foreign rulers.[43]

The slips of parchment commanding the Clerks of the Exchequer to pay out certain sums of money to various individuals in the E 404 series or to cancel certain individuals' debts to the king in E 208 files, some of

---

to an old age (see Furnivall and Gollancz, *Hoccleve's Works,* p. xxvii); the correct date of his death depended on new identification of the dedicatee of this poem as Edward Duke of York 1402–15, as argued by Schultz ("Thomas Hoccleve, Scribe," pp. 76–81).

[43] Brown, "The Privy Seal Clerks in the Early Fifteenth Century," 260–81, esp. 261. This same passage is quoted by Burrow, *Thomas Hoccleve,* p. 3.

which are now newly identified as being written by Hoccleve, would have been the simplest and most mundane of documents prepared by the Privy Seal. As a senior clerk of the Office, Hoccleve would probably be called on more often to prepare more unusual or sensitive documents in behalf of the king and the King's Council. The high number of Hoccleve's documents I have discovered for the single year, 1415, probably reflects Privy Seal activity that called for this particular type of document as much as it does Hoccleve's (and the other clerks') intense activity at that time. In the early summer of 1415, Henry V had just decided to go ahead with a French invasion with only a few months to prepare. As Christopher Allmand says, "He badly needed to carry out his attack by the summer of 1415 (or else lose almost a year before a suitable time presented itself again). This required a firm decision to be made by March or April of that year, at the very least. The failure of the February mission to Paris [of Henry's ambassadors seeking concessions from the French] gave him the chance to act within the same year, and to present its failure as offering him the go-ahead for war."[44] The eighteen documents in the E 404 series written by Hoccleve between 12 May and 13 June probably result from Henry's decision to go ahead, and his need to call upon his Privy Seal Clerks at that time to devote themselves to setting in motion the recruitment of commanders through indentures and advance payments for those who had agreed to accompany him on this military expedition.

Although this example suggests that many of E 404 documents by Hoccleve's hand are related as much to Privy Seal priorities as to his own involvement in work, the newly identified documents nevertheless help us to judge the duration of Hoccleve's career at the Privy Seal and might suggest periods when he was most active and least active. The earliest document definitely identifiable as Hoccleve's in this series of the Privy Seal files is dated 25 July 1391 (E 404/14, files 90–96, Part II).[45] Hoccleve says in his Prologue to the *Regiment of Princes* that he has

---

[44] Allmand, *Henry V*, p. 72.

[45] Other earlier documents may be Hoccleve's as well; for instance, E 404/13, file 84, document dated 6 April, 6 Richard II (or 1383), displays several characteristics in common with the hand we recognize as Hoccleve's from later years (as confirmed by Dr. A. I. Doyle when I showed him a photograph of it). This may represent early apprentice or assistant clerk work: if born in 1367, Hoccleve would have been sixteen in 1383. His reference to having "wryte ther . . . xxᵗⁱ yeer / And iiij" in the *Regiment of Princes* (lines 803–5) would then have to refer to some period after he had been an apprentice or assistant, that is, that he had been a clerk since 1387. Support for such an interpretation would come from the documents that show him with three other clerks (Robert Frye,

been writing for the Office of the Privy Seal for twenty-four years, come Easter.[46] Since the Prologue has generally been dated ca. 1411, it has been assumed that Hoccleve meant that he started work at the Privy Seal in 1387; thus this earliest document certainly by his hand would come four years later. It should be noted that many fewer Privy Seal documents survive in E 404 files from the reign of Richard II than from the subsequent reigns, so in the crucial period when Hoccleve began work, we cannot be certain based on the documents exactly when he entered service there, and there may well be other sorts of documents as yet unsearched that record his hand earlier. It is also possible that he was apprenticed to Guy de Rouclif even earlier than 1387 (Rouclif retired in 1389), and only began to write for the Privy Seal in his own name, as a Clerk, from 1387 onward.[47]

The newly discovered documents also show us that, like Chaucer, Hoccleve appears to have bridged the change of dynasty in 1399, writing for Richard II such important and delicate documents as the command, dated in Shrewsbury on 7 February 1397, commanding the Exchequer to pay Eleanor Duchess of Gloucester a thousand marks, as per the grant made to her in Northampton in July of the previous year; then in the first weeks of Henry IV's formal government, on 17 and 20 October 1399, writing the important command to the Exchequer to pay John Thorpe more than 270 pounds to reimburse those who had supplied him with food and lodging on the Marches in the preceding summer (E 404/15/37), and a second to pay for the expenses of Henry's

---

John Kethe, and William Flete) already receiving grants from the king in 1389 and 1391 as the "clerks" of the Privy Seal Office (the usual number of senior clerks was four): See Burrow, *Thomas Hoccleve*, Appendix, document 1 on page 33. Further support comes from Guy de Rouclif's naming Hoccleve as his underclerk ("*clerico meo*") in his will dated 1392: see Burrow, *Thomas Hoccleve*, document 3 on page 33. If Hoccleve had not begun work of some sort at the Privy Seal Office until 1387, that would leave only two years' apprenticeship before he presumably took de Rouclif's place as one of the clerks of the Privy Seal. See Burrow, p. 9 and Appendix documents numbers 1, 3, and 5 on pages 33–34. Locating him at the Privy Seal in the 1380s earlier than 1387, as an apprentice, probably under the elder clerk Guy de Rouclif, means that he was beginning life as a clerk at the Privy Seal before Chaucer left the city for Kent, and we believe that he was already expressing an interest in literature by this time since in his will in 1392 Guy de Rouclif left him a copy of a book on the Trojan War (Burrow's Appendix, document 3 on page 33). This would also place Hoccleve in the Office closer to the time that Rouclif sold two properties in East Anglia to John Gower, in 1382: See Burrow, *Thomas Hoccleve*, p. 10 and n. 34; E. M. Ingram, "Thomas Hoccleve and Guy de Rouclif," *Notes and Queries*, n.s. 20 (1973): 42–43.

[46] *Regiment of Princes*, lines 802–5. See Burrow, *Thomas Hoccleve*, p. 2.
[47] See note 45 above.

household *"costages et despenses par nous a faire en nostre Chambre auantdite,"* 4,000 pounds (E 404/15/40).

One document from this period may be taken as confirmation that Hoccleve knew Chaucer personally, as he claimed in his later writings. On the ninth of November 1399, Hoccleve himself writes the document that commands the Exchequer to pay Geoffrey Chaucer 10 pounds arrears of his 20-pounds-per-year annuity from Richard II, acknowledging that he has confirmed that annuity.[48] Given Hoccleve's claims to have been a disciple of Chaucer, this document may be interpreted as the Exchequer Clerk taking care that his mentor continues to receive his annuity from the crown after the change of dynasty; so Chaucer's speedy acknowledgment from Henry IV comes not just in response to Chaucer's "Complaint to his Purse," but also comes swiftly, a month after the coronation, because his disciple Thomas Hoccleve was on hand to write out the issue warrant.[49] At about the same time, on 12 November 1399, Hoccleve himself receives his first annuity from the crown, a grant of 10 pounds per annum awarded him by Henry IV.[50]

Hoccleve is active in writing Privy Seal issue warrants for Henry IV through the first ten years of the reign. Then abruptly after February 1410 he ceases for the most part, at least in writing these documents now archived in E 404 files, until after the first year of Henry V's reign: that is, he writes the last of these documents on 23 February 1410 (E 404/25/201) and writes only two documents at the very end of Henry

---

[48] Kew, National Archives E 404/15/62, dated 9 November 1399; see fig. 2. The text reads, "Henri par la grace de dieu Roi d'Engleterre & de ffrance & Seignur d'Irlande: As Tresorer & Chambreleins de nostre Eschequer, saluz. Nous voulons de nostre grace especiale & vous mandons que les dys livres que sont ariere a nostre ame Esquier Geffrey Chaucer a ce qu'il dit de l'annuitee de vynt livres a lui grantees par sire Richard nadgairs Roi d'Engleterre le second apres le Conquest a prendre a l'eschequer pur terme de la vie de mesme celui Geffrey, le quel grant nous avons confermez; facez liverer au dit Geffrey a avoir de nostre donn, donn souz nostre priue seel a Westminstre le ix jour de Novembre l'an de nostre regne Primer."

[49] See Crow and Olson, *Chaucer Life-Records,* 525–30. The relationship between Chaucer's "Complaint to his Purse" and the renewal of the annuity and payment(s) for it are detailed by Laila Z. Gross in the Explanatory notes to the "The Complaint of Chaucer to his Purse," in *The Riverside Chaucer,* gen . ed. Larry D. Benson (Boston: Houghton Mifflin, 1987), p. 1088.

[50] Recorded in the Patent Rolls, 12 November 1399 (Kew, National Archives, C 66/355 m. 21). See Burrow, *Thomas Hoccleve,* Appendix, item 6, on p. 34. The volume of work at the beginning of Henry IV's reign was apparently extraordinarily high, for in 1401, according to A. L. Brown, "Hoccleve asked for and obtained a reward with seven other s[ervitors] in the Privy Seal because of the great amount of work they had done since the beginning of the reign." (Brown, "Privy Seal Clerks," p. 267; he cites in a footnote National Archives E 28/9, dated 23 July 1401).

IV's reign (E 404/28/77 and E 404/28/227 in October 1412 and March 1413, respectively) until he becomes a more active clerk, at least in writing these kinds of documents, at the beginning of Henry V's second year, on 17 April 1414 (E 404/30/63). These last years of Henry IV's reign were turbulent, with many people being forced to take sides between the old king and the prince and Council. The fact that there are so few documents by Hoccleve's hand in these years suggests that he was not actively working at the Office of the Privy Seal or not being called upon by either Henry IV or the future Henry V and Council to write out royal commands under the Privy Seal. This absence is particularly remarkable in the first year of Henry V's reign, when, as usual in a new reign, the Office of the Privy Seal was otherwise particularly busy renewing grants and annuities and making other payments related to the new monarch.[51]

Besides not writing many of these writs and warrants for the Office of the Privy Seal (E 404 files), Hoccleve was also not being paid regularly in these years, his payments for the two years from Michaelmas 1411 until Michaelmas 1413 not having been made until the autumn of 1413.[52] The coincidence that Hoccleve seems not to be preparing issue warrants for the Privy Seal and appears to have had to wait until Henry V came to the throne for payment of his annuity for the preceding two years supports R. F. Yeager's argument that, whatever he felt about the king at the beginning of the reign, toward the end Hoccleve has taken the prince's side in the disputes between father and son and therefore slipped from favor with Henry IV.[53]

However it happened that he was not as active at the Privy Seal, Hoccleve appears to have taken advantage of the involuntary sabbatical, for these are exactly the years to which we assign the writing of the *Regiment of Princes* for Henry V. Again ten years later there is another gap in Hoccleve's activity in writing E 404 documents in the sixteen-

[51] There are many Privy Seal documents from the first year of Henry V's reign in the E 404 files, but none that I found to be clearly written by Hoccleve.

[52] Hoccleve's annuity payments from 1409 to 1413 (Henry V's regnal years beginning 21 March 1413) occurred as follows: 23 May 1409 for half-year to Easter 1409; 22 November 1409 for half-year to Michaelmas 1409; 17 July 1410 for half-year to Easter 1410; 8 July 1411 for half-year to Michaelmas 1410; 26 February 1412 for whole year to Michaelmas 1411; 28 September 1413 confirmation/renewal of annuity, saying Hoccleve has been paid arrears from the preceding Michaelmas (1411–12?) by the king's gift; 1 December 1413 for whole year up to Michaelmas 1413.

[53] R. F. Yeager, "Death is a Lady: *The Regiment of Princes* as Gendered Political Commentary," *SAC* 26 (2004): 147–93, pp. 150–52.

month period between 9 February 1420 and 3 June 1421, just the period to which we assign his writing of the *Series*. In the *Dialogue with a Friend,* too, he is visited by his friend in his chamber, rather than at the Privy Seal, and the Friend complains that it has been a quarter year since he has seen Hoccleve.[54] They discuss how Hoccleve could write to gain the patronage of a great lord, settling on Humfrey Duke of Gloucester as the most likely man to appreciate Hoccleve's writings. Hoccleve's devoting himself to writing in the periods of release from some activity at the Privy Seal fits a pattern we see in other writers of this and later centuries who take advantage of a period of enforced rest from their normal labors (imprisonment or dismissal from a job because of political alliances) to gain patronage and financial reward (or release) through their writings.[55] Writing at such gaps in his normal working routine would also help to explain why Hoccleve's works contain so many references to his need for money.[56]

The newly identified documents also show that Hoccleve was active at the Privy Seal through the remainder of his life. When he returns to writing these documents regularly, he is, as I said above, only writing the documents that will benefit those in high positions (or their immediate followers), and thus equally benefit himself through their fees or rewards. He also continues to write E 404 documents to repay himself for red wax and ink he purchased for use in the Office (e.g., E 404/39/ 303, dated 19 May, 1 Henry VI, that is, 1423). Hoccleve writes his last E 404 documents in March, April and June of 1425, this last fully eleven months after his previously supposed retirement on receipt of the corrody at Southwick Priory on 4 July 1424.[57] Even after the last docu-

[54] In the *Dialogue* his friend knocks at Hoccleve's chamber door, which suggests that Hoccleve is in some private space (*Dialogue,* lines 2–7).

[55] For example, Chaucer's begging poems written between periods of service to the crown; Charles d'Orléans's, James I's, George Ashby's, and Sir Thomas Malory's works written while imprisoned.

[56] A. L. Brown notes that "though Hoccleve often complained about money, the begging poems about his annuity may all relate to terms when he was not paid." ("Privy Seal Clerks," p. 271, n. 2.)

[57] As Burrow points out (p. 30 and n. 125), the latest datable piece in the Formulary is "a letter from Henry VI to his Chancellor concerning lands claimed by Sir John Lescrope," dated July 1424. I have found six documents written by Hoccleve in the third year of Henry VI's reign, that is, 1 September 1424 to 31 August 1425, the latest being the document named here dated 29 June, 3 Henry VI (1425). The others are E 404/41/158 (dated 3 December, 3 Henry VI [1424]); E 404/41/190 (dated 4 March, 3 Henry VI [1425]); E 404/41/191 (dated 4 March, 3 Henry VI [1425]); E 404/41/192 (dated 4 March, 3 Henry VI [1425]); and E 404/41/197 (dated 14 April, 3 Henry VI [1425]).

ment of this kind on 29 June 1425, he may have continued in the Privy Seal right up until his death in the following spring, for he received his annuity payment in February 1426, and was repaid still for purchase of wax and ink on the 4 March 1426. He is presumed to have died by 8 May 1426, when his Southwick corrody was granted to someone else.

Finally, one of the newly identified documents shows us Hoccleve's own personal seal. This is National Archives E 43/554,[58] a receipt for payment of his annuity written, signed, and sealed by Hoccleve himself (fig. 3). It may be that Hoccleve and other recipients of payments from the Lower Exchequer always wrote out such receipts, but that most have not survived or are buried among the still-uncatalogued documents at the National Archives. This one, as I noted above, has been enrolled in this category (E 43) because of the excellent condition of its seal, along with other documents whose seals are in good condition. The text reads,

Sachent toutes gens moye Thomas Hoccleve, Clerc, avoir recoit en nou[m] nostre tres redoute seigneur par les mayns du Tresorer le jour de la fesance de cestes cent soldz d'estre paiez pur le terme de seint Michel darein passez d'une annuitee de dys liures [*erasure*] a prendre en l'eschequer, des que ditz cent soldz [je] [me] cognoise estre paiez & mesme nostre seigneur le Roy eut aquite par

Figure 3   Kew, National Archives E 43/554. Reproduced with permission.

[58] This document is written on parchment, measuring 244 x 56 mm at left edge and 244 x 54 mm at right edge. It is folded tightly to fit a small box filed separately under this shelf number at the National Archives.

315

ces presentes, sealle par mon seal, don le vynt & septisme jour de Novembre, l'an du Regne de nostre dit seigneur le Roy le quart. (E 43/554)

Let all men know that I Thomas Hoccleve, Clerk, have received in the name of our most noble lord by the hands of the Treasurer the day of the writing of these [words] one hundred shillings paid for the term of St Michael just past, of an annuity of ten pounds [erasure] to be taken from the Exchequer, concerning which said hundred shillings I acknowledge myself to have been paid and also our lord the King to be acquit by these present [words], sealed by my seal on the 27th day of November, the fourth year of the reign of our said lord the King.

Hoccleve does not give a precise year at the end of this document, possibly forgetting to name which monarch, or more likely having confused the numbering of the regnal year (many of his E 404 documents end in this way, naming the year as the last word of the document) with the number attached to the king's name, that is, the fourth year of the reign of King Henry IV. The National Archives catalogue currently lists this document as datable to the fourth year of the reign of "[King Henry IV–VI],"[59] but the document must date from November 1402, the fourth year of the reign of Henry IV, since in this document Hoccleve acknowledges payment of 5 pounds (100 shillings) for the half-year payment of his annuity, and this would only have applied between 1399, when he was granted an annuity of 10 pounds, until 1409, when this was raised to 20 marks; thus 1402 would have been the only fourth year of a reign in the period when he was being paid 100 shillings per half year.[60] This document, Hoccleve's receipt, is dated 27 November 1402, but the Clerks of the Exchequer did not enroll the annuity payment until 7 December, ten days later.[61] The evidence this gives of delay on the part of the clerks to enroll payments on the Issue Rolls must force us to reevaluate the delays of payments of Hoccleve's annuities we

[59] It was previously listed as 4 Henry V, i.e., 1416.

[60] My grateful thanks to John Burrow for correcting my former dating of this document and pointing out that this amount of annuity would have been applicable only to this year.

[61] Burrow, *Thomas Hoccleve,* Appendix, no. 12, p. 36. The Issue Roll records payment of only 4 pounds, 18 shillings and 9 pence, so 15 pence must have been paid out of this to someone else, perhaps someone to whom Hoccleve owed this amount who accompanied him to the Exchequer to be paid. The discrepancy may account for Hoccleve's erasure in the receipt, noted in my transcription, just as he is to record the amount of his annuity.

have heretofore calculated, sometimes quite precisely, on the basis of the Issue Rolls.[62]

Attached to this document is Hoccleve's own personal seal, a small[63] round seal of red wax attached to a strip of parchment cut away from the bottom, with his motto, *"va illa voluntee"* written around a roundel, followed (or preceded) by a cross at the top, and with the signum of a pointing hand, or *maniculum,* in the middle of the roundel (fig. 4).[64] The language of the motto is French, the second word apparently an elision of the third person singular pronoun *"il"* and the adverb *"la,"* thus, "he goes there willingly." The *maniculum* pointing to a cross could indicate heaven, or simply any direction if we understand the hand to be the king's: thus a Privy Seal clerk willingly goes wherever the king commands. If we take this latter meaning, the motto would match the sentiments of the later writer *cum* Clerk of the Signet, George Ashby, who

Figure 4   Kew, National Archives E 43/554, detail. Reproduced with permission.

[62] See Brown, "Privy Seal Clerks," p. 271 and n. 2; discussed by Burrow, *Thomas Hoccleve,* 12, who calculates the delays in payments of Hoccleve's annuities by average numbers of days.

[63] The imprint of the seal is 10 mm in diameter; in red wax that varies from 20 to 22 mm in diameter.

[64] This was my best reading of the motto after much study of the original under a magnifying glass; the imprint of the seal is not absolutely sharp and the lettering is somewhat stylized.

makes a great point of his having been willing to go wherever he was bid to accompany the king (Henry VI) and Duke of Gloucester to write their commands from wherever they happened to be. In "Complaint of a Prisoner in the Fleet 1463," he says that he was ever ready

> Wrytyng to theyre sygnet full fourty yere
> As wel beyond the see as on thys syde,
> Doyng my servyce as well there as here,
> Nat sparyng for to go ne for to ryde,
> Havyng pen and inke evyr at my syde,
> As truly as I coude to theyre entent
> Redy to accomplysshe theyre commandment[65]

Appendix A:
Characteristics of Thomas Hoccleve's Handwriting

In an article in *Speculum,* 1937, H. C. Schulz described four characteristic features of Hoccleve's hand: his formation of the letters *A, g, w,* and *y.* As Schulz commented, however, "No one of these four can be said to be unique with Hoccleve, but as a group (and with identical slope, size, shading, position of pen, and degree of curvature) they have not been found to occur in any of the numerous Middle English hands so far examined."[66] In descriptions of these letters below, I quote A. I. Doyle's more detailed analyses from the EETS facsimile edition of the verse works written in Hoccleve's hand:[67]

1. The uppercase *A* has "a sweeping deep downwards stroke turning upwards counter-clockwise across itself as it turns clockwise either to a flattened head with an angular junction on the right with a straight broken downstroke or else continuing with a simple curve, in each with a more or less strongly seriffed foot" (for the square-topped version, see Figure 5, beginning of line 11, "And"; for the round-topped version, see Figure 6, lines 1, 3, 7, 12, "And").

---

[65] See *The Kingis Quair and Other Prison Poems,* ed. Linne R. Mooney and Mary-Jo Arn (TEAMS, Kalamazoo: Medieval Institute Publications, 2005), p. 155, lines 64–70.

[66] H. C. Schulz, "Thomas Hoccleve, Scribe," *Speculum* 12 (1937): 71–81; this quoted from p. 72.

[67] Thomas Hoccleve, *A Facsimile of the Autograph Verse Manuscripts: Henry E. Huntington Library, San Marino (California), MSS HM 111 and HM 744; University Library, Durham (England), MS Cosin V. III. 9,* intro J. A. Burrow and A. I. Doyle, EETS, s.s. 19 (2002), p. xxxiv.

2. The secretary *g* is "flat-topped . . . with variant tails, turning either tightly or in a wide sweep on the left to its head or else turning back more or less sharply to the right" (for the wider sweep, shaped like an old-fashioned coat-hanger hook, see Figure 5, second word of line 3, "purgatorie" or Figure 6, line 13, "mighte"; for the tighter version, see Figure 6, line 12, "thogh").

3. The *w* occurs in two forms: the most distinctive is "a round or oval *w* made usually with only two strokes, the second like a 2 within the circle"; the other is a "more complex three-stroke bipartite *w* with angular feet" (for the rounded form, see Figure 5, throughout exemplified by the second word in first line, "how," and Figure 6, line 2, "wall"; for the more complex form, see Figure 6 elsewhere, exemplified by line 1, "how" and "was").

4. Schulz's final characteristic letter was the *y,* "with its tail turning right up alongside or often back through the head as a hair stroke to make a dot or tick above" (see Figure 5, third word of line 1, "vnwys"; Figure 6, line 8, "kyng" and "ylion").

5. I would add that Hoccleve does much the same thing with tyronian *et,* which appears in his writing as a *z*-shape with continuation from the tail at the upper left to circle around under the letter and up toward the right ending in a hook to the right, toward the next letter (see Figure 5, three lines up from the bottom, "art / & haast").

6. In their description of the hand in "Production of Copies of the *Canterbury Tales* and the *Confessio Amantis* in the Early Fifteenth Century" (p. 185; repr. 223), Doyle and Parkes added the letter *h* to those formed characteristically by Hoccleve, where they noted that "the stem, shoulder and limb drop below the level of the other letters" (see Figure 5, sixth word of line 1, "haue"; Figure 6, third word of line 1, "how"). Still other features characteristic when found in conjunction with these are (7) an initial *V* with distinct spike to the left at the bottom of the initial downstroke (Figure 5, last word of line 5, "veyne"); and (8) an unusually pointed top of kidney-shaped final *s* (Figure 5, second word of line 9, "myndes"). His uppercase *N* has sharply angular feet and the stalk is often detached from the rising stroke to the shoulder (see Figure 6, last line, "No")

As Schulz noted, and Doyle and Parkes confirmed, Hoccleve sometimes used other forms for each of these characteristic features, so they cannot be sought as the only indicators of his handwriting; but the conjunction of three or more (with, as Schulz noted, the correct duct,

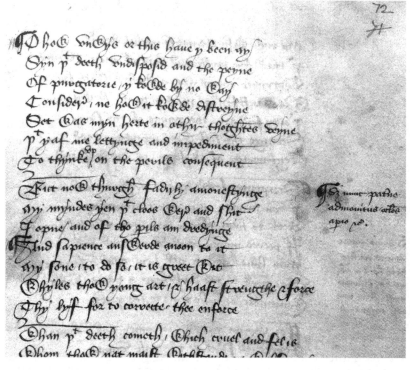

Figure 5   Durham, University Library, Cosin V. iii.9, folio 72^r, top half, reduced.
Reproduced with permission of Durham University Library.

angularity, etc., for Hoccleve's hand) is a strong indicator of his hand.
The documents newly identified have these characteristics together with
the overall appearance (duct, angularity, etc.) of Hoccleve's hand. In
Figure 7, Hoccleve characteristics are: the uppercase *A* in the ninth
word of the top line, "As Tresorer"; the coat-hanger tail of *g* in the
second word of the top line, "dengleterre"; the *y,* whose descender curls
back up through the letter to create the tick above it in the third word
of the last line, "Juyl"; the tyronian *et* with extension that creates a
circle under and to the right of it, ending in a hook to the right, sixth
word of the top line "&"; and the *h* with stem, shoulder, and limb
dropping below the line of the other letters, eighth word of the next-to-
bottom line, "Johan." Here and in all the documents I have identified
Hoccleve does *not* write the rounded form of *w* but rather the more
complex and formal form (sixth word of second line, "Welles"), which

320

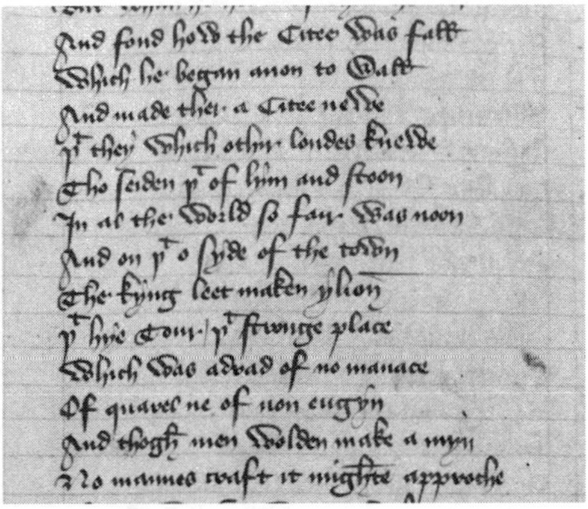

Figure 6   Cambridge, Trinity College, R.3.2, folio 82ᵛ, col. b, lines 9–21, reduced.
Reproduced with permission of the Master and Fellows of Trinity College, Cambridge.

he uses in his stint of writing in Trinity College, Cambridge MS R.3.2
(Figure 6 above). Doyle in the EETS facsimile edition (cited above) also
mentions Hoccleve's use of the long secretary *r* and the absence of
rounded anglicana *e* in this writing, both of which are illustrated in these
documents as well as in the examples of his literary hand.

In Figure 8, Hoccleve's characteristics are: the uppercase *A* (8b, second word of the top line, "As Tresorer"); the coat-hanger tail of *g* (8b,
last word of the second line, "vyngt"); the *y* whose descender curls back

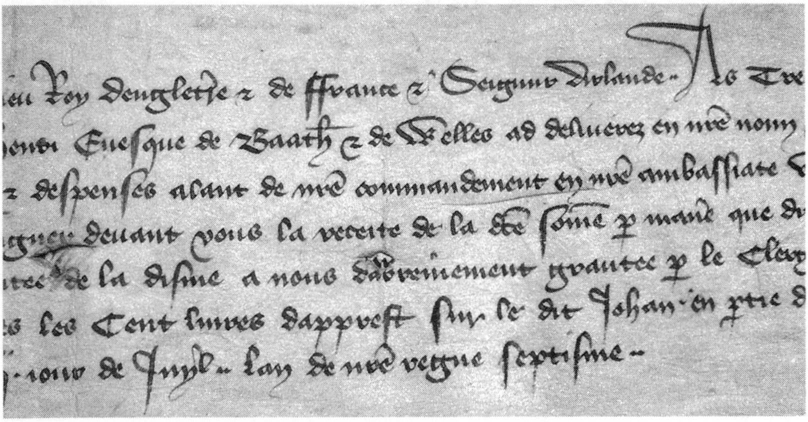

Figure 7   Kew, National Archives E 404/21/294 (dated 24 July, 7 Henry IV [1406]),
extract, reduced. Reproduced with permission.

321

up through the letter to create the tick above it (8a, seventh word of the top line, "Roy"); the tyronian *et* with extension that creates a circle under and to the right of it, ending in a hook to the right (8b, second word of the penultimate line, "&"); and the *h* with stem, shoulder, and limb dropping below the line of the other letters (8b, eighth word of the top line, "Eschequer"). Doyle also speaks of Hoccleve's graphs of *f* and long *s* with "characteristic overhanging curved or straightish heads" (p. xxxvii), which can be seen in this document (8b, third word of the top line, "Tresorer"). A tighter version of the uppercase *N* described above can be seen in 8b, the next-to-last word of the top line, "Nous."

Appendix B:
Documents Thus Far Identified as Written by Thomas Hoccleve

These documents have been arranged in chronological order, regardless of which collection of the National Archives contains them.

UNDATED?
E 28/29, item 30 First draft of letter / plea from Henry IV requesting aid for fighting war with France (identified as by Hoccleve in Doyle and Parkes, "Production of Copies," p. 182, repr. 222)

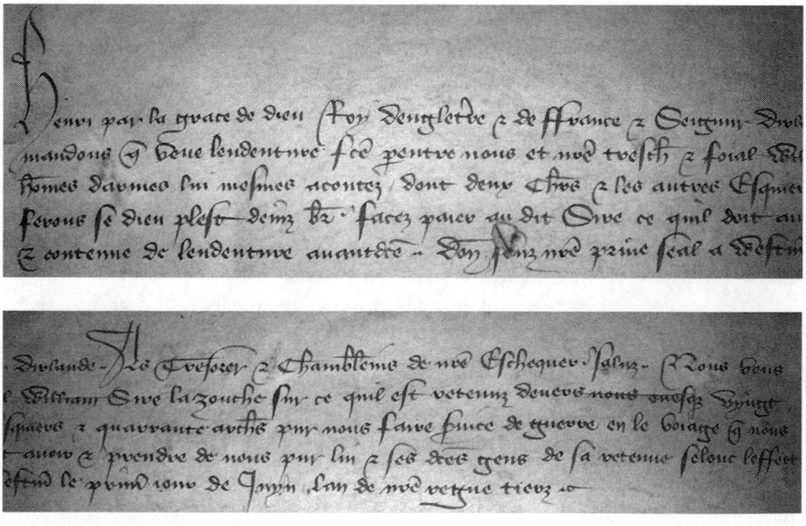

Figure 8a and b. Kew, National Archives E 404/31/351, left side and right side (reduced), dated 1 June, 3 Henry V (1415). Reproduced with permission.

Kew, National Archives E 404/14, file 96, part 1, the unnumbered document dated 25 July, 15 Richard II (1391): pay Raymon Guillam, one of the Judges of Aquitaine, his back wages and fees as seems reasonable

Kew, National Archives E 404/15/34 (dated 14 October 1 Henry IV [1399]): pay esquire Henry Betquenezell 20 pounds

Kew, National Archives E 404/15/37 (dated 17 October, 1 Henry IV [1399]): pay clerk John Thorpe 270 pounds, 8 shillings and 5 pence for purveying food and ?lodging for us on the Marches *"destor"*

Kew, National Archives E 404/15/40 (dated 20 October, 1 Henry IV [1399]): pay himself (Henry IV) 4,000 pounds in his Chamber for *"costages et despenses par nous a faire en nostre Chambre avantdite"*

Kew, National Archives E 404/15/45 (dated 30 October, 1 Henry IV [1399]): pay the clerks as accustomed for parchment purchased for use by our courts and offices

Kew, National Archives E 404/15/62 (dated 9 November, 1 Henry IV [1399]): pay esquire Geoffrey Chaucer the ten pounds in arrears for his annuity granted him by Richard II

Kew, National Archives E 404/15/69 (dated 13 November, 1 Henry IV [1399]): pay Thomas Mowbray his annuity granted by Richard II

Kew, National Archives E 404/15/78 (dated 19 November, 1 Henry IV [1399]): pay Clerk William Donne (or Doune?) annuity granted him by Richard II

Kew, National Archives E 404/15/81 (dated 19 November, 1 Henry IV [1399]): pay John West annuity granted by Edward III and Richard II

Kew, National Archives E 404/15/105 (dated 1 December, 1 Henry IV [1399]): pay Henry Percy 3000 pounds in accordance with indenture between him and Richard II for being warden of East Marches and of towns on the Scottish border, renewing this indenture and paying its annuity

Kew, National Archives E 404/15/109 (dated 3 December, 1 Henry IV [1399]): pay 200 pounds into hands of our brother the earl of Somers *"du donn"* 100 pounds by the hands of John Pull, knight, for defense of castles and Isle of Beaumaris to resist the insurrection in Wales, and 20 pounds for expenses of our Chambre

Kew, National Archives E 404/15/141 (dated 1 February, 1 Henry IV [1400]): pay Thomas Hynkeles, Constable of the Castle of Shrewsbury, 15 pounds for repair of said castle

Kew, National Archives E 404/15/154 (dated 19 February, 1 Henry IV [1400]): pay Bartholomew Bosane, esquire, 495 pounds, 13 shillings and 4 pence which is owed to him by the Earl of Huntington, as a gift from Henry

Kew, National Archives E 404/15/301 (dated 12 May, 1 Henry IV [1400]): pay Geraud Gautem Burgeois "de nostre citee de Burbeux" 95 pounds, 15 shillings for 27 tuns of Gascoigne wine

Kew, National Archives E 404/15/398 (dated 20 May, 1 Henry IV [1400]): pay John Cophill, esquire, 20 marks wages for carrying messages and also pay Geffrey Roos, Notary, for carrying messages

Kew, National Archives E 404/15/422 (dated 26 May, 1 Henry IV [1400]): pay John Norman Wqhelewright of London 15 pounds, 4 shillings and 7 pence for items he purchased for Richard II and Isabell when John Marchefeld was Keeper of the Great Wardrobe, and pay him a further 4 pounds for diverse things (*"choses"*) bought by him for Richard II and Isabel

Kew, National Archives E 404/16/325 (dated 13 January, 2 Henry IV [1401]): pay William Surcestre, haberdasher of London, as follows for goods purchased for the Privy Seal Office since Christmas in the first year of the reign (1399): *"cestassauoir quarrante & sys liures de cire rouge pris la liure dys deniers deux galons vn potel & vn quart de ynke pris le galon*

*quarrante deniers, quatre quaiers de papire pris le quaier oyt deniers & demy
quaier de papire roial pris le quaier dousze deniers"*

Kew, National Archives E 404/16/328 (dated 16 January, 2 Henry IV
{1401}): renew grant by Richard II to John Orewell and Peryn Lohar-
uauk(?)

Kew, National Archives E 208/11, Box 2, bundle 5, document 1—
though unnumbered, on top if knot at top (dated 4 March, 2 Henry IV
{1401}): acquit Piers Courteney, Constable of Windsor Castle, for costs
relating to this office in reign of Richard II

Kew, National Archives E 404/16/401 (dated 22 March, 2 Henry IV
{1401}): pay Clerk Alein Newerk for being of King's counsel and treating with the Scots

Kew, National Archives E 404/16/403 (dated 29 March, 2 Henry IV
{1401}): pay "nostre cher & loial Chiualier Her Nichol Ryvenytz" an
annuity granted him by Richard II

Kew, National Archives E 404/16/711 (dated 24 June, 2 Henry IV
{1401}): pay Thomas Bromflete, former Butler to King Richard II and
former controller of the household, for expenses incurred by him in this
office of Butler to Richard II

Kew, National Archives E 404/16/725 (dated 2 July, 2 Henry IV
{1401}): pay Clerk Henry Bowet who has paid William Monutendre,
Knight, in Guyenne

Kew, National Archives E 404/16/727 (dated 3 July, 2 Henry IV
{1401}): pay Clerk Henry Bowet and men who accompanied him to
Guyenne their expenses for the voyage

Kew, National Archives E 404/16/730 (dated 4 July, 2 Henry IV
{1401}): pay Knight, George Welbrigge, for expenses of a voyage in the
King's service

Kew, National Archives E 404/16/738 (dated 8 July, 2 Henry IV
{1401}): pay King's cousin Edward, earl of Rutland, who has been made
Lieutenant of Guyenne and Seneschall of Guyenne

Kew, National Archives E 404/16/746 (dated 19 July, 2 Henry IV [1401]): pay Sir Edward Hastyngs for expenses of service to the King

Kew, National Archives E 404/16/751 (dated 29 July, 2 Henry IV [1401]): pay Clerks of the Privy Seal for the extra service they have rendered

Kew, National Archives E 404/16/752 (dated 29 July, 2 Henry IV [1401]): pay creditors of the Duke of Norfolk who has died

Kew, National Archives E 404/16/766 (dated 30 August, 2 Henry IV [1401]): pay Henry's son Henry [later V] a thousand pounds for military expedition to put down rebellion by Owen Glendower

Kew, National Archives E 404/16/774 (dated 23 September, 2 Henry IV [1401]): pay Walter Longe of Southampton for passage of Earl of Pirregort *"lez capitain & Conestable de Curkuffyn"* and their men towards Guyenne

Kew, National Archives E 404/17/254 (dated 1 November, 3 Henry IV [1401]): pay William Surcestre, haberdasher of London, for parchment, paper, ink and wax purchased from him for use in the Office of the Privy Seal since last Christmas

Kew, National Archives E 208/11, Box 1, bundle 8, document 10—though unnumbered, 10th from top if knot at top (dated 6 November, 3 Henry IV [1401]): acquit Sergeant of Arms Robert Markelay of 101 shillings, 5 pence because he spent this much in arresting certain parties and in other commissions as ordered by our counsel

Kew, National Archives E 404/17/289 (dated 11 November, 3 Henry IV [1401]): hand over to our clerk John Legburn, Receiver of our Chamber 4000 pounds for expenses of our chamber

Kew, National Archives E 404/17/328 (dated 23 November, 3 Henry IV [1401]): hand over to Esquire Richard Cressy, usher of the king's Chamber, 40 pounds, 12 shillings and 3 pence for expenses for making a *"see roiale"* for Smithfield for the tournament that will be held there

Kew, National Archives E 404/17/344 (dated 1 December, 3 Henry IV [1401]): repayment (to clerk Richard Kingston who raised the sums) of large amounts to various noble persons, citizens of towns and abbeys etc. for loans to raise troops to fight against insurrection while King was fighting in Scotland

Kew, National Archives E 404/17/363 (dated 13 December, 3 Henry IV [1401]): pay 18 pounds, 9 shillings to Thomas Godestone, esquire, for provisions bought to safeguard the city of Caleys in time of predecessor Richard II

Kew, National Archives E 404/17/373 (dated 21 December, 3 Henry IV [1401]): gift of 100 marcs to Thomas, bishop of Bangor, in regard to possessions of church in Bangor being destroyed during uprising

Kew, National Archives E 404/17/377 (dated at Eltham, 28 December, 3 Henry IV [1401]): pay 24 pounds to John Stille and Richard Marcham of Sandwich for purchase of a ship called Juliane which they bought from John Kent and delivered to mariners of 'Bretaigne' at king's commandment

Kew, National Archives E 404/17/787 (dated 26 August, 3 Henry IV [1402]): write letters direct from us to Nicholas Usk, Treasurer of Caleys, commanding him to pay John Norbury, Captain of the castle at Guyennes, 1000 marcs to rebuild the keep called *"Cupe"* in said castle

Kew, National Archives E 404/18/207 (dated 26 October, 4 Henry IV [1402]): pay several men *"noz Somtermen du temps de nostre trescher Clerc Thomas Tuttebury nadgairs Tresorer de nostre houstel de lour gages chaucier & autres expenses faiz entour les chiualx quils ont gardez sicome par deux billes."*

Kew, National Archives E 43/554 (dated 27 November, 4 Henry IV [1402]) [kept in separate box, single document, kept for quality of its seal]: receipt from Hoccleve that he has received his annuity

Kew, National Archives E 404/18/255 (dated 29 November, 4 Henry IV [1402]): pay Thomas Beaufort as Warden of Ludlow Castle 100 marks to be repaid to the Abbot of Shrewsbury ['Salop.'] for 100 marks borrowed ['appresta'] from him for defense against rebels

Kew, National Archives E 404/18/260 (dated 3 December, 4 Henry IV [1402]): pay William Surcestre, citizen and haberdasher of London, for parchment, paper, ink and wax bought from him for use in Privy Seal Office from last day of October in 3rd year of reign until now

Kew, National Archives E 404/18/267 (dated 8 December, 4 Henry IV [1402]): pay king's cousin Elizabeth, countess of Salisbury, for accompanying King's daughter Blanche on travels abroad

Kew, National Archives E 404/18/285 (dated 8 February, 4 Henry IV [1403]): repay Bishop of Winchester

Kew, National Archives E 404/18/292 (dated 28 February, 4 Henry IV [1403]): pay annuities to John Overton, esquire, and John Dray, Sergeant of Arms

Kew, National Archives E 404/18/564 (dated 15 June, 4 Henry IV [1403]): pay William Surcestre, haberdasher of London, for parchment, paper, ink and wax bought by Privy Seal Office since 3 December most recently passed (29 shillings and 7 pence)

Kew, National Archives E 404/18/579 (dated 28 June, 4 Henry IV [1403]): pay Richard Garner merchant "de Pymont" for pearls purchased from him

Kew, National Archives E 404/19/163 (dated at Cirencester, 1 November, 5 Henry IV [1403]): pay Thomas Saunders, esquire, and others in order to pay mariners for passage to Cardiff

Kew, National Archives E 404/19/232 (dated at Westminster 15 November, 5 Henry IV [1403]): pay William Yerde and Thomas Prudence for information about deceits and damages by strangers against our people

Kew, National Archives E 404/19/273 (dated at Westminster 5 December, 5 Henry IV [1403]): award Thomas Talbot wardenship of Montgomery Castle

Kew, National Archives E 404/19/274 (dated Westminster 8 December, 5 Henry IV [1403]): reward Robert Leycestre, deputy of the "*Sercheour*" of the port of London for catching a vessel exporting without license (without paying export duty)

Kew, National Archives E 404/19/281 (dated 11 December, 5 Henry IV [1403]): pay Warden of the Wardrobe for buying vesture for clerks of Royal Chapel

Kew, National Archives E 404/19/284 (dated 20 December, 5 Henry IV [1403]): pay his brother John, Earl Somers, Captain of Calais, for keeping 500 men at arms and one hundred archers beyond the usual guard

Kew, National Archives E 404/19/285 (dated at the abbey of Abingdon, 27 December, 5 Henry IV [1403]): pay John Torrell of Bologne, merchant, 500 marks because he remains in London at King's wish and to repay him for monies ?borrowed from him by the king among others for wedding of his daughter Blanche

Kew, National Archives E 404/19/292 (dated Westminster 15 January, 5 Henry IV [1404]): pay John Selby and John Peek wages, etc., due to them as clerks during the time of Thomas Tuttebury, Clerk, who is now dead

Kew, National Archives E 404/19/450 (dated 18 June, 5 Henry IV [1404]): pay William Surcestre and John Pountfreit, haberdashers of London, for parchment, ink, and red wax for Privy Seal office

Kew, National Archives E 208/11, Box 1, bundle 3, uncatalogued document near top of pile on 25 May 2005 (dated 29 October, 6 Henry IV [1404]): acquit the abbot of [seint Dag . . . (Name illegible due to wear at end of parchment strip)], Cardigan, in Pembrokeshire, South Wales the collections of seconds and thirds from the clergy [of Cardigan?] under Richard II (2 March, 21 Richard II)

Kew, National Archives E 404/20/133 (dated 26 January, 6 Henry IV [1405]): give sufficient tailles to Richard Whittington that he be repaid 500 marks from the customs of wool at the port of Southampton

Kew, National Archives E 404/20/161 (dated 18 February, 6 Henry IV [1405]): pay Duchess of Ireland 100 pounds

Kew, National Archives E 404/20/164 (dated 18 February, 6 Henry IV [1405]): pay William Surcestre citizen and haberdasher of London 4 pounds, 3 shillings and 4 pence for parchment, ink, and red wax purchased for office of Privy Seal since 18 June just passed

Kew, National Archives E 404/20/165 (dated 18 February, 6 Henry IV [1405]): pay Thomas Clerc, John Oudeby, John Haddeley, Thomas Knolles, Richard Merlawe, treasurers of our wars(?) to pay to our son, lieutenant of Ireland, for expenses

Kew, National Archives E 404/20/294 (dated at Leicester 16 August, 6 Henry IV [1405]): as per letters signet, pay Gaillard, Provost of Bordeaux, 100 pounds

Kew, National Archives E 404/21/27 (dated 18 November, 7 Henry IV [1405]): give John Arundell 20 pounds gift from Henry

Kew, National Archives E 404/21/32 (dated 1 December, 7 Henry IV [1405]): pay Margerie Lodewyk 30 pounds which is overdue half of her annuity granted 31 October in first year of reign, not paid in last Easter half year payment

Kew, National Archives E 404/21/37 (dated 7 December, 7 Henry IV [1405]): pay the Queen 2500 marks due her and not paid last year from customs and subsidies of Southampton

Kew, National Archives E 404/21/40 (dated 11 December, 7 Henry IV [1405]): pay 100 shillings to Sibille Beauchamp for her services to his late sister the Duchess of Gloucester

Kew, National Archives E 404/21/54 (dated 9 February, 7 Henry IV [1406]): pay John Cristyn 25 pounds, 17 shillings and 4 pence due him for fresh fish provided in time of Thomas Tutbury who is now dead, which sum could not be paid because of the rebellion in Wales

Kew, National Archives E 404/21/73 (dated 24 March, 7 Henry IV [1406]): pay John Mortimer, esquire, 20 pounds toward ransom from the French since he was captured passing through France from Guyenne on king's business

Kew, National Archives E 404/21/104 (dated 3 May, 7 Henry IV [1406]): pay Lord Powys ('le sire de ?Powys?' indistinct because folded and rubbed) for term of Easter

Kew, National Archives E 404/21/254 (dated 12 June, 7 Henry IV [1406]): pay Lucas Feltham, esquire, past due wages of the household from when Thomas More was Treasurer

Kew, National Archives E 208/11, Box 1, bundle 8, document 41—though unnumbered, 41st from top if knot at top (dated 6 July in 7 Henry IV [1406]): acquit Margaret Sharnesfelde, our tenant of Eltham, of 100 shillings owed to John Cranborne who owes this amount therefore to the Exchequer

Kew, National Archives E 404/21/279 (dated 7 July, 7 Henry IV [1406]): pay John Wodecok and Thomas Knolles, citizens of London, in repayment for loans from each of 100 pounds

Kew, National Archives E 404/21/294 (dated 24 July, 7 Henry IV [1406]): repay Henry, Bishop of Bath and Wells, 100 pounds he paid to John Cheyne, knight, for his ambassadorial mission to Rome

Kew, National Archives E 404/22/100 (dated 16 October, 8 Henry IV [1406]): pay Lucas Feltham, esquire, 5 marks due of his wages earned "*deinz*" our household (*housteil*)

Kew, National Archives E 208/11, Box 1, bundle 3, uncatalogued document near middle of pile on 25 May 2005 (dated 27 October, 8 Henry IV [1406]): since king granted 200 pounds to the mayor and citizens of Southampton on 2 September, 2 Henry IV, to be given on feast of St Michael for next 6 years for making repairs and/or fortifying the town, if accounts for first 5 of these in order, then acquit(?) for 6th

Kew, National Archives E 404/22/271 (dated 26 February, 8 Henry IV [1407]): pay Hugh, Lord Burnell, for being of the King's council since 22 December in 7 Henry IV

Kew, National Archives E 404/22/374 (dated 16 April, 8 Henry IV [1407]): pay John Tiptoft, knight, Keeper of our Wardrobe, amounts he requires from time to time to run our household

Kew, National Archives E 404/23/297 (dated 27 February, 9 Henry IV [1408]): pay Richard Whittington, alderman of London, 100 marks for meeting Ambassiate from France and conducting them to King in Parliament at Gloucester

Kew, National Archives E 208/11, Box 2, bundle 2, document 2— though unnumbered, second from top if knot at top (dated 12 July, 9 Henry IV [1408]): since by great seal on 22 July in 7th year of reign granted to our esquire William Loueney Treasurer of our daughter Philippe queen of Denmark, Sweden and Norway to accompany her with knights, esquires, clerks, vallettes, etc. to said countries and back to London, acquit him of repaying money given him for these costs

Kew, National Archives E 404/23/536 (dated 31 July, 9 Henry IV [1408]): pay arrears of annuity to Hans Seintlinger, 40 pounds due on an annuity of 10 pounds per annum; and pay 40 pounds to his brother George Seintlinger as part payment of a large amount due to him in arrears of annuity of 20 pounds per annum

Kew, National Archives E 404/23/544 (dated 1 September, 9 Henry IV [1408]): pay Robert Duddebrook [by another name now rubbed out by wear] 26 pounds, 9 shillings and 8 pence for providing provisions ("*vitailles*") to the Castle of Coytif and other places

Kew, National Archives E 404/24/228 (dated 18 November, 10 Henry IV [1408]): pay Roger Trumpiton, knight, whatever is due and in arrears of his annuity of 100 marks per annum

Kew, National Archives E 404/24/236 (dated 22 November, 10 Henry IV [1408]): pay Thomas Bishop of Durham for expenses daily according to his rank for embassy (*"Ambassiate"*) to France on King's behalf

Kew, National Archives E 404/24/293 (dated 21 February, 10 Henry IV [1409]): pay Hoccleve 39 shillings and 9 pence for parchment, ink and red wax

Kew, National Archives E 208/11, Box 1, bundle 4 (this bundle labeled by modern hand "Augmentation Office"), document 28— though unnumbered, 28th from top if knot at top (dated 22 April, 10 Henry IV [1409]): since sheriffs of Canterbury and Huntingdon have not paid Marie de Seint Hillere her annuity as awarded by Richard II and confirmed by Henry, and in consideration of her advanced age and long service, Exchequer should insure that she is paid and he will acquit sheriffs this amount owed to him

Kew, National Archives E 208/11, Box 1, bundle 4 (this bundle labeled by modern hand "Augmentation Office"), document 29— though unnumbered, 29th from top if knot at top (dated 22 April, 10 Henry IV [1409]): ordering sheriffs of certain counties to pay annuities to those to whom Henry and his predecessors have granted them to be paid from counties, and Henry will acquit them this much owed to him

Kew, National Archives E 208/11, Box 1, bundle 4 (this bundle labeled by modern hand "Augmentation Office"), document 5— though unnumbered, fifth from top if knot at top (dated 27 May, 10 Henry IV [1409]): acquit Thomas Erpyngham 400 marcs that he spent as King's messenger to France in 9th year of reign, and do not charge him in future for this amount

Kew, National Archives E 404/25/177 (dated 9 December, 11 Henry IV [1409]): pay our clerk, Master Nicol Rixton, 100 pounds for his errand to the court of Rome

Kew, National Archives E 404/25/201 (dated 23 February, 11 Henry IV [1410]): that Ralph Ramsey esquire, formerly sheriff of Norfolk and Suffolk, should be pardoned 100 pounds on account which he spent in office (of which he can account for 60? and 40 more pounds to be given him by king's gift)

N.B. NONE IN 12 HENRY IV or 13 Henry IV

Kew, National Archives, E 404/28/77 (dated 10 October 14 Henry IV [1412]): pay 53 pounds, 6 shillings and 1 penny to William Marrowe, Chariotmaker of London, since he has been unable to collect against the order? (*"par une bille de debentur eut faite au dit William par John Carpenter"*) placed with him by John Carpenter, former Treasurer of the household of Richard II

Kew, National Archives, E 404/28/227 (dated 11 March, 14 Henry IV [1413]): pay Robert Hilliard, esquire, Warden of our *"Estanke"* de *ffosse* next to our city of York his wages granted when he took the Wardenship in 11 Henry IV, which were to be paid from issues, profits, and farms of the county of York by the Sheriff of same, but that Robert says have not been paid, so pay him 9 pounds, 2 shillings and 6 pence

N.B. NONE in 1 Henry V

Kew, National Archives E 404/30/63 (dated 17 April, 2 Henry V [1414]): confirming grant by his father to Richard Longe and Margaret his wife of an annuity of 22 pounds per year to be taken each year through the term of life of Margaret, and pay them arrears for last Easter term

Kew, National Archives E 404/30/191 (dated 29 January, 2 Henry V [1415]): pay John Burgh for self and ten men at arms and 20 archers for 50 days' service at sea , for each man at arms 12 deniers and for each archer 6 deniers, the term of the 50 days to begin when they set sail

Kew, National Archives E 404/31/219 (dated 12 May, 3 Henry V [1415]): according to the indenture between us, pay Thomas Chaucer what he needs to pay his retinue of 12 men at arms and 36 mounted archers to accompany Henry

Kew, National Archives E 404/31/225 (dated 12 May, 3 Henry V [1415]): pay Nichol Mountgomery 'le fitz' what he needs to pay his retinue of 3 men at arms and 9 mounted archers to accompany Henry

Kew, National Archives E 404/31/248 (dated 15 May, 3 Henry V [1415]): pay Thomas Dutton what he needs to pay his retinue of ten men at arms and 30 archers to accompany Henry

Kew, National Archives E 404/31/250 (dated 15 May, 3 Henry V [1415]): pay his brother Humfrey duke of Gloucestre for retinue of 200 men at arms, 6 knights, 193 esquires, 600 mounted archers

Kew, National Archives E 404/31/258 (dated 15 May, 3 Henry V [1415]): pay his cousin John Talbot, Lord Furnival, Lieutenant of Ireland, two thousand marks as his due for governance of Ireland

Kew, National Archives E 404/31/261 (dated 16 May, 3 Henry V [1415]): pay Richard Arundell to bring 10 men at arms and thirty mounted archers

Kew, National Archives E 404/31/264 (dated 16 May, 3 Henry V [1415]): pay sir Roger Fyenes to bring 8 men at arms and 24 mounter archers

Kew, National Archives E 404/31/266 (dated 16 May, 3 Henry V [1415]): pay Henry de Percy to bring 6 men at arms and 18 mounted archers

Kew, National Archives E 404/31/278 (dated 20 May , 3 Henry V [1415]): pay Thomas Earl of Dorset to bring six knights, 92 esquires, and 300 mounted archers under his banneret

Kew, National Archives E 404/31/296 (dated 23 May, 3 Henry V [1415]): pay our Esquires Robert Lacok, William Wightman, Richard Parker, John Kilner/Kilver, Thomas Lychebarowe and Robert Heton to come and bring three archers each

Kew, National Archives E 404/31/307 (dated 26 May, 3 Henry V [1415]): pay "nostre ame seruiteur" John Attilbrigge to come and bring three archers

Kew, National Archives E 404/31/322 (dated 27 May, 3 Henry V [1415]): pay members of Henry's household Thomas Tunbrigge, Wil-

335

liam Bangore, Hugh Bigge, Roger Chieff, Henry Shipley, Thomas Hampton, Richard Burton, John Botiller, John Northfolk, John Hille, Roger Seinper, John Birkyn, Thomas Swetenham, John Spaldy[ng], John Walssh, Richard Filongley, John Bannebury, William Alcok, John Mikelfeld, Henri Scalder, Gregory Scaldyr, William Shorn, Richard Breustere *et* Rauf Passenham what they need to accompany Henry

Kew, National Archives E 404/31/326 (dated 28 May, 3 Henry V [1415]): pay "vadletz de nostre houstel" Roger Draycote, William Wykeham, John Lynchelade, John Yaroughdale, Estiephene Frenssh, Laurence Combe, Thomas Walssh, Oliver Shorthale, Richard Castell, William Petham, Thomas Holme, Wauter Kendale, John Stokes, John Kirton, William Cryse, Alisandre Smetheley, William Malthous, John Sauky (or Sanky?), Thomas Thorp, John Peterburgh, John Elys, Richard Marchant, John Kexby, Robert Castelton, John Bukenham, William Lavender, Richard Lavender, John Dent, and John Hall what they need to accompany Henry

Kew, National Archives E 404/31/344 (dated 31 May, 3 Henry V [1415]): pay sir William Bourghchier to bring 30 men at arms and 80 mounted archers

Kew, National Archives E 404/31/351 (dated 1 June, 3 Henry V [1415]): pay William Lord Zouche to bring 20 men at arms among whom two knights and the rest esquires, and 40 archers

Kew, National Archives E 404/31/355 (dated 4 June, 3 Henry V [1415]): pay esquires William Brokesby and Bawdewyn Bugge for William to bring 2 men at arms and 6 archers and for Bawdewyn to bring *"sa propre lance"* and three mounted archers

Kew, National Archives E 404/31/364 (dated 5 June, 3 Henry V [1415]): pay Master Philip Morgan, Doctor of Laws, for bearing message to Calais in behalf of the King

Kew, National Archives E 404/31/383 (dated 13 June, 3 Henry V [1415]): pay John Cobyn Esquier to bring 2 mounted archers

Kew, National Archives E 404/31/452 (dated 1 September, 3 Henry V [1415]): pay Richard Berall Esquier who is made Warden of Rokesburgh Castle for a quarter year from taking over the Wardenship from Robert Dumfraville, Knight, former captain of the castle, and give him rights to arm the castle with as many men as needed to safeguard it if it is attacked by our enemies

Kew, National Archives E 404/32/262 (dated 9 December, 4 Henry V [1416]): pay Knight William Bourghchier, Constable of the Tower of London, all that is in arrears from 10 April just past for *"la sustenance"* of John Sire Destouteville put into his guard, that is to say 5 shillings per day and continue to pay him this for duration that the said is under his guard

Kew, National Archives E 404/33/194 (dated 10 December, 5 Henry V [1417]): turn over to the Ushers of our Chamber certain furnishings (e.g. *"tout lestuf de deux Chambres, vn drap destat deux lb de corde"* and a *"Charette pur la cariage des dites choses de nostre Garderobe tanque a nostre Palois de Westminster"*)

Kew, National Archives E 404/33/219 (dated 22 February, 5 Henry V [1418]): according to indenture between king and Thomas duke of Clarence by which he was to bring to France for an entire year 60 men at arms and 180 archers, and according to another indenture made between them in 4th year of reign, with set rates of pay for men, pay Thomas Duke of Clarence what he needs in accordance with these indentures

Kew, National Archives E 404/33/223 (dated 7 March, 5 Henry V [1418]): pay Hoccleve 42 shillings and 9 pence for red wax and ink bought by him from Walter Lucy of London for use in office of Privy Seal between 1 April in 4th year of reign and 6 March of this month

N.B. NONE IN 6 HENRY V

Kew, National Archives E 404/35/119 (dated 21 May, 7 Henry V [1419]): pay knight John Radclyf, Constable of Bordeaux, for guarding the Castle of Fronsac in the Duchy of Guyenne and the lands surrounding it (*"la paiis de ffrounsadeys"*) for six years, 1000 marks per year and for the first year [now] paying him 500 marks with another 500 to be paid at the time of his departure from England

Kew, National Archives E 404/35/123 (dated 28 May, 7 Henry V [1419]): pay esquire William Troutbek, king's Chamberlain of Chester, the expenses he has had in making trips from Chester to London each time carrying with him a large number of ?*"deniers"* (pennies) [badly rubbed and partly illegible]

Kew, National Archives E 404/35/131 (dated 10 June, 7 Henry V [1419]): pay Thomas Hoccleue 12 shillings and 2 pence for red wax and ink bought by him from Walter Lucy of London for use in the office of the Privy Seal from the 6th day of March in 5th year of reign up to now

Kew, National Archives E 28/97/9a (dated 29 December, 7 Henry V [1419]): from Henry V requiring Earl of Dorset to raise troops for service and be in attendance at council at Westminster the *"quinzeme de seint Hiller prochain"* with names of those enlisted

Kew, National Archives E 28/97/22A (dated 29 December, 7 Henry V [1419]): from Henry V requiring knights and esquires of county of Northampton prepare themselves for service and be in attendance at counsel at Westminster the *"quinzeme de seint Hiller prochain"* with names of those enlisted

Kew, National Archives E 28/97/25 (dated 29 December, 7 Henry V [1419]): from Henry V requiring knights and esquires of county of Rutland prepare themselves for service and be in attendance at counsel at Westminster the *"quinzeme de seint Hiller prochain"* with names of those enlisted

Kew, National Archives E 28/97/28 (dated 29 December, 7 Henry V [1419]): from Henry V requiring knights and esquires of county of Somerset prepare themselves for service and be in attendance at counsel at Westminster the *"quinzeme de seint Hiller prochain"* with names of those enlisted

Kew, National Archives E 404/35/272 (dated 9 February, 7 Henry V [1420]): pay Walter Hacluyt Esquier for service to King in the war in France with three men at arms and 9 archers brought by him

Kew, National Archives E 404/35/273 (dated 9 February, 7 Henry V [1420]): pay John duke of Bedford for service in the war in France for a year with 120 men at arms of which 6 knights and the rest esquires and men at arms and 300 mounted archers

Kew, National Archives E 404/35/274 (dated February, 7 Henry V [1420]): pay Ralph Langton Esquire for service in war in France for a year with 11 men at arms and 33 archers

Kew, National Archives E 404/35/275 (dated 9 February, 7 Henry V [1420]): pay John Lyuerpole Esquire for service in France in war for an entire year with 7 men at arms and 21 archers

N.B. NONE IN 8 HENRY V

Kew, National Archives E 404/37/102 (dated 3 June, 9 Henry V [1421]): pay to Louis duke of Bavaria, 300 marks due to him for the term of Easter just past, to pay into his hand or that of his attorney in his name [with name of attorney John Ladbaum written over "*au dit duc ou a son*"]

Kew, National Archives E 404/37/103 (dated 3 June, 9 Henry V [1421]): pay to Henry de Percy, Earl de Northumberland since the first of June when Henry was made Warden of the town of Berwick and all the Scottish marches for period of two years, and protect the said town [Berwick] and East March, in time of war being paid 5000 pounds and in time of peace or truce 2000 pounds

Kew, National Archives E 404/38/90 (dated 20 June, 10 Henry V [1422]): pay Geoffrey Yonge Guard of the "port" of the castle and park of Leeds Castle in Kent

Kew, National Archives E 404/39/268 (dated 4 May, 1 Henry VI [1423]): pay John Radclif Seneschal of Guyenne and his retinue with numbers of men and archers

Kew, National Archives E 404/39/269 (dated 4 May, 1 Henry VI [1423]): pay John [duke of Bedford] for guarding loyally to best of his power the Castle of Fronsac and land of Guyenne for six years, paying him now 500 marks and another 500 marks when he departs from England

Kew, National Archives E 404/39/285 (dated 11 May, 1 Henry VI {1423}): pay Esmon Conte de la Marche [Edmund Mortimer, Earl of Marche], who is made lieutenant of Ireland over which he shall have the governance for 9 years, for the first half-year 2500 marks, and paying him each quarter one month before the quarter, and paying him also for passages to and fro across the Irish Sea for himself and his retinue

Kew, National Archives E 404/39/303 (dated 19 May, 1 Henry VI {1423}): pay Thomas Hoccleve 23 shillings, 7 pence for red wax and ink purchased from Wauter Lucy of London and used in the office of Privy Seal from 9 February, 9 Henry V (= 1422) up to the present

Kew, National Archives E 404/40/162 (dated 8 February, 2 Henry VI {1424}): pay John Shilley and Thomas Denney, Esquires, fighting in France with Humfrey Duke of Gloucester

Kew, National Archives E 404/41/158 (dated 3 December, 3 Henry VI {1424}): pay Henry Percy, Earl of Northumberland

Kew, National Archives E 404/41/190 (dated 4 March, 3 Henry VI {1425}): pay Roger Fienes, knight for fighting in France with Duke of Bedford

Kew, National Archives E 404/41/191 (dated 4 March, 3 Henry VI {1425): pay John Grey, knight for fighting in France with Duke of Bedford

Kew, National Archives E 404/41/192 (dated 4 March, 3 Henry VI {1425}): pay Geffrey Whightyngton, Esquire for fighting in France with Duke of Bedford

Kew, National Archives E 404/41/197 (dated 14 April, 3 Henry VI {1425}): pay James Butler ("le Botiller"), Earl of Ormond, Lieutenant of Ireland

Kew, National Archives E 404/41/344 (dated 29 June, 3 Henry VI {1425}): pay Sir Robert Ogle, Custodian of Roxburgh Castle

N.B. NONE IN 4 HENRY VI [1425–26): Hoccleve died in 1426

The Professional: Thomas Hoccleve

Sarah Tolmie
University of Waterloo

No man ever writ, but for money.

—Samuel Johnson

THOMAS HOCCLEVE HAS UNDERGONE a lot of rehabilitation lately. Recent forms of historicism have saved him from lingering censure for dementia, effeminacy, and venality, and enlisted him instead as a participant in the larger social developments of his age: the bureaucratization of fifteenth-century society,[1] the drama of assimilating Lancastrian rule,[2] the fraught and contradictory rise of a money economy,[3] the task of domesticating Chaucer into a national icon.[4] He has been reassessed as an ideologue, a translator, a feminist,[5] a civil servant, an advi-

[1] See Ethan Knapp, "Bureaucratic Identity and the Construction of the Self in Hoccleve's *Formulary* and *La Male Regle,*" *Speculum* 74 (1999): 357–76, and his book *The Bureaucratic Muse: Thomas Hoccleve and the Literature of Late Medieval England* (University Park: Pennsylvania State University Press, 2001).

[2] See, for example, Paul Strohm, *England's Empty Throne: Usurpation and the Language of Legitimation 1399–1422* (New Haven: Yale University Press, 1998), pp. 141–48, 180–86, 197–214; and Derek Pearsall, "Hoccleve's *Regiment of Princes:* The Poetics of Royal Self-Representation," *Speculum* 69 (1994): 386–410.

[3] See Robert J. Meyer-Lee, "Hoccleve and the Apprehension of Money," *Exemplaria* 13 (2001): 173–214.

[4] Selected examples include J. A. Burrow, "Hoccleve and Chaucer," in *Chaucer Traditions: Studies in Honour of Derek Brewer,* ed. Ruth Morse and Barry Windeatt (Cambridge: Cambridge University Press, 1990), pp. 54–61; David R. Carlson, "Thomas Hoccleve and the Chaucer Portrait," *HLQ* 54 (1991): 283–300; Albrecht Classen, "Hoccleve's Independence from Chaucer: A Study of Poetic Emancipation," *Fifteenth-Century Studies* 16 (1990): 59–81; Ethan Knapp, "Eulogies and Usurpations: Hoccleve and Chaucer Revisited," *SAC* 21 (1999): 247–73 ; Jeanne E. Krochalis, "Hoccleve's Chaucer Portrait," *ChauR* 21 (1986–87): 234–45; James H. MacGregor, "The Iconography of Chaucer in Hoccleve's *De Regimine Principum* and in the *Troilus* Frontispiece," *ChauR* 11 (1977): 338–50; Tim William Machan, "Textual Authority and the Works of Hoccleve, Lydgate, and Henryson," *Viator* 23 (1992): 281–99.

[5] See Catherine Batt, "Hoccleve And. Feminism? Negotiating Meaning in the *Regiment of Princes,*" in *Essays on Thomas Hoccleve,* ed. Catherine Batt (London: Centre for Medieval and Renaissance Studies, Queen Mary and Westfield College, University of London, 1996), pp. 55–84; Ruth Nissé, "'Oure Fadres Olde and Modres': Gender, Heresy, and Hoccleve's Literary Politics," *SAC* 21 (1999): 275–99; Jennifer E. Bryan, "Hoccleve, the Virgin, and the Politics of Complaint," *PMLA* 117, no. 5 (2002): 1172–87; Anna Torti, "Hoccleve's Attitude toward Women: 'I Shoop Me Do My Peyne

sor to princes,[6] a sufferer of psychotic illness.[7] Evidence for such identifications has been drawn from his life records, and from the formulary he compiled for the office of Privy Seal during his tenure as a clerk, but chiefly from his poetry. Yet his specific status as a writer of poetry has remained secondary in much recent criticism: the poet has become a prisoner of context, administrative, political, or cultural. This does Hoccleve a particular disservice because the primary identity of his textual persona is that of poet; he is constantly and consciously engaged in the business of collecting, collating, translating, soliciting advice on, seeking patronage of, procrastinating over, and, above all, trying to sell,[8] poetry. The writing of poetic texts, and the implications of this action for the writer of them, and for the various readers, patrons, and buyers of them is the overriding concern of his work. My contention is that Hoccleve's mission was to create the secular poet, himself, as a professional subject and to figure him explicitly into the economy of representation.

No other Privy Seal clerk working in the first quarter of the fifteenth century has left a significant body of poetry; Prentys, Arondel, and the other colleagues Hoccleve mentions in his work shared a literate coterie culture but did not write poems about it, or about anything else, at

---

and Diligence / To Wynne Hir Loue by Obedience,'" in *A Wyf Ther Was,* ed. J. Dor (Liège: Université de Liège, 1992), pp. 264–74; K. A. Winstead, "'I Am Al Othir to Yow Than Yee Weene': Hoccleve, Women, and the *Series,*" *PQ* 72 (1993): 143–55.

[6] See Nicholas Perkins, *Hoccleve's Regiment of Princes: Counsel and Constraint* (Cambridge: D. S. Brewer, 2001).

[7] See Gordon Claridge, Ruth Pryor, and Gwen Watkins, *Sounds from the Bell Jar: Ten Psychotic Authors* (Basingstoke: Macmillan, 1990); R. Lawes, "Psychological Disorder and the Autobiographical Impulse in Julian of Norwich, Margery Kempe, and Thomas Hoccleve," in *Writing Religious Women* (Cardiff: University of Wales Press, 2000), pp. 217–43.

[8] Hoccleve, like Chaucer, was not paid for his poetic work as far as records indicate, and records are unusually good, as both were royal bureaucrats. Yet the kind of money poetry was worth—which was, I suspect, as often as not expressed in cash within the mixed economy of the royal offices—exposes the shortfall of relying on official bookkeeping to track emergent identities. Hoccleve's shorter poems frequently function as versified memos reminding people of his pay arrears in Privy Seal. Begging poems obviously serve an explicit purpose in the economy of the court and are shaped to bring the writer monetary gain, yet ambitious longer poems are likewise involved in the politics of visibility required to attract patronage, a patronage that was not grand feudal *largesse* expressed in kind (robes, wine, luxury items) but local pressure to produce cash. In a clerical atmosphere of continually late or absent payment for services, Hoccleve's own work makes clear the extent to which interest was for sale: see, for example, his discursus in the *Regiment* prologue, lines 1499–512, on the appropriation of fees owing to Privy Seal clerks (themselves off the books) by aristocratic retainers, discussed in Sarah Tolmie, "The *Prive Scilence* of Thomas Hoccleve," *SAC* 22 (2000): 281–309, (288–89).

least not poems that anyone deemed significant enough to preserve. If we are truly to comprehend the work of Hoccleve in its context, the fact that he was a poet while his friends and patrons were not needs to be considered: we must allow him a separate vocational commitment, if not a fully-fledged professional identity. Hoccleve's possible self-understandings as an *auctor,* compiler, translator, scribe,[9] petitioner, or autobiographical subject do not obviate his decision to compose poetry, a deliberately—and to many medieval writers and theologians, dangerously—artful form of language that had been the medium of serious aesthetic expression since the classical period. His investment in the mythos of Chaucer as a vernacular predecessor indicates a self-conscious interest in an emergent poetic vocation, and though much of his output is occasional and arguably written for the purposes of eliciting pay or assistance, it is likewise apparent that his petitionary rhetoric is also a means of poetic initiation, a self-authorizing strategy. Hoccleve's total *oeuvre* is a workshop of the self, and not just any self; his is an experiment not just in general late medieval, or Lancastrian, or even bureaucratic subjectivity, but in assembling a proprietary voice for himself as poet, a voice that models the disenchanted modernity of his Westminster.[10]

Hoccleve's attempt at vocational self-assembly would have been more recognizable to us had he organized it under the heading *poet,* but he does not do so.[11] He does not call himself a poet, nor does he use the

[9] For these and other ways of understanding the authorial project in the period, see Alastair Minnis, *Medieval Theories of Authorship: Scholastic Literary Attitudes in the Later Middle Ages* (Aldershot: Wildwood, 1988). For Hoccleve as petitioner, see John Burrow, "The Poet as Petitioner," *SAC* 3 (1981): 61–75. For his autobiographical subjectivity, see Albrecht Classen, "The Autobiographical Voice of Thomas Hoccleve," *Archiv für das Studium der Neueren Sprache und Literaturen* 228 (1991): 291–310; and John Burrow, "Autobiographical Poetry in the Later Middle Ages: The Case of Thomas Hoccleve," *Proceedings of the British Academy* 68 (1982) 389–412.

[10] For an overview of this working suburb, see Gervase Rosser, *Medieval Westminster: 1200–1540* (Oxford: Clarendon Press, 1989).

[11] Even the aggressively self-aware poets of troubadour tradition who arguably created the persona of vernacular poet for the medieval period rarely did so, for which see Olivia Holmes, *Assembling the Lyric Self: Authorship from Troubadour Song to Italian Poetry Book* (Minneapolis: University of Minnesota Press, 2000). Yet to withhold from them, or from Hoccleve, the title of poet, in which so much of our understanding of both the visionary and the vocational aspects of verse-writing are enfolded, is to relegate them to some subfield of premodern anonymity. Lee Patterson reviews the institutional schemes that have prevented medieval poets from joining the ranks of their progressive Renaissance inheritors in "On the Margin: Postmodernism, Ironic History, and Medieval Studies," *Speculum* 65 (1990): 87–108. I do not claim that Hoccleve's work lies along an express route to Romanticism and its claims for poets, only that he seriously addresses the embryonic social category of secular poet in the fifteenth century, a category so small as to be practically invisible.

more common Middle English word *makar.* No more did Chaucer when speaking of himself. Perhaps the chief problem of both poets is this default of nomenclature: Why is there no satisfactory word in their language for the job both men shared? Hoccleve describes his own work as *writyng*,[12] and uses the names of fixed or topical forms like *balade* or *complaynte;* he pictures his author figure reading his works aloud to an audience (e.g., in the *Dialogue*); he collects his works together into a single-author poetic anthology (in the holographs now in the Huntingdon Library); he reads and translates the texts of previous poetic authors and identifies them as authorities. Similarly, any reader of Chaucer sees immediately how seriously he took his poetic craft and even squibs like *Adam Scriveyn* reveal how concerned he was about his poetic posterity. Yet neither poet can encapsulate his activity with a single designation: both inhabit a professional vacuum.

While Chaucer shows various signs of discomfort in this space, Hoccleve's condition is more acute. Where Chaucer's poet-narrators suffer minor authorial maladies that prevent sleep and impel compulsive reading,[13] illnesses that could be confused with the universal aristocratic pathology of lovesickness, Hoccleve's poet-narrator risks specific and grave physical, mental, and moral breakdown as the result of the reading, writing, and composition attendant upon his poetic work. The high stakes involved in Hoccleve's poetic activity rather recall those of Langland. Like Langland, and unlike Chaucer, Hoccleve makes an effort to locate his poetry-writing in the spectrum of work,[14] and similarly fails to make it map on to any of the existing categories: it is not artisanal,[15] nor is it agricultural work,[16] yet it is a species of *labor;*[17] it is not endowed

[12] For example, "If that I do in my wrytynge foleye," "Balade to the Duke of York," line 46, *Hoccleve's Works: The Minor Poems,* ed. Frederick J. Furnivall and I. Gollancz, EETS, e.s. 61,73 rpt. 1970.

[13] Particularly the narrators of the dream visions; for an excellent study of the crisis of poetic authority in *The House of Fame,* see Jacqueline T. Miller, *Poetic License: Authority and Authorship in Medieval and Renaissance Contexts* (New York: Oxford University Press, 1986), pp. 34–72.

[14] An important volume on Langland's conception of authorial work is *Written Work: Langland, Labor, and Authorship,* ed. Stephen Justice and Kathryn Kerby-Fulton (Philadelphia: University of Pennsylvania Press, 1997).

[15] He distinguishes textual work from the work of manual laborers or artificers, *Regiment* Prologue, lines 1009–12. Citations from this text throughout are from *Thomas Hoccleve: The Regiment of Princes,* ed. Charles R. Blyth (Kalamazoo: Medieval Institute Publications, 1999).

[16] He discusses how he cannot plow or use agricultural implements, *Regiment* Prologue, lines 977–85.

[17] "It [writing] is wel gretter labour than it seemeth," *Regiment* Prologue, line 993.

with religious authority, which he disavows on various occasions, yet it is literate; it is not knightly, or even legal, although it relies on knowledge of ceremonial and institutional forms. Impossible as it is to place within the traditional boundaries of the three estates, aspects of Hoccleve's work nonetheless are palpable enough to create eyestrain, back pain, cramps,[18] anxiety, and paranoia[19] in their perpetrator, and to make him run the risk of *acedia*.[20] These signs of poetic hardship are not gratifying, but they are dramatic; for lack of a status for the poet, we get, instead, a story. This story, composed of details drawn from his disparate texts, is the one I will sketch out over the course of my argument.

John Bowers has recently offered a series of concrete local reasons why Hoccleve missed the boat of poetic fame, despite being one of the prime instigators of the whole idea of the English canon: commitment to the wrong genres, a risky partisanship with Prince Henry during his minority, ill-timed pacifism in *The Regiment of Princes* during a bellicose period, disinterest in Chaucerian narrative, a persistently low-level administrative career, an embarrassing personal breakdown, his choice of London and Westminster settings with their inevitable associations of factionalism.[21] The result was a poetics that even by the mid-fifteenth century was only readable as satire, yet it lacked the religious-didactic core that anchored the appeal of *Piers Plowman* and its tradition, the only similar exploration of urban blight in the English vernacular. Hoccleve's perspective, embodied as it was in his own historical person and with no more authority than that of literate poet-about-town, rapidly became unintelligible to later fifteenth-century readers. Hoccleve, determined to give the contemporary English poet a local habitation and a name, undoes himself even as he builds himself up, as people are not prepared to invest in this voice and its indeterminate social position.

The rejection of Hoccleve's bid for poetic posterity has everything to do with the disjointed persona who is so audible throughout his work and who fails to guarantee it, yet I stress that the implications of this

---

[18] He describes these physical hardships of scribal activity, *Regiment* Prologue, lines 995–1029.

[19] These are contemporary terms for the conditions he describes in the *Complaint*. Citations from this text throughout are from *Thomas Hoccleve's Complaint and Dialogue*, ed. J. A. Burrow (Oxford: Oxford University Press, 1999).

[20] The poet, indulging in tavern sins as well as purveying a parody of contrition, is certainly running this risk in the *Male Regle*.

[21] See John M. Bowers, "Thomas Hoccleve and the Politics of Tradition," *ChauR* 36, no. 4 (2002): 352–69.

rejection are more than merely personal, for the composite voice that is his dubious poetic achievement is actually the one most revelatory of the historical circumstances of the vernacular career poet of his period.[22] That is to say that in refusing to credit the nascent proprietary voice—frankensteinien monster though it is—of an urban, secular poet dedicated to staking out his professional territory, early readers of Hoccleve, and many critics, have failed to gain valuable insight into the professional situation not only of Hoccleve but also of his contemporaries like Chaucer and Langland. The strung-out and agonized voice of the poet, spliced together out of a variety of different outgrown genres made to contain quite other forms of subjectivity, expresses not just the individual weird personality of Hoccleve, but the crisis of genre with which any ambitious poet of the Ricardian/Lancastrian period had to contend: it is the poetic result less of acute problems of the person than of the persona. This generic instability in Hoccleve combines with another obsessive concern in his work, the network of patronage, to produce even more striated effects.[23] His is a highly interactive model of poetic production: he locates the poet's voice and initiative as only one among several complementary sites in a network of readers, patrons, and advisors who function jointly to produce textual meaning. His disparate corpus maps the system of cultural production that produced secular poetry in his period, recording its various transactions between source texts and their accumulated cultural capital, the labor of the living poet, and the purchasing and negotiating power of patrons, subpatrons, and wannabe patrons, all mediated by the quasi-hierarchical, quasi-cash economy of bastard feudalism. Hoccleve's decision to let this system show through, if not to govern, his work is another sore point; just as he has the nerve to expose how horribly interstitial any attempt at allowing the historical poet to speak *in propria persona* must be, he tactlessly reveals the extent

---

[22] For Chaucer's struggles with this series of problems, see Lee Patterson, "What Man Artow?": Authorial Self-Definition in *The Tale of Sir Thopas* and *The Tale of Melibee*," *SAC* 11 (1989): 117–75. These are obviously the correct tales to look at for a picture of the poet's self-image; what is curious is how long it has taken for anyone to compare them to the equally obvious site of professional poetic self-definition in Hoccleve's *Complaint* and *Dialogue*. See also the excellent discussion of "Selfishness and Selflessness" in Paul Strohm's *Social Chaucer* (Cambridge, Mass.: Harvard University Press, 1989), pp. 84–109.

[23] See John J. Thompson, "A Poet's Contact with the Great and the Good: Further Consideration of Thomas Hoccleve's Texts and Manuscripts," in *Prestige, Authority, and Power in Late Medieval Manuscripts and Texts,* ed. Felicity Riddy (York: York Medieval Press, 2000), pp. 77–101.

of his powerlessness by dwelling on the demanding and fragmenting system that constrains any serious poetic utterance at all.

His determination to provide too much information was meant, I contend, not only to elucidate his personal circumstances but also as an act of professional solidarity. The enfeebled persona of his work is actually a strong response to the tasteful silences of Chaucer and the guilty fulminations of Langland about a group to which they all belonged. His attempt to establish the poetic estate in all its circumscribed glory presumes to redress critical problems of voice that he found in the works of Chaucer, and arguably of Langland, in a way much more confident and thoroughgoing than Hoccleve is usually given credit for. Below I will examine his early poem *The Male Regle de T. Hoccleve* (circa 1406) as an initial exercise in what was to become the main preoccupation of his work: that is, trying to sort out the proprietary discourse of the vernacular poet whose authority is neither aristocratic-courtly nor religious-clerical. In doing so he cuts through a series of Gordian knots in voicing that trouble the productions of both Chaucer and Langland in using the same genre, the *exemplum* against tavern sins, to perform similar ends in *The Pardoner's Prologue and Tale* and the B-text Passus V confession of the Seven Deadly Sins, respectively. I begin, however, with the inevitable Hocclevean prologue.

Everybody Has to Be Somewhere:[24]
Hoccleve and the Poet's Prologue

Recent manuscript scholars have revealed much about the circumstances of poetic production and the London book trade that surrounded poets such as Chaucer, Gower, and Langland.[25] Hoccleve, however, himself

---

[24] This section title is from Douglas Adams, *The Long Dark Tea-Time of the Soul* (London: Pan Books, 1989), p. 195.

[25] For a comprehensive view of this trade, see Ralph Hanna III, *London Literature 1300–1380* (Cambridge: Cambridge University Press, 2005); Ralph Hanna III, A. S. G. Edwards, and Vincent Gillespie, *The English Medieval Book: Studies in Memory of Jeremy Griffiths* (London: British Library, 2000); Carol Meale et al., eds., *The Cambridge History of the Book in Britain, III: 1400–1557* (Cambridge: Cambridge University Press, 1999). Also helpful are Ralph Hanna III, "Miscellaneity and Vernacularity: Conditions of Literary Production in Late Medieval England," in *The Whole Book: Cultural Perspectives on the Medieval Miscellany,* ed. Ralph Hanna III, Stephen G. Nichols, and Siegfried Wenzel (Ann Arbor: University of Michigan Press, 1996), pp. 37–51; Carol Meale, "Patrons, Buyers and Owners: Book Production and Social State," in *Book Production and Publishing in Britain 1375–1475,* ed. Jeremy Griffiths and Derek Pearsall (Cambridge: Cambridge University Press, 1989), pp. 201–38.

concretizes the poetic and scribal producer and his consciousness within the boundaries of his texts, bringing the locus of the author down from the level of metanarrative, where he had lived comfortably for centuries, to that of narrative.[26] The composite picture of the insecure and complaining poet that emerges is not necessarily a pretty one. Yet by corporealizing the role of vernacular, secular, living author and contextualizing him within his urban, worldly environment, not only does Hoccleve create a refreshing verisimilitude, but he reorders the scattered structure of authorial voicing that he had inherited from Chaucer and other prestigious poets and places the historical poet, for the first time in Middle English, at the center of his own work.

Yet the poet figure in Hoccleve holds his central ground precariously and he does not perform his work alone. His shorter begging and occasional poems, such as the *Male Regle,* call attention to their petitionary functions and explicitly invoke particular patrons. Longer composite texts are produced piecemeal in front of the reader's gaze, changing course in response to imaginary laws of supply and demand brought into the text by advisor, critic, and patron figures who interact with the writer's persona: in the *Regiment of Princes,* by the old man in the prologue and patron he proposes, Prince Henry, and in the *Series,* by the anonymous friend in the *Dialogue.* Neither the poetic I of the text, nor the text itself, can stand on its own; both reach out and seek to form

[26] I concentrate here on the formation of Hoccleve's poetic voice as an indicator of his attempt to establish a professional or vocational identity. Manuscript studies have also yielded recent articles that record Hoccleve's attempts at professionalization. For codicological work that explores his contribution to the idea of an authorial collected works, see David Watt, " 'I This Book Shal Make': Thomas Hoccleve's Self-Publication and Book Production," *Leeds Studies in English* 34 (2003): 133–60 and J. A. Burrow, "Hoccleve's Huntingdon Holographs: The First "Collected Poems" in English," *Fifteenth-Century Studies* 15 (1989): 27–51. For a view of the perils of determining authorial identity from manuscript evidence, see A. S. G. Edwards, "Fifteenth-Century Middle English Verse Author Collections," in *The English Medieval Book: Studies in Honour of Jeremy Griffiths,* ed. Ralph Hanna III, A. S. G. Edwards, and Vincent Gillespie (London: British Library, 2000), pp. 101–12. For his pursuit of patrons, see Jennifer Nuttall, "Household Narratives and Lancastrian Poetics in Hoccleve's Envoys and Other Early-Fifteenth-Century Middle English Poems," in *The Medieval Household in Christian Europe C. 850–C. 1550: Managing Power, Wealth, and the Body,* ed. Cordelia Beattie (Turnhout, Belgium: Brepols, 2003), pp. 91–106; and Thompson, *A Poet's Contacts.* For the development of Hoccleve's poetic idiolect, see Judith A. Jefferson, "The Hoccleve Holographs and Hoccleve's Metrical Practice: More Than Counting Syllables?" *Parergon* 18 (2000): 203–26, and the prefatory matter on versification in Burrow's edition of the *Complaint and Dialogue,* as well as the introduction to the holograph manuscripts in Blyth's edition of the *Regiment.*

patronage relationships with everyone, including the reader, ceding to them a share in the work's direction. This picture of the historical poet as an embarrassing flunky is one some medievalists would prefer to be without, as it has the potential to compromise even Chaucer. Chaucer's reticence about his place in the system of patronage, which was not so very different from Hoccleve's (both were commoner bureaucrats, secular clerks in royal government within ten years of each other) cannot remove him from it. Indeed, first among the facts that Chaucer's greater success tacitly records must be a superior ability to negotiate with patrons, seconded perhaps by a higher initial status as the son of a rich city vintner,[27] with any aesthetic dimensions of his work making up a trailing third. Hoccleve unveils the spectacle of histrionic compliance that necessarily enabled Chaucer's poetic career, as well as his own, casting the father of the English poetic tradition back into the transitory world of transaction and interest.

Even when subjected to the pressure of recent historicist analysis, armed with sophisticated reading practices and a wealth of contextual information, Chaucer remains a courtly poet whose work reveals little about the historical court in which he was a functionary or about his own status as a poet within it. This may be because his higher status as a public servant (in customs, in diplomacy, in parliament) provided him with other, more discernible, identities. For those of us interested in the vocational history of poetry, this is not an advantage, merely a distraction. Here the resources of Hoccleve, whose bureaucratic star never rose and whose moderate success in the world of the court may actually have rested more on his poetry than Chaucer's ever did (as his administrative career was disrupted by a long leave of absence during his insanity), are ideally shaped to supplement his deficiencies. Yet so unthinkable is it that Hoccleve could be better than Chaucer at anything, that his extensive treatment of his own—and Chaucer's—identity as poet continues

---

[27] Nothing is known of Hoccleve's origins, except that he may have come from the village of Hoccleve in Bedfordshire. For his life and records, see J. A. Burrow, *Thomas Hoccleve* (Aldershot: Variorum, 1994). John and Agnes Chaucer of Vintry Ward, however, were able to place the young Geoffrey Chaucer in service as a page to Elizabeth de Burgh, Countess of Ulster, wife of Lionel, son of Edward III. See Martin M. Crow and Virginia E. Leland, "Chaucer's Life," in *The Riverside Chaucer,* 3rd., ed. Larry D. Benson (Boston: Houghton Mifflin, 1987), xv–xxvi. Chaucer citations are from this edition.

to play second fiddle to even the most fragmentary Chaucerian narratives.[28]

Additionally, Hoccleve, along with John Lydgate, has become so much a poster poet of Lancastrian unease that it is difficult to imagine him commenting profitably on the different political and poetic climate of the Ricardian period. Granted that the usurpation of Henry IV in 1400 and the usurping wars of his son in France in the next generation, as displays of naked power, did result in the unmetaphoring, and then the consequent anxious task of the remetaphoring, of many principles of social order, in which Hoccleve, like Lydgate, participated. Hoccleve, though, I contend, exploits the new nakedness of the Lancastrian atmosphere not primarily to expose the king, or even the civil servant, but to expose the poet, using the opportunity of political turmoil to accomplish poetic ends. The necessitous and calamitous world evoked in his work is one that provides distracting cover for the emergence of a voice previously unauthorized. Of all the various suppressions about persons of the court in Chaucer, the one that Hoccleve seized on was the omission of himself, the historical poet. His compensating project was the reinsertion of the poet into the court, a court reimagined from that lowly perspective, updated and scaled down, populated not by elegiac Black Knights, talking birds, or ancient Trojans but by proximate bureaucrats and distant patrons.

Spending a lifetime on the question of authority, textual and social,

---

[28] For example, in the recent volume *Theory and the Premodern Text* (Minneapolis: University of Minnesota Press, 2004), pp. 3–19, Paul Strohm creates a chapter on navigating social space in the city of London via a comparison of Chaucer's Scrope-Grosvenor testimony (describing his sighting of the contested arms of Sir Robert Grosvenor hanging in an inn in Friday Street), the appeal of Thomas Usk against former mayor John Northampton (in which he describes plotting that takes place in Willingham's tavern in Bow Street), and Hoccleve's description in the *Male Regle* of his travels between home and work, stopping in taverns on King Street. Two sources are documentary and one poetic. Chaucer never mentions the webs of affiliation and social pretension that are assumed in his court of chivalry deposition in his poetry; Usk discusses his factional London career in veiled and foreshortened terms later in his prose work *The Testament of Love;* Hoccleve alone chats openly about his personal life and suburban locale in the context of a poem directed to the public, or at least to the coterie of his fellow clerks. In my opinion this poetic packaging transforms the meaning of his itinerary; it cannot be confined to the shared symbolizations that are found in the three different narratives, rich as they are; it cannot be removed from "the category of the aesthetic" (p. 10) that Strohm is determined to overwrite with other social signifiers. This is not just to insist on the *Male Regle*'s status as a poem, but to claim that its focus is in fact on those "writerly experiences" that Strohm denies and that these define a new social role, that of poet: this is in fact the specific act of *social redefinition* (p. 10, Strohm's italics) that Hoccleve has in hand.

Chaucer asserted, continuously and obliquely, that wherever it might reside, it was not with him. This radicalization of the modesty topos is part of the charm of Chaucerian poetics; through juxtapositions of genre and systems of value, the masterful implied poet creates indeterminacy that both cloaks and reveals his own power, while occasionally providing brief caricatures of himself as a historical person—in *The House of Fame* and the *Canterbury Tales*—that seem to defy any possibility of agency. In the *House of Fame,* the Geoffrey persona is contained in a dream frame, the authority of which is generically doubtful, and he is literally swept off his feet by a force beyond his control in the form of an eagle (a rhetorical force that represents, at least in part, the overwhelming poetics of Dante). In the *Canterbury Tales,* the only occasion in which the authorial persona appears in the historical world, he is not the boss—the host Harry Bailly, likewise a named historical individual, runs the exchange of poetic tales. In the *General Prologue,* the poet himself is never described, and his tale is a debacle, in which he cannot sustain poetic language in the fragmentary *Tale of Sir Thopas* and soon collapses into the prose *Melibee.* This authorial peepshow is all very funny, but it is also a terrible *cri de coeur* about his professional status. The failed exchange of *Sir Thopas* encodes the fact that the secular poet had no place in the imagined order of the estates, even in his own revision of it. The tale conspicuously missing from his conspectus of later medieval trades in the *Canterbury Tales* is *The Poet's Tale.* Arguably, the entire work constitutes this tale, but if so, it remains a tale without a teller, that is, without a prologue identifying the narrative voice. Hoccleve bravely casts himself into this void left in Chaucer, producing a dilating series of poet's prologues throughout his work. So invested is he in these prologues that his invention often seems to flag when it comes to the tales over which he is so aggressively claiming propriety. The *Male Regle* is perhaps the most drastic case in point, as the entire poem consists of prologue, setting up the authority of the poet to utter moral truths that never transpire.

When we pause to compare the two most significant scenes of professional poetic reception in Chaucer and Hoccleve, respectively, the summary cutting off of *The Tale of Sir Thopas* by the host in the *Canterbury Tales,* and the critique of the *Complaint* by the anonymous friend in the *Series,* we are confronted by the surprising fact that Hoccleve's authorial persona comes off better in these critical exchanges in several key ways. The Geoffrey persona's poetic activity, which is comically egregious, is silenced by Harry Bailey in one of his most insulting utterances: "thy drasty ryming / is nat worth a toord!"[29] No voice speaks in Geoffrey's defense, as the other pilgrims evidently concur; his own protests about poetic competence are overridden. He is forced to begin again with the didactic allegorical prose *Tale of Melibee.* Geoffrey holds the floor for a long time with this tale, and its quality assessment has steadily risen among recent critics, following the evidence of its widespread positive reception among fifteenth-century readers, but the one thing we can say of it is that it is not a poem. The poet-persona must step out of his primary medium to gain credibility with his in-text audience. He forgoes his best opportunity for proprietary poetic performance: imagine what Dante, the self-advertising humanist of Chaucer's nightmare in the *House of Fame,* might have done with this opening. While Hoccleve does not produce a *tour de force* in his similar poetic test case of professional voicing in the lyric *Complaint,* the results are at least not embarrassing. The workmanlike *Complaint* is, moreover, in an up-to-date and sophisticated quasi-religious meditative genre as opposed to the rusticity of a tail-rhyme romance. Additionally, it is, at least in part, a translation, which endows it with status and credits Hoccleve's poetic scholarship.[30] Hoccleve also unabashedly appropriates the poem's meaning, using the text by Isidore of Seville to elucidate his own consciousness, bringing an old text forward in time and incorporating it into a contemporary poetic voice. This is the opposite of Chaucer's temporal maneuver, for example, in a similar instance of lyric insertion in *Troilus and Criseyde,* in which the aristocratic Trojan Troilus at the dawn of chivalric history composes a love poem, the *Canticus Troili,* that is actually a translation from Petrarch's *Canzoniere.*[31] Chaucer occludes and backdates poetry of his own period into the prestigious past (repeating in miniature the same process he enacts on Boccaccio's new poem *Il Filostrato* to present it as the work of the ancient author Lollius). Most important, by dint of persuasion, Hoccleve's poet-persona is able to arrange a positive reception for his work rather than having to abandon it. His unnamed friend is not initially enthused about Hoccleve's poem, although his grounds, being psychological instead of aesthetic, leave the poet's technical proficiency unchallenged:

[29] *Riverside Chaucer,* VII, 2120.
[30] See A. G. Rigg, "Hoccleve's *Complaint* and Isidore of Seville," *Speculum* 45 (1970): 564–74; and J. A. Burrow, "Hoccleve's *Complaint* and Isidore of Seville Again," *Speculum* 73 (1998): 424–28.
[31] Specifically number 132; see *Riverside Chaucer,* Explanatory Notes, p. 1028.

> Thy bisy studie about swich mateere
> Hath causid thee to stirte in-to the plyt
> That thow were in, as fer as I can heere;
> And thogh thow deeme thow be therof qwyt,
> Abyde, and thy purpos putte in respyt
> Til that right wel stablisshed be thy brayn:
> And ther-to thanne, I wole assente fayn.
>
> (*Dialogue,* lines 303–8)

The Hoccleve persona is intransigent, however, and insists on his personal and poetic proficiency. His friend is finally sufficiently assured of Hoccleve's professional poetic strength that he undertakes to recommend high-status patrons to him, and commissions a translation himself, for the instruction of his son. Far from shouting the poet down, as do the Canterbury pilgrims, Hoccleve's friend invests in his work.

Bowers claims that in general Hoccleve's generic choices did him disservice with early readers, but here we see them functioning to enable a successful poetic exchange. His admixture of the autobiographical and the religious-didactic creates a generic openness, allowing his reader-friend to witness an ameliorative process brought on by Hoccleve's poetic writing, one that he can buy into. The *Complaint* is produced both as a therapeutic utterance for the poet himself and as a specimen of his work: it establishes the credibility of its author, functions as an aesthetic sample, and demonstrates a restorative power that has already worked on the poet and so might assist in regulating the friend's unruly son. The other feature that is specifically enabling of a productive exchange is the explicit textuality of the *Series*. The documentary nature of the *Complaint* is never in question; the friend listens to Hoccleve read a written text,[32] and having one text conceptualized and commodified before him, is able to suggest—and even to provide, as he drops in later with a helpful manuscript coda to one of the translations the poet undertakes in the rest of the *Series*—others himself. Poetry in the *Series* is understood as quantifiable literate labor, and as such is both comprehensible to and tradable in the wider community.

No such point of access is available to the audience of pilgrims in the *Canterbury Tales* because of the nature of the frame narrative, which insists on the illusion of orality. As Geoffrey is only one speaker among

---

[32] "And right anon, I redd hym my "complaynte" explains the poet (*Dialogue,* line 17).

other speakers, Chaucer is unable to forge any privileged link between the living poet and poetic text. Likewise in the early dream poems, his narrators, ostensible writers of the texts they inhabit, are rhetorically overwhelmed by all characters they meet because of Chaucer's reluctance to break his frame: engulfed by dreamscapes that occlude their own textuality with the trope of vision, the narrators speak when spoken to and float otherwise unconnected to their own productions. There are important scenes of authorial reading in Chaucer, but none of writing, and this simple addition in Hoccleve makes a critical difference: moments at which the text crystallizes into a written commodity are flashpoints, underlining the unique communicative status of the poet and encouraging active reception by readers both fictive and real: we are invited at such junctures, in effect, to make patronage decisions. Such decisions are more interactive and binding than those involved in the posture of overhearing supposed oral discourse; they involve readers in snobberies, aesthetic, economic, and moral judgments and forms of display that in turn further concretize the role of the poet.

Hoccleve's poet-persona tells us his own personal *Historia Calamitatum* in episodes throughout his major works: his government pay chronically in arrears (*Male Regle,* lines 417–42; *Regiment Prologue,* lines 820–33) and with a wife to support (*Regiment Prologue,* lines 1226–29, 1450–59) along with a booze habit (*Male Regle,* lines 105–26),[33] he seeks patrons for poetic works that will function partly as purchasable items and partly as reminders of payments past due in Privy Seal; he consults various people on what kinds of works would be suitable for particular patrons (the old man in the *Regiment,* the friend in the *Series*); he complains that an episode of insanity five years in the past, from which he is now recovered by God's grace, continues to haunt his personal and professional life, as people will not believe in his rehabilitation (*Complaint,* lines 36–301). He describes the arduous technical process of his scribal work (*Regiment, Prologue,* lines 988–1029). He is fearful about his economic future once he has retired from court bureaucracy and loses the ear of the various people whom he has to remind in order to keep his annuity coming (*Regiment Prologue,* lines 834–47). This is as much information as is provided in the personality sketches of the *General Prologue,* and it is stylistically similar: anecdotal, local, incorporating rel-

---

[33] Citations from the *Male Regle* throughout are from *"My compleinte" and Other Poems,* ed. Roger Ellis (Exeter: Exeter University Press, 2001).

evant technical language, conveyed in a familiar vernacular. This racy cumulative text should qualify as a poet's prologue, filling in a gap in Chaucer's late work. Yet certain problems persist in making this identification. Hoccleve's version of the poet's prologue is consistently delivered in the first person to a variety of interlocutors. As such, it better resembles structurally the prologues of certain of the more self-aware Canterbury pilgrims, like the Pardoner or the Wife of Bath, prefatory to their tales. The main problem, however, is the shifting frame that surrounds this composite narrative, which makes it difficult to bring into generic focus.

In order to recover a linear narrative that might constitute Hoccleve's *Poet's Prologue* in its entirety, it is necessary to excavate it from a series of texts, beginning with *The Male Regle* (circa 1406). Here the Hoccleve persona, identified as a Privy Seal clerk by his association with two other clerks, Prentys and Arondel, overspends in bars and brings himself financial and bodily distress: generically, readers must determine if this is a historical or an exemplary narrative, autobiography or penitential set piece, in order to assess its meaning. Then we need to examine the extensive prologue to *The Regiment of Princes* (circa 1411), in which the poet-persona nerves himself up to write an advice text for Prince Henry of Lancaster by having a long conversation about his personal history and financial exigency with an unnamed old man whom he meets in a field at the edge of town: the task here is to extricate the poet's elaboration of his own identity from the rhetorical task of princely advising, in which a humble, truthful, and appropriately subordinated speaker is generically required. Finally, we need to work though the disparate structure of the *Series* (circa 1420–26) for evidence of the poet's selfhood: at the poet's description of his state of mind in the lyric *Complaint,* then at the peer assessment of text and poet by the bourgeois friend in the *Dialogue,* at the successful completion of which the friend recommends him to write a work on women for Duke Humphrey, as well as one against the evils of prostitution for his son. The idiosyncrasy of the *Series,* or at least of its frame narrative, based on the life of the historical poet in Chester's Inn in the Strand, initially makes readers wonder what genres they ought to be reading the work against; the most relevant one is probably the political complaint on the times, in which case it becomes possible to index the poet's narrative of insanity, recovery, and the necessity of social trust to the state of the commonwealth. Hoccleve's self is incomplete, intricately entangled with other selves and the discourses that constitute them textually. His poet is created intersubjectively—or more specifically, intergenerically. The suppletive model of the poetic self he presents in his texts reflects the lack of a discrete set of discourses to contain him, leaving him to cobble one together improvisationally in a sometimes inspired *bricolage*.

We might expect such a widely dispersed, reflexive self, serving so many generic masters (petitioner of the treasurer, needy friend, loyal subject of Prince Henry and a host of other roles) to be weak, but in fact Hoccleve's parasitic poetic self succeeds admirably in subordinating his generic hosts to his own requirements. In the *Male Regle,* the historical poet with his immediate needs, both for remuneration and self-expression, satirically appropriates and commodifies the universal voice of the penitent; in the *Regiment of Princes,* he uses the conventional humility topos required by the *speculum principis* to elaborate a detailed historical picture of himself; in the *Series,* in the course of ostensibly satisfying the demands of—in ascending order of social consequence—his own conscience, his friend's misapprehensions, and the wishes of high-status patrons, he provides readers with an elaborate proof of his personal and poetic competence and his working methods. His self operates like a vacuum, drawing other discourses toward it, and likewise other textual personae: over the course of his work, Lord Furnivall, the nameless old man, his friend, his friend's son, Prince Henry, Duke Humphrey, Lady Westmorland, and many others of varying degree in lesser poems all enable the poet's work, by forcing him to articulate himself and by encoding demand for his textual productions.

I Am Occasionally Here: The Male Regle de T. Hoccleve

Hoccleve picks up on Chaucer's initial setting of the *Canterbury Tales* in the Tabard Inn in Southwark by locating the *Male Regle* in a tavern in another London suburb, the Paul's Head in King Street, Westminster. In addition to revisiting the locale of the *General Prologue,* the poem is related to preacher's *exempla* concerning tavern sins, the territory of the *Pardoner's Tale* and of Passus 5 in Langland's *Piers Plowman,* and it performs similarly searching revisions of the allegorical technique inherent to the *exemplum* genre as are performed in those works. The *Male Regle* begins to explore the status of the tavern as a place of business rather than as a reflexive landscape of vice, as well as examining the nature of labor performed by urban service professionals. The nexus of regula-tions—personal, commercial, and hermeneutic—with which the poem is concerned, as well as its ludic tone, is encapsulated in the potential triple pun of its title. In this poem, the poet will address his own misrule (*mal regle*), a crucial subsection of which involves the regulation of his purse or "bagge" (*male*), which can contain, "in double wyse" (line 163) both money and semen, both of which he has been expending on whores in taverns, meaning that he fails, in his economic and sexual overexten-sion, to be a *mâle reglé* , a regulated man or male. The old goliardic joke about a man's *male* traditionally refers to a scrip or purse used for carry-ing not money, but pens, the (phallic) sign of clerical literacy. As is appropriate to the genre of the begging poem, the primary and empow-ering content of a purse here is cash, not writing utensils; however, the earlier meaning is not entirely elided, bringing the writer's scribal activ-ity obliquely into the formula and forging a latent connection between economic, sexual, and semiotic potency, which the remainder of the poem will exploit. After all, even as he disclaims his economic and erotic spending on prostitutes, he continues to write about them, expending his time and labor.

The *Male Regle* is a poem of 448 lines, addressed jointly to Furnivall, the royal treasurer, and to the allegorical Lord Health, whom Hoccleve has offended by his dissipated life; the poet narrator complains about his self-indulgence and its effect, the "penylees maladie" (line 130), and vows to reform, if only he can receive medicine, in the form of the pay he is owed for government work. The poem is occasional, a written instrument designed to draw attention to his financial plight and redress it; it functions like the bills or petitions he regularly drafted in Privy Seal. At the same time, the poet is empowered to speak at length about his own life—utterance otherwise difficult to justify for a commoner—specifically because of the institutional lag inherent in his bureaucratic job; rhetorically, poetic discourse itself is already a form of redress, a compensatory mechanism. What the civil servant cannot gain by his scribal labor, the professional poet can by his service as a moralist and entertainer; by changing hats, Hoccleve becomes his own initial inter-cessor, first in a series to which he appeals in the poem. This may seem like borrowing from Peter to pay Paul, but like many of Hoccleve's rhetorical strategies that are initiated by lack, to which he is expertly attuned, it is effective: he apparently elicited his pay[34]—and incidentally professionalized and laicized poetic discourse. The *Male Regle* presents a suffering initial self who is to be shucked off, not a sinning Everyman but an underpaid bureaucrat, superimposing upon it a corrected self who seeks redemption through the work of poetry, reward not heavenly but monetary, gained through earthly intercessory processes and based not on erasure of the sins of the tavern, but on their comical narrative reduplication. Both stages of this pseudo-Pauline self are urban secular writers: bureaucrat is saved by poet, and the drama of conversion remains wholly profane.

In the frame narrative of the *Canterbury Tales,* Chaucer uses the suburban commercial setting of the Tabard Inn as a plausible venue in which to collect his cross section of social types before moving them onto the road to St. Thomas's shrine. The socially leveling powers of commerce and pilgrimage are invoked to constrain a heterogeneous group, divided enough that they would not normally interact, into fictional togetherness. Chaucer needs this double whammy to perform an awkward act of translation in mode, from the fundamentally abstract estates satire that is his main generic inspiration for the *General Prologue,* to verisimilar narrative; he needs to create a naturalistic setting for a theoretically organized group, and to rearticulate its organizing principles so that they make sense narratively. In doing so, he places more emphasis on the idea of pilgrimage, one with a universal valence—and one that tends to tip the narrative balance toward allegory—than he does on the idea of commerce. Chaucer does not describe the workings of the inn other than as a backdrop for his character portraits, and rapidly leaves it behind, even taking the innkeeper away from his workplace to accompany the pilgrims on the road. The host Harry Bailly, in his guise as moderator of the tale-telling competition (and its automatic winner, as everyone is supposed to return and eat supper at his inn regardless of the outcome), is the sole lingering indicator of the topsy-turvy power of commercial exchange. Everyone is otherwise subordinated to the demands of the pilgrimage; it is the principle that keeps them together. Without it, the tales could simply have been told back at the inn. Chaucer, though, does not grant simple commerce—the joint status of all as

---

[34] After a year-long parliamentary suspension of annuities from Easter to Easter 1404–5, Hoccleve's annuity due at Michaelmas 1405 was finally paid in March 1406, a fairly speedy catch-up under the circumstances. His annuity was generally about fourteen weeks late. See Burrow, *Thomas Hoccleve,* pp. 12–15.

Harry Bailly's customers, chance met—to this kind of social agency. Rather, the chance-met pilgrims speak to one another because they are pilgrims, social hierarchy dissolved by the pressure of a universal status. Their long trip allows Chaucer the space to narrate their many tales, but his reason for choosing the pilgrimage road as his site of exposition is not really verisimilitude: it is because only this universalizing concept could discipline his diverse allegorical group and make them cohere in a historical situation.

In short, despite being widely praised for its verisimilar detail and mined for historical information, the opening of the *Canterbury Tales* loses its battle with allegory: needing to narrativize the polemical abstractions of estates satire, Chaucer's choice of a pilgrimage as the organizing principle relies not on particularity or historicity but on the religious ideal of salvation.[35] The poem is thus doubly pressured toward abstraction: characters retain the typiness of estates satire and tend to escape upward into a transcendental reality, against which the claims of the concrete experiential world cannot prevail. If he wanted to describe the historical world, he should have invested in Harry's bar and the regulatory powers of earthly commerce, the way Hoccleve does in the Paul's Head and other taverns of the *Male Regle*. The tavern and its *quid pro quo* values are the explanatory center of this poem. The tavern itself, not a remote shrine, is the site of desire, attracting customers and traders with "the outward signe of Bacchus and his lure" (line 121) and the clientele are locals, those who have some professional reason to be there—taverners and cooks, whores, ferrymen who taxi customers to and fro across the Thames. Hoccleve himself finds the tavern at the dangerously appealing midpoint of his daily commute to work, between Westminster gate, where he passed into the palace precinct to his office, and his Privy Seal lodging house along the river in the Strand. Tavern life is an end in itself, and while the poet comically bewails its deleterious effects on his purse, body, and reputation (although not his soul), satirizing both the confessional voice of penitential lyric and the preach-

---

[35] I do not mean to revive the specter of Robertsonian allegorical reading of the *Canterbury Tales,* or to deny the relevance of historicist criticism on the *General Prologue* with this remark, only to point out one effect of Chaucer's narrative decision to use pilgrimage as his expositional device. I do not consider the tales or their frame narrative to be religious allegories, or at least not primarily so, although I concede that Chaucer is the type of poet who prefers (or is compelled, chiefly because of the deficit of authority that I increasingly identify as the Ricardian-Lancastrian poetic problem) to have multiple narrative levels operating.

er's *exemplum* against tavern sins in so doing, the tavern is actually the locus of the poem's morality, the place where—in contradistinction to the court—people get what they pay for, and pay for what they get. The tavern succeeds in placing a discernible value on service, and on time expended in labor, where the king's government does not; it is the purveyor of what Jacques Le Goff has called "merchant's time."[36] In the *Canterbury Tales,* nobody does any work, as professions are temporarily suspended on the pilgrimage road; narration, which figures the elapse of time, occurs, in fact, in place of labor either temporal or spiritual. Hoccleve's poem is situated in a workplace, one that has the power to impose value on everything, including idleness, suffering, and pleasure; most important, its narration constitutes work, as it is the commodity— indeed, the timesheet—of a particular kind of worker, a professional poet.

The first eight-line stanza of the *Male Regle* is an exorbitant apostrophe of the "eerthely god" (line 8) Health, the onetime lord or "gouernour" (line 11) who has abandoned the ailing poet (identified by the name Hoccleve at line 351). Health is a specimen of personification allegory, an abstraction that stands in a symbolic relationship to the speaker: the poet, alienated from Health, is sick. Health is a god, therefore necessarily a figure of speech. Yet we rapidly pass over these symbolizations and the poet goes on to address Health in the contemporary terms of feudal subjection; he is Hoccleve's lord, who offers him scope to demonstrate the epideictic rhetoric appropriate to addressing historical superiors. Moreover, at the end of the poem in a final brief appearance, Health is addressed as "Hynesse" (line 419) and asked to release Hoccleve's back pay for Michaelmas to Lord Furnivall, the royal treasurer. This equates him, momentarily, with King Henry IV, the historical person with this power. A Lancastrian reading of this usage would claim this is flattery: Henry IV is a god, the figure of health and order to whom his subject appeals. The fact that Henry IV was anything but healthy circa 1406 would make this a typical Hocclevean malapropism, a Freudian slip that reveals the dangerous fact of the usurping king's illness and the opening this left for his ambitious son. Likewise, the fact that he goes on to inveigh specifically against flattery in the midsection of the poem would have to be taken as an instance of poetic bad faith,

---

[36] See Jacques Le Goff, *Time, Work, and Culture in the Middle Ages,* trans. Arthur Goldhammer (Chicago: University of Chicago Press, 1980), pp. 29–42.

the kind of misdirection typical of a disjointed royal administrative culture.[37] However, Health need not read this way at all; to do so is to impose a coherence on him that his slight figure will hardly bear. Rather, "Health" is a word, an item of poetic vocabulary, which Hoccleve moves quickly through a series of generic registers to obtain desired effects: as a god, he is the object of poetic invocation, a nice Chaucerian opening gambit; as a lord, he figures any patron who might be able to assist Hoccleve and earn his loyal service; as a king, he represents the point of last resort over the head of Furnivall, the named historical addressee. It is this kind of rapid, nonaccumulating movement of terms through generic settings that justifies comparisons with Langland.[38] In each case Health exists as an imaginary patron: his function is to give the poet someone to address. As such he is Hoccleve's servant, despite the poet-persona's protestations of suffering subjection.

Lancastrian mystique aside, there is little textual reason to grant the royal family and their interests hermeneutic primacy in any of Hoccleve's works, even the *Regiment of Princes* with its famous addressee, Prince Henry, and a persuasive one not to, namely that granting that place to the poet himself suddenly brings his whole *oeuvre* into focus, rather than yielding up a disconnected series of works with no unifying principle other than a pathetic and unsuccessful desire to please. The *Regiment* is a *speculum principis*, and is widely assumed therefore to be about the prince, who is supposed to constitute himself out of the body of advice given to him by the advisor, and differentiate himself from the subjected self of the advisor. In Hoccleve's case, I suggest that almost exactly the opposite is true: the figure of the patron, even the fascinating Prince Henry, functions as a site to which the poet continuously directs himself. The patron is a powerful object of desire, and as such a function of the poet's psychology. It is also possible to interpret the demanding, withholding, yet empty patron as a simple generic substitution, reiterating the role of the lady from courtly literature, the traditional arena for the enaction of poetic subjectivity. The contours of Hoccleve's work overall certainly repeat the familiar rhetorical outlines of courtly love

[37] For a Lancastrian-political reading of another begging poem, see Paul Strohm, "Saving the Appearances: Chaucer's 'Purse' and the Fabrication of the Lancastrian Claim," in *Hochon's Arrow: The Social Imagination of Fourteenth-Century Texts* (Princeton: Princeton University Press, 1992), pp. 75–94.

[38] For the antiteleological or nonaccumulating use of terms in Langland, see Sarah Tolmie, "Langland and the End of Language," *YLS* 21 (2006), forthcoming.

poetry, the abject posture of the lover-poet before the beloved, replaced by the professional poet and his patron. Even his reliance on intermediaries like the *Regiment's* old man, the anonymous friend of the *Series,* or Furnivall make sense in the context of the endless go-betweens required in courtly literature. Examining the transient figure of the lord Health allows readers to assess the patron-function in Hoccleve's work without undue distraction by Lancastrian or other historical claims.

It might seem as if, in Hoccleve's work generally, we hear entirely too much about patrons, hence the long-standing accusations of venality. Yet his approach to them evinces not braggadocio but a healthy caution. Hoccleve tends to communicate with patron figures strictly via intermediaries, creating bourgeois hypostases, second selves of a similar class, to interpose between the poet-persona and potential patrons. Here in the *Male Regle,* Furnivall, a government officer, even stands between him and the fictive Lord Health. This approach allows the poet to perform polyphonically, to model the kind of reception he hopes to achieve, but it also insulates his poetic voice from the potentially engulfing power of aristocratic-courtly subjectivity and language. Thus nowhere in Hoccleve's work is his narrator subjected to the kind of humiliating conversation that Chaucer's narrator has, for instance, with the Black Knight in the *Book of the Duchess,* in which the Knight's tortured chess metaphor confounds the plain-speaking poet completely. Hoccleve's name-dropping of his patrons appears servile, but in fact its consequences are liberating. As is always the case with name-dropping, it is not proximity to, but distance from, the patron that is revealed, and this distance is carefully mediated by poetic devices like the *Regiment's* old man or the friend in the *Series,* continuously foregrounding the poet's subjectivity at the expense of the remote patron.

The apostrophized Lord Health is finally impossible to locate, not least because he is so firmly annexed to the subjectivity of the poet. He barely coheres as an allegorical persona, or even as the addressee, being chronically described as an epiphenomenon of the poet's own experience and physicality, and often one that can only be inferred negatively: "While thy power, and excellent vigour / . . . Regned in me and was my governour / Than was I wel" (lines 9–12) or "My grief and busy smart cotidien / So me laboren and tormenten sore / That what thou art now wel remember I can" (lines 25–27). Hoccleve, in the past, participated in Health, just as he currently does in Health's evil twin, Sickness, who now holds him in wrongful subjection. Eight stanzas describing the poet's actions and symptoms follow. The poet-persona claims to be overmastered by both of these figures, patron and foe, yet in the narration they exist only as his subsidiaries. He is therefore talking not only about, but to, himself. Hoccleve is well aware of the extent to which his style figures himself as the primary audience: "Ey, what is, me, that to myself, thus longe / Clappid haue I" (lines 393–94), he exclaims before turning to his final address to Health at the poem's end.

Courtly discourse is an object of bathos in the *Male Regle*. The humble Hoccleve appears as Health's tenant-in-chief:

> From hennes foorth wole I do reuerence
> Un-to thy name and holde of thee in cheef,
> And werre make, and sharp resistence
> Ageyn thy fo and myn, that cruel theef,
> That undir foote me halt in mescheef,
> So thou me to thy grace reconcyle.
>
> (lines 49–54)

This embattled figure is the same Hoccleve who is so afraid of bar brawls that even when tipsily indiscreet he will only whisper criticisms (lines 171–72). He begs for "socour and relief" (line 55) against the "keene assautes" (line 58) of dyspepsia. Later we learn that his malady has several other, less comical, meanings: poverty, and possibly venereal disease. Knightly language is a delusion; it cannot describe Hoccleve's reality, only mockingly indicate his lack of status. Yet even this transient investment in pseudo-feudalism points out several features of Hoccleve's critical view of lordship: lords are fickle and easily alienated and it is incumbent upon the subject to take action and accept blame because of it. The poet does not blame Health for his predicament of abandonment, but rather his own spendthrift and overindulgent habits, just as, later in the *Regiment* prologue, he does not accuse the government, which had let his pay lapse into arrears, dwelling instead on the world's general uncertainty. In both cases the king, Hoccleve's ultimate employer, is responsible for the lack of coin that impels the poems and that is figured as the poet's disease in both of them, as physical sickness in the *Male Regle* and as mental anxiety in the *Regiment* prologue. No one external to the poet can be blamed for a disease, yet it provides a spectacle worthy of relief, hence the poet's self-pathologization. Hoccleve's somatic symptoms record his economic condition, and he writes about them in order to make a bid at workman's compensation without naming names. Hoccleve also expects Health, as a lord, to respond to the threat of aristocratic competition; the lowly poet might not appear on his radar, but his rival Sickness poaching his retainers must get his attention. Likewise, lordship is understood overall as a relationship cemented by cash, as the poet's new lord, Sickness, "habundantly . . . paieth [him] his wage" (line 119).

The segue he uses to make the transition from penitential autobiography to advice likewise points up the inadequacy of culturally sanctioned discourses, in this case classical stories, to capture the quotidian reality of the poet's fifteenth-century London life: the lazy Hoccleve, taking ferries he can ill afford across the river back to his lodgings from his nightly carousing, overtipping in his foolish delight at being called "maistir" by the flattering boatmen, is ridiculously, if obliquely, compared to Ulysses in his maritime encounter with the sirens (lines 185–208, 233–64). Failing to stop his ears with wax or tie himself to the mast in order to avoid succumbing to dangerously attractive and all-consuming utterances (as mermaids are cannibals, line 249), the poet becomes his own object lesson, enabling him to rebuke not only himself but assorted and unspecified "folk of hy degree" (line 210). The result of this dual address and its bathetic comparison is typically pointed: Hoccleve, lured only into overspending by the siren voices of the ferrymen, is a poor equivalent of Ulysses, where "lordes" whose rank would justify the comparison and have been taken in by similar "fauel" (line 244) may be "envolupid in cryme" (line 245) to an extent coterminous with their greater status.

The poet has the only convincing corporeality in the poem, a body that eats and drinks (line 106), has hands (line 115), a mouth (line 114) and a heart (line 131), suffers from heat (line 189), inclement weather (line 193), and the pains of overeating, blushes (line 159) and fears physical blows (line 175). At the same time, his bodily distress reflects his financial constraint. His lost lord Health is a "tresor" (line 1) initially rhymed with wealth (lines 6–8), and Hoccleve's body, isolated from Health, is empty and bare (line 14), like a purse; he suffers from the "penylees maladie" (line 130); he seeks to be "releeued / Of body and purs" (lines 386–87), and his "poore purs and peynes stronge" force him to utter his plea (line 395). His body is doubly instrumental, conveying his need by the drama of his suffering while simultaneously participating in a ludic metaphor. Where Chaucer, in the begging poem

Chaucer's Complaint to His Purse, simply addresses his purse in mock chivalric language, Hoccleve swallows his purse and becomes it, allowing its disabling emptiness to be part of him. This is a typically Hocclevean superimposition, and it generates a more complex poem, but more crucially, it generates a body for the poet that is not available in Chaucer. It is a paradoxical body, both experiential and metaphorical, present and absent, and crucial to both aspects of it is the supposed venality of the begging poem. The poet composes himself out of the occasion of his poem.

Hoccleve achieves here, and was to develop further in his later poems, an embodied historical persona that has enough weight to be the subject of a personal history and a narrative perspective. He extends to the poet the condition of "impersonated artistry," which H. Marshall Leicester claims that Chaucer created for the personae of the *Canterbury Tales.* Leicester admits that Chaucer did not grant the poet this privilege, instead expressing "the poet's desire to be and have a self of his own" indirectly by ventriloquizing and impersonating external characters.[39] Hoccleve does the inverse: he internalizes various preexisting voices, consecutively or simultaneously, seeking to constitute himself out of their resources. Both are responses to the impasse of the poet's estatelessness in later medieval England. In neither case has the poet's self wholly coalesced, but Hoccleve's formula at least offers a way forward and gives the poet some interiority, indeed, a virtual amphitheater, full of echoes. Speakers seem to cohere admirably in the *Canterbury Tales,* although they disperse under examination, composed as they are by multiple layers of voicing: Alison, for example, in *The Miller's Tale,* has a distinctive body and turn of phrase, but she is voiced by the Miller, reported by Chaucer the pilgrim, and all in turn are invisibly produced by the implied poet. She cannot speak herself. Hoccleve has trouble convincing us that he is all there, but his basically lyric identity, in which everything is marshaled behind the poetic I, means that if he is anyone, he must be himself. He deliberately breaks down the traditionally imagined body social—the three estates and the genres in which they are typically represented—into their constituent elements, so that they can be recombined to articulate the new poetic professional. This helps to explain the eerie floating quality of his work, in which voices fade in and

---

[39] H. Marshall Leicester Jr., *The Disenchanted Self: Representing the Subject in the Canterbury Tales* (Berkeley and Los Angeles: University of California Press, 1990), p. 412.

out, and narration veers between the general and the particular. Yet Hoccleve is less of a lone gunman in this deconstructive assault on the estates than we might think, if we look again at the drive toward compendiousness of other late medieval English poems—at the large cast of the *Canterbury Tales,* for example, or at *Piers Plowman.* Langland's poem totters under its own weight of social types, as Langland strives to externalize facets of himself via a veritable human zoo. Some of this is a quest to express Christian universality, but some of the impetus to multiply personae must also be compensation for the frustratingly inadmissible personhood of the poet.

The first thing Hoccleve does with his experimental new body is to take it out whoring. This is titillating, but also expedient and thematically relevant. Spending on prostitutes as well as victuals allows his persona to get even more acutely and embarrassingly into debt—and this debt is the ostensible reason for his utterance. Further, it allows him to demonstrate concupiscence, that changeable state of worldly appetite, more comprehensively, and locates the poem generically as a typical *exemplum* against the tavern sins of gluttony, lust, and sloth. The poet has hermeneutic interests in the concept of concupiscence and needs to highlight the motility of its objects of desire: food and drink, women, and, latterly, text. Finally, the ways in which the poet-persona interacts with the whores models appropriate financial behavior, of the kind that Hoccleve hopes to elicit from his patrons, Furnivall and Health.

Hoccleve opens his section on whores with the coy device of *occupatio,* claiming that he "dar nat telle" (line 137) how they attracted him frequently to the Paul's Head tavern (line 143). Incidentally, he manages to describe them:

> venus lusty femel children deere
> That so goodly, so shaply were, and feir,
> And so plesant of port and of maneere,
> And feede cowden al a world with cheere,
> And of atyr passyngly wel byseye
> (lines 138–42)

From this description it is difficult to distinguish these women—common women or prostitutes, who often sought customers in taverns in the liberties of Southwark and Westminster—from well-dressed and well-mannered bourgeois or noble women. We could be reading about aristocratic ladies in a romance, although the first line would likely force a readjustment toward bourgeois women in a fabliau. This potential confusion of status is typical of discourse about prostitutes in the medieval and early modern periods, as Ruth Mazo Karras and others have demonstrated: in principle, a whore or common woman was like all women in her fundamental licentiousness, demonstrating feminine appetite in her multiple sexual partners, from whom she might, or might not, accept money. In practice, prostitution in the London area was an informally regulated trade that urban authorities tolerated in the suburbs outside their jurisdiction, carried on by some identifiable individuals in *de facto* licensed establishments in Southwark as well as by a large and transient class of part-timers who worked taverns, alehouses, fairs and markets, and major thoroughfares or harvest periods, or out of private dwellings.[40] Never having achieved the recognition implied by schemes of municipal regulation into civic brothels, or court sanction by participating in state rituals, as in France and Italy, prostitution in England remained a gray area. The prostitute in fifteenth-century Westminster, like the poet, practiced an ill-defined profession. Hoccleve, recognizing their kinship as urban service providers, entertainers, and functionaries of a new moral order of consumer relations, seeks to make poet and whore mutually defining.

The whores appear to be primarily figured as consumers, as the poet describes the sweet wine and wafers (lines 145–46)—both deluxe commodities once reserved for the elite, but now more widely available to a commercial public—they devour at his expense, explaining that "this conpaignie / That I spak of been sumwhat likerous / Where as they

---

[40] For an overview of medieval English prostitution, see Ruth Mazo Karras, "Sex, Money, and Prostitution in Medieval English Culture; Proceedings of a Conference Held at the University of Toronto," in *Desire and Discipline: Sex and Sexuality in the Premodern West,* ed. Jacqueline Murray and Konrad Eisenbichler (Toronto: University of Toronto Press, 1996), pp. 201–16; Ruth Mazo Karras, "Theoretical Issues: Prostitution and the Question of Sexual Identity in Medieval Europe," *Journal of Women' s History* 11, no. 2 (1999): 159–78; Ruth Mazo Karras and David Lorenzo Boyd, " 'Ut Cum Muliere': A Male Transvestite Prostitute in Fourteenth-Century London," in *Premodern Sexualities,* ed. Louise Fradenburg and Carla Freccero (New York: Routledge, 1996), pp. 101–16. To compare the sex trade in medieval England and Europe, see Ruth Mazo Karras, "Prostitution in Medieval Europe," in *Handbook of Medieval Sexuality,* ed. Vern L. Bullough and James A. Brundage (New York: Garland, 1996), pp. 243–60; and Jacques Rossiaud, *Medieval Prostitution,* trans. Lydia G. Cochrane (Oxford: Basil Blackwell, 1988). For a defense of Chaucer's prioress against being involved in the trade in Southwark, see Henry Ansgar Kelly, "Bishop, Prioress, and Bawd in the Stews of Southwark," *Speculum* 75, no. 2 (2000): 342–88.

mowe a draght of wyn espie" (lines 146–48). He returns to the elevated pseudo-courtly language he had used in his address to the lord Health, continuing grandly that "to suffer hem paie, had been no courtesie: / That charge I took, to wynne love and thank" (lines 151–52); this bathetic "courtesie" points out that common women likewise have no place in language, as their transactions can merely and unflatteringly mime aristocratic ones. In a typical double usage, Hoccleve the commoner poet takes on their "charge," responsibility for their protection in magnatial terms, while prosaically accepting the real charge, paying. The language of lordship is hyperbolically meaningless and unquantifiable, but the cash transaction is ethically real, as it places Hoccleve in debt that he must now repay. The poet borrowed from friends due to his pay arrears (lines 369–70), and now Hoccleve is acting as his creditors' agent as well as his own in asking for his salary to be released. The money spent on the whores encodes a specific amount of obligation between men that cannot be dispelled (unlike the flimsy patronage of the Lord Health) and it records payment for a specific set of services, thus professionalizing them. As the whores are paid up front for their work, albeit in kind, and the taverners and ferrymen are paid cash, while Hoccleve remains unpaid waiting for his annuity, it is the value of their labor that lies at the heart of the poem, the labor that imposes value on all others. Compared to these tavern trades, Hoccleve's nebulous court patronage, the hierarchical system of relationships that was supposed to guarantee his government pay, is virtually worthless: thus he tries to redefine the terms, and employ the values of the former against the latter. The *Male Regle* exists as a record of his own apparent folly, but also as a record of labors duly performed and services dispensed, paid for justly, which now constitute a debt on the part of the poet that ought to be served by the government in the name of social order. Moral coherence breaks down at the level of the poet, that is, at the point of transition between one system and the other, the cash economy and the economy of feudal promises. Hoccleve comically offers himself up as the fall guy in a moral drama that is actually an indictment of the empty deferrals of noble patronage: everybody pays cash but princes. They just charge it.

Keen consumers as the whores are, they are also consumables; they "feede cowden al a world with cheere" (line 141) and are listed immediately after food and drink as objects of Hoccleve's overindulgence. Their own consumption of wine, "Sweete, and in wirkynge hoot for the maistrie / To warme a stomak with" (lines 149–50)—heating the section of the body closest to the genitals—renders them easily into objects of consumption, gluttony transforming in their bodies into lust, unifying two of the three so-called tavern sins. Yet while the whores are themselves products, they are producers, too: they attract the poet to the tavern "to talke of mirthe and to disporte and pleye" (line 144), retailing services, verbal and physical. Again the pseudo-courtly vocabulary highlights the lack of a specific status for this kind of transaction. The fact that the poet intends the notoriously double words "disporte" and "pleye" in their specifically sexual senses is confirmed in his protestation:

> Of loues aart yit touched I no deel;
> I cowde nat and eek it was no neede:
> Had I a kus, I was content ful weel,
> Bettre than I wolde han be with the deede.
>
> (lines 153–56)

We are less likely to believe Hoccleve in his disingenuous denials of full participation because he began this episode with an *occupatio* that resisted but performed full disclosure. He then continues in innuendo by concluding with airy generality: "Of him that hauntith tauerne of custume / At shorte wordes, the profyt is this / In double wyse, his bagge it shal consume" (lines 161–63) and leaves the topic with a final crashing pun, "my thank is queynte [i.e., extinguished/female genitalia], my purs, his stuf hath lore" (lines 349). Regardless of the precise nature of the services in which he partook, the poet-persona evidently paid the whores for their time and was satisfied with the justice of the transaction. His demands as a consumer were met. He acknowledges that he was paying for their labor, a joint product of their bodies and their intentions, both commodified: they work physically, but they also interact socially and deferentially with the customer. The address of the prostitute, the extent to which she is valued as an interlocutor, companion, subject, imaginary friend—as someone whose attention can be temporarily commanded—is a feature of her identity to which Hoccleve is attentive. Hoccleve, in fact, is one of the best literary witnesses of prostitution in the English Middle Ages; they are one of the most prominent categories of women he discusses throughout his longer works, especially in the *Series*. While some of this interest in their position might be prurient, or connected to their femininity and marginality—a potentially empowering rhetorical space for male poets in the later medieval period—I think that much of it reflects a sense of professional kinship. The *Male Regle,* at least, invests in the role of the whore because it models the role of the poet, the excessive consumer becoming the object of entertaining textual, if not sexual, consumption. The ways in which the prostitutes fluctuate from subject to object in the text map the similar processes going on in the poet's own persona, and for the same reason: professional invisibility. Hoccleve is doing his best to transform his patrons into johns, as he stands a better chance of getting paid that way than by waiting for his annuity. In fact, only those who perform whorishly will succeed in the service environment of Privy Seal, as he makes clear by claiming that his friends and fellow hard-living bureaucrats Prentys and Arondel only prosper because they "Lordes reconforten in sundry wyse" (line 336) and he has finally decided to follow their example.

The *Male Regle* is a poem that takes a ludic view of concupiscence, or at least of the tavern sins. Instead of eradicating worldly desires by confessing them, the poet reifies them by narrating them, and offering to exchange the result, the poetic text, for his pay. His patrons, Health and Furnivall, as well as readers, are brought into a circle of venal reduplication, in which worldliness is contained in, not expelled by, language. This is precisely the fear of representation, of imitation of life without transcending it, that exercised late medieval spiritual directors in discussing confession, and with which Langland grapples in Passus 5 of *Piers Plowman.*[41] There he has the Seven Deadly Sins unavailingly confess themselves; as personifications, whose meanings are contained in their names (i.e., coterminous with their forms of representation), they cannot leave themselves behind by verbal articulation. They cannot erase, but only repeat, themselves in language. Langland's horror at the inevitable surplus of linguistic representation is grossly evident in his own tavern scene in Passus 5, the bilious episode of Gluttony overeating, boozing, gossiping, and finally throwing up. The proverb that he alludes to in order to cap this episode—"Dogs always return to their own vomit"[42]—is sternly meant to apply both to wasted food and wasted

---

[41] A. V. C. Schmidt, ed., *William Langland: The Vision of Piers Plowman,* 2nd ed. (London: J. M. Dent, 1995), Passus 5, lines 65–461. Langland citations are from this edition.

[42] This proverb is the basis of Langland's lines: "Is noon so hungry hound in Hertfordshire / Dorste lap of that levynge, so unlovely it smaughte!" (B.5.356–57).

words, pointing up the dangerous materiality of language itself, his own medium. Language can be an object of desire; confession can be falsely cathartic. Hoccleve's *Male Regle* presupposes both, and adds the final insult of offering the resulting text as an object of commercial exchange. Langland's impaired sacrament reveals his anxiety about the worldly condition of human language; Hoccleve's satirical confession, on the other hand, embraces this condition and seeks to gain by it, incidentally allowing the historical world its legitimate place and allotting to the poet the task of representing it. It is the instrumentality of this poetry, its seemingly cheap admission of its own goal of remuneration, which is the precondition for committed verisimilitude: the historical world has value insofar as its poetic reflex does. The world as a place of valid occupation is built up around the figure of the poet.

It is Hoccleve's impersonation of himself in the tavern scene of the *Male Regle* that transforms and extends the traditional meanings of such scenes. By placing himself, a poetic I with the name of the historical poet, inside an *exemplum* against tavern sins—and within the conventions of allegorical reading, which render him into a static exemplification of vice in that context—the poet insists on his own powerlessness, apparent captive of the genre, doomed to repeat the same sins for others' moral edification. His increasingly urgent protestations of reform show the confessional voice associated with the dynamic process of penance apparently fighting the vicious hermeneutic circle of allegorical identity, the same battle that is staged in Langland's Passus 5. However, his confessional address is not to a priest, but to his supposed liege lord, Health, and his functionary, Furnivall; it is occasional rather than sacramental, part of a political rather than a spiritual economy. Confessional energy does not prevail against exemplary inertia: the poet-narrator, busily declaring withdrawal from excess and misrule, does so by producing a poem that is itself excessive—hyperbolical, full of puns, oxymoron,[43] and genre play—jumbled and unruly, and determinedly profane. However, this particular tavern sinner is the historical poet and Privy Seal clerk, Thomas Hoccleve, professional writer and person in service. He has justification for his performance that is not available to Langland's personifications: it is his trade. In his discussion of the prostitutes and other taverners, he has already established the ethical priority of

---

[43] For a study of this figure of speech in this poem, see W. A. Davenport, "Thomas Hoccleve's *La Male Regle* and Oxymoron," *ES* 82, no. 6 (2001): 497–506.

service trades, and the necessity of paying for services already dispensed. The superfluous, code-switching, self-serving language of the poem calls attention to its own status as service, and the chronic belatedness of representation that so worried Langland ensures that this work necessarily appears as service already performed: the poet has been debauched and indebted, corrected, made into a moral example and an entertaining spectacle, the result of which is this poem, which constitutes a bill for time already expended.

Chaucer's *Pardoner's Prologue and Tale* had previously ironized an *exemplum* against tavern sins by placing it in the mouth of an unreliable narrator. In Chaucer, the tale of tavern riot is told as a straight *exemplum* in the third person, generically separated from the confession of personal venality made by the Pardoner in the *Prologue* that destabilizes its interpretation. Hoccleve achieves a similar effect, but adds to it the professional bonus of establishing a proprietary discourse for the poet simply by changing its voicing. He does so by superimposing *The Poet's Prologue* and *The Poet's Tale,* introjecting the venal narrator into the *exemplum* and playing Pardoner and tavern rioter at the same time. Unlike Chaucer's Pardoner, a professional preacher with goals both transcendental and financial, the poet narrator of the *Male Regle* need not be condemned for his venal performance: it is part of his vocation, simply a kind of value-added service reminding his patrons of related bureaucratic services forgoing. The poem is allowed to be both instrument and artifice, produced openly by the poet for his professional ends. Chaucer the implied poet, neither preacher nor pardoner himself, likewise produces both the confessional Pardoner and his tale of the rioters in the *Canterbury Tales* as art, but he cannot step forward definitively to claim ownership of his own supervening and secular poetic vision because of his commitment to multiple levels of narration that necessarily diminish his own agency.

Hoccleve, by dint of his chronically complaining persona, keeps the secular poet front and center as the logical spokesperson for the disenchanted world. If we read the *Male Regle* and, in the words of H. Marshall Leicester, "attend consistently to the "I" of the text," we can arrive at: "a voice-oriented reading [that] would treat the second and third persons of a discourse (respectively the audience and the world), expressed or implied, primarily as indications of what the speaker maintains about audience and world and would examine how these elements are reflexively constituted as evidence of the character of this particular subject."[44] This reading yields us up not just impersonated artistry, but the impersonated artist, an enworlded self whose professional perspective rationalizes the buying and selling of commodities and services in the marketplace of the tavern into a legitimate system, upon which he models the conduct of his own poetic trade. While his drunk and disorderly persona carries with it an echo of the old voice of the goliard, available since the eleventh century, it also looks forward to other, more lionized, rebellious poet-personae of the late fifteenth century like Dunbar or François Villon. Hoccleve's resemblance to complaining courtier-poet Eustache Deschamps and some other Middle French predecessors has already been noted,[45] but Middle English scholars have hardly dared to compare Hoccleve proleptically to Villon, despite their common discourses of sex, money, disease, and disenfranchisement, and despite the fact that there is only one small step between presenting the secular poet as an oddball and presenting him as a rogue. Hoccleve's tavern is a profitable business rather than the resort of criminals, but it nonetheless helps him to provide a blueprint for a new form of counter-courtly subjectivity.

---

[44] *Disenchanted Self,* p. 10.

[45] See J. A. Burrow, "Hoccleve and the Middle French Poets," in *The Long Fifteenth Century: Essays for Douglas Gray,* ed. Helen Cooper and Sally Mapstone (Oxford: Clarendon Press, 1997), pp. 35–49; and William Calin, *The French Tradition and the Literature of Medieval England* (Toronto: University of Toronto Press, 1994), pp. 399–418.

English Poetry, July–October 1399, and Lancastrian Crime

David R. Carlson
University of Ottawa

"A MASTER OF LIES AND DISSIMULATION" is how J. W. Sherbourne characterized the person who made himself king of England by October 1399: "It is hard to think of another moment of comparable importance in medieval English political history when the supply of information was so effectively manipulated as it was by Henry IV on this occasion." Sherbourne has it further that the earliest "clear evidence" of a perjured intention to make himself king on Henry's part, his various solemn undertakings to the contrary notwithstanding, was in an effort to manage information. In August 1399, Henry dispatched writs ordering scrutiny of all *chronicae* "regni Angliae statum tangentes et gubernationem, a tempore Willelmi conquaestoris usque ad tempus praesens" ["touching on the status and governance of the realm of England from the time of William the Conqueror up to the present"], the intelligence gathered thereby—the pertinent chronicles themselves, under seal, in possession of persons "qui scirent respondere competenter et docere de chronicis supradictis" ["competent to explain the chronicles aforesaid and make answer"]—to be dispatched to Westminster for use of a committee there charged with considering the matter of Richard's deposition and Henry's accession to the throne ("deponendi regem Ricardum et Henricum Lancastrie ducem subrogandi in regem materia").[1]

For correction and advice, thanks are due the editor, as well as Steven Justice and R. F. Yeager; also, the other interlocutors of the "Lancastrian Politics of Culture" seminar in the University of Ottawa, especially Andrew Taylor, Siobhan Bly Calkin, and Geoff Rector; and finally, A. G. Rigg, who, *i. a.*, did the better part of the work of reconstructing the text in the appendix.

[1] James W. Sherborne, "Perjury and the Lancastrian Revolution of 1399," *Welsh History Review* 14 (1988): 218 and 239. The fundamental work on the various accounts of the deposition was that of Maude Violet Clarke and V. H. Galbraith, "The Deposition of Richard II," *Bulletin of the John Rylands Library* 14 (1930): 125–81 (rpt. in Clarke,

The chief product of the committee's portentous labors was the October 1399 "Record and Process of the Deposition of Richard II," with its stunning preambular deceit, narrating Richard's willing resignation of the crown ("vultu hillari"), twice, on separate occasions.[2] The "Record and Process" was enrolled in the rolls of parliament, as the state-official record of events, and then it was also broadcast about the kingdom in various forms—in English even, and with key passages put about in brief pamphlets—coming thereby to dominate the English historical record after the fact, through the work of the compliant chroniclers who used it.[3]

Fourteenth Century Studies, ed. Lucy S. Sutherland and May McKisack [Oxford: Clarendon, 1937], pp. 53–90), esp. 137–55, as Sherbourne acknowledges. Sherbourne's insight is the connection between the passage in Walsingham on the writs' dispatch and Adam Usk's participant's account of the committee work at Westminster, bespeaking regal ambitions on Henry's part (in *The Chronicle of Adam Usk 1377–1421,* ed. and trans. Chris Given-Wilson [Oxford: Clarendon, 1997], p. 62): "Item per sertos doctores, episcopos et alios, quorum presencium notator unus extiterat, deponendi regem Ricardum et Henricum Lancastrie ducem subrogandi in regem materia, et qualiter et ex quibus causis iuridice, committebatur disputanda. Per quos determinatum fuit quod periuria, sacrilegia, sodomidica, subditorum exinnanitio, populi in seruitutem redactio, uecordia, et ad regendum inutilitas, quibus rex Ricardus notorie fuit infectus, per capitulum *Ad apostolice,* extractus de *Re iudicata* in Sexto, cum ibi notatis, deponendi Ricardum cause fuerant sufficientes." Walsingham's complete remark is: "Litterae praeterea missae sunt ad omnes Abbathias regni, et majores ecclesias, ut praelati dictarum ecclesiarum perscrutari facerent cunctas Chronicas regni Angliae statum tangentes et gubernationem, a tempore Willelmi conquaestoris usque ad tempus praesens; ut mitterent certas personas instructas in chronicis, secum ferentes hujusmodi chronicas, sub sigillis communibus dictorum locorum, qui scirent respondere competenter et docere de Chronicis supradictis. Et hae quidem apices missae fuerunt sub nomine regis Ricardi, et privato sigillo suo": *Chronica maiora,* in "Annales Ricardi secundi," ed. Henry Thomas Riley, in *Johannis de Trokelowe, et Henrici de Blaneforde, monachorum S. Albani, necnon quorundam anonymorum Chronica et Annales,* Rolls Series 28, pt. 3 (London: Longmans, Green, Reader, and Dyer, 1866), p. 252. As it happens, all the quotations of Walsingham herein are from this portion of the *Chronica,* henceforth cited as *Annales.* On the peculiar editorial state in which the Rolls Series editions put Walsingham's work, see esp. Galbraith, "Thomas Walsingham and the Saint Albans Chronicle, 1272–1422," *EHR* 47 (1932): 12–30; also George B. Stow, "Richard II in Thomas Walsingham's Chronicles," *Speculum* 59 (1984): 68–102.

[2] Sherbourne, "Perjury and the Lancastrian Revolution," p. 218: "Who today believes a word of it?" The "Record and Process" is printed in *Rotuli parliamentorum: ut et petitiones, et placita in parliamento,* ed. Richard Blyke, John Strachey et al., 8 vols. (London: [s. n.], 1780–1832), III, 416–24, the portion here referred to and quoted being at III, 416–17.

[3] On the creation and recirculation of the "Record and Process," most instructive may yet be H. G. Richardson, "Richard II's Last Parliament," *EHR* 52 (1937): esp. 40–42, though on the poets see also Paul Strohm, "Saving the Appearances: Chaucer's 'Purse' and the Fabrication of the Lancastrian Claim," in *Hochon's Arrow: The Social Imagination of Fourteenth-Century Texts* (Princeton: Princeton University Press, 1992), pp. 75–94. On the excerpts surviving in the form of a single conjugate bifolium (London,

Poets of similar disposition may also have been enlisted to help fabricate the record, at just the same moment when the writs of research went out, in August 1399. The evidence is all indirect, only tractable by paranoiac inference: once or twice might be accidents of enthusiasm; more, it begins to look like conspiracy, and there survive five "English" poems, all sharing the same curious array of properties. All purport to have been written late in the summer of 1399, before the deposition of Richard II, castigating his regime and calling for the Lancastrian invasion and usurpation that were then only in progress. Despite generic differences among them suggesting different intended audiences, the poems concur in using the same odd enigmatic allegorical idiom, in a way otherwise unparalleled in the literature. And all also converge on exonerating Henry of murder and perjury, when he had acted as a king, while still promising publicly that he did not want to be one, by ordering execution of the Ricardian officers Scrope, Bussy, Green, and Bagot.

Helen Barr has suggested that poets "may even have been part of the Lancastrian aim of legitimation."[4] What follows attempts to develop such evidence as there may be for conspiracy on the occasion, or collaboration in some sense (though possibly still only coincidence): (1) the poems' statements about their own chronologies, false and true; (2) the matters of their generic distribution and peculiar style; (3) their contributions to politics, in the narrowest sense, concerned with the current struggle within the ruling elite for control of the surplus-extraction mechanisms, in land-tenure and the repressive apparatus of state; and (4) the context of the broad current effort to represent as righteous and lawful the lawlessness and crime used to put the Lancastrian regime in place—to make *Henricus pius*—with which, one way or another, the poets complied.

British Library, Stowe 66), see H. G. Wright, "The Protestation of Richard II in the Tower in September, 1399," *BJRL* 23 (1939): esp. 154–55; some of its contents are collated in G. O. Sayles, "The Deposition of Richard II: Three Lancastrian Narratives," *Bulletin of the Institute of Historical Research* 54 (1981): 264–66.

[4] In the chapter "Unfixing the King: Gower's *Cronica tripertita* and *Richard the Redeless*," in *Socioliterary Practice in Late Medieval England* (Oxford: Oxford University Press, 2001), p. 79. Other cases of royal enlistment of poets are known: the early case (1314) of Edward II and the poet "Baston" is discussed in A. G. Rigg, "Antiquaries and Authors: The Supposed Works of Robert Baston, O. Carm.," in *Medieval Scribes, Manuscripts and Libraries: Essays Presented to N. R. Ker,* ed. M. B. Parkes and Andrew G. Watson (London: Scolar, 1978), pp. 317–31; and recently, an early fifteenth-century attempt by Henry IV to employ Christine de Pizan has been argued, in R. F. Yeager, "Chaucer's 'To His Purse': Begging, Or Begging Off?" *Viator* 36 (2005): esp. 399–401 and 407–10.

The Poems and Their Imputable Dates

First comes a brief Latin verse oration, beginning "O deus in celis, cuncta disponens fidelis," in forty-two lines of Leonine hexameters.[5] The poem refers to Henry Bolingbroke repeatedly, never as anything greater than *dux,* moreover, as *dux Lancastrie* (27; also 30 "Henricus, Lancastrie"), a title apt for him only briefly, during some period in the interval between the death of his father, the duke of Lancaster John of Gaunt (d. 3 February 1399) and his own assumption of regal style, as Henry IV, publicly 30 September 1399, though when precisely in this period cannot be established: Henry was legally disbarred from doing homage for the ducal title after 18 March 1399 and in fact never formally acceded to it; likewise, though careful not to use regal style himself before 30 September, others may have been readier to entitle Henry somewhat sooner than he was.[6] In addition to complaining of common suffering and bad counsel around the throne (14 "Consilium tale pereat a sede regali"), "O deus in celis" calls specifically for Henry's invasion in force (31 "Scutis <patronus> nos protegat vndique pronus!") and for violent uprising on his behalf (28 "Huius consortes estote per omnia fortes!" and 38 "Expedit armare, nos a somno vigilare"), as if he had not yet invaded and gathered armed support to him.

Similarly brief, in ninety short-lined rhyming English verses, ballad-like, is a poem called "On King Richard's Ministers" by its earliest modern editor.[7] This item makes some allusion to earlier events, of the pe-

---

[5] A text and translation are essayed in the Appendix below. The poem was published by Thomas Wright, *Political Poems and Songs Relating to English History Composed During the Period from the Accession of EDW. III. to that of RIC. III.,* Rolls Series 14, 2 vols. (London: Longman, 1859–61), I, 366–68.

[6] The disbarment was implicit in parliament's revocation—itself later treated as perjured or otherwise illegal—of certain royal letters patent earlier granted Henry (see *Rotuli parliamentorum,* III, 372; also in S. B. Chrimes and A. L. Brown, *Select Documents of English Constitutional History* [London: Adam & Charles Black, 1961], p. 178), though the legal issues are involute; there is useful brief discussion in Nigel Saul, *Richard II* (New Haven: Yale University Press, 1997), pp. 403–4. The "Record and Process" itself is careful to call Henry *rex* only after he had claimed the formally vacated throne and been acclaimed or elected to it by the assembly (the first occurrence of the title applied to him comes at *Rotuli parliamentorum,* III, 423); earlier in the same document he is entitled only *dux.*

[7] Again, ed. Wright, *Political Poems and Songs,* I, 363–66. I cite the edition of the same poem, though under the title "There Is a Busch That Is Forgrowe," in James M. Dean, *Medieval English Political Writings,* Middle English Texts Series (Kalamazoo: Medieval Institute Publications, 1996), pp. 150–52. In Julia Boffey and A. S. G. Edwards, *A New Index of Middle English Verse* (London: British Library, 2005)—henceforth *NIMEV*—it is no. 3529.

riod of Richard's "Revenge" parliament, roughly August–September 1397, but to none later than Henry's landing in force at Ravenspur in the last few days of June 1399: Henry "is up and toke his flyt; / In the north contré he is light: / Thus here ye alle men saye" (43–45).[8] The same poem mentions the late duke of Gloucester's widow as still mournfully living and his son as missing, though the widow died 3 October 1399 and the son too, at uncertain date, though less than a month before his mother (he was still alive in August, apparently): Gloucester "is ded," says the poet, "his make is woo, / Her eldest bryd is taken her fro / In to an uncod place" (31–33).[9] By this its most definite evidence, the poem puts its own composition in July or possibly August 1399.

More complex and apparently some weeks later is the 857-line fragment now called *Richard the Redeless,* in English alliterative long lines, in the unique surviving manuscript distributed among four *passus,* as in *Piers Plowman.*[10] The poem's spatiotemporal scene setting is precise and clear enough at the outset (and the manuscript is evidently not defective here as it is elsewhere): from Bristol (1.2 "In a blessid borugh that Bristow is named"), the poet reports, Henry has returned to England, rallying support for professedly limited aims (not to make himself king, but only 1.13 "to rightyn his wronge"), while Richard is away campaigning in Ireland.

> So sore were the sawis of bothe two sidis:
> Of Richard that regned so riche and so noble,
> That wyle he werrid be west on the wilde Yrisshe,
> Henrri was entrid on the est half,
> Whom all the londe loued in lengthe and in brede,
> And rosse with him rapely to rightyn his wronge.
>
> (1.8–13)

Again, this was the situation in July 1399, and the poet is claiming that the outcome of such conflict as was in process could not yet be foreseen:

---

[8] The precise date of Henry's landing is not known; for discussion of the evidence, see Saul, *Richard II,* p. 408 and n.

[9] The deaths are reported, for example, in the *Vita Ricardi secundi,* ed. Stow, *Historia vitae et regni Ricardi Secundi* (Philadelphia: University of Pennsylvania Press, 1977), p. 155, though the various sources differ on particulars: see Stow's nn. 440–41, pp. 207–8, or Given-Wilson, *Chronicle of Adam Usk,* p. 61 n. 5.

[10] I cite the edition of Barr, in *The Piers Plowman Tradition* (London: Dent, 1993), pp. 101–33. On the setting and date, see Frank Grady, "The Generation of 1399," in *The Letter of the Law: Legal Practice and Literary Production in Medieval England,* ed. Emily Steiner and Candace Barrington (Ithaca: Cornell University Press, 2002), pp. 211–12.

"For it passid my parceit and my preifis also, / How so wondirffull werkis wolde haue an ende" (1.17–18).

These initial claims are not belied elsewhere in what survives of the poem. The poet describes Henry as leading his supporters regally one time—"In full reall aray he rood vppon hem euere"—though this does not amount to calling him king quite, and the preceding line entitles him *dux* only, albeit in similarly formulaic language: "a duke doughty in dedis of armes" (3.359–60). Also, from time to time, the poet tends to write as if Richard had already lost sovereignty, as a practical matter, beyond any hope of his recovering it. Twice, for example, the poet tells Richard, addressing him directly, that his manifold wrongdoings have "crasid youre croune for euere" (1.95; cf. 1.157): "But if God helpe, youre heruest is ynne" (1.166). Only the living are addressed in such terms, of course, and the poet is careful always to call Richard king, "oure crouned kynge" (pointedly, though, only "till Crist woll no lenger"):

> And as a [liage] to his [lord] though I lite hade,
> All myn hoole herte was his while he in helthe regnid.
> And for I [wuste] not witterly what shulde fall,
> Whedir God wolde [g]eue him grace sone to amende,
> To be oure gioure a[g]eyn or graunte it another,
> This made me to muse many tyme and ofte,
> Forto written him a writte to wissen him better,
> And to meuve him of mysserewle his mynde to reffresshe.
>
> (1.24–32)

The risks of admonishing a still-sovereign Richard II in this way must create suspicion of a postdeposition vantage point. It may be even probable that the poet was writing after the deposition, or was finishing up. Nevertheless, the poet's contrivances amount to avoidance of direct, unequivocal statements to the effect that Henry became king and Richard ceased to be, let alone that Richard was still later done to death. The summer of 1399 scene-setting at the outset may be a fiction, but it need not have been fictional by much time. There is no mention in the poem (allegorical or otherwise) of any event postdating the summer of 1399 by more than a few weeks.[11]

---

[11] The latest reference I find is to William Bagot's appearance in Henry's first parliament in October 1399, discussed below, pp. 397–8. Barr, "The Dates of *Richard the Redeless* and *Mum and the Sothsegger*," *N&Q* 235 (1990), esp. 271–72 (also, *Piers Plowman Tradition,* p. 261), suggests that the reference of *Richard* 2.17 is to events of January

The *Cronica tripertita* of John Gower (c. 1330–1408) ought not to be included here perhaps. It does not maintain consistently the same claim (fictional or otherwise) of predeposition composition.[12] Gower narrates a more extensive range of events than do the other poets—from the November 1386 establishment of the "Commission of Governance," chiefly, to the public obsequies for Richard II in February 1400—and often enough he seems clearly to be narrating with hindsight. Why else, for example, his assertion that the earl of Arundel's body had not yet reached its final place of rest (2.157–58 "Det deus hoc sciri, poterit quod adhuc sepeliri, / Eius et heredes proprias habeant sibi sedes" ["So he may rest in peace, God, let us know the place / And then his heirs may reacquire his proper space"]), unless Gower already knew that the body was to be moved again?

1400: the *Richard*-poet describes Richard's men's desertion of him at the time of the invasion, during July and August 1399, and comments that some at least of these liveried retainers, deerlike by virtue of their use of the Ricardian White Hart badge and their cowardice, kept some capacity to make trouble afterward or were allowed it: "But yet they had hornes half yere after." There was the rising against Henry in January 1400, occurring three months after he became king—at some point, say, between 30 September 1399 (the date of his public claim to the throne and acclamation) and 13 October 1399 (the date of the coronation)—though in the seventh month after his return to England, at roughly the beginning of July 1399. The *Richard*-poet's roundly vague dating-phrase "half yere after" appears formulaic, however, as is indicated by the evidence from *Richard* itself and other cognate poetry that Barr collects, "The Dates of *Richard the Redeless* and *Mum and the Sothsegger*," pp. 272–73, citing there also Elizabeth Salter's cautionary analysis of other parallels, "The Timeliness of *Wynnere and Wastoure*," *MÆ* 47 (1978), 40–65. The poet's phrase "But yet they had hornes half yere after" tends to suggest ignorance of January 1400 revolt, when such "hornes" as Richard's feral adherents had been left were no longer "had," but all lost, conclusively; the phrase may only mean what it says: at the moment of the invasion and usurpation, Henry was clement towards Richard's adherents (see below, pp. 402–4).

[12] See Grady, "The Generation of 1399," pp. 209–10. Often adduced in evidence on this point, erroneously, is *Cronica* 1.9 "Libro testante, stat cronica scripta perante," where the reference of *liber* and *cronica* must be to the *Vox clamantis,* treating events of the earlier period of Richard's rule, particularly its Book One on the Great Revolt of 1381 (*Cronica* 1.5 "Quomodo surrexit populus"). The *Vox clamantis* was written earlier ("perante") than the *Cronica tripertita,* and remained in circulation ("Libro testante, stat cronica scripta": also, the following line 1.10 "Est alibi dicta, transit nec ab aure relicta"), in some cases in manuscripts in which the *Cronica tripertita* followed it. In this prologue-like passage at the beginning of the *Cronica,* Gower is connecting his present work on the *Cronica* to the *Vox clamantis* by these references back to his earlier work. The line is mistranslated, "With this book as witness, the chronicle was written beforehand"—as if *liber* ("this book") and *cronica* ("the chronicle") refer to the *Cronica tripertita* itself—in Eric Stockton, *The Major Latin Works of John Gower* (Seattle: University of Washington Press, 1962), p. 290, adding a confused note on the passage, p. 471. For citing the *Cronica,* I use the text of G. C. Macaulay, ed., *The Latin Works,* in *The Complete Works of John Gower,* vol. 4 (Oxford: Clarendon, 1902), 314–43, though tacitly altering

Gower does intermittently invoke the notion that he was writing as events unfolded—journalism, in a fairly strict sense—even though the *Cronica*'s putatively current reportage often supersedes itself. For example, the second book pretends not to know what was to happen to the earl of Gloucester when he was arrested 11 July 1397 (2.50 "Nescit quo fine, sit vite siue ruine" ["He knows not whether life or death will be his fate"]). Soon, however, Gower goes on to tell what did happen: Gloucester was murdered in captivity, in late August 1397 (2.91–118), though in so doing Gower makes use of detailed information about the murder that came to light (or may have been fabricated) only long afterward, about October 1399. Then Gower ends his report of the murder with a prayer for Gloucester's proper burial, emphatically unisonant-couplet rhymed (2.117–18 "Det deus hoc fatum, sit adhuc quod corpus humatum, / Spiritus atque statum teneat sine fine beatum!" ["May God grant that his body find at last its rest, / And may his soul in heaven finally be blest!"]), as if it had not yet taken place. Gloucester had in fact been buried in England already by the end of September 1397, as Gower would already have known at the time of his writing this part of the *Cronica,* and the remains were reburied again about two years later, in late 1399, after Henry's accession. Still, at the end of this same Book Two, Gower announces a precise date for its composition, of September 1397 or immediately thereafter, claiming that it was current events of that moment that compelled him to pick up his pen:

> Anno bis deno primo, de sanguine pleno,
> Septembris mense feritas dominatur in ense!
> Tristis vt audiui, carmen scribendo subiui.
>
> [King Richard's reign, twice ten and one, a bloody year,
> September's moon—then sword and savagery ruled here!
> At this sad news to write my song I took my pen.]
> (2.340–42)

At the beginning of his final Book Three, to narrate events of early 1398 to early 1400, including the crucial revolutionary summer, Gower resumes the same fiction of current composition, as if at the later moment. The previous book had been written earlier, at the time of the

---

some of the edition's features of orthography and punctuation; the verse translations of it are courtesy of A. G. Rigg.

events it told, Gower reiterates; now he takes up his pen again, to write about more recent current events, as they too happen. Though Henry must in fact have been *rex* by the time these lines were written, Gower yet here calls him *dux;* the *rex* is still Richard:

> Regnum confractum, regis feritate subactum,
> Nuper defleui, lacrimas sed abinde quieui.
> Regnum purgatum, probitate ducis renouatum,
> Amodo ridebo, nec ab eius laude tacebo.

> [The kingdom torn apart and crushed by the king's rage
> I've recently bewailed, but now my grief's assuaged.
> For now I smile to see the kingdom purged and raised
> By the duke's prowess: now I'll always sing his praise]
>
> (3.3–6)

Genres and Allegorical Style

All these writings date themselves to the same period, July–October 1399, when even Gower claims to have been at work on the *Cronica tripertita;* despite this coincidence of occasion, the same poems yet embody a broad, even generic distribution, without overlapping one another much. The Leonine hexameter was the choice of both Gower and the "O deus in celis," which in fact shares a few other features, more unexpectedly, with the *Cronica tripertita.*[13] The meter was among the most elevate available—possibly the most elevate—and, especially in Gower's heavily spondaic treatment, it is stately: in Latin too, this was the antithesis of popular form.[14] The two poems deploy it in different generic registers, however. "O deus in celis" is a brief, simple oration, fit for the simplest sort of hand-to-hand circulation (if only among the clerically learned) by means of single-sheet copies. Gower's *Cronica,* on the other hand, is an ambitious narrative, grand in design, and also more costly to reproduce, copies of it necessarily built for longer-term storage rather than broadcast dispersal. Among the English-language poetry, by contrast, "On King Richard's Ministers" is strongly marked for generic popularity, broadside ballad-like in its length, line, and

---

[13] Verbal parallels are listed in the Appendix, nn. *ad* 1 and 15.

[14] There is comment in David R. Carlson, "A Rhyme Distribution Chronology of John Gower's Latin Poetry," *SP* 104 (2007): 15–55.

rhyme. Then *Richard the Redeless* is something else again: pamphlet-length, it seems, for putting about in single uncovered gatherings of a few sheets perhaps, not ballad-like but also not for storage by bound *volumen*. Significantly not a dream-vision, it is still deliberately in the *Piers Plowman* tradition, though it does not share the tradition's propensity for broad socioreligious criticism, learned but dissident: it uses the conventions apologetically rather, for castigating one faction of the great, to the benefit of another.[15]

What is missing is anything marked out, by language or genre, for the consumption of this same (nonclerical) elite social group itself—the titular nobility, including royals—whose hectic doings of 1399 provide the poems' subject matter. The genres not covered by the surviving poetry are the nobler ones: courtly lyric, dream-vision, and romance, in French or in English. With this exception of the local secular aristocracy (such persons as ought not to have required the sort of persuading undertaken by the surviving poems that their own antics were important), the poetry seems designed to reach out to a range of concerned niche-like audiences, with news of what was happening about the kingdom's governance, sometimes in the prophecy-like form of statements in advance of events, but one way or another in effect justifying, for nonnoble outsiders, what the Lancastrian regime did to put itself in power.

These choices imply a common authorial intention to address nontitled audiences—distinct, differing nontitled sectors, however, as the linguistic and generic differentiation of the poems one from another witnesses. Despite the sameness of non-noble address, the poems also share the peculiar allegorical conceit of referring to their chief figures by the same series of animal names, as well as other enigmatic forms of denomination, demonstrably aristocratic in bent or otherwise markedly nonpopular.

The poetry calls the victims of Richard's 1397 "Revenge" parliament *Olor* (or *Cignus, metri causa*), 'Swan' in English; *Vrsus* or 'Bear'; and *Equs,* 'Horse': respectively, Thomas of Woodstock (1355–97), duke of Gloucester; Thomas Beauchamp (c. 1339–1401), Earl of Warwick; and Richard Fitzalan (1346–97), Earl of Arundel and Surrey. No such appellation is used consistently for the king Richard in the same poetry, but for the invader Henry there are several: *Aquila* or 'Eagle' most often, though also 'Faulcon' (*Richard* 2.157) and 'Heron' (in "On King Rich-

---

[15] See Grady, "The Generation of 1399," esp. p. 210.

ard's Ministers")—comprehensively, "the blessid Bredd" or "the Fowle" (*Richard* 2.141 and 3.36 and elsewhere)—and possibly others.[16]

The Latin poems also feature a peculiar sort of riddling or punning interlingual denomination, recurrent in the English poems too but without the polyglot dimension. In the *Cronica,* for example, Gower calls Michael de la Pole "de puteo Michaelis" (1.109), literally, 'Michael of the pool' or 'pit,' as if translating French "de la" and English "pool" into Latin, simply enough. Likewise, though with a greater degree of difficulty, Gower uses "vestis stragulata"—literally, "burel cloth," after a coarse-grade of woolen fabric known as "burel" in English—in describing the 1388 execution of Richard's aged tutor Simon Burley, by decollation: "Corruit in fata gladii vestis stragulata" ["That burel-cloth fell to the sword, such was his fate"] (1.140). And so forth. Precisely the same sort of interlingual riddling occurs in the "O deus in celis" (30) too, where the poet uses "Ver"—Latin 'Spring' though here possibly also evoking French *vert*—and "Dumus"—Latin 'thorn-bush'—to refer to Henry Green and John Bussy, evidently pronounced like modern 'bushy.' The various references in the English poems to bushes ("Ther is a busch that is forgrowe"), for example, or even to the grass ("The long gras that is so grene")—discussed further below—work similarly, though without the linguistic complexities: to evoke names, by riddling references to stuff and things, allegorically.

Such manners of speaking were not common currency. An instructive contrast may be with the so-called John Ball Letters of 1381: in that case, there is evidence for popular circulation of the writings (multiple copies, independently derived, of widely variant, unstable texts that had been put about in oral and ephemeral written forms, like letters, such as could be folded up and put in pockets), in simple, irregular ("subliterary") English verse or rhymed prose, using largely self-evident allegorical codes (modeled after *Piers Plowman*), personification-like, drawn from popularly familiar processes of production, tilling, milling, and other varieties of quotidian making:

---

[16] Gower wrote an epigram too, inc. "H. aquile pullus"—ed. and trans. Yeager, *John Gower: The Minor Latin Works,* Middle English Texts Series (Kalamazoo: Medieval Institute Publications, 2005), p. 46—at about this same time. "Prophecia" is how the poem is labeled, and it does participate in a tradition of prophetic utterance by its use of the same enigmatic "Aquila" denomination for Henry, twice in its four lines. On it, see also Yeager, "Chaucer's 'To His Purse,'" p. 403.

Johon Schep, som tyme Seynte Marie prest of Yorke, and now of Colchestre, greteth wel Johan Nameles, and Johan the Mullere, and Johan Cartere, and biddeth hem that thei bee war of gyle in borugh, and stondeth togidre in Godes name, and biddeth Peres Ploughman go to his werk, and chastise wel Hobbe the Robbere, and taketh with yow Johan Trewman, and alle hiis felawes, and no mo, and loke schappe you to on heved, and no mo.

> Johan the Mullere hath ygrounde smal, smal, smal;
> The kynges sone of hevene schal paye for al.[17]

To the contrary, in the case of the 1399 poetry, the evidence is that contemporaries regarded the kind of riddling allegories the poems use as particularly difficult, fending off ready common apprehension. Gower himself wrote prose glosses to go with the *Cronica tripertita,* spelling out the tenor of the enigmatic appellations he uses ("Comes Northumbrie, cuius signum fuit luna crescens" ["The earl of Northumberland, whose device was a crescent moon"], e.g., is the gloss *ad* 1.55–56, "Hac sub fortuna presens aquilonica luna / Non fuit ad sortem, sequitur sed mente cohortem" ["The Northern Moon was not at hand among that group / By fortune's cast, but in his mind he joined their troop"]), in a way that also advertises the difficulties of the verse itself. Gower's earlier *Vox clamantis,* though allegorical also in long stretches, is provided with no such apparatus. Its allegories are simpler. Evidently, however, Gower believed that even the *Cronica*'s relatively adept audience, already impressed with his obscurity, might yet want help. Gower goes so far as to apologize for his recondite procedures:

> Si non directe procerum cognomina recte,
> Hec tamen obscura referam, latitante figura;
> Scribere que tendo si mistica verba legendo
> Auribus apportant, verum tamen illa reportant.

---

[17] Quoted from the editions in Richard Firth Green, "John Ball's Letters: Literary History and Historical Literature," in *Chaucer's England: Literature in Historical Context,* ed. Barbara Hanawalt (Minneapolis: University of Minnesota Press, 1992), pp. 193–95. On the letters' provenance, useful evidence is collected in Steven Justice, *Writing and Rebellion* (Berkeley and Los Angeles: University of California Press, 1994), pp. 15–23; a still earlier formal and substantive analogue, of c. 1311, is discussed in Margaret Aston, "*Corpus Christi* and *Corpus Regni:* Heresy and the Peasants' Revolt," *Past & Present* 143 (1994): 23–26. The phrase "sub-literary" is from John N. King, *English Reformation Literature* (Princeton: Princeton University Press, 1982), p. 4.

[I'll tell these nobles' names, but not direct, out loud;
I'll tell them in a riddle, veiled beneath a shroud.
The words I plan to write may seem mysterious
For ears to read, but still they're true and serious.]

(1.45–48)

The same occurs in *Richard the Redeless*. To end an especially obscure patch, the poet puts a rebuke, castigating an imagined reader or hearer ("Hicke Heuyheed"—using the other type of appellation, noteworthily a self-explanatory quasi-personification, *Piers Plowman*-like) for failure to penetrate; instead of explaining, the poet blames, insisting on the difficulty of the allegory and keeping it intact:

"What is this to mene, man?" maiste thou axe,
"For it is derklich endited for a dull panne.
Wherffore I wilne yif it thi will were,
The partriche propurtes by whom that thou menest?"
A! Hicke Heuyheed! hard is thi nolle
To cacche ony kunynge but cautell bigynne!
Herdist thou not with eeris how that I er tellde
How the egle in the est entrid his owen.

(3.62–69)

Fortunately (though not for "Heuyheed"), there survives a contemporary explanation of the allegorical techniques used for making up the 1399 poems. It may be useful to be told, perhaps, as a general rule of interpretation for this kind of enigmatic writing, that one of the types of "occultatio" it may dispose consists "in accendentali designatione propter aliquod accidens competens alicui in moribus vel dispositione corporali, vel ex nomine vel cognomine, vel ex armis sibi convenientibus" ["in denomination by accidental, by means of some accidental proper to a particular person, in respect of habit or bodily disposition, or from the person's Christian or family name, or from the blazons the person uses by convention"].[18] But the point is that such writing by "occultatio" required learned exegesis, *scholastico more,* even at the time. The manner of speaking at issue was emphatically not popular, at least in this sense: few, if any, could be expected to understand it without

---

[18] Ed. Wright, *Political Poems and Songs,* I, 126, cited in Barr, *Socioliterary Practice in Late Medieval England,* pp. 71–72 n. 47.

help. There are no examples of its use for contemporary topical poetry outside the 1399 summer poems.[19]

Some of the appellations chosen may have had a basis in heraldry;[20] the chief source for the kinds of allegories used in the poems of the summer of 1399, however, would have been the tradition of riddling "Galfridian" political prophecy, founded by Geoffrey of Monmouth in the twelfth century and proliferating thence. The chief examples are the various "Bridlington" prophecies, dating from the reign of Edward III and continuously reinterpreted, circulating most widely with the extensive exegetical apparatus of John Erghom, whose explanation of *occultatio in accendentali designatione* was quoted above, from his "Secundum praeambulum" to the prophecies—second of four. And there is other evidence for extensive clerical-academic cultivation of the enigmatic techniques involved at the same time.[21] Such evidence as there is for current knowledge of the particular allegories used in the 1399 poems— the beasts and birds, bushes and so forth—outside the poems themselves is restricted to this single, specific type of source. Contemporary annalists and memorialists—learned persons all, especially Thomas Walsingham (d. c. 1422) and Adam Usk (d. 1430)—cite (and then have to explicate) enigmatic Latin prophecies, of the sort associated with Bridlington's name, with which the 1399 poems would also have had some relation.

For example, on the occasion of the duke of Gloucester's arrest, in the early morning hours of 11 July 1397, Walsingham has it that a

---

[19] To my knowledge, the only analogues are a series of poems from the period c. 1450–c. 1464, another moment of intense partisan division within the ruling elite, which again did not have broader sociopolitical implications or ramifications except among the immediate dependents of the members of the royal family who were at odds with one another. The examples are cited in V. J. Scattergood, *Politics and Poetry in the Fifteenth Century* (London: Blandford, 1971), pp. 157–92.

[20] Heraldry too was already something of an occult science, with a castelike priesthood of initiates, the heralds and pursuivants charged with controlling proliferation of the enigmatic significations peculiar to the heraldic system; and the symbolism was legible or sensible only to a narrow social fraction, the armigerous few and their dependents: those immediately involved in the intraclass political adventures of this most elite secular group. Cf. Susan Crane, *The Performance of Self: Ritual, Clothing, and Identity during the Hundred Years War* (Philadelphia: University of Pennsylvania Press, 2002), pp. 108–11.

[21] On the "Bridlington" prophecies, see Rigg, "John of Bridlington's Prophecy: A New Look," *Speculum* 63 (1988): 596–613; and on the contemporary clerical interest in verbal enigmas, see Andrew Galloway, "The Rhetoric of Riddling in Late-Medieval England: The 'Oxford' Riddles, the *Secretum philosophorum,* and the Riddles in *Piers Plowman,*" *Speculum* 70 (1995): 68–105.

ten-year-old Latin verse prophecy ("per decennium ante vulgata") was fulfilled:

Impletaque fuit tunc prophetia comminatoria, metrice composita, et per decennium ante vulgata, quae talis est:

> Vulpes cum cauda caueat, dum cantat alauda,
> Ne rapiens pecus simul rapiatur, et equus.

"Vulpem cum cauda" vocauit ducem [sc. Gloucester], quia semper ferebatur super hastam, in eius prsesentia, cauda vulpis. "Dum cantat alauda" dixit, quia mane ad cantus alaudae, prout contigit, capiendus fuit; quo capto, imminebat et raptus pecudis rapientis, id est, comitis Warwici; et equi, id est, comitis Arundeliae; quia alter pro signo ferebat vrsum, alter equum.[22]

[Then was fulfilled that monitory prophecy composed in verse and published a decade earlier, reading "Let the tailed fox beware while the lark is singing, lest the devouring beast be devoured along with him, and the horse as well." It calls the duke "tailed fox" because he was in the habit always of having borne before him a fox's tail atop a spear. "While the lark is singing," it said, because in the morning, at lark's song, as it happened, he was to be arrested; and when he was arrested, seizure threatened "the devouring beast" too, namely, the earl of Warwick, as well as "the horse," namely, the earl of Arundel; for the one bore a bear for his device, and the other a horse.]

Such evidence makes manifoldly absurd Gower's assertion that, upon Richard's triumph over his enemies in the "Revenge" Parliament, the metropolitan *vulgus* sang:

> "Non Olor in pennis, nec Equs stat crine perhennis:
> Iam depennatus Olor est, Equs excoriatus.

[22] *Annales,* p. 206. Another version of the same prophecy and explication occurs in the "Dieulacres Chronicle," ed. Maude Violet Clarke and V. H. Galbraith, in "The Deposition of Richard II," *BJRL* 14 (1930): 169; and the *vulpis cauda* as another allegorical appellation for the *Olor* Gloucester recurs too in the *Cronica tripertita* 1.87–88 (also with the prohecy's *alauda*): "De vulpis cauda velox Aper est vt alauda; / Cauda ruit castra, que sunt numero velud astra," as Gower's marginal note *ad* 1.77 explains: "qui tunc vulpis caudam in lancea gessit." Of the use of the "Bridlington" prophecies by Adam Usk, there is instructive discussion in Strohm, *England's Empty Throne: Usurpation and the Language of Legitimation, 1399–1422* (New Haven: Yale University Press, 1998), pp. 9–14.

Vrsus non mordet, quem stricta cathena remordet."
Sic fatue turbe vox conclamabat in vrbe.

"The Swan is feather-free, the Horse has lost its mane,
The Swan's been plucked, the Horse is flayed (O what a shame),
The Bear can't bite, he's tethered by a biting chain!"
Throughout the town this silly rhyme the mob declaim.

(2.314–17)

No such celebration is otherwise in evidence, for one thing. Had Richard
tried some triumphal transit of the city, the *ciues* may have been less
supportive than Gower suggests, if people were at all interested in such
obscure squabbling among their betters, which had no import for the
class-struggle and little or none for daily living. Also, the evidence is
that such a crowd may have tended to use some other prosodic form, or
language even; and the peculiar allegorical idiom, compounding Galfridian prophetic utterance with quasi-heraldic emblems—*Olor, Equs,
Vrsus*—was not in popular use.[23]

The same considerations render the fifth "poem" in the corpus implausible too:

> Up on an hylle ys a greene.
> On the grene stondeþ a busch.
> Up on þe bussch hangeþ a bagge.
> Wh<erefore> the grene ys y-mowe,
> And the bussch ouere throwe,
> And the bagge y-schake:
> Þenne yt ys tyme, Engelond, to wake.

---

[23] Here as elsewhere, Gower may have been prey to an opaque Caesarism that occurs
elsewhere in the literature of the revolution, as, for example, in the pervasive imputation
to Henry of a Caesar-like clemency, discussed below, pp. 402–4. The analogue for the
kind of popular or vulgar scurrilous song that Gower attributes to the London *turba* on
the 1397 occasion is the verses Roman troops sang about their generals in formal triumphs in the city, as reported most famously about Caesar's quadruple triumph of 46
BCE (e.g., Suetonius, *Diuus Julius* 49.4, 51, 80.2–3); the people used trochaic tetrameter
catalectic, an old Roman meter, rather than hexameters or anything still more Helleniz-
ing, as well as their own peculiar ("sub-literate") vocabulary. For evidence of cultivation
of knowledge of Roman history and antiquities at Walsingham's St. Albans—at the
time that Gower too was writing—see now James G. Clark, "Thomas Walsingham
Reconsidered: Books and Learning at Late-Medieval St. Albans," *Speculum* 77 (2002):
832–60.

Hiis tres milites Buschey, Bagod et Grene, consiluerunt regi Ricardo ut trans-
fectaret in Hyberniam ut ipsi regerent regnum ad firmam. [These three sirs,
Bussy, Bagot, and Green, counseled King Richard to betake himself to Ireland,
in order that they might rule over the kingdom themselves, as a fee-farm.][24]

Its ventriloquism comes nearer a *vox populi* than Gower's does, by virtue
of its invocation of yet another noncoincident generic register: the
"subliterary" quasi-rhyming-poetic register of the 1381 John Ball Letters, with which this item probably shares more than provenance: it is
attested only by a marginal inscription in a copy of Walsingham's *Chronica maiora* from St. Albans (where John Ball was executed and copies
of the incriminating "Letters" were discovered about his person, to be
published by Walsingham).[25] With Gower and the rest of the corpus, it
uses the same nonpopular, enigmatic style of riddling denomination,
having even a Gower-like explanatory gloss in Latin spelling out answers.[26] In addition, this fifth item introduces the curious historical-

[24] Quoted from Clark, "Thomas Walsingham Reconsidered," p. 845 n. 84 (from
marginalia in the manuscript Cambridge, Corpus Christi College 7, fol. 47r)—the same
passage from the same manuscript was reported in *Annales,* ed. Riley, pp. 276–77 n.
5.—here introducing lineation as verse, though the item is not noted in the *NIMEV.*

[25] In the English, there may be some phrases that recall "On the King's Ministers"
(see above, n. 7): "up on þe bussch hangeþ a bagge" may recall 79–81 "The grete bage
is so ytoron, / Hit nyl holde neyther mele ne corn / Hong hit up to drye!" and "the
grene ys y-mowe" may recall 4–6 "The long gras that is so grene, / Hit most be mowe,
and raked clene—/ For-growen hit hath the fellde." But for two items using the same
allegorical conceit, both proleptically, to call for the same outcomes for the same current
events, the verbal parallels, not numerous, are also not close; it does not appear that the
one is a garbled recollection of the other, for example. The nearest parallels I find for
its particular terms are in the "John Ball Letters" (ed. cit., above n. 17). The concluding
English phrase of the marginalium, "Þenne yt ys tyme Engelond to wake," quotes a
refrain-like injunction that is the only feature common to all the "John Ball Letters": a
conclusion in three of them, "God doe bote, for now is time;" elsewhere, "For nowe is
tyme to be ware" or "Nowe is tyme." Cf. also the poem known as "The Insurrection
and Earthquake (1382)" (*NIMEV* 4268), ed. Rossell Hope Robbins, *Historical Poems of
the XIVth and XVth Centuries* (New York: Columbia University Press, 1959), pp. 57–60,
with a refrain, "This was a warnyng to be ware," including the variation (which Robbins, p. 277, calls "semi-proverbial") 79–80 "Vr bagge hongeth on a sliper pin, / Bote
we of this warnyng be ware."

[26] The Latin gloss with the English quotes a rumored allegation against Scrope that
only Walsingham transmits (*Annales,* p. 240), though the allegation is so wild that even
Walsingham qualifies, with "Dicebatur" and "imaginabatur": "Dicebatur praeterea,
quod Willelmus le Scrop, regis Camberlanus, et Comes de Wiltschire de novo creatus,
omnes escaetas regni Angliae de rege cepisset ad firmam per triennium; et ob hoc imaginabatur mortes plurimorum procerum et aliorum valentium, ut uberem faceret firmam." Of the *prosatores,* only Walsingham is concerned to inculpate the Bristol victims
in advance of the July executions, as the poets do (see pp. 394–6); here as elsewhere,
however, Walsingham is persistently oblique, only insinuating rather than specifying
malfeasance: at the news of Henry's landing, Walsingham has it, Scrope, Bussy, Green,

substantive common property of the 1399 poetry, by virtue of its relatively narrow concentration on just the one episode from the summer of 1399.

Scrope, Bussy, Green, and Bagot

The poems' shared disposition of the same deliberately veiled manner of speaking, in riddling and opaque allegories of a specialized type—not popular, but recondite, restricted in use to specialists purpose-trained in such idioms' vagaries—suggests coordination, at a culturally high level, as does the generic organization of the same poetry, by noncoincidence in a nevertheless relatively full range of the available nonaristocratic literary kinds. If the poetry were spontaneous or popular, both more and less coincidence would have occurred: more generic overlap, where the range of choice was restricted, especially in popular forms of writing; and less consistent recourse to the same strange allegorical idiom, where other commoner ways of representing the same events might have been disposed instead.

The other convergence of the poems is also telling: amid so many other conceivable points of focus, their coincident concentration on the same group of minor Ricardian place-holders—William Scrope (c. 1351–99), John Bussy (d. 1399), Henry Green (c. 1347–99), and William Bagot (c. 1354–1407). The five poems represent these men similarly, by means of the same allegorical appellations, prophecy-like, used also for Gloucester, Warwick, and the earl of Arundel, though Scrope, Bussy, Green, and Bagot were not personages of comparable eminence. Scrope was chamberlain of the royal household from 1395, and Richard's treasurer from 17 September 1398; for such services, he was created earl of Wiltshire on 29 September1397. And Bussy too had had a career of sorts, though it was strictly bourgeois: a former sheriff of Lincoln, and knight of the shire for Lincoln repeatedly from 1388, he was the speaker of commons for Richard's last three parliaments. Green and

---

and Bagot "timuerunt maxime, ita quod videbantur spiritum non habere" (*Annales,* p. 243); and again, Walsingham speculates, the same men left Westminster "conturbati et conterriti, utpote quos intus accusauit conscientia" (p. 244); cf. also the later passage where Walsingham says of them: "cernentes se inuisos patriae et patriotis, et metuentes quod si diutius starent cum duce Eboraci [sc., at Oxford], caperentur fortassis per manus communium [as Walsingham will go on to imply happened at Bristol], fugerunt ad villam Brystolliae sub magna festinatione" (pp. 245–46), again, without any imputation of actual crime, implying consciousness of guilt in them.

Bagot had still less public prominence, though both were intermittent parliamentarians, too. Then, however, Scrope, Bussy, Green, and Bagot were implicated in the episode that provided common topical matter for the poetry of the summer of 1399: Henry's illegal killing of as many of them as he could keep, at Bristol, on 29 July 1399.[27]

In modern historiography of the period, Scrope, Bussy, Green, and Bagot tend to be described as widely much hated; but the characterization is implausible. Who knew about their doings at the time? Who would have cared? The circle can only have been narrow, restricted to the few directly involved, for and against, with executive governance of the kingdom—peers and committee workers—in the brief period of Richard's tyranny, roughly from late 1397. Henry's Bristol victims had not acted in public, excepting hardly even the commons' speaker Bussy, but only at a level of consequential remove from the local and day-to-day, directing execution of policies made still higher up or mediating among the great, always away from the public scene. The notion that there could have been any spontaneous *clamor populi* against Scrope, Bussy, Green, and Bagot personally is difficult to credit. Only death made any of them more notable, somewhat, and only in retrospect, more by virtue of the circumstantial peculiarities that killed them than by any of their own doings or intrinsic consequence. What mattered was not the victims, but what Henry might have meant by killing them, or what might be inferred from his so doing.

The St. Albans "verse" is concerned exclusively with the prospect of executions; the other poems make more of the minions' earlier careers by way of justifying in advance what was to happen to them—especially *Richard the Redeless,* which has glancing references often, *per allegoria.* When Henry "the [hende] Egle" has returned to England, for example, gathering flock-like his supporters to him ("But the nedy nestlingis whan they the note herde / Of the [hende] Egle the heyer of hem all" [3.73–74]), the anti-Ricardian forces are said to light on Bussy ("Thei busked fro the busches and breris that hem noyed" [3.75]) and Green ("They gaglide forth on the grene for they greued were" [3.101]) in

---

[27] Scrope's career is delineated in the *Dictionary of National Biography,* vol. 51, ed. Sidney Lee (London: Smith, Elder, 1897), 148–50. For the others, I rely on the thoroughly documented brief biographies in *The House of Commons 1386–1421,* ed. J. S. Roskell, Linda Clarke, and Carole Rawcliffe, 4 vols. (Stroud: Sutton, 1992), on Bussy (by Rawcliffe), II, 449–54; on Green (by Colin Richmond and L. S. Woodger), III, 225–28; and on Bagot (by Woodger), II, 99–103.

particular: "busches and breris" can refer to Bussy, and Green's name appears again. Likewise, the poet makes allusion in course of faulting the wearers of King Richard's livery of the White Hart: "They bare hem the bolder for her gay broches, / And busshid with her brestis and bare adoun the pouere" (2.38–39), where Bussy appears to be blamed for a general popular oppression in fact beyond his capacity.

Most significant of these passing references in *Richard the Redeless* may be a passage in which the poet faults Bussy and Green for the malfeasances of the 1397 "Revenge" parliament, as if they were responsible for King Richard's vengeance then. The excessively young counselors around the king were blameworthy, the poet writes, addressing Richard directly, because

> They made you to leue that regne ye ne myghte
> Withoute busshinge adoun of all youre best frendis,
> Be a fals colour her caris to wayve.
>
> (1.185–87)

"Busshinge" appears to incorporate Bussy's name again, and the answer to the implicit riddle of the "fals colour" must be "green," the color of newfangledness, or falsity in the specific contemporary sense. The two are being apportioned blame for high crimes indeed, if the reference of "all youre best frendis" (1.186) is to the king's near-relatives, and long-time counseling benefactors, who were done various injuries in 1397, including death.

The "O deus in celis" too appears to allude to the same matter of the "Revenge" parliament, inexplicitly: "Dampnarunt forti iustorum corpora morti, / Sanguis <at> quorum vindictam clamat eorum" (23–24). Though these righteous, still crying out for vengeance, whose bodies were condemned to harsh death, are not named in the poem, the subject of the verb ("Dampnarunt"), here represented as the guilty parties, can only be "Scrope, Bagge, Ver, Dumus" (22): "Tales pomposi de stercore sunt generosi" (20).

Gower's only reference to the Ricardian minions other than his account of the executions in 1399 comes in similar context, where he too attempts to blame them for putative crimes of the period of the "Revenge" parliament. Once he has finished narrating the condemnations of Richard's enemies in that parliament, Gower goes on to tell that, afterward,

Omnia que dici poterant dicunt inimici,
Pluraque fingentes mendacia sunt parientes.
Grene, Scrop, Bussy, cordis sine lumine fusci,
Omne nephas querunt, quo ledere plus potuerunt.
Rex fuit instructus per eos, et ad omnia ductus
Que mala post gessit, quibus Anglia tota pauescit.
Intra se flebat populus, qui dampna videbat;
Cum non audebat vocem proferre, tacebat.

[The heroes' enemies dishonor their good name;
They fabricate their falsehoods, foully spreading shame.
Green, Scrope, and Bushy, black of heart, devoid of charm,
Search out all wickedness by which to do them harm.
By them the king to all the wicked schemes was led
That later he fulfilled, which caused all England's dread.
At heart the people wept for sorrows without cease,
But dared not say a word, and so they held their peace.]

(2.318–25)

Where Gower characterizes the minions' contributions to the 1397 business chiefly as giving malign advice afterward, "On King Richard's Ministers" is more direct. In turn, each personally is accused: Bussy of killing the *Cignus* Gloucester (13–14 "Thorw the busch a swan was sclayn; / Of that sclawtur fewe wer fayne"), Green of killing *Equs,* the earl of Arundel (19–20 "The grene gras that was so long, / Hit hath sclayn a stede strong"), and Bagot of bringing about the arrest and exile of *Vrsus,* the earl of Warwick:

A bereward fond a rag;
Of the rag he made a bag;
   He dude in gode entent.
Thorwe the bag the bereward is taken
Alle his beres han hym forsaken—
   Thus is the berewarde schent.

(25–30)

Incredible as these imputations in "On King Richard's Ministers" are (and must have been at the time, too, to anyone with the least intelligence of the events of the 1397 parliament), such assertions may yet have been expected to shift some weight, in some quarters, by way of justifying what was done with the minions at the moment, in July 1399: eye for eye, killers to be killed, as three of the four were, illegally.

The same poem "On King Richard's Ministers" refers to the executions themselves only *per allegoria* and in prospect, as what ought to be but has not yet been done. Two stanzas at its beginning (1–12) mirror three penultimate ones (67–84), symmetrically calling for the killings by turns of Bussy ("Ther is a busch that is forgrowe; / Crop hit welle, and hold hit lowe"; "But hewe hit downe, crop and rote, / And to the toun hit lede"), then of Green ("The long gras that is so grene, / Hit most be mowe"; "Til the roton be dynged ought, / Our lene bestes schul not rought, / Hur liflode to gete"), and finally of Bagot ("The grete bagge, that is so mykille, / Hit schal be kettord and maked litell"; "Hong hit up to drye!"). The proper agent for bringing these killings to pass is to be Henry Bolingbroke (a "heron" here rather than an "eagle"), this despite the legal problem of someone other than a king executing traitors:

> Upon the busch the eron wolle reste,
> Of alle places it liketh hym beste,
>   To loke aftur his paye.
> He wolle falle upon the grene;
> There he falleth hit wille be sene,
>   They wille not welle away.
>   (55–60)[28]

It is significant that there is no allusion in this crucial passage of "On King Richard's Ministers" to Henry killing Bagot. The St. Albans lines are verbally close but less equivocal on this point: "Wh<erefore> the grene ys y-mowe, / And the bussch ouere throwe, / And the bagge y-schake." Though "On King Richard's Ministers" pretends to be calling for the executions of the hated Ricardian minions, or prophesying—"the eron wolle," "He wolle," "hit wille," "They wille"—the poet also appears to know what happened: in fact, Bagot was to escape execution with the others.

The *Richard the Redeless* poet has the same kind of precise, detailed knowledge of what took place at Bristol, including the killings of Scrope, Green, and Bussy but not Bagot. Though again the writing

[28] At line 57 of this quotation, "paye" is a conjectural emendation, for both sound and sense, of ms. "pray."

needs be read allegorically, it narrates the three executions, as Henry's doing, rather than only calling for or predicting them:

> Thus baterid this bred on busshes aboughte,
> And gaderid gomes on grene ther as they walkyd
> That all the schroff and schroup sondrid from other.
> He mellid so the matall with the hand-molde
> That [they] lost lemes the leuest that they had.
> Thus foulyd this faukyn on fyldis aboughte,
> And caughte of the kuyttis a cartffull at ones,
> That rentis and robis with raveyn euere laughte.
> Yit was not the fawcon full fed at his likynge,
> For it cam him not of kynde kytes to loue.
> Then bated he boldeliche as a brid wolde,
> To plewme on his pray the pol fro the nekk.
>
> (2.152–63)

"Dux perlustrator, constans, sis tu dominator, / Et fac tractari fals<o>s et decapitari!" is how the same detail appears in "O deus in celis" (15–16), in the form of an imperative, as if for an action yet to be taken; and Gower, in narrative, has the same rhyme-word at the same point in his verse: 3.176 "statuit dux decapitari" ["the duke decided for decapitation"]. That decollation was how Scrope, Bussy, and Green were killed at Bristol appears here in *Richard the Redeless,* too, but *sub allegoria:* "Then bated he boldeliche as a brid wolde, / To plewme on his pray the pol fro the nekk."

The *Richard*-poet continues, in the same vein, with an account of what became of Bagot. He had been captured with the other three at Bristol but escaped, to be caught again later:

> But the blernyed boynard that his bagg stall,
> Where purraile-is pulter was pynnyd full ofte,
> Made the fawcon to floter and flussh for anger
> That the boy [nadd] be bounde that the bagge kept.
> But sone ther-after in a schorte tyme,
> As fortune folwith ech fode till his ende,
> This lorell that [ladde] this loby awey
> Ouere frithe and forde for his fals dedis,
> Lyghte on the lordschepe that to the brid longid.
>
> (2.164–72)[29]

[29] That Bagot was laid hold of somewhere in the Lancastrian patrimony (if that is the implication of 2.172 "on the lordschepe that to the brid longid") may be corroborated

Bagot's next public appearance after his disappearance from Bristol at the end of July appears to have been the one described here, in plain terms: he "was felliche ylaughte and luggid full ylle, / And broughte to the brydd and his blames rehersid / Preuyly at the parlement amonge all the peple" (2.173–75). Though the matter did not become part of the official parliamentary record—there was in fact no trial-like rehearsal of "his blames"—Walsingham too reports Bagot's appearance before Henry IV's first parliament as king, during October 1399.[30] The *Richard the Redeless* poet makes no further reference to him, however: evidently, Bagot's ultimate disposition, after his appearance in parliament, was not in public knowledge by the time *Richard the Redeless* was finished.[31]

---

by the account in Adam Usk, *Chronicle of Adam Usk*, ed. Given Wilson, p. 60, though the same passage has been taken to imply that Bagot was seized in Ireland, brought back under duress: "inuinculato ducto." Much about Bagot's post-capture doings remains uncertain.

[30] See *Annales*, pp. 303–6 and 308–9. Barr, *Piers Plowman Tradition*, p. 269, suggests that the last mention of Bagot in "On King Richard's Ministers" (80–85) hints at the pardon of him: calling out against "the grete bage"—"Hong hit up to drye!"—the stanza ends, "Wen hit is drye, then schalt thou se / Yif hit wil amended be, / A beger for to bye." The lines appear also to call for Bagot's execution, however, and it may be that the answer to the implicitly riddling remark ("then schalt thou se") is that, after execution, Bagot would prove not to have been "amended," even by so much as "A beger for to bye." As elsewhere in writings after this same fashion, the obscurity cannot be dissipated.

[31] Bagot was rehabilitated, to a remarkable degree, especially by light of what happened to his associates in Richard's late governance: at the time of Bagot's release from imprisonment, he was granted £100 per annum from the royal Exchequer, 17 November 1400 (*Calendar of the Patent Rolls Henry IV*, 4 vols. [London: HMSO, 1900–1986], cited by regnal-year coverage: *CPR 1399–1401*, p. 386); he was formally restored to law 8 June 1401 (*CPR 1399–1401*, p. 502) and returned to parliament in late 1402 (*Calendar of the Close Rolls Henry IV*, 5 vols. [London: HMSO, 1900–1986], also cited by regnal-year coverage: *CCR 1402–1404*, p. 125); 21–30 October 1404, he was in King Henry's company at Coventry, where he witnessed a series of royal writs (*CCR 1402–1404*, pp. 472–75); during this same period, from late 1400 to his death in 1407, Bagot was repeatedly a successful suitor to the king, in behalf of others (e.g., *CPR 1401–1405*, p. 468), and in his own, even in cases where recovery or retention of landed incomes that Bagot had obtained, by allegedly illegal means, during Richard's tyranny, were at issue (e.g., *CPR 1401–1405*, p. 96). Bagot was held imprisoned in the Tower of London from 22 November 1399 (*CCR 1399–1402*, p. 20), if not earlier, until 12 November 1400 (*CCR 1399–1402*, p. 224); and a royal order of 5 April 1400 allowing removal of Bagot's fetters during whatever might remain of his incarceration in the Tower (*CCR 1399–1402*, p. 78) may tell something of the conditions of his capture (corroborating the remark of Adam Usk quoted above, n. 29). Despite such evidence of Bagot's noncooperation—the point also, perhaps, of Walsingham's reports of what Bagot said when he appeared before Henry's first parliament in October 1399 (cited above, n. 30)—the fact remains, however, that Bagot was never tried or punished for his crimes in the reign of Richard II, unlike the Bristol victims; instead, he was rewarded

About this same sequence of events, Gower is briefer and less allegorically involute but has the same particulars:

> Dux probus audaci vultu cum plebe sequaci
> Regnum scrutatur, si proditor inueniatur;
> Sic tres exosos magis omnibus ambiciosos
> Regni tortores inuenerat ipse priores.
> Ense repercussi periunt Scrop, Grene, quoque Bussy:
> Hii quasi regales fuerant cum rege sodales.
> Scrop, comes et miles, eius Bristollia viles
> Actus declarat, quo mors sua fata pararet;
> Greneque sorte pari statuit dux decapitari;
> Bussy conuictus similes quoque <sus>tinet ictus.
> Vnanimes mente pariter mors vna repente
> Hos tres prostrauit, gladius quos fine vorauit.
> Sicut et egerunt aliis, sic hii ceciderunt,
> Quo dux laudatur regnumque per omne iocatur.

> [The worthy duke, bold-faced, with popular support,
> To search out treachery the whole of England sought.
> A hateful trio thus he found that led the rest,
> Tormenting all the realm, stirred by ambitious zest.
> The three were then beheaded: Bushy, Green, and Scrope,
> Three buddies of the king, a rascal royal group.
> Scrope was an earl and knight; his wicked deeds were shown
> At Bristol, where death claimed him as its very own.
> Green equally should lose his head, the duke declared,
> And Bushy was convicted too: he was not spared.
> These three were of one mind, and so one speedy death
> Took all at once: the sword devoured their final breath.

---

by the new king, who repeatedly protected Bagot from prosecutions concerning his
landed incomes even while Bagot was held under ostentatious duress in the Tower (*CCR
1399–1402*, pp. 31, 97, for royal protection; and, for the case against Bagot, *CPR
1399–1401*, p. 152). It must be possible that Bagot was let go from Bristol, rather than
escaping, in exchange for immediately useful intelligence, say, at a moment when all
were starved for information—or even that he had been a Lancastrian agent throughout—and that Bagot's subsequent nonpunishment and the rewards were payment to
him for services to the usurper, with Walsingham's stories and the Tower imprisonment,
chains or no, to cover. It would have been inimical, at least awkward, for Henry to
appear publicly lenient with the unpopular criminal Bagot at the same moment he also
still needed publicly to legalize his killings of the others at Bristol, on the basis of
popular outrage against the minions' crimes and his own divinely ordained rectitude
about meting out justice to them.

> As they had done to others, so they met their fate;
> For this the duke earned praise; the realm could celebrate.]

(3.168–81)

Gower's final assertion here, that the three *proditores'* executions were popular, widely even (3.181 "Quo dux laudatur regnumque per omne iocatur" ["For this the duke earned praise; the realm could celebrate"]), is repeated in Walsingham's *Cronica,* in remarkably similar terms, given the different verbal mediums: "laetantibus cunctis regni mediocribus, quod tam cito, tam gratiose, prout eis videbatur, de infestissimis liberabantur hostibus" ["all the lesser folk of the kingdom rejoiced at being freed so speedily, so graciously, from such evil wrongdoers, as it appeared to them"]. Walsingham also imputes Henry's doings to divine intercession—God himself "immisit igitur in cor domini Henrici" ["put it in Lord Henry's heart"], Walsingham has it: "repente Deus illius [sc. Ricardi] superbiam decreuit humiliare, et populo Anglicano succurrere, qui iam miserabiliter opprimebatur, et de spe releuationis et remedii omnino exciderat, nisi Deus manus porrigeret in adiutorium eorundem" ["of a sudden, God determined to put down his [sc. Richard's] pride, and to succor the English people, for long miserably oppressed, and altogether bereft of any hope of relief or remedy, had not God stretched out his hand to rescue them"][32]—as Gower does as well:

> O quam plura sinit deus, et cum tempora finit,
> Omnia tunc certe que sunt demonstrat aperte!
> Dux inspiratus tandem, quasi sit renouatus,
> Singula compensat perfecto cordeque pensat.

> God many things permits, but when He terminates
> All time, He'll surely show all things in their true state.

[32] The quotations are *Annales,* pp. 247 and 240–41. Walsingham makes this assertion repeatedly in the paragraphs he devotes to the revolution, typically with this same insinuation, that God's intervention was an answer to popular prayers. See *Annales,* p. 239: "Cum rex moram protelaret in Hibernia, communitas regni Angliae totis votis dominum precabatur, ne unquam sospes reverteretur; nempe in ore omnium voluebatur, quod iam terram Angliae idem rex habebat inuisam": p. 242: when rumors of Henry's approach begin to circulate, "fiebat magna communitatis exultatio, putantis veraciter quod Deus hunc mitteret ad dissoluendum jugum seruitutis eorum grauissimae": and p. 250, where Walsingham claims that Henry's miraculous success makes people want him to be king: "Et mirum quod totum regnum tantillo tempore sic pacificatum et stabilitum fuit, unanimi voluntate, ut nihil magis desiderarent incolae, quam Henricum, ducem Lancastriae, in regem suum, deiecto rege Ricardo."

> The duke, inspirited and, as it were, renewed,
> Considered carefully and everything reviewed.
>
> (3.122–25)

Support for such assertions is offered—ostensibly, tendentiously in fact—in the other poems, by way of their imprecations of the divine, as if the God of Walsingham and Gower were answering to the anti-Ricardian poets' prayers. The prayer begins the "O deus in celis" (3–4 "Ablue pennatos fallentes perfide natos, / Vt tormentorum noscant recepisse dolorem"), ends it (43–44 "Aquila dux austro saluabit nos alabaustro. / Illius cetum prestet, Christe, fore letum!"), and recurs in the middle (18 "clamat gens celitus"); and it finishes "On King Richard's Ministers" as well:

> Now God that mykelle is of myght,
> Grant us grace to se that syght,
>   Yif hit be thy wille.
> Our lene bestes to have reste
> In place that hem lyketh beste,
>   That were in point to spylle.
>
> (85–91)

In all cases—report, prophecy, prayer—the conceit is not that Henry wanted or needed to demonstrate his regal capacity by trying and killing *proditores,* nor that the killings satisfied some other mundane want of his, though three of the men had been Lancastrian retainers: Bussy a chief steward of the Duchy of Lancaster, and Bagot having been a close avuncular companion to Henry himself in youth, while Scrope was in receipt of incomes and holdings that had been redistributed from the Lancastrian patrimony after John of Gaunt's death. They were resisting the invasion, however, if only by fleeing it, so Henry, who did not want to be king, tried and killed them, as if he were.

Rather, the conceit is that ordinary folk were calling out to God for the executions, and Henry, as God's elect ("Quem deus elegit"), was in position to serve.[33] The Ricardian officers were persons "quos plebs communis reputaret hostes publicos" ["whom the common folk regarded as public enemies"], in Walsingham's account; "vrgebat nempe

---

[33] The quoted phrase is *Cronica tripertita* 3.320; cf. "In Praise of Peace" prol.1 "Electus Cristi."

dominos ad ferendum in eos tam repentinam sententiam clamor importunus communitatis, quae voluisset eos in frusta decerpsisse, si quomodolibet potuisset" ["the importunate clamor of the community—having long hoped in vain for them to be cut off by any means possible—compelled the lords to execute the sentence on them that had so quickly been handed down"]. In the circumstance, Henry could only yield to the popular sentiment: "et idcirco, ut praefertur, ad plebis importunam instantiam, tristem exceperunt sententiam" ["thus, as the story goes, they suffered the fatal decree, at the importunate insistence of the people"]; "hii namque capti sunt, et custodiae forti commissi vespere, et mane decapitati" ["for they were laid hold of, put in durance of an evening, and beheaded in the morning"].[34]

The poetry substantiates Walsingham's improbable assertions about the "plebs communis" at Bristol, that there was there "clamor importunus communitatis" and *plebis importuna instantia*. The poets' orations prove that there was *clamor populi* by representing themselves as the very *clamor populi* itself, in direct evidence. Spontaneously, as it were—howbeit with recondite poetic language, in even generic distribution, showing knowledge in detail of what happened—people were calling out to God for the murderous Henrician intervention against the king's men, while or even before it had occurred.

Henricus Pius, Murder, and Perjury

Gower mentions the fugitive Bagot only in a different connection, later, when narrating the doings of Henry's first proper parliament, in October 1399, and then only glancingly, in enumerating the surviving Ricardian favorites and servants treated mercifully by Henry at that time. Henry only deprived them of the titles (and incomes) they had acquired since the September 1397 death of the duke of Gloucester, leaving such persons otherwise unmolested.[35] Bagot too, though hateful, was spared:

> Est tamen ablatum, quod eis fuit ante beatum,
> Vocibus Anglorum venerabile nomen eorum.

[34] *Annales,* pp. 246–47.
[35] The pertinent parliamentary *acta* are in the *Rotuli Parliamentorum,* III, 449–52; see also the analysis of A. L. Brown, "The Reign of Henry IV: The Establishment of the Lancastrian Regime," in *Fifteenth-Century England, 1399–1509,* ed. S. B. Chrimes, C. D. Ross, and R. A. Griffiths (Manchester: Manchester University Press, 1972), pp. 2–7.

Corpora stant tuta, cecidit sed fama minuta;
Dux redit in comitem, quatit et sic curia litem.
Labitur exosus Bagot, quem rex pietosus
Erigit, et mite prolongat tempora vite.

[But now they lost their name that had before been sung
With reverence and awe upon the English tongue.
Their bodies were quite safe, their reputation mute;
Duke was reduced to earl—that settled that dispute!
The hateful Bagot fell; the king in mercy raised
Him up again, prolonging Bagot's living days.]

(3.384–89)

The conceit adumbrated in this passage was that the Lancastrian revolution had been accomplished "sine sanguinis effusione," the idea being that such events as had occurred could have been bloodless only "divina dispensacione," by God's special intervention.[36] So clement in victory toward his enemies was the *pius Henricus* that, according to both Walsingham and Gower, the people—crying out still for more vengeance—came to imagine that bribery must have been involved. After Richard's deposition and Henry's accession, "plebei constanter petebant, sisti in iudicio certos dominos pro prodicione et mala gubernacione regis et regni. Sed nouus rex, pius et misericors et generosus, noluit aliquem interire, rogauitque populum, vt omnem querelam, contra eos conceptam, dimitteret ad tempus" ["the people were petitioning urgently for a number of lords to be brought to trial for treason and ill-governance of the king and kingdom. But the new king—pious, merciful, well born—was unwilling to see anyone killed, and he besought the populace to set aside for a time the enmity they had conceived against them"].[37]

[36] Quoted from the somewhat more expansive version of Gower's gloss in the manuscript Oxford, Bodleian Library, Hatton 92, published in Carlson, "The Long Revolution Gloss *ad Cronica tripertita* 3.332," *John Gower Newsletter* 25, no. 1 (April 2006): 4–8. Application of the epithet *pius* to Henry—the cognate noun *pietas* yielding both MnE 'piety' and 'pity,' having also the benefit of equating the new king with the nation-founding Vergilian hero, *pius Aeneas*—is especially Gower's doing: at the conclusion of the *Cronica*, 3.462–77, the epithet recurs five times; the penultimate section of Gower's contemporary or slightly earlier "In Praise of Peace" 330–57—in which derivatives of *pius* and *pietas* occur ten times in under thirty lines—is built similarly.

[37] *Vita Ricardi Secundi,* ed. Stow, p. 163; and cf. *Annales,* p. 320: "Fiebat murmur in populo," Walsingham has it, "et obloquium de rege, et archiepiscopo, et comite Northumbriae, aliisque de consilio; quasi illi, caecati muneribus, saluassent vitam hominum, quos vulgus sceleratissimos et morte dignissimos reputabat."

403

Regia nam pietas sic temperat vndique metas,
Quod nil mortale datur illis iudiciale. . .
Sic pius Henricus, inimico non inimicus,
Gracius, vt debet, pro dampno commoda prebet.
Ipse pium frenum laxat, quia tempus amenum
Appetit, et Cristo placuisse putauit in isto.
Non tamen in gente placet hoc, sed in ore loquente
Publica vox dicit, leges quod mammona vicit.
Iusticiam queri plebs vult, rex vult misereri.

[For royal mercy moderates and modifies
Its power; there is no deadly judgment; no one dies. . .
Thus gentle Henry was not hostile to his foes,
But, as is right, to render good for evil chose.
He softly loosed the rein; he sought a time of peace,
For in this way he thought that he the Lord would please.
From gossip was clear the people disagreed,
And everyone declared that law was quashed by greed.
The mob sought justice, but the king for mercy tried.]
(*Cronica* 3.382–83 and 390–96)

"Pius et misericors et generosus," the new king "noluit aliquem interire," but of course there was killing: Richard himself, in February 1400,
for instance; and the Ricardian earls of the January 1400 "Epiphany
Rising," "quorum cadavera," wrote Adam Usk, "partita ad modum feri-
narum carnium venacione occupatarum, partim in sacculis, partim inter
duos super humeros in baculis, London' defferi et postea sale condiri,
vidi" ["and I saw their bodies, chopped up like the carcasses of beasts
killed in the chase, being carried to London, partly in sacks and partly
on poles slung across pairs of men's shoulders, where they were later
salted to preserve them"].[38]
     In addition to its evidences of Henry's clemencies to grander Ricardi-
ans, October 1399 saw also the brutal public execution—at London,
with a postmortem broadcast of the body parts, to assure the message
got about—of a more useful or convenient person, a man named John

---

[38] *Chronicle of Adam Usk,* ed. and trans. Given-Wilson, pp. 88–89. On the revolt, see
Alan Rogers, "Henry IV and the Revolt of the Earls," *History Today* 18 (1968): 277–83;
Peter McNiven, "The Cheshire Rising of 1400," *BJRL* 52 (1970): 385–92; also David
Crook, "Central England and the Revolt of the Earls, January 1400," *Historical Research*
64 (1991): 403–10.

Hall, *servus* of the late Thomas Mowbray, who may have withheld information about Gloucester's death in 1397, and whom Henry's parliament condemned: "le dit John Halle soit treinez del Tour Hill jesqes a les Fourkes de Tybourne, et la bowelez, et ses bowels arcz devaunt luy, et puis soit penduz, decollez, et quarterez, et son teste envoie a Caleys ou le mourdre fuist fait, et les quartres envoiez as autres lieux ou le roy plerra."[39]

The episode is excluded from the more partisan chroniclers; so too, almost, the "Decapitacio Perkyn de Lye," at Chester, the center of Ricardian real power since about 1387, where Henry did make extensive show of force in the summer of 1399: "ubi demonstravit se et miliciam suam magnifice coram civitate."[40] The killing is reported by Adam Usk, who witnessed it: Henry himself, Adam has it, "tercio die aduentus sui ibidem, magni malefactoris reputati Perkyn de Lye caput amputari, et in palo ultra portam orientalem affigi, fecit" ["on the third day after his arrival there, he gave orders that Perkyn de Leigh, who was reputed to be a great malefactor, should be beheaded, and his head set up on a stake outside the east gate"]. The justification was the popular opprobrium again, but lighting on a local Ricardian official, who liked to dress himself up as a monk, Adam alleges. So he was mocked while being tortured, killed, and mutilated:

Iste Perkyn in forestia regia de Lamari prinsipalis custos, et eius officii maiestate plures opressiones et extorciones pagensibus fecerat monacalia indutus, quia sub talibus uestium transfuguracionibus plura dampnosa, ut dicebatur, perpetrauerat, merito in eadem captus transmigrare extitit.

[This Perkyn was principal keeper of the royal forest of Delamere, where, puffed up with the majesty of his office, he had inflicted countless oppressions and extortions on the inhabitants of the region, in the course of which he used to dress up as a monk, for it was said that while thus disguised he could perpetrate even greater cruelties; it was thus fitting that following his capture, he was put to death in the same garb.]

[39] *Rotuli Parliamentorum,* III, 452–53.
[40] *Vita Ricardi Secundi,* ed. Stow, p. 155. On Richard and Cheshire, see R. R. Davies, "Richard II and the Principality of Chester 1397–9," in *The Reign of Richard II: Essays in Honour of May McKisack,* ed. F. R. H. Du Boulay and Caroline M. Barron (London: Athlone, 1971), pp. 256–79; also McNiven, "The Cheshire Rising of 1400," 379–96; and James L. Gillespie, "Richard II's Archers of the Crown," *Journal of British Studies* 18 (1979): 14–29.

"Vnum bene scio quod de eius morte neminem ad tunc dolere perpendi" ["One thing I know for sure, that I know of nobody at the time who lamented his death"] is Adam's claim;[41] but there is contrary evidence in this case, in a contemporary local memorial of the man as a Ricardian martyr ("That for Kyng Richard the dethe did die, / Betrayed for righteousnesse") and in the comment of the "Dieulacres Chronicle," which imputes unjust killing ("sine causa") to the duke Henry personally (also replacing the demeaning diminutive of the Lancastrian sources): "Quo in tempore Petri de Legh iudicio ducis sine causa est abscissum et super portam orientalem Cestrie positum, cuius anime propicietur Deus" ["At that time, Peter Leigh was killed without cause by judgment of the duke, and his head was set atop Chester Eastgate, may God have mercy on his soul"].[42]

Greater concern had to attach to the salient instance of the Lancastrian revolutionary killing, the executions of Scrope, Bussy, and Green, when only Bagot escaped to enjoy the new king's *pietas:* more numerous victims, who were not local (like Peter Leigh) or servile (like John Hall), but realm-level political actors, closest to Richard of all Henry's victims, killed first, earliest in the revolutionary cycle. Like the killing of Peter Leigh at Chester, again belying the regime's conceit of a revolution "sine sanguinis effusione," these were extra-judicial murders in fact, illegal for want of proper regal authority. A trial was staged, evidently, as Walsingham's reiteration of the term *sententia* in his account of what happened at Bristol implies: "Tandem capti sunt et inuiti ducti extra castrum ad ducem Lancastrie. Et primo quidem arestati sunt, deinde in crastino coram iudicibus, uidelicet constabulario et marescallo, iudicio sistuntur."[43] [Finally they were laid hold of and conveyed resisting to the duke of Lancaster outside the city. First, they were put under arrest, and then the next morning they were brought up for trial before judges,

---

[41] *Chronicle of Adam Usk,* ed. and trans. Given-Wilson, pp. 56–59. Chaucer describes his *custos*-like Reeve as disposed to similar dress-up, at *Canterbury Tales* 1.590 "His toppe was dokked lyk a preest biforn" and 621 "Tukked he was as is a frere aboute." I am not able to find that the parallel has been noted; Jill Mann, *Chaucer and Medieval Estates Satire: The Literature of Social Classes and the General Prologue to the Canterbury Tales* (Cambridge: Cambridge University Press, 1973), p. 284 n. 70, comments on the curiousness of Chaucer's characterization.

[42] Clarke and Galbraith, "The Deposition of Richard II," pp. 163–64 and 172. The verses (reportedly inc. "Here lyeth the bodie of Perkyn a Leigh") are not listed in the *NIMEV.*

[43] The quotations here and just below are from the *Vita Ricardi secundi,* ed. Stow, p. 154.

namely, the Constable and the Marshall.] In fact, the Constable and Marshall mentioned here were with King Richard in Ireland, and it may be only that Henry already had decided that he could hold or distribute such offices himself if he wanted.[44] Henry was still only *dux,* however, illegally in England, and he had no business trying traitors or executing them, though that is what he did: "dampnati et decollati" ["condemned and beheaded"] were the three at Bristol, "de prodicione et mala gubernacione regis et regni conuicti" ["convict of treason and ill-governance of the king and kingdom"].

Also fundamentally troubling about the episode—and so not even hinted at in the Lancastrian apologists—was the fact that Henry still had not yet publicly articulated any intention to be king, though at Bristol he was already acting as if in law he were one. He promised (and would continue to promise for some time after the executions)— swearing solemn oaths publicly to various parties—that he was come, not to make himself king, but only "sua iura petens" ["seeking what was rightfully his"], as one of the poets put it.[45] Oath-breaking was taken seriously among the Lancastrians, it would seem, and charges of perjury against Henry himself were to recur virulently later; nonetheless, the regime was founded, as K. B. Macfarlane concluded, "on a series of unconstitutional actions and upon at least three major acts of perjury."[46]

Hence, in the present case, the awkwardness of the Bristol killings remained great enough that, as the last item of business on the last

[44] On the stewardship Henry may already have been claiming for himself and the legal implications of it, see Sherbourne, "Perjury and the Lancastrian Revolution," esp. pp. 233–34.

[45] The phrase is from the c. 1400 *Metrical Historia regum Anglie Continuation* 260 "Appulit interea dux sua iura petens," ed. Rigg, *A Book of British Kings, 1200 BC–1399 AD,* Toronto Medieval Latin Texts 26 (Toronto: Centre for Medieval Studies, 2000); but it can be widely paralleled, in Gower, for example: *Cronica* 3.129 "Vt sua propria querat" and 3.167 "sua propria dumque resumit": "In Praise of Peace" prol.2 (addressing Henry directly) "Qui bene venisti cum propria regna petisti," as well as in the Lancastrian *prosatores,* e.g., Walsingham (*Annales,* p. 241): "vt reuerteretur in terram natiuitatis suae, et iura paterna repeteret." The "Dieulacres Chronicle" (ed. Clarke and Galbraith, pp. 170–71) qualifies significantly: "Ut dixit, ius sue hereditatis vendicaturus."

[46] *Lancastrian Kings and Lollard Knights* (Oxford: Clarendon, 1972), pp. 49–58, at 58; developed in Sherbourne, "Perjury and the Lancastrian Revolution," pp. 217–41. A perverse symptom of the Lancastrian concern is the number of times in the "Articles of Deposition" of the "Record and Process" that charges of perjury are brought against Richard. Richard's coronation oath is reproduced in full in it (*Rotuli parliamentorum,* III, 417), and he is then alleged to have been foresworn again and again.

day of Henry's inaugural parliament, 19 November 1399, the commons petitioned the king to impose a stipulated legality on the killings, in retrospect.[47] "Les ditz communes prierent au Roy, qe la pursuyte, l'arest, et les juggementz, et quant qe fuist fait envers William le Scrop, chivaler, Henry Green, chivaler, et John Bussy, chivaler, purroient estre affirmez en cest present parlement, et tenuz pur bones." In response, the king asserted that these three men only ("lesqueux taunt soulement") had been "encountre le bon purpos et commune profit de le roialme" "et coupablez de toute le male q'avoit venuz au roialme": patent fiction—"lies and dissimulation" again—but expeditious, so, "toutz d'une accord," all members of the assembly concurred, finding "Qe mesmes les pursuite, areste, juggementz, et quant qe fuist fait, come desuis est dit, furent bons, et les afferment pur bons et profitables."

This sophisticated rendition of the Henrician Bristol "juggement" "droiturel" *post festum* in parliament, implicitly acknowledging that Henry's doings were and had otherwise remained illegal, bespeaks a concern over the crimes necessary to put Henry in possession of the throne—murder and perjury, used again against Richard II in February 1400—that persisted among the Lancastrian activists into the postrevolutionary period. Hence too then, the effort to pretend such popular animus against the Bristol victims as is asserted in the summer 1399 poems, which appear to have come into circulation at about this moment (excepting the Gower), probably too *post festum.* The poetry also exculpates, asserting that the killings were not much Henry's doing, let alone the doing of a *Henricus rex,* to be lauded for his *pietas.* The duke only acquiesced to a *clamor populi* at Bristol, with the poems themselves

---

[47] *Rotuli parliamentorum,* III, 453, whence come the quotations following. Objection to the proceeding was raised in parliament by William Scrope's father, Richard, seeking guarantees to protect property rights (his own particularly) from a conqueror's malevolence or greed. Henry's response was the threat that the *acta* report. In claiming the throne, 30 September 1399, Henry himself had promised, or warned (*Rotuli parliamentorum* III, 423): "it es noght my will that noman thynk þat be waye of conquest I wold disherit any man of his heritage, franches, or other ryghtes that hym aght to haue, ne put hym out of that that he has and has had by the gude lawes and custumes of the rewme, except thos persons that has ben agan the gude purpose and the commune profyt of the rewme." The language Henry is reported to have used in parliament 19 November 1399, in course of the incident under discussion, carefully repeats these terms he had used earlier. Henry would now be content to warrant, in effect, that only these three men, Scrope, Bussy, and Green, had been "encountre le bon purpos et commune profit de le roialme," in exchange for retrospective parliamentary legalization of his murders of them.

to supply proofs that there had been such *clamor*. No murder, nor perjury, the coincident evidence provided by the poets' performances showed, concurring with Henry's parliament. God had answered the people's prayers, and parliament pronounced so much legal and right: "et sur ceo les ditz communes mercierent au Roy de son droiturel juggement, et de ceo qe Dieux lour avoit envoie tiel Roy et Governour."

There is no evidence of writs going out to the English poets in late summer 1399, as they did to the monastic chronicle-keepers at the time, ordering them too to do their part for the Lancastrian management of the information stream, nor are there receipts of payment and the like.[48] About the better-attested, more extensive writings of Gower, there is much to indicate that he wrote for the Lancastrian regime otherwise, with something like official sponsorship, in response to specific commissions—his inaugural effusion for Henry, "In Praise of Peace," for example—as he may have done earlier for other English monarchs, possibly as early as late in the reign of Edward III.[49] As Gaillard Lapsley suggested, Gower's *Cronica tripertita* is as much as another witness to the "Record and Process of the Deposition," like the pertinent sections of Walsingham's *Chronica maiora*.[50] Gower follows the parliamentary record so closely that it must be understood (again, even in the absence of direct evidence to this effect) that he came into possession of one of the relatively numerous copies of the "Record and Process" that the regime put about and based his work directly on it. Gower's only substantive departure from the "Record and Process" in the portions of the *Cronica tripertita* that correspond comes in the accounts he gives there of what happened with Scrope, Bussy, Green, and Bagot at Bristol.

[48] Receipts of payment to John Lydgate for poetry-writing survive: see Derek A. Pearsall, *John Lydgate (1371–1449): A Bio-bibliography,* English Literary Studies Monograph Series 71 (Victoria: University of Victoria, 1997), p. 59, nos. 13 and 13A; and there are fairly numerous later examples, from the last quarter of the fifteenth century onward. Earlier, the only direct evidence takes the form of poets themselves claiming to have been commissioned to write, though the poets are not invariably credible witnesses in such matters; a near-contemporary instance, c. 1367, is discussed in Carlson, "The Invention of the Anglo-Latin Public Poetry (*circa* 1367–1402) and its Prosody, esp. in John Gower," *Mittellateinisches Jahrbuch* 39 (2004): 392–93.

[49] On "In Praise of Peace," see Grady, "The Lancastrian Gower and the Limits of Exemplarity," *Speculum* 70 (1995): 552–75; also, on Gower's writing of the late years, see Yeager, "Chaucer's 'To His Purse,'" pp. 401–5; and for evidence from earlier in Gower's career, see Carlson, "Gower's Early Latin Poetry: Text-Genetic Hypotheses of an *Epistola ad regem* (c. 1377–80)," *Mediaeval Studies* 65 (2003): 293–317.

[50] Gaillard Lapsley, "The Parliamentary Title of Henry IV," *EHR* 49 (1934): esp. 438–40, also 596–600; cf. Grady, "The Generation of 1399," p. 223.

The poetry's coincidence of interest, in the profitable fiction of a *clamor populi* at Bristol—representing the *clamor* itself or report of it at the time—exonerating Henry, is too hard to imagine as accidental, as are the convergences of this peculiar substance and the peculiar allegorical idiom that the poetry all deploys. Finally also, the poetry was too particularly useful to the Lancastrian regime then in process of installing itself to pass now for spontaneous. Rather than popular effusions, clerical or lay, the contemporary English poems on the events of July and August are the more likely to be evidence again of the Lancastrian regime's disposition to manipulate the historical record, and its groundbreaking labors at public self-fashioning.

Appendix:
"O Deus in Celis" Text and Translation

<fol. 94r>   O deus in celis, disponens cuncta fidelis,
               Deprecor, exaudi reddentes nos tue laudi.
               Ablue pennatos fallentes perfide natos,
               Vt tormentorum noscant recepisse dolorem.

<5>   De regno flores nostros tollunt meliores:
               Taxas de gente, pro defectu moriente.
               Hii sunt inflati, pro nummis infatuati;
               Querunt ditari, pro gasis delapidari.

               Illustrent <fraude vulpes> <r>apidi sine laude.
<10>   Plus querunt aurum quam celi <f>erre tezaurum.
               Dissimulant, verba ponentes mortis acerba.
               Hos regni terra mactent et aspera fer<r>a!

               Gens male taxatur; p<er>ante furta sequatur!
               Consilium tale pereat a sede regali.
<15>   Dux, perlustrator constans, sis tu dominator,
               Et fac tractari fals<o>s et decapitari!

               Milleni fantur quod plures associantur.
               Priuatur vita, clamat gens celitus ita.
               Quondam peiores sunt facti iam meliores:
<20>   Tales pomposi de stercore sunt generosi.

               Fraus latet illorum propter <. . .> tezaurum.
               Scrope, Bagge, Ver, Dumus, tormentorum par<i>t humus.

Dampnarunt forti iustorum corpora morti,
Sanguis <at> quorum vindictam clamat eorum.

<25> Inuidia tentum reuocetur parliamentum,
Vt ciuitas digna, que plurima passa maligna.
Ad nostrum ducem Lancastrie reddite lucem!
Huius consortes estote per omnia fortes!

Heu! periunt iura, nisi sint beneficia plura.
<30> Lux, laus, Henricus, Lancastrie factus, amicus,
Scutis <patronus> nos protegat vndique pronus!
Taxa <. . .>

<. . .>
<Illo> regnante, semper post cesset, <u>t ante.
<35> Huius dux causa pateat! Sua ianua clausa;
<fol. 95v> Pannis indutus plusquam viuit modo mutus.

Mox suspendatur, si verum lingua loquatur.
Expedit armare, nos a somno vigilare.
Galli<a> per artes nostras vult perdere partes.
<40> Nos fallunt, illa que <palma fixa> sigilla.

Scriptum draconis verbum spernit Salamonis.
Gallus cantabit causas; caulis latitabit.
Aquila dux austro saluabit nos alabaustro.
Illius cetum prestet, Christe, fore letum!

[O God in the heavens, all-disposing, trustworthy,
Hear us, I pray, as we give ourselves to your praise.
Wipe out those befeathered boys, treacherously deceiving,
That they might know receiving the pain of torments.

<5> They pluck from the realm our better blossoms:
Taxes from the people, dying for want.
Such men are puffed up, infatuated with riches;
They seek to enrich themselves, to plunder for treasure.

Let their blazon be foxes, ravening in deceit, praiselessly.
<10> They want to carry off gold more than heaven's treasure.
They practice deceit, pronouncing bitter words of death.
Let the kingdom and hard steel punish them!

The people are wrongfully taxed, so let them try thievery
beforehand!

411

<15>
Such counsel from about the throne should be gone.
Duke, who shine constantly upon us, be you the master,
And cause false persons to be drawn and beheaded!

<20>
Many conspire, thousands are saying.
Life is laid waste, so the people cry out heavenwards.
Persons once lowly are now made superior:
Such pompous nobles are up from the dung-heap.

Their treachery lies hidden because of the riches they have.
A soil of torments engenders Scrope, Bagot, Spring-Green, and Thorn-Bush.
They condemn the bodies of the just to mighty death,
And their blood yet cries out for vengeance against them.

<25>
Held for spite, let the parliament be called anew,
Like a worthy city that has suffered many wrongs.
Return life again to our duke of Lancaster!
Be bold in all, you who are his followers!

<30>
But alas! laws die, if there be not many emoluments.
Splendour, praise, Henry, made duke of Lancaster, friend,
Eager shield-guardian, may he protect us on all sides!
Tax <. . .>

<. . .>
With him reigning, it would cease ever after, as before.
<35>
For the sake of this, let the duke come forth! His way is barred;
Dressed in rags, he lives now more in quiet.

Were a tongue to tell truth, straightaway would come a hanging.
It behooves us to arm, to rouse us up from sleep.
By ruses, France would lay waste our provinces.
<40>
They lead us astray, those armorial seals which are affixed by the palm.

The Dragon's script scorns the word of Salomon.
The Cock will crow its causes; in the sheep-folds will it hide.
The eagle-duke will save us from the alabaster-white south.
May it come to pass, Christ, that this man's company fare well!

TEXT:

Oxford, Bodleian Library, Ms. Rawlinson 4.429, fols. 94r–95v = *ms.*
Wr = ed. Wright, *Political Poems and Songs,* I, 366–68.

VARIANTS:

9 <fraude vulpes>] vulpes fraude *ms.*, *Wr* 9 <r>apidi] *fortasse* <r> a<b>idi : lapidi *ms.* : liuidi *Wr* 10 <f>erre] terre *ms.* 12 fer<r>a] *Wr* : fera *ms.* 13 p<er>ante] prouocante *ms.* 14 pereat] pareat *Wr* 15 tu] an *Wr* 16 fals<o >s] *Wr* : falses *ms.* 21 propter <. . .> tezaurum] propter tezaurum *ms.* 22 Ver] *fortasse* Ver<t> 22 par<i>t] parat *ms.* 24 <at>] que [= relative pronoun] *ms.* : qui *Wr* 24 vindictam] vindicta *Wr* 25 tentum reuocetur] centum reuocatur *Wr* 26 ciuitas] cunctas *Wr* 29 Periunt] Pereunt *Wr* 31 <patronus>] et armis *ms.* 31 pronus] pronos *Wr* 32–34] Taxa regnante semper post cesset et ante *ms.* 34 cesset] cessit *Wr* 34 <u>t] et *ms.* 35 Sua] sibi *Wr* (*non sine vi*) 39 Galli<a>] Gallica *ms.* 40 Nos] Rex *Wr* 40 <palma fixa>] fixa palma *ms.* : fixa penna *Wr* 44 Christe] Christus *Wr*

NOTES:

1: Cf. Gower, *Cronica tripertita* 1.109–10 "Sic deus in celis mala de puteo Michaelis / Acriter expurgat, ne plus comes ille resurgat," where the reference is to another, earlier much execrated favorite of Richard's, Michael de la Pole, earl of Suffolk (c. 1330–89), by means of the same sort of interlingual punning (see above, p. 385). Also, Gower, *Cronica tripertita* 1.54 "Sic quasi de celis interfuit, ille fidelis," where the reference is to Henry Bolingbroke. Gower did often rework or more simply reuse lines he had fashioned for another use; examples are discussed in "Gower's Early Latin Poetry," pp. 300–303 and 305, and "A Rhyme Distribution Chronology of John Gower's Latin Verse," pp. 25–7, 31–5, and 38–9.

3: *pennatos:* perhaps 'full-fledged,' like arrows properly fledged or fletched with feathers, in context 'over-grown,' boys who have gotten too big; or perhaps 'feathered,' like demons, who are sometimes depicted with feathered legs; or perhaps 'winged,' like the old god of cupidity itself, the boy Cupid.

4: Rhyme and meter fail in this line, which is nevertheless sensible. It may be that (unmetrical) *recēpisse* is a miswriting of *resipisse,* differing in sense but similarly pronounced.

8: *gasis:* > CL *gaza, -ae.*

8: *delapidari:* > CL *dilapido, -are,* but as a deponent for the sake of rhyme.

413

9: *Illustrent:* The translation interprets the verb as taking its sense from the cognate technical term *illustratio,* 'blazon,' in heraldry. The alternative interpretation ("Let foxes illuminate them") seems less pointed.

9: <*fraude vulpes*> the inversion of order restores rhyme.

9: <*r*>*apidi:* though the suggested reading may be somewhat strained in sense—"rabidi" might be more idiomatic—it has the attraction of being nearer manuscript "lapidi" than Wright's apparent conjecture "liuidi."

10: <*f*>*erre:* manuscript "terre" would be sensible, in chiasmus with "celi"—'aurum terre quam celi tezaurum'—but (with an ultimate longum) it is unmetrical.

10, 21: *tezaurum:* (in the same metrical position both times) > CL *thesaurum, -i.*

12: *terra:* the translation construes the noun as a nominative, taking its final longum in the position to be an instance of lengthening at the caesura, only *metri causa,* as is ubiquitous in contemporary prosody (e.g., the preceding line 11 *verbā*).

13: *p*<*er*>*ante:* manuscript "prouocante" will not construe (though a similarly dangling ablative may occur again below, 34 "regnante"), and it has too many syllables for the meter. The proposal supposes a lengthening of the final -*ē,* as if by analogy with regular adverbs.

15: *dux:* as confirmed later in the poem (26 and 30), the reference is to Henry Bolingbroke; for the implications for the date, see above, p. 378.

15: *Dux, perlustrator constans, sis tu dominator:* other constructions of the sequence of nominatives (differently punctuated) can be imagined. The line may recall (or be recalled by) Gower, *Cronica tripertita* 3.486 (with reference to Richard II): "Est qui peccator non esse potest dominator."

16: *tractari . . . et decapitari:* A precise description (in the correct legal terms) of what was in fact to happen: see above, pp. 396–7.

18: *clamat gens celitus:* For parallel conceits in the contemporary literature, see above, pp. 401–2.

19–20: *Quondam peiores sunt facti iam meliores./ Tales pomposi de stercore sunt generosi:* Adam Usk (ed. Given-Wilson, pp. 60–62) has similar comment, at the only point in his *Chronicle* where he mentions William Bagot.

21: *propter* <. . .> *tezaurum:* grammar and rhyme are satisfactory, despite the metrical shortness of the line, evidently just at this point: a word (or some combination of words) with the metrical values longum—longum—breve is wanted.

22: *Scrope, Bagge, Ver, Dumus:* On the careers of these four men, see above, pp. 392–402. On the interlingual synonymy peculiar to this corpus of poetry by which some are named here, see above, pp. 384–5. Wright's note (*Political Poems and Songs,* I, 367) essays an identification of "Ver" as "Robert de Vere, duke of Ireland," but this is an error (*vt puto*): though formerly a notorious victim of Richard's enemies, he had died at Louvain in 1392, having fled abroad after his defeat at Radcot Bridge in 1387 in the Appellants' coup, some years before the "O deus in celis" could have been written.

23: *Dampnarunt forti iustorum corpora morti:* For other contemporary attempts to blame these men for (or at least implicate them in) the "Revenge" parliament killings of 1397, see above, pp. 394–5.

24: *Sanguis* <*at*>: The manuscript's relative pronoun "que" (like Wright's "qui") does not make sense; an enclitic -*quĕ* ("Sanguisque") would be both sensible and close to the manuscript reading, perhaps enough so to tolerate its (unmetrical) brevity.

25: *Inuidia tentum:* The final parliamentary meetings before the deposition were the so-called Shrewesbury and Westminster continuations of the 1397 "Revenge" parliament, during early 1398, where parliamentary business of the "Revenge" parliament was carried forward by means of a subcommittee, of Richard's election, to which were appointed Scrope, Bussy, and Green, *inter alios,* but not Bagot (see *Rotuli parliamentorum* III, 368). The chief business of the continuations was additional prosecutions of Richard's enemies and the banishment of Bolingbroke; and their legality, not to mention their probity, was to form the basis of one of the "Articles of Deposition" in 1399 (Art. 8; cf. Art. 31: *Rotuli parliamentorum* III, 418 and 421). The issues are discussed in J. G. Edwards, "The Parliamentary Committee of 1398," *EHR* 40 (1925), 321–33.

26: *ciuitas:* Wright's "cunctas" would appear to be his representation of a manuscript spelling "cuntas" (a widely attested contemporary spelling), having the same number of minims. A similar line, perhaps clarifying the simile here ("vt ciuitas"), occurs in a poem of 1314 on the English defeat at Bannockburn, "Me cordis angustia," ed. Wright, *The Political Songs of England, from the Reign of John to that of Edward II*, Camden Society Old Series 6 (1839; repr. New York: Johnson, 1968), pp. 262–267, at p. 267, addressing "Anglia" now bereft of the earl of Gloucester, who was killed in the battle (110–113):

> Facta es vt domina viro viduata,
> Cuius sunt solamina in luctum mutata;
> Tu es sola civitas capite truncata;
> Tuos casus Trinitas faecundet beata!

31: *Scutis* <*patronus*> *nos:* manuscript "Scutis et armis," reasonably sensible, perhaps explicable as an intrusive cliché, will not scan ("et," not closed, is a breve) and does not rhyme; Wright's attempt to read "pronos" line-final, as if to make rhyme with "nos," will not do either: "nos" is post-caesural (and the "rhyme" would still be only monosyllabic). By light of the money-oriented immediate context (29 "beneficia," 32 "Taxa"), it might be possible (preferable) to take *scutum* as *écu,* the coin, understanding *scutis pronus* as "ready with coins, money."

32–34: The manuscript line, "Taxa regnante semper post cesset et ante," is troubling: it makes the final syllable of "Taxa" long, as if the word were to make an ablative absolute with "regnante"—and unlike the formally similar manuscript "prouocante" in 13, here "regnante" is confirmed by rhyme—but then the line leaves the verb "cesset" without an expressed subject; no other implicit subject can be supplied from the context, and resupplying "Taxa" itself for itself makes nonsense ("With tax reigning, tax would cease"), likewise taking the ablative phrase "Taxa regnante" as if somehow grammatically a subject. A possibility might be to construe the manuscript line's "Taxā" with the previous line 31, punctuating: "nos protegat . . . / Taxā!" ("he would protect us from tax!"), leaving "regnante" alone, to be construed with the rest of its line (loosely, perhaps, "eo" to be supplied, refering back to 30 "Henricus"): "Regnante, semper post cesset" "[With him] reigning, it [i.e., *taxa*] would cease ever after." The more extreme solution proposed here means to avoid some of these problems—the necessity of taking

32 "Taxa" as ablative case, and then resupplying the same term in the same line as a subject for 32 "cesset"; also, the related disconnection or incompletion about 34 "regnante"—by imagining a lacuna. So doing has the recommendation of preserving the otherwise consistent end-stopping of lines; also, of resolving the scribal division of the poem into quatrains, which otherwise comes up two lines short at the end in the manuscript's presentation. An alternative might be to treat the first two lines as a separate exordium-like injunction, shifting the beginning of the quatrain sequence to 3 (with line-space after 6, after 10, et cetera); but the attempt to do so would put an unacceptable quatrain division after 30, just about this hypothesized lacuna, where the one line oc-curs—the string of nominatives "Lux, laus, Henricus, Lancastrie factus, amicus"—that has a necessary (grammatical) connection with some-thing following: it needs the next line for completion. There is nothing in the poem itself, however, to indicate any quatrain (or other stichic or stanzaic) arrangement: no scheme of rhymes between (rather than within) lines or alternations of length of line, to provide *inter alia* some check on the scribal conduct; so it may be that any divisions of some groups of lines from others (couplets or quatrains) ought to be ignored. On the other hand, this same extrinsic nature of the quatrain divisions may indicate authority. Without prompting by the verse itself, a copyist would not trouble to impose an invented scheme; if such a premise is good—and it may well not be—the copyist here must be imagined to have been following the exemplar, at least to start; the (hypothesized) missing out of lines here would have put the exemplary scheme off, with the consequent stranding of the two lines 43–44 at the end of the surviving copy (as in Wright's representation).

35: perhaps instead: "Huius, dux, causa pateat sua ianua clausa" or, with Wright's conjecture, "sibi ianua clausa," "For the sake of this, O duke, let his closed door be open!" or "the door closed to him be open!"

37: *Mox:* emending to "<V>ox" might yield better sense: "were tongue to speak truth, that voice would be cut off." In any case, truth-telling was an especially vivid issue just at the moment, as witnesses contemporary poetry (from Chaucer's *Manciple's Tale* to *Mum and the Sothsegger*), but also as a specific legal charge against the Ricardian re-gime, which was regarded as having tried to criminalize speech: see Art. 20 of the "Record and Process" (*Rotuli parliamentorum* III, 420).

40: <*palma fixa*> *sigilla:* the reversal of the ms. word-order makes "palma" ablative and "fixa" nominative, to go with "sigilla." Whereas the grammatical relation in the ms. word-order cannot make sense, the reversal comes only somewhat closer to doing so. The translation interprets "palma" to mean "hand," by metonomy; an alternative might be to take it as an additional heraldic reference, to a "frond" of some sort: perhaps the fleur-de-lis of France, perhaps the *planta genesta,* or broomscod, of Richard's family. In either case, if the reference of "sigilla" is to armorial tokens, the use and abuse of them in retaining was a vivid contemporary issue: see John M. Bowers, *"Pearl* in Its Royal Setting: Ricardian Poetry Revisited," *SAC* 17 (1995): 136–37.

41–43: On the tradition of the enigmatic phraseology used here (*Scriptum draconis, verbum Salamonis, Gallus* apparently for France, *Aquila dux* for Henry Bolingbroke), see above, pp. 388–9. A similarly conceited stanza occurs in the "Me cordis angustia," ed. Wright, *The Political Songs of England,* at p. 267, allegorising the Scots' defeat of the English at Bannockburn (102-105):

> Quando saevit aquilum [= the north-east wind],
>   affricus [= the southwest wind] quievit;
> Et australi [= southern] populo dampnum
>   mortis crevit.
> Anglia victoria frui consuevit,
> Sed prolis perfidia mater inolevit.

43: *austro saluabit nos alabaustro:* Henry returned to England in the North (see above, p. 379, e.g.), so it seems likely or possible that the reference to the South is to the Ricardian regime based at Westminster, revealing an antimetropolitan or decentralizing bias often associated with the North in this period. Though *alabauster* is here taken as adj. modifying *auster,* it is not an especially instructive term; possibly some form of *arbalauster* (a loan-word from French, consequently spelled very variously in contemporary Latin) may lie behind the ms. reading: translate "The eagle-duke will save us from the south with his cross-bow."

44: *cetum:* the translation interprets as a spelling of CL *coetus, -i* "company, assembly," though CL *coeptum, -i* 'undertaking, purpose' (most commonly spelt in ML *ceptum, -i*) may also be possible.

Newfangled Readers in Gower's "Apollonius of Tyre"

Elizabeth Allen
University of California, Irvine

JOHN GOWER'S TALE OF "APOLLONIUS OF TYRE" begins with a strikingly explicit act of father-daughter incest perpetrated by a king. For Gower, however, "Apollonius" thematizes incest in order to meditate on audience reception: incestuous desire, repeatedly encountered and avoided throughout the narrative, necessitates a series of interpretive acts that figure the relation between king and subject as a relation of mutual audience. The interpretive effort that bolsters monarchy while attending to the needs of its subjects requires imagination on the part of both monarch and subjects. I argue in this essay that incest in "Apollonius" stages an exploration of such imaginative activity: a series of kings' daughters are figured as new audiences who reinterpret in order to reaffirm monarchical power. Far from the injunctive exemplary moralism with which Gower used to be associated, the interpretive process hypothesized in "Apollonius of Tyre" urges that readers invent, not just imitate, virtuous conduct. At the same time, moreover, Amans's reception in the framework of the *Confessio* complicates Gower's otherwise affirmative picture of active new audiences because he misunderstands the ways in which the story could apply to his life. Thus despite Book 8's embrace of imaginative fiction, in particular romance, the final action of the poem also points to severe constraints upon narrative's real-world applicability, as Amans is reconciled to John Gower and finally renounces love, "mak[ing] an ende" (8.2902) of stories. For what purposes does a poem that concludes with such renunciation generate eight books' worth of examples, in all their copiousness, applicability, and narrative variety? For what purposes does this poem end with the most frankly fictive of stories, the "Tale of Apollonius"? How does Gower

419

make this tale, and narrative generally, morally applicable?[1] Despite the accomplishments of recent scholarship, the poem's construction of moral influence remains problematic because, to my mind, our most recent and searching accounts of the poem's moral complexity tend to underplay the *Confessio*'s methods of anticipating, and even setting free, its own audience.

The *Confessio*'s conclusion seems particularly perverse because Book 8 already announces an explicit generic shift from exemplum to romance, as though abandoning the former and authorizing the latter. Exemplarity relies on a basic analogy between character and reader that, at its extreme, generates a fantasy of exact repetition: the ideal patient Griselda, for instance, should be possible for wives to imitate. Many readers have seen that Chaucer's Griselda may not, in fact, be imitable because of the resistance of real-world women, the imperfection of Walter's judgment, and the unbearable brutality of such suffering.[2] For Gower, as for Chaucer, the extreme version of exemplary repetition constitutes not a communicative ideal but a potential trap. Throughout the *Confessio,* in fact, Amans's responses generate discussion between himself and Genius about the applicability of stories to his own love affair.[3]

---

[1] The tag "moral Gower," which Chaucer bestowed on his contemporary, has been complicated by many critics since the work of John Fisher in *John Gower, Moral Philosopher and Friend of* Chaucer (New York: New York University Press, 1964). For classic explorations of the connection between morality and poetics in Gower, see Charles Runacres, "Art and Ethics in the Exempla of the Confessio Amantis," in *Gower's "Confessio Amantis": Responses and Reassessments,* ed. Alastair J. Minnis (Woodbridge: D. S. Brewer, 1983), 106–34; and R. F. Yeager, *John Gower's Poetic: The Search for a New Arion* (Cambridge: D. S. Brewer, 1990). On the morally formative powers of art in Gower, see James Simpson, *Sciences and the Self in Medieval Poetry: Alain of Lille's "Anticlaudianus" and John Gower's "Confessio Amantis"* (Cambridge: Cambridge University Press, 1995), esp. pp. 136–38. For recent treatments of the ways in which literary effects complicate clear moral truths and demand practical wisdom, see, for example, Patricia Batchelor, "Feigned Truth and Exemplary Method in the Confessio Amantis," in *Re-Visioning Gower,* ed. R. F. Yeager (Asheville, N.C.: Pegasus Press, 1998), pp. 1–16; J. Allan Mitchell, *Ethics and Exemplarity in Chaucer and Gower* (Cambridge: D. S. Brewer, 2004); and Diane Watt, *Amoral Gower: Language, Sex, and Politics* (Minneapolis: University of Minnesota Press, 2003).

[2] Particularly on the brutality of making an example of Griselda's suffering, see David Wallace, *Chaucerian Polity: Absolutist Lineages and Associational Forms in England and Italy* (Stanford: Stanford University Press, 1997), pp. 261–98.

[3] Application is my term more than Gower's: it is the folding of a narrative toward or into one's experience (Latin *ad* + *plicare,* to fold). In Book 1, Gower' "information" is related to application: "Mi Sone, as I thee schal enforme, / Ther ben yet of an other forme / Of dedly vices sevene applied, / Wherof the herte is ofte plied / To thing which after schal him grieve" (575–79). Here, application means naming, attaching a sign to, and thereby enabling comprehension of each deadly sin. In Chaucer, the word "applien"

Generally Amans embraces Genius's lessons most wholeheartedly when he can identify with a character—such as Canacee's enraged father, Aeolus, whose brutality against weaker members of the household Amans finds in himself as well (3.396ff.). Although moral application does not necessarily depend upon the affective dimension of such responses, identification is the emotional register in which Amans typically recognizes examples as analogous, hence relevant, to his own situation. When Genius turns to romance in Book 8, though, he leaves Amans's kind of exemplarity behind, in favor of an antique incest narrative with no direct correspondence to Amans's lovelorn condition.

Yet Gower has foregrounded Amans's vocabulary of correspondence throughout the *Confessio*. Amans, like the Host in the *Canterbury Tales,* consistently articulates a range of readings based on matching the story to his own life. To be sure, his methods make him a foil for the more sophisticated extratextual audience and, in that sense, a straw man with respect to actual habits of reading. Yet the exchange between Amans and Genius repeatedly stages exemplary morality in such a way as to make simple correspondence look initially attractive, summary morals seem incisive, and narratives themselves appear efficiently demonstrative of general truth. But both priest and lover repeatedly complicate the act of application, partly because Amans's emotional dissatisfaction contains him in a holding pattern throughout the book. His identification with moral narratives, moreover, can never be complete or exact, partly because it coexists with other effects of reading, like disapprobation or desire. In the "Tale of Virginia" near the end of Book 7, for instance, Genius's disapproval of Virginius calls into question the very value of storytelling itself. Earlier, at the conclusion of Book 6, Amans begs to hear the tales of kings—in particular, the tales used to educate Alexander—precisely as a distraction from his own amatory woes. Clearly this request inverts the usual relationship between recreational poetry and politics (poetry is usually an escape from politics, not vice versa), but Book 7's mirror for princes also emphasizes the distance between story and application, since Amans is not himself a prince. The Book relies upon but rarely states its implicit analogy between self-governance and kingship, leaving much to the reader's powers of analysis.

---

is used to mean combine (MED, s.v. "applien"). In demanding application, Gower's Genius suggests that narratives are not instrumental but constitutive of moral experience—that is, they work by activating readers, encouraging them, we might say, to "combine" the text with their own mental structures.

When toward the end of Book 7 the "Tale of Virginia" offers no clear monarchical ideal, the book lurches toward the conclusion that the meaning of power depends on those subject to it. Analogously, the meaning of authority depends on the reader.[4] In Book 8, we might expect Genius to reassert moral authority, providing a bulwark against utter relativism; we might expect him to announce Amans's resemblance to fictional characters, since the topic is now desire, the defining feature of Amans's predicament. But when Genius instead shifts from compressed exempla to dilated romance, spending almost the whole narrative energy of Book 8 on one story, he conclusively frustrates Amans's poetics of correspondence: the *Confessio*'s inscribed reader cannot create analogy between "Apollonius" and his own experience, fails to identify emotionally with the character, and therefore dismisses the whole narrative as irrelevant.

Book 8's expansion beyond the usual form of the exemplum, however, does not simply undo "the very analogical premises of exemplary reasoning."[5] Instead, Book 8 shows that Amans has fundamentally misapprehended the exemplary education that comprises the *Confessio*. Indeed, it is the task of the present essay to argue that Gower chooses father-daughter incest as the thematic focus of the book precisely because incest provides a figure for the coercive extreme in which stories demand a too-close alignment between moralist and audience: a figure, that is, for a poetics of correspondence. Indeed, Gower's final book dissuades readers from sheer imitation by examining the ways in which analogies created through literary repetition can, by virtue of their very analogical structure, negotiate moral transformation.[6] "Apollonius of

---

[4] I draw here on my account of the Virginia story in *False Fables and Exemplary Truth in Later Middle English Literature* (New York: Palgrave Macmillan, 2005), chap. 3.

[5] William Robins, "Romance, Exemplum, and the Subject of the *Confessio Amantis*," SAC 19 (1997): 157–81 (165). Robins finds that Amans refuses analogy *tout court*, whereas I would say that Amans actually expects stories to provide too close an analogy to his own life, and fails to accept the exemplary potential of romance. Larry Scanlon draws the opposition when he asserts that the tale is an exemplum, not a romance, as though the two necessarily ruled each other out. See "The Riddle of Incest: John Gower and the Problem of Medieval Sexuality," in *Re-Visioning Gower,* ed. R. F. Yeager (Asheville, N.C.: Pegasus Press, 1998), pp. 93–128 (112, 124).

[6] Analogy, for Aristotle a type of metaphor, implies proportional association: as *a* is to *b*, so *c* is to *d*. Analogies create associative, not causal structures: "When they tried to force his son who was under age to perform public services because he was tall, Iphicrates said that if they deem large boys men, they should vote that small men are boys" (*Rhetoric* 1399a). In Gower, the analogy between incest and political power (as fathers are to daughters, so kings are to their subjects) exposes the coercive potential of kingship. When a power relation resembling incest *doesn't* result in the sin, the analogy has succeeded in transforming a potential likeness into a differentiation. The analogy

Tyre" culminates the *Confessio*'s resistance to authoritative command— that of both kings and narrators—by emphasizing the changing stakes of narrator, characters, and audience in serial revisions of the incest act.[7] By stressing the increasingly willful separation of daughters from their fathers, Genius calls for a similar interpretive autonomy on the part of Amans and any audience. Far from a static alignment between characters and audiences, moreover, Book 8 insistently represents any interpreter's moral choice as an unpredictable and idiosyncratic process, a creative invention based on revising the past—a process that partakes in the imaginative dynamism of plot itself.[8]

Gower's Audiences: Women, Innovation, and Variety

Even at the beginning of the *Confessio,* in the outermost framework of quasi-dream vision, Gower depicts exemplarity as fundamentally dependent upon variety in audience response. Gower chose to write the poem in English, as opposed to Latin or French, to encode his text as a more accessible, contemporary, and "comun" one.[9] The *Confessio*'s "Prologue"

---

contained within "Apollonius" enters the framework of the poem when Amans denies his own likeness to the incestuous father, and readers are left to ask how incest (a relation between authority and subject) might be analogous to reading (a relation between author and audience). On analogy, see Aristotle, *On Rhetoric,* trans. and ed. George A. Kennedy (Oxford: Oxford University Press, 1991), 2:17, 3:10:4. The classic investigation of the analogy between self and king in Gower is Russell Peck, *Kingship and Common Profit in Gower's "Confessio Amantis"* (Carbondale: University of Southern Illinois Press, 1978).

[7] On incest as the plot that "keeps hanging over the story as a possibility . . . until nearly the end" (44), see Northrop Frye, *The Secular Scripture: A Study of the Structure of Romance* (Cambridge, Mass.: Harvard University Press, 1976), pp. 44–48, 52.

[8] Helen Cooper has recently argued that Shakespeare's *Pericles,* among other Gower reflexes that appear in the Early Modern period, helps construct Gower not as a moralist but as a generator of "willed imaginative magic" (113). See " 'This worthy olde writer': *Pericles* and Other Gowers, 1592–1640," *A Companion to Gower,* ed. Siân Echard (Cambridge: D. S. Brewer, 2004), pp. 99–113.

[9] Although critics vary in the kind of authority they ascribe to the Latin apparatus of the *Confessio,* the poem's moral equivocations have often been located in the relation between Latin and English, a question that I leave aside here in part because the Latin glosses are comparatively quite thin in the story of "Apollonius." For an argument that the two languages problematize the very notion of authority itself, see Batcheler, "Feigned Truth and Exemplary Method," in *Re-Visioning Gower,* and on Gower's multivalent latinity, see the work of Siân Echard, especially "With Carmen's Help: Latin Authorities in the *Confessio Amantis,*" *SP* 95 (1998): 1–40. For the view that Latin and vernacular authority continually conflict in the poem, see the seminal essay by Winthrop Wetherbee, "Latin Structure and Vernacular Space: Gower, Chaucer and the Boethian Tradition," in *Chaucer and Gower: Difference, Mutuality, Exchange,* ed. R. F. Yeager (Victoria, B.C.: English Literary Studies, 1991), pp. 36–74.

suggests that the whole poem refers directly to the social and political world of England. Book 1 then enters the oblique world of fiction, where Amans encounters Venus and the angry Cupid, and Venus sends him her priest. Genius launches his eight books of stories, throughout which Genius and Amans discuss successive acts of application to his particular situation. By the time readers reach the eighth book of the poem, the notion of application itself has come under serious scrutiny. Instead of systematic, authoritative moral direction, the *Confessio* offers a series of seductively transparent narratives that pull readers up short; an ostensibly authoritative guide, Genius, whose injunctions frequently fail to match his stories; and an embedded audience, Amans, who often points out that narratives with Genius's morals have only unpredictable relevance to his own love affair.[10]

At the same time, however, the fantasy of correspondence is continually activated, because Gower's purpose remains the creation of analogies between story and audience. This purpose is served by a rhetoric of plain-style accessibility.[11] Book 1 presents the *Confessio* as a new genre in a new language, intended to reach an audience Gower has not yet addressed:

> [T]he Stile of my writinges
> Fro this day forth I thenke change
> And speke of thing is noght so strange,
> Which every kinde hath upon honde, . . .
> And that is love.
>
> (1.8–11, 15)

[10] The diffuse authority of the *Confessio* has been remarked by many recent critics; for example, María Bullón-Fernández writes, "The *Confessio Amantis* has no single authoritative voice, but many different voices. Gower is more interested in the contrast among these voices than in the hegemony of one over the others," in *Fathers and Daughters in Gower's Confessio Amantis: Authority, Family, State, and Writing* (Cambridge: D. S. Brewer, 2000), p. 38. The critical tendency to privilege Gower's indeterminacy can sometimes lead to a celebration of copiousness that, in turn, raises the question of what moral determinations *are* in fact available in the text. Mitchell, *Ethics and Exemplary Narrative*, puts his finger on this problem: "Gower can be seen sorting out the benefits and liabilities of the case-ethics he employs to educate Amans, at the same time as he leaves it to Amans to make the best of . . . diverse moral examples" (p. 6). The aspiration toward moral directiveness remains a powerful impulse throughout the poem, expressed in claims of plainness and ethical certainty even as Bullón-Fernández's multiplicity of voices also emerges.

[11] For a suggestive account of the functions of the plain style in Gower, see John Burrow, "Gower's Poetic Styles," in *A Companion to Gower*, pp. 239–50. Burrow notes that "Stile" as used here refers to content, not just manner of writing (245).

The *Confessio* is designed, Gower claims, to be familiar and accessible; he chooses the discourse of love because it can include everyone, being less "strange," implicitly because of its association with vernacular poetry.[12] But in establishing the familiarity of his topic, he calls for readerly application: examples are designed to typify and affirm the shared—that is, the conventional—aspects of emotional experience, the repeatability of a familiar tale, and the modern relevance of past events. The new "Stile" is linked explicitly to a new theme, but both are designed to achieve legibility to "every kinde." Finally, the self-conscious change from strange to plain language suggests the potential for this poem to connect past and present, "Fro this day forth," in a narrative that will make stories of past virtue amenable to present-day experience.

It is well established that in his explicitly new literary language, Gower imagines an interpretive variety and multiplicity beyond what was possible in his French and Latin works.[13] Thus he opens the poem to "every kinde," a "comun" audience in the sense developed by Anne Middleton.[14] By embracing plural audiences, Gower acknowledges that he lives in a world full of "divisioun" for which he seeks order or coherence through writing; if his poem can reach many different audiences, then perhaps too it can make social differences cohere. Less well established is Gower's use of women to figure the remedial effects of such variety. Throughout the *Confessio,* in fact, division frequently arises from male anger and excess; and anger is either provoked or healed by female audiences, from the doomed Canacee to Florent's hag to Constance, and most explicitly Apollonius's daughter Thaise. For Gower, then, female audiences—those who hear, recognize, and redirect male aggression—do not just challenge norms but can represent the potential for

---

[12] "Strange" suggests not only foreignness or unfamiliarity but elaboration or ingenuity, and obscurity in language (MED, s.v. "straunge," 2[d]). Gower sets up the expectation that audiences will be able to find the familiar and, implicitly, the applicable in his poem.

[13] The contingencies of Gower's use of English are emphasized by Tim William Machan, "Medieval Multilingualism and Gower's Literary Practice," *Studies in Philology* 103 (2006): 1–25. Siân Echard complicates this view by reminding us that Gower's choice of English does not effect "a discarding of outdated languages or modes," but rather "an accumulation" of different voices, in "Gower's 'bokes' of Latin': Language, Politics, and Poetry," *SAC* 25 (2003): 123–56 (156).

[14] Anne Middleton, "The Idea of Public Poetry in the Reign of Richard II," *Speculum* 53 (1978): 94–114.

mending or healing social divisions.[15] As members of Gower's plural, "comun" audience, women become available as figures for new readership in general. Certainly not every female character throughout the *Confessio* thematizes innovative reception; in "Albinus and Rosemund," the lady offers no remedial counsel but simply takes her revenge upon the husband who has made her drink from a cup carved out of her father's skull; in "Constance," the lady's passive suffering eventually reveals, and remedies, masculine violence against her. But in "Apollonius," when female characters respond to faulty masculine aggression, they are figured as interpreters of men, and their role is both to identify violence and provide a new alternative to it.[16]

Women were, of course, vital members of fourteenth-century English vernacular literary culture. Jennifer Summit writes that "women became the privileged addressees of vernacular writing" and, indeed, that their roles as patrons and letter-writers call into question modern assumptions about book consumption as "passive and secondary."[17] Indeed, the fact that women partook in literate culture in various ways suggests the degree to which different levels of interpretive activity defined Gower's

[15] On women's rhetorical regulation of male anger, see David Wallace, "Household Rhetoric: Violence and Eloquence in the Tale of Melibee," in *Chaucerian Polity Absolutist Lineages and Associational Forms in England and Italy* (Stanford: Stanford University Press, 1997), pp. 212–46. Because of their conventional capacity to encourage mercy and restraint, women's presence can paradoxically encourage extremes of male violence, as when Florent's hag first prompts and then checks the hero's resentment about marrying her. The potential for women to challenge and (therefore) regulate excesses of male violence—and the ritualized way in which female counsel can be displayed so as to enhance male power even as a particular woman seems to hold it in check—is elucidated by Paul Strohm in "Queens As Intercessors," in *Hochon's Arrow: The Social Imagination of Fourteenth-Century Texts* (Princeton: Princeton University Press, 1992), pp. 95–120.
[16] Karma Lochrie, in *Covert Operations: The Medieval Uses of Secrecy* (Philadelphia: University of Pennsylvania Press, 1999), pp. 205–27, has argued that Gower's stance is consistently antifeminist. Diane Watt, however, insists on the sheer variety and contingency of Gower's moral judgments with respect to women. In "Gender and Sexuality in *Confessio Amantis*," *A Companion to Gower,* pp. 197–213, Watt also provocatively suggests that "sexual relationships also function in Gower's writing to articulate the writer's own language politics," including the tension between Latin authority and "vernacular, feminine" translation (211). This concern with gender as a figure for the power relations inherent in writing and reading can be understood still more broadly, as I hope to show.
[17] For a convenient brief discussion of the "authorship" of women, broadly construed, see Summit, "Women and Authorship," in *The Cambridge Companion to Medieval Women's Writing,* ed. Carolyn Dinshaw and David Wallace (Cambridge: Cambridge University Press, 2003), pp. 91–108 (104). As she points out, women participated in a range of ways in the English literary system, not for the most part as authors but as readers and patronesses. See also Carol M. Meale, ed., *Women and Literature in Britain, 1150–1500,* 2nd ed. (Cambridge: Cambridge University Press, 1996).

actual audience, female and male.[18] We can see both in his claim for a common "new stile" and in his version of "Apollonius" that he registered this variety and multiplicity. The fact that new audiences might include concrete female readers, however, is less important to my argument here than that the female figures within "Apollonius" signal variety among all new readers. The increase in historical female literacy lends Gower's female characters resonance; but he encodes their literacy as meaningful not on the basis of their sex per se but on the basis of their difference from scholarly and clerical male audiences. The female audiences in Gower's romance explicitly figure the good influence of audiences upon authority, ultimately allowing Gower to reimagine contemporary, variable, even unpredictable readers as forces of social and political coherence. "Apollonius" foregrounds female characters' engagement in interpretive activity of all kinds, not just textual but aural, physical and broadly artistic—Thaise can listen, speak, play instruments, set riddles, and "read" her father's countenance—in every case bringing about mutual recognition between author (or monarchical authority) and audience (or subject).

These developments reflect upon the developing self-awareness of the poem's central embedded audience, Amans. When Gower chooses love as his topic, he does more than choose an experience common to "every kinde": he implicitly engages the world of gendered discourse. Inasmuch as Amans's desire is defined by the stereotypical resistant lady, the poem itself aspires to be accepted by a woman. From this perspective, the *Confessio* explores the problem of how to call up a specific female audience, Amans's beloved. But that female audience is an imagined presence, whose recalcitrant actuality (in the form of her erotic refusal) Gower eventually has to acknowledge. When, at the end, the poem is revealed as applying to John Gower's life, we see, retrospectively, that the *Confessio*'s work lay in making Amans see not only himself but his lady clearly; the poem's tensions resolve as he accepts, regretfully, that his lady's reciprocal desire was only ever imagined.[19] Only then does

---

[18] The variety of women's "literate practice" is suggested by Rebecca Krug, *Reading Families: Women's Literate Practice in Late Medieval England* (Ithaca: Cornell University Press, 2002). On the variety of general literate practices Gower anticipates, see Joyce Coleman, "Lay Readers and Hard Latin: How Gower May Have Intended the *Confessio Amantis* to Be Read," *SAC* 24 (2002): 209–36.

[19] I differ from Kurt Olsson, who finds that the conclusion shows us an Amans/Gower who has a full capacity for intimacy; see "Love, Intimacy, and Gower," *ChauR* 30 (1995): 71–100.

Gower collapse his fictive will (Amans) and the figure of imaginative exploration (Genius) into a nonfictional author (John Gower) who closes the book.[20] When he relinquishes the fantasy that his lady's desire matches his own, John Gower becomes reintegrated, recognizes himself, realigns his character with his author; in temporal terms, he brings himself up to date, enacting psychologically the "change" he has already anticipated in his choice of plain, up-to-date English. Like any retraction, the moment expresses a profound ambivalence about storytelling that undergirds much of the Confessio, relegating the whole text to a potentially nugatory past, the realm of love fantasy, from which the reality of old age is utterly separate.[21] Indeed, by the end of the Book, even "Apollonius of Tyre"'s optimistic portrayal of idiosyncratic feminine audience has been set aside, since Amans's own feminine "audience" (the beloved) simply evaporates.

Yet "Apollonius" prepares and makes significant her disappearance. In response to the threat of incest—the merging of patriarch with subject—the tale shows how the education of women figures the liberation of audiences from authority, detaching Thaise from Apollonius, the beloved from Amans, exempla from Genius, and, ironically, Gower from the Confessio itself. Perhaps strangely for so traditional a poem—a poem designed to draw exempla from the memory into the present day (Prol. 51–60)—the conclusion frees the poet's present from its governing love story, and indeed from narratives imposed by the past. Gower's early assertion of a change "Fro this day forth" turns out to herald not so much an integrated narrative of poetic development as a narrative of

---

[20] Simpson, *Sciences and the Self,* glosses the *Confessio*'s characters in this helpful way. He argues that Genius is mistaken in his advice during the early parts of the *Confessio,* but that, "as Amans' own genius, [he] gradually moves Amans towards a reintegrated, rational self" (183). While I do not find this coherent steady progress in the *Confessio,* Genius's role as representative of Amans's imaginative capacity helps explain their different attitudes toward moral interpretation, which Amans views as so much more closed—and more constraining—than does Genius.

[21] There are certainly more sanguine readings of the poem's ending than this. Olsson, *John Gower and the Structures of Conversion: A Reading of the "Confessio Amantis"* (Cambridge: D. S. Brewer, 1992), finds that the fragmentation of the *Confessio* prepares readers for Amans/Gower's final self-recognition, itself one in a long line of "repeated conversions" (248). Simpson, too, characterizes the *Confessio* as a "narrative of the integration of the soul" (10), in particular the integration between reason and imagination. Ardis Butterfield's analysis in "*Confessio Amantis* and the French Tradition," *A Companion to Gower,* 165–80, which identifies a "mood of shame balanced against relief" and concludes that Amans and Gower have both "indulged in forgiveable fantasies" (180), comes closer to my own insistence on taking the retraction at face value.

rupture. In retrospect, then, the puzzle of Book 8 is how the overintimacy of incest produces differentiation and detachment, preparing and indeed enabling the whole work to come to an end.

Incest as Past

Until its ending, the *Confessio* centrally concerns the past, and in Book 8, Gower turns back to the Fall for an explanation of the social meaning of incest. He lays out a historical genealogy of incest prohibition, beginning with Lucifer's destruction and the expulsion of Adam and Eve from Paradise. Since there were no exogamous options after the Fall, incestuous procreation was fundamental to human origins: "Forthi that time it was no Sinne / The Soster forto take hire brother, / Whan that ther was of chois no other" (68–70). Later, in the time of Abraham, the practice of incest gave way to lawful endogamous relations within the tribe of Israel. Incest was never fully prohibited until after Christ, "For of the lawe canonized / The Pope hath bede to the men, / That non schal wedden of his ken / Ne the seconde ne the thridde" (144–47). This historical toleration, however, contrasts markedly with the vehemence of Genius's judgment against contemporary incest: in the present day, incest is "loves Rage" (150); incestuous men lack reason or discernment, behaving like animals:

> Bot as a cock among the Hennes,
> Or as a Stalon in the Fennes,
> Which goth amonges al the Stod,
> Riht so can he nomore good,
> Bot takth what thing comth next to honde.
> (159–63)

Incest is no longer the beneficial procreative relationship it once was, but has become an act of male domination committed by "a cock among the Hennes." As Thomas Aquinas claims, "incest" is derived from the Latin "in-castus": "For incest takes its name from defiling chastity."[22] Genius approaches incest as originally natural, but now fundamentally

---

[22] *Summa Theologica* 2a2ae.154.9, ed. and trans. Thomas Gilby, vol. 43 (London: Blackfriars, 1968), pp. 236–41. Based on this etymology, a number of critics argue that incest is a "blueprint" for love in the *Confessio,* most notably Georgiana Donavin, *Incest Narratives and the Structure of Gower's Confessio Amantis* (Victoria, B.C.: English Literary Studies 56, 1993).

unchaste, unnatural and inhuman—a sin that, like the rage of Virginius or the fury of Aeolus, denigrates man to the level of beast.

The introduction to Book 8 distills a medieval discourse that associates incest with not just moral or psychological but social problems of isolation and dominion.[23] Augustine discusses it in the context of the city as human community, where he concentrates on exogamy as a socially useful practice: "When, therefore, a man has one person for his father, another for his father-in-law, friendship extends itself to a larger number."[24] Aquinas's concern is more privately located and more graphic: he worries about the physical proximity of blood relations who grow up in the same "chambre." Nevertheless, he also argues that "incest would prevent people widening their circle of friends."[25] Incest, then, destroys social bonds; its implications are not primarily psychological but political, and its prohibition enables social organization. In father-daughter incest, the daughter is essentially kept in her chamber, an overclose sharing of physical space that suggests the collapse of distinctions among familial and dynastic roles.[26] As Larry Scanlon points out in his cogent exploration of the relationship between psychoanalytic and medieval discourses of incest, the law of exogamy (which prohibits incest) authorizes and upholds the patriarchal family.[27] Medieval discourse emphasizes the sociopolitical ramifications of incest, the way in which its fundamental misunderstanding of domestic authority affects

---

[23] On incest in medieval narrative, including a full account of the classical and medieval construction of incest, see especially Elizabeth Archibald, "Incest in Medieval Literature and Society," *FMLS* 25 (1989): 1–15, and *Incest and the Medieval Imagination* (Oxford: Clarendon Press, 2001). Archibald emphasizes ways in which incest can be viewed as either natural or culturally constructed, and even morally remediable in some circumstances. Although, as Bullón-Fernández details, Freud and Lévi-Strauss influentially maintained that incest-avoidance is a basis of human community, other contemporary scholars from anthropologists to psychologists have tended to emphasize the destructiveness (and pervasiveness) of incest acts within social networks. See, for example, contemporary anthropologist W. Arens's insistence that contemporary father-daughter incest is an expression of dominion in *The Original Sin: Incest and Its Meaning* (Oxford: Oxford University Press, 1986); as an example of modern clinical discourse in which incest is seen as a particularly gendered violation, see Judith Lewis Herman, *Father-Daughter Incest* (Cambridge, Mass.: Harvard University Press, 1981).

[24] *The City of God* 15.16, trans. Marcus Dods (New York: The Modern Library, 1950), 500.

[25] *ST* 2a2ae.154.9.

[26] Father-daughter incest, specifically, prevents the conventional exchange of women; see Pierre Roussel, "Aspects du père incestueux dans la littèrature mediévale," in *Amour, Mariage et Transgressions au Moyen Âge,* ed. Danielle Buschinger and André Crépin (Goppingen: Kimmerle Verlag, 1984), pp. 47–62.

[27] Scanlon, "The Riddle of Incest," p. 107.

the nature of a community. Incestuous kingship like that in "Apollonius of Tyre" figures a possessive and tyrannical failure of self-governance that shapes the king's entire realm.[28] Yet it grows out of his role as singular ruler of the realm as well. Historicizing incest, as Gower and his sources do, makes sense in this context because, far from providing a transhistorical structure, the practice emerges as deeply, even destructively, circumstantial. In the Middle Ages, incest is more than simply unchaste. It becomes a peculiarly monarchical failure of community, an expression of the extreme isolation of one ungoverned patriarchal will.

The historical account of incest, however, poses a conceptual problem for Genius and Amans precisely because of its basis in isolation. Genius enjoins Amans to confess if he has committed any such sin, but Amans denies any connection to incest, claiming he was never yet "So wylde a man" (171); his love is directed only to his lady. Amans in fact is impatient with Genius: "Ye mai wel axe of this and that, / Bot . . . / In al this world ther is bot on / The which myn herte hath overgon" (179–82). Amans wants applicable stories, and his experience does not resemble incest in any literal way. This desire for application raises a crucial problem of didactic narrative: How is the reader to "enfold" or combine his present experience with narrative? How does the present world find a "fit" with the past, and to what extent is that "fit" always metaphorical? The vocabulary of correspondence comes up against its limits here. Yet Mary Carruthers has shown how application can work even when the narrative seems distant from the recipient's experience: Heloise, in the act of taking religious orders on Abelard's wishes, cites Pompey's wife, Cornelia, as a "commonplace" character from the past whose words give the present meaning. She quotes Cornelia's greeting to her husband in Lucan's *Pharsalia*, when, after his shameful defeat in battle, Cornelia offers to commit suicide on his behalf. Carruthers writes that "what is so striking, or strikingly medieval, in Heloise's action is her articulation of her own present dilemma and decision by means of her memory of a text" (181).[29] Amans entertains the fantasy that he can

---

[28] Elizabeth Archibald notes the popularity of father-daughter incest romances in the Middle Ages, which tend to explore the link between incestuous fatherhood and kingship; see *Incest and the Medieval Imagination*, pp. 145–82.

[29] *The Book of Memory* (Cambridge: Cambridge University Press, 1990). Carruthers writes that such memorial activity shapes the self, who might be better construed as the "subject-who-remembers" (182). The interchange between Amans and Genius deeply troubles this notion of memorial activity because the "commonplaces" Genius offers are not always easily appropriated to Amans's memorial activity. In this sense, Amans does not measure up to the ethical self-awareness—or the opportunism—of Heloise.

trace just such analogies between his problem and those of characters Genius invokes from the past. Yet his skepticism about the relevance of Genius's characters exposes a kind of inflexibility—he is concerned with "bot on," and wants stories that correspond exactly to his erotic obsession. Carruthers's Heloise has a looser and more rhetorical idea of analogy. Despite her differences from Cornelia (Cornelia does not enter a convent; Heloise does not offer suicide), Heloise actively reinvents Lucan in order to contextualize her own action publicly, before an audience, as a sacrifice. Heloise appropriates and redirects her memory-text, an opportunistic act of reception that Amans refuses.

Genius responds to his interlocutor's skepticism by giving Amans an exaggerated version of what he appears to want: three compressed exempla, those of Caligula, Amnon, and Lot, in which concision encourages immediate outrage against incest. These exempla leave little room for narrative desire of any kind, especially sympathy. Caligula, after committing incest with his three sisters and exiling them, is summarily punished by God, "For evere his lust . . . overthrowe" (212). Amnon commits incest with his sister, and is killed in revenge by his own brother Absalom; the story accentuates both Amnon's violence and the symmetry of Absalom's vengeance in a brief and riddle-like ending that enwraps nature and kinship bonds, and the overcloseness of incest, into one highly charged pun: "thunkinde unkinde fond."[30] Finally, Lot's incest gives rise to the "ungoode" tribes of Israel. These three stories form a mini-compilation of exempla whose message about the incestuous abuse of intimacy is ostensibly transparent.

The compression of these exempla sets incest off from the ordinary and makes it almost inapplicable. Precisely because of their moral clarity, they form self-enclosed nuggets of past transgression; they close off

---

[30] These brother-sister acts are clearly figured as acts of domination, unlike the brother-sister incest in "Canacee and Machaire" (3.142–395), on the moral indeterminacy of which see C. David Benson, "Incest and Moral Poetry in Gower's *Confessio Amantis*," *ChauR* 19 (1984): 100–109. Winthrop Wetherbee suggests the tale exhibits a kind of amorality in "Constance and the World in Chaucer and Gower," *John Gower: Recent Readings,* ed. R. F. Yeager (Kalamazoo: Medieval Institute Publications, 1989), pp. 65–93. Diane Watt argues provocatively against such indeterminacy in "Gender and Sexuality in *Confessio Amantis*," *Companion to Gower,* 197–213 (198–203). Maura Nolan suggests that Lydgate dismantles the logic by which Gower portrays incest as motivated by human agency in "Lydgate's Literary History: Chaucer, Gower, and Canacee," *SAC* 27 (2005): 59–92. She links incest to problems of literary art and reception, finding in Lydgate an aesthetic "uselessness" (92) that reacts against both stringent moralism and radical contingency. For her, the Canacee story provides the occasion for searching questions about the sedimentation of literary forms and lessons.

narration. Correctively, Genius turns to a discussion of exemplary discourse generally, and incest now takes on the status of a kind of exemplary example:

> And every man is othres lore;
> Of that befell in time er this
> The present time which now is
> May ben enformed hou it stod,
> And take that him thenketh good,
> And leve that which is noght so.
>
> (256–61)

Genius reminds his audience that customs change over time, and that the past cannot be taken at face value; his audience can be "enformed" or given shape by the past, but must also contribute judgments of its own. He suggests audiences should act not according to given moral rules, but according to their own discretion, by deciding how other men's pasts might "give form to" their present lives. The content of the past matters less than what audiences will do with it, for "every man is othres lore"—anyone's experience has the potential to be read and learned by others. On one level, this theorizing disavows the rule-based content of the tales Genius has just related. As when Chaucer's narrator tells readers of the *Canterbury Tales* that if *The Miller's Tale* offends them they can "Turne over the leef and chese another tale" (I.3177), Genius here asserts that is up to readers to "take that him thenketh good, / And leve that which is noght so." On another level, though, Gower points out that his intent is less important than the effect of the "enformacioun" upon responsible audiences. Rather than relying on resemblance between a story's content and its readers' needs, Genius demands application in an extended sense, more than what can be contained in the frame of a story—perhaps more than "information" would suggest, even in Simpson's greatly expanded definition of the term. The "exemplary encapsulation[s]"[31] of Caligula, Amnon, and Lot are what we might call "devil's advocate" exempla: they encourage precisely the sort

---

[31] Robins, "The Subject of the *Confessio Amantis*," p. 159. Robins argues that exemplarity entails moral causality and fundamentally relies on the analogy between story and reader, whereas Gower "finds in romance an emplotment that leans toward a temporality of contingency" (162). Here, Robins's contrast between exemplum and romance is appropriate, because Gower sets up the contrast—but he does so precisely in order to blur any easy distinction between moral and imaginative storytelling.

of general, categorical condemnation of an aberrant act that fails to make incest available for use. The sin becomes an originary horror, like the rape of the Sabine women that established Rome—constitutive of modern society, yet ideally unrepeatable, a thing *only* of the past.[32] History itself looks like a kind of unbreachable alterity. The result, narratologically, is a need for more dilated plot in which to implicate the *Confessio*'s audience.

Repetition and the Wandering Cure

Before "Apollonius," then, Genius categorizes incest as historically past, static, and hence virtually inapplicable. When he turns to romance, he works against this impulse to relegate incest to the past, choosing a final narrative based on its continual repetition. The notion that repetition constitutes plot underpins narrative theory and genre theory alike, especially with respect to romance, that mode which Northrop Frye identifies as "the structural core of all fiction."[33] "Apollonius" consists of a succession of scenes that abstract from incest a set of associated problems: the father-monarch's isolation, singular will, and misapprehension of his subjects. Narratologically, the plot demonstrates the way in which incest applies to relationships of social and political power. Each new error stages the sin's continuing relevance, so that when the hero secretly absents himself from his kingdom, for example, or when he sends away his daughter, the text echoes the tensions between incestuous "privete" and feminine autonomy. Repetition works in retrospect, each new instance clarifying previous acts: Frye writes, "The beginning is a demonic parody of the end."[34] Seen in this light, "Apollonius" typifies

---

[32] For the rape of the Sabine women, see Livy, *Ab urbe condita,* ed. and trans. B. O. Foster (Cambridge, Mass.: Harvard University Press, 1922), 1.9.

[33] Frye, *The Secular Scripture,* p. 15.

[34] Ibid., p. 49. In romance, retrospective structural logic is very often expressed in a lack of apparent motivation or causal connection between events. Arthur Heiserman remarks in the context of late Greek romance that "the meaning of the plot emerges from the intrinsic plot"; see *The Novel Before the Novel: Essays and Discussions about the Beginnings of Prose Fiction in the West* (Chicago: University of Chicago Press, 1977), p. 202. On "backwards" motivation, see Morton W. Bloomfield, "Episodic Motivation and Marvels in Epic and Romance," in *Essays and Explorations: Studies in Ideas, Language, and Literature* (Cambridge, Mass.: Harvard University Press, 1970), pp. 97–128 (108–10). Frye calls attention to the impulse toward change embedded in this retrospective structure, which is "a spiral form, an open circle where the end is the beginning transformed and renewed by the heroic quest" (174); the plot's meaning hinges upon "creative repetition" (174–75).

romance in general, which continually and symbolically repeats an initial problem until it can be resolved through a sort of "wandering cure."

Several recent investigations of "Apollonius," however, raise questions about the degree to which these repetitions eventually resolve the problem of incest. María Bullón-Fernández has a relatively sanguine view: she examines the way in which the incest taboo, a fundamentally discursive construct, is ultimately reasserted in the tale, even as Apollonius enters a nonverbal world and then emerges from it to reinhabit his royal role. Bullón-Fernández points out the public discursive power achieved by Apollonius's wife and daughter Thaise—a power over language that enables Thaise to coax her father away from incest in the climactic recognition scene.[35] Larry Scanlon finds, in contrast, a precarious distinction between fatherly assertion and abject desire for the daughter, and for him the resolution emphasizes "the contingent nature of the [paternal] identity Apollonius recovers."[36] In Scanlon's analysis, the tale suggests that incestuous desire cannot fully be eradicated from familial or political power, and in fact, that incest underpins patriarchy; indeed, when Thaise helps Apollonius "into the liht" after the recognition scene, her quasi-parental role has a basic incestuous structure. These two analyses are closer than they first appear: Bullón-Fernández notes that even as the recognition scene displaces the possibility of incest, "it also creates the possibility of transgression."[37] What both scholars see is the peculiarly medieval way in which language not only creates the prohibition against incest but also expresses incestuous desire itself, in an uncanny return of something that modern psychoanalysis has repressed.[38] Incest, however awkwardly, provides both the basic framework for political power *and* the foil against which power (re)establishes itself.

In narratological terms, we might say that repetitions of incest serve successively to "romance" the act—turning from Frye's "demonic parody" toward well-regulated kinship, mutating the horror of the literal event into a fictionally resonant social metaphor. The plot enacts a process by which one tyrant's exemplary sin produces new fictions of change brought about by autonomous audiences, specifically the educated daughters who avert their fathers' tyrannical violence. A daughter,

---

[35] Bullón-Fernández , *Fathers and Daughters,* chap. 2.
[36] Scanlon, "The Riddle of Incest," p. 123.
[37] *Fathers and Daughters,* p. 59.
[38] Scanlon, "The Riddle of Incest," pp. 125–26.

this text asserts, cannot be wholly subsumed into her father's will any more than a subject can be wholly subsumed into the will of a king; the effective governor of self, household, and state will be the one who makes himself susceptible to the influence of his inferiors.[39] Diane Watt, though particularly attuned to the limitations of feminine will in the story, nevertheless argues that "[t]he resurrections of Thaise and her mother mark the posthumous redemption of Antiochus's [violated] daughter" and contribute to the renewal of Apollonius's power.[40] Watt views the restored Apollonius as far from an ideal king, and certainly the romance points as much to his flaws as to his ideality: as Scanlon also sees, romance mystifies, but also exposes, the incest-threat at the heart of monarchical power. But pragmatically, when women exert influence upon Apollonius, his very status as a moral and political ideal becomes itself susceptible to change: paradoxically the monarch best fulfills his role when he can change most drastically, indicating his constitutive imperfection. By emphasizing female influence over such change, Gower calls attention to the necessary flexibility of the patriarch. In this way, further, he makes the plot repetitions of "Apollonius" a structure for imagining the social and political benefits of idiosyncratic, unpredictable audiences.

This unpredictablity emerges with particular symbolic suggestiveness in romance. It has long been recognized that, through its use of an Otherworld, romance throws into relief the question of how fantasy applies to real life. Romance stages an oblique relationship between fiction

---

[39] Bullón-Fernández, *Fathers and Daughters,* provides both a good survey of the crucial analogy between familial and political authority in the fourteenth-century context and a sensitive assessment of Gower's use of father-daughter incest as a political metaphor, pp. 17–33. The analogy between individual moral governance and communal peace is a commonplace of medieval political theory in general, of course, and of Gower criticism in particular; besides Peck, cited in n. 6 above, see A. J. Minnis, "John Gower, Sapiens in Ethics and Politics," *MÆ* 49 (1980): 207–29; Elizabeth Porter, "Gower's Ethical Microcosm and Political Macrocosm," in *Responses and Reassessments,* pp. 135–62; for a skeptical reassessment of the analogy between ethics and politics in Gower, see David Aers, "Reflections on Gower as Sapiens in Ethics and Politics," in *Re-Visioning Gower,* pp. 185–201. The importance of counsel (the advice of inferiors) has been stressed in recent treatments of other authors as well; see, for example, Nicholas Perkins, *Hoccleve's Regiment of Princes: Counsel and Constraint* (Cambridge: D. S. Brewer, 2001).

[40] Watt, *Amoral Gower,* pp. 140–45, 147–48. Watt astutely observes that the role of women in "Apollonius" poses a challenge to oedipal interpretation in chapter 6, revised from "Oedipus, Apollonius, and Richard II: Sex and Politics in Book VIII of John Gower's *Confessio Amantis,*" *SAC* 24 (2002): 181–208. For her, Freud's analysis of "ruler taboos" in *Totem and Taboo* proves locally fruitful in analyzing the father-son dynamic between Antiochus and Apollonius (136), but she dodges the psychoanalytic account of incest as a foundation of human social organization.

and the lived reality inhabited by readers; it typically begins in an "actual" world from which the hero wanders into an "other" world—for Frye, this Otherworld is both a representation of the archetypal human unconscious and, at the same time, a realm of socially ritualized action.[41] Since any ritual relies on repetition for its meaning, the Otherworld repeats, in an explicitly fantastic register, ordinary action that has socially-charged meaning. To put this more dynamically, we might say that romance depicts ritualized action which could *apply* to the "actual" or "ordinary" world of the heroic individual, and, from there, the world of the reader. The adventures of the Otherworld echo and revise the initial status of the hero, and the Otherworld's relation to the ordinary within the romance implies an analogous relationship between the romance and the "actual" world of readers.[42] But even more than the conflicting moral impulses of exemplary narrative, the symbolic abstraction of romance foils any notion of exact correspondence. So how might we understand the "relevance" of incest in the narrative terms offered by Gower in Book 8?

Psychoanalysis provides one of the richest modern explorations of incestuous desire per se, and Bullón-Fernández, Scanlon, Watt and others have put it to work productively with respect to "Apollonius." I raid it here with a different purpose in mind, following Frye and more explicitly Peter Brooks in *Reading for the Plot,* for whom psychoanalysis provides a model for plot itself. In the process of psychoanalysis, when the patient narrates his or her life story, he or she repeatedly formulates the process of separation from the parents, a process, for Freud, fundamentally structured by the avoidance of incest.[43] In this sense, the fantasy of incest begins all family romance: it is the inception of the analytic plot. For Brooks, incest provides "the exemplary version of a temptation of short-circuit from which the protagonist and the text must be led away, into detour, into the cure that prolongs narrative."[44] However, my interest lies less in the psychological progress of Apollonius's desire than

---

[41] Frye, *The Secular Scripture,* pp. 56–58.

[42] A particularly rich account of this layering of analogy in the structure of romance is Matilda Tomaryn Bruckner, *Shaping Romance: Interpretation, Truth, and Closure in Twelfth-Century French Fictions* (Philadelphia: University of Pennsylvania Press, 1993).

[43] Freud, "Family Romances," in the *Standard Edition of the Complete Psychological Works of Sigmund Freud,* ed. and trans. James Strachey (London: Hogarth Press, 1953–74), 9:237–41.

[44] Peter Brooks, *Reading for the Plot: Design and Intention in Narrative* (Cambridge, Mass.: Harvard University Press, 1989), p. 109.

in Gower's deployment of the incest plot as a figure for narrative dynamics. As Brooks points out, plot shapes the relationship between narrative and audience. He writes that psychoanalytic transference provides a model for understanding the way plot *works* for readers.[45] Transference provides, in this case, a therapeutic model for the effects of the incest plot upon the Genius-Amans framework and the (anticipated) reception of the *Confessio* as a whole.

Transference, of course, is a particular kind of repetition based on a particular analogy. It occurs when the analysand's current situation merges with his story such that he essentially mistakes, or substitutes, the analyst for a figure from his past, reenacting with the analyst his past trauma and thereby revealing his own unconscious. When the analysand tells his story to the analyst, both content and style of telling are symptomatic: the analysand's retrospection, like romance plot, corresponds inexactly to the actual events of the past, so that "links are missing, chronologies are twisted, the objects of desire are misnamed."[46] The projection of familiar roles onto the therapist provides what Freud calls an "intermediate region" (between neurotic repression and healthy awareness) in which the analysand can move toward new understanding, a new ordering of past trauma.[47] This region resembles what Elizabeth Fowler calls romance's "stark landscape of 'suppose,'" where normal rules of time and place are temporarily suspended and characters become abstract actors in experimental vignettes.[48] The projected world of romance exists, as L. O. Aranye Fradenburg writes, "on the edge

---

[45] In Brooks's formulation, plot replays and reworks trauma, imposing new order upon it by means of "the productive encounter of teller and listener, text and reader" (p. 234). On transference generally as a model for the work of plot, see esp. pp. 216–37.
[46] Brooks, *Reading for the Plot*, p. 227.
[47] Freud, "Remembering, Repeating, and Working Through," in the *Standard Edition*, 12:154, qtd. in Brooks, 228.
[48] In her brillliant essay, "Lordship and Saracens in *Sir Isumbras*," in *The Medieval Spirit of Popular Romance*, ed. Ad Putter and Jane Gilbert (Harlow, England: Longman, 2000), pp. 97–121, Elizabeth Fowler writes that romances share with legal and philosophical discourse two features, generality and indefiniteness, which render their characters and events abstract. In her view, romances are "complex thought experiments" that take readers along a path of conceptual exploration about "crucial social formations such as lordship, marriage, and governance by setting such formations moving in a stark landscape of 'suppose'" (98–99). What Frye refers to as "socially ritualized action" Fowler sees as essentially theoretical: in romances, hypothetical or frankly fictive actions can be abstracted or isolated from their actual social content—we might say theorized—in order to examine their structural consequences. "Apollonius of Tyre" then becomes not simply an incest story but an exploration of the isolated will that both constitutes and threatens any monarch.

of the known and the unknown," "oscillat[ing] between archaism and 'novelrie.' "[49] For Fradenburg, this realm of innovation and suggestion calls attention to the creative potential of both writer and reader. Brooks writes that the text becomes a site of transference created "in the knowledge that the persons and relations involved are surrogates and mummers."[50] Especially in framed narratives, both author and reader become aware that the plot is substitutive, fictive, obliquely related to the "actual" just as the fantasy-exploration of an analytic session is only obliquely related to lived life.[51] Even in romance, the Otherworld is only provisional, and eventually the plot sends readers back "out" of its fantasy world into the world of application. But the work of plot lies in the reordering of events, so that instead of compulsive reenactment, the character (analysand) can come to understand the past intellectually, as past, and return both himself and his audience, as Brooks writes, "to a changed reality."[52]

Taking my cue from psychoanalytically informed accounts of "Apollonius," then, I am interested in how incest provides a model for desire in Gower; but veering away from other examinations of the tale, I emphasize the ways in which the story's plot, and its reception by Amans, demand the therapeutic work of readers. Amans's resistance signals the power of the story's call to application, but it also signals the transference, that highly charged affective bond between patient and doctor that is at once a barrier to and an instrument of cure. Moreover, the fact

[49] In another remarkable recent essay, "Simply Marvelous," *SAC* 26 (2004): 1–27, qtd. at pp. 6–7, Fradenburg argues that romance's approach to history is bound up with the unnecessary and frivolous, and urges scholars to place value on the seemingly outmoded, wacky, or wondrous in that genre.

[50] Brooks, *Reading for the Plot,* pp. 234–35.

[51] Brooks explores the model of transference with regard to Balzac's *Le Colonel Chabert,* where he investigates the relationship between narrator (analysand) and narratee (analyst) and implies that the reader of the text takes the role of analyst. There is some slippage here in Brooks's analogy, as when he writes, "Disciplined and subjugated, the transference delivers one back to a changed reality. And so does any text fully engaged by the reader" (235). Here the reader is implicitly more analysand, the subject of change, than analyst. This slippage actually somewhat leaves aside questions of authority and coercion that concern Gower in Book 8. When Gower calls for the reader's participation in plot, an engagement in transference, he too undermines the opposition between authority and audience that Amans, especially, finds so tempting. The psychoanalytic analogy, for Brooks, is most productive when least fixed; transference's work lies in the mutual engagement of character and narrator, narrator and narratee, so that the responsibility for the text's meaning lies in the dynamic transaction, not in one role or the other.

[52] Brooks, *Reading for the Plot,* 235.

that one very careful reader, Gower's editor G. C. Macaulay, finds incest an embarrassing subject suggests the extent to which Genius's approach to the sin implicates his readers in the effort of confronting and reworking it.[53] The problem that Amans and Macauley implicitly point out is that readers are not simply forces of "exogamy" here. Instead, every repetition of incest requires audience recognition and heightens audience desire. Even as Apollonius seeks to avoid incest—and thus loses kingdom, then wife, then daughter—every instance in which he seeks repair *resembles* incest. Both impulses of his plot (loss and repetition) continually attenuate human community within the story. Brooks remarks that compulsive repetition provides a bulwark against loss.[54] Certainly within the plot, Apollonius registers his deepest losses by seeking to repeat acts of secrecy, willfulness, and tyranny. Meanwhile readers, too, experience an ongoing equivocation. Despite readerly sympathy for the violated daughter of Antiochus, the initial transgression produces a readerly desire to see incest recuperated and even repeated; indeed, Scanlon ascribes to the "narrative itself" a "guilty pleasure" in imagining the violation of Thaise.[55] This guilty pleasure coincides uncomfortably with the arousal and sustaining of desire that defines any extended narrative.[56] In Gower, however, the continual presence of incest puts audience response under special scrutiny throughout the tale.

Desire for the plot, in fact, is constituted at least in part by the reader's heightened anticipation of repetitions, and the recognition of the dynamic between repetition and change. Such desire is a basis of audience involvement, and therefore of the kind of education that "Apollonius of Tyre" seeks to advance.[57] Book 8 enlists involvement to the point

[53] Scanlon, "Riddle of Incest," sees Macaulay's embarrassment manifested in critical attempts to understand incest figuratively, "as a typification or epitome of something else" (99). But surely the narrative everywhere accrues symbolic, not just literal, meanings around incest. Embarrassment, it seems to me, does not simply indicate modesty about sexual desire so much as register a call to audience activity, a kind of exposure of audiences to consciousness of their own judgment.

[54] Brooks, *Reading for the Plot*, p. 111.

[55] Scanlon, "The Riddle of Incest," p. 121.

[56] Brooks's central notion of "narrative desire" seeks to link content ("the narrative of desire") with structure ("the desire of narrative") in order to understand "the notion of desire as that which is initiatory of narrative, motivates and energizes its reading, and animates the combinatory play of sense-making" (48). In this model, the desire of characters puts in motion the desire of readers. Through Amans and through other framing techniques, Gower's "Apollonius" highlights in particular the morally equivocal role of its audience's desire.

[57] For Simpson, the *Confessio*'s structural incoherence calls for audiences to "participate in the construction of meaning" (*Sciences and the Self*, p. 14). Incoherence and elusiveness certainly do call upon readers' mental faculties throughout the poem; here,

of making readers anticipate incest—and even tempting them, figuratively, to submit to it themselves. Through calls for sympathy and moments of problematic stasis, Genius subjects readers to the incest act; through interruptions, narrative blanks or gaps, and other local formal effects, he makes incest both reprehensible and typical, both foreign and endemic to the civilized present. Moreover, incest becomes for Gower a figure for the errors of authority and identification to which any moralizing fiction can fall prey. The sin figures Amans's own fantasy of analogy, which confines literary authority to didactic message-making and subordinates readers to an author's command.

The "Apollonius" plot, then, becomes an instrument of conceptual shifts that implicate narrator, embedded audience, and readers in the problems associated with incest. Through repetition, the plot bridges narrative levels, because solitude and coercion implicitly define not just the plot's content, incest, but also the structure of the relationship between authority and audience. Amans, like an angry analysand, both disavows incest itself and rebels against the moral authority of his interlocutor. This rebellion, in turn, restructures the transaction between Gower and extratextual audiences. Readers are made aware of Genius's power to "enform" Amans and Gower's power to tell us what to think, and they are also made aware that Genius's story is available for some other use than Amans's strict imitation. Amans's resistance demands that the poem's extratextual readers engage in analysis, or what we normally call interpretation. Freud writes in "The Dynamics of Transference" that resistance challenges the analyst to recognize the unconscious urges that are made manifest.[58] Surprisingly, we are asked to take incest *more* seriously than does Amans, albeit in a figurative mode: like analysts, readers are to identify the resemblance between the therapeutic present and the traumatic past. Yet they are also partially responsible for making the distinction and providing an alternative to repetition, through awareness. Readers are asked to be authors of misprision; they are set up to be the provocation against the idealistic (or destructive) fantasy that stories should correspond precisely to their origins, or that

---

however, I find that a certain moral bossiness is both Gower's theme and Genius's method for demanding our engagement.

[58] Although transference presents the analyst with the "greatest difficulties," it does him the "inestimable service" of making the "hidden and forgotten erotic impulses immediate and manifest" ("The Dynamics of Transference," in the *Standard Edition*, 12:107–8).

lived existence should imitate stories exactly.[59] As we shall see, when Gower stages such provocation through women in "Apollonius," he makes female characters into analysts, heralds of general interpretive change. Thus, Book 8 brings to a head the argument that I take to be the basis of the whole of the *Confessio:* that exemplarity imposed by injunctive analogy rather than discovered through the transferential experience of interpretation constitutes a profound, even incestuous, abuse of authority.

Antiochus's Daughter

In contrast to the tales of Caligula, Amnon, and Lot, "Apollonius of Tyre" emphasizes the consequences of incest for daughters, thereby immediately involving audiences in the affective and moral process by which incest achieves meaning.[60] But the story opens with the perpetrator, Antiochus, king of Antioch. His queen has just died:

> The king, which made mochel mone,
> Tho stod, as who seith, al him one
> Withoute wif, bot natheles
> His doghter, which was piereles
> Of beaute, duelte aboute him stille.
>
> (283–87)

The loss of the queen debilitates the king, making him a victim of fortune and leaving him alone, a solitude that suggests that royal power needs affirmative and restraining company.[61] His daughter substitutes for the wife by living with him "still": her consistent presence formally resolves the disordered enjambments of the previous few lines. But still-

---

[59] "Misprision" is the term Harold Bloom uses in *Anxiety of Influence* (New York: Oxford University Press, 1973) to describe the productive deviations from his predecessors made by the "strong" poet.

[60] Elizabeth Archibald surveys various versions of the Apollonius story in her edition and translation of the Latin *Historia Appolonii,* likely a close cousin of Gower's story, if not his direct source. In her review of the literature, Archibald finds that most scholars have viewed the initial incest act as peripheral to the Apollonius story; she argues cogently for the integral role of incest in all versions of the tale. See *Apollonius of Tyre: Medieval and Renaissance Themes and Variations* (Cambridge: D. S. Brewer, 1991), pp. 15–18 and 98–100. The same narrative provides the basis of Frye's theory of romance in *The Secular Scripture.*

[61] In this Antiochus resembles the incestuous fathers described by W. Arens: in the face of social failure and isolation, "incest implies a sad and futile attempt to reconstruct a personal universe" (*The Original Sin,* p. 141).

ness also suggests a passivity or quietude that will subject her to her father's will. The daughter's stillness here indicates a plot defined by domestic and political "temptation to over-sameness," a resistance to progress through differentiation between king and subject toward the exogamous marriage that would widen Antiochus's circle of friends and produce a "cure."[62] Because the character seeks to stop historical change, the plot itself verges on the static encapsulation of Genius's earlier exempla.

Because politically Antiochus's incestuous desire is bound up with his patriarchal power, wealth, and leisure, Genius places blame squarely on the father:

> His doghter . . . duelte aboute him stille.
> Bot whanne a man hath welthe at wille,
> The fleissh is frele and falleth ofte,
> And that this maide tendre and softe,
> Which in hire fadres chambres duelte,
> Withinne a time wiste and felte:
> . . . he caste al his hole entente
> His oghne doghter forto spille.
> This king hath leisir at his wille
> With strengthe, and whanne he time sih,
> This yonge maiden he forlih.
> (286–92, 296–300)

As in early Latin versions of the story, Antiochus is so blinded by desire that his entire will focuses on his daughter.[63] Quite explicitly here, his status as king actually engenders his frailty: incest arises from his embat-

---

[62] Brooks, *Reading for the Plot,* p. 109.

[63] In the *Historia Apollonii* (HA), the father fights against his passion (pugnat cum dolore, 1.10), and the daughter is astonished by her father's immorality (miratur scelestis patris impietatem, 1.16–17). In both Godfrey of Viterbo and the *Gesta Romanorum* (GR), he burns with love and she weeps in agony. Gower's couplets expand and emphasize the deliberate violation of the father and the inner resistance of the daughter, arguably pointing already toward the enhanced problem of feminine will that defines his version. All quotations from HA are taken from the first recension (RA) in the edition by G. A. A. Kortekaas, *The Story of Apollonius King of Tyre* (Leiden: E. J. Brill, 2004), cited by paragraph and Kortekaas's line numbers; for translations I have also consulted Elizabeth Archibald's *Apollonius of Tyre.* Quotations from Godfrey are from S. Singer, *Apollonius von Tyrus: Untersuchungen über das Fortelben de antiken Romans in spätern Zeiten* (Halle: Max Niemeyer, 1895), pp. 150–76, my translations. Quotations from the *Gesta Romanorum* are taken from the translation by Charles Swan, rev. Wynnard Hooper (London: George Bell & Sons, 1905).

tled self-elevation, an attention to his individual power at the expense of his closest community, his daughter.[64] He seizes the goods of his subjects or, in Gower's words, enhances his "singulier beyete" (individual possession, 7.1996), in the form of his daughter's maidenhood. The "stille" / "wille" pair, echoed so soon in "spille" / "wille," emphasizes the degree to which he transgresses the consistent loyalty of his closest subject.

The daughter's stillness changes register as she responds to her predicament, seeking a cure that, immediately foiled, abandons the audience to an ineffectual sympathy for her entrapment. Throughout the passage, Genius encourages outrage against Antiochus through this sympathy:

> And thus this maiden goth to manne,
> The wylde fader thus devoureth
> His oghne fleissh, which non socoureth,
> And that was cause of mochel care.
> Bot after this unkinde fare
> Out of the chambre goth the king,
> And sche lay stille, and of this thing,
> Withinne hirself such sorghe made,
> Ther was no wiht that mihte hir glade,
> For feere of thilke horrible vice.
>
> (8.308–17)

The conventional expectation that every maid will "go to manne" highlights the perversity of the unnatural father: he acculturates her to wildness, a failure of both exogamous custom and natural law (kinde). The audience is shown what Antiochus does not recognize: that his daughter suffers, independent of him and his will. Her stillness, now embedded in the line ("and sche lay stille"), signals her inconsolability: it is "withinne hirself" that his violation has caused its ruin, precisely because her will has been negated, stilled. Stillness now suggests a failure of transformation through meaninglessly reiterated violation. She is victim of a sin for which she cannot be "wreke," avenged (323). The daughter's desire for

---

[64] According to many medieval formulations, tyranny comes about when a king fulfills his singular, idiosyncratic desires at the expense of the common profit rather than for its benefit. For a classic articulation of this structure, see Margaret Schlauch, "Chaucer's Doctrine of Kings and Tyrants," *Speculum* 20 (1945): 133–56.

"cure"—a desire engaged also by the sympathetic audience—will be met only through narrative displacement, since the incest itself is encoded as utter destruction, making a future impossible. In psychoanalytic terms, the tale's opening action establishes the traumatic foundation of the plot's symbolic development. In literary terms, the transference will take place with the "transfer" or doubling of the incestuous pair in the figures of Apollonius and Thaise.

Antiochus's transgression is no isolated act but an ongoing relation, and in contrast to Gower's sources, a political configuration to which the daughter must submit even as the situation resists narrative progress.[65] The permanence of the daughter's situation is confirmed when her nurse, startlingly, advises that she continue to submit to her father's will:

> Whan thing is do, ther is no bote,
> So suffren thei that suffre mote;
> Ther was non other which it wiste.
>
> (339–41)

By reiterating the daughter's helplessness, the nurse's proverbial language reveals the reductive, even recursive character of moral generalization itself.[66] The nurse's inadequate moral, however, solicits audience sympathy. Unlike the exempla of Caligula, Amnon, and Lot, this narrative encourages affective awareness of loss. By the time the nameless daughter speaks in direct discourse, she has been destroyed, so the story's audience is subject to a kind of narrative helplessness that mirrors hers. Having introduced the story in clear moral terms, Gower now stretches those terms—not by calling into question the sinfulness of the deed, but by suggesting we might sympathize with the experience of irremediable sin. The nurse's proverb, like analytic resistance, asks for complicity. Similarly Freud describes the angry analysand—or the one in love with the analyst—drawing the analyst into the structures of her

---

[65] In HA, the daughter has a horror that this disgrace might become public (2.8). Godfrey's extremely compressed version emphasizes the secrecy and hiddenness of the crime, omitting the nurse entirely (1–3). In GR, the horror is all internal: "I have no father; in me that sacred name has perished" (259). Gower highlights political nature of the transgression.

[66] In HA, she does "encourage . . . the reluctant girl to satisfy her father's desire" (2.12–15); in GR, she only begs the girl not to kill herself.

childhood.[67] Sympathetic response provides the initial step in creating a dynamic of transference, but risks an ambiguity in the daughter's moral status. She will later die with her father at the hand of God, as if to provide a retrospective moral clarity.

But this affective pressure amounts to a narrative method with Gower. On the one hand, the clear moral evil of incest engages a hermeneutics in which the father's transgression can be identified, recognized, and confirmed. Sympathy with the daughter serves to bolster this judgment. A certain moral clarity is also encouraged by style: Gower's octosyllabic rhymes and often repetitive, lengthy sentences encourage readerly assent, in contrast to Chaucer's remarkable disjunctions.[68] But Gower uses both stylistic shifts and moments of sympathy to call readers' attention to the problematic terms of their involvement. The nurse's proverbial language ("So suffren thei that suffe mote") sounds like acceptable social truth, but applied to incest, her language is revealed as smoothing over a horror. The nurse enhances the experience of loss and helplessness that the audience is encouraged to share with the daughter, even as the nurse's ineffectuality prompts us to seek a better cure—that is, produces a desire for the plot. Yet again, sympathy for the daughter becomes attenuated as the incest continues indefinitely, the suitors multiply, and finally the daughter is struck down by God along with her father. Sympathy is rendered temporary precisely because it initiates the desire to progress away from the violated daughter. In this way, Gower complicates any interpretation based on simply affirming moral wrongs, or even based solely on sympathy for the violated woman, instead issuing a challenge to readers' interpretive faculties, which can be employed to invent a cure. From within the narrative, that challenge is answered

[67] Freud writes of the temptation to requite or reject the love of the analysand, and advocates both sympathy and immunity from involvement. He concludes that "[the analyst] must keep firm hold of the transference-love, but treat it as something unreal, as a situation which has to be gone through in the treatment and traced back to its unconscious origins and which must assist in bringing all that is most deeply hidden in the patient's erotic life into her consciousness and therefore under her control. The more plainly the analyst lets it be seen that he is proof against every temptation, the more readily will he be able to extract from the situation its analytic content" ("Observations on Transference-Love," *Standard Edition,* 12:159–71 [166]). A narrative, like a patient, nevertheless demands something more than this ideal "immunity": and Freud's essay, directed against the temptations of patients, seems designed to register just how strong the demand for complicity must be.

[68] Kate Harris, "John Gower's Confessio Amantis: The Virtues of Bad Texts," in *Manuscripts and Readers in Fifteenth-Century England,* ed. Derek Pearsall (Cambridge: D. S. Brewer, 1983), pp. 27–40.

by Apollonius of Tyre, both analyst and patient, who explodes the Antiochan incest narrative only to become implicated in it himself. As Apollonius goes through his peregrinations, however, the story's audience is continually made aware of the ways in which his progress implicates ourselves, as well, in the problems of secrecy, recursion, and stasis that keep us seeking acts of incest.

"Privete" and Public Ritual

The world of public life encroaches upon the incestuous household in the form of Apollonius of Tyre, whose youthful energy drives through the careful rhetorical, social, and political barriers Antiochus has constructed around his act of domestic tyranny. Apollonius approaches the king full of passion—full of "mod" and "hote blod." When he gets to the court, Antiochus poses him the archetypal riddle, whose solution will win Apollonius his daughter's hand:

> "With felonie I am upbore,
> I ete and have it noght forbore
> Mi modres fleissh, whos housebonde
> Mi fader forto seche I fonde,
> Which is the Sone ek of my wif.
> Hierof I am inquisitif;
> And who that can mi tale save,
> Al quyt he schal mi doghter have;
> Of his ansuere and if he faile,
> He schal be ded withoute faile."
>
> (405–14)

Antiochus's sense of power depends on the nourishment of his daughter, by whom he is "upbore," even as the blurring of generational and gender lines characteristic of such incest enigmas confuses the direction of the violence he commits against her.[69] She is reduced to a vessel that contains his mother's flesh, his father, his wife's "Sone." Although the narrative earlier claimed that Antiochus "thoghte that it was no Sinne" (346), his own language marks his behavior as felonious and cannibalistic. But the riddle veils both act and morality by presenting the situation

---

[69] On enigmas in the literature of incest, see Archibald, "Incest in Medieval Literature and Society," pp. 3–4; and Roussel, "Aspects du Père," p. 50.

447

as a game, a rhetorical trick, one whose subjects and objects are impossibly confused. Father and mother, daughter and son, parents and offspring, are conflated in a description that defies logic: the "I" of the riddle eats his mother's flesh; he has simultaneously "fonde" his father as well; his father is, therefore, also his wife's son. These lines are finally insoluble.[70] The relative pronouns hopelessly confuse any actual kinship system: how can he eat both his mother and his father? How can his father become his offspring? Figuratively, Antiochus eats the flesh of both his parents, who are ancestors of his daughter; in this way, he has not only conflated his own parents with each other and with his offspring but also has merged his ancestry with his wife's (his father is the offspring of his wife) and thus conflated himself with his wife.[71]

The riddle, of course, is confused at the literal level precisely because it indicates the confusion of social roles that incest represents, and the failure of cure in the literal instance of the sin. Antiochus destroys the communicative value of language in the process of destroying the communal value of his kingship. If the riddle does communicate, as it will to Apollonius, the hearer destroys what the language signifies—by knowing the incest, he destroys the secret, private, sealed space that engenders it:

> "The question which thou hast spoke,
> If thou wolt that it be unloke,

[70] For three quite different, more sustained readings of this riddle's tortured syntax, see Donavin, *Incest Narratives*, pp. 71–72; Watt, "Oedipus, Appolonius, and Richard II," pp. 186–94; and Scanlon, "The Riddle of Incest," pp. 124–25.

[71] For a provocative reading of Apollonius's desire for the father as exactly what implicates him in Antiochan crime, see Watt, "Oedipus, Appolonius, and Richard II," pp. 191–98. Shakespeare solves the riddle by putting the words into the daughter's mouth, shifting blame toward her:

> "'I am no viper, yet I feed
> On mother's flesh which did me breed.
> I sought a husband, in which labor
> I found that kindness in a father.
> He's father, son, and husband mild;
> I mother, wife—and yet his child.'
> How they may be, and yet in two,
> As you will live, resolve it you."
> (*Pericles, Prince of Tyre*, 1.1.64–71)

Quotations from *Pericles* are from the Cambridge edition by Doreen Delvecchio and Anthony Hammond (Cambridge: Cambridge University Press, 1998).

It toucheth al the privete
Betwen thin oghne child and thee,
And stant al hol upon you tuo."
(423–27)

Apollonius exposes the incest by using the very word "privete": this answer is less a euphemism than a way of registering a lack of distinction between father and daughter. But all Apollonius has to do is indicate that underneath the riddling language lies an aberrant familial truth, and the barrier between the incestuous king and the rest of the world breaks down. Uncommunicative, irredeemable, and without any moral lesson, the riddle mystifies political power. Apollonius's plain language would seem to solve the narrative's initial problem here: when he destroys the riddle's mystification, he would seem to stage, within the plot, a refusal to apply the story to himself, like Amans's dismissal in the framework. Incest, he asserts, belongs wholly to Antiochus and not to himself.

Instead, however, unfolding the riddle only folds Apollonius into its dangers. Antiochus bestows upon the visiting prince the "grace" (437) of thirty days in which to escape. In response, Apollonius acts with his own version of cryptic behavior: he leaves "al prively" (451) in the dark of night. He has escaped, but has transferred to himself Antiochus's "privete," a spirit of incest for which he spends the rest of the story compensating.[72] Yet because Apollonius has recognized tyranny, his journeys will revise Antiochus's conflation of parent and child, sovereign and subordinate, and eventually, story and reader. For if Antiochus represents an excessive "privete" that encloses him within a circular system of kinship, nourishment, and corruption, Apollonius initially represents an excessive public drive that prevents him from settling within any kind of system at all for most of the story's duration. In fact he never does settle in one physical place but moves among several "otherworlds": Antioch, Tharsus, Pentapolis, Mitelene, Ephesis, and intermittently, his home of Tyre as well. Significantly, Apollonius does not end up in Tyre but in his wife's realm, Pentapolis—a kind of political exogamy.

[72] The echo of "privete" is Gower's innovation. In HA, the word "secretus" is associated with Antiochus and Apollonius later leaves Tyre "occulte," in secret (6.18), but does not depart form Antioch in secret. In GR, he leaves in the dark of night. In Godfrey, the incest is "occultum" (2) and Apollonius leaves Antioch "celeri," in secret (10).

Thus, in departing "al prively" from Tyre, Apollonius fails, like Antiochus, to attend to the common profit of his people, who love him:

> They losten lust, they losten chiere,
> Thei toke upon hem such penaunce,
> Ther was no song, ther was no daunce. . . .
> "Helas, the lusti flour of youthe,
> Our Prince, our heved, oure governour,
> Thurgh whom we stonden in honour,
> Withoute the comun assent
> Thus sodeinliche is fro ous went!"
> Such was the clamour of hem alle.
>
> (476–78, 490–95)

The community of Tyre will prove capable of self-governance in the course of the tale, deflecting any suggestion that Apollonius embarks upon his journey of self-exploration at his realm's expense. But here, as in Sir Orfeo's similar departure, royal abandonment causes grief, a cessation of leisure activity, and a breakdown of the community's function as "counsel," for he has left without their "comun assent." By depicting the grief of the abandoned citizens, Genius achieves something like the affective involvement that the account of Antiochus's daughter elicited, but here, readerly involvement is more interrogative: the citizens' grief prompts readers to call into question Apollonius's conduct as king. He holds his people at a remove, failing the vicarious relation through which his presence makes them "stonden in honour." Abandonment, the opposite of incestuous union and Apollonius's overcompensation for the threat of incest, leaves Tyre in a kind of limbo throughout the story. Ironically, the fierce distance Apollonius maintains from his subjects is itself a close cousin, if not an outgrowth, of incestuous coercion—a self-induced isolation that reveals the plot in which he has become involved.

As often during structural transitions, Genius's narration here calls attention to the plot's retrospective structural logic. He intervenes after Apollonius has left Tyre: "Bot se we now what is befalle / Upon the ferste tale plein, / And torne we therto ayein" (496–98). Repetition of the "plein" initial plot seems to mean that Genius will tell us the full story of Antiochus; he calls attention to the structural imbrication of the two kings, and suggests that the first may help interpret or make "plein" the second. But after relating that Antiochus plans to kill Apollonius, Genius immediately returns to Apollonius himself: "Bot over this now forto telle / Of aventures that befelle / Unto this Prince of whom I tolde" (537–39). The circular movement of these transitions calls attention to the plot's basis in repetition: the "Apollonius" plot continually reproduces the original scene, so that successive events enact the significance of earlier moments. Thus Genius's transitions also call attention to temporal changes, emphasizing shifts and "turning" to new scenes, reiterating the episodic structure of the plot, calling attention to narrative progress.

Moreover, Genius's interruptions call attention to the way in which plot bridges narrative levels. We have already touched upon the fundamental "backward motivation" of plot in romance. For Brooks, retrospection is a function of narrative per se: "prior events, causes, are so only retrospectively, in a reading back from the end."[73] This implies that the structural logic of the narrative produces the thematic material, rather than that the material or story-stuff (*fabula*) produces the narrative form (*sjuzet*): plot, the shape of events, gives rise to significant material, rather than vice versa. When Antiochus's double Apollonius "emplots" incest, he reinvents kingship through successive backward references, while Genius's presence in the "stages of our story" makes the extratextual audience recognize the character's restructuring of the plot.[74] The actions of the characters, that is, are always interpretive— not inasmuch as Apollonius reflects upon his own incestuous proclivities, but inasmuch as he carries out undermotivated repetitions that focus audience attention on the structure and narration of the story while he enacts it. Genius, like the analyst, calls attention to the arrangement of the plot. In his transitions, readers are made aware simultaneously of Apollonius's desire to reshape events, and of Genius's ability to provide transitions, beginnings and endings—to segment and organize action according to an anti-incestuous logic. His interruptions invite readers to assess the hero's interpretive efficacy by taking stock of the situation continually, recognizing also the reflexes of incest that still remain. Like the analyst in transference, Genius intervenes by momentarily halting sheer reenactment in order to put incest in its proper perspective— helping the action become conceptual, making mere action into meaningful revision.

[73] Brooks, *Reading for the Plot*, p. 29.
[74] It is in Shakespeare where Gower appears as Prologue and Narrator to "stand i' th' gaps to teach you / the stages of our story"; see *Pericles, Prince of Tyre*, Prologue to Act IV, lines 8–9.

Gower's "Apollonius," then, demands more from readers than affective involvement with the violated daughter. Plot repetitions, Genius shows, demand audience involvement by calling attention to the uneven and benighted progress of the story—that is, the episodic structure that calls for audiences to distinguish past from present to produce significance. The fits and starts of Apollonius's development, the plot's movement, and the narrator's interventions ask readers to experience constantly the tension between recursion and progress, a double vision that Freud repeatedly calls a struggle or "battle."[75] The analyst's challenge—and the task of readers here—lies in his recognizing the status of any given event *as* an echo or a memory, a thing of the past, rather than an actual return to the past. In the so-called "talking cure" of psychoanalysis, as Brooks describes it, "the narratee listens to narration for the implied plot of past desire as it shapes and disfigures the present discourse, looking for the design of the story it would tell, working toward the recovery of the past as past, syntactically complete and reconciled with the present."[76] This historicizes incest in an entirely different register from the one with which Gower began Book 8.

In this sense romance offers a generic perspective on exemplarity because it insists on the moral value of a kind of "wandering cure." Antiochus provides a negative example from which the journeying Apollonius has to escape. But whereas the ostensible purpose of an exemplum lies in the reader's imitation or avoidance, Apollonius must enter Antiochus's plot in order to take it to heart. When the romance calls attention to the doubling between Antiochus and Apollonius, and the constant threat that incest will arise from the hero's actions, it emphasizes the metonymic character of both plot and its interpretation by readers. The romance, again, differs markedly from the self-enclosed and static images of incest represented in Genius's stories of Amnon, Caligula, and Lot. The emphasis on narrative process discourages the simple alignment or correspondence between example and application that Amans, in his rejection of the relevance of incest to his own love, implicitly assumes. The problem with Amans's interpretive method arises from its essentially analogical structure; surprisingly like incest itself, his exemplary expectations rest on excessive "sameness" between narrative and reader, short-circuiting the detours of narrative.

[75] Freud, "Observations on Transference-Love," p. 170.
[76] Brooks, *Reading for the Plot,* p. 235.

452

Apollonius progresses through *privete* to publicity, and back to secrecy again, as the magnetic pull of incest exerts its pressure on his narrative. Midway through the plot, having married, lost his wife, and left his baby daughter at Tharsis, Apollonius actually returns to Tyre, a development unique to Gower.[77] In a public act that revises his earlier, "privee" departure, Apollonius summons a parliament and appeals to the assent of his lords to hold a funeral for his wife: "Solempne was that ilke office, / And riche was the sacrifice, / The feste reali was holde: / And therto was he wel beholde" (1561–64). The staging of a public ritual not only renders his exogamous marriage official (even though the kingdom knew nothing of his wife until now) but also makes himself, complete with personal grief, legible to his subjects. The "pleie" and "chiere" that they lost when he departed is transformed into a more solemn, ritualized expression, akin to a coronation or a marriage feast. Apollonius becomes "wel beholde," visible and highly regarded; he offers his community something to "holde," a focused and ethical act of ritual binding. His public act revises the royal grief that led Antiochus to solitude and incest, insisting that kingship itself is constituted through this emergence from solitude, which in turn entails submission to the interpretive activity of his subjects. This definition remains precarious, however: after the funeral, Apollonius requests that his lords accompany him to Tharsis to retrieve his daughter, affirming his public ties to his subjects. But the journey sends him back into a destructive solitude that makes public ritual and governance according to counsel look equally insufficient.

Innovation and the Influence of Audience

Interpretation may always fail to revise; repetition can always become recursion: the capacity for change hinges on such subtle shifts in meaning that, like many romances, "Apollonius of Tyre" ultimately seems to achieve its progress largely through happenstance, usually called "aventure." In the second half of "Apollonius," the impetus for transformation comes from a series of staged "readings" or interpretations of the king, first by his wife-to-be and later by his daughter. Thematically, as the tale progresses, the autonomous consent of subjects is increasingly figured through the educated will of these daughters. Structurally, the

[77] In HA, he goes to Egypt, and also in GR; in Godfrey, his travels are unknown.

daughters figure a kind of narrative exogamy, suggesting that an educated audience provides an innovative perspective on the past. Indeed, the tale's conclusion reveals that Tyre needs not Apollonius, but his daughter, who, married, will return to rule Tyre and produce a male heir, putting to rest the problem of incest's failure of succession. In the retrospective logic of romance, the return of the daughter to her father's kingdom suggests the degree to which *his* governance depends upon *her* autonomy for its continuance. Ultimately, far from compromising royal power, the two autonomous daughters shore up and publicize royal command. Their willed obedience—and their self-assertions beyond the framework of obedience—becomes identified with the productive misprision that the incest plot seeks.

At the height of his youthful travels, before wife and daughter have come on the scene, Apollonius is shipwrecked for the first of several times, and ends up destitute on the shores of Pentapolis. Invited to the king's hall, he sits "stille" at the feast, weeping for his loss of Tyre—a stillness and self-enclosed grief that have something of the recursiveness of his earlier "privete." This still grief may echo and overcompensate for the threat of incestuous violation, but it also leaves room for the king's daughter to express a desire unheralded by anyone else.[78] At the daughter's suggestion, Apollonius teaches her music and "tho sciences whiche he can" (810). To be sure, their shared recreation leads to the kind of moral frailty, connected with leisure, that led Antiochus astray:

> Bot as men sein that frele is youthe,
> With leisir and continuance
> This Mayde fell upon a chance,
> That love hath mad him a querele
> Ayein hire youthe freissh and frele.
>
> . . . .
>
> Thenkende upon this man of Tyr,
> Hire herte is hot as eny fyr.
> (834–38, 845–46)

In contrast to the incest scenario, however, here the daughter initiates desire. Although her love is attributed to "chance," and although her

---

[78] Bullón-Fernández notices that, whereas Artestrates's daughter initiates contact with Apollonius in HA, Gower has the relationship insistently mediated by her father (51). She finds that the privacy and secrecy of this new daughter's actions "do not require negative connotations" and hence revise Antiochan incest (52).

suffering, like the lovesickness more conventionally associated with male lovers, seems to afflict the girl from outside rather than being willed, nevertheless this passage marks a crucial development in the narrative's depiction of the wills of daughters. If incestuous suppression of a subject's will depends upon "privete" and stillness, then her fiery heart should derail the plot's recursion toward incest. Instead, however, such active desire risks violation in a new form, shaming or ill repute. Womanly "schame" demands secrecy here, so her father's careful "privete" becomes the defining feature of the marriage arrangement.[79] Her father asks her to choose a suitor by letter, a form at once public and "privee," expressive and conscious of shame. She writes:

> "The schame which is in a Maide
> With speche dar noght ben unloke,
> Bot in writinge it mai be spoke;
> So wryte I to you, fader, thus:
> Bot if I have Appolinus,
> Of al this world, what so betyde,
> I wol non other man abide."
> (894–900)

Like Antiochus's riddle, the apparently riddling language here emphasizes secrecy. Her negative declaration ("I wol non") protects her, so that syntactically, she unlocks only her shame, not her desire; by speaking privately through writing, she protects herself from plain expression. The father's conference with Apollonius, too, is secret, until the hero's assent is garnered and the "accord" publicly declared. The possibility of Apollonius's refusal and the girl's public disgrace hovers over the scene: modesty revises incestuous "privete," but only just barely.

Narratologically, this episode's immense effort to preserve the girl's honor results in exogamous marriage, which, in turn, makes way for the death of Antiochus and, eventually, Apollonius's return to Tyre. But

---

[79] In HA, the daughter writes on wax to preserve her modesty, presumably because wax can be erased. Gower expands the delicate conduct required for Thaise to navigate between the poles of secrecy and ill repute. He has Antiochus's daughter establish the initial link between ill repute and incest: "Thing which mi bodi ferst begat / Into this world, onliche that / Mi worldes worschipe hath bereft" (329–31). Her compressed, chiastic language signals not only the loss of "friendship" found in exogamy but also the loss of narrative progress itself. There is no solution to what she regards as an impossibly private, self-enclosed, and iterative event.

the tale's next sea storm reverts once again to incest, as his new queen apparently dies at sea, leaving him now "al one" (1103). This loss is almost immediately ameliorated for the reader by her marvelous revival when her casket washes ashore at Ephesus, marking a promise to the reader of "creative repetition" while also suggesting, in the retrospective logic of romance, that Apollonius has not quite yet learned to read well; he could solve the incest riddle, but plainer or more physical signs— signs of his wife's life—seem to escape him.[80] In his grief he temporarily avoids incest by leaving his daughter, Thaise, to be raised and educated in Tharsis, commanding that she be schooled.[81]

The education of daughters militates consistently against recursion, drawing first Thaise's mother and then the girl herself toward the possibility of public eloquence: as Thaise grows up at Tharsis, she becomes beloved of the people, like her father, and exerts a binding force in the "comun place" of the city. Her influence arises from her education: "Sche was wel tawht, sche was wel boked, / So wel sche spedde hir in hire youthe / That sche of every wisdom couthe" (1328–30). The explicit link here between book-learning and communal benefit recalls the terms of the *Confessio* itself, as established in Book 1, where Gower linked vernacular language, poetic style, and amatory theme in an effort to embrace a variety of readers. Thaise's education gives her wide knowledge, "every wisdom," creating social cohesion.[82] Nevertheless, Thaise remains at risk of violation: her stepmother tries to have her killed, and she is sold into prostitution in Mitelyne. Prostitution realizes and denigrates her "comun" status: she is "cried" about the city "In syhte of al the people aboute" (1421–22), suggesting a particularly visual mode of "divisioun" wherein her objectification divides her from the community. Yet Thaise refuses the interpretation of "comun" as sexually available. Her education enables her to refute publicly those who would understand her as erotic object, revising both the isolated suffering of

---

[80] "Creative repetition" is Frye's term, *The Secular Scripture,* pp. 174–75.

[81] Although in the narrative this demand is coded as novel, it may not have seemed entirely foreign to English readers. In the later fourteenth century, girls did receive some schooling at home, and this increased in the early fifteenth century. See Jo Ann Hoeppner Moran, *The Growth of English Schooling, 1340–1548: Learning, Literacy, and Laicization in Pre-Reformation York Diocese* (Princeton: Princeton University Press, 1985); and Nicholas Orme, *Education and Society in Medieval and Renaissance England* (London: Hambledon, 1989), esp. pp. 153–75.

[82] In HA, the citizens see Tarsia's beauty and finery (ornatum) as a marvel (31.3). In GR, she is praised for her beauty (282) and in Godfrey for she is beautiful (formosa, ornatus) and the populus reveres her (reveretur, 112–13).

Antiochus's daughter and the "schame" of Artestrates's daughter, her own mother.

Further, Thaise uses her rhetorical skills for economic advantage in this new, mercenary city. Having won the sympathy of her pimp's henchman, she begs him to let her earn his master money by leaving the brothel and establishing a school instead:

> "Let him do crie ay wyde where,
> What lord that hath his doghter diere,
> And is in will that sche schal liere
> Of such a Scole that is trewe,
> I schal hire teche of thinges newe,
> Which as non other womman can
> In al this lond."
>
> (1460–66)

Unlike the passive daughter of Antiochus, who is essentially "bereft" of her whole world, Thaise produces a novel social world. She demands a chamber where she can locate her school, suggesting an institutional stability and a feminine intimacy that revise the image of nurse and daughter trapped in the Antiochan chamber.[83] Thaise's new world re sponds to the communal need of lords who "will" that their daughters should learn "thinges newe." That is, she imagines a new audience of women, sanctioned and perpetuated by fathers.[84] Once she has estab-

---

[83] Unlike the more visible institutions for boys and men, the household seems to have provided a forum for the existence of communal reading among women. Felicity Riddy points out that "one of the features of convent life which is regularly criticised by the bishops is the way in which, from the thirteenth century on, religious communities were allowed to fragment into separate familiae or households." See "'Women Talking About the Things of God': A Late-Medieval Sub-culture," in *Women and Literature in Britain 1150–1500*, ed. Carol M. Meale, 2nd ed. (Cambridge: Cambridge University Press, 1996), pp. 104–27 (109). See also Mary Erler, *Women, Reading, and Piety in Late Medieval England* (Cambridge: Cambridge University Press, 2002). Both have argued that the difference between such convent households and the lay households of aristocratic women may not have been very great, and indeed that books regularly passed between them.

[84] This image of fathers sending their daughters to school anticipates the historical development that Michael Van Cleave Alexander attributes mainly to Thomas More, whose school for his daughters included Latin grammar and expanded to include others in the early sixteenth century. See Alexander, *The Growth of English Education, 1348–1648: A Social and Cultural History* (University Park: Pennsylvania State University Press, 1990), pp. 81–82. There is little evidence for regular grammar schooling for girls in the fourteenth century, but it does seem clear that either in individual households or in nunneries aristocratic girls received some education in vernacular and even the Latin

lished the school, "al the lond unto hir secheth / Of yonge wommen forto liere" (1496–97).[85] The new educational community draws from the whole land, suggesting a diverse public world. Moreover, the school focuses on the multiple *desires* of her pupils: "Now comen tho that comen wolde / Of wommen in her lusty youthe" (1480–81). The fathers' wishes authorize those of the daughters, who arrive in a state of intellectual desire to which Thaise responds with various disciplines, teaching music to some, proverbs and questions to others.

The school stages Thaise's adaptation to social circumstances. The image of female schooling suggests a female audience reflective of the communal nature of reading among women in fourteenth- and fifteenth-century England.[86] But again, Gower's notion of the eloquent woman is essentially an idealizing fiction. When he creates Thaise's peculiarly female institution, rather than advocating female education, he draws upon a relatively familiar picture of communal reading in order to idealize the *image* of female institutional literacy. Indeed, Thaise's adaptation to Mitelene's mercantile ethos resembles Gower's adaptation of his material to the wider audience that will appreciate his new style of English poetry. Her school, which teaches the disciplines she will later teach to her mourning father, depicts the structuring, even foundational function of audiences, with their novelty, variety, and eagerness to learn.[87]

Thaise's female community, then, figures innovation itself: her school demonstrates and carries out the purpose of romance, which renews its dark beginnings by turning over repeated motifs to new interpretations. The readaptation of incest motifs reaches its climax when Apollonius, believing the false account of his daughter's death at Tharsis, reenacts

---

psalter (Orme, *Education and* Society, pp. 170, 175; Moran, *Growth of English Schooling,* pp. 69–70).

[85] In other versions of the tale, Thaise (Tarsia) saves herself at first by telling her story to inspire pity in her potential sexual customers. Having avoided rape, she then earns money for her pimp by performing on the lyre in public and expounding upon philosophical questions (HA 34–36; GR 287–88; Godfrey 141–44). Only in Gower does Apollonius explicitly order her to be educated, "set to bokes lore" (1300), when he leaves her in Tharsis.

[86] Riddy suggests ways in which regular reading aloud formed a "reading community" for many women during the period (110–11); see also Mary Erler and Anne Clark Bartlett, *Male Authors, Female Readers: Representation and Subjectivity in Middle English Devotional Literature* (Ithaca: Cornell University Press, 1995).

[87] Bullón-Fernández similarly stresses Thaise's public function in this section of the story, arguing that "language as a social act displaces the threat of illegitimate sexuality," revising Antiochus's daughter's passivity (55).

the circumstances of Antiochan grief: he flees his ship's cabin and goes below, where "for the conseil of noman / Ayein therinne he nolde come" (1602–3). The pressure of misfortune has destroyed his precarious respect for counsel; when the ship drifts to Mitelene, he will not even greet the king, Athenagoras. This complete rejection of community brings to a head the story's divisions between singular desires and common profit. Apollonius is in danger of that animal regression that made the incestuous father look like the "Cok among the Hennes."[88] But unlike Antiochus, Apollonius will listen to the therapeutic narrative of lineage that Thaise tells him, which, properly understood, repeats but extends his own life's events.

Like the analyst in response to transference, Thaise both encourages Apollonius's expressions of desire and redirects them. Athenagoras sends the renowned teacher to coax the silent stranger with her scholarly puzzles and riddles.[89] When the resistant Apollonius finally asks her to leave, Thaise refuses to depart at his bidding. If royal power relies on the king's capacity to make his word law, then Thaise's refusal takes up his own and turns it around: his words are not the words of a king, so she will not allow him to command her:

> Bot as a madd man ate laste
> His heved wepende awey he caste,
> And half in wraththe he bad hire go.
> Bot yit sche wolde noght do so,
> And in the derke forth sche goth,
> Til sche him toucheth, and he wroth,
> And after hire with his hond
> He smot: and thus whan sche him fond
> Desesed, courtaisly sche saide,
> "Avoi, mi lord, I am a Maide;
> And if ye wiste what I am,
> And out of what lignage I cam,
> Ye wolde noght be so salvage."
> (1687–99)

---

[88] On the romance protagonist's descent away from his own identity (understood dynastically) into a kind of amnesia, and even animal metamorphosis, see Frye, *Secular Scripture,* pp. 95–126. "At the bottom is a memory which can only be returned to, a closed circle of recurrence; at the top is the recreation of memory" (183).

[89] In HA and GR, Athenagoras begins to figure out that Tarsia is Apollonius's daughter before he sends her in (HA 40; GR 289).

A number of critics have pointed out that Apollonius's rage and physical violence echo that of Antiochus; the enjambment of lines 1693–94 opens a brief space in which the activity of the prince's hand in the darkness is left to the reader's imagination.[90] Yet whereas Antiochus's riddle hid his crime, Thaise's narrative reveals her identity: she has a story, and suggests that the king learn to interpret it. In contrast to his Latin sources, where Thaise reveals her identity through riddles, Gower turns enigma into plain narration.[91] Her new narrative, in turn, "actualizes the past in symbolic form, so that it can be replayed to a more successful outcome."[92] Thaise teaches her father to interpret properly because she interprets his silence and rejection as itself an episode in a narrative—a contingent response rather than permanent separation. This mutual interpretive activity enables the series of adjustments that will result in recognition.

Genius governs the audience's response throughout this scene, undercutting the sense of precariousness that defined so many earlier revisions of incest. He establishes the entanglement of Apollonius's fate with that of Mitelene at a cosmic level: in the storm that drives Apollonius to his daughter's island, he is forced to follow Neptune's law (1595), and when he arrives the citizens of Mitelene are holding "hihe festes of Neptune" (1614) on the beach. Such gestures limit contingency by imposing a retrospective order on events. More concretely, the audience's foreknowledge is compounded by a reminder that Thaise at first knows nothing of the strange king's identity, even though readers do (1603). Genius assures us before the two have even recognized each other, "Bot of hem tuo a man mai liere / What is to be so sibb of blod" (1702–3). We are essentially guaranteed a successful recognition scene.

But we do not get it. Thaise begins her own story, a story she has told no one else except "this lord al one" (1728), but except for the potentially incestuous "he tho toke hire in his arm" (1732), Genius quickly removes the narrative into the realm of proverbial generality, where the "joie" of father and daughter illustrates the vicissitudes of

---

[90] I have made this observation before, in "Chaucer Answers Gower: Constance and the Trouble With Reading," *ELH* 63 (1997): 627–55 (638).

[91] Arthur Heiserman, *The Novel Before the Novel*, remarks that, in HA, "The recognition finally comes when Tarsia abandons art and weeps out her story in such prosaic detail that even her father cannot avoid seeing that this beautiful prostitute is his daughter" (215).

[92] Brooks, *Reading for the Plot*, p. 235.

Fortune: "So goth the world, now wo, now wel" (1738).[93] The gap at the recognition scene reminds us that plot, like Fortune's wheel, can always revert to the horrible origin, even as it moves toward renovation and what Brooks calls "lucid repose."[94] The end of Apollonius's isolation depends on his correct interpretation of the natural kinship bond. In the process of turning one thing into another, however, plot does not ultimately guarantee successful establishment of family and community; instead, Genius calls upon his audience to write the climax of Apollonius's plot ourselves—to distinguish between repetition and cure. Thaise's educated eloquence both enacts and calls for a reading that avoids incest, giving audiences the tools with which to understand the recognition scene as different from incestuous tyranny. That the scene avoids detailed performance leaves the story's conclusion adaptable to the idiosyncrasies of audience imagination.

After rediscovering Thaise, Apollonius finds a nearly sacral "grace" (1739) that allows him to ascend "into the liht" (1741), toward lucidity and royal authority. His kingship depends, in the end, on his ability to emerge from isolated grief into the imaginative realm of common profit—to enter the "common place" of his role as king, where he and his closest subject, Thaise, apply exemplary kinship relations to the wider political world. His kingship depends, that is, upon submission to his audience's influence. Thematically, the story's resolution here, in the public space of Mitelene, further depends upon the exogamy of Thaise, who, at her father's consent, promptly marries Athenagoras.

At first, the elision of an intimate recognition scene may disappoint; this is the kind of narration that gives Gower his reputation as a smooth and even skillful, but at times rather flat storyteller. Apollonius's reunion with his wife exhibits a fuller drama of recognition—she swoons upon hearing his voice and calls him husband, whereupon he "knew hire anon" (1862). But the story ends with a generalized account of Apollonius as ideal king. There are narrative and political reasons for the tactfulness of the recognition scene with the daughter and the distancing effects of the end of the tale. Gower calls attention to the necessity for audience involvement in the story's process of clarification, but

---

[93] Others have remarked on the recursive character of the recognition scene; Heiserman writes, "When the relationship between man and whore coincides with that between father and daughter, the tensions always sought by romances to vivify the paradoxical recognition and reversal become especially pleasing" (215).

[94] Brooks, *Reading for the Plot,* p. 61.

without enforcing particular audience response.[95] Familial and monarchical social bonds are not simply reestablished but also, because the language of the conclusion is impersonal, rendered natural. Apollonius's royal authority reaches past the circumstances of loss toward an image of steady, universal power.

When Genius depicts the recognition scene as an act of mutual interpretation, he implies that proper interpretation lies at the heart of moral experience, which grounds all political action. Amans, of course, responds by rebelling against the story of a sin he has never committed. In contrast to Thaise's recognition of contingency and change, he insists upon the consistency of his love (he puts all his love "in o place"). He complains that Genius has, from the beginning, misunderstood his situation: "Mi wo to you is bot a game, / That fielen noght of that I fiele" (2152–53). Disillusioned with stories, he is also impotent when it comes to rhetorical invention: no matter how many "thousand wordes on a rowe" (2050) he speaks to his lady, he says, her refusal overthrows them all. He wants advice on how to win her; the narrative dilations of the Apollonius story do not provide an instrument for success in love; the story does not rewrite *his own* story. Slowly, though, he learns that his resistance has disabled the affair, precisely because love demands a distinction between the lover's experience and the "love story"—or between the idealizing self and the actual beloved. When Amans recognizes his impropriety, he becomes reduced to his specific, mortal experience as John Gower, the poet looking at his aging self in Venus's harsh mirror.[96]

[95] On the liberation of readers available through the *Confessio*'s framework, see Kurt Olsson, "Rhetoric, John Gower, and the Late Medieval Exemplum," *M&H,* n.s. 8 (1977): 185–200.

[96] Even those critics inclined to argue that the *Confessio* strives for a single, specific, coherent goal rarely find that goal clearly articulated. Minnis writes, "But what is the total effect of the ending of the *Confessio Amantis;* how can we gauge Gower's shifting tone? . . . human love . . . is being celebrated even as it is being left behind, and in face of all the moral imperatives" ("*De Vulgari Auctoritate,*" pp. 60–61). For Wetherbee, although Genius provides some moral answers, "the project of the poem can never be brought to a satisfactory resolution, and must finally be abandoned. . . . it is [still] as if the instinctual energy of his verse were turning back toward the opening of the poem" ("Latin Structure and Vernacular Space," p. 31). Similar comments can be found in Yeager, *John Gower's Poetic: The Search for a New Arion* (Woodbridge: D. S. Brewer, 1990), pp. 262–68. Peter Nicholson, *Love and Ethics in Gower's "Confessio Amantis"* (Ann Arbor: University of Michigan Press, 2005), argues that concluding self-recognition allows Gower to see the design of events and order of the universe, despite the contingencies of love and "the elusiveness of moral certainty in our world" (394).

In this sense, the end of the *Confessio* becomes the story of John Gower's temporal existence: love becomes the stuff of memory. In the terms of transference, his unrequited love is the material that has finally been "worked through" and relegated to the past. In this context, we can look back on "Apollonius of Tyre" as the ultimate step in working through, a process to which readers are crucial. By emphasizing the fictive status of all the exempla compiled in the *Confessio*, "Apollonius" calls attention to its audience's involvement in the plot and, hence, in the structure of relations between authority and subject. Far from modeling exactly how readers should conduct themselves, subjecting them to morals, the story mediates on how readers garner authority and make therapeutic contributions to meaning. In the gap between incest and recognition lies the "exogamous" ethical work of reading, the confrontation of narrative changes as they unfold through time. Moral understanding thus comes to resemble textual repetition at its most generative: readers, rather than mirroring characters, reconceive them. For Gower, the efficacy of exemplary fiction depends upon an audience conscious of narrative desire. Looked at in this way, it is no wonder that he depicts his audience as a lover and fills his book with love stories.

When, in "Apollonius," Genius depicts readers not only as lovers or kings but women as well, the possibilities for novel and various readings increase dramatically. Nevertheless, the *Confessio* ends by reincorporating such variety. Because Genius emphasizes Thaise's education as an instrument of monarchy, "Apollonius" seems designed to argue for the normative benefits of female influence. Anxiety about new readership of many kinds was evident in fourteenth-century English texts, from conduct books seeking *gentil* audiences to mirrors for princes seeking to harmonize the will of king and subjects. In response to the possibilities of wayward reading, Gower's figure of what David Wallace calls "female eloquence" renders beneficial these potentially threatening new audiences.[97] Gower ends the *Confessio*, then, by realizing a form of feminine invention—and a shape for feminine desire—that calls attention to the affirmative possibilities of innovative vernacular reception. The various audiences featured in Thaise's school suggest that education perpetuates multiple desires in a "common place," drawing community together. Within the story's plot, then, female eloquence serves to confirm the

---

[97] Wallace, *Chaucerian Polity*, pp. 212–46. Bullón-Fernández argues that eloquence defines many of Gower's female characters throughout the *Confessio*.

communal ties that give fathers and monarchs hierarchical power.[98] Still, that power—and the authority of the narrative about its development—also depends intimately upon the experimentation, and the transformative influence, of its therapeutic audiences.

In the end, Gower imagines female audience hypothetically, and registers innovation in the explicitly fictive realm of romance. The central feminine audience of the *Confessio*—the beloved—never achieves the affirmative power hypothesized for Thaise in "Apollonius of Tyre." As Kurt Olsson has it, Amans's self-recognition in the end depends upon his dawning understanding that, in fact, his beloved has a separate existence and is not subject to his desires.[99] It seems to me that Gower makes "Apollonius" an imaginative experiment in cultivating an audience's autonomy in order to appropriate it to socially affirmative ends. In Gower's hands, the story investigates how the desires of those outside the self might be brought to bear on the ethical deployment of patriarchal power—an investigation that finally gestures beyond what the poem as a whole is able to achieve. Yet, if female eloquence can be an idealizing fiction only within the bounds of romance, and if the mental integration of Amans/Gower finally omits the lady entirely, nevertheless Gower has raised the serious possibility that newfangled audiences might contribute to the common good.

[98] Watt is similarly guarded about the affirmative nature of the tale's ending, finding in it an allegory of Richard II's failure to listen to good counsel; for her "it is far from clear that [Apollonius] has learnt much along the way" (207).

[99] Olsson, "Love, Intimacy, and Gower," p. 99.

REVIEWS

ANN W. ASTELL. *Eating Beauty: The Eucharist and the Spiritual Arts of the Middle Ages.* Ithaca: Cornell University Press, 2006. Pp. xiii, 296. $39.95.

Ann Astell's latest book studies the Eucharist not from a historical or social perspective, as much recent scholarship has done, but from an expressly theological one. In her own words, she is interested in the "theological aesthetics" of the Eucharist, a phrase that she defines via Robert Viladesau to describe the study of theological objects as aesthetic and of aesthetic objects as theological (p. 16). Specifically, she reads the Eucharist as the vehicle by which beauty enters the world and reads her subjects' eucharistic devotion as illustrative of their own understandings of beauty. As she does so, she refers to their own "theological aesthetics"—hence "Bonaventure's theological aesthetics" or, more broadly, "Cistercian theological aesthetics" (pp. 128, 72)—thus suggesting that her approach is their approach and that a fundamental continuity links the medieval past to the present. This justifies the extended historical scope of the project, which extends from Bernard of Clairvaux to the twentieth-century philosopher Simone Weil. It also bridges the spiritualities that Astell studies with her own, which is expressed directly in two of her own poems included in an appendix. Embodying the duality of the phrase "theological aesthetics," the book is both theology and literary criticism.

The basic argument of the book is that "every genuine spirituality" (though it's not clear what it takes for a spirituality to qualify as genuine, aside from its Christianity) seeks to restore the paradise lost through original sin, a restoration that the Eucharist enables (p. 257). The first chapter to explore this is also the strongest: Chapter 2 (Chapter 1 is the introduction) demonstrates compellingly that the eucharistic host was often figured as the antidote to the Edenic apple, making one form of eating a corrective to another. To eat the Eucharist is to eat from the Tree of Life, or Christ. This eating restores paradise by implanting in each person, through the Eucharist, a key virtue that is consonant with his or her religious vocation. This virtue, in turn, develops into a way of life that restores the beauty of paradise both to the individual and, though the individual, to others. Chapter 7, which Astell calls the other theoretical chapter, determines the relationship of the Eucharist to beauty in the aesthetics of Simone Weil and Hegel, locating beauty in Weil's Eucharistic devotion and siding with her against Hegel to conclude that the Eucharist is the basis of art which transmits beauty to the world.

Chapters 3–6 consider four virtues, each appropriate to a different religious order, that undo original sin. With reference to Bernard of Clairvaux and Gertrude of Helfta, chapter 3 identifies curiosity as original sin according to Cistercians, or elsewhere more generally to "monks," and humility as the virtue which reverses it. Chapter 4 uses Bonaventure's life of Francis to define concupiscence as original sin for Franciscans, and poverty as its virtuous antidote. Chapter 5 primarily focuses on Catherine of Siena, though it also discusses Dominic, Catherine of Genoa and the Peruvian saint Rose of Lima, to establish a Dominican concern with preaching as the remedy for the original sin of gluttony. Chapter 6 characterizes disobedience as original sin and obedience as its opponent according to Jesuits, focusing on Ignatius of Loyola and Michelangelo (who, she notes, was not a Jesuit). Throughout, she is interested in how the saints discussed embody a key virtue communicated to them through the Eucharist. In spite of the title of the book, however, the Eucharist generally remains in the background of the study, serving as the largely implicit source for each saint's virtue, which is Astell's true focus. One might object to the rigidity of the order-based distinctions, themselves not always faithful to order (again, Michelangelo is with the Jesuits), or to the grouping of figures separated by sometimes substantial temporal or spatial distance, but Astell does not pretend to describe the historical development of different spiritualities or even to offer a comparative study of early Christian religious orders. The book is organized by chronology and by religious order, but its fundamental goal, at least in my reading, is to demonstrate what Astell perceives as an essential and constant truth about Catholicism: that it seeks to restore paradise by the exercise of virtues, themselves embedded in and communicated through the Eucharist.

Astell's general instinct is to privilege unity and continuity over historical or political difference. In line with this, she consistently and self-consciously treats saints' lives as historically precise, reading Bonaventure's *Legenda Major,* for instance, as a faithful and nonpolemical account of Francis's spirituality and downplaying the political concerns that clearly impacted it. Further, because she seeks to link virtues, the Eucharist, and beauty as often as possible, the concepts of beauty, and even of the Eucharist, end up being quite broad. In order to keep attention focused on her central themes, she often appends phrases about beauty or the Eucharist to her quotations and paraphrases, but in such a way that implies that the original quotations explicitly address these themes. For instance, she claims that, for Bonaventure, "The substantial form of a thing unites its essence, nature and species, and its beauty consists in that harmonious unity of expression" (p. 105). Although Bonaventure does liken the three, he does not discuss them with respect to beauty (Astell often defines *species* as beauty, but in the passage she cites at the end of the sentence above, it connotes only "image"). Or, although a quotation from Catherine of Siena ends by describing Jesus as "the incarnate word and only begotten Son of God," Astell adds "present in the Eucharist" after the quotation, suggesting that Catherine drew attention to the Eucharist proper (p. 147).

This is not to detract from the sustained creativity of the work, which brings new and productive approaches to bear on the study of medieval (and later) spirituality. The book adds a crucial dimension to the study of the Eucharist in the Middle Ages by relating it to original sin, and its individual readings are often compelling, displaying Astell's ability to make unexpected connections between texts. This will be a useful read for anyone interested in the aesthetic content of medieval theology.

MICHELLE KARNES
University of Missouri–Columbia

ALCUIN BLAMIRES. *Chaucer, Ethics, and Gender.* Oxford: Oxford University Press, 2006. Pp. xii, 263. $90.00.

Having spent his recent career examining the role of women in medieval culture, Alcuin Blamires turns his attention to the nexus of moral and gender questions in Chaucer's work. Offering a set of examples of these questions in the Introduction (including "Does the Wife of Bath's discourse allege that women are mercenary, or generous, or profligate? What is the value of brotherhood in *The Knight's Tale*? If a female fortitude is projected in *The Clerk's Tale*, how much are we to admire it?"

[p. 1]), he notes that these questions derive from "a profound interest in dramas of personal morality—notably how people behave when making and justifying their choices in sexual matters" (p. 2). Noting the extensive discussion of gender issues in Chaucer's writings, Blamires points out that after a wave of both "capacious approaches" (p. 3) and more narrowly focused studies, "what is needed now is a period of consolidation, defining gender formulations in Chaucer's poetry with greater precision in relation to the various medieval discourses through and against which his formulations are positioned" (p. 3). *Chaucer, Ethics, and Gender* is his attempt to begin this consolidation, aiming both to historicize and to examine the doctrines that inform (correctly or incorrectly) Chaucer's works—certainly an ambitious task.

Blamires's introduction sets out his terms, noting the slippery nature of "ethics" and "morals." He attributes to Chaucer a particular interest in "the accommodations negotiated between ethical concepts and the moral systems into which Christianity sought to assimilate them" (p. 8), particularly in their relationship to gender. This fixing of terminology precedes an extended look at the moral treatises and dicta of Chaucer's age and an eclectic portrayal of their concepts. Drawing a metaphor from the assumptions of contemporary critical theory, he views Chaucer's narratives as showing a "creative awareness of ragged seams, and of overlaps where the nap of each cloth does not run quite in the same direction" (p. 19).

Blamires moves on to discuss individual texts and problems. His most overarching examination, "Fellowship and Detraction in the Architecture of the *Canterbury Tales:* from 'The General Prologue' and 'The Knight's Tale' to 'The Parson's Prologue,'" seeks to examine Chaucer's dramatization of friendship and community. This discussion also considers homosocial friendship, its potential for disturbance, and the "competitive and defamatory impulses" (p. 21) that build throughout the storytelling competition. Moral commentaries on friendship and defamatory speech frame this interrogation of the *Canterbury Tales* project (with *Troilus and Criseyde* brought in for good measure). "Credulity and Vision: 'The Miller's Tale,' 'The Merchant's Tale,' 'The Wife of Bath's Tale,'" takes up the morality of sight, foresight, and inquiry. Here the issues of gender come into play—sight, Blamires contends, is gendered "because in the misogynistic culture of the period women are sometimes held to act as decoys, disabling the faculty of prudence that should transcend credulity" (p. 47). In Chaucer's writings, women, as objects of the

468

male gaze, allow men to "'see' better." Within this reading, *The Wife of Bath's Tale* becomes the most intense example "of moral discovery and of revised perception of the Other engineered in an Everyman by an Everywoman" (p. 76).

The discourse and doctrines of desire follow in "Sex and Lust: 'The Merchant's Tale,' 'The Reeve's Tale,' and other *Tales*." Negotiating the often bizarre doctrines of sexual behavior, Blamires examines how the "established moral constraints on sex fare in Chaucer's writing" (p. 79). This chapter is particularly effective in its interrogations of assumptions about sexual double standards and the function of lust, demonstrating Chaucer's complex interactions with the prohibitions and limitations that informed the doctrines of his time. He shows Chaucer's own rhetoric of sexual vice and sexual permission, in both the heterosexual examinations of the Merchant and Reeve, as well as the same-sex representations found in the Pardoner and *The Miller's Tale*. This reading of the sodomic moment of the fabliau suggests that Chaucer's pastiche "leaves us amused but, so far as moral overtones are concerned, reeling" (p. 105). One of the most pointed statements in a book filled with intriguing assertions about the poetry we know and love, Blamires's analysis here seems unfortunately cursory.

Three chapters on specific moral issues follow: "The Ethics of Sufficiency: 'The Man of Law's Introduction' and 'Tale' and 'The Shipman's Tale'"; "Liberality: 'The Wife of Bath's Prologue' and 'Tale' and 'The Franklin's Tale'; and "Problems of Patience and Equanimity: 'The Franklin's Tale,' 'The Clerk's Tale,' 'The Nun's Priest's Tale.'" All three do essentially what they say they will, but they begin to seem a bit formulaic. However, "Men, Women, and Moral Jurisdiction: 'The Friar's Tale,' 'The Physician's Tale,' and the Pardoner" engages the issues of ethics, morality, and gender promised in the Introduction. Questions of authority govern this discussion. The *Canterbury Tales* thus becomes site for "developing the consequences of these evasions and distortions of moral jurisdiction" (p. 206).

"Proprieties of Work and Speech: 'The Second Nun's Prologue' and 'Tale,' 'The Canon's Yeoman's Prologue' and 'Tale,' 'The Manciple's Prologue' and 'Tale,' and 'The Parson's Prologue'" moves to the linguistic heart of Chaucer's project. The discourses of work and language, both fruitful and idle, become Blamires's focus. Interesting gender issues, he contends, arise because the Second Nun epitomizes dynamic linguistic and functional force, while a man stands for idle and useless activity.

Although he comes to the conclusion that "idle words may be the nearest thing to the besetting view of the Canterbury Pilgrimage game" (p. 228), Blamires also notes that "so-called idle words and vanities furnish the moral as well as imaginative core of his creative output" (p. 229). The book ends with a brief conclusion about Chaucer as a moral poet working "wonders" with moral analysis (p. 238).

The overall effect of *Chaucer, Ethics, and Gender* is an interesting one. While repeatedly making intriguing assertions and exploring complex questions, and certainly making a strong case for Chaucer as a poet deeply engaged with morality, the book seems to fall short in answering its own questions and exploring its own discoveries. In numerous cases, Blamires offers up readings with significant implications that he pulls back from investigating. The collection, for all its scope, leaves its readers wanting more. Yet if Blamires is correct in stating that in the investigation of Chaucer and gender "what is needed now is a period of consolidation" (p. 3), perhaps he has begun that challenge which succeeding critics will continue to answer. Certainly anyone interested in exploring "gender formulations in Chaucer's poetry . . . in relation to the various medieval discourses through and against which his formulations are positioned" (p. 3) will need to read this book, and in doing so will find a distinct combination of inspiration, frustration, and reward.

ANGELA JANE WEISL
Seton Hall University

ARDIS BUTTERFIELD, ed. *Chaucer and the City.* Cambridge: D. S. Brewer, 2006. Pp. xiv, 231. $80.00.

This diverse collection of essays works within the rich tradition of medieval London studies that flourished especially in the late twentieth century thanks to the work of Caroline Barron, Barbara Hanawalt, Sheila Lindenbaum, and David Wallace, among others. The individual essays (slightly more than half of which are versions of papers delivered at the 2002 London Chaucer Conference) frequently acknowledge their debt to this tradition through their methodologies or arguments, and sometimes extend beyond it in exciting and important ways.

The volume revolves most productively around the notions of residue, of conflagration, and of archive. That is, as Butterfield notes in her introduction, "Chaucer and the Detritus of the City," London famously does not exist in Chaucer's poetry; the text "rebuffs as much as invites our efforts to grasp its urban character" (p. 13). The essays collected here are often subtly sophisticated in their theoretical negotiation of the idea of "recovering" the medieval city. As Ruth Evans puts it in her contribution, "The Production of Space in Chaucer's London," we are well beyond "the critical game of hunt-the-London" (p. 56); instead, the contributors sift through the matter left over after the catastrophe of historical difference and find in Chaucer's poetry virtual spaces, along with alternative or oppositional discourses and ideas, in which medieval London can thrive.

Marion Turner's "Greater London," for example, argues that the geographical and cultural definitions of London exceed the boundaries of the walled city to include such diverse elements as the king, the country, the stews, the pubs, and even false words and gossip. Taking issue with David Wallace's formulation of London as an "absent city" in Chaucer's poetry, Turner demonstrates the city's frequently dangerous and noxious presence.

Evans's suggestion, in the course of her reading of Favent and the Rykener deposition, that London's multiple bodies are "energetic, sensual and defiant" (p. 52), is corroborated and extended in Barbara Nolan's "Chaucer's Poetics of Dwelling in *Troilus and Criseyde.*" Focusing on Chaucer's subtle and dynamic usage of the verb "to dwell," including its Old English senses of "seducing, wandering, erring, deluding" (p. 62), Nolan suggests that the city here is subject to "extreme rescaling" (p. 72) as its residents "habitually trop[e] whatever mortal spaces they inhabit for the sake of comfortable dwelling and love" (p. 74). Christopher Cannon, in his "Chaucer and the Language of London," similarly focuses on the broken, or diminished, body of the "citee," a term (Cannon notes) Chaucer uses some eighty-seven times in the *Canterbury Tales.* Cannon's discussion demonstrates how Chaucer's use of the language of craft rivalries, the defining (and divisive) discourse of the capital, locates London not as a "place someone might actually live in" but instead as "an idea *about* such living"(p. 89) that never fulfills its promise.

Derek Pearsall, in his essay on "The *Canterbury Tales* and London Club Culture," develops the notion that "women were not important members of Chaucer's post-1387 audience" (p. 9). Imagining the appeal of a " 'clubby' kind of male coterie audience" (p. 99) to Chaucer, Pearsall conjures that audience's delight in the "easy-tempered misogyny" (p. 101) he finds throughout the *Tales*. Helen Cooper suggests another constituent excluded or neglected by Chaucer. Her "London and Southwark Poetic Companies: *'Si tost c'amis'* and the *Canterbury Tales*" includes as an appendix an edition and translation of Renaud de Hoiland's *"Si tost c'amis"*; this Anglo-Norman song seems to derive from the London *puy,* a group that was founded in the late thirteenth century and based on continental "fraternities or confréries . . . devoted to the competitive writing of poetry" (p. 109). But Cooper claims that both stylistically and culturally the *Tales* would not suit such a Francophilic brotherhood (even if it did exist contemporaneously: there is no documentary evidence to indicate that the London *puy* survived into Chaucer's lifetime); the *puy,* Cooper argues, like other London institutions, traded in forms and discourses deliberately rejected by Chaucer when he wrote in English and had his pilgrims ride out of the city.

C. David Benson, in "Literary Contests and London Records in the *Canterbury Tales,*" relies on London court records (as found in the *Letter Books* and *Plea and Memoranda Rolls)* to draw out comparisons with Chaucer's representation of crime and punishment in the city, particularly with reference to *The Cook's Tale.* Elliot Kendall's contribution, "The Great Household in the City: The *Shipman's Tale,*" similarly exploits documentary culture while contrasting the famous commercialism of the merchant against the noncommercial forms of social capital modeled by the aristocratic household. Surprisingly, as Kendall notes, Chaucer's tale resists the easy polarization such a division seems to present, showing instead that "values and traits commonly attributed to one social group are neither invariably nor exclusively the property of that group" (p. 154). John Scattergood, in "London and Money: Chaucer's *Complaint to His Purse,*" suggests that when Chaucer asks his purse to help him "out of this toune" (line 15), a phrase usually glossed as "out of this situation," he actually means he wants to leave London, which Scattergood shows was not only unsavory but also expensive.

Paul Davis's "After the Fire: Chaucer and Urban Poetics, 1666–1743" and Helen Phillips's "Chaucer and the Nineteenth-Century City" extend the volume out of the Middle Ages and into some fascinating realms of inquiry. Davis traces how Chaucer's poetry changed (or at least served as a catalyst to change) Dryden's view of London, and Phillips deconstructs the motivated view of Chaucer as a rural poet, singing the life of the countryside (with its attendant associations of health, cleanliness, masculinity, and Englishness—in other words, everything the city is not). This pair of essays inspires a number of questions both about this current volume and about our contemporary critical practices. Why is the idea of London currently (or recently) so central to Chaucer studies? Where does our interest in the city place us? And what, or where, might be next?

SYLVIA FEDERICO
Bates College

CAROLYN P. COLLETTE. *Performing Polity: Women and Agency in the Anglo-French Tradition, 1385–1620.* Turnhout, Belgium: Brepols, 2006. Pp. 218. $75.00.

Powerful and original in its insights, richly detailed and suggestive in its readings of individual texts, Carolyn Collette's *Performing Polity* will almost certainly become required reading for any Chaucerian interested in women's writing and history, late medieval political theory and its relation to literary culture, or Chaucer and French literature. It's impossible within the confines of a short review to do justice to the complex and various arguments of the eight chapters that make up the book, so I will focus my detailed discussion to the first three chapters as containing material most likely to be of immediate interest to Chaucerians.

Chapter 1 discusses how Christine de Pizan's *Livre des Trois Vertus* maps the routes to agency a culturally authorized social androgyny made possible for late medieval women. Even while the default template of action and being is male, and a woman must prove herself as an ideal woman, nonetheless, Collette argues, women, "particularly of the aristocracy and the merchant classes, regularly perform successfully as socially androgynous members of society who are fully able to step into male positions and roles, fully able to function as men" (p. 24). Thus, in order to act successfully as surrogate men, Christine advises women to use speech as an offensive and defensive weapon, to preserve the good reputation that will afford her power and leverage over others, to cultivate the foundational social and political virtue of late medieval French culture, *Prudence*. Exploring the social construction of gender as powerfully as she does thus allows Christine to articulate women's goals, properly defined, as social goals advancing the common good and to thus assert that "men and women demonstrate an equal capacity to engage in the same range of human activity" (p. 39).

Chapter 2 addresses the tradition of female conduct literature from which Christine's more radical interventions develop, focusing in particular on Philippe de Mézières' *Le Livre de la vertu du sacrament de marriage*. In contrast to Christine, and her emphasis on a female agency and access to power that could be constructed via a culturally sanctioned social androgyny, Philippe's stories of married women center on the connections to be made among virtue, marriage, and the public good. Thus Philippe emphasizes the role of "*Prudence* as an important female virtue . . . in the private life of the individual woman rather than as part of the strategies that enable her public life" (p. 42), or emphasizes the Saint Cecilia story as an exemplum of marriage as much as of martyrdom. And his narrative endpoint, the story of Griselda, casts her as the most exalted exemplar of female virtue—greater even than any of the nine ancient worthy women—because she conquers herself and manifests an unwavering self-control. Philippe's work, Colette argues, epitomizes a larger ideology of women as participants in shaping polity, one influential on both sides of the Channel, and thus one that "helps define the field of reference and the literary *sociolect* in which Chaucer's stories of Prudence, Cecilia, and Griselda were written and received."

Chapter 3 reads the late fourteenth-century play *L'Estoire de Griseldis* through the lens of contemporary French political theory, notably Nicole Oresme's translation and commentary on Aristotle's *Politiques* (completed at the request of Charles V). In a detailed and fascinating close analysis of the play, Collette notes that the play's emphasis on dialogue and the scenes it selects for inclusion "re-presents the story of Gautier and Griselda within a wider social context than the terms of an individual, if exemplary, marriage found in most prose versions" (p. 62). This is accomplished through extended scenes of action and conversation between Gautier and his huntsmen and courtiers; through conversations between Griselda and a nurse that establish a context of nurture and maternal solicitude for Griselda's virtue; through portrayals of the court as a chorus for an elite class with a particular interest in advancing the common good; and most important, through a pastoral motif established in the exchanges between two shepherds who abandon dreams of escaping their class like Griselda to choose duty and the care of sheep as their highest calling. Throughout, Collette traces the close correspondences between these features of the play and elements of Oresme's political theory in order to demonstrate how "rather than being ends in themselves, the virtues Griselda manifests serve a greater purpose, the establishment of social harmony in a hierarchical yet integrated society" (p. 78).

Chapters 6 and 8 engage with the Early Modern afterlife of the Griselda story: first, with William Forrest's *History of Grisild the Second* (written during the last months of Mary Tudor's reign), which reads Catherine of Aragon's Griselda-like patient resistance to the tyranny of a Walter-like Henry VIII by womanly force of will; and second, with a series of Elizabethan and Stuart pamphlets and plays. The latter, especially, chart the shift in interest from a late medieval Griselda embodying the ideals of *Prudence* and constancy that Collette sees offering potential agency to medieval women to an Early Modern Griselda that emphasizes patient obedience to authority as the essential virtue of the good subject, a representation of woman now capable of responding to and helping to disseminate "an emerging Tudor-Stuart ideology of ready obedience in which previously separate spheres of household and state craft become conjoined in one model of absolute authority." A similar shift in the relationship of women and agency and the performance of polity is mapped in the discussion of the power of medieval representations of the Virgin Mary as intercessory queen, along with the agency gained through intercession by earthly queens such as Richard II's Anne of Bohemia, in chapters 4 and 5, giving way to the Protestant despoliation of the Virgin's power and celebration of her absolute obedience and abject humanity as simple womb receiving and giving birth to the Godhead (in Chapter 7's "'*Nowe leaft of*': The York Pageants of the Death, Assumption, and Coronation of the Virgin").

Performing Polity makes an important and substantial contribution to a growing body of work that brings together conduct literature, conjugality, the household, and political theory. Its picture of a vibrant and innovative social, literary, and political Anglo-French tradition developing in the late fourteenth and early fifteenth centuries around women's agency and the common good should also go a long way to challenging some long-standing assumptions about where Chaucer's literary influences are derived.

GLENN BURGER
Queens College and The Graduate Center, CUNY

ROBERT M. CORREALE and MARY HAMEL, eds. *Sources and Analogues of*
The Canterbury Tales, *Vol. 2.* Chaucer Studies, 35. Cambridge:
D. S. Brewer, 2005. Pp. xvi, 824. $145.00.

With this second volume, Robert Correale and Mary Hamel complete
the long-delayed updating of Bryan and Dempster's *Sources and Ana-*
logues of Chaucer's Canterbury Tales (hence *B&D*). Like Volume 1 (reviewed
by Helen Phillips, *SAC* 26 [2004]: 372–75), all Chaucerians will want
this book at their "beddes heed." In general, the contributors improve
the new *S&A* by addition, subtraction, or substitution. "The General
Prologue," for instance, which *B&D* omitted, now has a very welcome
chapter by Robert Raymo. After briefly surveying opinion about the
frame narrative, Raymo offers concise yet rich surveys of each pilgrim,
the narrator's apology for his unseemly language, Harry Bailly's tale-
telling proposal, and the drawing of lots. Although Raymo sometimes
uses the word "influence" loosely (e.g., Chaucer owes the sexual overtones of the first eighteen lines to the *Georgics*), his synopses should become the starting point for future studies of the "Prologue."

In *B&D,* Robert Pratt was able to provide only brief summaries of
Boccaccio's *Teseida;* no passages from the *Thebaid* or any of the lesser
sources of *The Knight's Tale* were cited. These omissions are brilliantly
remedied by William Coleman. With Edvige Agostinelli he has prepared an excellent edition and translation of all passages in the tale that
come from the version of the *Teseida* closest to the one Chaucer knew.
Coleman's comments on the manuscript tradition of the Italian poem
contain an extraordinary amount of information about important issues.
Coleman also prints relevant passages from Statius, Ovid, and Boethius.
His chapter is indispensable.

Peter Beidler's contribution on *The Miller's Tale* improves by subtraction. Of the five analogues Stith Thompson published in *B&D,* only a
newly edited version of the Middle Dutch *Heile van Beersele* remains.
Beidler casts doubt on the long-held belief that Chaucer modeled *The*
Miller's Tale on one or more lost French fabliaux. Based primarily on
seventeen words in the Tale that "have Middle Dutch origins," Beidler
goes on to argue that the *Heile* is a "hard analogue with near source
status"—that is, Chaucer could have known and used it. Although I feel
"parallels" describes more accurately than "origins" the relation between Chaucer's English and the *Heile*'s Dutch, Beidler strengthens our
understanding of Chaucer's connection to Flanders.

Robert Correale usefully prints the passages from Innocent III's *De Miseria* that the Man of Law mangles in his prologue and provides a newly edited and translated text of Trevet's tale of Constance from the manuscript whose version is closest to Chaucer's (in contrast to the manuscript Schlauch made her base text in *B&D*). Correale also includes Gower's rendering of the tale and judiciously summarizes opinion about its relation to Chaucer's.

Ralph Hanna and Traugott Lawler draw on their excellent *Jankyn's Book of Wicked Wives: The Primary Texts* to revise Whiting's chapter on *The Wife of Bath's Prologue*. They helpfully separate Theophrastus from Jerome and add passages from the *Roman de la Rose*. New are short passages from five minor sources and an ample excerpt from Matheolus's *Lamentations*. Their introduction succinctly covers all major issues; they are especially good in pointing the reader to more general sources like the Bible or Jean de Meun's *Nature*.

John Withrington and P. J. C. Field give new transcriptions of the three analogues of the Wife's tale that appeared in *B&D*. Christine Richardson-Hay reprints the "Priest's Bladder" analogue of *The Summoner's Tale* and wisely replaces Seneca's *De Ira* with passages from John of Wales's *Communiloquium* as the source for Friar John's three exempla.

By adding selections from Jerome, Albertano of Brescia, and the *Sarum Manual* to the selections Dempster printed from Deschamps's *Miroir*, N. S. Thompson sharpens the picture of advice about marriage in *The Merchant's Tale*. Thompson follows Dempster in citing passages from Boccaccio's *Comedia delle ninfe fiorentine*, which, "if not a direct source, may have exerted a strong influence" on Chaucer's description of January and May in the boudoir; he adds *Decameron* 2.10, which he believes may have shaped January's portrait. As for the pear-tree story, Caxton's version now represents the ultimately Far Eastern analogues, all of which Chaucer probably did not know. Thompson provides good translations of the closer analogue from the *Novellino,* and of *Decameron* 7.9, which he includes because, "more richly elaborated" than preceding versions, it perhaps provided a model for the intricacy of Chaucer's.

Kenneth Bleeth demurs from Edgar Shannon's conclusion that Livy was Chaucer's direct source in *The Physician's Tale;* he quite properly prints the story as an analogue. In place of passages from Saint Ambrose, Bleeth quotes excerpts from the *Communiloquium* as the more likely source of the Physician's comments on the education of children and comportment of women. Bleeth's arguments are all carefully considered and fully persuasive.

John Scattergood casts doubt on the widespread belief that a lost French fabliau stands behind *The Shipman's Tale*. He also rejects a story John Spargo had printed from Sercambi's *Novelle,* since Chaucer almost certainly did not know this collection. Scattergood disagrees with Spargo as well by accepting *Decameron* 8.1 and 8.2 as "possible sources" for *The Shipman's Tale,* even though they contain "much that was not used and, indeed, much that was incompatible." Scattergood's translations of both stories are very good.

Carleton Brown's chapter on the many analogues of *The Prioress's Tale* was a highlight of *B&D*. Laurel Broughton improves it by adding a very good section on the Prioress's prologue, by documenting the liturgical sources of the Tale, and by setting the analogues in the larger context of miracles of the Virgin. Broughton also provides brief descriptions of six new analogues and gives convincing reasons why "The Child Slain by Jews" (C5) is a better choice than Brown's (C1) for the closest analogue to the Tale.

Joanne Charbonneau briskly summarizes the critical history of *Sir Thopas* as satire, identifies tail-rhyme romance as the main butt of Chaucer's irony, supports Chaucer's familiarity with the Auchinleck manuscript (as well as with Cotton Caligula A.2 and Thornton), discusses Thopas's name, and comments on the progressive halving of the number of stanzas in each fit. She then balances the richness of her introduction by providing numerous analogues of various motifs in all three fits, many but by no means all of which Loomis had included in *B&D*.

In the absence of any major source or analogue for *The Canon's Yeoman's Tale,* Carolyn Collette and Vincent DiMarco cite texts that establish the intellectual tradition of alchemy and allow the reader to see how Chaucer fully incorporated its subjects and discourse in the Tale. In their introduction, they effectively discount the old belief that *The Canon's Yeoman's Tale* is autobiographical and cite historical records that ground details of the story in fourteenth-century London life. Collette and DiMarco then print fascinating texts that exhibit a combination of skepticism and fascination similar to the Canon Yeoman's.

Edward Wheatley endorses accepted opinion that *The Manciple's Tale* is an amalgam of stories about Phoebus and the crow. He therefore reprints the five versions that James Work assembled for *B&D* but judiciously drops the brief passages of proverbial wisdom or etiological material, which Chaucer could have recalled from memory.

Anita Obermeier adds a welcome concluding chapter on the "Retraction." After discussing the medieval understanding of *retractio* as "retreatment" or "revision" rather than recantation, she prints an example from Bede, four analogues of Chaucer's profession of authorial humility, twenty-three analogues of the idea of worldly vanity, and three analogues that include lists of works by the author.

In the texts and information it provides, this *S&A* is a worthy successor to *B&D*. As a work of criticism, it is far more heterogeneous. In 1940, the contributors were unified less by the editors' mandate to refrain from interpreting their material than by shared, unstated assumptions about what makes a text a source or an analogue. With few exceptions (e.g., Bleeth, Beidler), these assumptions remain unanalyzed in the new *S&A*. Some contributors cleave to old conceptions, others take a more expansive view, still others combine elements of both. Too often defining terms, such as "possible source," which need comment, are adopted without it; too often assertions about textual affiliation made in their name pass without interrogation. What does it mean, I found myself asking, to consider a text a source in the absence of direct verbal imitation? Can we not develop a theory of cultural translation that speaks meaningfully of the influence of analogues by acknowledging the full weight of their differences? Like the old, the new *Sources and Analogues* is an invitation to revisit ideas about the purview and practice of source criticism; meanwhile, for the many treasures it does contain, we owe the editors and contributors our heartfelt thanks.

WARREN GINSBERG
University of Oregon

CATHERINE C. COX. *The Judaic Other in Dante, the Gawain Poet, and Chaucer.* Gainesville: University of Florida Press, 2005. Pp. 265. $65.00.

Catherine Cox's *The Judaic Other* is, by turns, illuminating and exasperating. Her overall framework—that "supersessionist hermeneutics, as both concept and method, informs the poetry and poetics of the late medieval period" (p. 1)—is one with which I profoundly agree. Cox's readings of textual "confiscatory hermeneutic gestures"—founded on "Christianity's [conflicted] relationship to its originary matrix" (p. 3), leading to "platitudinous rehearsal" (p. 21) of anti-Judaic stereotypes, "performative utterances of the faithful" (p. 23), and "[u]surpative appropriation [that] erases the identity of those whose heritage is co-opted in the guise of respect and inclusiveness" (p. 16)—are thoroughly argued in her analyses of "the hermeneutic Jew in Dante's *Commedia*" (chapter 2), "the Hebrew truth in *Sir Gawain and the Green Knight*" (chapter 3), and "the Jewish Pardoner and Chaucer's *Canterbury Tales*" (chapter 4). However, I find these readings to be ultimately unconvincing, based as they are on the assumption that these poets knew and knowingly drew upon some specific Hebrew traditions, particularly the talion code and the Mishnah Sotah (p. 7). Cox elaborates at length on the misinterpretation of talion and the Sotah in the Christian tradition, and her arguments that such misinterpretations fitted Christian supersessionist purposes are entirely convincing. However, that Cox is able to bring such misinterpretations and revaluations to our attention is not the same as saying the poets knew and used them. Cox's book, therefore, also raises, albeit unintentionally, the question with which all readers are plagued, medievalists perhaps more than most: How much of what we read out of a text is purely an effect of what we read into it?

As her epilogue makes clear, Cox is intent on putting "the Jew" and "the Judaic" back into the Christian tradition from which they have been deliberately erased even to the present day (for one instance, see the classroom episode described on page 152), rather than on showing that the specific traditions she cites are those with which the writers on whom she focuses had knowledge, familiarity, or even passing acquaintance. And if they did have such traditions in mind, how did they obtain them? I don't doubt that we can—and should—read medieval texts with our own knowledge, ideas, biases, and preferences intact, for how could we avoid them? Like other modern-day theoretical readings of medieval texts, anti-anti-Judaic readings reveal possibilities that without those perspectives could never be seen. Yet, at some point, such possibilities, however intriguing, must remain possibilities only. Accepting those possibilities allows the texts to speak more interestingly to us; their meanings shift according to our interests and fashions. But those interests and fashions are always our own.

In *The Judaic Other,* Cox gestures in this direction when she asserts that "[r]eaders who assume that the texts are intended to appeal to a unified, homogeneous audience with anti-Judaic evangelical beliefs, or, conversely, who consider these authors to be prescient spokesmen for current multicultural agendas and popular issues of tolerance, miss the subtly destabilizing compromises and contradictions that generate the texts' numerous and intricate subtextual engagements with scripture and alterity in context, an opportunity to explore asymmetrical hierarchies and the ideologies that produce and sustain them, specifically the tensions inhering in Jewish-Christian contiguity and conflict" (pp. 33–34). (This sentence is, unfortunately, typical of Cox's style.) Cox is consistent on this point: in their use of Christian scripture and Christian scriptural rewritings of Hebrew scripture, the poems are more complex than scholars have yet seen. But such complexity is very different from the poets' direct use of the Hebrew tradition, which is something Cox also asserts. Speaking of *Gawain,* for instance, she writes: "the construction and articulation of identity in the course of the penitential sequence can be analyzed in relation to the creation and expulsion sequences of both the Vulgate Genesis and the Hebrew בראשית, Ber'eshit" (p. 77). Scholars might reasonably assume that the *Gawain*-poet knew the Vulgate Genesis, but Cox offers no evidence for any acquaintance with the Hebrew Ber'eshit. Similarly, Cox states that "Gawain's dilemma can be elucidated by way of the Green Chapel's allusive relationship to the land of Cain's exile, ארץ נוד, 'erets-Nod, a highly symbolic biblical and narrative space" (p. 78). But, as Cox herself would likely agree, the Christian "land of Nod" is *not* the same as the Jewish "'erets-Nod," for the difference in naming brings with it a host of other connotations; these are never shown to have been known to the *Gawain*-poet himself. Nonetheless, Cox concludes that "*SGGK*'s poetics . . . are based upon its intertextual and intercultural engagement with not only Christian but also Jewish exegetical modes." This is an exciting assertion, but no evidence is adduced in support of it.

Despite the stylistic heaviness and a tendency toward theoretical and conceptual slippage—to give just one example, Cox's Pardoner is simultaneously "hermaphroditic," "androgynous," "neuter" (p. 119), and "gay" (p. 124), terms that are decidedly *not* synonymous—Cox does valuable work by bringing forward ways of reading and texts that have not previously been known or known well enough by medievalists in general. It is a tribute to her extensive analyses that a poem like *Sir Gawain and the Green Knight* now seems Christian at its core in ways I would not have previously recognized. But still, I am left with some difficult questions: How do we use texts and traditions in ways that illuminate but not exasperate? How do we consider past cultural productions so as to speak fairly to the conditions of writing and reading in the fourteenth century as well as to the conditions in the twenty-first? How do we, as modern readers who resist the naturalization of supersessionist rewritings, nonetheless respect the power of such interpretations in our own attempts to understand poems that are, in many ways, as foreign to us as the Hebrew texts were to medieval poets? I don't have the answers, except that I know we must take such texts, such modes of interpretation, and such questions seriously, and we must be very careful in doing so.

SYLVIA TOMASCH
Macaulay Honors College of the City University of New York

MARILYN DESMOND. *Ovid's Art and the Wife of Bath: The Ethics of Erotic Violence.* Ithaca: Cornell University Press, 2006. Pp. xiii, 206. $52.50 cloth. $20.95 paper.

One might not think that "free speech and academic freedom" as "principles that have come under enormous political pressure in the few short years since September 2001" have much to do with Ovid and the Wife of Bath. However, in an opening excurses on a Woman's Studies conference that included a session on S/M, Marilyn Desmond relates contemporary cultural politics to sex and violence in medieval authors. Desmond generalizes from this incident that S/M is today "intensively policed" (p. 4), while maintaining that today in Britain and the United States "domestic violence has generally been tolerated . . . as part of the status quo" (ibid.). The transition from S/M to Chaucer is achieved through a citation from "one S/M practitioner" who "longingly writes" that "(f)or years I was actually unhappy about the civilized times I lived in, full of envy for people who had lived in the Middle Ages, in the days of witch-hunts and the Inquisition" (p. 5). The medieval, in other words, has always been a fantasy space psychologically. Desmond hopes, therefore, that "perhaps the constructs of the medieval past might elucidate specific performances of contemporary heterosexualities in terms of erotic violence." Cant overwhelms this section ("category maintenance work," "heteroerotic performance," "cultural scripts," etc.). Desmond then turns to an overview of the chapters: Ovid's *Ars* "ironically explicates the potential of violence in the heterosexual contract as facilitated by Roman colonial power," while the medieval citations and adaptations of Ovid "elaborate on violence as a formative component of eros." Put more hauntingly: "The structures of medieval desire thus carry the traces of ancient Mediterranean sexual regimes" (p. 7).

Desmond then traces a series of medieval commentaries on Ovid's erotic poetics by Heloise, Jean de Meun, Chaucer, and Christine de Pizan, moving toward the argument that the two female authors "expose the gendered nature of the French and Ovidian traditions that produced the Wife of Bath's *Prologue*" (p. 9). Desmond first addresses the icon of "woman on top" enacted by the Wife of Bath as one that nonetheless "[a]s in contemporary cultures, obscures everyday violences, particularly marital violence, a quotidian feature of medieval cultures" (p. 13). The cumulative picture she paints, as she "articulate[s] the cultural intelligibilities of erotic violence" (ibid.), is that marriage is inherently, then and now (cf. "[a]s in contemporary cultures"), tied to violence, with the modulation of that violence benefiting male pleasure and control. Despite this control, men fantasize their own humiliation as Desmond notices in images of "leather thongs furnished with metal studs" that she relates to "contemporary dominatrix pornography" and "pony training" (p. 27).

Chapter 2 addresses Ovid's *Ars,* a "handbook for heterosexual desire within a hierarchical dynamic," which formulates "categories of erotic violence," offers violence as an "effective option for heterosexual performance," and "crudely proposes the sexual pursuit of women with the goal of achieving dominance over them." Accordingly Desmond associates the "male conquest of women" with colonialism, war spectacle, and even the "homoerotic spectacle of gladiators," all of which give that conquest an "imperial value" (p. 37). One's reaction to Desmond's argument will hinge on whether *Ars* 1, 673–78 is "rape," as Desmond asserts absolutely, or the performance of rape required by the complex indirect expressiveness of female will. The third book of the *Ars* Desmond reads as a "heterosexual script" outlining "heterosexual obligations," noting also the connections between Roman "colonial dominance" and the arts of beauty in its production of "exotic commodities."

The next chapter addresses Heloise's reactions to the Ovidian scripts. Desmond depicts a pedagogical setting that "situate[s] Heloise as the object of desire precisely because she is the object of violence. Thus Heloise, as a pupil, encounters a *magister* armed with an Ovidian amatory arsenal—both the rhetoric and the violence associated with erotic violence" (p. 59). Except for noting the "privileged categories of Christian doctrine" (p. 67) that would like to keep Heloise repressed, Desmond ignores the couple's religion and their ultimate unity of spiritual and pastoral purpose. The cumulative effect of her chapters is to render Christianity, like heterosexuality, as little more than a hegemonic structure of violence and oppression of women.

In the next chapter on the *Rose,* the "imperial ethos" of Rome becomes the "commodity fetishism" of the "mercantile economic structures of the late medieval world" (p. 73). The bibliographic survey of the *Ars Amatoriae* in Medieval French that follows displays Desmond's scholarship at its best and is a helpful archival and bibliographic guide for any readers interested in the vernacular *Ars* tradition. She then moves through the *Rose* and through the glosses to the *Art d'amours,* highlighting passages that link force to sex and other misogynist moments such as Jaloux's "performance of verbal abuse that is crude and offensive" (p. 82). A score of miniatures, mostly of "Jaloux beats his wife," are at odds with the text's indictment of his attitudes, but the powers of visual memory allow these illustrations to cast "a long shadow over the remainder of the allegory" (p. 95), which culminates in Amant's "hyperheterosexual discourse" (p. 112) and conquest. But Desmond does not conclude rape here, arguing rather that the "conclusion to the *Rose* is emblematic of the Ovidian discourse of *eros* that depends on the erotics of violence as a means of rendering heterosexual desire legible" (p. 115). By legible she means that some attribution of "implied consent" (p. 114) (in this case female ejaculation) is needed to complete the performance of masculinity.

Manuscript depictions of the Wife and her studded whip relate her to the "mounted Aristotle tradition," while her clothing reveals the "commodity fetishism of medieval trade and economic exchange" (p. 123), resulting in a "gendered fantasy of sexual and even imperial dominance" (p. 124). Desmond does a good job showing why we are captivated by the Wife's powerful confessional performance, while she adjusts our personal engagement with her by focusing on textual sources and history, closely explicating her debt to the *Vieille.* Discussion of the

Trotula is particularly insightful. But some may question Desmond's reading of the stories of Clytemnestra and Pasiphaë as exempla of "female agency and even sexual autonomy" (p. 139). Likewise her contention that the Wife "can knock [Jankyn] down; he can—and does—knock her out" misreads the Wife's Ali-esque ring mastery. For Desmond, that the Wife is ever "on top" is only a momentary illusion.

The last chapter explores Christine's "vehement correction to the textual tradition of misogyny" (p. 146). Desmond's study of Christine's relations with her sources and her peers displays first-rate scholarship on the *Querelle* and on medieval literary ethics. This excellent chapter (revising an earlier publication) has nothing to do with Foucault or with the modern "policing of S/M," though they return for an unearned bow in a two-page "afterword" that attempts to unify all the discrete chapters and bring home the thesis that the "erotics of sexual difference . . . achieves legibility through violence" in Roman culture (colonial, "slave-owning," and imperial) and in "medieval marriage and desire" (p. 166).

At its best, Desmond's book reveals details in the history of culture and erotic violence in Ovid and his medieval disciples, offering generous quotations from all the primary texts, useful to students and scholars alike. Those who see the function of criticism as the indictment of "heteropatriarchy" throughout time will likely agree with the narrative Desmond constructs in linking these amatory texts. But others might find that Desmond's book, with its reductive narratives and in its exclusionary discourses of antiheterosexuality, risks becoming an instance of what Frank Lentricchia has called "pre-reading," in which political and theoretical arguments, bound up with theory-speak and jargon, predetermine meaning and overwhelm the act of reading.

MICHAEL CALABRESE
California State University–Los Angeles

STEVE ELLIS, ed. *Chaucer: An Oxford Guide.* Oxford: Oxford University Press, 2005. Pp. xxiv, 644. $38.00 paper.

Steve Ellis's hefty *Chaucer: An Oxford Guide* contains thirty-six essays plus an Introduction and Postscript, each by a different authoritative specialist. The essays are grouped in five sections: "Historical Contexts" on biographical, historical, and cultural topics; "Literary Contexts" on sources and contemporary texts; "Readings" on theoretical approaches; "Afterlife" on editions and imaginative responses; and "Study Resources," a guide to printed and electronic reference works. With a caveat or two, it is a useful reference anthology, and its reasonable price makes it a volume that students and others can afford.

The book's essays sometimes are and sometimes are not a sign of the times. Saddam Hussein is in the *Oxford Guide* (under "The Carnivalesque"!), but Adam Pinkhurst is not. The writing acknowledges the calamitous war in Iraq but not torture in its unofficial or federally sanctioned forms. The new millennium also hovers behind the anthology in that several essays evaluate Chaucer with the confidence of the twentieth century completed while recognizing the continuing validity of arguments made then. However, some essays express interest in tales and topics that haven't recently garnered much scholarly attention. For instance, the essayists most frequently discuss the *Canterbury Tales,* with *The Wife of Bath's Prologue* and *The Pardoner's Tale* mentioned often. The guide confirms that *The Parson's Tale*'s reputation is firmly restored. If the guide is a register of critical interest, it's therefore somewhat unusual that *The Knight's Tale* is repeatedly discussed as a test case and example.

The "Historical Contexts" section voices the current refrain of how difficult it is to tie Chaucer, with any simple confidence, to specific historical events. The descriptions of other scholars' historical studies and the essays themselves model the tentative and subjunctive language that's necessary when we try to draw connections between Chaucer's poetry and his contemporary world. The entry on "Nationhood" in this section is another register of recent interest (one that would now include David Wallace's more recent work), while the chapter on "Chivalry" seems to belong to a former age.

The book also registers present-day sophisticated uses of literary theory to study Chaucer in section three, "Readings." Some terms in this part of the book are now appropriately plural: "feminisms," "sexualities." It is odd that postmodernism has a chapter in "Readings" and is repeatedly mentioned elsewhere since it does not seem of importance to recent scholarly inquiry. Also, there's some concern with the spirit of D. W. Robertson throughout, which reflects the age and training of the writers more than current criticism or the undergraduate reader's expectations of Chaucer. It is also a sign of the present moment that

Jacques Derrida doesn't need mentioning, deconstruction is only invoked, knowledge of poststructuralism can be presumed, and Cultural Studies also doesn't need to be named.

The back cover (the only guide to the book's apparatus) doesn't quite make clear that "Readings" contains unpublished and provocative applications of theory to texts. These are new, brief essays that stand alone as contributions to the field of scholarship: Marion Turner discusses the *Parliament of Fowls's* polyphony, Sylvia Federico (coining the useful term "new Chaucerian historicism") provides a fascinating fresh reading of rape in Chaucer's works, Glenn Burger intervenes with a subtle historical interpretation of *The Shipman's Tale* in relation to marriage in the bourgeois household, Jeffrey Cohen offers a new reading of *The Prioress' Tale* in a chapter on "Postcolonialism," and Patricia Ingham analyzes the "uncommon wisdom" of psychoanalysis and *The Knight's Tale*. Part Four, "Afterlife," makes the study of the reception of Chaucer's works and reputation after his death in 1400 more accessible and organized.

Another register of present-day Chaucer studies is the common thread throughout the book—an attempt to reach across the divide between academic and popular receptions of Chaucer: adaptations, translations, guides, and other writings. For example, Stephanie Trigg employs Pierre Bourdieu's ideas about literature's institutional roles and cultural uses in order to discuss some recent appearances of Chaucer in popular culture, including the "now defunct but once very popular Chaucer's wedding reception and banquet venue in the Melbourne suburb of Canterbury" (p. 539).

A book with this much in it will inevitably have some faults. A few essays make tendentious and misleading points, which teachers are likely to find frequently and enthusiastically quoted in student essays. Can we really still assert that Chaucer's pilgrims "display a remarkable tolerance and generosity of spirit toward one another" (p. 94)? It's particularly unfortunate that the "Feminisms" chapter contains an eccentric history of feminism, inaccuracies, simplifications, and odd interpretations. Elsewhere, readings of the Cambridge, Corpus Christi College MS 61 *Troilus and Criseyde* are potentially deceptive, especially in the List of Illustrations and the label that accompanies the reproduced image (also on the cover, though flipped left to right), which suggest it shows "The Poem being read before a court audience" (pp. xix, 114). The "Chaucer's Language" section is intended to "help change a hurdle into a gate," but it is fairly technical, with perhaps necessary use of the International Phonetic Alphabet but also unexplained terms such as "fricative" and "fronting." Titles of essays in the "Literary Contexts" section—"The English Background," "The Italian Background," and so on—are potential misnomers if the reader takes "background" to mean Chaucer's use of sources rather than the more broad contemporary milieux of English, Italian, and other literatures, languages, and cultures. In a few places, including the introduction, there's a slightly annoying defensiveness about teaching Chaucer at this moment in time. Four substantial online articles on pedagogy accompany the book, but these tend to be more on the current status of Chaucer in university and high school curricula rather than offering lesson suggestions or specific teaching plans and utilitarian suggestions for resources; these are included, but the emphasis is on politics. The Index contains no *sees*, only *see also*s, so readers will not find the *Canterbury Tales* anywhere under the main heading "Chaucer, Geoffrey." Separate headings for the tales do not distinguish between a pilgrim portrait and tale.

In terms of utility, the guidebook's essays fall along a continuum of tones from the polemical to the more presentational. Past critics named and discussed in the essays are usually the more important ones. Many of the best entries contain excellent summaries of books, articles, and arguments; also, at the end of each essay is a "Further Reading" section, and in each case the books and articles are astutely selected and clearly reviewed. The length of every essay, about fourteen pages, feels just right; each is succinct but complex.

The volume is explicitly aimed at undergraduates. Each essay supposes knowledge of several of Chaucer's texts, so students might read parts of it near the end of a course. The book is otherwise difficult to assign in the sense that it's hard to pair the essays with individual poems or tales, and my guess is that most teachers have their students work through Chaucer's texts one by one. Perhaps the thinking within Oxford University Press was that the Oxford Guides might take care of individual works; for example, Helen Cooper's guide to the *Canterbury Tales* is helpfully organized by tale. Ultimately, the book suggests that students take one approach to a number of texts—a historical one, a study of literary influence, or an explicitly theoretical line—rather than studying an individual poem. Writing across Chaucer's texts seems very fruitful and a move away from close reading, but it is a more accomplished approach. The book fortunately provides several exciting models for how to read across works, and it might therefore be just as useful in graduate classes as well as of interest to other scholars.

MATTHEW BOYD GOLDIE
Rider University

LIANNA FARBER. *An Anatomy of Trade in Medieval Writing: Value, Consent, and Community.* Ithaca: Cornell University Press, 2006. Pp. x, 235. $39.95.

Trade and deceit go hand in hand, according to early medieval commentators such as Cassiodorus, who proclaimed that merchants "burden their wares with lies even more than with prices" (p. 15). But, by the High Middle Ages, increasing commerce led to discourses challenging that negative stereotype of the deceptive trader. Typically drawing on Aristotle, writers increasingly affirmed the social benefits of trade, describing it as an activity that provides goods to individuals incapable of independently producing all necessities. Such justifications of trade constitute the likely primary reading for scholars interested in the history of economic ideas in the Middle Ages. But as Lianna Farber's valuable book demonstrates, we would do wrong to rely only on such explicit discussions of trade. While accounts of trade may seem descriptive, they are actually "falsely reassuring" justifications (p. 2). Not unlike the dishonest merchant derided early on by Cassiodorus and others, later medieval commentators on trade also mislead.

According to Farber, commentators deceive in their uncritical stance toward three components that invariably constitute trade in official accounts: the *value* of the objects exchanged, the *consent* of the traders to the commensurate worth of those goods, and the *community* that trade makes possible. While value, consent, and community emerge in accounts of trade as unproblematic assumptions, they are subject to substantial critique in less predictable primary sources. Farber's study exposes the deceptive qualities of medieval accounts of trade by moving from the texts that traditionally have informed the history of economic ideas across disciplinary lines to a rich variety of texts, among them legal tracts, city records, and English vernacular poetry. By tracking trade as it explicitly emerges in official accounts *and* as it indirectly is queried by other kinds of writing, Farber has generated an analysis that is groundbreaking in its methodology and exemplary in its balanced, nuanced, and scholarly approach to the problem of the medieval economy.

Farber lays out the argument, scope, and methodology of her project in her introduction. The introduction ends with a reading of Ambrogio Lorenzetti's frescoes on good government. The frescoes, to which Farber returns in her conclusion, serve as a visual counterpart to her own effort at linking trade with activities seemingly beyond the purview of commerce.

Chapter 1 offers a lucid synthesis of explicit discussions of trade, from the derogatory writings produced up to the twelfth century to the legitimizations of trade that begin to appear during the High Middle Ages. Aristotle emerges as the "touchstone for scholastic writing about the value of trade," thanks to Latin translations of the *Nicomachean Ethics* and the *Politics* (p. 18). Here, as elsewhere, Farber's clarity and knack for likening old ideas to contemporary examples makes *An Anatomy of Trade* a good choice for undergraduate reserve lists.

The rest of the book is divided into three chapters on value, consent, and community, respectively. The first, on value, should prove invaluable for scholars working on material culture, insofar as it delineates a "surprisingly large number of ways to understand the value of goods" in writings on value that appear in Aristotelian commentaries, Roman legal tracts, and theological treatises (p. 49). Of special interest is Farber's account of Augustine's distinction between natural and economic scales of value, which affirms the justness of the natural valuation of all living things over inanimate objects (i.e., a mouse is naturally valued above a pearl). That chapter concludes with new and persuasive readings of *The Shipman's Tale, The Franklin's Tale,* and Henryson's "The Cock and the Jasp," all of which demonstrate how literature troubles the supposedly clear distinction of natural and economic value. In the case of *The Shipman's Tale,* Farber powerfully counters the critical tendency to claim that the Shipman represents the degradation of the natural world by commerce, by showing how human relations in the tale are "structured like those of commodities" before their apparent abasement by trade (p. 75). Turning to *The Franklin's Tale,* Farber contends that while Arveragus's belief in "absolute, noneconomic" value ultimately is embraced by all other male characters, that final assertion of "trouthe" in the romance only narrowly avoids the fabliau ending that Aurelius's trick looks toward, thus demonstrating "how precarious absolute values can be" (pp. 89, 83). Finally, Henryson's rooster points to the particular problem of "knowing the realm of valuation," when he happens upon a jewel and, unaware of the gem's absolute valuation as a symbol of wisdom, values the object only along economic lines (p. 88).

Farber's next chapter, on consent, is requisite reading for anyone working on medieval marriage. Cognizant of the fact that, more than any other topic, marriage inspired medieval writers to scrutinize issues of consent, Farber devotes the bulk of the chapter to an examination of the history of Church law on marriage formation. After carefully describing the framework for ascertaining consent that arose in Church cases on the legality of marriages, Farber turns to *The Physician's Tale*. Farber demonstrates how Chaucer offers what the courts cannot: a meditation on the nurturing processes that might lead a person to consent, as Virginia does, to her own death. A highlight of the chapter is Farber's response to scholarly complaints that the Physician's emphasis on guardianship clashes with Virginia's moral independence. Farber convincingly argues that those contradictions merely reflect Chaucer's decision to create an "inclusive list" of elements—Nature, individual agency, parents, and governesses—any or all of which could account for good behavior (p. 135). By going on to point out that among those various causes, "only the influence of parents is left . . . as a locus for behavior that might seem, to us, wrong or ill-considered" in the particular case of Virginia, Farber shrewdly shores up the crucial role that the Physician's apparent digression plays in his tale (p. 135).

If accounts of trade claim that the practice benefits the community, Farber queries in her final chapter just what constitutes a community by using late medieval London as her test case. The chapter includes a fine reading of *St. Erkenwald* as a poem in which the community of London is a noisy gathering of "people, clerical and lay, from all stations of London life" who are united by both their initial empathy for a fellow Londoner, a righteous heathen from the past who has been denied heaven, and their eventual celebration of his miraculous baptism and salvation (p. 156). Farber turns next to London craft guild charters, which query the community "depicted so fulsomely in *St. Erkenwald*" by both dividing the community into buyers and sellers, and tacitly excluding certain craftspeople from the communality they construct (p.

161). The chapter ends with a look at the good-humored satire of commerce in *London Lickpenny*.

Painstakingly alive to the nuances of the texts she describes, Farber admirably realizes the difficult goal she sets out to attain in her book: to describe accurately how writers understood trade during a time when the category of the "economic" was nonexistent. This sensible, jargon-free, and evenhanded study makes an impressive contribution both to literary criticism and to the history of ideas.

KATHY LAVEZZO
University of Iowa

JUDY ANN FORD. *John Mirk's "Festial": Orthodoxy, Lollardy, and the Common People in Fourteenth-Century England.* Cambridge: D. S. Brewer, 2006. Pp. 168. $80.00.

John Mirk's *Festial,* a collection of vernacular sermons probably written between 1382 and 1390, was a "popular" text in both senses of the word. It seems to have been designed for the rural, "lewde" majority rather than members of the urban, educated elite; moreover, as studies by Alan Fletcher, Susan Powell, and H. L. Spencer have shown, the *Festial* was one of the most widely copied and printed English sermon compilations during the latter half of the fifteenth century. Nevertheless, the *Festial* has met with a rather subdued response from contemporary scholars. As the first full-length interpretation of the work, Ford's analysis provides a much-needed introduction to the complexity of the *Festial* and its contributions to medieval debates concerning clerical power, class relations, and religious narrative itself.

Scholars have long agreed that Mirk, an Augustinian canon writing for a lay audience in Shropshire, positions himself firmly on the orthodox side of late medieval religious controversies. Ford persuasively argues that although Mirk refers to Lollards only twice in his text, the *Festial* as a whole attempts to provide lay people with an alternative to heresy. A crucial dimension of Ford's book, however, involves reading the *Festial* in light of other developments of the late fourteenth century, including the rebellion of 1381 and the general evolution of literate culture in England during the period. Emphasizing the exclusionary effects of this latter factor, Ford regards Lollardy as a relatively elitist movement. Given the continued prevalence of illiteracy in late medieval England, her first chapter contends, "cultural movements associated with literacy can hardly be labeled 'popular'" (p. 29). Because the *Festial* resists "bibliocentric" (p. 113) approaches to Christianity, it may have been perceived as "attractively inclusive" (p. 114) by uneducated audiences.

According to Ford's second chapter, Mirk also affirms the culture of the illiterate laity by recounting saints' lives and miracle stories. Even as Mirk upholds the indispensability of clerical mediation in lay people's lives, he empowers his audience by telling stories in which the sacraments take place "off stage" (p. 40), and in which ordinary men and women often directly encounter the divine. Ford perceives a similar dynamic within Mirk's discussions of social class, the subject of her third chapter. Although Mirk advocates submission to temporal authority in this world, his frequent criticisms of higher learning and empathetic discussions of the poor uphold a positive view of lay people's abilities.

Ford's fourth chapter highlights Mirk's treatment of biblical material; once again, she feels that Mirk does so in a manner that privileges non-literate forms of spirituality. By comparing Mirk's treatment of the evangelists to that of his main source, Jacobus de Voragine's *Legenda Aurea,* Ford demonstrates that Mirk stresses the Gospel-writers' talents as preachers, saints, and recipients of divine inspiration, rather than as writers. By doing so, Ford argues, Mirk implicitly allows for "lay agency" even among those Christians who cannot read. A brief concluding chapter reiterates this point. Instead of responding to either Lollardy or rebellion through "heavy-handed condemnation," Mirk offers his audience "compelling images of lay agency functioning within established orthodoxy" (p. 150).

Ford's approach to the *Festial* has many strengths. She keeps a close eye on the educational, social, and cultural differences separating members of the laity from one another, and maintains a healthy skepticism toward any medieval writer's claim to represent the true voice of the people. Her close readings of Mirk's narratives are often effective as well; she convincingly demonstrates, for example, that Mirk says as little as possible about the textual dimensions of the four evangelists' achievements. By carefully tracing Mirk's additions and omissions to his source material in such sections, Ford highlights the distinctive authorial "voice" within narratives that might seem merely derivative or disjointed after an initial reading.

Contextualizing the *Festial* within a broader analysis of exemplary literature might have allowed Mirk's ideas to emerge even more forcefully. In addition to comparing Mirk's text to the *Legenda Aurea*, Ford explores analogues to his narratives found in Woodburn O. Ross's *Middle English Sermons Edited from British Museum MS. Royal 18 B xxiii*, the *Gesta Romanorum*, and *The Book of Margery Kempe*. She also alludes to other scholars' discussions of Jacques de Vitry and of *Handlyng Synne*. Engaging more fully with these last two works, as well as with other Latin and vernacular narrative collections of the period (*Speculum Laicorum, Alphabetum Narrationum, Jacob's Well*, and so on) could have provided Ford with useful touchstones for her arguments. When analyzing the narrative of a monk whose severed hand is restored by the Virgin, for instance, Ford notes that the tale is not found in *Legenda Aurea*, Mirk's primary source; she does not, however, address the many versions of this story found in other exemplum collections to which Mirk might have had access. It would also have been salutary for Ford to have considered Mirk in light of other late medieval works regarded as strongly orthodox in their presentation of Christianity. To cite just one example, the emphasis on envisioning (rather than reading about) biblical events in Nicholas Love's *The Mirror of the Blessed Life of Jesus Christ* would have provided a fascinating counterpart to Mirk's many depictions of people's direct encounters with God.

Finally, Ford could have been more precise about the forms of "agency" made available to lay people within the *Festial*. Although Ford evenhandedly explores Mirk's emphasis on clerical intervention in lay spirituality, she does not quite do justice to his insistent opposition to what we might consider "grassroots" religious practices. Mirk not only reminds his listeners that prayers are best formulated in church, but he also spells out complicated intercessory chains of command that these petitions should follow: "ȝe schul now knele adowne," he tells his audience at one point, "and pray Saynt Anne to pray to her holy doghtyr, our lady, þat scho pray to her sonne þat he ȝeue you hele yn body and yn sowle" (*Festial*, p. 216). He describes himself as divinely inspired, without ever indicating that such illumination might be open to his audience; he chastises those who overdo fasting and other nonliturgical forms of commemorating saints. In one instance he even quotes a proverb used by his listeners, only to demonstrate its inadequacy: "ȝe haue a comyn sayng among you, and sayn þat Godys grace ys worth a new fayre . . . Godys grace ys more worþy þen any fayre" (*Festial*, p. 86).

How *should* we categorize a writer who employs populist forms even while manifesting great distrust for "the people"? Although Ford's book may not offer the final word on this question, it successfully highlights the *Festial* as a rich resource for ongoing scholarly investigation.

MOIRA FITZGIBBONS
Marist College

KATHLEEN FORNI, ed. *The Chaucerian Apocrypha: A Selection.* Kalamazoo: Medieval Institute Publications, Western Michigan University, for TEAMS in association with the University of Rochester, 2005. Pp. vii, 169. $15.00, paper.

DANA M. SYMONS, ed. *Chaucerian Dream Visions and Complaints.* Kalamazoo: Medieval Institute Publications, Western Michigan University, for TEAMS in association with the University of Rochester, 2004. Pp. vii, 293. $22.00, paper.

The Middle English Texts Series began modestly in 1990 with the prospect of inexpensive student editions designed for classroom use, but many of these paperbacks quickly established themselves as the new standard editions for scholarly citation. This has been particularly true for works of the "Chaucer Apocrypha" previously available only in outdated EETS editions and Walter W. Skeat's still-useful *Chaucerian and Other Pieces: Being a Supplement to the Complete Works of Geoffrey Chaucer* (1897), with its assembly of thirty-one of these spurious texts. The previous TEAMS volumes *The Floure and the Leafe* (1990), *Six Ecclesiastical Satires* (1991), *The Canterbury Tales: Fifteenth-Century Continuations and Additions* (1992), *Poems of Robert Henryson* (1997), Thomas Usk's *Testament of Love* (1998), and John Lydgate's *The Siege of Thebes* (2001) placed most of the longer texts in print according to editorial standards much more exacting than would normally be expected in undergraduate textbooks. Original manuscripts and early printings have been consulted for establishing base texts and assessing variant readings. Introductions and annotations as well as textual notes maintain high standards of professional rigor. Bibliographies are comprehensive and timely. Nowhere are these dual commitments to scholarship and pedagogy so beautifully balanced perhaps than in the two volumes under review here.

Kathleen Forni's *The Chaucerian Apocrypha: A Selection* arrives as a valuable supplement to her critical study *The Chaucerian Apocrypha: A Counterfeit Canon* (2001). Her volume includes some well-known pieces by named authors as well as the flotsam and jetsam of the ancillary tradition, mostly preserved in the folio editions of William Thynne (1532), John Stow (1561), and Thomas Speght (1598). The determination of Chaucer's genuine productions and the gradual removal of inauthentic pieces from the canon started with Thomas Tyrwhitt's landmark edition of *The Canterbury Tales* (1775–78), continued with the enterprises of the nineteenth-century scholars such as Bradshaw, Ten Brink, Furnivall, and Skeat, and was still being hashed out by Robinson in his first *Riverside Chaucer* (1933). Here we can revisit some of the texts that contributed to Chaucer's early reputation and continue, almost on a subliminal level, to color the ways that we conceive of the personality and productions of the Father of English Poetry.

After a welcome new edition of *The Court of Love,* Forni proceeds by grouping shorter texts under three general headings. "Literature of Courtly Love" includes *The Floure of Curtesye* written by John Lydgate, "The Antifeminist Tradition" offers *Beware (The Blynde Eteth Many a Flye)* newly attributed to Lydgate, and "Good Counsel, Wisdom, and Advice" brings the collection to a close with John Gower's *In Praise of Peace* and Henry Scogan's *Moral Balade.* There are many happy surprises in these groupings. For example, Shakespeare's anti-Petrarchan Sonnet 130—"My mistress' eyes are nothing like the sun"—clearly had a native precedent in the seven-stanza verse (pp. 105–6) preserved only in Cambridge Trinity MS R.3.19 and the more recently discovered Leiden MS Vossius 9:

> I have a Lady, whereso she be,
> That seldom ys the soverayn of my thought;
> On whos beawté when I beholde and se,
> Remembryng me how well she ys wrought,
> I thanke fortune that to hyr grace me brought,
> So fayre ys she but nothyng angelyke –
> Hyr bewty ys to none other lyke.

These new editions play catch-up, in a sense, with recent critical interests in these long-neglected texts by John Fisher, Paul Strohm, Frank

Grady, and others investigating the textual underpinnings of Lancastrian political culture and, simultaneously, Lancastrian efforts at fostering a vernacular poetic tradition, conspicuously Chaucerian, that long outlasted the regime itself.

Directly addressing Henry IV, Gower's *In Praise of Peace* worked hard at legitimating the usurper monarch as *Electus Christi*—"God hath thee chose in comfort of ous alle" (p. 4)—while casting him in the role of a king open to moral counsel, unlike Richard II, who was accused of not accepting advice according to the Articles of Deposition. This rhyme-royal work anticipates Thomas Hoccleve's *Regiment of Princes* as an inside job recycling well-worn bromides while making its recipient seem a wise Alexander welcoming the counsels of his sage but subservient Aristotle. Much interest resides in what Gower merely implies. The warfare that actually threatened England during the period 1399–1404 did not take the form of military campaigns against foreign enemies or Saracens, but rather the numerous uprisings and rebellions that Henry IV's usurpation had unleashed upon England. The story of Emperor Constantine being cured of leprosy because he rejected violence—"And al his lepre it hath so purified / That his pité forever is magnified" (pp. 349–50)— helps confirm the long-standing rumor that Henry IV's own mysterious illness was in fact leprosy.

Henry Scogan's *Moral Balade* has also attracted recent interest for what the poem has to suggest about the early context for Chaucerian poetry in Lancastrian London. John Shirley's headnote in Ashmole 59 indicates that the poem was written for a guild dinner attended by Henry IV's four teenage sons in the Vintry. Himself the recipient of Chaucer's *Lenvoy*, the courtier Scogan (d. 1407) was clearly a member of the poet's immediate circle of readers, and his allusions to *Boece* and *The Monk's Tale*, as well as his incorporation of the three-stanza *Gentilesse*, indicate an early appreciation for the poet's more sententious works. Scogan became one of the first, if not *the* first, to use "Chaucer" as a brand-name, to invoke the guild language of "master," and to grant the poet the status of "father" later employed to construct a genealogy of literary tradition. It seems no accident that those charged with fulfilling their filial duties, the future Henry V and the future Duke of Gloucester, would also become the key supporters of the Chaucerian tradition, particularly as patrons of Hoccleve and Lydgate.

Chaucerian Dream Visions and Complaints by Dana Symons takes fullest advantage of Julia Boffey's work on the manuscript anthologies and

497

miscellanies such as Bodleian MS Fairfax 16, where nearly all of these shorter texts survive, as well as the critical insights on lamenting lovers and eavesdropping narrators provided by A. C. Spearing's *The Medieval Poet as Voyeur* (1993). Better known perhaps as *The Complaint of the Black Night*, Lydgate's poem provides fascinating insights into the monastic writer's response to Chaucer's *Book of the Duchess* with its "courtly" themes and poetic diction that would define a particular strand in the Chaucerian tradition that extends to his Tudor heirs Wyatt and Surrey. *La Belle Dame sans Mercy* has been edited from the superior Longleat MS 258 not known to Skeat, who had an unfortunate tendency to prefer Thynne's printed versions for these works. *The Quare of Jelusy* has long deserved more attention as the traveling companion with James I's *The Kingis Quair* in Bodleian MS Arch. Selden B.24. And we have very much needed *The Boke of Cupide* in a critical edition more up to date than V. J. Scattergood's excellent *Works of Sir John Clanvowe*, published in 1975 by D. S. Brewer.

Now come the quibbles. Symons does much in her General Introduction to critique the artificial construction of a Chaucerian tradition by Renaissance editors like Thynne and poets like Spenser, while exposing direct French influences from fifteenth-century poets such as Alain Chartier not filtered through Chaucer's own dream-visions. But even this volume's title has the effect of reenacting the modern critical practice of categorizing much late medieval English poetry as Chaucerian and then simultaneously esteeming it as "like Chaucer" and devaluing it as "not enough like Chaucer." The table of contents further obscures individual talents by omitting the names of the three known poets Sir John Clanvowe for *The Boke of Cupide, God of Love,* John Lydgate for *A Complaynte of a Lovers Lyfe,* and Sir Richard Roos for *La Belle Dame sans Mercy.*

The force of the received tradition is obviously difficult to resist. Symons's designation of Clanvowe as the eldest "son of Chaucer" falls prey to the patrilineal construction of literary tradition and misses the likelihood that he was instead "brother of Chaucer," an exact contemporary influencing as well as being influenced by his more accomplished fellow poet. Scattergood dated Clanvowe's poem as early as 1386 because the first two lines were quoted from the 1380s version of the Knight's Tale known as *The Love of Palamon and Arcite*—"The God of Love, a benedicité! / How myghty and how grete a lorde is he!" (cf. *CT,* I, 1785–86)—and Clanvowe died outside Constantinople in 1391 after two years of nonstop international travel that probably prevented any literary endeavors. The G Prologue of the *LGW* was certainly revised after Queen Anne's death in 1394, and it seems likely that the F Prologue was composed after Richard II's royal entry into London in 1392. Therefore Clanvowe did not copy his irascible God of Love from the *Legend* Prologue but, the other way around, Chaucer took his God of Love from *The Boke of Cupide*. So, too, Clanvowe's commendation to Queen Anne at one of the royal residences in 1389—"Before the chambre wyndow of the quene / At Wodestok upon the grene lay" (pp. 284–85)—suggested to Chaucer a similar commendation with reference to *two* royal residences in a playful gesture of one-upmanship—"And whan this book ys maad, yive it to the quene / On my behalf at Eltham or at Sheene" (F.496–97)—in lines deleted from the G Prologue following the queen's sudden death at Sheene.

Scholars and teachers alike will welcome these two editions for making available more of the poetry that helped define the Chaucer tradition, and even passed under the name of Chaucer, throughout most of our literary history.

JOHN M. BOWERS
University of Nevada, Las Vegas

FRANCIS INGLEDEW. *Sir Gawain and the Green Knight and the Order of the Garter.* Notre Dame: University of Notre Dame Press, 2006. Pp. xi, 307. $40.00 paper.

Sir Gawain and the Green Knight and the Order of the Garter is a densely argued, provocative book. The poem, according to Ingledew, critiques Edward III's court, specifically the relationship between chivalric achievement and sexual misconduct and, as such, should be relocated to the 1350s or early 1360s. Ingledew begins with the assumption that the appearance of the Garter motto at the end of the poem, whether authorial or by a later glossator, invites "a reading of the poem as a reading of history whose point of departure is the founding of this order" (p.3). Not every reader will accept every facet of Ingledew's thesis, particularly his claim that *SGGK* is Edwardian rather than Ricardian in both outlook and date, but his close and careful reading will certainly spark debate on the topicality of Sir Gawain's adventure at Hautdesert.

After a brief introduction, the book is divided into three chapters, the first two establishing a historical and historiographical context in which to read *SGGK* and the third focusing on the poem itself. Chapter 1 discusses Jean le Bel's *Chronique* and Froissart's *Chronicles*. Both texts consistently praise Edward as the paragon of contemporary chivalry on an Arthurian model, but, oddly, le Bel is also the earliest and most complete witness to the accusation that Edward fell in love with and subsequently raped the Countess of Salisbury. Ingledew pays particular attention to the structure of le Bel's narrative (a technique of reading used throughout the book), noting that his account of the rape is placed between Edward's announcement of a new Arthurian chivalric order (1344) and the establishment of the Order of the Garter (1349). For Ingledew, le Bel's rearrangement of chronological order places the foundation of the Garter within a context of sexual scandal. Froissart, in an early version of his text, claims that the scandalous story was false. Despite this, he still includes an account of Edward's love for the countess and a detailed scene in which the two play chess while Edward attempts to force the countess to accept a token, thus potentially compromising her reputation. Chapter 2 examines other contemporary texts, including *Tirant lo Blanc,* the *Scalacronica, Wynnere and Wastoure,* and the *Vows of the Heron,* and their concern over sexual misconduct within Edward's court. Whether that misconduct is a general licentiousness or (as in the *Vows)* a veiled reference to an inappropriate passion for the Countess of Salisbury, it is again associated with the Order of the Garter, and this leads Ingledew to conclude that the motto of the order, "Hony soyt qui mal y pense," does not (as has been recently argued) refer to Edward's claim to the throne of France, but to the potentially dishonorable garter that serves as an emblem for the order. While the word "garter" invites thoughts of hidden and eroticized feminine clothing, the actual image of a small belt more closely depicts an item of masculine dress used in the knighting ceremony. Motto and emblem therefore interact in a powerful rebuttal to those who disapproved of Edward's rumored sexual misdeeds: "The viewer is dared to think ill of a garter (the word) through visual confrontation with a (knightly) belt (the image); what is sexualized, profaned and rendered contingent as an item of intimate dress or a verbal sign is purified and sacralized as the displaced sign of the liturgized girdle or belt that meets the eye" (p. 152). Ingledew's insertion of the word "girdle" here is obviously not accidental. Throughout these chapters he argues for a close association between Arthurian and Edwardian chivalry generally, and between Gawain's green girdle and the blue garter specifically. Gawain thus inverts the Edwardian pattern by wearing a token he gained while defending his chastity. While Edward attempts to transform a possible token of shame into a token of honor, Gawain recognizes the personal shame inherent in the green girdle, which the Round Table adopts as a mark of honorable membership.

Chapter 3 turns to the poem itself. Ingledew convincingly argues that *SGGK* is a fundamentally religious poem consistent with the other texts in Cotton Nero A. x, particularly *Cleanness*. Reading the pentangle within a context of penitential and liturgical traditions, Ingledew suggests that all five points of the device emphasize Gawain's own commitment to a Christian model of courtesy. The hero, however, is distracted by the historical and romance narratives in which he finds himself, and the romance reputation that he finds difficult to shake. Only after he recognizes his faults and their cause (i.e., love of life) is Gawain able to reevaluate the discourse within which he defines himself. Thus the so-called misogynistic speech is not a confused attempt to shift blame, but an example of Gawain facing "his discursive misallegiance when he turns to the greatest of all history books, the Bible, and not to romance or national historiography, for the exempla he needs to live his life by" (p. 187). The "fylþe" with which Gawain is tainted, according to this reading, is not simply his disloyalty to Bertilak, but original sin. What I find perplexing about this chapter is that its thoughtful analysis is enriched by, but not contingent upon, the theory espoused in chapters 1 and 2. Additionally, I am not convinced of the need to redate the poem to the Edwardian period, even if the Edwardian interpretive context is accepted. Surely if, as Ingledew argues, Edwardian scandal was still resonant when Froissart sought to hide it in the Rome MS. of his *Chronicles* (c. 1400), a poet working anywhere in the last half of the century could còmment on an Edwardian chivalric past undercut by licentiousness. If the motto in the Cotton ms. is indeed a late fourteenth-century gloss, it could easily indicate that at least one reader responded to the text as Ingledew suggests.

Technically, the lack of translations from Latin and French sources will make the book inaccessible to the nonspecialist, and the odd relationship between this book and the forthcoming companion volume,

Romance as History, means that some texts, most notably the *Bridlington Prophecy,* do not receive as clear an analysis as they may have otherwise. I trust, however, that this will be rectified in that project, and I particularly look forward to the promised expansion of the discussion of the relationship between romance and historiographic discourses. A short review, however, cannot do justice to the depth of Ingledew's scholarship. His careful reading will enrich our understanding of the penitential and liturgical aspects of the poem and renew debate about its historical context and references.

RICHARD J. MOLL
University of Western Ontario

STEVEN F. KRUGER. *The Spectral Jew: Conversion and Embodiment in Medieval Europe.* Minneapolis: University of Minnesota Press, 2006. Pp. xxx, 320. $26.00 paper, $78.00 cloth.

Steven Kruger has been writing important and innovative articles on the topic of representations of Jews in the Middle Ages for over a decade now. This background shows in the breadth and erudition of this book, which is not simply a reprinting of earlier articles, but a significant and thoughtful expansion of this earlier work. The study draws upon an unusually wide range of sources and locations and thereby fulfills its goal of presenting changes and continuities over time and geographical region.

Kruger opens with a reading of a visual representation of "The Living Cross," engaging questions of gender as well as religious difference. This is a real strength of the book; although the title focus is on Jews, Kruger never loses sight of the intersection of this category not only with gender but also with sexuality and with other forms of religious difference, including representations of Islam and of heresy. This opening reading is later echoed by an equally compelling reading of Chagall's *White Crucifixion.* Kruger's readings maintain a firm basis in specific historical times and settings, but he also never loses sight of the relevance of his readings to contemporary issues and debates.

The book's title concept, "spectrality," is a very effective tool for understanding what Kruger rightly terms the "strong ambivalence" in medieval Christian representations of and treatment of Jews and Judaism (p. 5). Kruger's theoretical frame draws primarily on Derrida's *Specters of Marx,* but it is also influenced by work on sexuality (Terry Castle) and race (Kathleen Brogan). Kruger begins by examining the importance of temporality to Christian formulations of the role of Jews and Judaism; the notion of supersession posits that Judaism is the Old Law, but this ancestor cannot be completely discarded, since it is upon this Jewish foundation that Christianity's claims to truth lie. In order to deal with this paradox, Kruger argues, Christianity attempts to "conjure" away the Jewish past, but this very conjuring perpetuates a haunting Jewish presence. As Kruger observes, "In being summoned up for burial, Jewish corporeality is also paradoxically preserved and invested with a transgressive, polluting power" (p. 13).

In describing this phenomenon of an "absent presence," Kruger takes care not to erase actual Jews from his argument. The book continually attempts to take into the account the impact of their spectral representational role on actual Jews, particularly through focusing on the debate genre and the question of conversion, which, as Kruger shows, are often interrelated historically and textually.

Chapter 2 focuses on what Kruger calls the "long twelfth century," a period marked by increased and significant cultural and intellectual exchange between Christians and Jews as well as a significant negative shift in the nature, tone, and magnitude of polemic against Jews and Judaism. Focusing on the writings of Guibert de Nogent, Kruger shows the ways in which the new formulations of Christian identity developed in the "twelfth-century Renaissance" were dependent on conceptions of Jews and particularly of Jewish bodies as a site through and against which Christian identity was defined. Kruger also demonstrates how the figure of the Muslim was seen as a different, but related, form of threat and reads Guibert against contemporary Jewish writings, specifically responses to the pogroms of the first Crusade, which constructed models of martyrdom in response to persecution.

Chapter 3 builds on the theoretical work of the previous two chapters with a focus on conversion. Kruger asks a brilliant question about figurations of Jewish conversion to Christianity: "If Jews, in the very stuff of their corporeality, are somehow essentially different from Christians, what happens when they undergo a religious conversion?" (p. xxviii). He first addresses this question through a smart and important discussion of conversion that draws upon theories of performative identity. Kruger

503

shows the ways that medieval notions about religious identity were intimately bound with questions of gender and sexuality and also with early conceptions of "race." Because Jewish and Muslim men are represented as feminized, one might conclude that their conversion to Christianity would masculinize them. But Kruger demonstrates that representations of such a conversion are usually far more complex, involving "a 'gender trouble' and a 'queerness' that continue to circulate around the figure of the convert even after religious conversion has been fully achieved" (p. 100).

In Chapter 4, Kruger uses historically situated readings of Petrus Alfonsi's *Dialogi* and the disputations of Ceuta and Majorca, which, strikingly, represent Jews as losing in religious debates not to trained clerics, but to Christian merchants (p. 145). Here Kruger introduces another important strand to his complex argumentation, showing how the figure of the Jew came to be used not only to define Christian identity, but to define the figure of the proper "Christian merchant." By contrasting what Ora Limor has called "the motif of the merchant as hero" against the negative type of the "treacherous" Jewish merchant, Christians can better come to terms with their own engagement with materialism, an engagement that works against the typical association of Christianity as concerned with the spiritual over the material (pp. 149, 156).

Chapter 5 examines the disputations at Paris, Barcelona, and especially Tortosa, carefully situating this last debate within the context of Spanish mass conversions and expulsion. Kruger shows how these debates highlight a key problem in the representation of the Jew. If Jews are stubborn and unchangeable, how can conversion be possible? What does this possibility for Jewish identity say about "the instability of *Christian* identity" (p. 180)? Kruger also shows how these disputations, while fundamentally uneven and unfair, can still be seen as important sites of Jewish resistance to Christian misrepresentation and coercion.

In its use of such a wide range of sources and intricate and synthetic argumentation, this book calls to mind James Shapiro's landmark study, *Shakespeare and the Jews*. Kruger's book is not only essential reading for anyone interested in the history of anti-Semitism and medieval Jewish-Christian relations, but his theoretical formulations, particularly of conversion, have important implications not only for medievalists, but for anyone working on questions of gender, sexuality, and race.

LISA LAMPERT-WEISSIG
University of California, San Diego

WILLIAM KUSKIN, ed. *Caxton's Trace: Studies in the History of English Printing*. Notre Dame: University of Notre Dame Press, 2006. Pp. xxvii, 394. $60.00 cloth, $33.50 paper.

This collection of newly commissioned essays is a substantial attempt at a new version of the early history of printing in England. Its ten contributions explore not just Caxton's own activities as printer and translator, but the various ways in which the technology of printing was to be absorbed into the commercial structures of late medieval and early modern book production, and the kinds of impact it was to have on reading, reception, the formation of a literary canon, and cultural history in the broadest sense. The concerns of the essays stretch from the manuscript transmission of fourteenth-century texts forward to sixteenth-century printing of the works of Chaucer and Langland, and onward still, in a "coda" provided by Seth Lerer's overview of "Caxton in the Nineteenth Century," to the formalizing of Caxton's reputation in enterprises like Blades's *Life and Typography of William Caxton* and the *Oxford English Dictionary*.

The essays are grouped in sections ("The Introduction of the Press: The Culture Machine," "Manuscript and Print Strategies," and "Language, Book, and Politics") whose titles flag the political, economic, and social emphases that are foregrounded in Kuskin's own lengthy introduction. Kuskin opens with a quotation from Adorno on the paradox that books can be both material things and vehicles for ideas, and goes on to explore the varieties of "trace" (best understood here as "following," perhaps, without implications of continuity or replication) in the practices of the English book producers who worked alongside Caxton and after him. After summarizing Elizabeth Eisenstein's concentration on the new mechanical fixity of printing and Adrian Johns's arguments about the social relations of the printshop, Kuskin moves to an investigation of the variety of ways in which "trace" informs the transmission of Chaucer's "Gentilesse"—a short poem about ancestry and inheritance—whose successive copyings and printings in the course of the fourteenth, fifteenth, and sixteenth centuries (alongside Chaucer's other works) offer a model of the ways in which "the trace of the first stock" can filter through time and change. This is deftly done, and it makes clear that the book will not be simply about book production, but about the production of culture, and more specifically the production of literary history. The contributors are all professors of English, with a take on the history of English printing visibly shaped by their practices as readers and sometimes as literary or cultural theorists, and their essays are in the main less about printing than about "the symbolic layer of early English books" (p. 7), and the ways in which "English literary history . . . is constructed by a variety of readers, each consolidating previous readers' efforts in different material conditions" (p. 18).

The essay that broaches most directly here the mechanical practicalities of early printing is David R. Carlson's informative survey of Caxton's practice of weaving the printing of ephemera into his work on longer, more labor-intensive volumes, provocatively entitled "A Theory of the Early English Printing Firm: Jobbing, Book Publishing, and the Problem of Productive Capacity in Caxton's Work." Carlson urges the abandonment of a sentimental attachment to Caxton's translations and his large folio volumes, and recommends instead the study of his handbills, indulgences, and smaller pamphlets, giving much enlightening detail on the working practices that enabled them to be turned around between more challenging undertakings. For Carlson, such study illuminates "the class-based means of production current at the time" and indeed the "class struggle" itself, as Marx and Raymond Williams are invoked. Whatever the terminology, exploration of these areas of Caxton's activities is indeed revealing, and Carlson's suggestions that Caxton may have had to revise his initial overinvestment in "the potential of the elite, courtly market for his products" (p. 52), taking on the printing of more remunerative service books and devotional works, seems plausible. Upturning the more conventional view of Caxton's enterprises also highlights the sheer novelty of printing something like the *Morte D'Arthur,* and clarifies the ways in which a concern with productive capacity was probably to determine de Worde's and Pynson's relocation from Westminster to Fleet Street.

Material features of printed books, and some of the relationships between their production and their use, form the core of Alexandra Gillespie's essay, " 'Followynge the trace of mayster Caxton': Some Histories of Fifteenth-Century Printed Books," prompting questions about what can be determined about printers' intentions from physical evidence like book size or provision of paratext. Gillespie describes some of the means by which printers seem to have produced books both large and small for collection into *Sammelbände* or composite volumes. For comparative purposes, she uses a folio volume compiled by the mercer Roger Thorney, and a smaller composite book (the "Fisher" *Sammelband*), which includes some of the same material. Thorney's book incorporates both manuscript and print, and may well have been put together in consultation with de Worde, with whom he had close connections. The Fisher compilation, in contrast, is made up of constituent parts that reflect commercially influenced decisions to design books specifically for serial collection. This is an important topic, and Gillespie's well-illustrated examples open the way for further study.

The other essays here are less overtly concerned with the economy or practicalities of production, directing their energies toward individual texts, or trends in the selection and promotion of particular genres and modes of writing. Both the editor (in " 'Onely imagined': Vernacular Community and the English Press") and Patricia Clare Ingham ("Losing French: Vernacularity, Nation, and Caxton's English Statutes") cover the potential of print for the symbolic production of national identity, contributing, respectively, a large-scale overview and a detailed, text-specific study. Jennifer Goodman ("Caxton's Continent") and A. E. B. Coldiron ("Taking Advice from a Frenchwoman: Caxton, Pynson, and Christine de Pizan's Moral Proverbs") offer valuable insights into the wider European context of early printing, Goodman by comparing Caxton's English romances with analogues printed abroad in other vernaculars, and Coldiron by tracing the transmission, in both manuscript and print, of a translation of one of Christine de Pizan's shorter works, and its incorporation into the nascent Chaucer canon. Tim William Machan ("Early Modern Middle English") also writes on the printing of Chaucer and pseudo-Chaucer, considering late fifteenth- and early sixteenth-century printings of earlier works by Chaucer and his contemporaries and immediate successors as a definable genre, newly "authorized" with prefatory material or special apparatus. The concept of the edition is explored in more abstractly theorized ways, with reference to Bourdieu, in William N. West's "Old News: Caxton, de Worde, and the Invention of the Edition," and Bourdieu features too in Mark Addison Amos's study, "Violent Hierarchies: Disciplining Women and Merchant Capitalists in *The Book of the Knyght of the Towre*," where Caxton's status as a mercer serves as a way into analyzing the economy of familial relationships at the heart of this text.

Taken together, these essays distill a history of English printing very much of our time, mapping onto this history a number of issues and concerns that are current preoccupations across many disciplines: England and Europe; markets and economies; canon formation and literary history; printing and state power; genealogy and succession. "History of the book" is here proposed and explored as a branch of cultural theory, and with often interesting results, although sometimes a vague sense that evidence is sought to demonstrate the truth of particular models, rather than responded to for what it can suggest on its own terms. The best of the essays ask new questions and suggest some new approaches, particularly in their understanding of the complicated relationships between manuscript and print, between printers and the markets they both cultivated and responded to, and between Englishnesses of various sorts.

JULIA BOFFEY
Queen Mary, University of London

KATHY LAVEZZO. *Angels on the Edge of the World: Geography, Literature, and English Community, 1000–1534.* Ithaca: Cornell University Press, 2006. Pp. xiv, 191. $65.00 cloth, $29.95 paper.

With Kathy Lavezzo as a guide, one feels in capable hands—even in a landscape of daunting proportions. *Angels on the Edge of the World* brings together a swath of understudied material, orders it with a clean argument, and, in so doing, provides a compelling introduction to three discourses whose "subtle [intertwining]" (p. 73) has grown in importance to medievalists of late. Lavezzo's focal concerns are "geography" (including cartography), "literature" (most often historical writing), and "English community," a category whose limitations are communicated in the interrogative section title—"A Medieval English Nation?" (p. 8)—that serves as her point of departure. The book's dates are daringly splayed, but each chapter takes as its focus a carefully historicized textual location. Starring roles go to Aelfric, Anglo-Saxon homilist (c. 950–1010); Gerald de Barri (a.k.a. Gerald of Wales), in his capacity as ethnographer of Ireland (c. 1187–89); Ranulph Higden, compiler of the *Polychronicon* (c. 1327–60); the ubiquitous Geoffrey Chaucer, as represented by *The Man of Law's Tale* (c. 1394); and—an outlier in disciplinary terms, since his "texts" are processions—Cardinal Thomas Wolsey (c. 1472–1530), adviser to Henry VIII.

Angels on the Edge of the World argues that "for medieval English writers and mapmakers . . . the image of their geographic otherworldliness contributes to the production of national identity" (p. 14). Refinements on this core idea of England's "geographic marginalization" (p. 82) proliferate, the valence of each being determined by local interpretive needs. Thus we encounter the radical "geographic alterity" of the English (p. 10), their special status as a "people set apart from the world" (p. 82), their "geographic remoteness" (p. 53), "privileged placement" (p. 50), "exceptional strangeness" (p. 11), "vulnerability" (p. 37), and more. From a textual standpoint, none of these claims rings false. This comment says much about the critical due-diligence of *Angels,* yet Lavezzo's literary and cartographic readings do not impose so much as suggest themselves. Her most arresting claim concerns the persistence of England's investment in its "geographic otherness" (p. 104). As the book hammers home, a counterintuitive attachment to the concept of their island-realm's constitutive marginality (dare one call this spatial essentialism?) continues to haunt insular imaginations long after events such as the discovery of America "should have demolished the notion of English geographic isolation" (p. 25). *Angels* dwells less on establishing England's marginalized identity than on articulating the "two-fold meaning" (p. 76) inherent in this formulation.

Lavezzo is ferocious in her attention to the profound "geographic ambivalence lying at the heart of England's emergent identity" (p. 70). Indeed, ambivalence drives her argument (itself quite clear, paradoxically). Many readings begin by tracing a line in which the disenfranchised English are maligned as barbarous or backward (pp. 37, 104) only to double-back and pursue a course that seizes upon the "advantages of England's border positioning" (p. 82). But Lavezzo's interpretive tacking is neither indulged without cause (her works *are* highly polysemous) nor conducted without payoff. Century after century, "marginality and exceptionalism" emerge as sides of the same coin: the "two mutually constitutive traits that define England" (p. 73). An evolving geopolitical exceptionalism coupled with abiding belief in their spiritual and ethnic "election" (pp. 28, 31) would eventually suggest to the English "how [they] should be the rightful masters of the earth itself" (p. 21). Yet the "ambivalent responses to English otherworldliness" that Lavezzo discovers throughout her long premodern period "foreshadow as well the ironies that mark the modern geographic production of English imperial identity" (p. 26).

Contemporary maps play supporting roles in this account. Thus the Cotton/Anglo-Saxon map of the world (c. 1000) illustrates Aelfric's Rome-centric but Anglo-partisan thinking; Gerald's textual designs on Ireland sharpen against his Map of Europe, "the fiction of [whose] cartography authorizes a geographic vision of England as expansionist world center" (p. 69); the *mappamundi* that fronts the Ramsey Abbey copy of Higden's nationalist universal chronicle "privileges the English world border" to suggest that his native island "merits the same historical prominence" accorded Rome (p. 73); and so forth, down to two (medieval?) maps inventoried among Cardinal Wolsey's household goods (p. 116). (The Chaucer chapter—published in earlier form in *SAC* 24 [2002]—treats cartography metaphorically.) Map-habits aside, another tactic of Lavezzo's chapters is to take some radical diachronic flight, veering to consider William Godwin's 1803 musing upon "what [Chaucer] and Petrarch would have made of each other had they ever met" (pp. 93–94), or Elizabeth Elstob's 1709 deployment of an anecdote from Aelfric to "enable colonial empathy for slaves of color" (pp. 44–45). Such moments symbolize Lavezzo's work. Her theoretical, textual, and historical fluency allows her to cross borders with aplomb.

As glances toward "national hobbies such as the English garden and . . . World Cup football" (p. 10) signal, Lavezzo stretches her temporal canvas taut. She proffers the year 1534 as historical terminus, yet the territorializations sketched by *Angels on the Edge* hardly dissolve with the Middle Ages. (If anything, their importance increases during the high-colonial and arch-nationalist centuries to follow.) As with "1534," the round originary date of "1000" misleads, for the anecdote launching *Angels* concerns Pope Gregory the Great (540–604), who is smitten at the Forum by some heathen slave-boys, "white of body and . . . of noble hair" (p. 38). "Rightly are they called Angles [*angli*]," he puns, "since they have the beauty of angels [*angeli*]." Lavezzo's title derives from the wordplay whereby Gregory transmutes his bodily attraction to such "angels" into a missionary desire to draw their homeland, situated at the world's top edge or "angle" (per later punning), within the authorizing spiritual embrace of Rome. The "white angels" of Aelfric's account flirt with blackness (pp. 38–40), then return as "Irish Angels on the Edge of the World" (p. 54), later to become "Angels at the Center of the World" (p. 87). The Man of Law makes Custance virtually "an angel of

God," "set apart from Rome yet possessed of Christian law" (pp. 97, 103). (Cardinal Wolsey manages no such trick.) Such touches are indicative of the book's crafting.

Angels on the Edge trains its focus on England. Yet while the category that dare not speak its name (the term "nation" is absent from the index) stays foregrounded, the perspective of our surveying shifts. Lavezzo's chapters will appeal according to the interests individual readers bring. My heightened moments came during her original analysis of understudied maps, but personal proclivities aside, most outstanding is Lavezzo's virtuoso introduction. Grounded in medieval evidence yet leavened by theoretical prompts, these lucid pages will become required reading for many. If one consequence of the introduction's success is that it steals some thunder from ensuing chapters, this seems a fair exchange for a performance of such verve and erudition.

There are times, during what follows, when one desires this book to be other than it is. Lavezzo entertains many questions, but others arise: How does this Higden *mappamundi* compare to others that survive? What challenges to English and Irish marginality does Gerald's work on Wales introduce? And what about the rest of the far-flung *Canterbury Tales?* Much might be gained through increased attention to each text's synchrony of complications; yet compromised, by consequence, would be the sleek verticality that makes *Angels on the Edge* literally a trailblazing study. No meandering here: this book takes us places.

DANIEL BIRKHOLZ
University of Texas at Austin

SETH LERER, ed. *The Yale Companion to Chaucer.* New Haven: Yale University Press, 2006. Pp. ix, 420. $65.00

The most obvious reason for the flood of companions to Chaucer and medieval literature in recent years is economic. Universities have largely renounced their commitment to underwriting the costs of academic publishing, demanding of their presses that they publish with an eye firmly fixed on the bottom line. Since companions can be marketed for something akin to "textbook adoption," they are potentially more profitable than books whose intellectual or scholarly agenda is, to use the derogatory commercial idiom, "narrowly specialist." The danger of this situation—and one that reaches far beyond the "companion" phenomenon—is that organizing academic publishing around market conditions is not exactly the best recipe for the production of good and useful work.

This is not to say that companions serve no purpose beyond helping to right the balance sheets of academic presses. Perhaps a more useful way to think about the companion phenomenon is to ask what pedagogical purpose they might serve that would not be as well or easily served by assigning critical essays or chapters on the works being studied. The answer most companions give, at least implicitly by way of their format, is that our students need a large number of snapshots of various kinds of historical, cultural, and literary backgrounds—a few pages on the Three Estates, a few pages on medieval science, a few pages on Boethius, and so on. Such a format produces a rhetorical pressure toward dispensing information rather than exhibiting and teaching an interpretive relation to the text, if only because it is hard to build much of an interpretive relation in a small amount of space dedicated to a topic that can be easily marked out and named. The *Yale Companion to Chaucer* gives a different and more interesting answer. As Seth Lerer says in his Introduction, the idea of this companion is to provide a small number of scholars the full space of a thirty-page-or-so essay to explore topics, not only in greater depth than is typical, but in ways that model for students various kinds of interpretive skills and thoughtful consideration of substantive critical concerns. To facilitate a more interpretive relation to the material, the volume construes its topics much more loosely than do other companions.

James Simpson's contribution, for instance, is titled "Chaucer as a European Writer." As Simpson takes it, this topic means something quite different from a sketch of Chaucer's debts to French and Italian poetry; it involves capaciously reimagining what it meant for Chaucer to inhabit an international literary and intellectual culture. Among other things, this includes tracing a relation between Chaucer and Ovid that has less to do with assessing Chaucer's Ovidian borrowings than with understanding a shared mode of intellectual and cultural critique and a characteristic rhetoric—a "poetry of rough surfaces," as Simpson nicely puts it. As Simpson unfolds his account of this poetic mode, he engages the usual targets of his topic—the relation between Boccaccio's *Filostrato* and Chaucer's *Troilus and Criseyde*, for instance—in ways that combine acute attention to the text with a keen sense of the critical and cultural stakes of Chaucer's engagements with his sources. The result of this more capacious formulation of a topic is that the essay actually does what companions always advertise but rarely deliver, namely, provide a guide to major issues that is accessible to undergraduates while still being useful to graduate students and offering new insights to specialists in the field.

Paired with Simpson's reassessment of Chaucer's Europeanness is D. Vance Smith's reassessment of "Chaucer as an English Writer," a topic that might not make it into a more traditional companion at all. If it did, it would almost certainly mean a focus on Chaucer's relation to English society and politics, perhaps in comparison to Gower, rather than as here, a broader imagining of Chaucer's relation to the scene and the traditions of writing in English. Among the topics Smith provocatively considers is the question of what it might mean to understand Chaucer's work as a response to Langland. Smith's consideration of the question begins by exploring sites of rhetorical contact between the two writers, in ways that expand a sense of what rhetorical contact might consist in and what might be at stake in it. The essay then builds to a wonderful characterization of how the difference between Chaucer and Langland, a difference any student who is paying attention will be struck by, is less a matter of differences of epistemology (a topic to which bright students so frequently leap too quickly) than of how the two writers understand the import of the epistemology they share. Here again, then, we have a major issue that has been inadequately addressed in the critical literature on Chaucer, taken up in a way that meets students on intellectual ground to which they can be expected to go, but which they are likely to misconstrue on their own.

The intellectual engagement and pedagogical care of Simpson's and Smith's essays is characteristic of the volume as a whole. Since I don't have time to give a similar description of the contributions of each of the other essays in the volume, I will conclude by registering a surprise and a disappointment. The surprise is that, despite the structural and editorial encouragement of an essayistic, interpretive mode of engagement by the contributors, the volume as a whole paints a remarkably unified sense of Chaucer, and does so with a critical voice that varies little from essay to essay. This is not in itself a bad thing, and one might imagine many reasons for it, including the simple fact that everyone, rightly enough, is aiming for maximum accessibility. But the way the similarity plays out here has the unfortunate effect of making critical differences seem largely a matter of generational shifts. There is discussion, for instance, of what it meant for the field of Chaucer studies to be organized around a split between historicism in a Robertsonian mode and a New Critical formalism, and what it means for those critical modes to have been supplanted by new kinds of historicism. This is all good and useful, but it does tend to underemphasize the question of critical difference today, and it is misleading about the reasons for critical difference as such. Both undergraduates and graduate students are already subject to the temptation to imagine critical difference as a matter of distinctions between different schools or "camps" defined by competing beliefs and methodologies. This only reinforces students' tendency to think that one of their main tasks is to decide what critical school or methodology to subscribe to, and that doing so will tell them what to do when faced with a text. It is pedagogically crucial to help students see that they cannot overcome their own difference from themselves by becoming recruits to a school or methodology; that signification is endlessly productive and endlessly problematic; and that both Chaucer's poetry and our critical engagements with it are organized around problems rather than "positions." I would not expect the contributors to this volume to take issue with such claims. In fact, there are many moments in the volume that capture just such a sense of what drives poetry and criticism. But then perhaps it would have been useful, and truer to the mission of the volume, for it to have given more space—to invoke Simpson's phrase again—to developing its own rhetoric of "rough surfaces." Marking the discontinuities and ongoing questions arising not only between but within each contribution might more fully model for students the idea that criticism, far from issuing from a position of mastery and sureness, is an unfolding project continually troubled both by its objects and by itself.

MARK MILLER
University of Chicago

KATHERINE C. LITTLE. *Confession and Resistance: Defining the Self in Late Medieval England.* Notre Dame: University of Notre Dame Press, 2006. Pp. vii, 196. $27.50.

On the top-ten list of the scholarly obsessions of our field over the last twenty years, Lollardy and the nature of the subject must be at or near the head. Seminal studies on these topics from the late 1980s and early 1990s—such as, respectively, Ann Hudson's *The Premature Reformation* (1988) and Lee Patterson's *Chaucer and the Subject of History* (1991)—have shaped the direction of much research and continue to serve as touchstones. In this regard, Katherine Little's first book arrives as a shrewd intervention into critical history, one that offers something new by showing how two familiar areas of research bear on each other in ways surprisingly little noticed. In arguing that "Wycliffites and the controversy they engendered . . . should be understood in terms of the history and the sources of the self" (p. 1) and, in turn, that the vernacular literature of the period responds to the "Wycliffite concerns" of "the ideological power of identification and the capacity of language to represent the interior" (p. 80), the book uncovers a relatively untrodden path through scholarly domains that have begun to feel crowded. While readers may not always agree with how Little defines the nature of the Wycliffite impact on subject formation (or, as she prefers, self-definition), or with how she describes poets such as Chaucer, Gower, and Hoccleve responding to this impact, she nonetheless succeeds at opening up a productive new strand of inquiry.

As the book's title indicates, the Wycliffite critique of auricular confession serves as the historical fulcrum that the study, as a whole, investigates. Between the Fourth Lateran Council (1215) and the late fourteenth century, Little sees normative self-definition as largely the product of verbal technologies associated with confession in particular and pastoral instruction of the laity in general. More specifically, the principal means of institutional production and maintenance of the self consisted of the taxonomies of sin, through which individuals were to understand their interiorities, and the exempla that both gave these taxonomies embodied form and directed self-understanding toward practice. When Wycliffites rejected both auricular confession and the use of extrabiblical narrative in lay instruction, then, they also rejected the normative technologies of self-definition, and what they offered in place, Little argues, was strangely without content. Wycliffite selfhood—whether it took the form of identification with Christ, or with a Lollard martyr, or with a generalized Truth—was inevitably self-identical and outward faced. It was, indeed, more a form of resistance to establishment control over self-definition than a form of self-definition per se (hence the second term of the book's title).

After an introduction that situates the book's argument theoretically and critically, Little provides two chapters that together draw a portrait of the impact of Wycliffism on normative self-definition. The focus of the first is lay instruction, and, of the second, confession; the principal texts under investigation include sermon collections, penitential treatises, and *The Testimony of William Thorpe*. With this portrait in place, the next two chapters take up the response of vernacular poets: chapter 3 (an earlier version of which appeared in *SAC* 23 [2001]) focusing on Chaucer's Parson and his tale, and chapter 4 contrasting the role of confession in Gower's *Confessio Amantis* with that in Hoccleve's *Regiment of Princes*. Following a brief afterword offering a glimpse into the early modern period, the study concludes with a list of references and index.

The book's proportions create some difficulties. On a mechanical level, its 46 pages of notes result in too-frequent interruption of its 131 pages of text. More consequentially, in taking on such large topics in a relatively small space, the book will seem to many underdeveloped in certain aspects and to have made odd choices of coverage in others. For example, the study's concept of self-definition strikes this reviewer as somewhat undertheorized. Although Little maintains a dialogue with many prominent recent theorists of subject formation, in practice her notion of self-definition seems largely the structuralist one of grammatical substitution, and in this way keeps complex—but, I think, crucial—questions of power and desire mostly, if not entirely, at bay. One might also look for more evidence that the Wycliffite critique of auricular confession and lay instruction possessed the cultural potency Little ascribes to it—that it in fact led to, or signaled, a crisis regarding the language of self-definition and consequent shift in this language. Since the verbal machinery of penitence remained firmly in place into the sixteenth century, the evidence for this cultural potency is often of the indirect sort, consisting of texts that appear somehow to respond to the Wycliffite critique. But the natures of these texts' responses are frequently quite contestable. Little's reading of Hoccleve's *Regiment of Princes,* for example, understands the idiosyncrasies of the poem's long confessional prologue, as well the "generic fissure" (p. 128) between that prologue and the following exempla-filled advice text, as enacting, in its response to Lollardy, a "retreat from confession as it has been traditionally defined" (p. 117). And yet, while her comments on the role played in the poem by Lollard John Badby are undoubtedly valuable, there are so many other possible explanations for the odd characteristics of the poem (as Little acknowledges) that it seems rather tendentious to see these characteristics as determined by (and therefore evidence for) a shift, spurred by Wycliffism, in the normative techniques of penitential self-definition. Moreover, the absence of considerations of other seemingly relevant works by Hoccleve—such as the more purely confessional *Male Regle*—makes such assessment of Hoccleve's concerns provisional. More generally in regard to coverage, in a book investigating the discursive relays between penitential self-definition and religious reform, one fairly expects *Piers Plowman*, especially the figure of Will, to make more than the brief appearance it does, and the same may be said about the famously complex and ecclesiastically entangled selves of the *Canterbury Tales,* such as the Pardoner (to whom Little devoted a chapter in her 1998 Duke dissertation).

These criticisms, however, are not intended to put either the book's achievement or value into question. Indeed, inasmuch as they represent a call for further investigation and corroboration, they underscore the importance of the research direction Little's book so auspiciously opens up. To those interested in the discourses of religious reform and self-definition—most readers of this journal, I wager—this book is a must read.

ROBERT J. MEYER-LEE
Goshen College

KARMA LOCHRIE. *Heterosyncrasies: Female Sexuality When Normal Wasn't.* Minneapolis: University of Minnesota Press, 2005. Pp. xxviii, 178. $60.00 cloth, $20.00 paper.

Lochrie's Introduction and first chapter ("Have We Ever Been Normal?") offer smart, informed discussions of the impact of statistical science and the concept of the "average man" on sex research in the late nineteenth and early twentieth century. This is still, even in our modern times, a surprising way to begin a book about the Middle Ages. But Lochrie means to distinguish contemporary from medieval knowledge-production, and accordingly it behooves her to explain why she sees the "norm" as a modern artifact. "Heterosyncracy" is Lochrie's term, indicating "diverse forms of desire, sexual acts, medical technologies, and attendant theologies" bound neither to the "procreative model of heterosexuality" (p. xix) nor to recent notions of number. In brief, *Heter-*

osyncrasies claims that there was a time when normal "wasn't," and that time was premodernity. The book goes further: there was a time when "norms," "normality," and "normativity" did not rule discussions of sexuality.

Lochrie wants "to imagine a preheteronormative past that is neither hopelessly utopian nor inveterately heteronormative," awakening us "to the medieval residues [in our present] that must now be accounted for in the way we will imagine sexualities in the future" (p. 25). There is actually not a lot of future talk in this book. But it is incontrovertibly visionary. The uncanniness of the Middle Ages emerges from its pages with joyous clarity. Lochrie's ability to think variously challenges many of the timelines sacred to contemporary historians of sex, for example, the discussion in chapter 4 of the "medieval ignorance of the clitoris," its "discovery" by Renaissance anatomists, and the consequent breakdown of the "one-sex model of sexual difference" and "emergence of the lesbian" (p. 72). Now, one might reasonably find risible the idea that the clitoris was ever unknown to anybody anytime, the organ really not being as difficult to locate as all that. Do today's female infants owe their masturbatory pleasure to centuries of anatomical study? But life is funny, morphology is cultural, and knowledges differ, so it is useful to learn that "anatomists had already begun dissecting corpses at the end of the thirteenth and beginning of the fourteenth century," and that the Middle Ages "had two clitorises instead of one and . . . both of them were dangerous" (pp. 74–75). (As Lochrie observes, "to see . . . a clitoris does not necessarily amount to . . . less confusion about it.")

Although I'm still not sure why we can't question Suger's allegations against the behavior of the nuns at Argenteuil (an assertion made in Lochrie's second chapter, "Untold Pleasures"), her exploration of Heloise's remark to the effect that "women are most vulnerable to seduction from each other" is all you need to make you appreciate how important the convent was in medieval culture, and why. It was an exceptional, extraordinary way of life that was in theory open to all women, and nothing has ever replaced it in Western culture. Chapter Three, "Far from Heaven," persuasively argues that Chaucer's Prioress is a Lollardish satire of "a late medieval spirituality associated with women that emphasized affective devotion"—Chaucer as Dominick Dunne sticking it to the Hollywood wife who adopts unfortunate African children and dresses them up like jockeys for garden parties. Finally, "Amazons at the Gates" (chapter 5) establishes once and for all the queerness of the

Christian West's fascination with the *jouissance* of paganism, and the weird centrality of the nonetheless rarefied figure of the Amazon in medieval Britain. Amazons meant many things to the medieval imaginary: "nostalgia for a masculinity that exceeds feminine nature, and even male masculinity" (p. 112); "a sort of gendered erotics outside heterosexuality" (p. 114); "a masculinity that is not male" (p. 115); "a courtly lover" (p. 116); "a sexual, masculine female body split between axes of maternity and martiality," for which "there is no word," though Lochrie obligingly (if only to expose the limitations of "available sexual terminology" [p. 121]) offers "stone butch" along with "virilophilia," "highly developed procreative selection," "bello-eroticism," and "a virginal identity and lifestyle." Lochrie's critical gifts derive to a considerable degree from her ability to help us imagine extraordinarily, to show us how layered, complex, and surprising the most powerful fantasies— the ones that achieve a certain social "consensus" (in Lacan's term)— always are.

Heterosyncrasies is a short book that would have profited from a more generous format. Long-term readers of Lochrie will recognize a degree of compression that can leave an argument less persuasive than it might otherwise be. In chapter 2, for example, Lochrie contends that "in spite of the fact that Heloise's sexology of the convent taps medieval misogyny, it nevertheless also condenses a cultural anxiety as a form of female sexuality, one that fosters unlimited forms of female eroticism and fellowship" (p. 29). Is this still subversion/containment, or some homology thereof? Why *wouldn't* a sexology of the convent condense a cultural anxiety? What does it mean to condense a cultural anxiety anyway, and to whom does this anxiety belong? What is at stake in this distinction between tapping medieval misogyny and condensing a cultural anxiety, if distinction it in fact be?

Heterosyncrasies displays some occasionally rattletrap argumentation on the level of its historicism as well. The book invokes multiple timelines—including its ethical commitments to contemporary imaginative activity—but draws nonetheless some perplexingly definitive boundaries between the medieval past and modernity, on the score of the exceptionalism of the Middle Ages. One is made nervous by a claim that implies a bit of binarism, however likeable. That is to say, one would like to know what's really so uncanny about a historiography that seems to equate the Middle Ages with uncanniness? When Lochrie multiplies her timelines, moreover, one often goes away with more questions than answers. Are all the centuries before statistics premodern? Would eighteenth-century formulations of sexuality, for example, libertinism, be heterosyncratic but also modern? Is de Sade's Gothic revivalism an identification with those strains of Catholicism that despise "nature," or with an Enlightenment preference for natural law stripped of sentiment? Did Elizabeth I preserve or even extend, as well as redefine, the parameters of medieval chastity? Although Lochrie is not obliged to address matters beyond the scope of her book, one would like more guidance as to how such matters *could* be addressed. But *Heterosyncracies* is required reading nonetheless, for the growing number of ethnographers interested in sex as well as the growing number of medievalists aware of its historicity. If the eclecticism of its uses of periodicity is inadequately explored, the book is nonetheless a wonderful example of how rich historiography can become when it takes multiple timelines into account. *Heterosyncracies* is a curious, flexible, humane inquiry, open to anomaly on all levels, and perhaps could not have enchanted me as much as it did, or achieved so much in the arena of "re-thinking," if it had insisted on dotting every methodological "i" and crossing every meta-discursive "t." Countering the notion that significance resides in the majority, the widespread, and the enduring, Lochrie extends a generous welcome to heterogeneity, on the level of practice as well as content. The result is a marvelous challenge and addition to the way we appreciate the Middle Ages and the history of its reputation for danger.

ARANYE FRADENBURG
University of California, Santa Barbara

TIM WILLIAM MACHAN, ed., with the assistance of A. J. Minnis. *Sources of the Boece.* The Chaucer Library. Athens: University of Georgia Press, 2005. Pp. xiv, 331. $85.00.

The stated aim of the Chaucer Library is to present modern editions of the medieval works that Chaucer "knew, translated, or made use of in his writings in versions that are as close as possible to those that were in existence, circulating, and being read by him and his contemporaries" (p. ix). The complexities surrounding the sources of the *Boece* render such a task especially difficult, necessitating, in the words of general editor Robert E. Lewis, a sort of third way in editorial procedure: a "hypothetical source text created by drawing readings from various manuscripts according to what Chaucer had in his translation" (p. ix). That is, working backward from the *Boece,* Machan creates hypothetical French and Latin source texts, using other French and Latin manuscripts to justify his emendations.

Machan's texts are based on the manuscripts apparently closest to the ones Chaucer used: for the Latin, the text in Cambridge University Library, MS Ii.3.21; for the French, both the very corrupt text in Besançon, Bibliothèque Municipale, MS 434 and V. L. Dedeck-Héry's 1952 edition, in *Mediaeval Studies,* based on Paris, Bibliothéque Nationale, MS Fr. 1097 (from the *a* tradition of manuscripts of Jean de Meun's prose translation of Boethius's *Consolatio Philosophiae*). None of these texts or any other extant French or Latin text was the exact copy Chaucer used for his translation. Further, as Machan points out, following his book-length analysis of the *Boece* in *Techniques of Translation* (1985), Chaucer's uses of his sources are "seldom predictable" (p. 12). In Machan's opinion, Chaucer viewed translation as "a fairly fluid activity" (p. 13), which makes it even more challenging to reconstruct his source texts. At each point where the French or Latin texts deviate from readings in the *Boece* (of which, of course, there is no holograph), Machan must decide whether to emend the Latin, the French, or both, with reference to other manuscripts and, in the case of the Latin, the traditional text as opposed to the Vulgate represented in the Cambridge manuscript. For the text of the *Boece,* Machan uses the text in C^2 (Cambridge University Library, MS Ii.3.21) as opposed to that of C^1 (Cambridge University Library, MS Ii.1.38), which Ralph Hanna and Traugott Lawler used as the base for their edition of the *Boece* in the *Riverside Chaucer.* He justifies his use of C^2, the best witness of the ß group of *Boece* manuscripts, with the claim that the scribal sophistication in the α manuscripts indicates the further distance of the α tradition from Chaucer's original translation (p. 14). In his notes Machan signals those places where C^1 and C^2 diverge in such a way as to influence his presentation of the French or Latin texts.

A further complicating factor is Chaucer's incorporation of material from the extensive tradition of commentaries on the *Consolatio Philosophiae.* Machan's introduction is most helpful here. He sorts through the various claims made in the last century regarding the possibility, for example, that Chaucer relied on Trevet's commentary entirely rather than on an independent text of the *Consolatio,* that he had only excerpts of Trevet rather than the full text, or that he relied at any point on the commentary of William of Conches. Following A. J. Minnis, Machan concludes that Chaucer primarily used Trevet's commentary and the Remigian glosses rather than that of William of Conches. (Alas, scholars hoping for a reliable edition of Trevet must still rely on the unpublished, incomplete edition of E. T. Silk, which, as Machan notes, relies on too small a sample of the many manuscripts of this commentary. Machan quotes extensively from the Silk edition in his notes to the text.)

An example of how Machan's editorial strategy works in practice: in the French text of I.pr.4, he prints: "Se tu atens [l'aide] de ton mire" (p. 35). Dedeck-Héry reads (according to Machan's note) "l'entente." In the *Boece,* the word is "helpe" (*Riverside,* I.pr.4.4). In this case, Chaucer's source manuscript seems to have followed the reading in the Besançon text. Later in I.pr.4, Machan's text reads: "Mais [ce meismes n'avions nous pas deservi] des peres des senateurs" (p. 41), again the reading in the Besançon text (as opposed to "deservions nous donques aussi ce meismes" in Dedeck-Héry). The corresponding text in Chaucer reads: "yit hadde I nought disservyd of the faderes (that is to seyn, of the senatours) that they schulden wilne my destruccioun" (I.pr.4.206–9). Elsewhere Machan allows the Dedeck-Héry reading to stand, as in II.pr.5: Chaucer "joies" (II.pr.5.69), Dedeck-Héry "joies" (p. 71), Besançon "gloire" (p. 254). Such evidence as this supports the claim of Machan and others about the French manuscript Chaucer used—that the Besançon manuscript corresponds in many readings with the *Boece,* but that elsewhere the latter seems to correspond more closely to other manuscripts in the *a* tradition of Jean's translation. But it also does something to undermine his claim regarding Chaucer's fluid notion of translation. If his practices as a translator were really so unpredictable, would it be so clear in readings such as the above (and many others) which French words Chaucer must have encountered?

The editorial procedure of creating a hypothetical source text perhaps merits further discussion. It may prove problematic, for example, for those trying to ascertain where Chaucer rejected particular readings in his sources. However, Machan makes his methods perfectly transparent. As he remarks, "Given the collation banks, readers are in a position to evaluate any of my editorial decisions and to alter accordingly this reconstruction of the sources of the *Boece*" (p. 15). In any case, scholars examining Chaucer's translation practices need no longer rely on the

Loeb or other editions of the traditional Latin text of the *Consolatio,* and
they now have another source of information regarding where and how
Chaucer used material from Trevet and the Remigian commentary tradition.

JENNIFER ARCH
Washington University in St. Louis

WILLIAM PERRY MARVIN. *Hunting Law and Ritual in Medieval English
Literature.* Cambridge: D. S. Brewer, 2006. Pp. ix, 198. $75.00.

Did we really need another book on hunting in medieval literature?
William Marvin makes a good case that his book is indeed needful. The
originality of his contribution lies in his attention to the political and
ideological dimensions of the hunt. The basic tenet of Roman law, that
wild game is nobody's property and everyone is free to hunt, accorded
with the practices of Germanic tribes; but, over the course of the medieval period, hunting in England gradually became a privilege of the
few—of kings, who after the Conquest began privatizing vast tracts of
land as "royal forests," or of noblemen, who soon followed the trend by
converting land into private hunting reserves. The tensions between
these processes of "afforestation" and "imparking" and the old customs
of "free capture" provide the unifying thread in the best parts of this
book.

The worst part is the first chapter on *Beowulf.* Anyone maintaining
that hunting is central to this poem would have to be most ingenious.
And Marvin is. He argues that the building and naming of Heorot
("Hart") are symbolic of the institution of a particular social order (hier-
archically organized) and of the hunting ethos of "delayed return" hunters (who act as a corporate body). By contrast, Grendel's attack on
Heorot symbolizes the backlash of the ruthless individualism associated
with the older "immediate return" hunters (who hunt for instant self-
gratification). The fact that *Beowulf* is not about hunting does not deter
Marvin. There are, after all, plenty of other critics who talk about things
that are *not* in a text. Marvin's model is David Aers, who "illustrates in
the case of *Sir Gawain and the Green Knight* how a socio-economic factor
such as the agricultural labor of the peasantry is critical to the represen-

523

tation of élite chivalric subjectivity" (p. 33). *Illustrates?* And, of course, some other interpretations of Heorot's meaning are equally wild. Marvin says he is "encouraged" by the fact that his interpretation "can hardly be more speculative than what has already been said about the pagan stag cult" (p. 21). I agree that there are many tenuous interpretations about in the field, but that should not encourage anyone to produce more.

The second chapter is valuable, for there Marvin looks at texts that really do share his interests. "Bloodsport and the Symbolic Order of the Forest" is devoted to writers at the court of Henry II, in particular John of Salisbury, the great critic of the hunt, and Richard FitzNigel, a royal apologist. Marvin sees and shows clearly that the stakes in the twelfth-century hunting debate are very high. The royal forests were subject to the king's arbitrary rule. The common law did not apply in this domain, and so Henry II's policy of afforestation and his enthusiastic pursuit of the hunt came to be seen as indicative of his absolutist aspirations. The invention of "forest law" politicized hunting in novel ways.

The third chapter deals with the *Artes venandi* of England, and contains some thoughtful observations about the point of hunting rituals. Practical considerations may have mattered rather less in these rituals than did the competition for social distinction. Marvin is right to emphasize that English hunting manuals are as much about "correct speaking" as they are about "doing," but I doubt that this insistence was peculiar to English hunting manuals. The same fussiness about terminology can be found in French authors: witness Henri de Ferrières, who (c. 1375) wrote that all things related to the hunt should be done and named properly, "for words well spoken proceed from understanding, especially since the manner of words has been ordered in accordance with the art of venery." Marvin also exaggerates the "Frenchness" of the Englishman's hunting terms. He imagines that while "the gentleman's converse is congested with [French] hunting jargon, the yeoman can talk the talk but has things to say in English as well" (p. 104). This is not borne out by the gentlemen he cites, namely, Sir Thomas Malory and Edward of York, translator of Gaston Phoebus's *Livre de chasse*. Malory's "terms of venery" are predominantly Germanic ones, and while it is true that Edward of York retains many French terms, he explicitly says that he does so to acquaint readers with terms used "beyond the sea," and *not* with the intent that his readers should use these terms in England.

The next chapter deals with Gottfried's *Tristan* and *Sir Gawain and the Green Knight*. Marvin has some interesting things to say about the "curialization" of the hunt. These ceremonies offered participants symbolic and material "rights" and "fees" in a context where the actual freedom to hunt had been ceded to the monarch (or baron). "Ritualization therefore recuperated a semantic of free estate in a legal context within which a man could not freely hunt" (p. 141). The arrival of Tristan amid King Mark's primitive huntsmen is the inaugural moment of this new "civilized" order of refinement and subjection. This might seem a promising basis from which to approach *Gawain,* but Marvin tries too hard to make the hunting scenes thematically relevant to the rest of the story. He argues, for example, that the "assay" of the deer (to determine its fatness) is relevant to Gawain's attempted seduction by the lady (for she was sent to "assay" him) and to Gawain's nick in the neck (another "assay"). I am aware (as Marvin seems not to be) of many similar attempts to integrate the hunting scenes with Gawain's adventures, but think that all such readings, however "historicized," beg the fundamental *historical* question of whether "unity of action" was something that medieval writers set as much store by as their modern interpreters.

The final chapter, "Slaughter and Romance," focuses on *Sir Degrevant,* a chivalric romance about love, hunting, and raids on other men's hunting parks. Marvin truly illuminates the romance by setting it into the context of the late medieval privatization of hunting grounds by the nobility, and by reading the story alongside historical documents that similarly record the passions and troubles fueled by "imparking."

I should finally note that there is some important scholarship that Marvin does not refer to. For example, the authority on the history of *Artes venandi* is Badouin van den Abeele, *La littérature cynégitique* (Turnhout: Brepols, 1996). The hunting scenes in Gottfried have been carefully studied by William Sayers, "Breaking the Deer and Breaking the Rule," *Oxford German Studies* 32 (2003): 1–52. Marvin unwittingly echoes observations about *Gawain* made by Felicity Riddy, "The Speaking Knight and Other Animals," in Martin B. Shichtman and James P. Carley, eds., *Culture and the King* (Albany: SUNY Press, 1994), 149–62, and Dorothy Yamamoto, in *The Boundaries of the Human in Medieval English Literature* (Oxford: Oxford University Press, 2000), 99–131.

AD PUTTER
University of Bristol

525

GRETCHEN MIESZKOWSKI. *Medieval Go-Betweens and Chaucer's Pandarus.* New York: Palgrave Macmillan, 2006. Pp. x, 218. $69.95

Sometimes lovers need a helping hand to overcome the obstacles blocking their path. If a young man is struck motionless by the force of his passion, or if social class boundaries hinder love from blossoming, or if any other of a number of impediments make love impossible, a go-between—or pander or pimp—serves a necessary purpose in joining together lovers who could never sate their passions on their own. Gretchen Mieszkowski addresses the medieval incarnations of this pandering tradition in *Medieval Go-Betweens and Chaucer's Pandarus,* tracing its history through its classical roots to its medieval incarnations in a variety of comic and courtly genres and then reading Chaucer's *Troilus and Criseyde* through a pandering hermeneutic.

The monograph is organized simply and effectively. Part I, "Choreographing Lust: Go-Betweens for Sexual Conquest," concentrates on the role of the pander in Latin comedies (*De nuntio sagaci, Pamphilus, Baucis et Traso, Lidia,* and *Alda*), fabliaux (*Le Prestre teint, Auberee, Dame Sirith, Constant du Hamel,* and *Le Prestre et Alison*), and other texts, including *Roman de la Rose,* that foreground lust over love in their depiction of pandering. Typically, panders in these comic and bawdy tales use deception and trickery to dupe a woman into bed with a randy young man. Part II, "Choreographing Love: Idealized Go-Betweens," addresses the go-between's role in the more rarefied world of courtly romance, in which the aim is to assist lovers to come together in celebration of their ennobling passion. The panders addressed in this section of the book include Guinevere in *Cligés,* Alexandrine in *William of Palerne,* Galehot and Guinevere in the Prose *Lancelot,* Blancheflor's governess in *Tristan,* Cypriane and Delfin in *Florimont,* Herland in *Romance of Horn,* Glorizia in Boccaccio's *Filocolo,* Pity in Renzee d'Anjoy's *Le livre du cuer d'amour,* Urake in *Partonope of Blois,* Lunete in Chrétien de Troyes's *Yvain,* the eponymous protagonists of *Claris et Laris,* the numerous go-betweens in *Protheseläus,* and the Old Woman of *Éracle.* This analysis of the literary history of panders in the Middle Ages illuminates their multiple cultural meanings, and then, in the final unit of the monograph, "Choreographing Lust and Love: Chaucer's Pandarus," Mieszkowski demonstrates how the two traditions of the go-between intersect in Chaucer's Pandarus. Mieszkowski's scholarship on *Troilus and Criseyde,* including her famous article "Chaucer's Much Loved Criseyde" (*Chaucer Review* 26, no.

2 [1991]: 109–32) and her book, *The Reputation of Criseyde: 1155–1500,* has established her as a leading authority on the function of gender in the text, and her analysis of masculinity and male trafficking in women promises to transform the ways that scholars view Pandarus and Troilus in a similar manner to her groundbreaking work on Criseyde. Miesz-kowski's interpretation of Pandarus as a go-between who merges the opposing traditions of pandering for lust and pandering for love clearly explains many of the fundamental inconsistencies of his character. Also, Mieszkowski reclaims and problematizes Troilus's masculinity, especially in regard to the ways in which some scholars dismiss his swooning man-hood in the bedroom scene; in contrast, Mieszkowski outlines how his extreme emotions establish his genteel nobility. The sweep of Miezkow-ski's survey of medieval pandering and her trenchant analysis of its im-pact on *Troilus and Criseyde* enable readers to look at familiar texts with new eyes, which is certainly one of the most compelling effects of literary scholarship.

I will limit my criticisms of *Medieval Go-Betweens and Chaucer's Panda-rus* to three main points. First, Mieszkowski takes a rather bleak view of the going-between in comic texts, arguing that many of the tales of deception should be read as rapes: "*Pamphilus* was so popular in the Middle Ages because it fed readers' appetite for reading about rape" (p. 31). Such an assertion seems remarkably difficult to prove, and it ig-nores the ways in which reprehensible acts, when presented in comic texts, shed the social disapproval in which they are normally shrouded. Many a comic text humorously endorses outrageous cruelty, but that does not mean that a fabliau about sexual conquest endorses rape any more than a fabliau such as *The Sacristan* endorses killing monks. Sec-ond, Mieszkowski establishes a dichotomy between go-betweens for lust and go-betweens for idealized love, but this binary appears to crumble in some instances. For example, in her analysis of *Claris et Laris,* Miesz-kowski suggests that "despite making love to his comrade's beloved, Claris remains within the conventions of idealized going between" (p. 120). Surely such moments belong more to the humorous tradition of deceptions and trickery in courtship, or are at least heavily inflected by such comic forebears. As with many binaries, this dualistic structure allows for a simplified organizational schema, but this advantage is un-dermined by a concomitant loss of complexity. Finally, with such detail given to the various incarnations of the pander in medieval literature, Mieszkowski can be readily forgiven for not addressing the ways in which erotic tensions circulate so messily in most of these tales (save for her extensive analysis of *Troilus and Criseyde*). With so much desire slopping about in these triangulated affairs of man, woman, and pander, the analysis begs for a queer theoretical approach to map out the ways in which the heterosexual and the homosexual merge with the heterosocial and homosocial to the ultimate confusion of many gendered categories. Mieszkowski addresses these tensions in her analysis of Pandarus, but such an examination could be fruitfully expanded to virtually every other text addressed in *Medieval Go-Betweens and Chaucer's Pandarus.* Scholars interested in queer theory should mine through Mieszkowski's wonderful monograph; she has established a new territory of pandering scholarship that will benefit from additional investigations.

In sum, Mieszkowski has written a glorious book in *Medieval Go-Betweens and Chaucer's Pandarus,* one that illuminates a fascinating literary tradition and then shows its relevance to one of the masterworks of the English literary tradition. I am confident that her monograph will make a lasting contribution to medieval studies of gender, romance, and the messy cultural work of love.

TISON PUGH
University of Central Florida

J. ALLAN MITCHELL. *Ethics and Exemplary Narrative in Chaucer and Gower.* Cambridge: D. S. Brewer, 2004. Pp. viii, 157. $75.00.

Scholars have long seen that the contingent voices of Chaucer's *Canterbury Tales* pose a sophisticated poetic challenge to readerly judgment, while Chaucer's moral tenor has often been taken as implicit rather than explicit. In Gower's *Confessio Amantis,* on the other hand, contingent morality has often been understood as a poetic liability. J. Allan Mitchell sets out to redress this imbalance by foregrounding the ways in which both poets reveal the circumstantial nature of ethical decision-making. By situating both poets in an ethical context that stretches from Aristotelian rhetoric to modern moral philosophy, Mitchell makes a learned and suggestive case for reading Gower and Chaucer as "exemplary genealogists of morals rather than just representative moralizers" (p. 7).

Chapter 1, "Reading for the Moral: Controversies and Trajectories," sets aside the awkward marriage between general and particular (moral and story) which commonly characterizes moral discourse, emphasizing instead the act of reception: drawing on exegetical terminology, Mitchell writes that readers reduce stories to individually applicable truths, engaging in "tropological" understanding of exemplary texts. He defends the value of reading for moral messages, insisting that in the Middle Ages, "reductive moralization represented an acceptable and in fact indispensable way of putting exemplary narrative to use" (p. 17). Narrative cases are essentially incomplete until applied in action: "Until it is realized in the conscience or conduct of a practitioner as a form of life, exemplary morality exists only *in potentia*" (p. 17). Chapter 2, "Rhetorical Reason: Cases, Conscience, and Circumstances," charts the history of inductive judgment in moral casuistry, tracing connections from Aristotelian rhetoric to Cicero, through *ars predicandi* to Aquinas and Giles of Rome. This chapter foregrounds the way that exemplary rhetoric demands responsiveness to particular cases. The first two chapters, then, cogently set aside any notion of exemplary discourse as a stable code of sociopolitical norms. Mitchell's emphasis on audience response is refreshing, less because he embraces the apparent naïveté of reading for moral nuggets (p. 142) than because his central argument raises important questions about the relation between narrative poems and lived lives.

In practice, Mitchell's focus on reductiveness and pragmatic action provides grounds for celebrating the contradictions in Gower's moral discourse. Chapters 3 and 4 focus on the *Confessio,* and chapters 5, 6, and 7 offer readings of the *Canterbury Tales.* The Gower chapters argue, first, that contradictory messages do not detract from moral clarity but prompt ethical decision-making; and, second, that Gower's vocabulary of experiential proof provides a comprehensive, not coherent, array of instances to draw upon. The argument strongly resists any notion that readers simply accede to exemplary injunctions, asserting instead that Genius teaches contradictory lessons precisely because "life demands more than a system of neat and tidy normative distinctions" (p. 56). The survey of criticism in chapter 4, if belated, nevertheless effectively refutes recent accounts (by Copeland, Simpson, and Scanlon) that place insufficient value on the text's incongruities. This chapter traces further the ways in which the reader's activity consists of memorial reconstruction through awareness of "mesure" in both perception and internal judgment (conscience).

Mitchell's contention that the real test of moral philosophy lies in the extratextual world of contingent action is irrefutable, and calls salutary attention to Gower's sense of urgency; yet his appeal to the extratextual begs the question of how we get from text to action, how the poem's narrative form shapes its audience's reflections—and how, therefore, reading itself might constitute a moral experience. For example, Mitchell cites the "Tale of Capaneus" as evidence of the vice of forgetfulness while the case of Nebuchadnezzar foregrounds forgetfulness as a step in the process of redemption (pp. 68–71). To what extent can we say that a narrative of change embraces the value of every step in the *process* of change? Isn't the figure of Nebuchadnezzar exemplary only when he becomes the humbled king? Moreover, isn't Nebuchadnezzar exceptional, precisely in his vaulting ambition, and inimitable, in his temporal dislocation from the present? Mitchell explicitly disavows an interest in viewing narrative as ideologically authoritative, but in practice, his readings could make more of the gap between narrative contingency and moral authority—a gap that leaves enormous space for reader response. Mitchell's reading of Nebuchadnezzar supports his general claim that "Gower is not always confident that good judgment will prevail" (p. 66) but could further specify the causes, or the plausible effects, of such authorial anxiety about his audience.

The chapters on Chaucer begin with a helpful if somewhat overdrawn insistence on the moral seriousness of Chaucer, for whom, according to Mitchell, overt failures of exemplary authority provoke reflection on exemplarity per se. Although Mitchell explicitly resists the usual hierarchy of value between the two poets, his argument in practice gives Chaucer more credit than Gower for meta-ethical reflection. Chapter 5 argues that the Wife of Bath demonstrates the adjustability of examples to various situations, and that her situation "literalizes" antifeminist exempla. Chapter 6 examines the "meta-homiletics" (p. 95) of the Friar, Summoner, and Pardoner, whose storytelling Chaucer uses to condemn the storytellers for treating exemplarity so cavalierly. By far the strongest analysis in the Chaucer section comes in the last chapter on the Clerk's Tale. Mitchell struggles with the "monstrosity" of Griselda's actions and argues, using Derrida and Levinas, not simply that she sacrifices motherly tenderness to a principle of obedience, but that *any* moral responsibility entails sacrifice because decision reduces the possibilities for action. Moreover, explanations are always insufficient to account for the resulting violence, calling attention to the gap between moral contemplation and ethical action. Thus when readers are faced with the undecidability of the tale—marriage exemplum vs. spiritual exemplum—"no explanation is totally persuasive, no decision sufficiently justified, no response good enough . . . so that responsibility will have about it an air of irresponsibility" (p. 135). The problem Mitchell delineates in the Clerk's Tale might productively be extended to the rest of the book, to enrich that difficult problem of how one gets from text to action. Perhaps Mitchell's answer, like that of Gregory the Great in his homilies, is that examples work on the mysterious energy of inspiration—an answer that might lend strength and complexity to his argument about the circumstantial nature of exemplary discourse.

Gower is the governing presence in *Ethics and Exemplary Narrative,* even though Chaucer occupies more chapters. The book joins an ongoing critical exploration of contradiction in the *Confessio:* from systematic accounts in which particular tales resolve into moments of conversion (Olsson) or the conflict between reason and will brings about an integrated identity (Simpson), scholarship has moved toward an emphasis on Gower's moral contingency (Bullón-Fernández, Watt, myself). Mitchell lays out a useful basis for this emphasis in philosophy and rhetoric, lends credibility to the medieval method of reducing stories to their moral nuggets, and makes a welcome contribution to the developing conversation about narrative and ethics in the Middle Ages.

ELIZABETH ALLEN
University of California, Irvine

NIGEL MORTIMER. *John Lydgate's "Fall of Princes": Narrative Tragedy in Its Literary and Political Contexts.* Oxford: Oxford University Press, 2005. Pp. vx, 360. $110.00.

A recent spate of critical productivity has placed Lydgate at the forefront of Middle English literary criticism and history, a position he has not occupied for almost six centuries, since his days as "Laureate Lydgate" (Derek Pearsall's memorable label), when he wrote poetry for kings, princes, abbots, lords, and ladies. In part this flowering of interest reflects a recalibrated understanding of the relationship between medieval and Renaissance literary cultures, with Lydgate now recognized not only as a crucial link between Chaucer and Shakespeare but also as an important influence in his own right on sixteenth-century poetry and drama. Nigel Mortimer's reassessment of the *Fall of Princes* adroitly places Lydgate in both his medieval and early modern contexts; it is a study that will be inestimably valuable, not only for medievalists but also for those Renaissance literary critics who take seriously the influence and persistence of medieval traditions in the early modern period.

After an introductory survey of the state of play in Lydgate studies and a summary of Lydgate's career, Mortimer turns to the major source texts for the *Fall of Princes,* Giovanni Boccaccio's *De casibus virorum illustrium* and Laurent de Premierfait's *Des Cas des nobles hommes et femmes.* In so doing, he sets in place a principle for reading the *Fall* to which he will adhere throughout the book: Lydgate's text cannot be understood without a very precise knowledge of its sources, particularly Laurent's *Des Cas.* We see this intertexual method begin to pay off in chapter 3, which addresses Lydgate's position as a Lancastrian court poet and focuses on a varied assortment of texts, ranging from the *Serpent of Division* to Lydgate's treatment of Lucretia to the role of Caesar more generally in the *Fall of Princes.*

But it is in chapter 4 that Mortimer's intertextual work and his concern for historical context come together and illuminate the *Fall of Princes* in an entirely new way. As he tells us, Lydgate was particularly concerned in the *Fall* to address the relationships between spiritual and secular authority, so much so that he altered his sources a good deal in order to emphasize the importance of Church hegemony over secular rule. Throughout the chapter, Mortimer builds a convincing case for this claim by painstakingly comparing Lydgate's exemplars to his sources and showing minutely how those source texts were altered and reshaped in order to make the Benedictine case. Taken alone, these examples would be convincing evidence that Lydgate sought to assert the authority of the Church over secular rulers. But Mortimer also includes a long discussion, largely unprecedented in work on Lydgate's poetry, of the place of his monastic community at Bury St. Edmunds in the England of the 1420s and 1430s, and the importance of that community as a context for the *Fall.* That discussion includes extensive consideration of Lydgate's abbot, William Curteys, and the records of his abbacy, which show how the issues of spiritual and secular authority were being contested at Bury during the very decade in which Lydgate was writing the *Fall of Princes*. Whether or not all scholars agree that Lydgate is as orthodox and as Benedictine as Mortimer describes, his scholarly synthesis of material in this chapter will be essential reading for everyone interested in Lydgate's poetry and its contexts, and will provide the groundwork for all future study of his religious writing.

In his penultimate chapter, Mortimer addresses head-on the major philosophical issue at the heart of the *Fall of Princes:* the role and definition of tragedy as a genre in relation to the status of Fortune and the question of human agency. He argues, through extensive close reading, that when Lydgate is considered in relation to Laurent's aggressive disavowals of Fortune's power, it becomes clear that the *Fall* reinstates a vision of Fortune as a willful and capricious agent. Further, when Lydgate navigates the complexities of the battle between Fortune and Poverty in Book 6, a scene taken from Boccaccio and rewritten by Laurent, he narrates the scene in such a way that he leaves room for both a vision of personal responsibility *and* a notion of arbitrary Fortune. Mortimer concludes that Lydgate did not present readers with a formulated thesis about Fortune and agency, but rather displayed a set of "habitual responses and casts of mind," that led him to envisage tragedy as both a story about the punishment of evil and a narrative of innocent suffering.

This temperate conclusion leads directly to Mortimer's final chapter, in which the influence of the *Fall* in both the fifteenth and sixteenth centuries is described, with extensive discussion of manuscript versions of the text as well as of the works of Lydgate's imitators and followers, coupled with useful historical contexts for all three. Mortimer examines several manuscripts in which the *Fall* was excerpted and shows that far from being randomly or carelessly chosen, these excerpts were specifically selected by compilers and arranged in such a way that they made moral claims—indeed, perhaps claims that Lydgate himself might not support. Mortimer goes on to discuss the work of Peter Idley and George Cavendish, as well as the *Mirror for Magistrates* and its continuations, showing that over the course of the fifteenth and sixteenth century and beyond, attitudes to Fortune and tragedy shifted several times. In conclusion, Mortimer includes an appendix containing a "Conspectus of the Narratives," which carefully maps, in table form, each episode in the *Fall,* along with corresponding episodes in Boccaccio and Laurent's texts. From start to finish, Mortimer's book is useful to the reader; it sets out not only to advance theses about the poem but also to enable and encourage future work. Such scholarly generosity makes this book essential reading for medievalists and Renaissance critics alike.

MAURA NOLAN
University of California, Berkeley

PETER NICHOLSON. *Love and Ethics in Gower's* Confessio Amantis. Ann Arbor: University of Michigan Press, 2005. Pp. x, 461. $80.00.

It may seem unusual at this point in Gower scholarship that a book should be written to affirm, explore, and defend, as the poet's purpose in the *Confessio,* the construction of an ethics of human love. Nicholson prepares us, however, with an equally unusual prefatory comment: this is a book that should have been written forty years ago, but wasn't. To supply what other major Ricardian poets have had, but Gower has lacked—a "shared understanding" of the poetic text, "the product of a preceding generation of scholars" (p. v)—he returns to this core subject and makes a case that he thinks may benefit us even now. Indeed, he warns that he will stop short of questions that one might justifiably also raise, about how the poem, for example, may be "either subversive of or blind to its own ideological foundations" (p. vii). Nevertheless, this book, he suggests, could also provide a basis for such study.

Having shown the differences between the *Confessio* and Gower's two other major poems, Nicholson challenges those who interpret the poet's treatment of love—the "newe thing" of this work—from the perspective of "a watered down neo-Augustinianism." The "received view" of the poem, deriving largely from this approach, serves to demarcate Nicholson's uniquely contrasting perspective. In his judgment, Amans is not "an embodiment of human sinfulness," but an "ordinary mortal"; the task of Genius is not "to win [Amans] away from his love," but to show him "how he might become a more virtuous lover"; "the underlying moral structure of the poem" is not "the opposition between *caritas* and concupiscence, or in broadest terms, between the love of God and human love," but "the fundamental harmony . . . between God's ethical demands and love's" (pp. v–vi).

Nicholson lays the foundation for his own approach and book-by-book analysis by initially examining the framework of the lover's confession. Among Gower's sources for that framework, Guillaume de Machaut provides the closest models, and Nicholson's survey of the *dits amoureux* in relation to the *Confessio* is one of the strengths of his book. The effect of his analysis is to draw Gower's poem back into the realm of courtly fictions and to focus our attention on matters such as the dialogue form, inherited from Machaut, in which the god Love or associated allegorical figures attempt to guide the lover-narrator to a new perspective on love worthiness. In his adaptation of this material, however, Gower "takes a far broader view," exploring a greater diversity of lovers, situations, and moral choices, and "he chooses to face . . . issues that Machaut ignores" (p. 44). Given the expanse and variety of Gower's work, Nicholson's approach is fittingly comprehensive: he combines close readings with a helpful mapping of the argument and unique structure of each book. He also pays particularly close attention to about 20 of the 150 tales in the collection. Given the subject, his choice of some of these, such as Canace, Rosiphelee, and Apollonius, is expected, and of others, such as Constance, Nero, and Nectanabus, is less so, but such variety enriches the inquiry. Throughout, the interpretations are insightful; often they are provocative.

Space will not permit looking closely at Nicholson's treatment of any single narrative, but a few of his premises regarding the poem require comment. He insists, for example, that Genius is a reliable teacher, one who "speaks for the poet most of the time" (p. 7). Whereas many recent critics, observing Genius's lapses and inconsistencies, treat them as also forming part of Gower's design, Nicholson does not. Either this is a nonissue—"For every problematic tale," he argues, "there are dozens with completely straightforward lessons"—or, because "moral choices are not always clear-cut," the "incomplete lessons," "unresolved paradoxes," and "seeming contradictions" cannot be seen to "detract from the reliability of the instructor" (pp. 36–37). Furthermore, while Nicholson recognizes Genius's "dual allegiance, as a priest in the service of Venus" (p. 7), he perceives no conflict in his "serving his goddess and also serving God" (p. 39), and that is because, in his view, only one of the multiple Venuses in the poem is relevant to Genius's instruction: the goddess in the frame narrative is a "morally regulatory" character, an earnest proponent of virtuous love. By contrast, the Venus depicted by Genius in his excursus on the pagan gods, knowing only what "unto lust belongeth" (5.1425), incites to promiscuity. Genius had tried to avoid speaking about her in this excursus, but when Amans confronts him with the omission, he explains, "I have it left for schame, / Be cause I am here oghne prest" (5.1382–83). Nicholson keeps his Venuses separate and here shifts focus, in an interesting but distracting observation arguing that in Genius's denouncing the goddess he serves, "the fiction denies its own reality" (pp. 301–2). At the literal level, however, Genius sees but one goddess and admits to her dual nature: that in turn directs us back to possible conflict in his own "dual allegiance." There is complexity here that Nicholson has not adequately addressed. Finally, he has insisted throughout that love is a site of moral choices, but he appears to deny that when he charges Genius with eventually "stepping outside of his character" (p. 37) to advise Amans to abandon his love. His speech, Nicholson argues, is "a dismissal of everything that precedes" (p. 382). It is hardly that. At a particular site of moral choices, Genius concludes that Amans's choice to persist in his love would be a wrong choice—"it is a Sinne" (8.2088). The judgment does not invalidate the ethics of love Genius has been developing and Nicholson describing, but affirms it through the application.

One may dispute some of Nicholson's premises and readings, then, and yet we must not forget that he has done something not yet attempted on such a scale in Gower studies, and in many ways he has done it well: this book will form a useful "companion" to the *Confessio* not only for its comprehensiveness but also for its organizational clarity as well as its detail in guiding readers through Gower's long and often difficult poem. That Nicholson never shirks introducing major points of controversy, moreover, is commendable. He does not provide answers on every occasion, to be sure, nor will his book assuredly produce "shared understanding," but he has written a work that will do something just as important: newly challenge us to engage in a form of *pley* that Gower appears to have valued—a play of diverse readings.

KURT OLSSON
University of Idaho

MAURA NOLAN. *John Lydgate and the Making of Public Culture.* Cambridge: Cambridge University Press, 2005. Pp. x, 278. $90.00.

Maura Nolan's book is an ambitious and challenging addition to the reappraisal of John Lydgate's work that began in the 1990s as an adjunct to the new historicism and has since taken several directions. Those directions include recent contributions in textual scholarship such as Alexandra Gillespie's *Print Culture and the Medieval Author: Chaucer, Lydgate, and Their Books, 1473–1557* and interpretive studies like Nigel Mortimer's *John Lydgate's "Fall of Princes": Narrative Tragedy in Its Literary and Political Contexts.* A larger agenda emerges in Larry Scanlon and James Simpson's essay collection *John Lydgate: Poetry, Culture, and Lancastrian England,* which fashions Lydgate's writing as the vast, uncharted territory whose critical mapping is key to a full understanding of Middle English literature. Nolan stakes out a smaller territory by focusing on selected texts from Henry VI's minority—specifically, the *Serpent of Division,* the mummings written for the mercers and goldsmiths, the disguisings at London and Hertford, and Lydgate's retrospective poem on Henry's triumphal entry into London. Historically and politically, her texts represent the decade between Henry V's death at Vincennes in 1422 as he sought to establish the dual monarchy envisioned by the Treaty of Troyes and Henry VI's return to London as King of England and France in 1432, a title already preempted by Charles VII's coronation at Rheims in 1429. In Lydgate's career, these texts are minor works situated between two monuments, *Troy Book* (1412–20), commissioned by Henry V, and *Fall of Princes* (1431–38), commissioned by Humphrey, Duke of Gloucester. The claim Nolan makes for them, however, is not at all minor: the texts, she argues, register the crisis of a child ruler and conciliar government, and they remake the available forms of public culture to offer "imaginary and symbolic resolutions to critical cultural problems and contradictions" (p. 3).

One challenge that Nolan implicitly raises is to the category "minor works" within Lydgate's career as a writer. As she rightly notes, scholars regard the period she examines as the high point of Lydgate's influence among his contemporaries, when he writes occasional pieces across multiple genres on both aristocratic and civic commissions. Within the dynamics of Lancastrian cultural exchange, minor work proves to be a hard currency. Nolan is more explicit in her challenging formulation of public culture, the object (and objective) of Lydgate's writerly making in higher and lower genres. The prose, paradramatic, and poetic texts she analyzes are public in the dual sense of commemorating public occasions and appealing to a hierarchical and exclusive audience. The public culture they embody inevitably suggests Habermas's public sphere, but the contrast is more instructive. The "public" Lydgate addresses is not, as in Habermas, a third term between the state and society, a body of citizens at once private and reflective; if anything, the state and society, particularly its elites, have collapsed into each other. The works of Lydgate's so-called laureate phase command our interest for the ways that power speaks to itself.

A further challenge that Nolan makes is to our expectations and tactics of reading. The public and topical nature of Lydgate's texts leads us to anticipate overtly didactic and exemplary works, rhetorically framed to point a moral or address the philosophical issues beneath public and ceremonial occasions. Nolan insists, however, that Lydgate works against the grain, complicating didacticism and exemplarity with the nuanced, allusive, and resistant discourse that we recognize as distinctly literary. The life of Julius Caesar in *Serpent of Division,* for example, reveals the limitations of moralized history and the failure to integrate human agency and Fortune within a coherent explanation of tragic action. The mummings and disguisings, Nolan demonstrates, are insistently literary in their images and references as well as their invocations of classical and vernacular authorities. Henry VI's entry into London becomes legible as Lydgate's readers draw on the cultural information about the classical past transmitted to them by exempla and sermons. One might want to argue, with Warren Ginsberg in *Chaucer's Italian Tradition,* that for the late Middle Ages a sense of the radical alterity of the past originates with Petrarch and is transmitted by Chaucer, but Nolan stresses the divide between past and present specific to secular exemplarity, for which Gower serves as a powerful model for Lydgate.

Readers looking for a sustained narrative that links Lydgate's writing in 1422–32 to its occasions and historical contexts seek a different kind of literary history from what Nolan undertakes. The empty throne that Paul Strohm has made the informing figure of earlier Lancastrian political anxiety recurs periodically in Nolan's discussion as a reminder after Henry V's death of the trauma of lost heroic kingship and perhaps, too, as an anticipation of Henry VI's later collapses as a reigning monarch. But Henry's minority and the problems of conciliar government do not structure the historical dimension of Nolan's account, nor do they make an ongoing connection between Nolan's principal texts and others related to the events and their themes. Nolan's history lies, rather, in literary form as the vehicle by which historical forces and cultural anxieties break into public consciousness. And literary form implies, in turn, a rich layering of reference and meaning. For this reason, Nolan devotes considerable attention to both authorial sources and the generic back-grounds of mummings, disguisings, and the triumph. History thus be-comes legible through intertextuality as royal, aristocratic, and civic elites, schooled by vernacular learning in particular, recognize the liter-ary framing of exemplary and ceremonial discourse.

Nolan's book reflects wide reading in late medieval literature and culture, at the same time that it insists on bracketing Henry VI's minor-ity as a distinct moment within Lydgate's literary career. Her detailed analysis of the texts suggests that our understanding of Lydgate's career needs to move beyond the taxonomies of major and minor works if we are to understand the full scope of his writing as cultural practice as well as poetic composition. Nolan's book also tells us something about our own moment of critical practice, which, if history depends on literary form and intertextuality, might have already become recognizably post-historicist.

ROBERT R. EDWARDS
The Pennsylvania State University

KELLIE ROBERTSON. *The Laborer's Two Bodies: Labor and the "Work" of the Text in Medieval Britain, 1350–1500.* New York: Palgrave Macmillan, 2006. Pp. ix, 276. $65.00.

The punning subtitle on the dust-jacket, cited above, differs from the more concise subtitle listed on the book's title page: *Literary and Legal Productions in Britain.* The discrepancy perhaps testifies to the last-minute challenge of selecting just the right brief description for a much-labored-over manuscript. It may also indicate the difficulty of capturing the essence of a complex argument about an unstable term like "work."

Kellie Robertson's study of the "cultural logic" governing both the material discourses of labor law and the symbolic discourses about labor during a historical period (1350–1500) when defining and regulating work were high on the national agenda is a tour de force of medieval cultural studies. This intricately constructed and densely argued book should be read by all interested in late medieval English society, but it has postmedieval implications also, which are indicated in the epilogue about sixteenth-century discussions of labor and in a coda about contemporary theoretical developments. The central argument of the book is that there is an intimate—if complex and changing—relationship between material and immaterial worlds, between labor laws, laboring bodies, and the social imaginary of labor. Thus, "juridical discourse produced significant semiotic and epistemological shifts in areas far removed from the immediate concerns of policing labor shortages" (p. 3).

Each of the book's five chapters provides an in-depth exploration of a development in medieval labor history with its discursive implications for both law and literature. Chapter 1 explains the punning titular reference to Kantorowicz's concept of the "king's two bodies" by arguing that the period also identified two laboring bodies—one theologically and the other juridically defined. Through new regulatory strategies such as branding and corporal punishment, the government attempted to produce a laboring body whose identity could be controlled in response to labor shortages, plague, and rebellion. "Good" and "bad" workers were represented in the visual arts and the flourishing cult of St. Walstan, patron saint of agricultural workers. Robertson argues that the cult was "an orchestrated use of a hagiographical symbol to help enforce labor obligations at a time of drastically changed master-servant relations" (p. 33). The chapter ends by looking at fourteenth-century poets, who entered into the day's dominant discourse by emphasizing the social usefulness of their labor. Most provocatively, Robertson sees Langland construing writing as a "hybrid third term" (or type of labor between material and immaterial) that was called on to "enforce the difference" between good and bad labor.

Chapter 2 focuses on Chaucer's "social imaginary" in the 1380s, a time when he was justice of the peace in Kent and, in Robertson's view, would have spent the bulk of his time enforcing labor regulation. This neglected period becomes a key example of "how regulation of material labor influences the production of immaterial literary labor"— specifically Chaucer's Prologue to the *Legend of Good Women*. Intellectual labor becomes in the process both an instrument of enforcement and a suspect in need of regulation. The chapter offers a fascinating reminder of the "fraught" position of a rural peace commissioner in the fates of Chaucer's peers (contrary to biographers who see the Kent sojourn as a respite from urban political pressures). It also argues that the courts of love in which the poet is tried had more than a passing resemblance to the king's courts in which Chaucer served, as both were sites where the "hermeneutic limits of truth" could be investigated. The chapter ends with the trenchant suggestion that Chaucer was "Pre-Raphaelitized" by William Morris, who created for posterity a childlike court poet at odds with the worlds of industrialization and mercantile production and consumption.

Chapter 3 examines the popular phrase the "common profit" used in various texts, both civil and religious, through the fifteenth century. Robertson calls it the very "trope of immateriality," which simultaneously conjured up the opposing idea of all that was selfish in the material realm. In the "struggle for social legitimacy," she says, "one had to capture the common profit" (p. 79); it was the "metadiscourse of medieval community" that represented society as a "corporate body that depended on the work of all estates for its well-being" (p. 80). Late medieval labor legislation and moral treatises tended to subdivide the three traditional estates into more and more categories of workers, and gradually the phrase "common profit" was appropriated by marginal social groups like rebels, heretics, and urban merchants. Robertson is at her most persuasive showing how common profit comes to refer to a culture of consumption and civic monopolism when it is used by London guilds for their ordinances or associated with the fiscal interests of mercantile exporters. Eventually, in the early Tudor period, the ruling elites came to prefer the concept of the "commonwealth" as expressive of the new political theology.

Chapter 4, which engages with gender and Foucauldian theory, is the most unexpected in the book. It studies the household as a site of production and consumption, a "unit of economic regulation," and a microcosm of the state, with the housewife as privileged laborer. Using the Paston letters, the chapter explores the "ideological contradiction" of the gentry wife, who was figured as part of the household whose labor she regulated, but at the same time was expected to be capable of representing "the legal and financial interests of her frequently absent husband" (p. 119). There is a fascinating examination of Margaret Paston's letters not just as functional documents but as conscious self-representations that through "performative speech acts created and maintained the household itself" (p. 121). The discussion of Margaret's lists of necessities argues for a rhetoric, a "narrativized mode" of inventorying that mimicked her husband's legal training and embodied the mediating place of her labor in the household—between private and public, and between material and immaterial.

Chapter 5, more predictably, connects the preoccupations of the mo-

STUDIES IN THE AGE OF CHAUCER

rality play *Mankind* with mid-fifteenth-century East Anglian social unrest, suggesting that both were responses to the 1445–46 regulation of agrarian labor. The densely historical discussion concludes with analysis of how a play may "stage rebellion." Robertson focuses on "performative" language that (in J. L. Austin's sense) may be identical to action; the linguistic play and mockery of legalities in *Mankind,* she claims, dramatically reveal the implicit (usually invisible) coercion in familiar juridical situations.

In sum, this is a perspicacious study that will deepen our understanding of late medieval literary and historical references to labor. The theoretical acumen and care with which the book's arguments are made will certainly generate new insights into familiar texts. As a demonstration of what a cultural studies methodology can bring to medieval studies, *The Laborer's Two Bodies* is exemplary and can be highly recommended.

KATHLEEN ASHLEY
University of Southern Maine

LARRY SCANLON and JAMES SIMPSON, eds. *John Lydgate: Poetry, Culture, and Lancastrian England.* Notre Dame: University of Notre Dame Press, 2006. Pp. 314. $65.00 cloth, $30.00 paper.

In the first essay proper in this fascinating and significant volume, Phillipa Hardman remarks upon the quality of "connectedness" that characterizes John Lydgate's verse, the many conjunctions that create the "perceived effect of an unstoppable narrative flow" (pp. 23–24) in the prolix poet's work. If this reviewer had to pick one way to characterize the overall impression created by the sum of the parts that make up this rich, varied, and critically nuanced collection, it would be in just these same terms of connectedness and flow. Despite the many texts discussed and complex issues raised by eleven contributors, the editors have succeeded in assembling a collection remarkable for the ease—indeed, the seeming inevitability—with which each essay leads to the next. And just as Hardman asks us to look past our stylistic predilections in order to appreciate the function and even the beauty of Lydgate's seemingly aberrant syntax, so too does this collection ask us to look past the critical predilections that, until very recently, have left Lydgate standing in "the shadow of Chaucer" (p. 6) in order to appreciate the multiple functions—poetic, social, political—and, yes, the beauty of a much-undervalued and still relatively understudied *corpus*. While this volume is not the only participant in the recent and steadily-expanding effort to firmly reestablish Lydgate's work as an object fully deserving of serious scholarly attention, it is certainly the most multifaceted and capacious contribution to that effort to date.

In their introduction, Scanlon and Simpson provide an excellent overview not only of the critical misfortunes that have afflicted the study of Lydgate, but also sketch the critical fortunes of the discipline of medieval literary studies. Noting that Lydgate's work remains "the largest, most underexplored area of Middle English studies," they suggest that the time has now come to "take Lydgate seriously as a major poet" (p. 6). The most important part of this argument for the shape of the rest of the volume is the observation that Lydgate "often served as the mediating voice between one institution and another" (p. 8). In the essays that follow we often find Lydgate standing in the middle—whether in terms of literal structure (as one who, in Hardman's terms, "places himself at the center of meaning in the sentence" [p. 21]), or else, more metaphorically, as one positioned between people and prince (Meyer-Lee, Scanlon, Straker, Simpson), commons and nobility (Simpson, Benson, Nolan), cloister and city (Benson, Nolan), visual performance and verbal text (Nolan), medieval and Renaissance (Summit, Copeland), secular and sacred (Somerset, Nisse), and life and death (Nisse).

Hardman's contribution makes sense of the puzzling mechanics of Lydgate's style in a way few others have been able. Four subsequent essays pick up in a broader sense on her insistence that Lydgate's poetics, rather than an impoverished Chaucerianism characterized by a series of blunders, is in fact a calculated stance designed to produce particular effects. Robert J. Meyer-Lee points to the way Lydgate carves out the role of poet-laureate for himself through a deliberate pose of subjection before his declared (but notably dead) master, Geoffrey Chaucer, and shows how Lydgate fashioned the laureate as "the king's double in the realm of the aesthetic" (p. 52). Larry Scanlon argues for historicizing fifteenth-century poetics so that we see Lydgate's self-advertised dependence on Chaucer on its own terms rather than through our post-Kantian model of aesthetic originality. Scott-Morgan Straker proffers a valuable critique of the truism that Lydgate wrote propaganda for the Lancastrians; in a careful and revisionary reading of three occasional poems, he demonstrates that what looks like royalist propaganda may actually be cautionary advice or civic celebration. James Simpson reads a little-studied poem, the *Churl and the Bird,* against the usual critical grain; he shows that while it *is* a political allegory, an attentive reading uncovers not a reflection of the glories of power, but rather a meditation both on the problems of the poet whose duty it is to speak truth to power as well as on the troubles of those born to carry power's heavy weight upon their shoulders.

With C. David Benson's essay the volume turns from Lydgate's epic and more occasional productions for and about the monarchy to his somewhat more narrowly-focused urban verse. Benson notes that several of Lydgate's short poems do not so much satirize the city as they do those who would undermine its stability. Maura Nolan's essay compares his royal and London mummings and finds the latter operating in the service of an aspiring merchant class as a vehicle for the display of cultural capital; this contribution is especially compelling for the way it raises pressing theoretical questions about the status of the performed and the read, the oral and the written, in the fifteenth century as well as in our own critical practice. A consideration of critical practice past and present also lies at the heart of the essays by Jennifer Summit and Rita Copeland. Summit reads Humphrey of Gloucester's collection of England's first humanist library and his commission of Lydgate's *Fall of Princes* in tandem to show that these were not only chronologically parallel projects but "mutually dependent productions" (p. 208). Just as the ducal library provided a fictional context (as well as literal content) for the poem, she argues, so did the poem provide an English context for the Italian humanism of the library. Where Summit places the medieval and the early modern in dialogue across the institutional space of the library, Copeland positions them vis-à-vis one another within the longer history of rhetoric.

If there is any complaint one might make about this excellent volume, it is that it gives Lydgate's religious poetry rather short shrift; but, no single volume of essays, however varied its set of approaches or choice of texts, could possibly account for the whole of Lydgate's output. In addition, we might take to heart Fiona Somerset's gently made but trenchant point that the critically accepted divide between Lydgate's secular and sacred verse is at best artificial and at worst a barrier to effective reading. Somerset makes this critique through a skillful analysis of the ideologies that motivated Lydgate's production of *St. Edmund and St.*

Fremund for Henry VI. In the volume's final chapter, Ruth Nisse also considers the intersection of the secular and the sacred, but this time from the perspective of Lydgate's monastic career. Nisse's essay is as neat an ending to this collection as one could wish, since it considers the way that Lydgate considered his own end. Arguing that Lydgate's "later works reveal . . . a growing tension between courtly eloquence and contemplative silence" (p. 282), Nisse sees Lydgate, in his *Testament,* perform a renunciation of politics and poetry that trumps anything Chaucer may have been attempting in his *Retraction.* Nisse points out, however, that it is actually the poet's absence from the *Norton Anthology of English Literature* that has silenced him in a way that little else could; this concluding remark, like this volume as a whole, may serve as a clarion call for John Lydgate's reinstatement not only in medieval studies, but also in our discipline as a whole.

LISA H. COOPER
University of Wisconsin–Madison

JAMES SIMPSON. *The Oxford English Literary History, Volume 2, 1350–1547: Reform and Cultural Revolution.* Oxford: Oxford University Press, 2002; paperback, 2004. Pp. xviii, 661. $74.00 cloth, $35.00 paper.

Such a late review of a book that has already received concentrated attention may seem superfluous, but Oxford's earlier reluctance to part with a copy has hitherto left a gap in the review section of *SAC.* The volume was the subject of the Winter 2005 issue of the *Journal of Medieval and Early Modern Studies,* where an impressive group of experts applauded and took potshots in equal measure, and James Simpson responded unapologetically, conceding some details but insisting on his central thesis. For, unlike many literary histories, this book has a central thesis, though it is disguised by his counter-intuitive definitions of the words in the title. "Reform" means not change for the better, or even change, but multiform; "revolution" not the overthrowing of the old but a unifying process of centralization. The multiformedness is exemplified by the period leading up to the Henrician Reformation, and the Revolution is the Reformation in a new guise. What is at issue is far more than just a change of nomenclature, however, and more too than the increasing insistence (evident in David Wallace's much-compared multiauthor *Cambridge History of Medieval English Literature*, or the anthologies edited by Douglas Gray and Derek Pearsall) that early Tudor literature is continuous with late medieval; Simpson argues for a reversal of values, by which he would see, not a literary recession after Chaucer into a dullness reversed only by the advent of humanism, but the fifteenth century as a discursive powerhouse extinguished in the succeeding decades. "Discursive" is his favorite word, and it focuses attention on who controls what is written, proclamations and parliamentary bills as much as the more conventional kinds of literature. The book represents the culmination of Simpson's thinking over many years—half the chapters have had a previous existence in article form—but their convergence here makes it more than the sum of its parts.

So what is in this book for Chaucerians? As Chaucerians, at first glance, less than they might expect: but that is part of its point. Among the applecarts it sets out to overturn is the view of literary history represented by H. S. Bennett's *Chaucer and the Fifteenth Century,* which devoted most of its space to Chaucer; and if Bennett is not much read now, the attitude behind that book still holds too much sway. Chaucer can look after himself; it is the fifteenth century that needs rehabilitation, and Simpson sets out to provide it. The sections on Chaucer are nonetheless important for Simpson's larger thesis, and for his reformulation of the generic divisions of late medieval writing—divisions that cast *Troilus* as tragic, *The Parliament of Fowls* and *The House of Fame* as elegiac, and the *Canterbury Tales* as comedy. The very spread of Chaucer's works across the chapters therefore gives him a key role in the argument about high medieval multiformedness. The new hero of Simpson's book is John Lydgate, whose merits he has been promoting for some years, and who is the only author to get a chapter to himself (though John Leland provides the organizing idea for the opening chapter). Even those of us who believe Lydgate should enjoy a higher profile and an improved reputation may find it hard to follow Simpson all the way here, but given the entrenched nature of the opposition, overstatement may be what is needed to shift opinion. Chaucerians will thus find above all a readjustment of context that makes Chaucer look very different from the traditional figure. His French background effectively disappears (the emphasis on English is dictated by the principles of the series, but it results in some marked distortions); the later poems most closely linked to the "Chaucer tradition," such as *The Flower and the Leaf* and *The Assembly of Ladies,* are reduced to single sentences. He emerges as much attenuated, a supporting actor in a larger discursive drama whose directing energies are those of Lydgate.

If the "literary" aspect of this literary history is displaced by the discursive, the "history" is treated with equal originality. Simpson eschews any kind of chronological organization. Instead, six of the ten chapters offer broad generic divisions—the tragic, elegiac, political, comic, biblical, and dramatic—that run across the grain of a fully historical reading, insofar as perhaps only the biblical, and to a less extent the tragic, would have been recognizable under those names to the original authors and audiences. They thus also go against any understanding of genre as conformity to a horizon of expectation: or rather, the horizon is a modern one, and nonetheless challenging for that. Three of the terms, however, evoke a classicism that the evidence does not really support. In the cases of the tragic and comic, Simpson offers redefinitions that make good sense in medieval terms; but in the case of the elegiac, he stresses an Ovidianism that is fully applicable only to a handful of the texts he discusses and that tends to distort much of the poetry that he draws into his purview. Here too the erasure of the French context tends to skew the chapter away from a full historical contextualization. Simpson's concern with the engagement of literature with its historical moment can indeed sometimes militate against an engagement with how it presented itself at the time. Ecclesiology is a major theme—inevitably so, given the current interest in Lollardy (well evidenced in Simpson's own earlier work) and the book's larger thesis about the role of the Henrician Reformation; but piety, the everyday practice of devotion, largely disappears. Arundel's suppression of discursive freedoms also gets discussed surprisingly late in the work, perhaps because it is at odds with the argument that Henry's comparable suppression was unprecedented. Simpson's reading of at least some of the cycle plays as evidence for the continued vibrancy of religious literature outside direct church control is, however, surely right (as is his carrying the story of biblical drama through to John Bale), though he is reluctant to make the same argument for their survival into the later sixteenth century.

It will be evident that the book invites argument, in a way that few other literary histories either desire or could dream of achieving. The swarm of reviewers and commentators around it, myself included, resemble iron filings trying not to realign themselves too perfectly with the new magnetic field that Simpson has created. The book is hugely well informed, genuinely illuminating, full of sharp *aperçus,* and challenging in inspirational ways. His thesis, however, does not seem to leave any possibility for the Elizabethan reflorescence of literature to happen: his surprise at the long survival of the cycle plays, for instance, is witness to a reluctance to allow that multiformedness had not become extinct by 1547, and according to this account romance died out with Henry's censorship of the press. That was not how Spenser and Shakespeare experienced their English literary history—though that would require another volume to explore.

HELEN COOPER
Magdalene College, Cambridge

A. C. SPEARING. *Textual Subjectivity: The Encoding of Subjectivity in Medieval Narratives and Lyrics.* New York: Oxford University Press, 2005. Pp. vi, 273. $95.00.

A. C. Spearing's new book revises, develops, and collects a series of articles published from 1992 to 2001 into a general theory about who is addressing the reader(s) in medieval narrative and lyric poetry. Twentieth-century criticism, following the influential readings of Chaucer by G. L. Kittredge and E. T. Donaldson, has sought to identify and interpret a unique spoken voice in the text such as "Chaucer the Pilgrim" in the *Canterbury Tales,* a fictional persona whom the perceptive reader supposedly distinguished from "Chaucer the Poet." Spearing sets out to show how, in search of supposed irony at the expense of a "fallible narrator," such readings often distort and diminish the richness and subtlety of medieval narrative.

Spearing begins by defining his title, which refers not to the way "poems express or represent individual subjectivities, whether of their writers or of fictional characters, but how subjectivity is encoded in them as a textual phenomenon" (p. 1). The introductory chapter introduces readers unfamiliar with "the theoretical landscape" (presumably these include most of the subscribers to *SAC*). Following Derrida, Spearing challenges Saussure's dictum that "writing is nothing but the representation of speech" (p. 5) and the assumption that any "narrative" necessarily presupposes a "narrator." Medieval authors, he reminds us, are constantly referring to old stories told or written by storytellers in a distant and indefinite past.

A chapter on "Romances" demonstrates convincingly that nothing in *King Horn,* where the storyteller's "I" addresses the audience only at the beginning and end, "serves to individualize any narrating person as part of the poetic text" (p. 45). The more frequent interventions of the first person in *Havelock* reveal "less a single narrator than a series of narrating 'I's enacting a variety of different roles" (p. 52).

Troilus and Criseyde, of course, has inspired a vastly larger body of criticism following E. T. Donaldson's influential writings. With respectful attention to Donaldson's own nuanced readings of the "narrator," Spearing effectively demonstrates through close readings of the poem that "we find not a single shaping subjectivity but the traces of many different centres of consciousness" (p. 95). To reduce these to the fallible consciousness of a single "narrator" is to weaken and diminish Chaucer's work.

The *Canterbury Tales* is primarily represented by *The Man of Law's Tale,* one that, Spearing suggests, some Chaucerians do not much care for and have sought to salvage by arguing that the tale conveys the shortcomings of its narrator. Spearing points to the textual evidence that "Chaucer had not settled on a pilgrim teller" for the tale, which he ultimately assigned to the Man of Law. And he demonstrates that critics spoil one of Chaucer's better tales of "moralitee and hoolynesse" by forcing upon it ironies found in the Sergeant of the Law's portrait. In an aside, Spearing mentions that "Chaucer was truly interested in the possibility of connections between stories and their tellers, and voiced narratives and unreliable narrators are the ultimate outcome of the process he set going" (p. 120). A reader might wish Spearing had analyzed at least one such voiced narrative, say *The Miller's Tale* or *The Wife of Bath's Prologue* and *Tale.* To what extent were these texts told in the pilgrim's own voice?

The chapter "Narration in the *Pearl* Poet" introduces a distinction in "first person" narrative between "heterodiegesis," where the "I" represents different subjectivities as it does in *The Man of Law's Tale* or *Sir Gawain and the Green Knight,* and "homodiegesis" ("same-narrating"), where a unique "I" represents a character narrating the story of his own experience (p. 148). The distinction is made primarily for the sake of *Pearl,* where the profound emotional impact of that work is lost when a critic tries to turn the grieving father into an obtuse narrator unable to grasp how his beloved child has become a heavenly queen. Spearing movingly shows how the true power of *Pearl* depends on our identification with the dreamer and, at the end, the realization of our own inability, except in dream or poetry, to cross the stream and to experience the ultimate communion except "in the forme of bred and wyn."

The final two chapters deal, respectively, with courtly lyrics and specifically with those in epistolary form, particularly the poetry of Charles of Orleans. Here there is not much commentary to argue against— except for Chaucer's *Complaint unto Pity,* which is, for a change, given credit for wit that does not come at the expense of a persona invented by Chaucer or one of his critics.

"Studies questioning the validity of the narrator theory," writes Spearing, "have largely fallen on deaf ears" (p. 76), and at times he sounds slightly exasperated at having to deal with the proliferation of articles promoting that theory: "No reader need ever be at a loss for new theories about the connections between a tale and its teller, and thus the supply of original articles and books need never dry up—an obvious advantage when the great majority of readers of Chaucer (again especially perhaps in America) are academics whose careers depend on their production of articles and books that purport to give original readings" (p. 105).

One study of Chaucer's works "questioning the validity of the narrator theory" that has fallen upon a deaf ear in Spearing happens to be my own book *The Strumpet Muse* (1976). In the chapter entitled "Cracks in the Frame of Illusion," I argued at length against the theory that Chaucer assumes a consistent narrative persona in the *Canterbury Tales,* although, like many authors who present their works to a live audience, Chaucer tends to assume a stage presence that need not be consistent or serious and is also capable, as in the ending of *Troilus,* of expressing deep feeling. But *The Strumpet Muse* has apparently fallen through the cracks of *Textual Subjectivity.*

The same thing has happened to Donald R. Howard's concept of "Unimpersonated Artistry" (in *The Idea of the Canterbury Tales,* 1976). There is, of course, a difference between what Spearing is advocating here, namely. that the encoding of subjectivity is textual and virtual—as is certainly true—and Howard's position and mine that it could also be phenomenal and human. In short, I have long agreed with the essence of Spearing's attack on "narrator theory," though at the time the theoretical sophistication of "Textual Subjectivity" was not yet available, and my disagreement with that theory had a different basis.

In fairness, I must quote a disclaimer Spearing makes in a footnote to his chapter on *The Man of Law's Tale:* "My purpose here is not to demonstrate my superiority over these scholars (I must be guilty of at least as many errors), but to argue that failure to achieve perfection is characteristic of human authors, not merely of fictional narrators" (p. 116). To that we may all say, "Amen!"

ALFRED DAVID
Indiana University

PAUL STROHM. *Politique: Languages of Statecraft between Chaucer and Shakespeare.* Notre Dame: Notre Dame University Press, 2005. Pp. ix, 298. $27.50 paper, $55.00 cloth.

Chaucer and Shakespeare, like parallel mountain ranges, have cast a deep shadow over everything between them. In recent years, critical exploration has discovered that this territory is not uniformly dark and arid. The period's reputation for "dullness" has been revealed as a mask for writing that is anything but dull. Paul Strohm's new volume contributes to the illumination and irrigation of this hidden territory, revealing it to contain fertile ground for critical inquiry. The particular focus of *Politique* is on "mainly vernacular English political texts" (p. 1) and on "performative or action-seeking languages" and "symbolic deeds and events" that "create something new" (p. 9).

Politique, the word that gives the book its title, is the focus of the first chapter, "*Politique* Perjury in the *Arrivall* of Edward IV." *The Historie of the Arrivall of King Edward IV* (usefully reprinted here in an appendix) is an English prose account of the return in 1471 of Edward IV from exile to take the throne again. In Strohm's analysis, *politiqwe* in the *Arrivall* means "shrewd," "diplomatic," rather than (as previously) "pertaining to governance"; it is part of an analytical vocabulary that enables the *Arrivall* author to pursue his own and his audience's interests in "calculation and naked self-interest" (p. 44), interests that anticipate those of Shakespeare's histories. Like Henry Bolingbroke, Edward landed at Ravenspur and evaded resistance by maintaining that he only intended to claim his dukedom. But whereas earlier pro-Lancastrian chroniclers were embarrassed by Bolingbroke's subterfuge, the *Arrivall* author depicts Edward's parallel action as "politically astute behaviour" (p. 32), exemplifying, Strohm claims, a "pre-Machiavellian moment" (p. 35).

In "Lydgate and the Rise of *Pollecie* in the *Mirror* Tradition," Strohm analyses responses to Boccaccio's *De Casibus Virorum Illustrium* and its genre. The pilgrims' response to Chaucer's *Monk's Tale* has often been used to confirm that misfortune makes tedious narratives (Greg Doran's Royal Shakespeare Company production of the complete *Tales* brilliantly had the Monk recite during the interval; when the audience returns, the Monk is still performing and the pilgrims are asleep). In Strohm's analysis, far from being boring, the genre was "disturbing" for readers in the fifteenth and sixteenth centuries who wished to analyze the practical steps (*pollecie,* now "prudence" as much as "good governance") that they might take to remedy the effects of Fortune. Strohm locates the first signs of the shift of perspective on Fortune in Laurent de Premierfait's version of Boccaccio's text, and in Lydgate's reworking of Laurent. He suggests that an unbroken tradition stretches from Lydgate to the sixteenth century; to the *Mirror for Magistrates,* the updated sequel to Lydgate published in 1559 and 1563, and to Shakespeare's *Henry VI, part 3.*

A chapter on Fortescue and Pecock identifies both as "parcyalle" men who described the state in the language of natural reason and were forced to recant their writings. Fortescue was able to retract his support for the Lancastrians by claiming that his political writings about the Yorkist claim to the throne were shaped by partisan interests. Partisanship and self-interestedness are the dark side, according to Strohm, of the state as described in Fortescue's reasoned analysis. The parallel with Pecock seems a little strained, since in Pecock's writings descriptions of governance and society are figures illustrating his theological arguments rather than his primary focus, and, though there is plenty of evidence that Pecock's prosecution was politically interested—that he had to contend with *parcyalle* men—Strohm does not, I think, provide conclusive evidence that Pecock's opponents represented him as *parcyalle.*

While chapter 3 treats two huge corpora of vernacular prose, chapter 4 focuses on two short political poems, *Balat set upponne the yates of Caunterbury* and *The Holkham Verses.* Like the *Arrivall,* neither text is particularly well known or easy of access, and Strohm sensibly reprints them in appendices to the chapter. The focus of analysis is on their representation of a Yorkist king's accession to the throne. Each poem deploys "ideologically charged materials" (liturgy, the royal entry symbolism, prophecy) to attempt to call into existence a political community, with varying success. The *Balat,* dated 1460, anticipates the coming of Richard Duke of York; the Holkham verses, dated 1461, although written after Richard's death and the coronation of his son as Edward IV, still finds the accession of a Yorkist king "unrepresentable."

Chronicle accounts of the death of Richard Duke of York in which Richard's decapitated head is displayed at York wearing a "paper crown" (in earlier texts variously a *carta,* and a circlet made of reeds) are the subject of chapter 5. Tracing accounts of this legend through "Holinshed" to Shakespeare and the seventeenth-century *Eikon Basilike,* Strohm explores how the religious (the Christological reference to the crown of thorns) continues to permeate the realm of secular politics.

Each chapter does service by bringing to attention neglected texts and subjecting them to searching, deeply considered, and highly original analysis. They deserve the serious attention of all literary scholars—and historians—of the period. I have, though, some reservations about the way the material has been structured as a book. The volume is based on Strohm's three Conway Lectures, which he delivered at the University of Notre Dame in 2003, augmented with other material. The volume has been provided with the features of a monograph—an introduction that sets out starting points, questions, and an agenda, a postscript, a glossarial index of vernacular political terminology, and an index—but these elements are in tension with the clear signs of its genesis as separate pieces. In the introduction we are promised that we shall be shown "the beginnings of a new language of politics" (p. 13), "the barest beginnings . . . [of] a separation of the political and religious realms"(p. 16), and "the contours of an emerging fifteenth-century public sphere." These topics are present in the chapters that follow, but there is no overarching thesis, narrative, or theory, such as the Lacanian program that underpins Strohm's book on the earlier fifteenth century, *England's Empty Throne.* Cross-references between chapters are minimal; for example, the chapter on the Yorkist verses recapitulates material on Bolingbroke's perjury without reference to the discussion of this material in the first chapter (p. 184), and the chapter on the paper crown returns to the *Arrivall* and the *Mirror for Magistrates* without properly acknowledging that there has been extensive discussion of these texts in earlier chapters. Notre Dame's series editors may have been better advised not to try to turn a series of lectures into a monograph, but to have published them as a collection of independent essays. For the chapters of *Politique* are, in the fullest sense, "essays." Individually, they bring into brilliant focus some of the most neglected and little-known texts of the period. Collectively, they illustrate the difficulties future scholars will face when they try to find a compelling framework within which to view this challenging material as a whole.

WENDY SCASE
University of Birmingham

CAROLYNN VAN DYKE. *Chaucer's Agents: Cause and Representation in Chaucerian Narrative.* Madison and Teaneck, N.J.: Fairleigh Dickinson University Press, 2005. Pp. 371. $63.50.

Carolynn Van Dyke justly observes that, although examinations of agency and subjectivity have been productive for Chaucer critics, such studies often slide into generalizations or vaguely psychoanalytic interpretations of either character or author. She sets out to redress this problem by synthesizing a concept of agency from a stimulating variety of critical contexts, including literary theory, philosophy, computer science, legal studies, social sciences, and business (no doubt relying partly on her own varied experience as a scholar of computer science as well as literary studies). Agency, as Van Dyke conceives it, "need not be human, social, or even animate" (p. 17), nor does it need to be intentional or autonomous. Ultimately, however, this definition of agency is so capacious that it becomes less rather than more useful. While it does allow consideration of an array of unusual agents, this inclusive notion of agency is difficult to pin down in any meaningfully specific way and, as a result, exercises of agency often escape detailed examination. Van Dyke's individual readings tend to focus instead on Chaucer's multivalent characterizations of various agents.

The first chapter establishes this definition of agency and examines its theoretical and historical contexts. Van Dyke identifies several crises of agency in late medieval culture, including divisions of power within spiritual and secular hierarchies, the philosophical debate between Scholastic Realism and Nominalism, and conflicting ideas about authorship and textual authority. She concludes somewhat reductively that Chaucer's representations of agency, which are multiple and shifting, reflect these contemporary circumstances.

Each of the subsequent chapters takes up a different type of agent in relation to the particular genres within which Chaucer deployed it; the three immediately following the introduction exploit the space opened up by a broader definition of agency to consider allegorical figures, animals, and pagan gods. Chapter 2 focuses on allegory, tracing Boethius's influence on Chaucer's polysemous allegorical narratives and insisting that they are among his most artistically mature and aesthetically accomplished works. Van Dyke uses three dream visions—the *House of Fame,* the *Parliament of Fowls,* and the *Legend of Good Women*—to demonstrate that Chaucer employs allegory to represent universal agency even as he particularizes such agency and problematizes it through parody, ambiguity, and irony.

The third chapter engages provocatively with the literary and philosophical debate during the Middle Ages over animal agency as either completely absent or anthropomorphically complex, suggesting that Chaucer's representations of animals draw not on human characteristics but on "zoological reality" and that, "paradoxically, he thereby blurs the boundaries between their agency and ours" (p. 106). Van Dyke shows that *The Squire's Tale* translates the falcon and her agency so completely into the human world that any meaningful avian equivalent is lost, whereas *The Nun's Priest's Tale* reveals Pertelote and Chauntecleer to have an agency that seems both familiarly subjective and fundamentally appropriate to their animal natures. The chapter concludes with *The Manciple's Tale,* reading it as an example of how human and animal agents can fall or fail but may thereby gain a kind of liberty.

Chapter 4 takes up the acknowledged problems that medieval Christian authors faced when working with pagan elements of classical literature, but views those problems through the filter of agency. Van Dyke argues that pagan gods were treated with a kind of "theological ambivalence" even in classical texts and that Chaucer recognizes and re-creates this (p. 114). She examines a wide variety of texts, including dream visions, two of the *Canterbury Tales,* and *Troilus and Criseyde,* but can draw only speculative conclusions about the relationship between paganism and Christianity, Chaucer's attitude toward divinity, and medieval readers' reception of such portrayals.

The next pair of chapters returns to more familiar ground by emphasizing human agents. Van Dyke is particularly interested in representations of female agency, contending that it disproves "the assumption that individual intention is the fundamental level of agency in Chaucerian narrative" (p. 148). Chapter 5 concerns what she terms "exemplary agents," including figures from tales by the Clerk, Franklin, Man of Law, Prioress, and Second Nun, while chapter 6 treats two "subjective agents," the Wife of Bath and Criseyde. The consideration of female agency begins with a survey of historical representations of femininity, which Van Dyke oversimplifies as "monolithic" (p. 154). However, chapter 5 demonstrates that Chaucer's romance heroines perform as both literary stereotypes and individual subjects and that, among his martyrs and female saints, only Cecilia acts directly (albeit as a conduit for divine agency); the others actively disclaim agency and then paradoxically act through passivity. These exemplary agents thus disrupt their own stories. Similarly, chapter 6 examines the ways in which the Wife of Bath and Criseyde act as both objects and subjects. Van Dyke concludes that these shifts also disrupt readers' subjectivity by encouraging and then undermining our empathy for and identification with these ambiguous female characters.

Chapter 7 examines Chaucer's authorial agency. Van Dyke suggests that agency offers a way to reconsider the status of authorship in the wake of poststructuralism and argues that authorial agency is marked off by "its inherent claim to an impossible hegemony," a claim with which Chaucer plays (p. 224). She examines the interactions of poet and persona in the *Book of the Duchess* and the *Canterbury Tales,* tracing the attribution of particular narrative or descriptive elements to different voices; the issue becomes particularly relevant, she demonstrates, in those tales that critics have judged to be distasteful, inferior, or anomalous. The concluding chapter reaffirms the multiplicity of Chaucerian agency and relates it to the debate over free will. Chaucer uses what Van Dyke names "representational agency," which both acts directly and confers agency on other figures. This agency also acts on Chaucer's readers and, the book concludes, "Because he shapes what binds us, he is our agent of freedom" (p. 275).

As its title indicates, this project is more about agents than agency. But its focus on agents renders the analysis vulnerable to the very weakness that Van Dyke identified in earlier studies by reducing the complicated concept of agency to questions of characterization and voice. Throughout, however, the book is enlivened by the comprehensive context within which it positions its explorations of agency. In the final analysis, *Chaucer's Agents* demonstrates that broadening our set of critical and theoretical references can inform as well as challenge our interpretive practices.

TARA WILLIAMS
Oregon State University

DAVID WALLACE. *Premodern Places: Calais to Surinam, Chaucer to Aphra Behn*. Oxford: Blackwell Publishing, 2004. Pp. ix, 342. $34.95, paper and $73.95, cloth.

It is impossible not to reflect on the process of reading David Wallace's *Premodern Places*. Umberto Eco famously commented that the first hundred pages of *The Name of the Rose* served as a kind of initiation rite for his readers: if you could only get through these, you were somehow fitted, or trained, to read the rest of the novel. Reading *Premodern Places* provides almost the opposite experience: I almost felt I had to unlearn how to read.

Reading this book in my formal academic way (what are the assumptions and arguments that drive the work? what does it omit or repress? how can I use it for my own work?) initially led to some anxiety, since at one level the book proceeds by suggestive indirection rather than conventional argument, by mimesis rather than diegesis. The introduction does, however, provide all the clues one needs to become Wallace's ideal reader. These pages range from autobiographical (transatlantic) narrative to theoretical reflections on times and places within the rough geographical and historical limits set out in the title: Calais to Surinam, Chaucer to Aphra Behn. We might, indeed, add a third, methodological frame: Benjamin to Barthes. Wallace articulates a relationship between Barthes's *punctum* and Benjamin's emphasis on the constellation of past and present in a "flash" of illumination, to frame his meditations on places chosen in part—and this is crucial to the book's organization—because they no longer produce the symbolic resonance they once did. "Narratives of outward expansion and homeward return, of translation and conversion, have designs on these places, but each place interpellates or buttonholes us with its own images and tales, distracting us from grander visions of geographical space and historical process" (p. 2).

Admitting to the ease of becoming distracted, of bringing our own feelings and emotions about places (p. 16) into play, releases the reader into the pleasurable Barthesian leisure of following the movement of texts, people, and ideas as Wallace, our time-travel tour guide, takes us to his six locations—Calais, Flanders, Somerset, Genoa, the Canary Islands, and Surinam—and back and forward across the medieval, the early modern, and the modern, frequently exceeding the chronological boundaries implied in his title. For example, chapter 3, "Dante in Somerset," begins with traces of a lost manuscript of Giovanni Bertoldi's Latin translation (1416) of the *Commedia* that, according to John Leland, once graced the Cathedral library at Wells; considers the Council of Constance, where Bertoldi completed the translation, as a center for cultural exchange; tracks Bertoldi's consciousness of England and northern Europe as an important reception context for Dante and the ironic complexities of using Latin as the means for such dissemination; explores the depths of readership and literacy at Wells (Polydore Vergil was appointed archdeacon there in 1508); ponders the possibility of a twinned English reception of Dante as both Catholic and proto-Wycliffite; describes the "psychotic demands" (p. 161) of John Leland's adulation for the king, who causes the destruction of the books he loves; and finally, via Coleridge's admittedly rather tenuous links with the Bristol-based slave trade, offers a meditation on the means by which "certain ghostly figures—Dante, black slaves—fade from the scene" of Somerset (p. 166), leaving only the impoverished cultural stereotype of provincial England.

For *Premodern Places* is a book about cultural memory, but it is also about cultural forgetting. What do we remember and forget, from the Middle Ages through to the present, about all these places? One of the most powerful threads running through the whole book is the forgotten history of premodern slavery in Europe. The history of Genoa and its trafficking in goods and people, for example, becomes a compelling example of what we repress about the Renaissance: "The study of Genoa continually confronts us with historical practices (enslavement, forced conversion, colonization) upon which cultural history has chosen not to dwell. If Florence—with its glorious efflorescences of painting, building, humanism, and literature—represents the superego of an emergent Renaissance, Genoa—always present, if out of sight—forms the id" (p. 187).

Wallace's practical method is dizzying, as he moves through what must be an extraordinary archive of filing cabinets filled with photographs, maps, references and allusions to events, emotions and memories of these six locations across several centuries, and from many different kinds of writing. He lays a rich and fascinating wealth of material before us in this book as he traces the patterns of remembering and forgetting that influence the cultural histories of place and period.

This is not a narrative strategy without risk, however. *Premodern Places* is a wonderful and practical exercise in the multiple temporalities invoked by postcolonial criticism, in critiques of periodization, and especially by scholars working in the fascinating territory between the late medieval and the early modern, a problem neatly solved by the inclusive "premodern" of its title. It is a book preeminently concerned with the shaping power of broad cultural forces, and many will find it an inspiring, even liberating project in uncovering multiple forgotten histories, places, and voices. Wallace is interested, after all, in the way literary scholars can sometimes fall silent, and let texts speak "in the past's own idiom"; indeed, he gives the last word of his book to the pseudonymous poet "Tryphossa," writing in 1973, in the hybrid language Sranan: "Èn beybi-Jesus krey a fosi: yè-è-è."

Nevertheless, the book depends on an extraordinary mastery in marshaling and organizing its materials. Wallace's narrative voice is engagingly candid and modest, but the hand of the *compilator* remains firmly in control. Moreover, the impulse to write of the superego and the id of the Renaissance, for example, to speak so broadly of what history, or cultural history, represses, skirts dangerously close to reinstituting the unfashionable grand narratives of modernism and colonialism. Perhaps it is impossible to write this kind of long history without such perspectives. *Premodern Places* will undoubtedly stand for a long time as an important test case for this method.

STEPHANIE TRIGG
The University of Melbourne

559

Books Received

Adams, Jenny. *Power Play: The Literature and Politics of Chess in the Late Middle Ages*. Philadelphia: University of Pennsylvania Press, 2006. Pp. 250. $49.95.

Altmann, Barbara K., and R. Barton Palmer, ed. *An Anthology of Medieval Debate Poetry*. Gainesville: University Press of Florida, 2006. Pp. xii, 393. $39.95.

Birkholz, Daniel. *The King's Two Maps: Cartography and Culture in Thirteenth-Century England*. New York: Routledge, 2004. Pp. xxxv, 254. $70.00.

Blumenfeld-Kosinski, Renate. *Poets, Saints, and Visionaries of the Great Schism, 1378–1417*. University Park: Penn State University Press, 2006. Pp xiii, 240. $45.00.

Bolduc, Michelle. *The Medieval Poetics of Contraries*. Gainesville: University Press of Florida, 2006. Pp. xv, 304. $65.00.

Clarke, Catherine A. M. *Literary Landscapes and the Idea of England, 700–1400*. Cambridge: D. S. Brewer, 2006. Pp. xii, 160. $80.00.

Cohen, Jeffrey Jerome. *Hybridity, Identity, and Monstrosity in Medieval Britain: On Difficult Middles*. New York: Palgrave Macmillan, 2006. Pp. viii. $75.00.

Glaser, Joseph, trans. *Le Morte D'Arthur, Or the Whole Book of King Arthur and of His Noble Knights of the Round Table, By Sir Thomas Malory*. Chandler, Ariz.: Pegasus Press, 2005. Pp. xviii, 357. $19.95 paper.

Gil, Daniel Juan. *Before Intimacy: Asocial Sexuality in Early Modern England*. Minneapolis: University of Minnesota Press, 2006. Pp. xvi, 187. $66.00 cloth, $22.00 paper.

Hamaguchi, Keiko. *Chaucer and Women*. Tokyo: Eihosha, 2005. Pp. xii, 168.

————. *Non-European Women in Chaucer: A Postcolonial Study*. Studies in English Medieval Language and Literature 14. Frankfurt-am-Main: Peter Lang, 2006. Pp. ix, 194. $43.95.

Hamer, Richard. Edited with the assistance of Vida Russell. *Gilte Legende*, vol. 1. EETS, o.s., 327. New York: Oxford University Press, 2006. Pp. xvi, 496. $115.00.

Horner, Patrick J. *A Macaronic Sermon Collection from Late Medieval England: Oxford, MS Bodley 649*. Toronto: Pontifical Institute of Mediaeval Studies, 2006. Pp. viii, 544. $94.95.

Kerby-Fulton, Kathryn. *Books Under Suspicion: Censorship and Tolerance of Revelatory Writing in Late Medieval England*. Notre Dame: Notre Dame University Press, 2006. Pp. lii, 562. $50.00.

Kibler, William W., and Leslie Zarker Morgan, ed. *Approaches to Teaching the "Song of Roland."* New York: Modern Language Association of America, 2006. Pp. viii, 317. $37.50 cloth, $19.75 paper.

Lees, Claire A., and Gillian Overing, ed. *A Place to Believe In: Locating Medieval Landscapes*. University Park: Penn State University Press, 2006. Pp. vix, 272. $65.00 cloth, $25.00 paper.

Lutton, Robert. *Lollardy and Orthodox Religion in Pre-Reformation England*. Woodbridge, Suffolk, and Rochester, N.Y.: Boydell Press for The Royal Historical Society, 2006. Pp. ix, 236. $80.00.

Lynch, Kathryn L., ed. *Geoffrey Chaucer: Dream Visions and Other Poems*. New York: W. W. Norton, 2007. Pp. xx, 396. $10.50 paper.

McDonald, Nicola. *Medieval Obscenities*. York: York Medieval Press, 2006. Pp. viii, 210. $80.00.

Mann, Jill, and Maura Nolan, ed. *The Text in the Community: Essays on Medieval Works, Manuscripts, Authors, and Readers*. Notre Dame:

Notre Dame University Press, 2006. Pp. xv, 296. $75.00 cloth, $37.00 paper.

Masciandaro, Nicola. *The Voice of the Hammer: The Meaning of Work in Middle English Literature*. Notre Dame: Notre Dame University Press, 2006. Pp. xii, 209. $25.00 paper.

Millett, Bella, ed. *Ancrene Wisse: A Corrected Edition of the Test in Cambridge, Corpus Christi College, MS 402, With Variants From Other Manuscripts*. EETS, o.s., 325. New York: Oxford University Press, 2005. Pp. lxxiv, 254. $125.00.

Patterson, Lee, ed. *Geoffrey Chaucer's Canterbury Tales: A Casebook*. New York: Oxford University Press, 2007. Pp. x, 241. $35.00 paper.

Poor, Sara S., and Jana K. Schulman, ed. *Women and Medieval Epic: Gender, Genre, and the Limits of Masculinity*. New York: Palgrave Macmillan, 2007. Pp. xii, 299. $74.95.

Schibanoff, Susan. *Chaucer's Queer Poetics: Reading the Dream Trio*. Toronto: University of Toronto Press, 2006. Pp. x, 365. $75.00.

Sargent, Michael G., ed. *Nicholas Love: The Mirror of the Blessed Life of Jesus Christ: A Full Critical Edition*. Exeter: University of Exeter Press, 2005. Pp. 433. $100.00.

Stein, Robert M. *Reality Fictions: Romance, History, and Governmental Authority, 1025–1180*. Notre Dame: Notre Dame University Press, 2006. Pp. ix, 294. $30.00 paper.

Strohm, Paul. *England's Empty Throne: Usurpation and the Language of Legitimation, 1399–1422*. 2nd ed. Notre Dame: Notre Dame University Press, 2006. Pp. xviii, 274. $27.50 paper.

Tavormina, M. Teresa, ed. *Sex, Aging, and Death in A Medieval Compendium: Trinity College Cambridge MS R.14.52, Its Texts, Language, and Scribe*. Medieval and Renaissance Texts and Studies, 292. Vols. 1 and 2. Tempe: Arizona Center for Medieval and Renaissance Studies, 2006. Pp. xxvi, 454, and Pp. iii, 930. $110.00.

Trigg, Stephanie, ed. *Medievalism and the Gothic in Australian Culture*. Turnhout, Beligium: Brepols, 2005. Pp. xxiii, 302. $75.00.

Turner, Marion. *Chaucerian Conflict: Languages of Antagonism in Late Fourteenth-Century London*. Oxford: Clarendon Press, 2007. Pp. ix, 213. $95.00.

Watson, Nicholas, and Jacqueline Jenkins, ed. *The Writings of Julian of Norwich*. University Park: Penn State University Press, 2006. Pp. xii, 474. $65.00.

Whitelock, Jill, ed. *The Seven Sages of Rome (Midland Version)*. EETS, o.s., 324. New York: Oxford University Press, 2005. Pp. lxxx, 182. $90.00.

Winstead, Karen A. *John Capgrave's Fifteenth Century*. Philadelphia: University of Pennsylvania Press, 2007. Pp. xiii, 231. $55.00.

Yeager, R. F., ed. and trans. *John Gower: The Minor Latin Works* with *In Praise of Peace* edited by Michael Livingston. Kalamazoo: Medieval Institute Publications, 2005. Pp. vii, 139. $14.00 paper.

An Annotated Chaucer Bibliography 2005

Compiled and edited by Mark Allen and Bege K. Bowers

Regular contributors:

Bruce W. Hozeski, *Ball State University* (Indiana)
George Nicholas, *Benedictine College* (Kansas)
Marilyn Sutton, *California State University at Dominguez Hills*
Gregory M. Sadlek, *Cleveland State University* (Ohio)
David Sprunger, *Concordia College* (Minnesota)
Winthrop Wetherbee, *Cornell University* (New York)
Elizabeth Dobbs, *Grinnell College* (Iowa)
Teresa P. Reed, *Jacksonville State University* (Alabama)
William Snell, *Keio University* (Japan)
Denise Stodola, *Kettering University* (Michigan)
Brian A. Shaw, *London, Ontario*
William Schipper, *Memorial University* (Newfoundland, Canada)
Martha Rust, *New York University*
Warren S. Moore, III, *Newberry College* (South Carolina)
Amy Goodwin, *Randolph-Macon College* (Virginia)
Cindy L. Vitto, *Rowan College of New Jersey*
Richard H. Osberg, *Santa Clara University* (California)
Brother Anthony (Sonjae An), *Sogang University* (South Korea)
Anne Thornton, *Tufts University* (Massachusetts)
Martine Yvernault, *Université de Limoges*
Margaret Connolly, *University College, Cork* (Ireland)
R. D. Eaton, *Universiteit van Amsterdam* (the Netherlands)
Mary Flowers Braswell and Elaine Whitaker, *University of Alabama at Birmingham*
Stefania D'Agata D'Ottavi, *University of Macerata* (Italy)
Cynthia Ho, *University of North Carolina, Asheville*
Richard J. Utz, *University of Northern Iowa*
Rebecca Beal, *University of Scranton* (Pennsylvania)

Mark Allen, R. L. Smith, and Elaine Wong, *University of Texas at San Antonio*
Joerg O. Fichte, *Universität Tübingen* (Tübingen, Germany)
John M. Crafton, *West Georgia College*
Robert Correale, *Wright State University* (Ohio)
Bege K. Bowers, *Youngstown State University* (Ohio)

Ad hoc contributions were made Brian S. Lee (University of Cape Town) and Jesús L. Serrano-Reyes. The bibliographers acknowledge with gratitude the MLA typesimulation provided by the Center for Bibliographical Services of the Modern Language Association; postage from the University of Texas at San Antonio Department of English, Classics, and Philosophy; and assistance from the library staff, especially Susan Mc-Cray, at the University of Texas at San Antonio.

This bibliography continues the bibliographies published since 1975 in previous volumes of *Studies in the Age of Chaucer*. Bibliographic information up to 1975 can be found in Eleanor P. Hammond, *Chaucer: A Bibliographic Manual* (1908; reprint, New York: Peter Smith, 1933); D. D. Griffith, *Bibliography of Chaucer, 1908–1953* (Seattle: University of Washington Press, 1955); William R. Crawford, *Bibliography of Chaucer, 1954–63* (Seattle: University of Washington Press, 1967); and Lorrayne Y. Baird, *Bibliography of Chaucer, 1964–1973* (Boston: G. K. Hall, 1977). See also Lorrayne Y. Baird-Lange and Hildegard Schnuttgen, *Bibliography of Chaucer, 1974–1985* (Hamden, Conn.: Shoe String Press, 1988); and Bege K. Bowers and Mark Allen, eds., *Annotated Chaucer Bibliography, 1986–1996* (Notre Dame, Ind.: University of Notre Dame, 2002).

Additions and corrections to this bibliography should be sent to Mark Allen, Bibliographic Division, The New Chaucer Society, Department of English, Classics, and Philosophy, University of Texas at San Antonio 78249-0643 (Fax: 210-458-5366; e-mail: mark.allen@utsa.edu). An electronic version of this bibliography (1975–2005) is available via The New Chaucer Society Web page at <http://artsci.wustl.edu/~chaucer/> or directly at <http://uchaucer.utsa.edu>. Authors are urged to send annotations for articles, reviews, and books that have been or might be overlooked.

Classifications

Abbreviations of Chaucer's Works

ABC	*An ABC*
Adam	*Adam Scriveyn*
Anel	*Anelida and Arcite*
Astr	*A Treatise on the Astrolabe*
Bal Compl	*A Balade of Complaint*
BD	*The Book of the Duchess*
Bo	*Boece*
Buk	*The Envoy to Bukton*
CkT, CkP, Rv–CkL	*The Cook's Tale, The Cook's Prologue, Reeve–Cook Link*
ClT, ClP, Cl–MerL	*The Clerk's Tale, The Clerk's Prologue, Clerk–Merchant Link*
Compl d'Am	*Complaynt d'Amours*
CT	*The Canterbury Tales*
CYT, CYP	*The Canon's Yeoman's Tale, The Canon's Yeoman's Prologue*
Equat	*The Equatorie of the Planetis*
For	*Fortune*
Form Age	*The Former Age*
FranT, FranP	*The Franklin's Tale, The Franklin's Prologue*
FrT, FrP, Fr–SumL	*The Friar's Tale, The Friar's Prologue, Friar–Summoner Link*
Gent	*Gentilesse*
GP	*The General Prologue*
HF	*The House of Fame*
KnT, Kn–MilL	*The Knight's Tale, Knight–Miller Link*
Lady	*A Complaint to His Lady*
LGW, LGWP	*The Legend of Good Women, The Legend of Good Women Prologue*
ManT, ManP	*The Manciple's Tale, The Manciple's Prologue*
Mars	*The Complaint of Mars*
Mel, Mel–MkL	*The Tale of Melibee, Melibee–Monk Link*
MercB	*Merciles Beaute*
MerT, MerE–SqH	*The Merchant's Tale, Merchant Endlink–Squire Headlink*

MilT, MilP, Mil–RvL	*The Miller's Tale, The Miller's Prologue, Miller–Reeve Link*
MkT, MkP, Mk–NPL	*The Monk's Tale, The Monk's Prologue, Monk–Nun's Priest Link*
MLT, MLH, MLP, MLE	*The Man of Law's Tale, Man of Law Headlink, The Man of Law's Prologue, Man of Law Endlink*
NPT, NPP, NPE	*The Nun's Priest's Tale, The Nun's Priest's Prologue, Nun's Priest's Endlink*
PardT, PardP	*The Pardoner's Tale, The Pardoner's Prologue*
ParsT, ParsP	*The Parson's Tale, The Parson's Prologue*
PF	*The Parliament of Fowls*
PhyT, Phy–PardL	*The Physician's Tale, Physician–Pardoner Link*
Pity	*The Complaint unto Pity*
Prov	*Proverbs*
PrT, PrP, Pr–ThL	*The Prioress's Tale, The Prioress's Prologue, Prioress–Thopas Link*
Purse	*The Complaint of Chaucer to His Purse*
Ret	*Chaucer's Retraction {Retractation}*
Rom	*The Romaunt of the Rose*
Ros	*To Rosemounde*
RvT, RvP	*The Reeve's Tale, The Reeve's Prologue*
Scog	*The Envoy to Scogan*
ShT, Sh–PrL	*The Shipman's Tale, Shipman–Prioress Link*
SNT, SNP, SN–CYL	*The Second Nun's Tale, The Second Nun's Prologue, Second Nun–Canon's Yeoman Link*
SqT, SqH, Sq–FranL	*The Squire's Tale, Squire Headlink, Squire–Franklin Link*
Sted	*Lak of Stedfastnesse*
SumT, SumP	*The Summoner's Tale, The Summoner's Prologue*
TC	*Troilus and Criseyde*
Th, Th–MelL	*The Tale of Sir Thopas, Sir Thopas–Melibee Link*
Truth	*Truth*
Ven	*The Complaint of Venus*

WBT, WBP, WB–FrL	The Wife of Bath's Tale, The Wife of Bath's Prologue, Wife of Bath–Friar Link
Wom Nob	Womanly Noblesse
Wom Unc	Against Women Unconstant

Periodical Abbreviations

AdI	*Annali d'Italianistica*
Anglia	*Anglia: Zeitschrift für Englische Philologie*
Anglistik	*Anglistik: Mitteilungen des Verbandes deutscher Anglisten*
AnLM	*Anuario de Letras Modernas*
ANQ	*ANQ: A Quarterly Journal of Short Articles, Notes, and Reviews*
Archiv	*Archiv für das Studium der Neueren Sprachen und Literaturen*
Arthuriana	*Arthuriana*
Atlantis	*Atlantis: Revista de la Asociacion Española de Estudios Anglo-Norteamericanos*
BAM	*Bulletin des Anglicistes Médiévistes*
BJRL	*Bulletin of the John Rylands University Library of Manchester*
C&L	*Christianity and Literature*
CarmP	*Carmina Philosophiae: Journal of the International Boethius Society*
CE	*College English*
ChauR	*Chaucer Review*
CL	*Comparative Literature* (Eugene, Ore.)
CLS	*Comparative Literature Studies*
CML	*Classical and Modern Literature: A Quarterly* (Columbia, Mo.)
CollL	*College Literature*
Comitatus	*Comitatus: A Journal of Medieval and Renaissance Studies*
CQ	*Cambridge Quarterly*
CRCL	*Canadian Review of Comparative Literature/Revue Canadienne de Littérature Comparée*
DAI	*Dissertation Abstracts International*
DR	*Dalhousie Review*
ÉA	*Études Anglaises: Grand-Bretagne, États-Unis*
EHR	*English Historical Review*
EIC	*Essays in Criticism: A Quarterly Journal of Literary Criticism*

ELH	*ELH: English Literary History*
ELN	*English Language Notes*
ELR	*English Literary Renaissance*
EMS	*English Manuscript Studies, 1100–1700*
Encomia	*Encomia: Bibliographical Bulletin of the International Courtly Literature Society*
English	*English: The Journal of the English Association*
Envoi	*Envoi: A Review Journal of Medieval Literature*
ES	*English Studies*
ESC	*English Studies in Canada*
Exemplaria	*Exemplaria: A Journal of Theory in Medieval and Renaissance Studies*
Expl	*Explicator*
Fabula	*Fabula: Zeitschrift für Erzählforschung/Journal of Folktale Studies*
FCS	*Fifteenth-Century Studies*
Florilegium	*Florilegium: Carleton University Papers on Late Antiquity and the Middle Ages*
FMLS	*Forum for Modern Language Studies*
Genre	*Genre: Forms of Discourse and Culture*
Hortulus	*Hortulus: The Online Graduate Journal of Medieval Studies <http://www.hortulus.net/>*
HudR	*Hudson Review*
IJES	*International Journal of English Studies*
JAIS	*Journal of Anglo-Italian Studies*
JEBS	*Journal of the Early Book Society*
JEGP	*Journal of English and Germanic Philology*
JELL	*Journal of English Language and Literature* (Korea)
JEngL	*Journal of English Linguistics*
JGN	*John Gower Newsletter*
JHiP	*Journal of Historical Pragmatics*
JMEMSt	*Journal of Medieval and Early Modern Studies*
JML	*Journal of Modern Literature*
JNT	*Journal of Narrative Theory*
JRMMRA	*Quidditas: Journal of the Rocky Mountain Medieval and Renaissance Association*
L&LC	*Literary and Linguistic Computing: Journal of the Association for Literary and Linguistic Computing*

L&P	*Literature and Psychology*
L&T	*Literature and Theology: An International Journal of Religion, Theory, and Culture*
Lang&Lit	*Language and Literature: Journal of the Poetics and Linguistics Association*
Lang&S	*Language and Style: An International Journal*
LeedsSE	*Leeds Studies in English*
Library	*The Library: The Transactions of the Bibliographical Society*
MA	*Le Moyen Age: Revue d'Histoire et de Philologie* (Brussels, Belgium)
MÆ	*Medium Ævum*
M&H	*Medievalia et Humanistica: Studies in Medieval and Renaissance Culture*
Manuscripta	*Manuscripta* (St. Louis, Mo.)
Marginalia	*Marginalia: The Journal of the Medieval Reading Group at the University of Cambridge* <http://www.marginalia.co.uk/journal/>
Mediaevalia	*Mediaevalia: An Interdisciplinary Journal of Medieval Studies Worldwide*
MedievalF	*Medieval Forum*
MedPers	*Medieval Perspectives*
MES	*Medieval English Studies*
MFF	*Medieval Feminist Forum*
MichA	*Michigan Academician* (Ann Arbor, Mich.)
MLQ	*Modern Language Quarterly: A Journal of Literary History*
MLR	*The Modern Language Review*
MP	*Modern Philology: A Journal Devoted to Research in Medieval and Modern Literature*
N&Q	*Notes and Queries*
Neophil	*Neophilologus* (Dordrecht, Netherlands)
NLH	*New Literary History: A Journal of Theory and Interpretation*
NM	*Neuphilologische Mitteilungen: Bulletin of the Modern Language Society*
NML	*New Medieval Literatures*
NMS	*Nottingham Medieval Studies*
NOWELE	*NOWELE: North-Western European Language Evolution*

Parergon	*Parergon: Bulletin of the Australian and New Zealand Association for Medieval and Early Modern Studies*
PBA	*Proceedings of the British Academy*
PBSA	*Papers of the Bibliographical Society of America*
PLL	*Papers on Language and Literature: A Journal for Scholars and Critics of Language and Literature*
PMAM	*Publications of the Medieval Association of the Midwest*
PMLA	*Publications of the Modern Language Association of America*
PoeticaT	*Poetica: An International Journal of Linguistic Literary Studies*
PQ	*Philological Quarterly*
R&L	*Religion and Literature*
RCEI	*Revista Canaria de Estudios Ingleses*
RenD	*Renaissance Drama*
RenQ	*Renaissance Quarterly*
RES	*Review of English Studies*
RMRev	*Reading Medieval Reviews* <www.rdg.ac.uk/ acaDepts/In/Medieval/rmr.htm>
SAC	*Studies in the Age of Chaucer*
SAP	*Studia Anglica Posnaniensia: An International Review of English*
SAQ	*South Atlantic Quarterly*
SB	*Studies in Bibliography: Papers of the Bibliographical Society of the University of Virginia*
SCJ	*The Sixteenth-Century Journal: Journal of Early Modern Studies* (Kirksville, Mo.)
SEL	*SEL: Studies in English Literature, 1500–1900*
SELIM	*SELIM: Journal of the Spanish Society for Medieval English Language and Literature*
ShakS	*Shakespeare Studies*
SIcon	*Studies in Iconography*
SiM	*Studies in Medievalism*
SIMELL	*Studies in Medieval English Language and Literature*
SMART	*Studies in Medieval and Renaissance Teaching*
SN	*Studia Neophilologica: A Journal of Germanic and Romance Languages and Literatures*

SoAR	*South Atlantic Review*
SP	*Studies in Philology*
Speculum	*Speculum: A Journal of Medieval Studies*
SSF	*Studies in Short Fiction*
SSt	*Spenser Studies: A Renaissance Poetry Annual*
TCBS	*Transactions of the Cambridge Bibliographical Society*
Text	*Text: Transactions of the Society for Textual Scholarship*
TLS	*Times Literary Supplement* (London, England)
TMR	*The Medieval Review* <http://www.hti.umich.edu/t/ tmr/>
Tr&Lit	*Translation and Literature*
TSLL	*Texas Studies in Literature and Language*
UTQ	*University of Toronto Quarterly: A Canadian Journal of the Humanities* (Toronto, Canada)
Viator	*Viator: Medieval and Renaissance Studies*
WS	*Women's Studies: An Interdisciplinary Journal*
YES	*Yearbook of English Studies*
YWES	*Year's Work in English Studies*
YLS	*The Yearbook of Langland Studies*

Bibliographical Citations and Annotations

Bibliographies, Reports, and Reference

1. Allen, Mark, and Bege K. Bowers. "An Annotated Chaucer Bibliography, 2003." *SAC* 27 (2005): 381–470. Continuation of *SAC* annual annotated bibliography (since 1975); based on contributions from an international bibliographic team, independent research, and *MLA Bibliography* listings. 304 items, plus listing of reviews for 68 books. Includes an author index.

2. Allen, Valerie, and Margaret Connolly. "Middle English: Chaucer." *YWES* 84 (2005): 222–55. A discursive bibliography of Chaucer studies for 2003, divided into four subcategories: general, *CT*, *TC*, and other works.

3. Johnson, James D. "Identifying Chaucer Allusions, 1991–2000: An Annotated Bibliography." *ChauR* 39 (2005): 436–55. Tabulates and annotates fifty-seven studies that identify or discuss allusions to Chaucer, presented as a continuation of Caroline Spurgeon's *Five Hundred Years of Chaucer Criticism and Allusion* (1925). Includes a name and title index for the studies.

4. Oizumi, Akio, ed. *A Bibliography of Writings on Chaucer's English*. New York: Olms-Weidmann, 1995. xxv, 81 pp. A selective bibliography of Chaucer studies, covering linguistic approaches through 1993, arranged topically under ten headings: Bibliographies (30 items); Manuscripts, Facsimiles, and Editions (26); Textual Criticism (53); English Linguistic Background (53); Medieval Rhetoric and Poetics (26); Dictionaries and Concordances (55); Phonology and Grammar (111); Lexicon (142); Meter and Versification (80); and Style and Rhetoric (130). Updates versions published in 1989 and 1990.

5. Tajima, Matsuji. *Waga Kuni no Eigogaku: Kaiko to Tenbo 100-wen* [*One Hundred Years of English Philology: Retrospect and Prospect*]. Tokyo: Nanundo, 2001. 225 pp. Tajima discusses the status of English study in Japan, providing a discursive bibliography of studies on linguistic topics: parts of speech, metrics, onomastics, etc. Addresses Old English to Modern English, with significant attention to Chaucer. Includes an index.

See also nos. 108, 137.

Recordings and Films

See nos. 60, 150.

Chaucer's Life

6. Taggie, Benjamin F. "Chaucer in Spain: The Historical Context." *Mediterranean Studies* 3 (1992): 35–44. Describes political and military events involving Edward, the Black Prince, Pedro of Castile, and his rivals that led up to the military campaign of 1366. Suggests the nature and timing of Chaucer's likely participation in these events, perhaps as an emissary to Anglo-Gascon forces in Navarre.

See also nos. 48, 118, 122, 131.

Facsimiles, Editions, and Translations

7. Beidler, Peter G. "Where's the Point? Punctuating Chaucer's *Canterbury Tales.*" In T. L. Burton and John F. Plummer, eds. *"Seyd in Forme and Reverence": Essays on Chaucer and Chaucerians in Memory of Emerson Brown, Jr.* (*SAC* 29 [2007], no. 96), pp. 193–203. Repunctuates several passages from *CT* and comments on the implications, encouraging classroom attention to modern editorial punctuation.

8. Bordalejo, Bárbara. "The Text of Caxton's Second Edition of the *Canterbury Tales.*" *ILES* 5.2 (2005): 133–48. Bordalejo compares variant readings of Caxton's first and second editions of *CT*, explores affiliations of these variants in the manuscript tradition of the poem, and argues that the readings in the second edition are useful for understanding the textual tradition of the poem and the construction of a reliable text.

9. Costa Palacios, Luis, trans. *El parlamento de las aves.* Córdoba: Astur, 1982. 137 pp. A facing-page Middle English/Spanish verse translation of *PF*, with notes and introduction by the translator.

10. Erne, Lukas. "Words in Space: The Reproduction of Texts and the Semiotics of the Page." *Swiss Papers in Language and Literature* 17 (2005): 99–118. Exemplifies how various aspects of the "bibliographical space" (e.g., format, typography, layout, paper, binding) of manuscripts and early editions challenge modern editors to represent the semiotic value of such space. Examples include the Ellesmere manuscript of *MLT* with its accompanying glosses.

11. Glaser, Joseph, trans. *Geoffrey Chaucer: "The Canterbury Tales" in Modern Verse*. Indianapolis: Hackett, 2005. vi, 348 pp. Verse translation of *CT* with several tales abridged or excerpted (*KnT*, *MLT*, *ClT*, *SqT*, *FranT*, *MkT*) and several summarized (*Mel*, *CYT*, *ManT*, *ParsT*), based on the Riverside edition. Converts Chaucer's pentameter couplets into octosyllabic couplets to increase the pace but maintains the original verse forms elsewhere. The introduction emphasizes Chaucer's vitality and social realism, and occasional glosses and notes identify terms, quotations, and unfamiliar concepts.

12. Howard, Donald R., ed. *The Canterbury Tales: A Selection*. Signet Classics. New York: New American Library, 2005. 400 pp. Reprint of the 1969 edition, with a new foreword (pp. 7–15) by Frank Grady.

13. Jung, Verena, and Angela Schrott. "A Question of Time? Question Types and Speech Act Shifts from a Historical-Contrastive Perspective: Some Examples from Old Spanish and Middle English." In K. M. Jaszczolt and Ken Turner, eds. *Meaning Through Language Contrast*. 2 vols. Pragmatics and Beyond, n.s., nos. 99–100. Amsterdam and Philadelphia: John Benjamins, 2003, 2:345–71. Combines historical pragmatics and translation studies, using them to clarify issues fundamental to both. Examines translations of questions in *Cantar de mio Cid* and translations of lines from *WBP* (ll.1–3 and 149–51), assessing in the latter case how Modern English and Modern German translations change the illocution of the lines.

14. Karita, Motoshi, trans. *Koi no Toriko: Toroirusu to Kuriseide* [*Prisoners of Love: Troilus and Criseyde*]. Tokyo: Hon no tomo sha, 1998. 311 pp. Reprint of Japanese translation of *TC* with notes and commentary, based on F. N. Robinson's edition. First published in 1948.

15. Klitgård, Ebbe. "Chaucer Reception and Translation in Denmark." *ChauR* 40 (2005): 207–17. Surveys Chaucer's reception in Danish scholarship, curricula, and translations, emphasizing the need for a Danish translation of *CT* that does not lose Chaucer's "subtlety and poetic forcefulness."

16. Kolve, V. A., and Glending Olson, eds. *The "Canterbury Tales": Fifteen Tales and the General Prologue. Authoritative Text, Sources, and Backgrounds, Criticism*. 2nd ed. Norton Critical Edition. New York: W. W. Norton, 2005. xix, 600 pp. Revised version of the 1989 Norton critical edition, with expanded selection and apparatus. Includes *GP*, *KnT*, *MilPT*, *RvPT*, *CkPT*, *WBPT*, *FrPT*, *SumPT*, *ClPT*, *MerPT*, *FranPT*, *PardPT*, *PrPT*, *ThP,* and *Th* and selections from *MelP* and *Mel*, *NPPT*,

ManPT, and *ParsPT*. Notes and glosses accompany the texts. Also includes a selection of sources and analogues, nine previously published essays by various authors, a chronology, and a selected bibliography.

17. Mann, Jill, ed. *The Canterbury Tales*. London: Penguin, 2005. lxxii, 1254 pp. New edition of *CT*, based on both the Hengwrt and Ellesmere manuscripts, with on-page glosses, explanatory notes (pp. 795–1111), and glossary (pp. 1112–1254). The introduction (pp. xvii–lxx) comments on the importance of Chaucer and *CT*, Chaucer's language, and major themes and techniques of the work. Headnotes to the explanatory notes discuss sources and genres.

18. Mason, Tom. "Chaucer and Other Earlier English Poetry." In Stuart Gillespie and David Hopkins, eds. *The Oxford History of Literary Translation in English. Volume 3: 1660–1790*. Oxford and New York: Oxford University Press, 2005, pp. 427–39. Mason surveys English translations and modernizations of Chaucer's works (and apocrypha) between 1660 and 1795, commenting on Dryden's and Pope's versions and the imitations they inspired. Includes a list of "Chaucer's Translations 1660–1795."

19. Mayer, Lauryn S. "Caxton, Chaucerian Manuscripts, and the Creation of an *Auctor*." In Lauryn S. Mayer. *Worlds Made Flesh: Reading Medieval Manuscript Culture*. Studies in Medieval History and Culture, no. 28. New York: Routledge, 2004, pp. 121–54. Mayer examines Caxton's edition of *HF* and de Worde's edition of *TC* to explore "strategies of authorial construction."

20. McCaughrean, Geraldine. Victor G. Ambrus, illus. *The Canterbury Tales*. Oxford: Oxford University Press, 1991. 118 pp. Color illus. Free adaptation of *CT* for children: *GP, KnT, MilT, NPT, RvT, ClT, WBT, PardT, Th, FranT, ManT, CYT, FrT*, and *MerT*. Provides links for the *Tales* in the above order and concludes with an arrival at Canterbury. First published in 1984.

21. Miyata, Takeshi, trans. *Turoirasu to Kuriseide [Troilus and Criseyde]*. Tokyo: Kobian Shoten, 1987. 311 pp. Reprint of a Japanese translation of *TC* with notes and commentary, based on F. N. Robinson's second edition. First published in 1979.

22. Mosser, Daniel W. "William Caxton's First Edition of the *Canterbury Tales* and the Origin of the Leaves for the Caxton Club's 1905 Leaf Book." In Christopher de Hamel and Joel Silver, with contributions by John P. Chalmers, Daniel W. Mosser, and Michael Thompson. *Disbound and Dispersed: The Leaf Book Considered*. Chicago: Caxton Club,

2005, pp. 24–51. 10 color illus. A portion of a copy of Caxton's first edition of *CT* was "harvested" to make a run of "leaf books" for the Caxton Club. Mosser describes the project, the known portions of the dismembered book, the known copies of Caxton's first edition, collectors' efforts to reconstruct a "perfect" version of Caxton's original, and the codicological implications of such efforts. Includes two appendices.

23. Oka, Saburo, trans. *Toroirusu* [*Troilus*]. Toroia Sosho [Troy Series], no. 4. Tokyo: Kokubunsha, 2005. 584 pp. Japanese translation of *TC*, based on the Windeatt edition, with commentary.

24. Richmond, E. B., trans. Steve Ellis, ed. *The Parliament of Birds*. London: Hesperus Poetry, 2004. xv, 151 pp. Facing-page translation of *PF* and nineteen short poems and lyrics by Chaucer, with introduction and brief notes. The translations maintain Chaucer's metrical forms and, where possible, original rhymes, while normalizing spelling and modernizing diction and syntax. Short poems include *Form Age*, *Pity*, *Lady*, *Mars*, *Venus*, *Ros*, *Wom Nob*, *Adam*, *For*, *Truth*, *Gent*, *Sted*, *Scog*, *Buk*, *Purse*, *Prov*, *Wom Unc*, *MercB*, and *ABC*.

25. Richmond, Velma Bourgeois. "Edward Burne-Jones's Chaucer Portraits in the Kelmscott *Chaucer*." *ChauR* 40 (2005): 1–38. The thirty-one portraits in the Kelmscott Chaucer show Burne-Jones's development as a painter and his identification with Chaucer as an artist. Burne-Jones represents Chaucer as a tall and slender man, similar to his own self-portraits. The emotions he captures in Chaucer—happy to melancholy to almost deathlike—roughly parallel events in the artist's own life and reflect changes in his own philosophy, as well as tensions in late Victorian England.

26. Serrano Reyes, Jesús L., trans. *El parlamento de las aves y otras visiones del sueño*. Madrid: Ediciones Siruela, 2005. 191 pp. An anthology of Spanish translations of Chaucer's dream visions. Includes previously published translations of *BD* and *HF*, plus new translations of *PF* and *LGW*. Notes and introduction by the translator.

27. Sherbo, Arthur. "From the Sale Catalogue of the Library of Samuel Rogers." *N&Q* 52 (2005): 25–32. Lot 1543 is "Chaucer (black letter): printed by Wyllyam Bonham, at the sign of the Reed [*sic*] Lyon," given to Rogers (1763–1855) by his friend Horne Tooke.

28. Shiomi, Tomoyuki, trans. *Chaucer no Yume Monogatari Shi* [*Chaucer's Dream Poetry*]. Tokyo: Kobundo, 1981. 295 pp. Japanese translation of *BD*, *HF*, and *PF*, based on Robinson's and Skeat's editions.

29. Snell, William. "A Note on Dr. Samuel Johnson and the Recep-

tion of Chaucer in Eighteenth-Century England." *Hiyoshi Review of English Studies* (Keio University) 44 (2004): 157–72. Explores why Samuel Johnson did not carry out his publicized intention to produce an annotated edition of Chaucer's works. If he had relied on Urry's edition, the annotated edition would have proved a sorry rival to Tyrwhitt's.

30. Tanaka, Sachiho, trans. *Toritachi no Kokkai, G. Chaucer {Saku}* ["*The Parliament of Fowls*" by G. Chaucer]. Tokyo: Eihosha, 2004. 161 pp. Japanese translation of *PF*, based on Derek S. Brewer's 2nd edition (1972) and *The Riverside Chaucer*. Includes Japanese translation of Brewer's commentary.

31. Tokunaga, Satoko. "Early English Printing and the Hands of Compositors." *IJES* 5.2 (2005): 149–60. Explains the value of variant type faces in establishing the process and sequence of composition in Caxton's Westminster print house, focusing particularly on the two compositors of the first edition of *CT* and on evidence of their involvement in other early Caxton volumes. Computer-aided analysis enables specific surmises about the process of composition in *Mel* and *ParsT*.

32. Ullyot, Michael. "English *Auctores* and Authorial Readers: Early Modernizations of Chaucer and Lydgate." In Ian Frederick Moulton, ed. *Reading and Literacy in the Middle Ages and Renaissance* (*SAC* 29 [2007], no. 129): 45–62. Assesses how two seventeenth-century modernizations reflect the reception of their Middle English originals. Jonathan Sidnam's modernization of the first three books of *TC* (ca. 1630) offers respectful tribute to Chaucer and seeks to preserve his legacy, while *The Life and Death of Hector* (1614), an anonymous modernization of Lydgate's *Troy Book*, seeks to replace the original.

33. Walker, Greg. *Writing Under Tyranny: English Literature and the Henrician Reform*. Oxford: Oxford University Press, 2005. xi, 556 pp. Walker seeks to understand reactions to the rise of tyranny during the rule of Henry VIII—the "unprecedented changes of the 1530s and 1540s"—seen through records left by "poets, prose-writers, scholars, and dramatists who wrote, revised, edited, or printed works of fiction and advice" during this period. Chapters 4–5 (pp. 56–99) emphasize Sir Brian Tuke's involvement with William Thynne's 1532 edition of Chaucer's works, considering the "politics" of editing and the implications of the apocrypha included in the edition, the importance granted to *CT*, and the recurrent emphasis on peace. Other works considered at length are John Heywood's *Play of the Weather*, Sir Thomas Elyot's *Book*

Named the Governor, and works of Sir Thomas Wyatt and Henry Howard, Earl of Surrey.

See also nos. 58, 108, 158, 193, 270, 281, 311, 329.

Manuscripts and Textual Studies

34. Blake, N. F. "Editorial Assumptions and Problems in *The Canterbury Tales*." *PoeticaT* 20 (1984): 1–19. Considers textual issues that pertain to the "Host stanza" at the end of *ClT* (4.1212a–g) and several passages in *MkT* and *NPT*: the "Adam stanza" (7.2007–14), the "Modern Instances" (7.2375–2462), and the short versus long versions of *NPP*. Discusses manuscript evidence and the likely sequence of composition.

35. ———. "The Manuscripts and Textual Tradition of *The Canterbury Tales* Again." *PoeticaT* 28 (1988): 6–15. Argues for new attention to the complexities of textual issues in critical discussions of *CT*, suggesting that many recent studies ignore or only gesture toward such complexities.

36. ———. "The Text of the *Canterbury Tales*." *PoeticaT* 13 (1982): 27–49. Comparison of manuscripts of *CT* enables inferential conclusions about their exemplar (which does not survive), but the complexity of these conclusions justifies reliance on the Hengwrt manuscript. Blake considers the likelihood that the manuscripts of most of Chaucer's works, especially those of *CT* and *TC*, may be the products of an "editorial committee."

37. Brewer, Derek. "Root's Account of the Text of *Troilus*." *PoeticaT* 12 (1981): 36–44. Brewer critiques Root's explanation of relationships among *TC* manuscripts, arguing that Root's explanation is inconsistent and commenting on the possibilities of discovering the process of Chaucer's revisions.

38. Edwards, A. S. G. "Collation and Its Misuses in Some Middle English Texts." In Christa Jansohn and Bodo Plachta, eds. *Varianten— Variants—Variantes*. Tübingen: Max Niemeyer, 2005, pp. 79–90. Edwards comments on the conceptualizations and uses of variants in textual studies of *CT* and *Piers Plowman*, particularly those by Manly and Rickert and by Kane and Donaldson, arguing that some manuscripts are better regarded as separate versions of texts than as sources of individual

variants. Edwards considers in this light an excerpted version of the *GP* description of the Parson found in British Library MS Additional 10340.

39. ————. "A New Text of *The Canterbury Tales?*" In Anne Marie D'Arcy and Alan J. Fletcher, eds. *Studies in Late Medieval and Early Renaissance Texts in Honour of John Scattergood* (*SAC* 29 [2007], no. 103): 121–28. Transcribes a version of *CkT* from Oxford, Bodleian Library, MS Ashmole 45, previously unnoticed or ignored. Accompanied by the apocryphal *Tale of Gamelyn*, the text was copied by Elias Ashmole (1617–92), probably from a manuscript now lost.

40. ————. "The Text of Chaucer's *House of Fame*: Editing and Authority." *PoeticaT* 29–30 (1989): 80–93. Edwards clarifies the indeterminacies of the "editorial process" by questioning several textual issues pertaining to the manuscripts of *HF*: uncertain authority of individual manuscript and manuscript groupings, and the implications of this uncertainly for individual readings.

41. Horobin, Simon, and Daniel W. Mosser. "Scribe D's SW Midland Roots: A Reconsideration." *NM* 106 (2005): 289–305. The authors analyze the spelling and dialect evidence of manuscripts attributed to Scribe D (including *CT*) and argue that the southwestern dialect features derive from exemplars rather than from the scribe's own dialect. This argument, in turn, raises questions about the relative chronology of the manuscripts and challenges assumptions that scribes converted copy-texts into their own dialects. More generally, the rise of a London standard may have been slower than previously thought.

42. Pouzet, Jean-Pascal. "Quelques aspects de l'influence des chanoines Augustins sur la production et la transmission littéraire vernaculaire en Angleterre (XIIIe–XVe siècles)." *Comptes-rendus de l'Académie des Inscriptions et Belles-lettres* 1(2004): 169–213. Pouzet surveys the late medieval activities of Augustinian canons in the production of Anglo-Norman and Middle English manuscripts and texts. Considers evidence of the commitment of members of the order to the transmission of Chaucer material.

43. Robinson, Peter. "Where We Are with Electronic Scholarly Editions, and Where We Want to Be." *Jahrbuch für Computerphilologie* 4 (2002): 123–42; *Jahrbuch für Computerphilologie Online* 1 (2005): n.p. Robinson surveys developments in electronic editing and comments on the strengths and limitations of electronic scholarly editions, calling for greater collaboration among scholars and for increased fluidity and in-

teractivity in the editions. Draws examples from several projects, including *The Canterbury Tales Project* e-version of *MilT*.

44. Sánchez-Martí, Jordi. "Longleat House MS 257: A Description." *Atlantis* 27.1 (2005): 79–89. 5 b&w illus. Considers the date and provenance of the Longleat 257 manuscript, describes its contents, and offers a full codicological analysis of collation and compilation, hands, and illustrations.

45. Windram, Heather F., Christopher J. Howe, and Matthew Spencer. "The Identification of Exemplar Change in the *Wife of Bath's Prologue* Using the Maximum Chi-Squared Method." *L&LC* 20 (2005): 189–204. Uses a statistical technique derived from DNA research to reexamine the possibility of exemplar changes in the copying of *WBP*. Results agree with earlier studies, indicating the usefulness of this method.

See also nos. 8, 10, 86, 97, 112, 116, 168, 186, 193, 244, 281.

Sources, Analogues, and Literary Relations

46. Correale, Robert M., and Mary Hamel, eds. *Sources and Analogues of the "Canterbury Tales."* Vol. 2. Chaucer Studies, no. 35. Woodbridge, Suffolk; and Rochester, N.Y.: D. S. Brewer, 2005. xvi, 824 pp. An anthology of the sources and analogues for selections from *CT*. Each section comments on source-and-analogue relations, edits the materials in a form close to what Chaucer might have known, and provides facing-page translations of non-English material. Sections include *GP* (Robert R. Raymo), *KnT* (William E. Coleman), *MilT* (Peter G. Beidler), *MLPT* (Robert M. Correale), *WBP* (Ralph Hanna and Traugott Lawler), *WBT* (John Withrington and P. J. C. Field), *SumPT* (Christine Richardson-Hay), *MerT* (N. S. Thompson), *PhyT* (Kenneth Bleeth), *ShT* (John Scattergood), *PrPT* (Laurel Broughton), *Th* (Joanne A. Charbonneau), *CYT* (Carolyn P. Collette and Vincent DiMarco), *ManT* (Edward Wheatley), and *Ret* (Anita Obermeier). The volume includes an index of names and titles. For vol. 1, see *SAC* 26 (2004), no. 47.

47. Griffiths, Eric, and Matthew Reynolds, eds. *Dante in English.* New York: Penguin, 2005. cxxxvi, 479 pp. An anthology of selections from Dante's works adapted or translated into English, including several examples from Chaucer's works (*WBT*, *MkT*, *SNT*, *HF*, and *TC*). Focusing on the *Commedia* and arranged chronologically, the selections range

from Chaucer to works of the late twentieth century, with about one hundred writers included. The extensive introduction addresses the challenges of translating Dante.

48. McTurk, Rory. *Chaucer and the Norse and Celtic Worlds*. Aldershot, Hampshire; and Burlington, Vt.: Ashgate, 2005. ix, 218 pp. Revives the idea that Chaucer visited Ireland between 1361 and 1366, placing new emphasis on the date of the Statute of Kilkenny. Identifies sources for Chaucer's works in Irish and Norse literatures. Observes parallels for *HF* in the *Topographia Hibernie* of Gerald of Wales, Snorri Sturluson's *Edda*, and the Old Irish sagas *Fled Bricrend* and *Togail Bruidne Da Derga*. Compares the journey as framework for a collection of tales in *CT* with Snorri's *Edda* and the Middle Irish saga *Acallam na Senórach*. Argues that *Laxdæla Saga* and *WBT* descend from an Irish version of the Loathly Lady story and surmises that Chaucer's five-stress line may derive from the tradition of Irish song known as *amhrán*.

49. Minnis, Alastair. "'I speke of folk in seculer estaat': Vernacularity and Secularity in the Age of Chaucer." *SAC* 27 (2005): 25–58. Biennial Chaucer Lecture, The New Chaucer Society, Fourteenth International Congress, 15–19 July 2004, University of Glasgow. Traces late medieval "vernacular secularity," particularly the influences of Aristotle's *Ethics*, *Politics*, and *Economics* and Boethius's *Consolation* as transmitted to England by Giles of Rome, Nicole Oresme, Nicholas Trevet, Jean de Meun, Guillaume de Machaut, etc. Comments on issues of audience and patronage. Explores the secularity of Chaucer's "renegotiations of Boethian matter" in *KnT*, *FranT*, and *TC*, as well as his representation of the Aristotelian virtue of magnificence in Theseus of *KnT*.

50. Tripp, Raymond P., Jr. "On the Continuity of English Poetry Between *Beowulf* and Chaucer." *PoeticaT* 6 (1976): 1–21. Argues for the continuity of English literary tradition from *Beowulf* to the present by exploring several "great speeches" in Chaucer's works and in previous literature. No one disputes the continuity from Chaucer to the present, and the presence in these speeches of similar rhetorical and thematic devices indicates a common English tradition up to and including Chaucer.

51. Wetherbee, Winthrop, III. "Chaucer and the European Tradition." *SAC* 27 (2005): 3–21. The Presidential Address, The New Chaucer Society, Fourteenth International Congress, 15–19 July 2004, University of Glasgow. Explores Chaucer's idea of "serious poetry," derived from French and Italian models. Comments on Chaucer's treat-

ments of heroism and tragedy, the political implications of poetry, and Chaucer's fusion of courtly and classical traditions. Discusses *TC*, *KnT*, and *NPT* and gives particular attention to *MkT* (especially Hugolino) as Chaucer's exploration of inadequate poetry.

52. Williams, Deanne. "Gower's Monster." In Ananya Jahanara Kabir and Deanne Williams, eds. *Postcolonial Approaches to the European Middle Ages: Translating Cultures.* Cambridge: Cambridge University Press, 2005, pp. 127–50. Compares Nebuchadnezzar in Gower's *Confessio Amantis* with his depictions in Chaucer's *HF* and *MkT*.

See also nos. 73, 87, 106, 108, 126, 155, 160, 166, 168, 181, 184, 191, 197, 202, 203, 205, 206, 210–12, 216, 226, 243, 246, 247, 267, 271, 282, 288, 295, 312, 317, 324.

Chaucer's Influence and Later Allusion

53. Beidler, Peter. "Louise Erdrich's Lulu Nanapush: A Modern-Day Wife of Bath?" *Studies in American Indian Literature* 15 (2003): 92–103. Comments on the possible influence of *CT* on the frame-tale structure of Erdrich's *Tales of Burning Love* and considers to what extent parallels between the Wife of Bath and Lulu Nanapush (*Love Medicine*) indicate that Chaucer's work is a source for Urdich's. Identifies eight parallels between Alison and Lulu.

54. Crocker, Holly A. "Manufacture in the Archive: Impingham's Chaucer in MS BL Harley 7333." *MFF* 39 (2005): 29–37. The proverbs signed "Impingham" in Harley 7333 derive from Chaucer, but the emphases and arrangement of the proverbs present a more reductive view of women than is found in Chaucer's works.

55. D'Agata D'Ottavi, Stefania. "Dunbar's 'The Goldyn Targe' and the Question of the *Auctoritates*." In Marco Fazzini, ed. *Alba Literaria: A History of Scottish Literature.*" Venice: Amos Edizioni, 2005, pp. 45–63. Chaucer's four dream poems, especially *PF* and *LGWP* (both the F and G versions), are sources of Dunbar's "Golden Targe," although Dunbar's imagery owes much to *CT*, *Anel*, and *Rom*. Dunbar seeks innovation within tradition, and the praise he bestows on Chaucer shows that he wishes to have in Scottish literature the place that Chaucer has in English.

56. Edminster, Warren. "Fairies and Feminism: Recurrent Patterns in Chaucer's 'The Wife of Bath's Tale' and Brontë's *Jane Eyre*." *Victorian*

Newsletter 104 (2003): 22–28. Similar concerns with fairies and male oppression encourage comparison of *WBT* and *Jane Eyre*; they reflect either Brontë's familiarity with Chaucer's work or a significant coincidence.

57. Ellis, Steve. "Framing the Father: Chaucer and Virginia Woolf." *NML* 7 (2005): 35–52. Virginia Woolf's discussions of Chaucer have "the effect of cutting him down to size." This effect reflects her reaction to High Modernist affection for the Middle Ages and her "subversive and anti-canonical approach to literary history."

58. Ganim, John M. "Chaucer and Free Love." In Robert M. Stein and Sandra Pierson Prior, eds. *Reading Medieval Culture: Essays in Honor of Robert W. Hanning* (SAC 29 [2007], no. 146): 344–65. Explores the reception of Chaucer by William Morris (the Kelmscott *Chaucer*) and Virginia Woolf ("The Pastons and Chaucer"), arguing that the responses of both individuals are deeply autobiographical and indications of how "modernity privatizes the premodern." Woolf's essay is a "dry run" for "*Orlando* and its imagining of a subversive past," while Morris's edition (especially in Burne-Jones's illustrations) combines innocence and fatalism in ways that reflect Morris's troubled marriage.

59. Jack, R. D. S. "Robert Henryson." In Marco Fazzini, ed. *Alba Literaria: A History of Scottish Literature*. Venice: Amos Edizioni, 2005, pp. 33–44. Comments on Henryson's biography, relations with medieval tradition, and stylistic range. Though he admired Chaucer, Henryson criticizes *TC* in the *Testament of Cresseid* because at the end of Chaucer's poem nothing more is known about Criseyde.

60. Johnston, Andrew James. "Filming the Seven Deadly Sins— Chaucer, Hollywood, and the Postmodern Middle Ages." In Thomas Honegger, ed. *Riddles, Knights, and Cross-Dressing Saints: Essays on Medieval English Language and Literature* (SAC 29 [2007], no. 119): 1–32. Johnston compares uses of medieval details, anachronisms, and hermeneutic concerns in two films (Brian Helgeland's *A Knight's Tale* and David Fincher's *Seven*) and Umberto Eco's *The Name of the Rose*. Includes attention to Chaucer references and allusions.

61. Lynch, Kathryn L. "The Three Noble Kinsmen: Chaucer, Shakespeare, Fletcher." In Yvonne Bruce, ed. *Images of Matter: Essays on British Literature of the Middle Ages and Renaissance. Proceedings of the Eighth Citadel Conference on Literature, Charleston, South Carolina, 2002*. Newark: University of Delaware Press, 2005, pp. 72–91. Lynch posits that Shakespeare had an "anxious" relationship with Chaucer as a model, a

source, and a father figure. She reads *Two Noble Kinsman* against *KnT* for evidence of this "nervous" relationship and similarly assesses Fletcher's "revisionary adaptation" of Chaucerian and Shakespearian material.

62. McCleary, Joseph Robert, Jr. "Locality, Patriotism, and Nationalism: Historical Imagination and G. K. Chesterton's Literary Works." *DAI* 66 (2005): 1009A. Considers Chesterton's literary criticism of Chaucer as a means to understanding Chesterton's conception of locality as part of his philosophy of history.

63. Nolan, Maura. "Lydgate's Literary History: Chaucer, Gower, and Canacee." *SAC* 27 (2005): 59–92. Reads Lydgate's tale of Canacee (*Fall of Princes*, Book 1) as a subtle response to its source (Gower's *Confessio Amantis*), complicated by several allusions to Chaucerian narratives (*ClT, MLT, PrT*). Lydgate's confrontations with various kinds of "Ovidianism" are epitomized in the silence of Canacee's child and in Canacee's own complaint, which via further allusions to Chaucer (*TC, HF*) poses competing views of fortune and of the value of poetry in representing fortune and history.

64. Phillips, Helen. "Scott and Chaucer: Ekphrasis, Politics, and the Past in *The Antiquary*." *PoeticaT* 61 (2004): 25–42. Explores Sir Walter Scott's knowledge of Chaucer and the novelist's use of themes and techniques reminiscent of those in *BD* and the apocryphal *Flower and the Leaf*. Alluding to these works in *The Antiquary*, Scott emphasizes their concerns with gender and feudalism and imitates such devices as juxtaposition, ekphrasis, genre shift, and insertion.

65. Robbins, Rossell Hope. "Chaucer and the Lyric Tradition." *PoeticaT* 15–16 (1983): 107–27. Arguing that "Chaucer changed the direction of the Middle English lyric," Robbins comments on Chaucer's lyrics, on fifteenth-century lyrics, and on the influence of *TC* on the latter.

66. Sallfors, Solomon, and James Duban. "Chaucerian Humor in *Moby Dick*: Queequeg's 'Ramadan.'" *Leviathan* 5 (2003): 73–77. Sallfors and Duban contend that *MilT* "informs the dramatic setting, humor, and tension of Ishmael's response to Queequeg's 'Ramadan'" in Chapter 17 of Melville's *Moby Dick*. Specifically, the characterization of John the Carpenter underlies Ishmael's skeptical response.

67. Sayers, William. "Gat-Toothed Alysoun, Gaptoothed Kathleen: Sovereignty and Dentition." *Hypermedia Joyce Studies* 6.1 (2005): n.p. Explores the complex workings of an allusion to the Wife of Bath in

591

Joyce's *Ulysses* that resonates with Irish mythology, Yeats, and Irish political power.

68. Steinberg, Glenn A. "Spenser's *Shepheardes Calendar* and the Elizabethan Reception of Chaucer." *ELR* 35.1 (2005): 331–51. Spenser's adoption of Chaucerian humility should be understood in light of Elizabethan debates about Chaucer. Although Chaucer is universally listed as preeminent among English poets, his detractors find him lacking in moral or stylistic weight, while his defenders—especially those associated with Cambridge—praise his morality and poetic richness. Spenser's imitation of Chaucerian humility reflects positive assessments of Chaucer.

69. Terrell, Katherine Hikes. "Translating the Past, Scripting the Nation: Poetry, History, and Authority in Late Medieval Scotland." *DAI* 66 (2005): 1350A. In a larger discussion of Scottish attempts to form national and literary identities, Terrell mentions William Dunbar's and Gavin Douglas's "myths of Chaucerian inheritance" as grounds for a Scots poetics.

70. Torti, Anna. "The Poetry of Gavin Douglas: Memory, Past Tradition, and Its Renewal." In Marco Fazzini, ed. *Alba Literaria: A History of Scottish Literature*. Venice: Amos Edizioni, 2005, pp. 65–81. Consciousness of the importance of the Scottish literary tradition characterizes Douglas's work. Although *The Palice of Honour* is grounded in Chaucer's *HF*, Douglas makes it clear that his aim is different, and the latter compares Fame to Honour unfavorably. In *Eneados* and in the *Prologues* to the individual books of the poem, Doublas shows interest in tradition and in the theoretical aspects of translation.

See also nos. 50, 108, 182, 197, 264, 272, 286, 316, 325.

Style and Versification

71. Murphy, James J. "A New Look at Chaucer and the Rhetoricians." In James Jerome Murphy. *Latin Rhetoric and Education in the Middle Ages and Renaissance*. Variorum Collected Studies Series; Collected Studies, no. 827. Burlington, Vt.: Ashgate, 2005. First published in 1964, the essay is reprinted here with original pagination, along with a number of other essays by Murphy. Murphy argues that Chaucer was not likely to have been directly influenced by rhetoricians such as Geoffrey of Vinsauf.

72. Windeatt, B. A. "'Most conservatif the soun': Chaucer's *Troilus* Metre." *PoeticaT* 8 (1977): 44–60. Examines manuscript evidence and compares the verse of *TC* with that of Boccaccio's *Filostrato*, arguing that Chaucer's decasyllabic lines, adapted to rhyme-royal stanzas, are characterized by greater flexibility of caesura than in English four-stress verse and by more varied syllable numbers and stress patterns than in strict iambic pentameter.

73. Windeatt, Barry. "Pace in Chaucer. 'The proverbe seith: "He hasteth wel that wisely kan abyde'" (*Melibee*, 1054)." *PoeticaT* 14 (1983): 51–65. Windeatt compares several of Chaucer's works and their sources to show that through variations in narrative pace and increased attention to pinpointing time, Chaucer makes something quite new. Considers *PF*, *MLT*, *TC*, *KnT*, and several of the tales in *LGW*.

74. Zonneveld, Wim. "Constraining S and Satisfying Fit." In Paula Fikkert and Haike Jacobs, eds. *Development in Prosodic Systems*. Berlin and New York: Mouton de Gruyter, 2003, pp. 197–247. Zonneveld examines factors associated with iambic stress in the octosyllabic Dutch poem *Het Leven van St. Lutgart* [*Life of St. Lutgart*], comparing them with conditions in early English. Considers the "uncertain status of schwa syllables" in Chaucer's poetry and in Shakespeare's plays.

See also nos. 48, 244, 302.

Language and Word Studies

75. Boggel, Sandra. "*Nou ondertsand wel*—Metacommunicative Directives in Middle English and Early Modern English Religious Texts." In Thomas Honegger, ed. *Riddles, Knights, and Cross-Dressing Saints: Essays on Medieval English Language and Literature* (*SAC* 29 [2007], no. 119): 193–222. Metacomnmunicative markers are more frequent in Middle English religious texts than in Early Modern English religious texts. Boggel focuses on such structural and directional markers as "you must remember this" or "let us first examine." Examples include passages from *ParsT*.

76. Burnley, J. D. "Geoffrey Chaucer." In D. Alan Cruse et al., eds. *Lexikologie: Ein Internationales Handbuch zur Natur und Struktur von Wörtern und Wortschätzen/Lexicology: An International Handbook on the Nature and Structure of Words and Vocabularies*. 2 vols. Handbooks of Linguistics and Communication Science, nos. 21.1–2. Berlin and New York: Walter

de Gruyter, 2002, 2:1468–71. Describes the historical and regional characteristics of Chaucer's vocabulary, his particular uses of various registers, and how he adapts them to circumstances and contexts.

77. Dor, Juliette. "Les bons comptes font les bons amis: Variations sur *quite(n)* dans *Les contes de Canterbury*." In Marie-Françoise Alamichel, ed. *La complémentarité: Mélanges offerts à Josseline Bidard et Arlette Sancery à l'occasion de leur départ en retraite (SAC* 29 [2007], no. 85): 165–76. Analyzes Chaucer's polysemous uses of *quite(n)* in *CT* in light of late fourteenth-century concerns with contracts and debts, disclosing various tensions among the tellers' origins, professions, and ranks.

78. Eitler, Tamás. "Some Dialectical, Sociolectal, and Communicative Aspects of Word Order Variation and Change in Late Middle English." In Michael D. Fortescue et al., eds. *Historical Linguistics 2003: Selected Papers from the 16th International Conference on Historical Linguistics, Copenhagen, 11–15 August 2003*. Philadelphia: John Benjamins, 2005, pp. 87–102. Eitler studies the development of the "incipient standard" syntactic pattern (subject-verb-object), comparing data from Chaucer's prose works with data from other ME prose, characterizing his idiom as the "(relatively) upper class sociolect" of London and suggesting that syntactic analysis encourages us to accept Chaucer's authorship of *Equat.*

79. Honegger, Thomas. "'And if ye wol nat so, my lady sweete, thane preye I thee, [. . .]': Forms of Address in Chaucer's *Knight's Tale*." In Irma Taavitsainen and Andreas H. Jucker, eds. *Diachronic Perspectives on Address Term Systems*. Philadelphia: John Benjamins, 2003, pp. 61–84. Honegger argues that analyses of international forms of address would gain depth if critics considered "situational" factors and even "competing interactional" factors along with traditional considerations of *ye/thou* pronouns. He focuses on addresses to the gods in *KnT* to demonstrate such complicating factors. See also no. 406.

80. Kokorian-Coutureau, Nathalie. "Le rôle du discours homilétique dans l'émergence de la valeur additive de *also* en moyen-anglais." *BAM* 67 (2005): 1–24. Examines the evolution of *also* from a marker of comparison in Old English to a marker of addition in Middle English.

81. Laing, Margaret, and Roger Lass. "Early Middle English *Knight*: (Pseudo)metathesis and Lexical Specificity." *NM* 106 (2005): 405–23. Surveys a wide range of occurrences and developments for [kn], a cluster with a number of uncommon properties. Examination of the lexical and phonetic idiosyncrasies demonstrates that observed figural representa-

tion in <cin-/kin-> is not at odds with a rational literal and phonetic interpretation.

82. Pakkala-Weckström, Mari. "Genre, Gender, and Power: A Study of Address Forms in Seven *Canterbury Tales*." In Karind Aijmer and Britta Olinder, eds. *Proceedings from the 8th Nordic Conference on English Studies*. Göteborg: Göteborg University Department of English, 2003, pp. 121–36. Pakkala-Weckström applies linguistic "politeness theory" to the use of pronouns as "forms of address in male/female dialogue" in *MilT*, *MerT*, *ShT*, *ClT*, *Mel*, *WBT*, and *FranT*. Usage is similar in the romances and religious tales but differs in the fabliaux; social class complicates patterns of usage in male and female speech.

83. Tajima, Matsuji. "The Gerund in Chaucer, with Special Reference to the Development of Its Verbal Character." *PoeticaT* 21–22 (1985): 106–21. Examines Chaucer's use of gerunds, observing that his usage is generally not unusual for his time except in two respects: he more frequently uses the construction "determiner + gerund + of-adjunct"; and seemingly "modern" gerunds with verbal properties occur in his works, especially his prose works.

84. Twomey, Michael W. "Reading Chaucer's Latin Aloud." In T. L. Burton and John F. Plummer, eds. *"Seyd in Forme and Reverence": Essays on Chaucer and Chaucerians in Memory of Emerson Brown, Jr.* (*SAC* 29 [2007], no. 96): 181–90. Guide to pronouncing the Latin words and phrases in *CT*, presented in International Phonetic Alphabet; includes a brief introduction on historical phonology.

See also nos. 5, 116, 128, 165, 221, 239, 253, 255, 256, 280.

Background and General Criticism

85. Alamichel, Marie-Françoise, ed. *La complémentarité: Mélanges offerts à Josseline Bidard et Arlette Sancery à l'occasion de leur départ en retraite.* Publications de l'Association des Médiévistes Anglicistes de l'Enseignement Supérieur. Hors série, no. 11. Paris: AMAES, 2005. 290 pp. Includes seven essays that pertain to Chaucer; see nos. 77, 93, 163, 199, 202, 283, and 327.

86. Allen, Elizabeth. *False Fables and Exemplary Truth in Later Middle English Literature.* New York: Palgrave, 2005. viii, 225 pp. Explores issues of exemplarity and applicability in examples of Middle English literature—*Book of the Knight of the Tower*, Gower's *Confessio Amantis*,

Lydgate's *Fall of Princes*, Henryson's *Testment of Cresseid*, and *CT* and *TC*. Chaucerian topics include the function of the frame in *ClT;* history, fiction, and exemplarity in *PhyT*; Northumberland MS 455 and how the *Canterbury Interlude (Tale of Beryn)* reflects fifteenth-century audience reaction to *PardT*; and Criseyde's multivalent exemplarity in *TC*.

87. Battles, Dominique. *The Medieval Tradition of Thebes: History and Narrative in the OF "Roman de Thèbes," Boccaccio, Chaucer, and Lydgate.* New York: Routledge, 2004. xix, 235 pp. Examines the Chaucerian treatment of Theban matter. Unlike Boccaccio's *Teseida*, *Anel* represents Thebes as a viable urban center even after the siege, while *KnT* disentangles Theban from Trojan history and re-creates Thebes as a pagan site. Both texts reinstate Statius's fatalistic sense of a criminal Theban identity. In addition, *TC* dramatizes the failure of historical transmission and reception to avert tragedy. All three Chaucerian texts construct an intimate, subjective, multivalent portrait of Theban history that Lydgate attempts to reenvision in politically utilitarian terms.

88. Böker, Uwe, et al., eds. *Of Remembraunce the Keye: Medieval Literature and Its Impact Through the Ages. Festschrift for Karl Heinz Göller on the Occasion of His 80th Birthday.* Frankfurt am Main: Lang, 2004. 378 pp. Twenty-one essays by various authors and a bibliography of Göller's publications. The essays focus on medieval romances and their reception in later traditions, German and English. Four essays pertain to Chaucer. See nos. 121, 141, 243, and 299.

89. Braswell, Mary Flowers. "The Chaucer Scholarship of Mary Eliza Haweis (1852–1989)." *ChauR* 39 (2005): 402–19. Haweis's two books—*Chaucer for Children* (1877) and *Chaucer for Schools* (1881)—reveal much about Victorian Chaucerians, their conversations, and their research. A scholarly popularizer, Haweis supported Chaucer's reputation during the formative years of his Victorian revival.

90. Brewer, D. S. "Chaucer's Attitudes to Music." *PoeticaT* 15–16 (1983): 128–35. Brewer surveys the presence (and absence) of music in Chaucer's work, suggesting that Chaucer knew its celestial, theoretical underpinnings and enjoyed its zesty, earthy pleasures.

91. Brewer, Derek. "The Nature of Romance." *PoeticaT* 9 (1978): 9–48. Seeks to define "romance" in Western literary tradition, commenting on its development from classical roots up to modern fantasy literature. Common formal features help to define the term, along with recurrent narrative patterns and themes. The article treats a wide range of literature, including Arthurian romance and works by Chaucer.

92. ———. "Some Notes on 'Ennobling Love' and Its Successor in Medieval Romance." In Corinne Saunders, ed. *Cultural Encounters in the Romance of Medieval England*. Studies in Medieval Romance, no. 2. Cambridge: D. S. Brewer, 2005, pp. 117–33. Chaucer indicates that same-sex friendship is threatened when complicated by issues of "sexual love" (127). Considering *TC, PF, WBPT*, and *FranT*, Brewer calls for reinstatement of friendship "as a recognizable, uncontentious area of love" and praises Chaucer for recognizing the value of friendship in marriage.

93. ———. "A Test of the Nature of Friendship: Lydgate, Chaucer, and Others." In Marie-Françoise Alamichel, ed. *La complémentarité: Mélanges offerts à Josseline Bidard et Arlette Sancery à l'occasion de leur départ en retraite* (*SAC* 29 [2007], no. 85): 155–64. Examines the portrayal of friendship in works by Chaucer, Lydgate, and Petrus Alfonsi.

94. Brown, Peter. "Chaucer and Medieval Studies in Canterbury." Colloquium: Administrative Perspectives on Chaucer Studies. *SAC* 27 (2005): 261–67. Brown describes a "recent crisis" that threatened the survival of the Canterbury Centre for Medieval and Tudor Studies at the University of Kent at Canterbury.

95. Burger, Glenn, and Steven F. Kruger. "Queer Chaucer in the Classroom." In Tanya Agathocleous and Ann C. Dean, eds. *Teaching Literature: A Companion*. New York: Palgrave Macmillan, 2003, pp. 31–40. Argues for an expansion of the notion of queer readings of Chaucer, encouraging a broad concern with questions of identity and its formulations. Comments on possible queer approaches to Chaucer the Pilgrim and the "Marriage Group" of *CT*.

96. Burton, T. L., and John F. Plummer, eds. *"Seyd in Forme and Reverence": Essays on Chaucer and Chaucerians in Memory of Emerson Brown, Jr.* Provo, Utah: Chaucer Studio Press, 2005. xix, 249 pp. Eighteen essays by various authors; a professional biography of Emerson Brown Jr.; and a list of his academic publications. For the essays, see nos. 7, 84, 115, 134, 166, 179, 196, 204, 232, 234, 252, 259, 276, 282, 316, 317, 322, and 326.

97. Caie, Graham D. " 'I do not wish to be called auctour, but the pore compilatour': The Plight of the Medieval Vernacular Poet." *Miscelánea* 29 (2004): 9–21. Caie describes features of manuscript *ordinatio*, material, glossing, etc. to show how late medieval English vernacular manuscripts (especially those of Chaucer and Gower) lay claim to authority even while their authors assert that they are only compilers.

Clarifies "scribe," "compiler," "author," and related terms as they are used by the poets.

98. Camargo, Martin. "The State of Medieval Studies: A Tale of Two Universities." Colloquium: Administrative Perspectives on Chaucer Studies. *SAC* 27 (2005): 239–47. Recounts the author's experiences as chair of the English departments at the University of Missouri and the University of Illinois.

99. Cannon, Christopher. *The Grounds of English Literature*. Oxford: Oxford University Press, 2004. xi, 247 pp. Cannon combines Marxist and Hegelian ideas of "form" to argue that *"form is that which thought and things have in common"* (5), enabling a valuation of form as a record of thinking in and about a culture. Formalist criticism (in this sense) of Middle English literature reveals a poverty of categories in literary history and encourages an expansion of our ideas of literary potential and of the idea of form itself. Cannon challenges the traditional division of Old and Middle English literatures and explores the "body of learning that informed" particular texts (Layamon's *Brut*, the *Ormulum*, *The Owl and the Nightingale*, *Ancrene Wisse* and the *Katherine*-group, and several romances). He discusses romance in light of the "closing down of formal possibilities," considering Chaucer's uses of this "holographic" form or genre in *BD* and *Th* and his awareness that literature projects particularities into forms.

100. Carruthers, Leo, and Adrian Papahagi, eds. *Jeunesse et vieillesse: Images médiévales de l'âge en littérature anglaise*. Paris: Harmattan, 2005. 199 pp. Eleven articles in French and English by various authors exploring the themes of youth and age in Old and Middle English literature. For two essays that pertain to Chaucer, see nos. 198 and 328.

101. Carruthers, Mary. "Our 'crafty science': Institutional Support and Humanist Discipline." Colloquium: Administrative Perspectives on Chaucer Studies. *SAC* 27 (2005): 269–76. Encourages medievalists to recognize the realities of academic institutions and to participate in administrative processes.

102. Crane, Christopher Elliott. "'Now mendys oure chere from sorow': The Rhetoric of Humor in Middle English Drama, Spiritual Instruction, and Chaucerian Religious Comedy." *DAI* 65 (2005): 3377A. Examines the relationship between humor and religious rhetoric in a variety of texts, including *CT*, *BD* and *TC*.

103. D'Arcy, Anne Marie, and Alan J. Fletcher, eds. *Studies in Late Medieval and Early Renaissance Texts in Honour of John Scattergood: "The key*

of all good remembrance." Dublin: Four Courts, 2005. 416 pp. Twenty-four essays by various authors and a bibliography of Scattergood's publications. For eight essays that pertain to Chaucer, see nos. 39, 169, 227, 273, 319, 325, 330, and 332.

104. Denny-Brown, Andrea B. "Beyond the Fig Leaf: Sexuality, Consumption, and the Clothed Medieval Self." *DAI* 65 (2005): 2981A. Considers Chaucer's vernacular poetry as part of the discourse on "vestimentary appearance and consumption."

105. Duncan, Thomas G. *A Companion to the Middle English Lyric.* Woodbridge, Suffolk, and Rochester, N.Y.: D. S. Brewer, 2005. xxv, 302 pp. An introduction and twelve essays by various authors survey critical issues related to Middle English lyrics—courtly, popular, religious, political, etc. Individual essays consider topics such as manuscripts, meter and editing, carols, lyrics in sermons, gender issues, and Middle Scots lyrics. The book contains recurrent references to Chaucer's stand-alone and embedded lyrics, with one essay that pertains directly to his works. See no. 318.

106. Economou, George D. "Chaucer and Langland: A Fellowship of Makers." In Robert M. Stein and Sandra Pierson Prior, eds. *Reading Medieval Culture: Essays in Honor of Robert W. Hanning* (*SAC* 29 [2007], no. 146): 290–301. Economou considers a range of possibilities—that Chaucer and Langland knew each other, knew each other's works, or shared the same literary context. Focuses on *GP* and *Ret* of *CT*.

107. Edwards, David L. *Poets and God: Chaucer, Shakespeare, Herbert, Milton, Wordsworth, Coleridge, Blake.* London: Darton, Longman, and Todd, 2005. xv, 256 pp. Appreciative criticism of seven major poets, aware of academic theory (formalist, psychoanalytic, feminist) but addressed to a nonacademic audience. Chapter 1, "Chaucer" (pp. 1–33), considers Chaucer's characterization, moral tolerance, comedy, tragedy, and Christian humanism. See also no. 353.

108. Ellis, Steve, ed. *Chaucer: An Oxford Guide.* Oxford: Oxford University Press, 2005. xxiv, 644 pp. 14 b&w illus. Thirty-six essays on individual topics, plus an introduction (by Ellis) and a postscript (Julian Wasserman). Part 1 (historical contexts): Chaucer's life (Ruth Evans), society and politics (S. H. Rigby), nationhood (Ardis Butterfield), London (C. David Benson), religion (Jim Rhodes), chivalry (Mark Sherman), literacy and literary production (Stephen Penn), Chaucer's language (Donka Minkova), philosophy (Richard Utz), science (J. A. Tasioulas), visual culture (David Griffith), sexuality (Alcuin Blamires), identity and

subjecthood (John M. Ganim), love and marriage (Bernard O'Donoghue). Part 2 (literary contexts): classical (Helen Cooper), English (Wendy Scase), French (Helen Phillips), Italian (Nick Havely), biblical (Valerie Edden). Part 3 (readings): modern criticism (Elizabeth Robertson), feminisms (Gail Ashton), carnivalesque (Marion Turner), postmodernism (Barry Windeatt), new historicism (Sylvia Federico), queer theory (Glenn Burger), postcolonialism (Jeffery J. Cohen), psychoanalytic criticism (Patricia Clare Ingham). Part 4 (reception): editing (Elizabeth Scala), 1400–1700 (John J. Thompson), 1700–1900 (David Matthews), 1900–present (Stephanie Trigg), translations (Malcolm Andrew), performance (Kevin J. Harty), guides (Peter Brown). Part 5 (study resources): printed (Mark Allen), electronic (Philippa Semper). See also no. 356.

109. Fichte, Jörg O. "Chaucer's Work in German Literary Scholarship." *PoeticaT* 29–30 (1989): 93–101. Surveys studies of Chaucer written in German from the mid-nineteenth century until World War I.

110. Galloway, Andrew. "Middle English Prologues." In David F. Johnson and Elaine Treharne, eds. *Readings in Medieval Texts: Interpreting Old and Middle English Literature* (*SAC* 29 [2007], no. 120): 288–305. Galloway examines the claims to authority—traditional and innovative—found in prologues to Middle English works, with special attention to Chaucer's *HF*, *LGWP*, *GP*, and other prologues in *CT* (e.g., *WBP*). The essay identifies four types of prologues in Middle English: the "redactor's prologue" (which emphasizes the writer's role as collector or compiler), the "testimonial" prologue, the "commentary" prologue, and the "literary autobiographical" prologue.

111. Gildow, Jason R. "Origin and Adaptation of the Medieval Theban Narrative from Gildas to Shakespeare." *DAI* 65 (2005): 2981A. Examines the treatment of Theban/Oedipal myth in Chaucer, Lydgate, and Shakespeare.

112. Gilles, Sealy, and Sylvia Tomasch. "Professionalizing Chaucer: John Matthews Manly, Edith Rickert, and the *Canterbury Tales* as Cultural Capital." In Robert M. Stein and Sandra Pierson Prior, eds. *Reading Medieval Culture: Essays in Honor of Robert W. Hanning* (*SAC* 29 [2007], no. 146): 364–83. Describes the "scientific humanism" that underlies the scholarship of Manly and Rickert and that prompted them to construct Chaucer as "an ideal bourgeois." Their efforts to establish Chaucer as an originary ideal through a wholly authoritative text failed because of a shift in cultural valuation.

113. Haas, Renate. "From the *Vormärz* to the Empire: The Socio-Political Context of the Golden Age of German Chaucer Scholarship." *PoeticaT* 29–30 (1989): 102–14. Assesses the sociopolitical assumptions and implications of mid-nineteenth-century German study of Chaucer, especially pre-academic translations and commentary.

114. Hamaguchi, Keiko. *Chaucer and Women*. Tokyo: Eihosha, 2005. xiv, 168 pp. Eight previously printed essays, seven on Chaucer and one on Shakespeare's Cressida. See *SAC* 11 (1989), no. 186; *SAC* 12 (1990), no. 124; *SAC* 17 (1995), no. 203; *SAC* 20 (1998), no. 248; *SAC* 21 (1999), no. 108); *SAC* 24 (2002), no. 282; and *SAC* 29 (2007), no. 184.

115. Hanks, D. Thomas, Jr. "Chaucer, Auctoritas, and the Problem of Pain." In T. L. Burton and John F. Plummer, eds. *"Seyd in Forme and Reverence": Essays on Chaucer and Chaucerians in Memory of Emerson Brown, Jr.* (*SAC* 29 [2007], no. 96): 219–36. Surveys Chaucer's concern with the coexistence of a beneficent God and the suffering of humans in *KnT*, *MLT*, *ClT*, and *FranT*. Chaucer often poses this issue by alluding to Job.

116. Hanna, Ralph. *London Literature, 1300–1380*. Cambridge Studies in Medieval Literature, no. 57. Cambridge: Cambridge University Press, 2005. xxi, 359 pp. Analyzes the cultural conditions of literary production and the books produced in England, 1300–1380, focusing on English vernacular works but also attending to Latin and French ones, seeking to understand the textual communities defined by such texts. Hanna considers linguistic features (the transition from Type II to Type III English, Anglo-Norman, etc.), as well as literary genres such as romance, biblical commentary, history, and legal discourse, with extended attention to the Auchinleck Manuscript, Laud miscellaneous 622, Pepys 2498, the Chandos Herald, and Langland's *Piers Plowman*. Comments on ways that Chaucer helped to displace earlier traditions, with attention to *Th*, the *GP* description of the Parson, and Chaucer's status as a court poet. See also no. 367.

117. Hansen, Elaine Tuttle. "Response: Chaucerian Values." Colloquium: Administrative Perspectives on Chaucer Studies. *SAC* 27 (2005): 277–87. Expresses concerns about contemporary higher education—from "prevailing careerism to the overall decline in literary reading"—and encourages "Chaucerian values" among university administrators.

118. Helterman, Jeffrey. "Geoffrey Chaucer (1340?–1400)." In Jeffrey Helterman and Jerome Mitchell, eds. *Old and Middle English Literature*. Dictionary of Literary Biography, no. 146. Detroit: Gale, 1994, pp.127–44. 5 b&w illus. Introduces Chaucer's life and works, summa-

rizing historical context, plots, relations to sources, themes, and critical issues. Includes a brief bibliography of manuscripts, editions, and critical works.

119. Honegger, Thomas, ed. *Riddles, Knights, and Cross-Dressing Saints: Essays on Medieval English Language and Literature*. Bern: Lang, 2004. 222 pp. Eight essays by various authors, selected from the papers presented at SEM (Studientag zum Englisches Mittelalter) 4 and 5, held in Potsdam in 2002 and 2003, respectively. Three essays pertain to Chaucer; see nos. 60, 75, and 315.

120. Johnson, David F., and Elaine Treharne, eds. *Readings in Medieval Texts: Interpreting Old and Middle English Literature*. Oxford: Oxford University Press, 2005. [xii], 400 pp. Twenty-five essays by various contributors, addressing individual works or genres and designed for "students undertaking courses in Old and Middle English." The book includes recurrent references to Chaucer's works, with two essays that pertain to them directly. See nos. 110 and 279.

121. Kaylor, Noel Harold, Jr. "Karl Heinz Göller's Essay 'Geoffrey Chaucer: *Troilus and Criseyde.*'" In Uwe Böker et al., eds. *Of Remembraunce the Keye: Medieval Literature and Its Impact Through the Ages. Festschrift for Karl Heinz Göller on the Occasion of His 80th Birthday* (*SAC* 29 [2007], no. 88): 17–45. English translation of a German essay that was first published in 1969, assessing the narrative techniques, structure, characters, and major themes of *TC*.

122. Kelly, Henry Ansgar. "Jews and Saracens in Chaucer's England: A Review of the Evidence." *SAC* 27 (2005): 129–69. Compiles evidence for the presence of Jews, Muslims, and other non-Christians in late medieval England, using as sources public records, sermons, and toponyms. Chaucer likely had significant contact with non-Christians—or recently converted Christians—while at home in England, as well as abroad.

123. Kendrick, Laura. "'In bourde and in pleye': *Mankind* and the Problem of Comic Derision in Medieval English Religious Plays." *ÉA* 58 (2005): 261–75. Includes references to Chaucer's fabliaux.

124. Knapp, Peggy A. "Aesthetic Attention and the Chaucerian Text." *ChauR* 39 (2005): 241–58. Knapp argues that a historicized, aesthetic appreciation of Chaucer is possible, despite recent tendencies to focus on ideological issues only. The aesthetic theories of Kant and Gadamer help to explain the roles of subjectivity, universality, and ge-

nius in the perception of aesthetic value. The article comments on *Bo*, *CT*, and *TC*.

125. Liu, Jin. "Chaucer's Dream Poetry and the Medieval Tradition of Dream Vision." *Wai Guo Wen Xue Yan Jiu* [*Foreign Literature Studies*] 6.116 (2005): 112–17, 174 (in Chinese, with English abstract). Describes adaptations of dream-vision conventions in Chaucer's early works, arguing that Chaucer transcends the genre.

126. Masi, Michael. *Chaucer and Gender*. New York: Peter Lang, 2005. 165 pp. Masi investigates depictions of women in Chaucer's works compared to depictions in works of other authors, including Christine de Pizan, Aquinas, and Boethius. He links Chaucer's *LGW* and Pizan, suggesting that Eustace Deschamps may have been a mediator; also suggests that Chaucer's use of the incubus figure is pivotal in his Lucretia account in *LGW*. Assesses the Wife of Bath's central role in the Marriage Group, her role in *ShT*, and her uses of logic as it is found in Boethius. Discusses Cecilia's feminine discourse in *SNT* in relation to medieval stereotypes, suggesting contrasts with Pertelote of *NPT*, Prudence of *Mel*, the Wife of Bath, and Criseyde. Also considers the feminine and masculine aspects of Criseyde's logical discourse.

127. McCarthy, Conor. *Marriage in Medieval England: Law, Literature, and Practice*. Woodbridge, Suffolk: Boydell, 2004. [viii], 185 pp. McCarthy explores how marriage is represented in medieval English literary and legal texts and the "relationship of these representations to actual practice." Subjects range from *Beowulf* and Old English laws to late medieval ecclesiastical statutes and the works of Chaucer and his contemporaries, including such topics as marital consent, property rights, love and sex, the family, and more. McCarthy comments on *LGW* and portions of *CT*, especially *KnT*, *WBP*, *MerT*, *FranT*, and *ParsT*. See also no. 385.

128. Moore, Colette. "Representing Speech in Early English." *DAI* 65 (2005): 3815A. Moore shows that medieval poems (including Chaucer's) "exploit the less-determined systems of medieval speech marking for aesthetic and rhetorical purposes."

129. Moulton, Ian Frederick, ed. *Reading and Literacy in the Middle Ages and Renaissance*. Arizona Studies in the Middle Ages and the Renaissance, no. 8. Turnhout: Brepols, 2004. xviii, 193 pp. Nine essays by various authors on reading habits and the trope of reading in the late Middle Ages and the Early Modern period. The introduction by Moulton (ix–xviii) comments on evidence of reading practice in *GP* and other

literature and summarizes the essays included in the volume. For two essays that pertain to Chaucer, see nos. 32 and 306.

130. Nachtwey, Gerald R. " 'Swete harm': Chivalry and the Consent to Violence in the Works of Geoffrey Chaucer and Jean Froissart." *DAI* 66 (2005): 1680A. Nachtwey argues that chivalry was "a pragmatic institution" that created a framework for understanding/controlling knightly violence. He further argues that this concept of chivalry is apparent in the works of Froissart and Chaucer (especially in *TC* and *CT*), as well as in a host of chivalric manuals.

131. Pugh, Tison. "Chaucer's Rape, Southern Racism, and the Pedagogical Ethics of Authorial Malfeasance." *CE* 67 (2005): 569–86. Consideration of authorial agency enables professors and students to explore relationships between personal ethos and literary texts. Ethical criticism frames discussions of whether Chaucer raped Cecily Chaumpaigne or whether Flannery O'Connor was a racist and thus enables students to develop a more critically sophisticated and ethically engaged analysis.

132. ———. *Queering Medieval Genres.* The New Middle Ages. New York: Palgrave Macmillan, 2004. x, 226 pp. Pugh assesses the "nonnormative" features of several genres in medieval literature—lyric, fabliau, tragedy, and romance—exploring not only representations and suggestions of homosexual behaviors but also how these behaviors disrupt readers' expectations of genre and ideological power. One chapter considers Latin lyrics; another, *Sir Gawain and the Green Knight.* Two chapters pertain to Chaucer: one focuses on adaptations of genre expectation compelled by heteronormativity in the fabliaux of *CT* (especially *MilT* and *WBPT*, but others as well); the other, on how Pandarus's relations with Troilus in *TC* suggest resistance to courtly codes, Christian teleology, and the genre of tragedy.

133. Quinn, William A. "Harriet Monroe as Queen-Critic of Chaucer and Langland (*viz.* Ezra Pound)." *SiM* 14 (2005): 200–216. Monroe's essay "Chaucer and Langland," published in her journal *Poetry* in 1915, argued that Chaucer's preference for French forms and rhythms had cut off later English poetry from the true native tradition represented by Langland's alliterative verse. The essay was intended to counter the strong critical influence of her sometime collaborator in *Poetry*, Ezra Pound, who "adored" Chaucer, and to remind him of native qualities he himself had captured in his "truly wonderful paraphrase" of the *Seafarer*.

134. Ransom, Daniel J. "Annotating Chaucer: Some Corrections and

Additions." In T. L. Burton and John F. Plummer, eds. *"Seyd in Forme and Reverence": Essays on Chaucer and Chaucerians in Memory of Emerson Brown, Jr.* (*SAC* 29 [2007], no. 96): 205–15. Offers adjustments or expansions to explanations of several of Chaucer's allusions: the labors of Hercules, Lucia, Xantippe, Chrysippus, a number of place names, etc.

135. Raybin, David, and Susanna Fein. "Chaucer and Aesthetics." *ChauR* 39 (2005): 225–33. Raybin and Fein introduce the six essays included in this "special issue" of *ChauR*, all pertaining to Chaucer and aesthetics; see nos. 124, 249, 265, 275, 303, and 304.

136. Richardson, Catherine. *Chaucer: A Beginner's Guide.* London: Hodder & Stoughton, 2001. v, 90 pp. Introduces Chaucer and his works, with focus on *CT*, and provides commentary on context, themes, and critical approaches. The guide is aimed at high school students or students early in college.

137. Richmond, Velma Bourgeois. *Chaucer as Children's Literature: Retellings from the Victorian and Edwardian Eras.* Jefferson, N.C.: McFarland, 2004. viii, 255 pp. Richmond studies British and American adaptations of Chaucer's *CT* for children, from Charles Cowden Clarke's *Tales from Chaucer in Prose* (1833) until World War I. She examines the selections and adaptations of the *Tales* and the accompanying illustrations, exploring didactic and pedagogical values that underlie the texts and illustrations, as well as relationships with the contemporary book trade, artistic traditions, educational reforms, and cultural nostalgia. Also considers the inclusion of Chaucer's works in schoolbooks and the development of his status as "Father" of English poetry. The book includes a bibliography of "Victorian and Edwardian Books of Chaucer for Children," plus several tables that identify which *Tales* were selected and illustrated in these books. See also no. 393.

138. ———. "Ford Madox Brown's Protestant Medievalism: Chaucer and Wycliffe." *C&L* 54 (2005): 363–96. Four historical paintings by Ford Madox Brown (1821–93) exhibit the interplay among literature, art, and religion in Victorian medievalism. Chaucer is the primary focus in *The Seeds and Fruits of English Poetry* (1845) and *Chaucer at the Court of Edward III* (1851, 1867–68). In addition, Chaucer is a witness to Wycliffe in *Wycliffe Reading His Translation of the Bible to John of Gaunt, in the Presence of Chaucer and Gower* (1847–48, 1859–61) and in *Wycliffe on His Trial* (1884–86). Brown saw Chaucer and Wycliffe, through their development of English poetry and prose, respectively, as crucial to

breaking the hold of the Catholic Church in England and establishing national identity.

139. Sadlack, Erin A. "'In Writing It May be Spoke': The Politics of Women's Letter-Writing, 1377–1603." *DAI* 66 (2005): 1782A. In a larger discussion of women's letter-writing, Sadlack notes that "Ovid, Chaucer, and Gower suggest that letters are often the best means for women to communicate."

140. Saunders, Corinne. "Chaucer's Romances." In Corinne Saunders, ed. *A Companion to Romance: From Classical to Contemporary*. Malden, Mass.: Blackwell, 2004, pp. 85–103. Chaucer transcended and transgressed the commonly accepted conventions of "romance": *Th* parodies the genre, while *BD* elevates its status by associating romance with classical works. *Th*, *KnT*, *SqT*, *FranT*, and *WBT* reflect a variety of approaches to romance. In *TC*, Chaucer combines realism and romance and raises "existential questions relating to free will, faith, and transience."

141. Schleburg, Florian. "Role-Conformity and Role-Playing in Troilus, Pandarus, and Criseyde." In Uwe Böker et al., eds. *Of Remembraunce the Keye: Medieval Literature and Its Impact Through the Ages. Festschrift for Karl Heinz Göller on the Occasion of His 80th Birthday* (*SAC* 29 [2007], no. 88): 79–93. The three main characters of *TC* "embody three widely different ways of handling the roles they want to be judged by": total identification (Troilus), total detachment (Pandarus), and acceptance with reservations (Criseyde). Although Chaucer could not have had role-playing theory in mind, he was sensitive to "what happens when three persons of so incompatible views on reality are let loose on each other."

142. Shiomi, Tomoyuki. *Chusei Goshikku Kaiga to Chosa* [*Medieval Gothic Art and Chaucer*]. Tokyo: Kobundo, 2005 (in Japanese, except for pages 179–200). 206 pp.; illus. Assesses Chaucer's works in the light of medieval English and European art.

143. Spearing, A. C. *Textual Subjectivity: The Encoding of Subjectivity in Medieval Narratives and Lyrics*. Oxford: Oxford University Press, 2005. viii, 273 pp. Spearing counters the assumption that all medieval narration implies a narrator. Medieval literature is permeated with subjectivity, but it is often "subjectless subjectivity," better compared to painting than to oral storytelling. Similar to twentieth-century experiments in disembodied perception, medieval fiction was just beginning to explore the possibility of representing unified consciousness. Examination of linguistic phenomena, such as deixis, shows how subjectivity is encoded in

medieval lyrics and narratives, even though it is not represented as the product of a unitary speaking voice. Spearing considers *TC, MLT*, and *Pity,* as well as other works of Middle English literature.

144. Staley, Lynn. *Languages of Power in the Age of Richard II*. University Park: Pennsylvania State University, 2005. xiv, 394 pp. Explores how late medieval English literature helps us to understand contemporary political events and aristocratic efforts to develop a successful rhetoric of power amid shifts in control. Chapter 1 focuses on Richard I, political discourse, and the discourse of courtly love in Gower, Usk, Clanvowe, and Chaucer (*TC, LGWP, KnT, FranT*). Chapter 2 considers the Merciless Parliament to be a watershed that changed the discourses of the court and courtliness, documented by chroniclers and here paralleled with political address in Valois France; considers in this light Part 7 of *CT*, especially *NPT* and *ManT*. Chapter 3 explores patronage, John of Gaunt, and Thomas of Woodstock; and chapter 4 assesses the household as a political metaphor in French literature, courtesy books, several romances, and *CT (MLT, ClT, Mel)*. See also no. 401.

145. Stanley, E. G. "Parody in Early English Literature." *PoeticaT* 27 (1988): 1–69. Surveys parody and parodic devices in Middle English literature, arguing that, though there is much that is coarse in this literature, there is little actual parody outside of liturgical texts. *Th* is Chaucer's only true parody, although elsewhere (e.g., in portions of *PF, MilT, NPT*) he approaches parody while lampooning or satirizing.

146. Stein, Robert M., and Sandra Pierson Prior, eds. *Reading Medieval Culture: Essays in Honor of Robert W. Hanning*. Notre Dame: University of Notre Dame Press, 2005. ix, 505 pp. Twenty essays by various authors and a bibliography of Hanning's publications. The essays are divided into three sections: history and romance, Chaucer's works, and Italian contexts. For nine essays that pertain to Chaucer, see nos. 58, 106, 112, 185, 209, 226, 242, 262, and 305.

147. Stévanovitch, Colette, and Henry Daniels, eds. *L'Affect et le jugement: Mélanges offerts à Michel Morel à l'occasion de son départ à la retraite.* 2 vols. xiv, 574 pp. Publications de l'Association des Médiévistes Anglicistes de l'Enseignement Supérieur. Collection GRENDEL, no. 6. Paris: AMAES, 2005. xiv, 574 pp. Includes two essays that pertain to Chaucer; see nos. 214 and 297.

148. Thompson, N. S. "Geoffrey Chaucer (c. 1340–1400)." In Jay Parini, ed. *British Writers. Retrospective Supplement II*. New York: Scrib-

ner's, 2002, pp. 33–50. Surveys Chaucer's reception, life, and works, with recurrent attention to Chaucer's nascent realism.

149. Tomasch, Sylvia. "Searching for a Medievalist: Some (Generally Positive) News About the State of Chaucer Studies." Colloquium: Administrative Perspectives on Chaucer Studies. *SAC* 27 (2005): 249–59. Characterizes the "scholarly interests" of the more than 150 applicants for a 2003 tenure-track job in medieval studies at Hunter College of the City University of New York.

150. Trigg, Stephanie. "Walking Through Cathedrals: Scholars, Pilgrims, and Medieval Tourists." *NML* 7 (2005): 9–33. Distinguishes among "various ways in which medieval English religious sites are mediated for visitors," from cathedrals (including Canterbury) to the Canterbury Tales Visitor Attraction. Assesses the authenticity of visitors' experiences in light of theories of tourism, comments on Brian Helgeland's movie *A Knight's Tale*, and concludes that there is no pure "medieval" separate from medievalism.

151. Van Dyke, Carolynn. *Chaucer's Agents: Cause and Representation in Chaucerian Narrative*. Madison, N.J.: Fairleigh Dickinson University Press, 2005. 371 pp. Examines agency as theme and narrative technique throughout Chaucer's corpus, considering the "multifariousness" of the topic. Agency does not refer exclusively to the human will; it also "embraces innumerable forces that operate interdependently"—not only "multiple but also bidirectional." Chaucer's works present for consideration the agency of nonhuman forces as they affect human affairs (birds, gods, universals), with parallel attention to humans as both "instigators and instruments"—producers of art and social constructs and respondents to such forces. Often gendered female, Chaucer's protagonists are at times paradoxically passive, suggesting that human freedom "arises from our ability to confer freedom on our own agents, human and non-human."

152. Weisl, Angela Jane. *The Persistence of Medievalism: Narrative Adventures in Contemporary Culture*. The New Middle Ages. New York: Palgrave Macmillan, 2003. ix, 277 pp. Weisl explores residual traces in contemporary American popular culture of medieval narrative structures and patterns—e.g., pilgrimage, veneration of relics, conversion, heroic accomplishment, romance, fabliau—identifying such patterns in sports (especially baseball), popular news scandals, film, and television. Recurrent references to Chaucer. Includes bibliography and index.

153. Yandell, Stephen. "Concealed Revelation: The Work of the

Prophet in Late Medieval Britain." *DAI* 65 (2005): 2983A. Argues that Chaucer "uses prophecy as a way of proposing alternate, flexible modes of reading."

154. Yuko, Tagaya, and Masahiko Kanno, eds. *Words and Literature: Essays in Honour of Professor Masa Ikegami*. Tokyo: Eihosha, 2004. iii, 293 pp. Includes three essays that pertain to Chaucer; see nos. 194, 207, and 230.

The Canterbury Tales—General

155. Behrman, Mary Davy. "Chaucer, Gower, and the Vox Populi: Interpretation and the Common Profit in *The Canterbury Tales* and *Confessio Amantis*." *DAI* 65 (2005): 2981A. *CT*—in part a reaction to Gower's conservative conception of vernacular literature in *Confessio Amantis*—is a text encouraging interpretive autonomy.

156. Chicote, Gloria B. "La construcción ficcionel en las colecciones de cuentos medievales: *Libro del conde lucanor*, *Decameron*, y *Canterbury Tales*." In Lillian von der Walde Moheno, ed. *Propuestas teórico-metodológicas para el estudio de la literatura hispánica medieva*. Publicaciones de Medievalia, no. 27. Mexico: Universidad Nacional Autónoma de México, 2003, pp. 165–89. Three features characterize the collections of tales of Don Juan Manuel, Boccaccio, and Chaucer, especially as they relate to cultural context: marks of realism or authentication, thematic concern with unity and diversity, and the presence of the author and his relationship with his audience.

157. Cornelius, Michael G. "Geoffrey Chaucer's *Canterbury Tales*: Gender in the Middle Ages (ca. 1388–1400)." In Jerilyn Fisher and Ellen S. Silber, eds. *Women in Literature: Reading Through the Lens of Gender*. Westport, Conn.: Greenwood, 2003, pp. 69–71. The stereotypes depicted in Cecilia, the Wife of Bath, and Griselda reflect the continuing conflict between women who want to escape submissive roles and those who accommodate abusive relationships. Cornelius encourages classroom discussion of *SNT*, *WBPT*, and *ClT* in quantitative and qualitative terms.

158. DeSpain, Jessica. "A Book Arts Pilgrimage: Arts and Crafts Socialism and the Kelmscott *Chaucer*." *Journal of the William Morris Society* 15.4 (2004): 74–90. In his Kelmscott *Chaucer*, Morris presents Chaucer as a proponent of anticapitalist socialism, consistent with Morris's own arts and crafts movement. The essay comments on the heteroglot

voices of the Canterbury pilgrims and the Kelmscott illustrations of Chaucer that frame *CT* in this edition; compares these features with Morris's own interests and activities.

159. Ganze, Alison L. "Seeking Trouthe in Chaucer's *Canterbury Tales.*" *DAI* 65 (2005): 4189A. Ganze discusses concepts and manifestations of "trouthe" in *MLT*, *ClT*, and *FranT*.

160. Gariano, Carmelo. *Juan Ruiz, Boccaccio, Chaucer*. Explicación de Textos Literarios, no. 13.2. Sacramento: Department of Foreign Languages, California State University, 1984 (in Spanish). 175 pp. Comparative analysis of the themes, techniques, and intertextual relationships of Ruiz's *Libro de buen amor,* Boccaccio's *Decameron*, and *CT*. Topics include worldview, love and passion, nascent humanism, satire and irony, and narrative structures. Recurrent emphasis on the innovations of Ruiz.

161. Griffith, John Lance. "Anger in the *Canterbury Tales.*" *DAI* 66 (2005): 173A. Anger "rises to the level of a philosophical and ethical problem for Chaucer." An understanding of the role anger plays in the formation of self and community is useful in understanding the communities Chaucer creates and examines in *CT*.

162. Mertens-Fonck, Paule. "*Les contes de Canterbury* et la querelle des universaux." In Colette Stévanovitch, ed. *L'Articulation langue-littérature dans les textes médiévaux anglais*. Collection GRENDEL, no. 5. Nancy: Association des Médiévistes Anglicistes de l'Enseignement Supérieur, 2005, pp. 99–116. *CT* reflects the medieval philosophical debate over universals, posing traditional literature in tension with more fully actualized characterization.

163. ———. "Les deux débats complémentaires des *Contes de Canterbury.*" In Marie-Françoise Alamichel, ed. *La complémentarité: Mélanges offerts à Josseline Bidard et Arlette Sancery à l'occasion de leur départ en retraite* (*SAC* 29 [2007], no. 85): 177–85. Two intertwined debates underlie *CT*: (1) a tension between traditional literature and individualizing contemporary details, and (2) the realist/nominalist debate over universals.

164. Miller, Mark. *Philosophical Chaucer: Love, Sex, and Agency in the "Canterbury Tales."* Cambridge: Cambridge University Press, 2004. x, 289 pp. Although Chaucer is often considered a poet of love or of philosophy, an examination of the philosophical facets of *CT*—especially practical reason, individual agency, and autonomy—illuminates the ideologies of sex, gender, and love within his works. This analysis encourages a reformulation and broadening of our understanding of ideol-

ogy and practical reason and their relationship to normativity. In *MilT* and *KnT*, natural impulses are in tension with practical reason. A reading of the *Consolation of Philosophy* provides a foundation for understanding "why normativity resists grounding in a comprehensive theory," illustrating in the Prisoner a tension between desire and action and thus exploring the mutually shaping forces of practical rationality and psychological phenomena. A close reading of *Rom* provides a better understanding of how these forces shape eroticism in Chaucer, especially as it appears in *WBP*, *WBT*, and *ClT*. See also no. 388.

165. Pakkala-Weckström, Mari. *The Dialogue of Love, Marriage, and "Maistrie" in Chaucer's "Canterbury Tales."* Mémoires de la Société Néophilologique de Helsinki, no. 67. Helsinki: Société Néophilologique, 2005. 265 pp. Explores the relationships between power ("maistrie") and gender in *CT* as these relationships are reflected in conversation and the dialogue of spouses and lovers in seven *Tales*: *MilT*, *WBT*, *ClT*, *MerT*, *FranT*, *ShT*, and *Mel*. Using techniques of historical pragmatics, Pakkala-Weckström examines such matters as politeness strategies, forms of address, pronoun usage, and speech acts—especially as they operate under a variety of conditions, including literary genre and the status of medieval women.

166. Plummer, John F. "Tables, *Cupiditas,* and Vessels of Tree: Chaucer's Use of The Epistles to Timothy." In T. L. Burton and John F. Plummer, eds. *"Seyd in Forme and Reverence": Essays on Chaucer and Chaucerians in Memory of Emerson Brown, Jr.* (*SAC* 29 [2007], no. 96): 237–45. Considers citations of Paul's epistles to Timothy in *WBPT*, *PardPT*, and *ParsPT*, reading them in light of late fourteenth-century concerns with preaching and pastoral care—Lollard and anti-Lollard, mendicant and antimendicant. Chaucer was concerned with the performative force of language.

167. Shiomi, Tomoyuki. *Chaucer Kenkyu* [*Studies in Chaucer*]. Tokyo: Kobundo, 2004 (in Japanese). vi, 255pp. A selection of essays on Chaucer's works, with attention to structure and meaning, focusing on *CT*.

168. Vaughan, Míceál F. "Chaucer's *Canterbury Tales* and the Auchinleck MS: Analogous Collections?" *Archiv* 242 (2005): 259–74. Manuscript compilations, especially the Auchinleck MS, are structural analogues to *CT*. Manuscripts segmented into booklets parallel the fragments in *CT* in four ways: segments vary considerably in size and shape; common subjects and themes link portions that are not contiguous; seg-

ments evince multiple "voices" in scribal hands and literary styles; and portions are incomplete or unfinished.

See also nos. 7, 11, 12, 16, 17, 20, 33, 35, 36, 46, 48, 55, 77, 82, 95, 102, 124, 137, 140, 185, 266.

CT—The General Prologue

169. Allen, Valerie. "Playing Soldiers: Tournament and Toxophily in Late-Medieval England." In Anne Marie D'Arcy and Alan J. Fletcher, eds. *Studies in Late Medieval and Early Renaissance Texts in Honour of John Scattergood* (*SAC* 29 [2007], no. 103): 35–52. Allen explores the showiness and ideology of tournaments in late medieval England, not only for knights but also for archers, focusing on Roger Ascham's *Toxophilus* for information about the latter. Allen comments on Chaucer's *GP* Yeoman as an absent presence.

170. Hodges, Laura. *Chaucer and Clothing: Clerical and Academic Costume in the General Prologue to "The Canterbury Tales."* Chaucer Studies, no. 34. Rochester, N.Y.; and Woodbridge, Suffolk: D. S. Brewer, 2005. xiv, 316 pp. 16 b&w illus.; 8 color illus. Assesses the details and implications of the clothing and accoutrements of the clerical and academic pilgrims in *GP*, discussing the Prioress, Monk, Friar, Clerk, Physician, Parson, Pardoner, and Summoner. More richly symbolic than secular dress, clerical dress must be understood in terms of social and literary values developed over time and exploited by Chaucer. Hodges introduces historical, linguistic, sartorial, and literary contexts as backgrounds to the descriptions. She examines each detail of the descriptions (and illustrations surviving in the manuscripts) to explain how "costume rhetoric" is fundamental to Chaucer's creation of character in *GP*.

171. Kendrick, Laura. "Lives and Works: Chaucer and the Compilers of the Troubadour Songbooks." In Teodolinda Barolini, ed. *Medieval Constructions in Gender and Identity: Essays in Honor of Joan M. Ferrante*. Tempe: Arizona Center for Medieval and Renaissance Studies, 2005, pp. 103–15. Kendrick compares *GP* to the vernacular compilations of lives of the troubadours in fourteenth-century songbooks. A revised version of *SAC* 25 (2003), no. 170.

172. Steiner, Emily. "*Piers Plowman*, Diversity, and the Medieval Political Aesthetic." *Representations* 91 (2005): 1–25. Assesses the political character of late medieval English poetry, arguing that it extends the

political thinking found in contemporary legal writing. Focuses on the notion of "diversity" in *Piers Plowman* and other alliterative verse as an extension of Continental legal thought and explores contrasts between Langland's "field of folk" and Chaucer's "sundry folk" in *GP*.

See also nos. 38, 106, 110, 116, 129, 176, 177, 183, 200, 201, 230, 239, 252, 255, 256.

CT—The Knight and His Tale

173. Boehler, Karl E. "Heroic Destruction: Shame and Guilt Cultures in Medieval Heroic Poetry." *DAI* 66 (2005):1348A. Boehler employs the concept of "shame culture" (which emphasizes satisfaction and honor over personal happiness, or even survival) as a means to examine medieval heroes (including those in *KnT*.) Ultimately, shame culture contributes not only to the death of heroes but also to the death of their societies; it is eventually supplanted by "guilt culture," as seen in *Sir Gawain and the Green Knight*.

174. Greenwood, Maria. "The Discourses of Chivalry and Courtly Love in Chaucer and Malory: With Particular Reference to *The Knight's Tale* and *The Book of Tristram*." In Colette Stévanovitch, ed. *L'Articulation langue-littérature dans les textes médiévaux anglais*. Collection GRENDEL, no. 5. Nancy: Association des Médiévistes Anglicistes de l'Enseignement Supérieur, 2005, pp. 133–56. Greenwood contrasts Chaucer's and Malory's uses of models and antimodels in depictions of chivalry and courtly love.

175. Greenwood, Maria. "Theseus and His 'Manly' Fight in Chaucer's *The Knight's Tale*." In Colette Stévanovitch, ed. *L'Articulation langue-littérature dans les textes médiévaux anglais*. Collection GRENDEL, no. 5. Nancy: Association des Médiévistes Anglicistes de l'Enseignement Supérieur, 2005, pp. 157–75. Greenwood examines the meaning of *manly* as applied to the character of Theseus in *KnT*.

176. Keen, Maurice. "Chaucer and Chivalry Re-Visited." In Matthew Strickland, ed. *Armies, Chivalry, and Warfare in Medieval Britain and France: Proceedings of the 1995 Harlaxton Symposium*. Harlaxton Medieval Studies, no. 7. Stamford, Lincolnshire: Watkins, 1998, pp. 1–12. Keen surveys a range of late medieval attitudes toward chivalry, knighthood, and warfare, especially a "streak of puritanism" that criti-

cized the vainglory of chivalry. He considers a range of texts, including Chaucer's *ParsT* and the *GP* description of the Knight.

177. Krochalis, Jeanne. "'And ridden in Belmarye': Chaucer's General Prologue, Line 57." *ANQ* 18.4 (2005): 3–8. In *GP*, "Belmarye," one of the Knight's destinations, might well be glossed as a reference to Almerin (a province between Granada and Algezir), spelled "Balmarie" in a mid-fifteenth-century manuscript.

178. Stretter, Robert. "Cupid's Wheel: Love and Fortune in *The Knight's Tale*." *M&H*, n.s., 31 (2005): 59–82. Discusses the "amatory fatalism" of *KnT* as Chaucer's means to explore "problems of chance, destiny, and Providence." Somewhat different from *TC* in this regard, *KnT* poses love as analogous to fate. Chaucer uses the analogy to focus on human perception of experience as well as on the order that frames it.

179. Thomas, Paul R. "Chaucer's *Knight's Tale*: Were Arcite and Emelye Really Married? Why It Matters." In T. L. Burton and John F. Plummer, eds. *"Seyd in Forme and Reverence": Essays on Chaucer and Chaucerians in Memory of Emerson Brown, Jr.* (*SAC* 29 [2007], no. 96): 19–35. Argues that Palamon and Arcite in *KnT* are very carefully balanced, "even equivalent" as warriors, lovers, and husbands to Emelye. Explains aspects of the symmetry by means of *fin amor*, or courtly love.

180. Williams, Tara Nicole. "Inventing Womanhood in Late Medieval Literature." *DAI* 65 (2005): 4190A. In exploring development of the word/concept *womanhood*, Williams discusses *KnT* and *ClT*, as well as works by Gower, Lydgate, Henryson, Kempe, and Julian of Norwich.

See also nos. 49, 51, 61, 73, 79, 87, 115, 127, 130, 144, 164, 181, 182, 250, 257.

CT—The Miller and His Tale

181. Arner, Timothy D. "No Joke: Transcendent Laughter in the *Teseida* and the *Miller's Tale*." *SP* 102.2 (2005): 143–58. Examines Chaucer's use of Boccaccio's *Teseida* as a source for *KnT*. Also argues that by having the Miller parody the story of Palamon and Arcite, Chaucer transforms his own work, as well as Boccaccio's text, into a fabliau.

182. Biggs, Frederick M. "The Miller's Tale and *Heile van Beersele*." *RES* 56 (2005): 497–523. Difficulties in dealing with the role of the three tubs (along with other issues) suggest that Chaucer's *MilT* is the

source for the Flemish version. Chaucer may have originated this *Tale* to reflect on the theme of God's control, an idea also important in *KnT* and *ParsT*.

183. Bredehoft, Thomas A. "Middle English 'Knarre': More Porcine Imagery in the Miller's Portrait." *ELN* 43.2 (2005):14–18. In calling the *GP* Miller a "knarre," Chaucer probably draws on an iconographic tradition illustrated in a pilgrim badge depicting a boar playing a bagpipe and inscribed "Laet knorren."

184. Hamaguchi, Keiko. "The Adoption of Conventions in 'Alysoun' in the Harley Lyrics 2253, f. 63 and in *The Miller's Tale*." *Tosa Women's Junior College Journal* 12 (2005): 57–66. Chaucer's descriptions of Alison and of Absolon's love of her in *MilT* parody the courtly diction and conventions found in "Alysoun" of the Harley lyrics. Possibly, Chaucer was influenced by the lyric. Also printed in *SAC* 29 (2007), no. 114.

185. Pappano, Margaret Aziza. "'Leve Brother': Fraternalism and Craft Identity in the Miller's Prologue and Tale." In Robert M. Stein and Sandra Pierson Prior, eds. *Reading Medieval Culture: Essays in Honor of Robert W. Hanning* (*SAC* 29 [2007], no. 146): 248–70. Pappano characterizes late medieval craft guilds and the roles they play in *CT*, particularly the recurrent concern with "male artisan identity." Through *MilPT*, Chaucer critiques the exclusionary nature of "craft fraternalism."

186. Robinson, Peter. "The Identification and Use of Authorial Variants in the *Miller's Tale*." *IJES* 5.2 (2005): 115–32. Selection from among variant readings should be based on both literary judgment and variant distribution. In the case of *MilT*, the richest readings are likely to be Chaucer's own. Analysis of them leads to greater appreciation of *MilT*, "of the processes that shaped the tale," and "of what is distinctive about Chaucer." Robinson examines sets of variants in *MilT*.

See also nos. 43, 66, 132, 164.

CT—The Reeve and His Tale

187. Morris, Andrew Jeffrey. "Representing the Countryside in Fourteenth-Century England." *DAI* 65 (2005): 4555A. As part of a larger discussion of medieval estate management and its literary representations, Morris examines the character of Piers Plowman and Chaucer's Oswald the Reeve.

CT—The Cook and His Tale

188. Stanley, E. G. "'Of This Cokes Tale Maked Chaucer Na Moore.'" *PoeticaT* 5 (1976): 36–59. Stanley comments on the inconclusive endings of several Chaucerian narratives and argues that *CkT* is complete as it is, developing the theme of *herbergage* (taking in lodgers) that runs throughout Part 1 of *CT*.

See also nos. 39, 193.

CT—The Man of Law and His Tale

189. Cordery, Leona. "A Medieval Interpretation of Risk: How Christian Women Deal with Adversity as Portrayed in *The Man of Law's Tale*, *Emaré*, and the *King of Tars*." In Gudrun M. Grabher and Sonja Bahn-Coblans, eds. *The Self at Risk in English Literatures and Other Landscapes: Honoring Brigitte Scheer-Schäzler on the Occasion of Her 60th Birthday*. Innsbrucker Beiträge zur Kulturwissenschaft, no. 29. Innsbruck: Institut für Sprachwissenschaft, 1999, pp. 177–85. Spiritual stalwartness makes heroines of the protagonists in *MLT*, *Emaré*, and the *King of Tars*; the active quality of their faith makes them agents in the conversion of others.

190. Ingham, Patricia Clare. "Contrapuntal Histories." In Patricia Clare Ingham and Michelle R. Warren, eds. *Postcolonial Moves: Medieval Through Modern*. New York: Palgrave Macmillan, 2003, pp. 47–70. Ingham urges a "contrapuntal" postcolonial approach to premodern texts—i.e., an approach that observes differences and distinctions that are oppositional without overdetermining them. She explores how Chaucer's *MLT* and Conrad's *Heart of Darkness* invite and resist colonialist attitudes. See also no. 375.

191. Kisor, Yvette. "Moments of Silence, Acts of Speech: Uncovering the Incest Motif in the *Man of Law's Tale*." *ChauR* 40 (2005): 141–62. Unlike the character in the sources and analogues, Custance in *MLT* forcefully confronts her father's authority at times. This confrontation and her willingness to disclose her past inscribe a "lesser version of the incest motif that has supposedly been excised from the tale."

192. Lee, Brian S. "Family Values and the Boundaries of Christendom in Chaucer's *Man of Law's Tale*." *Southern African Journal of Medieval and Renaissance Studies* 14 (2004): 23–38. Discusses three top-

ics—Ford Madox Brown's painting of Chaucer reading from *MLT* to a decadent court at a time of dynastic crisis, the current Middle Eastern situation, and the story of Noah's Flood—in relation to Chaucer's portrayal of Custance's wanderings between the extremes of Islamic "heresy," to Northumbrian paganism and Christian apostasy, and to the portrayal of the triumph and continuity of Christianity in *MLT*, signified by water.

193. Morse, Ruth. "Chaucer's Man of Law in Sequence." *PoeticaT* 28 (1988): 16–31. *MLT* extends the concerns with wooing and governance that are developed in Part 1 of *CT*, especially when considered in light of the extended version of *CkT* found in Bodley MS 686, which is edited and appended to "Chaucer's Man of Law in Sequence."

194. Shimodao, Makoto. "Devotion and the Passion as Seen in Chaucer's *Man of Law's Tale*." In Tagaya Yuko and Kanno Masahiko, eds. *Words and Literature: Essays in Honour of Professor Masa Ikegami* (*SAC* 29 [2007], no. 154): 181–97 (in Japanese). Discusses the religious significance of *MLT*.

See also nos. 10, 73, 115, 143, 144, 159, 228.

CT—The Wife of Bath and Her Tale

195. Alexander, Laura. "'Thanne Have I Gete of Yow Maistrie': Power and the Subversive Body in Chaucer's Wife of Bath." *Hortulus* 1 (2005): n.p. Traditonal mind (male)/body (female) distinctions are insufficient for discussing *WBPT* because the Wife celebrates "reason, learning, and open sexuality as rights given to women." In the Wife's relations with Jankin and in the Loathly Lady of *WBT*, Chaucer anticipates feminist efforts to redefine marriage as a free relationship between the sexes.

196. Burton, T. L. "Sir Gawain and the Green Hag: The *Real* Meaning of the *Wife of Bath's Tale*." In T. L. Burton and John F. Plummer, eds. *"Seyd in Forme and Reverence": Essays on Chaucer and Chaucerians in Memory of Emerson Brown, Jr.* (*SAC* 29 [2007], no. 96): 75–80. A playful send-up of literary criticism, especially efforts to psychoanalyze characters. Explains features of *WBT* in terms of *Sir Gawain and the Green Knight* and vice versa.

197. Carter, Susan. "Duessa, Spenser's Loathly Lady." *Cahiers Élisabéthains* 68 (2005): 9–18. Assesses Spenser's Duessa in light of *WBT*

and its Middle English analogues, exploring how Spenser turned the Irish sovereignty motif against the Irish.

198. Cigman, Gloria. "Excavating Alison." In Leo Carruthers and Adrian Papahagi, eds. *Jeunesse et vieillesse: Médiévales de l'âge en littérature anglaise* (*SAC* 29 [2007], no. 100): 93–101. Imaginative re-creation of the Wife of Bath's life and times from childhood onward, expanding on hints in *WBP*.

199. ————. *"Sentence and solaas: visitaciouns . . . to pleyes of myracles."* In Marie-Françoise Alamichel, ed. *La complémentarité: Mélanges offerts à Josseline Bidard et Arlette Sancery à l'occasion de leur départ en retraite* (*SAC* 29 [2007], no. 85): 267–79. Explores the character of the Wife of Bath, focusing on complementary dualities, particularly moral instruction and enjoyment.

200. Goldbeck, Janne. "The Teeth of Desire." *Rendezvous* 38 (2003): 31–33. Personal comments on being gap-toothed, related to the Wife of Bath (*GP* 1.468; *WBP* 3.603). Also comments on having a "colt's tooth.

201. Haines, Simon. *Poetry and Philosophy from Homer to Rousseau: Romantic Souls, Realist Lives.* New York: Palgrave Macmillan, 2005. xiii, 214 pp. Haines surveys interactions between realist and romantic thought in Western literary and philosophical discourse, commenting on a range of writers but focusing on Homer, Sophocles, Plato and Aristotle, Augustine, Aquinas, Dante, Shakespeare, and Descartes. In "Chaucer: The Wife and the Clerk" (pp. 84–89), he discusses Chaucer's *GP* and the Wife of Bath as manifestations of "appetitiveness" and the poet's essential realism, cast into relief by the Clerk.

202. Kendrick, Laura. "Deschamps' Anonymous 'Belle' and Chaucer's Wife of Bath: Complementary Experiments in Feminine Audacity." In Marie-Françoise Alamichel, ed. *La complémentarité: Mélanges offerts à Josseline Bidard et Arlette Sancery à l'occasion de leur départ en retraite* (*SAC* 29 [2007], no. 85): 203–19. Contrasts Chaucer's Wife of Bath with Belle, who is constructed from the tradition of masculine discourse on feminine attractiveness.

203. Kennedy, Thomas C. "The Wife of Bath as St. Jerome." *Mediaevalia* 23 (2002): 75–97. Close reading of Jerome's "Against Jovinian" indicates that in *WBP* the Wife of Bath agrees with Jerome, even though she shifts the emphasis from the superiority of virginity to the acceptability of marriage. At Jankyn's death, she becomes, like her fifth

husband, a student of patristic texts, although her interpretations are affected by her own experiences.

204. Koster, Josephine A. "The *Vita Sancte Alicie Bathoniensis*: Transgressions of Hagiographic Rhetoric in the *Wife of Bath's Prologue* and *Tale*." In T. L. Burton and John F. Plummer, eds. *"Seyd in Forme and Reverence": Essays on Chaucer and Chaucerians in Memory of Emerson Brown, Jr.* (SAC 29 [2007], no. 96): 35–45. Reads *WBP* as an example of genre-bending: a parody of female saints' lives. Surveys Chaucer's uses of the conventions of female hagiography in *CT* and argues that Alison of Bath "acts in *precisely* the opposite way to an orthodox saint." The essay gives little attention to *WBT*.

205. McTurk, Rory. "Guðrún Ósvífrsdóttir: An Icelandic Wife of Bath?" In Ásdís Egilsdottir and Rudolf Simek, eds. *Sagnaheimur: Studies in Honour of Hermann Pálsson on His 80th Birthday, 26th May 2001*. Studia Medievalia Septentrionalia, no. 6. Vienna: Fassbaender, 2001, pp. 175–94. McTurk argues that *Laxdaela Saga* is an analogue to *WBPT*, although the two derive independently from the Irish tale of the Loathly Lady.

206. Minnis, Alastair. "'Dante in Inglissh': What *Il Convivio* Really Did for Chaucer." *EIC* 55 (2005): 97–116. The Loathly Lady's lecture on "gentilesse" in *WBT* goes beyond sexual sovereignty to encompass *dominium*, a concept central to Wyclif's challenge to authority. Without naming his source, Chaucer channels orthodox, Boethian ideas about "gentilesse" through Dante's vernacular *Convivio* to allow for observations without the taint of Lollardy.

207. Noji, Kaoru. "A Woman Who Talks: The Wife of Bath." In Tagaya Yuko and Kanno Masahiko, eds. *Words and Literature: Essays in Honour of Professor Masa Ikegami* (SAC 29 [2007], no. 154): 99–207 (in Japanese). Noji examines the Wife of Bath as a marginalized woman.

208. Passmore, S. Elizabeth. "The Loathly Lady Transformed: A Literary and Cultural Analysis of the Medieval Irish and English Hagbeauty Tales." *DAI* 65 (2005): 4556A. Passmore engages *WBT* as part of a longer examination of the Loathly Lady motif in English and Irish texts, stories, and fabula.

209. Robertson, Elizabeth. "'Raptus' and the Poetics of Married Love in Chaucer's Wife of Bath's Tale and James I's *Kingis Quair*." In Robert M. Stein and Sandra Pierson Prior, eds. *Reading Medieval Culture: Essays in Honor of Robert W. Hanning* (SAC 29 [2007], no. 146): 302–23. The representations of rape (sexual assault and abduction) in *WBT* and

Kingis Quair invite consideration of free will and agency as part of a
critique of late medieval social formulations of male/female relationships. In *WBT*, Chaucer indicts contemporary social structures; James I
locates the problem in poetics.

210. Smith, Warren S. "The Wife of Bath and Dorigen Debate Jerome." In Warren S. Smith, ed. *Satiric Advice on Women and Marriage
from Plautus to Chaucer*. Ann Arbor: University of Michigan Press, 2005,
pp. 243–69. In *WBP* and *FranT*, the uses of Jerome's antifeminist treatise *Adversus Jovinianum* as source material are ironic. *WBP* presents a
more centrist Augustinian tradition than does her acerbic predecessor,
and Dorigen's lament prefigures the gentle "resolution of her dilemma."

211. Zaerr, Linda Marie. "*The Weddynge of Sir Gawen and Dame Rag-
nell*: Performance and Intertextuality in Middle English Popular Romance." In Evelyn Birge Vitz, Nancy Freeman Regalado, and Marilyn
Lawrence, eds. *Performing Medieval Narrative*. Cambridge: D. S. Brewer,
2005, pp. 193–208. Zaerr explores the concept of *mouvance* (textual
variation) as reflected in a performance of *The Weddynge*, commenting
on the process of performance and adaptation and tabulating variants
between the manuscript of the poem and a recorded memorized performance. Briefly contrasts the flexibility of *Weddynge* with the relative
metrical fixity of *WBT* and Gower's *Tale of Florent*.

See also nos. 13, 45, 48, 53, 56, 67, 92, 110, 126, 127, 132, 157,
164, 166, 245, 310.

CT—The Friar and His Tale

212. Finlayson, John. "Art and Morality in Chaucer's *Friar's Tale* and
the *Decameron*, Day One, Story One." *Neophil* 89 (2005): 139–52. Finlayson reads *FrT* as anticlerical comic satire rather than a moral exemplum, exploring similarities between the *Tale* and Boccaccio's story of
Ciapellatto in *Decameron* 1.1. The probable source of *FrT* is a sermon by
Robert Rypon, but Boccaccio may have influenced its structure, characterization, narrative stance, and anticlerical outlook.

CT—The Summoner and His Tale

[No entries]

CT—The Clerk and His Tale

213. Filios, Denise Keyes. "Rewriting Griselda: From Folktale to Exemplum." *Mediaevalia* 24 (2003): 45–73. Filios compares the folktale of

Griselda with four medieval versions, exploring their adaptations. Boccaccio's tale is eroticized, with the teller Dioneo disagreeing with the conventional happy ending that reinforces dangerous power relations; Petrarch valorizes both Griselda and her husband, reinforcing dominant power structures; *ClT* ironically celebrates unruly wives; and Christine de Pisan's version is a feminist reappropriation in which Griselda's strength leads to her husband's reform.

214. Greenwood, Maria. "Skirting Damnation, or the Speech and Speechlessness of Griselda in Chaucer's *The Clerk's Tale*." In Colette Stévanovitch and Henry Daniels, eds. *L'Affect et le jugement: Mélanges offerts à Michel Morel à l'occasion de son départ à la retraite* (*SAC* 29 [2007], no. 147), 1:33–256. Surveys recent criticism of *ClT*, focusing on Griselda as allegory, as "a figure of divinity," and as a flat figure. Concludes that Griselda may simply be read as a real person.

215. Hernández Pérez, María Beatriz. "Griselda's Heritage: Ancestral Family Bonds in *The Clerk's Tale*." In Manuel Brito and Juan Ignacio Oliva, eds. *Traditions and Innovations Commemorating Forty Years of English Studies at ULL (1963–2003)*. Tenerife, Canary Islands: RCEI, 2004, pp. 273–80. Hernández Pérez explores kinship models implicit in the cultural "memory" of *ClT*, especially those that involve Walter's sister and the sending of children to a relative's household. Griselda's class and deference may reflect vestiges of marriage to a "strange woman" of the wild. Told by the Clerk, the *Tale* may also include vestiges of the Church's opposition to endogamy.

216. Klein, Joan Larsen. "'Ne suffreth nat that men yow doon offence': The Griselda Figure in Boccaccio, Petrarch, and Chaucer." In Rhoda Schnur, gen. ed.; J. F. Alcina et al., eds. *Acta Conventus Neo-Latini Bariensis: Proceedings of the Ninth International Congress of Neo-Latin Studies, Bari, 29 August to 3 September, 1994*. Medieval & Renaissance Texts & Studies, no. 184. Tempe: Arizona Center for Medieval and Renaissance Studies, 1998, pp. 361–69. *ClT* is, in some ways, more like Boccaccio's version of the Griselda story than like Petrarch's, and it goes even further than its predecessors in eliciting pity for Griselda and her children.

217. McClellan, William. "'Ful Pale Face': Agamben's Biopolitical Theory and the Sovereign Subject in Chaucer's *Clerk's Tale*." *Exemplaria* 17 (2005): 103–34. McClellan relates Giorgio Agamben's theory of the ambiguity of political sovereignty and his ideas on "gesture" and "shame" to Walter's sovereignty and Griselda's submission in *ClT*. Argues that these are key to understanding the *Tale*: "The paradoxes of sovereignty, the medium of gesture, and the disarray of shame [are]

the cruxes of a political allegory that has long disturbed and baffled readers."

218. Mitchell, J. Allan. "Chaucer's *Clerk's Tale* and the Question of Ethical Monstrosity." *SP* 102.1 (2005): 1–26. Mitchell examines the polyvalent meanings of *ClT* and reflects on the processes of moral deliberation and the polarities that possible meanings represent. The *Tale* invites us to think hard about the nature of moral thinking.

219. Patterson, Lee. "Freedom and Necessity: History and Performance in the Clerk's Tale." *SIMELL* 20 (2005): 35–58. Considers *ClT* in light of historical context, particularly the events of Richard II's marriage to Isabel of France.

220. Shutters, Patricia Lynn. "Gendering Histories: Representations of Pagan Cultures in Middle English Literature." *DAI* 65 (2005): 3401A. In an argument that medieval writers gendered undesirable aspects of pagan beliefs as feminine, Shutters examines Griselda in *ClT*.

221. Williams, Tara. " 'T'assaye in thee thy wommanheede': Griselda Chosen, Translated, and Tried." *SAC* 27 (2005): 93–127. In *ClT*, Chaucer expands notions of female power, helping to shape an idea of womanliness, especially as manifested in submissiveness, production of heirs, and self-sacrifice. Williams analyzes the linguistic and cultural category of "womanhood" in late medieval England.

See also nos. 34, 86, 115, 144, 157, 159, 164, 180, 201.

CT—The Merchant and His Tale

222. Bodden, M. C. "Via erotica/via mystica: A *Tour de Force* in the 'Merchant's Tale.' " In Susannah Mary Chewning, ed. *Intersections of Sexuality and the Divine in Medieval Culture: The Word Made Flesh*. Burlington, Vt.: Ashgate, 2005, pp. 51–73. The carnal quest in *MerT* has as its goal an erotic union in the "paradys terrestre." This desire is fulfilled in an inverted *via mystica*, enforcing the ambiguity of mystical language as a mode of knowing. See also no. 344.

223. Eadie, John. "Chaucer's *Merchant's Tale* Reviewed." *PoeticaT* 21–22 (1985): 25–47. In light of the mythological tradition of Janus and connections between January and Adam, January's self-deception in *MerT* is less bitter than funny. In general, the *Tale* "is one of the great literary celebrations of marriage, albeit a comic one."

224. Sheridan, Christian. "Commodification and Textuality in the

Merchant's Tale." *SP* 102.1 (2005): 27–44. Discusses how readers of *MerT* are encouraged to view all texts in mercantile terms and how texts (medieval texts in particular) are formed in the interactions among reader, author, and language. Both a product (a text to be consumed) and a producer (retelling the events in the pear tree), May exemplifies how characters are made into commodities.

See also nos. 127, 250.

CT—The Squire and His Tale

225. Bloomfield, Morton W. "Chaucer's *Squire's Tale* and the Renaissance." *PoeticaT* 12 (1981): 28–35. Bloomfield considers natural law, an interest in distant geography, and the similarities between magic and technology in *SqT* as evidence of the "new spirit of the Renaissance" in Chaucer's works.

CT—The Franklin and His Tale

226. Ginsberg, Warren. " 'Gli scogli neri e il niente che c'è': Dorigen's Black Rocks and Chaucer's Translation of Italy." In Robert M. Stein and Sandra Pierson Prior, eds. *Reading Medieval Culture: Essays in Honor of Robert W. Hanning* (SAC 29 [2007], no. 146): 387–408. Ginsberg considers Boccaccio's tale of Menedon (*Filocolo* 4) as a "translation" of *FranT*, as well as vice versa, exploring the "mode of meaning" particular to each version. Differences in ideology between *trecento* Italy and Chaucer's London encourage us to recognize how the plot and details would have been read differently in these different contexts.

227. Lucas, Angela M. " 'But if a man be vertuous withal': Has Aurelius in Chaucer's *Franklin's Tale* 'lerned gentilesse aright?' " In Anne Marie D'Arcy and Alan J. Fletcher, eds. *Studies in Late Medieval and Early Renaissance Texts in Honour of John Scattergood* (SAC 29 [2007], no. 103): 181–200. Surveys approaches to *FranT* and discusses it as "an exemplum on a young man's learning of *gentillesse*, by way of serving an apprenticeship in love." Set against actions in other Breton lays, Aurelius's behavior reflects the *gentillesse* that the Franklin hopes his son will learn.

228. Tajiri, Masaji. *Studies in the Middle English Didactic Tail-Rhyme Romances.* [Tokyo]: Eihosha, 2002. x, 232 pp. Examines several aspects

of Middle English tail-rhyme romances, contrasting them with couplet romances, comparing them with Japanese "sekkyo," and exploring their relations with the "cult of the Virgin," the Holy Family, and contemporary visual art. Includes a survey of previous criticism and gives sustained attention to "the hero on the beach" motif, women in the Breton lays, and individual romances such as *Le Bone Florence of Rome, Sir Gowther,* and *Sir Orfeo.* Recurrent comments on *Th* and *MLT,* plus discussion of *FranT* as a Breton lay in couplets that show "some orientation to Celtic tradition." See also no. 407.

229. Wright, Edmond. "Faith and Narrative: A Reading of *The Franklin's Tale." Partial Answers* 3.1 (2005): 19–42. Wright argues that the conditional faith and reciprocal acceptance of narrative reception are intrinsic to human communication and that *FranT* explores similar principles and their relations to love. The love between Dorigen and Aurelius gives way to the love between Dorigen and Arveragus, depicting Chaucer's ideal of marriage—ideal insofar as it "confronts its own imperfections" by accepting the risks that are intrinsic to all acts of human communication.

See also nos. 49, 92, 115, 127, 144, 159, 210.

CT—The Physician and His Tale

230. Asakawa, Junko. "Chaucer's Physician and Astronomy." In Tagaya Yuko and Kanno Masahiko eds. *Words and Literature: Essays in Honour of Professor Masa Ikegami (SAC* 29 [2007], no. 154): 209–18 (in Japanese). Examines the *GP* description of Chaucer's Physician, assessing the extent to which the Physician's astrological medicine is satiric when seen in relation to such works as Nicholas of Lynn's *Kalendarium.*

See also nos. 86, 235.

CT—The Pardoner and His Tale

231. Cox, Catherine S. *The Judaic Other in Dante, the "Gawain" Poet, and Chaucer.* Gainesville: University Press of Florida, 2005. x, 239 pp. Four chapters and an epilogue. Chapter 1 establishes the background for exploration of "the late medieval legacy of early Christianity's appropriation of the Hebrew scriptures." Chapters 2–3 assess Dante's *Comme-*

dia and *Sir Gawain and the Green Knight*, respectively. Chapter 4, "The Jewish Pardoner and Chaucer's *Canterbury Tales*" (pp. 111–44), explores how in *PardPT* and *PrT* Christian appropriations of the Old Testament are cast into relief by the conflicts and contingencies of scriptural interpretation. In this way, the appropriations "betray a reliance upon the legitimacy and currency of the original precepts."

232. Harwood, Britton. "Chaucer on the Couch: The Pardoner's Performance and the Case for Psychoanalytic Criticism." In T. L. Burton and John F. Plummer, eds. *"Seyd in Forme and Reverence": Essays on Chaucer and Chaucerians in Memory of Emerson Brown, Jr.* (*SAC* 29 [2007], no. 96): 47–57. "Parapractic" repetitions in *PardPT* indicate that the Pardoner may be an "unconscious inversion" of Chaucer's own desires for home and for his absent father.

233. Leasure, T. Ross. "Belial, Belialism, and the Diabolic Power of Rhetoric from Cynewulf to Milton." *DAI* 65 (2005): 2982A. Examines the development of Belial as a personification of the power of rhetoric to deceive; discusses Chaucer's Pardoner as an example.

See also nos. 86, 166.

CT—The Shipman and His Tale

234. Crocker, Holly A. "Wifely Eye for the Manly Guy: Trading the Masculine Image in the *Shipman's Tale*." In T. L. Burton and John F. Plummer, eds. *"Seyd in Forme and Reverence": Essays on Chaucer and Chaucerians in Memory of Emerson Brown, Jr.* (*SAC* 29 [2007], no. 96): 59–73. The wife in *ShT* refuses to submit to the "comprehensive masculine dominance" of the competitive world of her husband and the monk. The two men understand their manliness in terms of the "*image* of potency"; like commerce, manliness is based on appearance only.

235. Lee, Brian S. "The 'Mayde Child' in *The Shipman's Tale*." *Southern African Journal of Medieval and Renaissance Studies* 15 (2005): 55–68. Comments on the upbringing of young people in *CT*. Mentioned in only three lines, the "mayde child" in *ShT* exemplifies the late medieval practice of wardship. The words signify the callous immorality of the guardian who, like the governesses castigated in *PhyT*, fails to set a good moral example.

See also nos. 126, 249.

CT—The Prioress and Her Tale

236. Bauer, Renate. "Der Antijüdische Diskurs im Mittelalter am Beispiel Mittelenglischer Dramen und der *Prioress's Tale.*" In Thomas Honegger, ed. *Authors, Heroes, and Lovers: Essays on Medieval English Literature and Language.* Bern and New York: Peter Lang, 2001, pp. 47–71. Bauer compares examples of anti-Jewish discourse in the *Ludus Coventriae* ("deicide"), *PrT* ("ritual murder"), and the *Croxton Play of the Sacrament* ("desecration of the host"). All three texts criminalize, victimize, and dehumanize Jews, demonstrating that anti-Jewish discourse did not depend on the presence of a Jewish minority within Christian society but could be memorialized by stereotypes in literary texts from generation to generation.

237. Besserman, Lawrence. "Chaucer, Spain, and the Prioress's Anti-semitism." *Viator* 35 (2004): 329–53. The anti-Semitism of *PrT* is attributable to the Prioress, not to Chaucer, who would have known Jews through the courts of Castile (referred to in *MkT*) and who presents Jews as "renowned historians and transmitters of knowledge in the field of astronomy" (in *HF* and *Astr*). Besserman examines critical responses to *PrT* and the reactions of the other pilgrims to the *Tale.*

238. Dahood, Roger. "The Punishment of the Jews, Hugh of Lincoln, and the Question of Satire in Chaucer's *Prioress's Tale.*" *Viator* 36 (2005): 465–91. Chaucer's ties to Lincoln and the reference to Hugh of Lincoln in *PrT* make it unlikely that Chaucer was satirizing anti-Semitism in the *Tale.* The punishment of drawing and hanging in *PrT* refers to historical cruelty and reflects an attitude prevalent among important members of Chaucer's audience, including John of Gaunt and his circle.

239. Eaton, R. D. "Sin and Sensibility: The *Conscience* of Chaucer's Prioress." *JEGP* 104 (2005): 495–513. In the *GP* description of the Prioress, the term *conscience*, used to describe her mental operations, implies not sensibility or emotion but rather prescription or governance. The Prioress's display is not emotive but mimetic, and her performance reveals the moral disengagement of the court and cloister.

240. Tripp, Raymond P., Jr. "Ignorance, System, and Sacrifice: A Literary Reading of the *Prioress's* Tale." *PoeticaT* 15–16 (1983): 136–53. Reads *PrT* as satiric, an exposé of the horrors of "institutional ignorance," both Christian and Jewish.

241. Wilsbacher, Greg. "Lumiansky's Paradox: Ethics, Aesthetics and Chaucer's 'Prioress's Tale.'" *CollL* 32 (2005): 1–28. The linked anti-

Semitism and poetic virtuosity of *PrT* confront medievalists with a paradox, in which accurately representing the past and combating bigotry in the present are pitted against each other. Resolving this paradox by ignoring aesthetics in favor of historicism is not a solution; engaging it illuminates the possibility of an ethical aesthetics.

See also no. 231.

CT—The Tale of Sir Thopas

242. Askins, William. "All That Glisters: The Historical Setting of the Tale of Sir Thopas." In Robert M. Stein and Sandra Pierson Prior, eds. *Reading Medieval Culture: Essays in Honor of Robert W. Hanning* (*SAC* 29 [2007], no. 146): 271–89. Askins reads *Th* for details that reflect Anglo-Flemish relations during the Hundred Years' War. He identifies heraldic details, commercial concerns, and echoes of the Ghent war of 1379–84.

243. Markus, Manfred. "The Holy War in the Popular 'Romances of Prys': Intertextuality in Chaucer's 'The Tale of Sir Thopas.'" In Uwe Böker et al., eds. *Of Remembraunce the Keye: Medieval Literature and Its Impact Through the Ages. Festschrift for Karl Heinz Göller on the Occasion of His 80th Birthday* (*SAC* 29 [2007], no. 88): 95–108. Explores the often-submerged relations between Middle English romances and the Crusades, reading *Th* as Chaucer's rejection of the "pleasure of indoctrination directed against the pagan enemy." Considers *Th* "modern, partly even postmodern," in its intertextuality, metafictive qualities, and fragmentary nature.

244. Purdie, Rhiannon. "The Implications of Manuscript Layout in Chaucer's *Tale of Sir Thopas*." *Forum* 41 (2005): 263–74. Purdie demonstrates that the layout of *Th* in several key early manuscripts derives from the traditional layout of Middle English tail-rhyme poetry. Chaucer intended to contribute to the *Tale*'s humor with this arrangement, which reflects his fascination with book culture.

245. Symons, Dana Margaret. "Literary Pleasure, Popular Audiences, and Middle English Romance." *DAI* 65 (2005): 2983A. Symons compares and contrasts "literary" works (including *Th* and *WBT*) with popular romances, considering the differing appeals of the forms.

See also nos. 99, 116, 145, 228.

CT—The Tale of Melibee

246. Grace, Dominick. "Telling Differences: Chaucer's *Tale of Melibee* and Renaud de Louens' *Livre de Mellibee et Prudence*." *PQ* 82 (2003): 367–400. *Mel* interprets and transforms its source. Chaucer's alterations, although slight, tend to undercut the allegorical reading, qualifying Prudence's authority and conclusions. *Mel* makes explicit concepts that are implicit in the original: the limitations of human knowledge and the difficulty of deciding on proper authoritative bases for reaching any decision.

247. Harding, Wendy. "Contradiction and Conciliation in Chaucer's *Tale of Melibee*." In Colette Stévanovitch, ed. *L'Articulation langue-littérature dans les textes médiévaux anglais*. Collection GRENDEL, no. 5. Nancy: Association des Médiévistes Anglicistes de l'Enseignement Supérieur, 2005, pp. 177–89. Contradictions inherent in medieval social order are evident in the sources of *Mel*, but Chaucer reconciles these contradictions through his treatment of pity.

248. Kennedy, Kathleen Erin. "Maintaining Injustice: Literary Representation of the Legal System c. 1400." *DAI* 65 (2005): 3398A. Discusses *Mel* as a medieval critique of the interplay between the justice system and the practice of livery and maintenance.

249. Taylor, Karla. "Social Aesthetics and the Emergence of Civic Discourse from the *Shipman's Tale* to *Melibee*." *ChauR* 39 (2005): 298–322. Taylor reads *ShT* and *Mel* as an opposed pair. In *ShT*, puns indicate the failure of human attempts at community; in *Mel*, doublets encourage and iterate a linguistic and aesthetic community. Civil society comes into order in and through *Mel*, which expresses a "civic vocabulary for a community of English speakers."

250. Tchalian, Hovig. "Noble Counsel in the Age of Chaucer and Langland: Authority, Dissent and the Political Community." *DAI* 66 (2005): 1011A. Considers representations of noble counselors to royalty in *GP* (the Knight), *MerT*, and *Mel*, among others, arguing that writers such as Chaucer and Langland demonstrate faith in this "traditional institution."

251. Walling, Amanda. "'In Hir Tellyng Difference': Gender, Authority, and Interpretation in the *Tale of Melibee*." *ChauR* 40 (2005): 163–81. *Mel* is "very much about what happens when texts are taken out of one context and put to work in another." Prudence invokes gender in shaping her arguments, and her presentation of her authorities

reminds us that the "processes of textual engendering and reproduction" are not simple transmission. Her "work" as a compiler and interpreter "mirrors Chaucer's own role" in compiling his tales, as well as his concern about the relationship between authority and authorship.

See also nos. 31, 126, 144.

CT—The Monk and His Tale

252. Chickering, Howell. "'And I seyde his opinion was good': How Irony Works in the Monk's Portrait." In T. L. Burton and John F. Plummer, eds. *"Seyd in Forme and Reverence": Essays on Chaucer and Chaucerians in Memory of Emerson Brown, Jr.* (*SAC* 29 [2007], no. 96): 3–18. Provides a close reading of the *GP* description of the Monk to show how a "complex interaction of the reader with Chaucer's text" produces a more satisfactory reading than does the positing of a naïve narrator.

253. Gillmeister, Heiner. "Zenobia's *Vitremite*, or The Case of the Unidentified Headdress." *PoeticaT* 17 (1984): 22–26. Gillmeister explains "vitremite" as a combination of "uistre" (oyster) and "ermite" (hermit), a Chaucerian coinage for a kind of headwear the poet may have associated with monasteries.

254. Hamaguchi, Keiko. "Transgressing the Borderline of Gender: Zenobia in the *Monk's Tale*." *ChauR* 40 (2005): 183–206. *MkP* reflects the Monk's anxiety about cross-dressers such as Zenobia, whom he orientalizes in *MLT* as a monstrous threat to traditional authority. Eventually humiliated and punished, Zenobia trades her helmet for a woman's headdress.

255. Morrison, Stephen. "*Les contes de Canterbury* A.1675: La signification de *manly man*." In Colette Stévanovitch, ed. *L'Articulation langue-littérature dans les textes médiévaux anglais*. Collection GRENDEL, no. 5. Nancy: Association des Médiévistes Anglicistes de l'Enseignement Supérieur, 2005, pp. 117–32. Explores the combination of *manly* and *man*, as well as the meaning of *manly*, in reference to the *GP* description of the Monk.

256. Scott-Macnab, David. "'Of prikyng and of huntyng for the hare': General Prologue to The Canterbury Tales, I 191." *JEGP* 104 (2005): 373–85. As used to describe the Monk in *GP*, the term *pricking* should not be understood in a sexual sense; review of sources, the *OED*, and the *MED* indicates that the term means "hard galloping."

257. Strohm, Paul. *Politique: Languages of Statecraft Between Chaucer and Shakespeare*. Notre Dame, Ind.: University of Notre Dame Press, 2005. 298 pp. Explores the political discourse of fifteenth-century England, identifying a "pre-Machiavellian moment" in which awareness of political upheaval and the unreliability of Fortune influenced or produced a variety of vernacular texts. Assesses the relations between these texts and their contextual ideologies and events. Includes discussion of *MkT* and the Knight's interruption of it in relation to Boccaccio's *De casibus virorum illustrium*, Lydgate's *Fall of Princes*, and later works in the tradition of *Mirror for Magistrates*.

See also nos. 6, 34, 51, 52, 237, 262.

CT—The Nun's Priest and His Tale

258. Finlayson, John. "Reading Chaucer's 'Nun's Priest's Tale': Mixed Genres and Multi-Layered Worlds of Illusion." *ES* 86 (2005): 493–510. *NPT* can best be approached by focusing on form and style rather than on theme and narrator. Attempting to define a central theme or message is frustrated by the *Tale*'s allusive richness and multiplicity of perspectives, and the narrator is largely generated by the *Tale*. An example of Chaucer's "virtuoso comic art at its height," *NPT* leaves central matters of interpretation to the reader.

259. Gaylord, Alan T. "Chaucerian Sentences: Revisiting a 'Crucial Passage' from the *Nun's Priest's Tale*." In T. L. Burton and John F. Plummer, eds. *"Seyd in Forme and Reverence": Essays on Chaucer and Chaucerians in Memory of Emerson Brown, Jr.* (*SAC* 29 [2007], no. 96): 167–80. A close reading of *NPT* 7.4347–61 (Chauntecleer on women as men's confusion), seeking to clarify subtleties via "prosodic criticism," i.e., reading the lines as a spoken performance.

260. Hazell, Dinah. "Poverty and Plenty: Chaucer's *Povre Wydwe* and Her *Gentil Cok*." *Mediaevalia* 25 (2004): 25–65. The widow's poverty in *NPT* indicates the cloistered clergy's failure to practice humility, poverty, and charity. Altering his source materials, Chaucer highlights the contrast between the lifestyle of the Prioress and that of the widow and creates links between the Nun's Priest, on the one hand, and Chauntecleer, the Monk, and the Friar, on the other. Reference to the "Peasants' Revolt" and the ambiguous moral of *NPT* reflect clerical insensitivity to the impact of extravagance on the impoverished.

261. Houwen, L. A. J. R. "Fear and Instinct in Chaucer's *Nun's Priest's Tale.*" In Anne Scott and Cynthia Kosso, eds. *Fear and Its Representations in the Middle Ages and Renaissance.* Arizona Studies in the Middle Ages and the Renaissance, no. 6. Turnhout: Brepols, 2002, pp. 17–30. Chauntecleer's responses to the fox in his dream and in his initial sighting of the beast are rooted in Aristotelian traditions of psychology and natural antipathy, here traced from their classical roots through their medieval adaptations. The presence of such erudite depictions of instinct and enmity in *NPT* heightens its "contrast between the animal and human."

262. Travis, Peter W. "The Body of the Nun's Priest, or, Chaucer's Disseminal Genius." In Robert M. Stein and Sandra Pierson Prior, eds. *Reading Medieval Culture: Essays in Honor of Robert W. Hanning* (*SAC* 29 [2007], no. 146): 231–47. Travis explores the Host's "hypermasculine vision of literary genius" in Part 7 of *CT*, especially the Host's comments in *MkP*, *NPP*, and *NPE*. Using parody rather than satire, Chaucer gently exposes the "phallocentric presuppositions" of Western aesthetic tradition in which writing is associated with insemination.

See also nos. 34, 51, 126, 144.

CT—The Second Nun and Her Tale

263. Biscoglio, Frances. "St. Cecilia: Chaucer's Valiant Woman." *Mediaevalia* 23 (2002): 123–35. Like the Valiant Woman of Proverbs 31:10–31, Cecilia brings honor to her husband, manages her household well, works untiringly, and faces danger with fearless self-confidence. In contrast to Harry Bailly, who sets up the rules and pragmatic externals of the pilgrimage, Cecilia points the way to a transformative pilgrimage.

264. Edwards, A. S. G. "Fifteenth-Century Collections of Female Saints' Lives." *YES* 33 (2003): 131–41. Compares the contents of Cambridge University Library MS Additional 4122 with similar contemporary compilations, encouraging further study of such devotional collections. The presence of Chaucer's *SNT* in such anthologies may indicate his shaping influence on the tradition, later modified by Lydgate, Bokenham, and Capgrave.

See also nos. 126, 157.

CT—The Canon's Yeoman and His Tale

[No entries]

CT—The Manciple and His Tale

265. Astell, Ann W. "Nietzsche, Chaucer, and the Sacrifice of Art." *ChauR* 39 (2005): 323–40. Reads *ManPT*, *ParsPT*, and *Ret* in light of the Dionysian/Apollonian opposition posed by Nietzsche in "The Birth of Tragedy Out of Music." Whereas Nietzsche treated the two as irreconcilable, Chaucer combines them in "an ethical aesthetics and an aesthetic ethics."

266. Jost, Jean E. "Chaucer's Vows and How They Break: Transgression in *The Manciple's Tale*." In Albrecht Classen, ed. *Discourses on Love, Marriage, and Transgression in Medieval and Early Modern Literature*. Medieval and Renaissance Texts and Studies, no. 278. Tempe: Arizona Center for Medieval and Renaissance Studies, 2004, pp. 267–87. Explores vows and vow-breaking in *CT*, arguing that *ManT* brings to tragic crescendo a concern with the transgression of marital vows and presents consequences as horrific as any in Greek drama.

See also no. 144.

CT—The Parson and His Tale

267. Twu, Krista Sue-Lo. "Chaucer's Vision of the Tree of Life: Crossing the Road with the Rood in the *Parson's Tale*." *ChauR* 39 (2005): 341–78. Although *ParsT* relies heavily on Raymond de Penaforte's *Summa de poenitentia et matrimonio*, Chaucer extracts one chapter from the treatise and substitutes a "tree of life" for Raymond's pilgrimage metaphor. By indicating that one can live a life of religion here in this world, Chaucer adapts his work to the fourteenth century.

268. Watson, Nicholas. "Chaucer's Public Christianity." *R&L* 37.2 (2005): 99–114. Chaucer's religion is important even in his secular tales, a reflection of his public stance as a lay penitent, a member of the *mediocriter boni*, a category of the religious to be distinguished from the contemplative path of the *perfecti*. Reads *ParsT* as a virtual autobiography of Chaucer's view of religion and as indication of how the Pilgrims reflect the values of the "lay religious."

See also nos. 31, 38, 75, 116, 127, 166, 176, 182, 265.

CT—Chaucer's Retraction

See nos. 106, 265.

Anelida and Arcite

See nos. 55, 87.

A Treatise on the Astrolabe

See nos. 237, 284.

Boece

269. Bourgne, Florence. "Le vocabulaire savant du *Boece* est-il universitaire?" In Colette Stévanovitch, ed. *L'Articulation langue-littérature dans les textes médiévaux anglais*. Collection GRENDEL, no. 5. Nancy: Association des Médiévistes Anglicistes de l'Enseignement Supérieur, 2005, pp. 247–68. Studies Chaucer's *Bo* to determine which texts, versions, and commentaries Chaucer might have used and which modifications he might have introduced and to what purposes.

270. Lewis, Lucy. "The Tavistock Boethius: One of the Earliest Examples of Provincial Printing." In John Hinks and Catherine Armstrong, eds. *Printing Places: Locations of Book Production and Distribution Since 1500*. Newcastle, Del.: Oak Knoll; London: British Library, 2005, pp. 1–14. Lewis assesses challenges confronted by printer Thomas Richard when, in 1525, he produced John Walton's translation of Boethius's *Consolation of Philosophy*, especially those challenges that resulted from interspersing intermittent commentary in a smaller typeface. The commentary derives from *Bo*, and the volume may have been modeled on Caxton's edition of *Bo*.

271. Machan, Tim William, ed., with the assistance of A. J. Minnis. *Sources of the Boece*. The Chaucer Library. Athens: University of Georgia Press, 2005. xiv, 311 pp. The book presents hypothetical source texts for *Bo*, seeking to reconstruct as closely as possible what was accessible to Chaucer when he translated Boethius into Middle English. Provides an edition of Boethius's Latin original and, on facing pages, Jean de Meun's French translation of the Latin. Accompanying notes include selections from Nicholas Trevet's Latin commentary and various inter-

linear glosses "from the Remigian tradition," i.e., those attributed to Remigius himself and "later expansions thereof." The introduction surveys critical discussions of the sources of *Bo*, describes pertinent manuscript traditions, and explains textual methods. Includes collations for the Latin and French texts and a bibliography.

272. Summers, Joanna. *Late-Medieval Prison Writing and the Politics of Autobiography*. Oxford: Clarendon Press, 2004. x, 229 pp. Summers assesses the commonalities and differences among Usk's *The Testament of Love*, *The King's Quair* of James I of Scotland, Charles d'Orléans' *English Book of Love*, the *Testimony* of William Thorpe, the *Trial* of Richard Wyche, and George Ashby's *A Prisoner's Reflections*. Explores the influences on these of Boethius's *Consolation of Philosophy*, often mediated by Chaucer's translation, *Bo*. Also explores the influences of Chaucer and Gower on the creation of narrative personae in these works, raising questions about how and to what extent prisoner literature can be thought to constitute a genre or to contribute to the development of literary creations of identity. See also no. 404.

See also nos. 49, 124.

The Book of the Duchess

273. Burrow, J. A. "Politeness and Privacy: Chaucer's *Book of the Duchess*." In Anne Marie D'Arcy and Alan J. Fletcher, eds. *Studies in Late Medieval and Early Renaissance Texts in Honour of John Scattergood* (*SAC* 29 [2007], no. 103): 65–75. Explores the concept of "civil inattention" ("a desire not to intrude on privacy") as it helps to explain the behavior of the dreamer toward the Black Knight in *BD*. The concept is described in modern sociology and occurs in several medieval romances besides *BD*: *TC*, Chretién's *Yvain*, and the work of Malory.

274. Foster, Michael. "Chaucer's Narrators and Audiences: Self-Deprecating Discourse in *Book of the Duchess* and *House of Fame*." In Janne Skaffari et al., eds. *Opening Windows on Texts and Discourses of the Past*. Pragmatics and Beyond, n.s., no. 134. Philadelphia: John Benjamins, 2005, pp. 199–213. Chaucer constructed a self-deprecating narrator in *BD* and in *HF* in response to audience expectations. These constructions, in turn, shaped how people in Chaucer's own society regarded Chaucer and how his personality has been recorded historically.

275. Horowitz, Deborah. "An Aesthetic of Permeability: Three

Transcapes of the *Book of the Duchess." ChauR* 39 (2005): 259–79. Horowitz assesses the aesthetic value of *BD* by focusing on three "transcapes" (through visions): that of the narrator as a literary medium; that of the work's interwoven sources and time spans; and that of the gendered landscape, which is both unstable and constant. The transcapes constitute a closely woven (but simultaneously open) work that is always open to interpretation and in a constant state of flux.

276. Kensak, Michael. " 'My first matere I wil yow telle': Losing (and Finding) Your Place in Chaucer's *Book of the Duchess." In T. L. Burton and John F. Plummer, eds. "Seyd in Forme and Reverence": Essays on Chaucer and Chaucerians in Memory of Emerson Brown, Jr. (SAC* 29 [2007], no. 96): 83–96. Assesses the narrator's digressions and "digression-returns" in *BD*, arguing that they are part of Chaucer's indications of the inexpressibility of grief.

277. Long, Rebekah. "Apocalypse and Memory in *Pearl." DAI* 66 (2005): 2206A. Considers *BD* and *Pearl* as case studies in the search for "an appropriate, adequate language of commemoration," as opposed to prior models of elegiac language.

278. North, John. "Arithmetic and Chaucer." In Giancarlo Marchetti et al., eds. *Ratio et Superstitio: Essays in Honor of Graziella Federici Vescovini*. Textes et Études du Moyen Âge, no 24. Louvain-la-Neuve: Fédération Internationale des Instituts d'Études Médiévales, 2003, pp. 263–83. North summarizes medieval arithmetic theory and practice, describes Chaucer's professional familiarity with arithmetic, and explores arithmetic allusions and structuring in *BD*, particularly its shape as an abacus.

279. Quinn, William A. "Medieval Dream Visions: Chaucer's *Book of the Duchess." In David F. Johnson and Elaine Treharne, eds. Readings in Medieval Texts: Interpreting Old and Middle English Literature (SAC* 29 [2007], no. 120): 323–36. Quinn defines the genre of dream vision, surveys "standard readings" of *BD*, and offers a "re-vision" of the poem that reconciles its humor and sadness by imagining it as a performance some years after the death of Blanche. The poem may have been performed on the occasion of Gaunt's betrothal to Constanza of Castile or in acknowledgment of his love of Katherine Swynford.

280. Scott-Macnab, David. "Polysemy in Middle English *Embosen* and the Hart of *The Book of the Duchess." LeedsSE* 36 (2005): 175–94. Critics generally gloss "embosen" as either "concealed in the woods" or "exhausted from the hunt." Examination of the word determines its

precise meaning as a hunting term and also sheds light on Octovyen's hunt.

281. Seymour, M. C. "Chaucer's *Book of the Duchess*: A Proposal." *MÆ* 74 (2005): 60–70. Examines the manuscript and editorial traditions of *BD* to argue for a new edition, based on MS Tanner 346, sensitive to the poem's octosyllabic meter and aware of scribal contamination. Suggests a number of emendations.

282. Stock, Lorraine Kochanske. "'Peynted . . . text and [visual] glose': Primitivism, Ekphrasis, and Pictorial Intertextuality in the Dreamers' Bedrooms of *Roman de la Rose* and *Book of the Duchess*." In T. L. Burton and John F. Plummer, eds. *"Seyd in Forme and Reverence": Essays on Chaucer and Chaucerians in Memory of Emerson Brown, Jr. (SAC* 29 [2007], no. 96): 97–114. Reads descriptions of the bedchamber in the *Roman de la Rose* as a source for the bedchamber scene in *BD*, arguing that Chaucer's "visual/verbal intertextuality" reveals his preference for civilization over primitivism.

283. Yvernault, Martine. "Le chevalier, le poète, et le petit chien: La présence animale dans *Le livre de la duchess*." In Marie-Françoise Alamichel, ed. *La complémentarité: Mélanges offerts à Josseline Bidard et Arlette Sancery à l'occasion de leur départ en retraite* (*SAC* 29 [2007], no. 85): 187–95. Considers *BD* as a partition between the mythical and fictional worlds and reality, as a textual space of transition where poetic experience and real life are intertwined.

See also nos. 26, 28, 55, 64, 99, 102, 140.

The Equatorie of the Planetis

284. Arch, Jennifer. "A Case Against Chaucer's Authorship of the *Equatorie of the Planetis*." *ChauR* 40 (2005): 59–79. Differences in prose style, in syntactic and conceptual organization, and in levels of technical expertise between *Astr* and *Equat* indicate that Chaucer did not write the latter. *Equat* shows more skill in calculation, but *Astr* demonstrates more careful planning.

See also no. 78.

The House of Fame

285. Ambrosini, Richard. "Self-Remembrance and the Memory of God: Chaucer's *House of Fame* and Augustinian Pschology." *Textus* 2.1–2

(1989): 95–112. Summarizes the Augustinian psychology of memory and its relationship to language, arguing that these concepts underlie the narrator's "'educational' pilgrimage" in *HF*. The end of the poem reflects the transformation of fiction into reality.

286. Bellamy, Elizabeth Jane. "Slanderous Troys: Between Fame and Rumor." In Alan Shephard and Stephen D. Powell, eds. *Fantasies of Troy: Classical Tales and the Social Imaginary in Medieval and Early Modern Europe*. Toronto: Centre for Reformation and Renaissance Studies, 2004, pp. 215–35. Bellamy considers Paridell's undermining of Britomart's "nostalgia for the fallen Troy" in Spenser's *Faerie Queene*, Book 3, and argues that the "slippages" between fame and rumor in *HF* influenced Spenser's presentation. See also no. 398.

287. Bennett, Alastair. "Ambition and Anxiety in *The House of Fame* and *The Garlande of Laurell*." *Marginalia* 2 (2005): n.p. Compares the attitudes toward fame and poetic fame in *HF* and in Skelton's *The Garlande of Laurell*, arguing that Chaucer's willingness to accept the Boethian transience of fame contrasts a greater desire for certainty in Skelton.

288. Minnis, A. J. "'Figures of Olde Werk': Chaucer's Poetic Sculptures." In Phillip Lindley and Thomas Frangenberg, eds. *Secular Sculpture: 1300–1550*. Stamford: Shaun Tyas, 2000, pp. 124–43. Minnis considers possible sources or inspirations for Chaucer's techniques of describing the architecture and statuary in the Temple of Venus of *HF*, surveying previous scholarship. Despite the possible influence of actual art and architecture or the descriptions in guidebooks to Rome, descriptions in mythographic tradition are the most likely sources, although Chaucer did not include the allegorizations found there.

289. Simeroth, Rosann. "Lady Philosophy and the Construction of Poetic Authority in Jean de Meun, Dante, and Chaucer." *DAI* 66 (2005): 2207A. Beginning with Boethius's feminine Philosophia, Simeroth examines "her" transformation in such texts as the *Roman de la Rose* (where she becomes Reason); Boccaccio's *Convivio* (where she is a gentle lady); and *HF*, where Chaucer merges Philosophia with "a monstrous Lady Fame," revealing a "dark vision of Boethius."

290. Yvernault, Martine. "The *House of Fame:* Unfamous Fame. La maison de papier, une enterprise de (dé)construction." In Colette Stévanovitch, ed. *L'Articulation langue-littérature dans les textes médiévaux anglais*. Collection GRENDEL, no. 5. Nancy: Association des Médiévistes Anglicistes de l'Enseignement Supérieur, 2005, pp. 229–46. Yvernault

explores the representation of space(s) and the problem of deconstruction in *HF*, focusing on the poem as textual architecture.

See also nos. 19, 26, 28, 40, 48, 52, 55, 70, 110, 125, 237, 274.

The Legend of Good Women

291. Brown, Sarah Annes. "Philomela." *Tr&Lit* 13 (2004): 194–206. Surveys versions and adaptations of the Philomela-Procne-Tereus story from Euripides through Timberlake Wertenbaker's *Love of the Nightingale* (1988), observing overt and submerged motifs of incest and lesbianism. In *LGW*, the motifs are underscored by a concern with speech and speechlessness.

292. Horsley, Katharine Frances. "Poetic Visions of London Civic Ceremony, 1360–1440." *DAI* 65 (2005): 3796A. As part of a larger consideration of dream poems and medieval ritual, Horsley argues that Chaucer intended liturgical elements of *LGWP* to evoke saints' day ceremonies recorded in the *Sarum Missal*.

293. Renda, Patricia A. "Mythopoesis and Ideology in Late Medieval and Early Modern Versions of 'Lucrece' and 'Philomela.'" *DAI* 66 (2005): 1759A. Considers Chaucer's rendition of Lucrece (in *LGW*) as part of a series of narratives that transform Lucrece's story into a text that "reveal[s] an evolving patriarchal ideology."

See also nos. 26, 55, 73, 110, 125–27, 144.

The Parliament of Fowls

294. Bidard, Josseline. "Animaux et distanciation dans *The Parliament of Fowls*." In Colette Stévanovitch, ed. *L'Articulation langue-littérature dans les textes médiévaux anglais*. Collection GRENDEL, no. 5. Nancy: Association des Médiévistes Anglicistes de l'Enseignement Supérieur, 2005, pp. 217–28. Analyzes Chaucer's characterization of the birds in *PF* to explore the process of "distanciation," stemming from two coexisting viewpoints in the poem: the author's and the dreamer's.

295. Morgan, Gerald. "Chaucer's Adaptation of Boccaccio's Temple of Venus in the *Parliament of Fowls*." *RES* 56 (2005): 1–36. Following Aristotle, medieval poets consider poetry a branch of moral philosophy. Whether or not Chaucer knew Boccaccio's own glosses on the *Teseida*,

he adapts the Italian work to his own treatment of allegorical figures and so justifies Usk's description of Chaucer as a noble, philosophical poet.

296. Yvernault, Martine "Horticulture et orties: Le paradis contrarié du *Parlement des oiseaux*." In Colette Stévanovitch, ed. *L'Articulation langue-littérature dans les textes médiévaux anglais*. Collection GRENDEL, no. 5. Nancy: Association des Médiévistes Anglicistes de l'Enseignement Supérieur, 2005, pp. 191–215. Posits that uncertainty and ambiguity are structuring stylistic techniques of Chaucer's descriptions in *PF*.

297. ———. "Paroles d'oiseaux, paroles oiseuses: Le discours amoureux et l'arbitrage du cœur dans *Le parlement des oiseaux*." In Colette Stévanovitch and Henry Daniels, eds. *L'Affect et le jugement: Mélanges offerts à Michel Morel à l'occasion de son départ à la retraite* (*SAC* 29 [2007], no. 147), 2:563–71. Yvernault explores various levels of the love discourse in *PF* in relation to the roles played by reflection and silence.

See also nos. 9, 24, 26, 28, 30, 55, 73, 92, 125.

The Romaunt of the Rose

See nos. 55, 164.

Troilus and Criseyde

298. Barbaccia, Holly G. "Kalendes of Chaunge: Thinking Through Change in Middle English Poetry." *DAI* 66 (2005): 2205A. Examines the concepts of "change and eschaunge" in Middle English poetry, with particular attention to Langland's Lady Meed, Gower's Constance, Criseyde from *TC*, and Lady Bertilak in *Sir Gawain and the Green Knight*. Considers instability and epistemology.

299. Brewer, Derek. "Some Notes on the Nature of Medieval Romance and the Modern Novel." In Uwe Böker et al., eds. *Of Remembraunce the Keye: Medieval Literature and Its Impact Through the Ages. Festschrift for Karl Heinz Göller on the Occasion of His 80th Birthday* (*SAC* 29 [2007], no. 88): 47–59. Traces the history of romance as a genre as it adumbrates the modern novel. Includes recurrent references to *TC*.

300. Einersen, Dorrit. "Shakespeare's *Troilus and Cressida*: Tragedy, Comedy, Satire, History of Problem Play?" *Angles on the English-Speaking*

World 5 (2005): 45–55. Einersen examines genre markers in versions of the story of Troilus and Criseyde (including Chaucer's claims for tragedy in *TC*) as background to a discussion of Shakespeare's play as a "historical-tragical-comical-satirical problem play."

301. Garner, Lori Ann. "The Role of Proverbs in Middle English Narrative." In Mark C. Amodio, ed. *New Directions in Oral Theory*. Medieval and Renaissance Texts and Studies, no. 287. Tempe: Arizona Center for Medieval and Renaissance Studies, 2005, pp. 255–77. Contrasts uses of proverbs in *TC* and in *Havelock the Dane*. In the latter, proverbs affirm traditional wisdom and elicit the reader's trust. Chaucer uses proverbs in more complex ways, presenting them as contradictions or in striking juxtapositions that help to create rich characters while undercutting traditional wisdom.

302. Gaylord, Alan. "Chaucer's Tragic Romance: Imagining Voices in *Troilus and Criseyde*." Plenary Address, 20th Annual Meeting of the Medieval Association of the Midwest. *PMAM* 11 (2004): 1–25. An extended example of "prosodic criticism," which comments on several passages of *TC* (1.1–21, 53–56, 99–133, 981–87, 1016–29; 2.109–47, 190–217, 309–28, 407–28, 443–48; and 3.1198–1211). Gaylord explains how Chaucer's poetry invites readers to be conscious of form and details, while compelling them to read "backwards" as well as "forwards" as they respond to the dexterous rhyme-royal stanzas, possibilities beyond editorial punctuation, implication, ambiguity, pronoun shift, and other aspects of imagined voices.

303. Ginsberg, Warren. "Aesthetics *Sine Nomine*." *ChauR* 39 (2005): 234–40. Although we know of no sustained aesthetic treatise dating from the Middle Ages, medieval people were lovers of beauty who conceived of worldly beauty as a reflection of divine perfection. Ginsberg comments on Chaucer's leave-taking of his poem in *TC*, where the Trinity is the paradigm of love that Troilus, Criseyde, and Pandarus unwittingly emulate.

304. Hill, John M. "The Countervailing Aesthetic of Joy in *Troilus and Criseyde*." *ChauR* 39 (2005): 280–97. Hill argues that Troilus's pagan, earthly joy in the second half of Book 3 of *TC* is Chaucer's representation of "the maximum of good and beauty to be found outside of Christian belief and the dispensations of faith." The intense joy experienced by the lovers is the apex of worldly sufficiency, temporarily safe from worldly threat and rendered powerful through Chaucer's indications of universality.

305. Howes, Laura L. "Chaucer's Criseyde: The Betrayer Betrayed." In Robert M. Stein and Sandra Pierson Prior, eds. *Reading Medieval Culture: Essays in Honor of Robert W. Hanning* (*SAC* 29 [2007], no. 146): 321–43. Chaucer presents Criseyde as a victim of several betrayals—by Calchas, by the Trojan parliament, by Pandarus, and by the narrator—and prompts the possibility of readers' betrayal of her as well. Obedient to her father but unfaithful to her lover, Criseyde is trapped between two opposed sets of expectations, social and literary, that shape our complex response.

306. Kimmelman, Burt. "The Trope of Reading in the Fourteenth Century." In Ian Frederick Moulton, ed. *Reading and Literacy in the Middle Ages and Renaissance* (*SAC* 29 [2007], no. 129): 25–44. Surveys representations of reading in literature from Abélard and Héloïse to Margery Kempe and Julian of Norwich, including commentary on *TC*. The "autonomy of the reader" developed in the fourteenth century.

307. Mitchell, J. Allan. "Romancing Ethics in Boethius, Chaucer, and Lévinas: Fortune, Moral Luck, and Erotic Adventure." *CL* 57.2 (2005): 101–16. Emmanuel Lévinas's *Time and the Other* indicates how Fortune or contingency is constitutive of ethics in Chaucer's *TC*. In contrast to Boethian readings of *TC*, a Lévinasian reading shows how Troilus's subjection to love and his passivity before an uncertain future—not his autonomy or agency—make him a figure of the ethical human. *TC* also provides a way of evaluating Lévinas's medievalism.

308. O'Brien, Timothy. "Brother as Problem in the *Troilus*." *PQ* 82 (2003): 125–48. O'Brien examines the theme of brotherhood in *TC* as portrayed through the relationships of Troilus and Pandarus, Troilus and Criseyde, Diomedes and Criseyde, and the narrator and readers. The poem's ending portrays brotherly relationships as no remedy for loss.

309. Pugh, Tison. "Christian Revelation and the Cruel Game of Courtly Love in *Troilus and Criesyde*." *ChauR* 39 (2005): 379–401. Pugh explores the "performative cruelties" of *TC*—the ways the three major characters are willing to "resort to tactics of cruelty to advance their individual agendas" and the way the narrative itself displays the "pleasures of salvation" that are unavailable to the pagan characters.

310. Ramsburgh, John S. "Writing Medieval Lives in Dante and Chaucer." *DAI* 65 (2005): 3797A. Suggests that *TC* and *WBP* argue for a diachronic understanding of time-as-phenomenon, as opposed to the religious emphasis on eternity over temporality.

311. Ryan, Lawrence V. "Chaucer's Criseyde in Neo-Latin Dress." *ELR* 17 (1987): 288–302. Francis Kynaston's translation of *TC* in Latin rhyme-royal stanzas was influenced by Henryson's and Shakespeare's depictions of Criseyde. Substantial omissions in Books 4 and 5 of the translation simplify the character and reduce readers' sympathy by emphasizing her coquetry.

312. Thompson, Diane P. *The Trojan War: Literature and Legends from the Bronze Age to the Present.* Jefferson, N.C.: McFarland, 2004. vi, 241 pp. Fourteen chapters on the cultural legacy of the Trojan War, from archaeology through literary versions to recent popular culture. Includes chapters on Latin and Roman classics (the works of Homer, Aeschylus, Euripides, and Virgil), the medieval romance tradition, Chaucer, Shakespeare, Racine, and more. Chapter 10, "Chaucer's *Troilus and Criseyde*: The Christian Synthesis" (pp. 154–64), includes a plot summary of *TC*, descriptions of the main characters, and commentary on courtly love, Boethian influence, and the legacy of the poem. See also no. 408.

313. Tournoy, Gilbert. "Apollo and Admetus: The Forms of Classical Myth Through the Middle Ages and the Renaissance." In George Hugo Tucker, ed. *Forms of the "Medieval" in the "Renaissance": A Multidisciplinary Exploration of a Cultural Continuum.* Charlottesville, Va.: Rookwood, 2000, pp. 175–203. Traces the developments and distortions of the classical myth of Apollo's service to Admetus and its association with love; includes discussion of the allusion in *TC* 1.659–65.

314. Urban, Malte. "Chaucer's *Troilus and Criseyde* as a Critique of Medieval Historiography." *CarmP* 12 (2003): 75–90. Reads *TC* as a critique of the Augustinian Christian view of providential historical teleology.

315. ———. "Myth and the Present: Chaucer's *Troilus* as a Mirror for Ricardian England." In Thomas Honegger, ed. *Riddles, Knights, and Cross-Dressing Saints: Essays on Medieval English Language and Literature* (*SAC* 29 [2007], no. 119): 33–54. Presenting Troy in *TC* as the mirror image of London in the 1380s, Chaucer engages conflicting notions of history and historiography. In particular, his depiction of the Trojan parliament is a warning to his contemporaries. Chaucer embraces wholeheartedly neither Christian teleology nor pagan cyclicity.

316. Wetherbee, Winthrop. "Cresseid vs. Troylus in Henryson's *Testament*." In T. L. Burton and John F. Plummer, eds. *"Seyd in Forme and Reverence": Essays on Chaucer and Chaucerians in Memory of Emerson Brown, Jr.* (*SAC* 29 [2007], no. 96): 133–41. In its bleak presentation of love,

Henryson's *Testament of Cresseid* responds in a complex way to Chaucer's characterization of Criseyde in *TC*, making apparent the "spiritual and ethical limitations of the world view that frames the experience of Chaucer's lovers."

317. Wittig, Joseph S. "Tereus, Procne, and Her Sister: Chaucer's Representation of Criseyde as a Victim." In T. L. Burton and John F. Plummer, eds. *"Seyd in Forme and Reverence": Essays on Chaucer and Chaucerians in Memory of Emerson Brown, Jr.* (*SAC* 29 [2007], no. 96): 117–32. Reads Chaucer's allusion to Tereus, Procne, and Philomela in *TC* as an "ethical and moral" gloss on his own poem, generating tensions between the refined love of Troilus and Criseyde and the raw passions in Ovid. Also comments on source relations between *TC* and both Petrarch's "Zephiro torna" and Dante's *Purgatorio*.

See also nos. 14, 19, 21, 23, 32, 36, 37, 49, 51, 59, 65, 72, 73, 86, 87, 92, 102, 121, 124, 126, 130, 132, 140, 143, 144, 273.

Lyrics and Short Poems

318. Gray, Douglas. "Middle English Courtly Lyrics: Chaucer to Henry VIII." In Thomas G. Duncan, ed. *A Companion to the Middle English Lyric* (*SAC* 29 [2007], no. 105): 120–49. Sketches the French backgrounds and courtly functions of late medieval English lyrics, surveying representative samples from Chaucer, Gower, Hoccleve, Lydgate, Charles d'Orléans, Skelton, the Findern manuscript, and Humphrey Newton's collection. Clarifies Chaucer's foundational role.

See also nos. 24, 65.

An ABC

319. Thompson, John J. "Patch and Repair and Making Do in Manuscripts and Texts Associated with John Stow." In Anne Marie D'Arcy and Alan J. Fletcher, eds. *Studies in Late Medieval and Early Renaissance Texts in Honour of John Scattergood* (*SAC* 29 [2007], no. 103): 353–61. Considers the omission of *ABC* from Chaucer's canon and what it reflects about the editorial habits of John Stow and Thomas Speght; religious-political pressures on editors of the time; and the reception of the Marian devotion of *ABC* in Protestant England.

Adam Scriveyn

320. O'Connell, Brendan. "Adam Scriveyn and the Falsifiers of Dante's *Inferno:* A New Interpretation of Chaucer's *Wordes.*" *ChauR* 40 (2005): 39–58. Associates *Adam* with Dante's "counterfeiter," Adam of Brescia. The two characters share a name, the same thematic occupation, and a disease: *scale.*

The Complaint of Chaucer to His Purse

321. Yeager, R. F. "Chaucer's 'To His Purse': Begging or Begging Off?" *Viator* 36 (2005): 373–414. Yeager reads *Purse* as a political poem rather than a begging poem, addressed initially to Richard. When Chaucer added the envoy, he was under duress from the court of Henry, not financial distress. The poem undermines Lancastrian legitimacy and if decoded might have contributed to Chaucer's death.

322. ————. "'Saving the Appearances' II: Another Look at Chaucer's 'Complaint to His Empty Purse.'" In T. L. Burton and John F. Plummer, eds. *"Seyd in Forme and Reverence": Essays on Chaucer and Chaucerians in Memory of Emerson Brown, Jr.* (*SAC* 29 [2007], no. 96): 151–64. Yeager finds a partisan second level of meaning underneath the sycophantic surface of the envoy of *Purse*—one that challenges Henry's right to rule.

The Complaint of Mars

323. Takada, Yasunari. "*The Brooch of Thebes* and *The Girdle of Venus*: Courtly Love in an Oppositional Perspective." *PoeticaT* 29–30 (1989): 17–38. Takada complicates traditional notions of "courtly love" by adducing Continental examples of marital love and English examples of extramarital sex outside of nonfabliau settings, focusing on the two motifs of the brooch and the girdle. Argues that the depiction of adultery in *Mars* is unique in many ways.

The Complaint unto Pity

See no. 143.

The Former Age

324. Stock, Lorraine Kochanske. "Past and Present in Chaucer's 'The Former Age': Boethian Translation or Late Medieval Primitivism?" *CarmP* 2 (1994): 1–37. Explores the late medieval traditions of the Wild

Man and idealized primitivism, arguing that they are useful in understanding and interpreting Chaucer's additions to the Boethian materials
in *Form Age*.

Fortune

325. Boffey, Julia. "Chaucer's *Fortune* in the 1530's: Some Sixteenth-
Century Recycling." In Anne Marie D'Arcy and Alan J. Fletcher, eds.
*Studies in Late Medieval and Early Renaissance Texts in Honour of John Scat-
tergood* (*SAC* 29 [2007], no. 103): 53–64. Discusses William Calverley's
Dyalogue Bitwene the Playntife and the Defendaunt (c. 1530–35?) in light
of the "Boethian motif of the prisoner of fortune," discussing Chaucer's
influence, especially among printers interested in religious or political
commentary.

Gentilesse

326. Hill, Thomas D. "Adam, 'The First Stocke,' and the Political
Context of Chaucer's 'Gentilesse.'" In T. L. Burton and John F. Plummer, eds. *"Seyd in Forme and Reverence": Essays on Chaucer and Chaucerians
in Memory of Emerson Brown, Jr.* (*SAC* 29 [2007], no. 96): 145–50. Argues that "fader" in the first line of *Gent* refers to prelapsarian Adam,
evidence of Chaucer's "modest egalitarianism."

Chaucerian Apocrypha

327. Dauby, Hélène. "La complémentarité du prologue de *Beryn* et
des *Canterbury Tales*." In Marie-Françoise Alamichel, ed. *La complémentarité: Mélanges offerts à Josseline Bidard et Arlette Sancery à l'occasion de leur
départ en retraite* (*SAC* 29 [2007], no. 85): 197–201. Though posed as a
continuation of *CT*, the Prologue to the *Tale of Beryn* emphasizes a return from Canterbury to London, from the sacred to the profane. *Sentence* and *solaas* are reduced to the merely "glad and merry."
328. ———. "Parcours initiatique d'un jeune truand: Beryn." In
Leo Carruthers and Adrian Papahagi, eds. *Jeunesse et vieillesse: Médiévales
de l'âge en littérature anglaise* (*SAC* 29 [2007], no. 100): 103–15. The *Tale
of Beryn* shows that bargaining is essential in the mercantile world. It
uses the "biter bit" pattern and—unusual in *CT*—reflects the moral
growth of an individual. First shown misbehaving like the rioters in
PardT, Beryn undergoes a true initiation process.

329. Patterson, Paul L. "Reforming Chaucer: Margins and Religion in an Apocryphal *Canterbury Tale*." *Book History* 8 (2005): 11–36. Patterson studies the marginalia printed with the 1606 edition of *The Plowman's Tale*, arguing that it challenges both papal authority and the Church of England, encouraging Puritanism. He also discusses the place of this edition in the tradition of Chaucer reception.

330. Pearsall, Derek. "The *Flower and the Leaf* and the *Assembly of Ladies*: A Revisitation." In Anne Marie D'Arcy and Alan J. Fletcher, eds. *Studies in Late Medieval and Early Renaissance Texts in Honour of John Scattergood* (*SAC* 29 [2007], no. 103): 259–69. Reads the two title poems in the context of contemporary court activities and conventions as "attempts to present a moralized version of love within an allegorical framework."

331. Vásquez, Nila. "The Need for 'Re-editing' *Gamelyn*." *IJES* 5.2 (2005): 161–73. Justifies the need for a new edition of the *Tale of Gamelyn* on the grounds that previous editions rely on limited manuscript authority and reflect various editorial biases.

332. Walker, Greg. "The Textual Archaeology of *The Plowman's Tale*." In Anne Marie D'Arcy and Alan J. Fletcher, eds. *Studies in Late Medieval and Early Renaissance Texts in Honour of John Scattergood* (*SAC* 29 [2007], no. 103): 375–401. Argues that *The Plowman's Tale* was composed in a complex process of interpolations and revisions (evident in various metrical schemes) that reflect various political and doctrinal agendas. Walker suggests a five-stage process of composition that began c. 1400 and extended into the 1530s.

333. Weinstock, Horst. "(K)ein Chaucer-Sonett?" In Horst Weinstock. *Kleine Schriften: Ausgewählte Studien zur Alt-, Mittel- und Frühneuenglischen Sprache und Literatur*. Heidelberg: Winter, 2003, pp. 99–109. Weinstock constructs a pseudo-sonnet from Chaucerian couplets and submits it to translation, analysis, and commentary. See also no. 414.

See also nos. 39, 64, 86.

Book Reviews

334. Akbari, Suzanne Conklin. *Seeing Through the Veil: Optical Theory and Medieval Allegory* (*SAC* 28 [2006], no. 59). Rev. Norman Klassen, *MÆ* 74 (2005): 333–34; John North, *N&Q* 52 (2005): 525–27.

335. Amtower, Laurel. *Engaging Words: The Culture of Reading in the*

Later Middle Ages (*SAC* 24 [2002], no. 131). Rev. Glenn Wright, *ES* 86 (2005): 371–73.

336. Benson, Robert G., and Susan J. Ridyard, eds. *New Readings of Chaucer's Poetry* (*SAC* 27 [2005], no. 90). Rev. Thomas Honegger, *Anglia* 123 (2005): 296–98; Glending Olson, *Speculum* 80 (2005): 514–16.

337. Bernau, Anke, Ruth Evans, and Sarah Salih, eds. *Medieval Virginities* (*SAC* 27 [2005], no. 197). Rev. Jennifer N. Brown, *MFF* 40 (2005): 143–45.

338. Black, Nancy B. *Medieval Narratives of Accused Queens* (*SAC* 27 [2005], no. 190). Rev. Laura Barefield, *MFF* 39 (2005): 64–65; Jennifer Britnell, *Speculum* 80 (2005): 837–39; Julia C. Deitrich, *NWSA Journal* 17.3 (2005): 207–8.

339. Boffey, Julia, comp. *Fifteenth-Century English Dream Visions: An Anthology* (*SAC* 28 [2006], no. 41). Rev. Donald C. Baker, *ELN* 42 (2005): 68–70; Louise M. Bishop, *TMR* 05.06.02, n.p.

340. Boitani, Piero, and Jill Mann, eds. *The Cambridge Companion to Chaucer*. 2nd ed. (*SAC* 27 [2005], no. 92). Rev. Mary Theresa Hall, *SCJ* 36 (2005): 514; Scott Lightsey, *TMR* 05.01.08, n.p.

341. Bowers, Bege K., and Mark Allen, eds. *Annotated Chaucer Bibliography, 1986–1996* (*SAC* 26 [2004], no. 3). Rev. Marion Turner, *N&Q* 52 (2005): 395–96 and 522–23.

342. Brown, Sarah Annes. *The Metamorphosis of Ovid: From Chaucer to Ted Hughes* (*SAC* 23 [2001], no. 230). Rev. Judith Woolf, *CQ* 33 (2004): 294–97.

343. Burger, Glenn. *Chaucer's Queer Nation* (*SAC* 27 [2005], no. 143). Rev. Karma Lochrie, *SAC* 27 (2005): 294–97.

344. Chewning, Susannah Mary, ed. *Intersections of Sexuality and the Divine in Medieval Culture: The Word Made Flesh* (*SAC* 29 [2007], no. 222). Rev. Nancy Bradley Warren, *MFF* 40 (2005): 113–17.

345. Cohen, Jeffrey J., ed. *Medieval Identity Machines* (*SAC* 27 [2005], no. 171). Rev. Susan Crane, *SAC* 27 (2005): 297–300.

346. Cooper, Helen. *The English Romance in Time: Transforming Motifs from Geoffrey of Monmouth to the Death of Shakespeare* (*SAC* 28 [2006], no. 65). Rev. Susan Crane, *MÆ* 74 (2005): 130–31; Richard Moll, *TMR* 05.09.29, n.p.

347. Copeland, Rita, David Lawton, and Wendy Scase, eds. *New Medieval Literatures* 5 (*SAC* 26 [2004], nos. 240 and 258). Rev. Leo Carruthers, *MÂ* 111 (2005): 192–93; Richard Utz, *Anglia* 123 (2005): 519–20.

348. Correale, Robert M., and Mary Hamel, eds. *Sources and Analogues of the "Canterbury Tales."* Vol. 1 (*SAC* 26 [2004], no. 47). Rev. Jill Mann, *JEGP* 104 (2005): 103–29.

349. Dalrymple, Roger, ed. *Middle English Literature: A Guide to Criticism* (*SAC* 28 [2006], no. 66). Rev. Suzanne M. Yeager, *N&Q* 52 (2005): 390–91.

350. Dawkins, Richard. *The Ancestor's Tale: A Pilgrimage to the Dawn of Evolution* (*SAC* 28 [2006], no. 96). Rev. Harold Fromm, *HudR* 58 (2005): 519–27.

351. Delany, Sheila, ed. *Chaucer and the Jews: Sources, Contexts, Meanings* (*SAC* 26 [2004], no. 129). Rev. John C. Hirsh, *MÆ* 74 (2005): 133–34.

352. Di Rocca, Emilia. *Letteratura e Legge nel Trecento Inglese* (*SAC* 27 [2005], no. 101). Rev. James H. McGregor, *Speculum* 80 (2005): 1262–63.

353. Edwards, David L. *Poets and God: Chaucer, Shakespeare, Herbert, Milton, Wordsworth, Coleridge, Blake* (*SAC* 29 [2007], no. 107). Rev. John Whale, *TLS,* April 15, 2005, p. 27.

354. Edwards, Robert R. *Chaucer and Boccaccio: Antiquity and Modernity* (*SAC* 26 [2004], no. 49). Rev. Claes Schaar, *ES* 86 (2005): 457–58.

355. Eisner, Sigmund, ed. *A Treatise on the Astrolabe.* Vol. 6, The Prose Treatises, pt. 1, of *A Variorum Edition of the Works of Geoffrey Chaucer* (*SAC* 26 [2004], no. 25). Rev. Kari Anne Rand, *ES* 86 (2005): 458–61; Chauncey Wood, *Speculum* 80 (2005): 536–39.

356. Ellis, Steve, ed. *Chaucer: An Oxford Guide* (*SAC* 29 [2007], no. 108). Rev. Lisa Clark, *RMRev,* n.p.

357. Farmer, Sharon, and Carol Braun Pasternack, eds. *Gender and Difference in the Middle Ages* (*SAC* 27 [2005], no. 193). Rev. Alison Gulley, *MFF* 40 (2005): 108–12.

358. Federico, Sylvia. *New Troy: Fantasies of Empire in the Late Middle Ages* (*SAC* 27 [2005], no. 280). Rev. Patricia Clare Ingham, *SAC* 27 (2005): 303–6.

359. Fenster, Thelma S., and Clare A. Lees, eds. *Gender in Debate from the Early Middle Ages to the Renaissance* (*SAC* 26 [2004], no. 212). Rev. Emma Cayley, *MÆ* 74 (2005): 125–26.

360. Finley, William K., and Joseph Rosenblum, eds. *Chaucer Illustrated: Five Hundred Years of the "Canterbury Tales" in Pictures* (*SAC* 27 [2005], no. 105). Rev. Bert Dillon, *PBSA* 99 (2005): 317–19; E. A. Jones, *Journal of the William Morris Society* 15.4 (2004): 165–67.

361. Fradenburg, L. O. Aranye. *Sacrifice Your Love: Psychoanalysis, Historicism, Chaucer* (*SAC* 26 [2004], no. 133). Rev. Bruce Holsinger, *SAC* 27 (2005): 306–9; Elizabeth B. Kaiser, *Speculum* 80 (2005): 870–72; Mark Miller, *MP* 103 (2005): 243–48.

362. Ginsberg, Warren. *Chaucer's Italian Tradition* (*SAC* 26 [2004], no. 50). Rev. Piero Boitani, *Speculum* 80 (2005): 228–30.

363. Godsall-Myers, Jean E., ed. *Speaking in the Medieval World* (*SAC* 27 [2005], no. 110). Rev. Laurie Shepard, *SCJ* 36 (2005): 1125–26.

364. Goldie, Matthew Boyd. *Middle English Literature: A Historical Sourcebook* (*SAC* 27 [2005], no. 111). Rev. Sarah Downey, *N&Q* 52 (2005): 527–28.

365. Gray, Douglas, ed. *The Oxford Companion to Chaucer* (*SAC* 27 [2005], no. 5). Rev. Suzanne Conklin Akbari, *N&Q* 52 (2005): 114–15; Derek Brewer, *SAC* 27 (2005): 309–12.; Michael Kuczynski, *TMR* 05.03.05, n.p; R. F. Yeager, *MÆ* 74 (2005): 344–36.

366. Hagedorn, Suzanne C. *Abandoned Women: Rewriting the Classics in Dante, Boccaccio, and Chaucer* (*SAC* 28 [2006], no. 35). Rev. Michael A. Calabrese, *JEGP* 104 (2005): 400–03; Carolyn P. Collette, *SAC* 27 (2005): 312–15; Robert R. Edwards, *MP* 103 (2005): 240–43; Jamie C. Fumo, *Speculum* 80 (2005): 1291–93; Mathilde Skoie, *TMR* 05.01.15, n.p.

367. Hanna, Ralph. *London Literature, 1300–1380* (*SAC* 29 [2007], no. 116). Rev. Tom Shippey, *TLS,* March 31, 2006, p. 25.

368. Harding, Wendy, ed. *Drama, Narrative, and Poetry in the "Canterbury Tales"* (*SAC* 27 [2005], no. 114). Rev. Elizabeth Scala, *TMR* 05.02.06, n.p.

369. Heffernan, Carol F. *The Orient in Chaucer and Medieval Romance* (*SAC* 27 [2005], no. 115). Rev. Helen Moore, *TLS,* July 8, 2005, p. 5; Brenda Deen Schildgen, *SAC* 27 (2005): 315–18.

370. Heng, Geraldine. *Empire of Magic: Medieval Romance and the Politics of Cultural Fantasy* (*SAC* 28 [2006], no. 127). Rev. Christine Chism, *SAC* 27 (2005): 318–21; Laurie A. Finke, *Arthuriana* 15.2 (2005): 71–72; Kathy Lavezzo, *MFF* 40 (2005): 104–7; Helen Moore, *TLS,* July 8, 2005, p. 5.

371. Hilmo, Maidie. *Medieval Images, Icons, and Illustrated English Literary Texts: From Ruthwell Cross to the Ellesmere Chaucer* (*SAC* 28 [2006], no. 99). Rev. Catherine E. Karkov, *N&Q* 52 (2005): 111; Charlotte C. Morse, *JEBS* 8 (2005): 288–89; Susan Yager, *TMR* 05.02.07, n.p.

372. Hirsh, John C. *Chaucer and the "Canterbury Tales": A Short Introduction* (*SAC* 27 [2005], no. 151). Rev. Christopher Stout, *RMRev*, n.p.

373. Holsinger, Bruce W. *Music, Body, and Desire in Medieval Culture: Hildegard of Bingen to Chaucer* (*SAC* 26 [2004], no. 136). Rev. Judith Dale, *Parergon* 22.1 (2005): 239–41; Annette Kreutziger-Herr, *Music & Letters* 86.1 (2005): 100–04.

374. Horobin, Simon. *The Language of the Chaucer Tradition* (*SAC* 27 [2005], no. 74). Rev. John H. Fisher, *SAC* 27 (2005): 321–23; Derek Pearsall, *Speculum* 80 (2005): 885–87; Jacob Thaisen, *ES* 86 (2005): 188–89.

375. Ingham, Patricia Clare, and Michelle R. Warren, eds. *Postcolonial Moves: Medieval Through Modern* (*SAC* 29 [2007], no 190). Rev. Cristina Sandru, *English* 54.209 (2005): 162–69.

376. Johnston, Andrew James. *Clerks and Courtiers: Chaucer, Late Middle English Literature, and the State Formation Process* (*SAC* 25 [2003], no. 111). Rev. David N. DeVries, *TMR* 05.01.24, n.p.

377. Jones, Sarah Rees, ed. *Learning and Literacy in Medieval England and Abroad* (*SAC* 28 [2006], no. 159). Rev. Andrew Galloway, *Speculum* 80 (2005): 659–61.

378. Jones, Terry, Robert Yeager, Terry Dolan, Alan Fletcher, and Juliette Dor. *Who Murdered Chaucer? A Medieval Mystery* (*SAC* 27 [2005], no. 14). Rev. Glending Olson, *Speculum* 80 (2005): 900–901; Derek Pearsall, *SAC* 27 (2005): 326–28.

379. Knapp, Ethan. *The Bureaucratic Muse: Thomas Hoccleve and the Literature of Late Medieval England* (*SAC* 26 [2004], no. 73). Rev. Richard K. Emmerson, *Speculum* 80 (2005): 1315–16.

380. Krier, Theresa M. *Birth Passages: Maternity and Nostalgia, Antiquity to Shakespeare* (*SAC* 27 [2005], no. 276). Rev. Dolora Chapelle Wojciehowski, *MP* 102 (2005): 410–13.

381. Lambdin, Laura Cooner, and Robert Thomas Lambdin, eds. *A Companion to Old and Middle English Literature* (*SAC* 26 [2004], no. 142). Rev. Andy Orchard, *N&Q* 52 (2005): 518–19.

382. Lampert, Lisa. *Gender and Jewish Difference from Paul to Shakespeare* (*SAC* 28 [2006], no. 157). Rev. Matthew Biberman, *Shakespeare Yearbook* 15 (2005): 397–404; Marilyn Francus, *Shakespeare and Renaissance Association of West Virginia* 28 (2005): 111–13; John C. Hirsh, *MÆ* 74 (2005): 133–34; William Chester Jordan, *SAC* 27 (2005): 329–31; M. Lindsay Kaplan, *ShakS* 33 (2005): 277–84.

383. Lavezzo, Kathy, ed. *Imagining a Medieval English Nation* (*SAC*

28 [2006], no. 76). Rev. Chris Jones, *Comitatus* 36 (2005): 245–50; Paul Strohm, *SAC* 27 (2005): 331–34.

384. Machan, Tim William. *English in the Middle Ages* (*SAC* 27 [2005], no. 77). Rev. Norman F. Blake, *Archiv* 242 (2005): 420–23; Christopher Cannon, *Speculum* 80 (2005): 629–31; Simon Horobin, *SAC* 27 (2005): 334–37.

385. McCarthy, Conor. *Marriage in Medieval England: Law, Literature, and Practice* (*SAC* 29 [2007], no. 127). Rev. Emma Lipton, *TMR* 05.07.17, n.p.

386. McDonald, Nicola F., and W. M. Ormrod, eds. *Rites of Passage: Cultures of Transition in the Fourteenth Century* (*SAC* 28 [2006], no. 175). Rev. Leo Carruthers, *MÂ* 111 (2005): 357–58.

387. Meyerson, Mark D., Daniel Thiery, and Oren Falk, eds. *"A Great Effusion of Blood"? Interpreting Medieval Violence* (*SAC* 28 [2006], no. 138). Rev. Anna Klosowska, *TMR* 05.06.04, n.p.

388. Miller, Mark. *Philosophical Chaucer: Love, Sex, and Agency in the "Canterbury Tales"* (*SAC* 29 [2007], no. 164). Rev. Sammie McGlasson, *WS* 34 (2005): 706–7; Thomas Joseph O'Donnell, *Comitatus* 36 (2005): 261–64; H. L. Spencer, *RES* 56 (2005): 780–81.

389. Mitchell, J. Allan. *Ethics and Exemplary Narratives in Chaucer and Gower* (*SAC* 28 [2006], no. 101). Rev. Georgiana Donavin, *TMR* 05.08.01, n.p.

390. Osborn, Marijane. *Time and the Astrolabe in the "Canterbury Tales"* (*SAC* 26 [2004], no. 176). Rev. Chauncey Wood, *Speculum* 80 (2005): 536–39.

391. Prendergast, Thomas A. *Chaucer's Dead Body: From Corpse to Corpus* (*SAC* 28 [2006], no. 46). Rev. Helen Cooper, *SAC* 27 (2005): 342–45; Joel Fredell, *TMR* 05.08.07, n.p.

392. Rhodes, Jim. *Poetry Does Theology: Chaucer, Grosseteste, and the "Pearl"-Poet* (*SAC* 25 [2003], no. 129). Rev. Elizabeth Robertson, *Journal of Religion* 85.1 (2005): 185–86.

393. Richmond, Velma Bourgeois. *Chaucer as Children's Literature: Retellings from the Victorian and Edwardian Eras* (*SAC* 29 [2007], no. 137). Rev. Gillian Adams, *Children's Literature Association Quarterly* 30 (2005): 131–32; Gary Schmidt, *Lion and Unicorn* 29 (2005): 276–80.

394. Rosenthal, Joel T. *Telling Tales: Sources and Narration in Late Medieval England* (*SAC* 27 [2005], no. 15). Rev. Charles F. Briggs, *Journal of British Studies* 44 (2005): 607–8; Carl Lindahl, *Journal of British Studies* 44 (2005): 364–66; Lee Patterson, *SAC* 27 (2005): 353–55.

395. Sadlek, Gregory M. *Idleness Working: The Discourse of Love's Labor from Ovid Through Chaucer and Gower* (*SAC* 28 [2006], no. 84). Rev. Audrey DeLong, *SCJ* 36 (2005): 1147–48.

396. Saunders, Corinne. *Chaucer* (*SAC* 25 [2003], no. 136). Rev. Sophie van Romburgh, *ES* 86 (2005): 370–71.

397. Serrano Reyes, Jesús L., and Antonio R. León Sendra, trans. *Geoffrey Chaucer: Cuentos de Canterbury* (*SAC* 28 [2006], no. 21). Rev. Jordi Sánchez-Martí, *SAC* 27 (2005): 350–52.

398. Shepard, Alan, and Stephen D. Powell, eds. *Fantasies of Troy: Classical Tales and the Social Imaginary in Medieval and Early Modern Europe* (*SAC* 29 [2007], no. 286). Rev. Sylvaine Bataille, *Cahiers Élisabéthains* 68 (2005): 88–91; Charles Russell Stone, *Comitatus* 36 (2005): 227–29.

399. Smith, D. Vance. *Arts of Possession: The Middle English Household Imaginary* (*SAC* 27 [2005], no. 225). Rev. Elizabeth Robertson, *Speculum* 80 (2005): 1366–68; Claire Sponsler, *SAC* 27 (2005): 355–58.

400. Somerset, Fiona, Jill C. Havens, and Derrick G. Pitard, eds. *Lollards and Their Influence in Late Medieval England* (*SAC* 27 [2005], no. 134). Rev. Kalpen Trivedi, *SAC* 27 (2005): 358–61.

401. Staley, Lynn. *Languages of Power in the Age of Richard II* (*SAC* 29 [2007], no. 144). Rev. Robert Barrett, *TMR* 05.09.05, n.p.

402. Steinberg, Theodore L. *Reading the Middle Ages: An Introduction to Medieval Literature* (*SAC* 28 [2006], no. 88). Rev. John C. Hirsch, *Speculum* 80 (2005): 332–34.

403. Steiner, Emily, and Candace Barrington, eds. *The Letter of the Law: Legal Practice and Literary Production in Medieval England* (*SAC* 26 [2004], no. 154). Rev. John M. Ganim, *SAC* 27 (2005): 364–67.

404. Summers, Joanna. *Late-Medieval Prison Writing and the Politics of Autobiography* (*SAC* 29 [2007], no. 272). Rev. Fiona Somerset, *MÆ* 74 (2005): 347–48.

405. Symons, Dana M., ed. *Chaucerian Dream Visions and Complaints* (*SAC* 28 [2006], no. 218). Rev. Kathryn L. Lynch, *TMR* 05.05.02, n.p.

406. Taavitsainen, Irma, and Andreas H. Jucker, eds. *Diachronic Perspectives on Address Term Systems* (*SAC* 29 (2007), no. 79). Rev. Manfred Markus, *Anglia* 123 (2005): 490–96.

407. Tajiri, Masaji. *Studies in the Middle English Didactic Tail-Rhyme Romances* (*SAC* 29 [2007], no. 228). Rev. Eve Salisbury, *Speculum* 80 (2005): 336–38.

408. Thompson, Diane P. *The Trojan War: Literature and Legends from*

the Bronze Age to the Present (*SAC* 29 [2007], no. 312). Rev. Sylvaine Bataille, *Cahiers Élisabéthains* 68 (2005): 88–91.

409. Treharne, Elaine, ed. *Writing Gender and Genre in Medieval Literature: Approaches to Old and Middle English Texts* (*SAC* 26 [2004], no. 156). Rev. Annette Kern-Stähler, *Anglia* 123 (2005): 296–98.

410. Utz, Richard. *Chaucer and the Discourse of German Philology: A History of Critical Reception and an Annotated Bibliography of Studies, 1793–1948* (*SAC* 26 [2004], no. 159). Rev. Jerold Frakes, *TMR* 05.01.09, n.p.

411. Vaught, Jennifer C., ed., with Lynne Dickson Bruckner. *Grief and Gender: 700–1700* (*SAC* 28 [2006], no. 143). Rev. Robin Norris, *N&Q* 52 (2005): 514–15.

412. Waters, Claire M. *Angels and Earthly Creatures: Preaching, Performance, and Gender in the Later Middle Ages* (*SAC* 28 [2006], no. 93). Rev. Lawrence Besserman, *Speculum* 80 (2005): 1393–95; Catherine Cox, *MFF* 40 (2005): 87–90; Katherine Little, *SAC* 27 (2005): 367–70; Alison Tara Walker, *Comitatus* 36 (2005): 312–14; Nancy Bradley Warren, *TMR* 05.01.20, n.p.

413. Watt, Diane. *Amoral Gower: Language, Sex, and Politics* (*SAC* 27 [2005], no. 51). Rev. María Bullón-Fernández, *SAC* 27 (2005): 370–73; Graham Drake, *TMR* 05.01.39, n.p.

414. Weinstock, Horst. *Kleine Schriften: Ausgewählte Studien zur Alt-, Mittel- und Frühneuenglischen Sprache und Literatur* (*SAC* 29 [2007], no. 333). Rev. Hans-Jürgen Diller, *Anglia* 123 (2005): 104–6.

415. West, Richard. *Chaucer, 1340–1400: The Life and Times of the First English Poet* (*SAC* 24 [2002], no. 13). Rev. Peter Beidler, *SIMELL* 17 (2002): 101–5.

416. Williams, Deanne. *The French Fetish from Chaucer to Shakespeare* (*SAC* 28 [2006], no. 94). Rev. A. Kent Hieatt, *RenQ* 58 (2005): 1037–38.

417. Wogan-Browne, Jocelyn, et al., eds. *Medieval Women: Texts and Contexts in Late Medieval Britain: Essays for Felicity Riddy* (*SAC* 24 [2002], no. 194). Rev. Kate Jackson, *Bulletin of International Medieval Research* 9–10 (2005, for 2003–4): 70–72.

418. Zeikowitz, Richard E. *Homoeroticism and Chivalry: Discourses of Male Same-Sex Desire in the Fourteenth Century* (*SAC* 28 [2006], no. 214). Rev. William Burgwinkle, *SAC* 27 (2005): 373–76; Allen J. Frantzen, *N&Q* 52 (2005): 241–43.

Author Index—Bibliography

The New Chaucer Society
Fifteenth International Congress
July 27–31, 2006
Fordham University

THURSDAY, JULY 27

10:00 am–5:30 pm
Registration

11:00 am–2:00 pm
Trustees' Meeting

2:00–3:00 pm
Session 1 (Plenary)
Business Meeting

3:00–3:30 pm
Session 2 (Plenary)
Presidential Address: David Wallace, University of Pennsylvania
"New Chaucer Topographies"

3:30–4:00 pm
Coffee, tea, and cookies

4:00–5:30 pm
Concurrent Paper Sessions (Sessions 3–7)

Session 3: What Is Happening to the Middle Ages?
Session organizer: Stephanie Trigg, University of Melbourne
Session chair: Tom Prendergast, College of Wooster
- "Making History Whole: Diachronic History and the Shortcomings of Medieval Studies," James Simpson, Harvard University
- "Cultural Memory and the Middle Ages: What Is the Future of Medievalism?", Stephanie Trigg, University of Melbourne
- "Bridging the Gap: Two Worlds, One Poet," Philip Thiel, University of York
- "Never, Always, Now, Again: The Temporalities of Medieval Studies," Carolyn Dinshaw, New York University

Session 4: Adaptations: Chaucer and Julian in the Modern World
Session organizer: Program Committee
Session chair: Russell Peck, University of Rochester
- "Screening *The Canterbury Tales*," Laurie Finke, Kenyon College

- "Reinventing Chaucer Onstage for an Early Twentieth-Century Audience: Percy Mackaye's 1908 Play and Reginald De Koven's 1917 Opera, *Canterbury Pilgrims*," Lorraine K. Stock, University of Houston
- "Tongue to Tongue: An Afro-Caribbean Response to Chaucer's *Canterbury Tales*," Tamara F. O'Callaghan, Northern Kentucky University
- "Julie Norwich and Julian of Norwich: Annie Dillard's Theodicy in *Holy the Firm*," Denise Baker, University of North Carolina

Session 5: Dream Visions
Session organizer: Program Committee
Session chair: Lisa Kiser, The Ohio State University
- "The Disposition of the Bed Chamber," Elizabeth Fowler, University of Virginia
- "Vernacular Style and the Scene of Reading," Thomas Hahn, University of Rochester
- "Imagining Women's Spaces and Women's Voices in *The Floure and the Leafe*," Tim Turner, University of Texas at Austin
- "Emotion, Motion, and Transformation in the *Legend of Good Women*," Suzanne Conklin Akbari, University of Toronto

Session 6: Reading Antiquity
Session organizer: Program Committee
Session chair: Elizabeth Archibald, University of Bristol
- "An Anti-Homeric Ethic: Translating Truth in the *Destruction of Troy*," Alex Mueller, University of Minnesota, Twin Cities
- " 'To Be Trewe to Her Nacioun': *Troy Book* and Fifteenth-Century Chaucerian Nationhood," Wolfram R. Keller, Philipps Universität Marburg
- " 'Petrarke, Ariosto, and Gaufredus Chaucer': How Speght and Thynne Translated Chaucer into a Classical Author," Roberta Magnani, Cardiff University
- "The *Legend of Good Women* and the Latin Glosses to Ovid's *Heroides*: Some Approaches," K. P. Clarke, University College, Oxford

Session 7: Chaucer in Theory
Session organizer: Program Committee
Session chair: Peggy Knapp, Carnegie Mellon University
- "Quitting the 'Manciple's Tale,' " Krista Sue-Lo Twu, University of Minnesota, Duluth

- "Ethics in the Event of the *Canterbury Tales*," Allan Mitchell, University of Kent
- "Chaucer's Liminal Ethics: The Other as Test Case," Leonard Koff, University of California, Los Angeles
- "Post-Philology for Chaucer," Michelle R. Warren, University of Miami

5:30–6:30 pm
Reception 1
Sponsored by Hunter College and The Graduate Center, The City University of New York

FRIDAY, JULY 28

8:30 am–6:30 pm
Registration

8:30 am–5:00 pm
Book Exhibit
Sponsored by SUNY Stony Brook

9:00–10:30 am
Session 8 (Plenary): Exhibiting Medieval Art: A Discussion with Directors and Curators
Organizers: Daniel R. Rubey, Hofstra University, and John M. Ganim, University of California, Riverside
Presiding: David Lawton, Executive Director, New Chaucer Society, and Washington University
- Peter Barnet, Michel David-Weill, Curator in Charge, Department of Medieval Art and The Cloisters, The Metropolitan Museum of Art
- Consuelo W. Dutschke, Curator, Medieval and Renaissance Manuscripts, Columbia University
- Nancy Netzer, Director, McMullen Museum of Art and Professor of Art History, Boston College
- Moderators: Daniel R. Rubey, Dean of Library and Information Services, Hofstra University, and John M. Ganim, University of California, Riverside

This panel is in conjunction with tours of the Morgan Library and the Metropolitan Museum of Art.

10:30–11:00 am
Coffee, tea, and pastries

11:00 am–12:30 pm
Concurrent Paper Sessions (Sessions 9–13)

Session 9: Reading Aloud as Interpretation
Session organizer and chair: David Fuller, University of Durham
- "Audible Sincerity Increases Unheard Ironies," Howell Chickering, Amherst College
- "Aurality/Orality: What's a Poor Reader to Do?", Alan Gaylord, Dartmouth College
- "Chaucerians, Don't Do It with Pronounced '-e's," Michael Murphy, CUNY
- "An Echoic Reading of the 'Canticus Troili,'" William Quinn, University of Arkansas

Session 10: Finding Adam Scriveyn: Scribes, Manuscripts, and Texts
Session organizer and chair: Toshiyuki Takamiya, Keio University
- "The Linguistic Implications of Adam Pinkhurst," Jeremy Smith, University of Glasgow
- "Dr. Jekyll and Mr. Pinkhurst: The Under-the-Counter Literature of Adam Scriveyn," Alan J. Fletcher, University College, Dublin
- "The Making of Corpus 198 and the Ellesmere Tradition: Evidence from the *Melibee* Glosses," Stephen B. Partridge, University of British Columbia
- "Adam Pinkhurst in Context," Linne Mooney, University of York

Session 11: Ethics: History
Session organizer: Richard Newhauser, Trinity University, San Antonio
Session chair: Nicolette Zeeman, King's College, Cambridge
- "The 'Stalke' and the 'Balke': The Ethics of Reproof in *The Canterbury Tales*," Edwin D. Craun, Washington and Lee University
- "Queer After All: Toward an Historically Responsible, Philologically

Nuanced, and Otherwise Thoroughly Unimpeachable Reading of the Pardoner's Sexuality," Larry Scanlon, Rutgers University
- "The Remedy Against Temptation: Moral Theology and the Problem of Despair," Nicholas Watson, Harvard University

Session 12: The University
Session organizer and chair: Warren Ginsberg, University of Oregon
- "The University in Ruins? Scholastic Argot, Vernacular Writing, and Arundel's Constitutions," Thomas Goodmann, University of Miami
- "Politics, Rape, and the Intellectual in Chaucer's 'Reeve's Tale': From Fabliau to the Classics," Nicole Nolan Sidhu, East Carolina University
- "Taking Chaucer to School," William Askins, Community College of Philadelphia

Session 13: Performing Emotion
Session organizer and chair: Sarah McNamer, Georgetown University
- "On Being 'Sober': Hiding Emotion in Chaucer and Other Middle English Contexts," Lawrence Besserman, Hebrew University of Jerusalem
- "Cacophony and Silence: Performing Emotion in *The Parliament of Fowls*," Denis Renevey, Universities of Fribourg and Neuchâtel
- "'How Sholde I Singe Mor?': Lyric Conjunctions of Emotion and Performance in Medieval England," Seeta Chaganti, University of California, Davis
- "Feeling Like Saints: Affect, Martyrdom, and Performance in Late Medieval England," Fiona Somerset, Duke University

12:30–2:30 pm
Lunch / Free Time

2:30–4:00 pm
Concurrent Paper Sessions (Sessions 14–18)

Session 14: Historicism as Close Reading
Session organizer and chair: Tom Stillinger, University of Utah
- "Historicizing Sir Thopas's Jewish Armorer," Miriamne Krummel, University of Dayton

- "'What Man Artow?' Lee Patterson's Gradual Self-Definition as a New Historicist," Kathy Cawsey, Wilfrid Laurier University
- "Close Reading, History, and Genre: Can Cecilia Tell a Lollard Joke?", Thomas J. Farrell, Stetson University
- "Joke, Sermon, 'Gaude': Reading the Pardoner's Approach," Warren Ginsberg, University of Oregon

Session 15: London and Textual Culture: Chaucer in the City
Session organizer and chair: Marion Turner, King's College London
- "The Word and the Street: Sexual and Civic Negotiation in the Ward Mote Records, *Troilus and Criseyde*, and the Annunciation," Nicola McDonald, University of York
- "The Word on the Street: Chaucer and the Regulation of Nuisance in Post-Plague London," Sarah Rees-Jones, University of York
- "Chaucer and Ricardian Pamphlet Poetry in London," Joel Fredell, Southeastern Louisiana University
- "Marchantz, Mercurie,and Markyng: Gower, Chaucer, and the London Goldsmiths," Jonathan Hsy, University of Pennsylvania

Session 16 Ethics: Narrative
Session organizers: Elizabeth Allen, University of California, Irvine, and Catherine Sanok, University of Michigan
Session chair: Elizabeth Allen, University of California, Irvine
- "Experimenting with the Real: The Griselda Story as Ethical Narrative," Glenn Burger, Queens College and The Graduate Center, CUNY
- "Hard-Boiled Hagiography, or Looking Awry at *St. Erkenwald*," Frank Grady, University of Missouri, Saint Louis
- "'With that Word': Making Examples in the *Legend of Good Women*," Walter Wadiak, University of California, Irvine
- "Chaucer, Reading, and Remedies," Rebecca Krug, University of Minnesota

Session 17: Chaucer and Architecture
Session organizer and chair: Martine Yvernault, Université de Limoges
- "Chaucer's New Ekphrasis," Florence Bourgne, Paris IV-Sorbonne
- "Architecture and Nature in the 'Knight's Tale': Action Overt and Covert," Claire Jardillier, Paris IV-Sorbonne

- "The Prioress and the Privy," Kathy Lavezzo, University of Iowa
- "Visions of the Grotesque in *The House of Fame*," Tatjana Silec, Paris IV-Sorbonne

Session 18: Friendship and Desire
Session organizer and chair: Corinne Saunders, University of Durham
- "The Dynamics of Friendship and Desire in *Troilus and Criseyde*," Andreea Boboc, University of Michigan
- "The Desire of Friendship—Chaucer's Two Shields of Arcite," Simon Meecham-Jones, University of Cambridge
- "Friend or Foe: Discerning Friendship in Chaucer's *Canterbury Tales*," Rebecca Leeper, University of California, Los Angeles
- "Loyalty among Wives: Desire and Same-Sex Friendship in the *Canterbury Tales*," Tara Williams, Oregon State University

4:00–4:30 pm
Coffee, tea, and cookies

4:30–6:00 pm
Concurrent Paper Sessions (Sessions 19–23)

Session 19: Aurality and the Written Text
Session organizer: Joyce Coleman, University of Oklahoma
Session chair: Evelyn Birge Vitz, New York University
- Presentation of a short film: "Reading in a Paved Parlor," Joyce Coleman, University of Oklahoma
- "Misreading as Introit to Book II of *Troilus and Criseyde*," Eugene Green, Boston University
- "Criseyde's Romance Community: Shared Readings, Shared Values?", Cathy Hume, University of Bristol
- "Chaucer's Only Text for Readers? Aurality, Genre, and the 'Second Nun's Tale,'" Michael Foster, Åbo Akademi University

Session 20: Langland and His Contemporaries
Session organizer and chair: Simon Horobin, University of Glasgow
- "Langland in London, c. 1385? John of Northampton and the Production of *Piers Plowman*," Lawrence Warner, University of Adelaide
- "The Scribe of HM 114: Nearly Contemporary with Langland and Chaucer," Bryan P. Davis, Georgia Southwestern State University

- "Langland's Search for a Reader: London Manuscripts and the Construction of Textual Histories," Stephen Kelly, Queen's University, Belfast
- "*Piers Plowman* on Paper," Orietta Da Rold, University of Leicester

Session 21: Ethics: Theory
Session organizer and chair: D. Vance Smith, Princeton University
Session chair: Larry Scanlon, Rutgers University
- "Illiberal Chaucer," Mark Miller, University of Chicago
- "The Pardoner's 'Anxiety toward Death' vs. the Parson's Path of Penitence: Two Ways toward a Levinasian Chaucer," Ann Astell, Purdue University
- "Toward a Chaucerian Ethics of the Same," George Edmondson, Dartmouth University
- "Chaucerian Object Relations," Kellie Robertson, University of Pittsburgh

Session 22: Shame
Session organizer and chair: Alcuin Blamires, Goldsmiths College, London
- "Shaming Fame," Susan E. Phillips, Northwestern University
- "Conditions Shameful and Unshameful in the 'Franklin's Tale,'" Wan-Chuan Kao, The Graduate Center, CUNY
- "'In wyfhod I wol use myn instrument / As frely as my Makere hath it sent': The Wife of Bath's Shameless Sexuality," Sue Niebrzydowski, University of Warwick
- "'Maydens shamefastnesse': Shame as Honour in the Middle Ages," Mary Flannery, Pembroke College, Cambridge

Session 23: Exemplarity
Session organizer: Program Committee
Session chair: Elizabeth Allen, University of California, Irvine
- "'I,' Art, Melibee: Prudent Poetics and the Ethics of Self-Representation," Stephen Yeager, University of Toronto
- "Gower and the Anxiety of a Career-Ethicist," Steele Nowlin, Pennsylvania State University
- "Resisting and Revising Exempla in Late Medieval Religious Writing," Moira Fitzgibbons, Marist College
- "Exemplars and Exemplarity: Compilation as Narrative in Thomas Hoccleve's *Series*," David Watt, University of Manitoba

6:00–7:00 pm
Reception 2
Sponsored by Fordham University

7:00–7:40 p.m.
Tour of the J. P. Morgan Library

8:00 pm
Present Tense: Literary Artists and Performers Engaging Chaucer
Organized by David Wallace, University of Pennsylvania
Host: Charles Bernstein, University of Pennsylvania
Co–sponsored by Poets House and the Medieval Club of New York
- "The Loathly Lady: An Animated Opera," Wendy Steiner, University of Pennsylvania
- "Dreaming After Chaucer," Susan Stewart, Princeton University
- " 'Thy likerous mouth': Short Chaucer Tales," Caroline Bergvall, Bard College

9 pm–midnight
Reception for Graduate Students
Columbia University
Sponsored by Columbia Medieval Guild

SATURDAY, JULY 29

8:30 am–4:30 pm
Registration

8:30 am–5:00 pm
Book Exhibit
Sponsored by SUNY Stony Brook

9:00–11:00 am
Concurrent Panel Sessions (Sessions 24–28) and Teachers' Forum (Session 29)

Session 24: From Crux to Theory (E-seminar and panel)
Session organizer and chair: Robert J. Meyer-Lee, Goshen College

- "Masculine Mimicry? Another Look at the 'Shipman's Tale,' VII.11–19," Holly A. Crocker, University of South Carolina
- "Chaucer's 'Complaint Unto Pity' as a Crux of Form and Narrative," Matthew Giancarlo, Yale University
- "Chaucer's Parson in MS BL Add. 10340," Erick Kelemen, University of Missouri, Columbia
- "Textual Variance and Lay Devotion in the Notre Dame Mirror MS," Paul J. Patterson, University of Cincinnati
- "Lost Books and Leprous Bodies," Christian Sheridan, Saint Xavier University
- "'Incestus Paridis, Ypolitique pudor' and the Ellesmere Gloss to Lines 197–202 of the 'Man of Law's Tale,'" Andrew Taylor, University of Ottawa
- "Authorship in the Margins: The Auctor Annotations in Chaucer Manuscripts," Carolynn Van Dyke, Lafayette College

Session 25: Time, Measure, and Value in Chaucer's Art and Chaucer's World
Session organizer and chair: Carolyn Collette, Mt. Holyoke College
- "Counsels of Attemperance in the *Canterbury Tales*," Nancy Bradbury, Smith College
- "Chaucer's Time Signatures," Dan Ransom, University of Oklahoma
- "Quantifying the Unquantifiable: Farting, Geometry, and Theology in the 'Summoner's Tale,'" Glending Olson, Cleveland State University
- "Tricks of Time: The Power of Time Reckoning in the *Canterbury Tales*," Dawn Simmons Walts, Ohio State University
- "The Subject of Art in an Age of Alchemical Non-Production: Self-Appraisal and the Canon's Yeoman," Eleanor Bayne Johnson, University of California, Berkeley
- "'Knowledge of the Files': Subverting Bureaucratic Legibility in 'The Franklin's Tale,'" Cara Hersh, Duke University
- "Business and Pleasure: Measuring Value in the 'Shipman's Tale,'" Robert Epstein, Fairfield University

Session 26: Institutions and Objects (E-seminar and panel)
Session co-organizers and chairs: Andrea Denny-Brown, University of California, Riverside, and John M. Ganim, University of California, Riverside

- "Daedalus, Domesticity, and Disaster: 'The Knight's Tale' (*et alia*)," Lisa H. Cooper, University of Wisconsin, Madison
- "'Vive la bele!': 'Galaunts' and Goods in Late Medieval England," Andrea Denny-Brown, University of California, Riverside
- "Material Culture Displayed: The Processions in the 'Knight's Tale,'" Laura Hodges, Independent Scholar, Houston
- "Chaucer's Vows and How They Break: Marital Transgression in the 'Manciple's Tale,'" Jean Jost, Bradley University
- "Mirrors, Interiority, and the High Style in 'The Merchant's Tale,'" Thomas O'Donnell, University of California, Los Angeles
- "Chaucer and the Language of Property: An Analysis of Late Medieval Terms for 'House' in Literary and Historical Sources," Jayne Rimmer, University of York

Session 27: Honor as a Commodity

Session organizer and chair: Edwin Craun, Washington and Lee University
- "Honour in Chaucer," Derek Brewer, Emmanuel College, Cambridge
- "Chaucer's Second Hector," Tim Arner, Pennsylvania State University
- "Book Borrowing, Honor, and the Circulation of Medieval Texts," Tom Prendergast, College of Wooster
- "Honor Among Thieves and Nobles: Social Class and 'Saving Face' in Chaucer's Works," Laura Getty, North Georgia College and State University

Panel Session 28: Fabliaux

Session organizer: Program Committee
Session chair: John Fyler, Tufts University
- "Destabilizing Fabliau in the 'Miller's Tale,'" Jerome Mandel, Tel Aviv University
- "'Myn hous is streit': The Phenomenology of Place in the 'Reeve's Tale,'" John F. Plummer, Vanderbilt University
- "Space, Desire, and the Wife of Bath," Kenneth Bleeth, Connecticut College
- "Chaucer's Thirteenth-Century Songbook: A Key to Understanding the 'Miller's Tale,'" Charlotte Allen, Catholic University of America
- "'A Myle Brood of Twenty Foot of Space': Physical and Social Space in Fragment I of the *Canterbury Tales*," W. Joseph Taylor, University of Texas at Austin

- " 'House of Mean': Vindictiveness in the 'Reeve's Tale,' " Gregory J. Darling, John Jay College of Criminal Justice, CUNY, and Fordham University, Lincoln Center
- "Deceptive Enclosures: Chaucer's Use of Domestic Space in the Fabliaux," Dhira B. Mahoney, Arizona State University
- "When Bodies Count: Resistance to Exchange in the 'Shipman's Tale,' " Alyssa Meyers, Columbia University

Session 29: Teachers' Forum 1: Opening Session
Session organizer and chair: Larry Scanlon, Rutgers University
- David Raybin, Eastern Illinois University
- Mary Flowers Braswell, University of Alabama, Birmingham
- Anne Prescott, Independent Scholar
- Samantha Rayner, University of Wales, Bangor
- Stephanie Sanchez, Tesoro High School
- Wim Lindeboom, Hilversum Gymnasium

11:00–11:30 am
Coffee, tea, and pastries

11:30–12:30 pm
Session 30 (Plenary): Biennial Chaucer Lecture
Susan Crane, Columbia University
"For the Birds"

12:30– 2:30 pm
Lunch / Free Time

2:30–4:30 pm
Concurrent Panel Sessions (Sessions 31–35) and Teachers' Forum (Session 36)

Session 31: The Value of Close Reading: Theory
Session organizer and chair: Christopher Cannon, Girton College, Cambridge
- "Close Reading, Style, and History," Charles Muscatine, University of California, Berkeley
- "What Would a Post-Historicist Formalism Look Like?", Bruce Holsinger, University of Virginia

- "A Close Reading of the Idea of Close Reading," Peter Travis, Dartmouth College
- "Crossing the Pond: Diversities of Close Reading in North American and British Criticism," Ethan Knapp, Ohio State University
- "Enjoying the Signifier," Aranye Fradenburg, University of California, Santa Barbara
- "Close Words," Ardis Butterfield, University College, London

Session 32: Emotions (E-seminar and panel)
Session organizer and chair: Matthew Boyd Goldie, Rider University
- "Natural Passion and Moral Virtue: Pecock and 'Truth,'" Louise M. Bishop, University of Oregon
- "The Rhetoric of Emotions: From Aristotle to Chaucer and Gower," Georgiana Donavin, Westminster College
- "Grief and Grievance for Chaucer's Forsaken Women," Elizabeth Edwards, University of King's College
- "'With Gam and with G[u]ile': Floods of Emotion in The Wakefield 'Noah' Play," Kari Gillesse, Indiana University
- "Chaucer, Penitence, and the Pleasure of Sacrifice," Cathryn Meyer, University of Texas at Austin
- "Pathos and Anti-Clericalism in the 'Clerk's Tale,'" Derrick Pitard, Slippery Rock University
- "Performing Emotions," Sylvia Tomasch, Hunter College, CUNY

Session 33: New Light on Thomas Usk
Session organizer and chair: David Wallace, University of Pennsylvania
- "New Evidence of Usk," Caroline Barron, Royal Holloway, University of London
- "Usk's Middle English," Ronald Waldron, King's College London
- "Usk and the 'Shepy-People': Rhetoric, Reform, and the Commons in the Writing of Thomas Usk," Maria Cristina Santos Pangilinan, University of Pennsylvania
- "Usk and Faction," Paul Strohm, Columbia University
- "Holding Usk," Steven F. Kruger, Queens College and The Graduate Center, CUNY

Session 34: Chaucer's English: A Creole?
Session organizer and chair: Fabienne Toupin, Université de Tours

- "Chaucer's Diversity of Language," Lindsey Jones, Pennsylvania State University
- "Chaucer's English: A Fusion Language?", Jennifer G. Wollock, Texas A&M University
- "Chaucer's Multilingual Nation," Mary Catherine Davidson, University of Kansas
- "Chaucer's Borrowing and Macaronic Writing," Judith Tschann, University of Redlands

Session 35: Contexts of Reading in Late Medieval England
Session organizer: Program Committee
Session chair: H. A. Kelly, University of California, Los Angeles
- "The 'Comene Course of Prayer': Julian of Norwich and Late Medieval Death Culture," Amy Appleford, Harvard University
- "Chaucer and the Female Audience: Manuscripts of *Troilus and Criseyde*," Kara Doyle, Union College
- "Text and Image in the Ellesmere Manuscript: Reading the Portraits in the *General Prologue*," Anne Mulligan, Bishop Kearney H.S. and Saint Joseph's College
- "The Alien Boy," Jeffrey Cohen, George Washington University
- "Chaucer, the Church, and the Man of Law," Jim Rhodes, Southern Connecticut University
- "More than a Metaphor: The Horizontal Orientation of the 'Franklin's Tale,'" Mark Sherman, Rhode Island School of Design

Session 36: Teachers' Forum 2: Break-out Meetings
Session organizer and chair: Larry Scanlon, Rutgers University

5:30 pm
Excursion: Metropolitan Museum

SUNDAY, JULY 30

9:00 am–5:30 pm
Registration

9:00 am–5:00 pm
Book Exhibit

Sponsored by SUNY Stony Brook

9:30–11:00 am
Concurrent Paper Sessions (Sessions 37–41) and Teachers' Forum
(Session 42)

Session 37: Spoken Voice and the Illusion of Presence
Session organizer and chair: Aranye Fradenburg, University of California, Santa Barbara

- "Citation, Erasure, and Trope," Patricia Clare Ingham, Indiana University
- "The Living Thing," Christopher Cannon, Girton College, Cambridge
- "The Variant Voice: Aestheticized Politics in the *Piers Plowman* Tradition," Randy Schiff, SUNY Buffalo
- "A Tongue Purloined: Creseyde's Unspeakable Entente and Its Ovidian Intertexts," James R. Simpson, University of Glasgow

Session 38: Digital Chaucer
Session organizer and chair: Ruth Evans, University of Stirling

- "Learning Technology and Chaucer Pedagogy: The Wiki," Susan Yager, Iowa State University, and Kenneth Tompkins, Richard Stockton College of New Jersey
- "*The Book of the Duchess*: Towards a Digital Model for Variorum Editions," Laurel Broughton, University of Vermont, and Murray McGillivray, University of Calgary
- "Phenomenology of a CD," Valerie Allen, John Jay College of Criminal Justice, CUNY
- "As We May Read Chaucer," Peter Robinson, Institute for Textual Scholarship and Electronic Editing, University of Birmingham

Session 39: Give and Take
Session organizers: Margaret Pappano, Queen's University, and Nicholas Perkins, St. Hugh's College, Oxford
Session chair: Margaret Pappano, Queen's University

- "Gifts and Greeks in *Troilus and Criseyde*," Emily Reiner, Centre for Medieval Studies, University of Toronto
- "The Function of Give and Take in the 'Wife of Bath's Tale,'" Lawrence Beaston, Pennsylvania College of Technology

- "The 'Pardoner's Tale' and the Economics of Sociability," Jenny Adams, University of Massachusetts, Amherst
- "'Sadde Tokenes and Wordes Bolde': Speech-act and the Properties of Words in the 'Franklin's Tale' and the 'Manciple's Tale,'" Nicholas Perkins, St. Hugh's College, Oxford

Session 40: John Gower
Session organizer and chair: Elliot Kendall, University of Exeter
- "Picturing Women in Pierpont Morgan MS M. 126," Martha W. Driver, Pace University
- "Lady Wool and the Lombards: John Gower's Mirour of Trade," Brantley Lloyd Bryant, Columbia University
- "The Father's Two Bodies: Gower's Treatments of Incest between the Familial and the Dynastic," Sebastian Sobecki, University of Cambridge

Session 41: The Bible As, In, or Against Literature: Medieval to Early Modern I
Session organizer and chair: James Simpson, Harvard University
- "Reading as Rewriting in *Piers Plowman*," Laura Bradford, Harvard University
- "Biblical Writing/Literary Writing: The Chester Plays as Test Case," Theresa Coletti, University of Maryland
- "The Story of Susanna in the Vernacular: Examples from the Thirteenth to the Fifteenth Century, including Chaucer," Susanna Fein, Kent State University
- "Susanna's Voice," Lynn Staley, Colgate University

Session 42: Teachers' Forum 3: Wrap-up Session
Session organizer and chair: Larry Scanlon, Rutgers University

11:00–11:30 am
Coffee, tea, and pastries

11:30–1:00 pm
Concurrent Paper Sessions (Sessions 43–47)

Session 43: Reiteration: Repetition in the Chaucerian Text
Session organizer and chair: Mark Miller, University of Chicago

- "The 'Thral to Whom That He Hath Seyd': The Power of Hearing Chaucer's *Canterbury Tales*," Elizabeth Scala, University of Texas at Austin
- "The Cutting Edge of the Mother's Tongue," Disa Gambera, University of Utah
- "'The Word Moot Nede Accorde with the Dede': Creative Speech and Necessary Silence in the 'Manciple's Tale,'" David Coley, University of Maryland
- "From 'Wikked' to 'Perilous': A Reading of the Manciple's Dame's Advice on Lingua," Michaela Grudin, Lewis and Clark College

Session 44: Chaucer and Fifteenth-Century Humanism
Session organizer: Daniel Wakelin, Christ's College, Cambridge
Session chair: James Simpson, Harvard University
- "John Whethamstede: Monastic and Humanist Reading," Brandon Alakas, Queen's University
- "'The Blosmes Fresshe of Tullius Garden': Humanist Rhetoric and the Preface to *The Court of Love*," Annika Farber, Pennsylvania State University
- "English Humanism: The Fifteenth Century Reconsidered," Alessandra Petrina, Università di Padova
- "Reading Chaucer: The Limitations of Humanist Reading?", Daniel Wakelin, Christ's College, Cambridge

Session 45: Julian of Norwich in Medieval and Post-medieval Perspectives
Session organizer: Sarah Salih, University of East Anglia
Session chair: Anthony Bale, Birkbeck College, University of London
- "Playing Julian: The Cell as Theatre in Contemporary Culture," Jacqueline Jenkins, University of Calgary
- "Julian in Contemporary Norwich," Sarah Salih, University of East Anglia
- "From Anchorhold to Lady's Closet: Julian of Norwich in 1670," Jennifer Summit, Stanford University
- "History in a Hazelnut: A Sociological Consideration of Julian of Norwich's Function in Contemporary Christian Spirituality," Christiania Whitehead, University of Warwick

Paper Session 46: The Astrolabe
Session organizer and chair: Jennifer Arch, Washington University
- "The Morals and Metaphysics of Astrolabes," Edgar Laird, Texas State University, San Marcos
- "'I N'am but a Lewd Compilator of the Labour of Olde Astrologiens': Chaucer's *Treatise on the Astrolabe* as a Bridge between Cultures and Languages," Gila Aloni, New York University
- "Chaucer's Use of the Astrolabe as Metaphor in *Troilus and Criseyde*," Noel Harold Kaylor Jr., Troy State University
- "Technical Writing in English and Latin: Chaucer and His Contemporaries on Astrolabes, Sundials, and Quadrants," Catherine Eagleton, The British Museum

Paper Session 47: Romances
Session organizer: Program Committee
Session chair: James Dean, University of Delaware
- "Chaucer and *Kyng Alisaunder*," Helen Phillips, Cardiff University
- "*Raptus* and Justice: Narratives of Sexual Violence and Marriage in the West Petitions and the 'Wife of Bath's Tale,'" Suzanne M. Edwards, University of Chicago
- "Cross-Cultural Movements in the Late Middle Ages: A Study of the Middle English and Old Norse Versions of *Partonopeu de Blois*," Sif Rikhardsdottir, Washington University
- "Uglier than Honorable Death: Old Age and the Hag," Sandy Feinstein, Pennsylvania State University, Berks

1:00-3:00 pm
Lunch / Free Time

3:00–4:30 pm
Session 48 (Plenary): Peasantry
Session organizer: David Wallace, University of Pennsylvania
Session chair: Maryanne Kowaleski, Fordham University
- "The Curse of the Plowman," Judith Bennett, University of Southern California
- "Serfdom in England and Elsewhere in Medieval Europe," Paul Freedman, Yale University
- "Official and Vernacular Traditions in Religion and Politics," James C. Scott, Yale University

4:30–5:30 pm
Reception 3
Sponsored by Rutgers University

6:30–10:30 pm
Banquet: World Yacht Princess
Includes music by Houston Person, winner of the Eubie Blake Jazz Award, and swing dancing.

MONDAY, JULY 31

8:30 am–3:00 pm
Registration

8:30 am–1:00 pm
Book Exhibit

9:00–10:30 am
Concurrent Paper Sessions (Sessions 49–53)

Session 49: John Lydgate
Session organizer and chair: Anthony Bale, Birkbeck College, University of London
- "Fear and Loathing in Lydgate's Short Poems," Maura Nolan, University of California, Berkeley
- "John Lydgate and the Curse of Genius," Stephanie Kamath, University of Pennsylvania
- "Lydgate and Chaucerian Performance in *The Hertford Mumming*," Emma Lipton, University of Missouri, Columbia
- "Patronage at the Periphery," John Sebastian, Loyola University New Orleans

Session 50: London and the Conventions of Writing
Session organizer: Program Committee
Session chair: Lisa Cooper, University of Wisconsin, Madison
- "The Mercers' Tale: The Production and Purpose of the 'Petition of the Folk of Mercerye,'" Wendy Scase, University of Birmingham
- "'In Deception of the People and to the Scandal of the Entire Mys-

tery': The Canon, The Pardoner, and Fraud Litigation in Late Medieval London," Craig E. Bertolet, Auburn University
- "A Political Pamphleteer in Chaucer's London: Thomas Fovent, Geoffrey Chaucer, Thomas Usk, and the Merciless Parliament of 1388," Clementine Oliver, California State University, Northridge

Session 51: The Bible As, In, or Against Literature: Medieval to Early Modern II
Session organizer and chair: James Simpson, Harvard University
- "'Among Psalms to Fynde a Cleer Sentence': The Psalmody of John Lydgate and Eleanor Hull," Shannon Gayk, Indiana University
- "Biblical Narrative and Literary Representation in *Troilus and Criseyde*," William Robins, University of Toronto
- "*The Historye of the Patriarks*: A Fifteenth-Century Vernacular Translation of the Book of Genesis," Mayumi Taguchi, Osaka Sangyo University
- "'It Is No Tyme for to Studien Heere': Reinterpreting Biblical Authority in the 'Clerk's Tale,'" Brandon Tilley, Harvard University

Session 52: Religious Cultures
Session organizer: Program Committee
Session chair: Lynn Staley, Colgate University
- "Spiritual Friendship, Conversation, and the Visit," Mary C. Erler, Fordham University
- "Ethical Frames, Ethical Practices," Nicolette Zeeman, King's College, Cambridge
- "The Lost Lives of Osbern Bokenham," Simon Horobin, University of Glasgow
- "Affective Piety, Private Devotion, and the Reformation of Faith," Michelle Karnes, University of Missouri, Columbia

Session 53: Words, Speech, and Style
Session Organizer: Program Committee
Session chair: Mary-Jo Arn, Medieval Academy of America
- "Som Honeste Thyng," Karla Taylor, University of Michigan
- "'With Nede Artow So Woundid': Revisiting Narrative Voice in the 'Man of Law's Prologue and Tale,'" Cristina Maria Cervone, Villanova University

- "Pilgrims' Pride: Penance, 'Janglynge,' and the Parson," Ellen Ketels, Columbia University
- "Ambiguity in Chaucer's Language with a Focus on *Troilus and Criseyde* 3.587: 'Syn I Moste on Yow Triste,'" Yoshiyuki Nakao, Hiroshima University

10:30–11:00 am
Coffee, tea, and pastries

11:00 am–1:00 pm
Concurrent Panel Sessions (Sessions 54–58)

Session 54: Gender and Historicism in Chaucer Studies
Session organizer and chair: Elizabeth Scala, University of Texas at Austin
- "Chaucer in the All-Woman Classroom: Emasculating the Father, Empowering the Mother," Kathryn Lynch, Wellesley College
- "(Un)Holy Alliances: Gender, Historicism, and Religion in the Study of Middle English Literature," Claire Waters, University of California, Davis
- "Women Chaucerians and the Academy," Jane Chance, Rice University
- "Chaucer and the Masculinity of Historicism," Sylvia Federico, Bates College
- "Embodied History, Engendered History, Reception History: The Legend and Its Readers," Betsy McCormick, Mount San Antonio College
- "'That Semeth Oon and Ys Not Soo': Historicism's Boethian Heritage," Brooke Hunter, University of Texas at Austin

Session 55: Manuscripts and Textual Culture—Responses and Reassessments
Session organizer and chair: Alexandra Gillespie, University of Toronto
- "Does Adam Pynkhurst Matter?", Barbara Bordalejo, University of Birmingham
- "Offshoots or Offspring? Reconsidering Chaucer's Children," Myra Seaman, College of Charleston
- "The Mercers' Petition and the *House of Fame* in the 1380s," Marion Turner, King's College London

- "Jean d'Angoulême and John Duxworth: Chaucer's Captive Audience," John Bowers, University of Nevada, Las Vegas
- "Copying Adam Scriveyn," Alexandra Gillespie, University of Toronto

Session 56: Translating Ethics (E-seminar and panel)
Session organizer and chair: Jessica Rosenfeld, Washington University
- "Chaucerian 'Proces,' Ovidian 'Usus': *Habitus* in *Troilus and Criseyde*," Colin Fewer, Purdue University, Calumet
- "The Moral Balade: Chaucer, Deschamps, Boethius," Laura Kendrick, Université de Versailles
- "The Invisible Other: *Dux Moraud* and the Vagaries of Textual Transmission," Julie Paulson, San Francisco State University
- "Translating Enjoyment in Chaucer," Jessica Rosenfeld, Washington University
- "Pastoral Ethics and Translation in Late-Medieval England," Elizabeth Schirmer, New Mexico State University
- "Legal Personification in the Examination of William Thorpe," Jamie Taylor, University of Pennsylvania
- "The Translator's Behalves," Meg Worley, Pomona College

Session 57: The Value of Close Reading: Practice
Session organizer and chair: Christopher Cannon, Girton College, Cambridge
- "The Poetics of Sainthood: Vernacular Hagiography and Literary Form," Jennifer Jahner, University of Colorado, Boulder
- "Reading Closely a Close Reading: The Problem of Translation," Ivana Djordjevic, Dalhousie University
- "Reading 'Singing by Rote' in the 'Prioresse's Tale,'" Helen Barr, Lady Margaret Hall, Oxford
- "Too Close for Historicism? Topicality," Andrew Cole, University of Georgia
- "Chaucer, Boethius, and the Erotics of Close Reading," Deanne Williams, York University, Toronto
- "*Digressio Intra* in the 'Franklin's Tale,'" Jorge Alcázar, Universidad Nacional Autónoma de México
- "Close Reading on the Couch," Sarah Stanbury (respondent), College of the Holy Cross

Session 58: Chaucerian Connections
Session organizer: Program Committee
Session chair: Robert F. Yeager, University of West Florida
- "A Gower *Exemplum*, *Dame Sirith*, and *Troilus and Criseyde*," Gretchen Mieszkowski, University of Houston, Clear Lake
- "Maidstone's *Concordia* and Chaucer," Charles R. Smith, Colorado State University
- "The Rural Community in *Piers Plowman* and *The Canterbury Tales*," Sandra Pierson Prior, Columbia University
- "Bonaventure's Ecclesiastes and the Ending of the *Troilus*," Rebecca Beal, University of Scranton
- "Indeterminacy in Lydgate's *Temple of Glass*," Bernadette Vankeerbergen, Ohio State University
- "'He Myghte Seyn He Were a Conquerour': Diomede's Battle for Renown," Kimberly Jack, Loyola University, Chicago
- "'I Sleep Nevere on the Mount of Pernaso': Fragment V of *The Canterbury Tales* and the Claims of Humanism," Jamie C. Fumo, McGill University
- "Sound and Silence: Retrospection in the 'Manciple's Tale,'" Mel Storm, Emporia State University

1:00–3:00 pm
Buffet Lunch and Session 59 (Plenary): Wrap-up
Session chair and moderator: David Lawton, Executive Director, New Chaucer Society, and Washington University
Conference Perspectives:
- Nicholas Watson, Harvard University
- Jennifer Summit, Stanford University
- Responses from Teachers' Forum
- Responses from Graduate Students
- Open Forum

Index